Banner of the Fenhall Drift Lodge, Lanchester, now in custodianship of Lanchester Parish Church. It was made in 1960 by Tutill of Chesham to designs by Ernie Reay and George Thomas. Reproduced courtesy of Lanchester Parish Council and the Durham Miners' Association.

A PEOPLE'S HISTORY OF CLASSICS

A People's History of Classics explores the influence of the classical past on the lives of working-class people, whose voices have been almost completely excluded from previous histories of classical scholarship and pedagogy, in Britain and Ireland from the late 17th to the early 20th century.

This volume challenges the prevailing scholarly and public assumption that the intimate link between the exclusive intellectual culture of British elites and the study of the ancient Greeks and Romans and their languages meant that working-class culture was a 'Classics-Free Zone'. Making use of diverse sources of information, both published and unpublished, in archives, museums and libraries across the United Kingdom and Ireland, Hall and Stead examine the working-class experience of classical culture from the Bill of Rights in 1689 to the outbreak of World War II. They analyse a huge volume of data from individuals, groups, regions and activities, in a huge range of sources including memoirs, autobiographies, Trade Union collections, poetry, factory archives, artefacts and documents in regional museums. This allows a deeper understanding not only of the many examples of interaction with the Classics, but also what these cultural interactions signified to the working poor: from the promise of social advancement, to propaganda exploited by the elites, to covert and overt class war.

A People's History of Classics offers a fascinating and insightful exploration of the many and varied engagements with Greece and Rome among the working classes in Britain and Ireland, and is a must-read not only for classicists, but also for students of British and Irish social, intellectual and political history in this period. Further, it brings new historical depth and perspectives to public debates around the future of classical education, and should be read by anyone with an interest in educational policy in Britain today.

Edith Hall is Professor of Classics at King's College London, UK and is leader of a campaign to introduce Classical Civilisation and Ancient History qualifications across the UK state-school sector. She has published 30 books on ancient Greek and Roman civilisation and its continuing influence, and in 2015 was awarded the Erasmus Medal of the European Academy.

Henry Stead is Lecturer in Latin at the University of St Andrews, UK. His research project 'Brave New Classics' explores the relationship between the Greek and Roman classics and world communism. He is the author of *A Cockney Catullus* (2015), a translator of Latin poems and co-editor of *Greek and Roman Classics in the British Struggle for Social Reform* (2015).

A PEOPLE'S HISTORY OF CLASSICS

Class and Greco-Roman Antiquity in Britain and Ireland 1689 to 1939

Edith Hall and Henry Stead

Routledge
Taylor & Francis Group
LONDON AND NEW YORK

First published 2020
by Routledge
2 Park Square, Milton Park, Abingdon, Oxon OX14 4RN

and by Routledge
52 Vanderbilt Avenue, New York, NY 10017

Routledge is an imprint of the Taylor & Francis Group, an informa business

British Library Cataloguing-in-Publication Data
A catalogue record for this book is available from the British Library

Library of Congress Cataloging-in-Publication Data
A catalog record has been requested for this book

ISBN: 978-1-138-21283-1 (hbk)
ISBN: 978-0-367-43236-2 (pbk)
ISBN: 978-1-315-44660-8 (ebk)

DOI: 10.4324/9781315446608

Typeset in Bembo
by Deanta Global Publishing Services, Chennai, India

For Product Safety Concerns and Information please contact our EU representative: GPSR@taylorandfrancis.com
Taylor & Francis Verlag GmbH, Kaufingerstraße 24, 80331 München, Germany.

For Richard and Becky

CONTENTS

MAPS

FIGURES

MAPS OF LOCATIONS DISCUSSED IN THE TEXT

0.1 South of England

0.2 North of England

ORKNEY
Stornoway
MORAY FIRTH
Cromarty
Fort George
BANFF
Buckie
Rathven
Inverboyndie
Moray Parish
Peterhead
HIGHLANDS
ABERDEEN
Gilcomston
SCOTLAND
Laurencekirk
Fort William
DUNDEE
River Tay
PERTH
FIFE
Madras College
St Andrews
Falkland
Broomhall Estate
STIRLING
Alloa
Dunfermline
FIRTH OF FORTH
Bó ness
Greenock
River Clyde
EDINBURGH
Dunbar
Haddington
Rothesay
GLASGOW
Linlithgowshire
EAST LOTHIAN
Paisley
BUTE
LOWLANDS
BERWICKSHIRE
New Lanark
Peebles
Annbank
Leadhills
Jedburgh
Kirkconnel
Wanlockhead
Alloway
Sanquhar
AYRESHIRE
Langholm Academy
BORDER WITH ENGLAND
DUMFRIESSHIRE
GALLOWAY
Annan
KIRKCUDBRIGHTSHIRE

0.3 Scotland

ANGLESEY
Llandudno
Colwen Bay
Abergele
Rhyl
BANGOR
Caernarfon
Llanberis
Snowdon
Denbigh
DENBIGHSHIRE
Porthmadog
Harlech
Aberdaron
Bala
BORDER WITH ENGLAND
WALES
ABERYSTWYTH
Pisgah
Bryndu
Trecastle
Brecon
Talgarth
PEMBROKESHIRE
Carmarthan
Haverford West
Abergaveny
Brynamman
Lower Brynamman
Llanelly
Monmouth
Kidwelly
Gwaun Cae Gurwen
Nant-y-glo
Penllergaer
Banwen
Llettyshenkin
Rhymni
Morriston
SWANSEA
Aberdare
Ponthir
Mountain Ash
Caerleon
Nantymoel
Trealaw
Pontypridd
NEWPORT
Tonypandy
Rhondda
Gwent
Ogmore
GLAMORGAN
CARDIFF
Glamorgan
Barry

0.4 Wales

0.5 Republic of Ireland and Northern Ireland

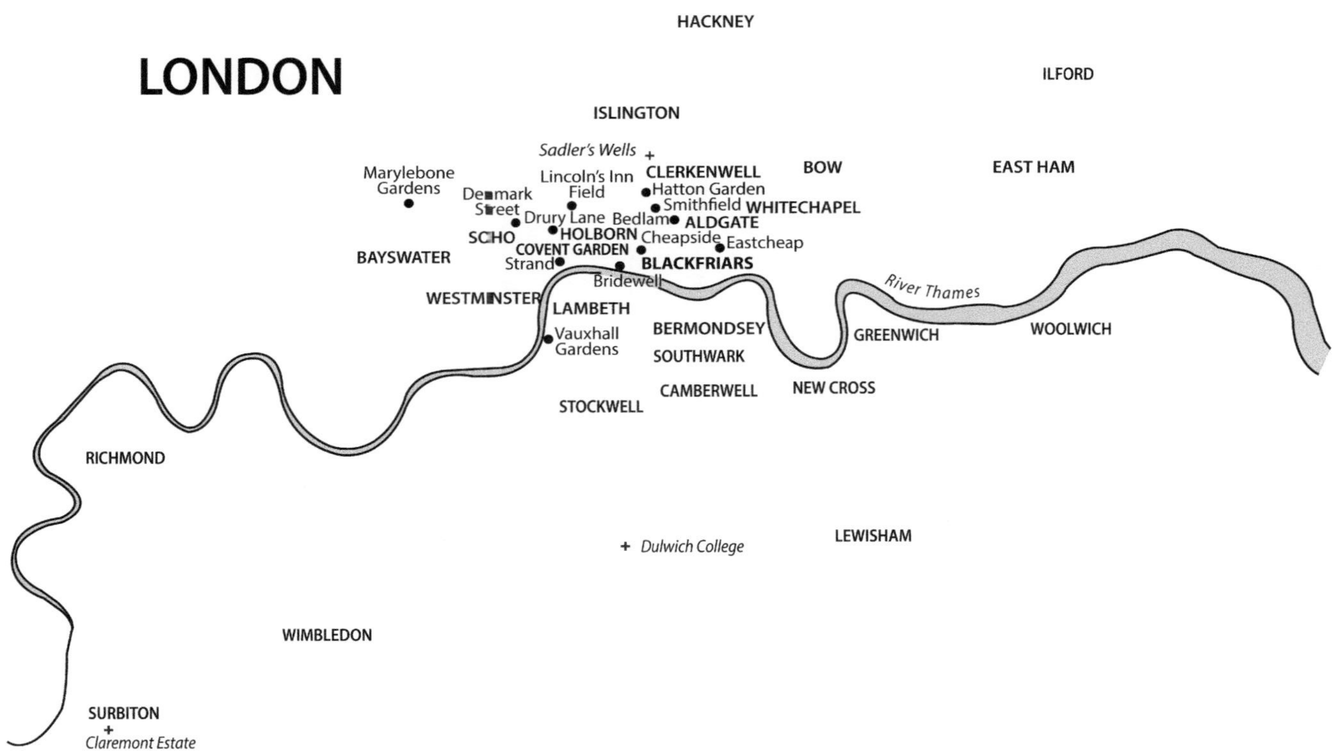
LONDON
HACKNEY
ILFORD
ISLINGTON
Sadler's Wells
Marylebone Gardens
Denmark Street
Lincoln's Inn Field
CLERKENWELL
Hatton Garden
Smithfield
WHITECHAPEL
BOW
EAST HAM
Drury Lane
Bedlam
ALDGATE
SOHO
HOLBORN
Cheapside
Eastcheap
BAYSWATER
COVENT GARDEN
Strand
BLACKFRIARS
Bridewell
River Thames
WESTMINSTER
LAMBETH
Vauxhall Gardens
BERMONDSEY
SOUTHWARK
GREENWICH
WOOLWICH
CAMBERWELL
NEW CROSS
STOCKWELL
RICHMOND
Dulwich College
LEWISHAM
WIMBLEDON
SURBITON
Claremont Estate

0.6 London

PREFACE

This book began life in the 1980s when Edith Hall was trying to find conceptual links between her academic study of Classics at Oxford University and her lifelong interest in Labour history. Its eventual appearance was made inevitable when she was employed in the towage industry in Cardiff and Liverpool docks in 1983, before meeting some miners from Maerdy Colliery in the Rhondda during the 1984–1985 miners' strike. From them, especially National Union of Mineworkers activist Mike Edwards, she learned about the extraordinary tradition of miners' libraries in South Wales. The shape and scope of the book were conceived at a conference on the theme of Classics and Class financed by and hosted at the British Academy in 2010. The intensive research was made possible when the AHRC offered a major research grant for three years' explorations in libraries and archives between 2013 and 2016, and Henry Stead, who had written a doctorate on radical receptions of Catullus in the late 18th and 19th centuries, agreed to join the project as chief collaborator. It was originally intended to be made freely Open Access from the date of its original publication, but unfortunately this has had to be postponed until 2023.[1]

During the lengthy gestation of the book, debts have been incurred to a wide range of individuals and organisations. But we record our very special gratitude to Paul Cartledge, who read the entire book before it went into production and made many helpful suggestions. Thanks are also owed to the late Margot Heinemann; Oswyn Murray; Robert Lister; Jo Balmer, Rosie Wyles; Emma Bridges; the Miners of Maerdy Colliery; Liz Dobbin; Sarah Poynder; Georgie Poynder; Tony Harrison; Sian Thomas; David Braund; Michele Ronnick; Jonathan Rose; Charlotte Higgins; Peggy Reynolds; William Fitzgerald; Margaret Malamud; Emily Greenwood; Greg Thalmann; Stephen Hodkinson; Brycchan Carey; Leanne Hunnings; David Lupher; Elizabeth Vandiver; Ahuvia Kahane; Laura Proffitt; Matt Shipton; Elinor Taylor; Ben Harker; Hanna

Paulouskaya; Zara Torlone; John Hilton; Anthony Ellis; Wallace Kwong and Mr Anthony of the British Library Rare Books and Music Reading Room; the Leverhulme Trust, who awarded Stead an Early Career Fellowship, during the term of which the book was completed; Matt Halliday; Newcastle University's Robinson Library, Special Collections; National Library of Wales; The John Gray Centre, Haddington; The Family of Vulcana; Helen Lindsay; Durham University Library, Archives and Special Collections; Melvin Murray, actor and archivist of the Theatre Royal, Stratford East; Arlene Holmes-Henderson; Peter Thonemann; Sam Richardson; Miranda Goodby; Alexandra Geary; Andrew Jameson; Leigh Taylor; Christopher Stray; Evelien Bracke; Lorna Hardwick; Adam Roberts; Edmund Richardson; Sarah Butler; Peter Kruschwitz; Justine McConnell; Alexia Petsalis-Diomidis; P.J. Rhodes; John Roger; Sara Monoson; Christele Machut; Fiona Macintosh; Neil Leeder; Robert Templing; Ceri Davies; Andrew Green; Christopher Pelling; Stephen Harrison; Patrice Rankine; Janett Morgan; Mark Humphries; Barbara Goff; Paula James; Annie Ravenhill-Johnson; Richard Alston; Neville Morley; Sharon O'Connor and all the volunteers at Bell House, Dulwich; Selina Todd; Michael Simpson; Emma Stafford; Phiroze Vasunia; Helen Eastman and the Actors of Live Canon; Tony Harrison; Sian Thomas; Melvyn Bragg; Lee Hall; Barrie Rutter; Simon Armitage; Paul R Ternent; Adam Roberts; Hugh Bowden; Alexandra Geary; Chris Bishop; Guy Moody; Conor Kerr; Andrew Cracknell; Tom Geue; Will Harris; Shafquat Towheed; Edmund King; Charlie Stead; Kevin Morgan; Urve Opik; Colin Chambers; Paul Gillen; Anne Cranny-Francis; the cooks and waiters at Pizza Express on the Euston Road and Daniel Orrells. We have received tremendous support from Elizabeth Risch and especially Amy Davis-Poynter at Routledge and our copy-editor Stephen Riordan at Deanta Global. But the book could never have been completed without the uncompromising and determined support of our partners in life, Richard Poynder and Becky Brewis, to whom it is gratefully dedicated.

Note

1 See the interview with Richard Poynder posted at https://poynder.blogspot.com/2019/08/the-open-access-interviews-edith-hall.html

PART I

Canons, media and genres

Pictures of romance and beauty I had never dreamed of suddenly opened up before my eyes. I was transported from the East End to an enchanted land.

[Will Crooks MP, quoted in 1917, on reading Homer][1]

The upper classes, from their first day at school, to their last day at college, read of nothing but the glories of Salamis and Marathon, of freedom and of the old republics. And what comes of it? No more than their tutors know will come of it, when they thrust into the boys' hands books which give the lie in every page to their own political superstitions.[2]

[Charles Kingsley, 1850]

A student of classical influence and of the interest felt in Greek and Latin authors in successive periods cannot but feel surprised, and sometimes even startled, at the different points of view to which he must adjust himself in order to follow the thought of past generations about the classics.[3]

[Henry Lathrop, 1933]

Notes

1 Labour MP Will Crooks on reading a translation of the *Iliad*, quoted in Haw (1917) 22.
2 Kingsley (1898 [1850]) vol. I, 143.
3 Lathrop (1933) 9.

DOI: 10.4324/9781315446608-1

1

MOTIVES AND METHODS

In *Reflections on the Revolution in France* (1790), Edmund Burke laments that all is lost if the aristocracy and the church lose their authority: 'Along with its natural protectors and guardians, learning will be cast into the mire and trodden down under the hoofs of a swinish multitude'.[1] To fan the flames of moral panic about the consequences of mass education, Burke here invokes the King James Bible's translation of a famous passage of Matthew's Gospel (7:6): 'Give not that which is holy unto the dogs, neither cast ye your pearls before swine, lest they trample them under their feet, and turn again and rend you'.[2]

Classicists and theologians dispute the meaning of Matthew's pearls, *margarites*, which in the New Testament Greek may imply crumbs from the rite of the Eucharist.[3] But, in Burke's polemic, the pearls are not crumbs of communion bread. Burke's pearls are learning, and the swine are the uneducated masses. Since the education of the French ruling class revolved around classical languages, Burke's pearls of learning meant—and were understood to mean—learning in those tongues.

His sentence resonated with his contemporaries.[4] Its impact can be seen in the new frontispiece engraving entitled 'Homer casting pearls before swine', supplied to a 1797 edition of a bawdy burlesque of the *Iliad* books 1–12. (Figure 1.1) It was entitled *A New Translation of Homer's Iliad, adapted to the Capacity of Honest English Roast Beef and Pudding Eaters* and ascribed to Thomas Bridges, who treated Virgil's *Aeneid* to a comparable subversion in his *Dido*, a comic opera produced at the Haymarket Theatre in 1771.[5] The first four books of this burlesque *Iliad* had originally been published in 1762 under the pseudonym of Junior Cotton.[6] It creates humour through stylistic bathos and social demotion of its personnel,

DOI: 10.4324/9781315446608-2

FIGURE 1.1 Homer casting pearls before swine, frontispiece from Bridges (1797), reproduced from copy in Hall's personal collection.

presented as plebeian Britons who speak uncouth rhyming iambic tetrameters. Book X, for example, begins thus:

> The Greeks, though sorely drubb'd all day,
> Asleep before their scullers lay—
> All but poor Agamemnon, who
> Could only nod a spell or so.
> His fears did such a rumbling keep
> Within his guts, he could not sleep.
> As when a barrel of small-beer,
> No matter whether foul or clear,
> Begins to leak, drop follows drop
> As fast as wanton schoolboys hop.[7]

The author revels in the burlesque's swinification of the Homeric pearls, requiring a knowledge of Alexander Pope's *Iliad* (1715–1720) rather than of Homer's.

Pope's translations had brought Homer to a larger audience, including workers and women, than ever had the opportunity to learn Greek. Take Esther

Easton, a Jedburgh gardener's wife, visited by the poet Robert Burns in 1787. He recorded that she was

> a very remarkable woman for reciting poetry of all kinds ... she can repeat by heart almost everything she has ever read, particularly Pope's 'Homer' from end to end ... and, in short, is a woman of very extraordinary abilities.[8]

Pope's Homer captured the childhood imagination of another Scot, Hugh Miller, to whom the discussion will return in Chapter 5. A stonemason and a distinguished autodidact, Miller grew up to become a world-famous geologist (Figure 1.2). Even as a boy he saw the *Iliad* as incomparable literature. He wrote in *My Schools and Schoolmasters* (1854) that he had learned early 'that no other writer could cast a javelin with half the force of Homer. The missiles went whizzing athwart his pages; and I could see the momentary gleam of the steel, ere it buried itself deep in brass and bull-hide'.[9] The working-class Esther and Hugh,

FIGURE 1.2 Hugh Miller (1802–1856), from Miller (1885), reproduced from copy in Hall's personal collection.

whom Burke would no doubt have regarded as swine, could easily have understood what Bridges was doing with his *Iliad*.

Burke's swine made defiant appearances in the 1790s during the trials of British republicans.[10] Joseph Gerrald, a revolutionary democrat and member of the London Corresponding Society, used the swine trope in a speech he delivered in a court in Edinburgh when charged with sedition. Perhaps his democratic ardour had been fostered when, two decades before, he had acted the role of Sophocles' tyrant of Thebes in a Greek-language production of *Oedipus Tyrannus* at Stanmore School, run by the 'Whig Dr Johnson', Dr Samuel Parr.[11] Gerrald attacks Burke in his Edinburgh oration partly by presenting the 14th-century Henry Knighton as Burke's predecessor. Knighton was outraged by the popularity of translations, usually known as the Wycliffe Bible, of the Latin Vulgate Bible into Middle English.[12] Gerrald therefore reminds his audience of their contemporary, Burke, by pairing him with the medieval Knighton, as twin enemies of the Reformation/Reform. He refers to Knighton's lament concerning the translation of the Scriptures: 'Pity it is, that this evangelical pearl should be trodden down under the foot of swine'.[13] Knighton, Gerrald implies, was complaining about popular literacy as well as popular access to the word of God. Gerrald accurately presents both Knighton and Burke as enemies of social inclusion.

Gerrald was not the only democrat of the 1790s who used classical material to advance the cause. A collection of works in the public journals during that decade shows how much satirical response Burke's 'swinish multitude' had elicited, from radicals including the controversial Regius Professor of Greek at Cambridge, Richard Porson.[14] The sympathy with the lower classes apparent in the pig-theme central to Percy Bysshe Shelley's *Oedipus Tyrannus; or, Swellfoot the Tyrant*, published and almost immediately suppressed in 1820, along with the pirating of *Queen Mab* in 1821, first attracted a large working-class readership to his poetry.[15] The theme of the swinish multitude and their vexed relationship with ancient languages will recur repeatedly in this volume.

Conventional histories of Classics always discuss Thomas Gaisford, Dean of Christ Church, Oxford and Regius Professor of Greek (1811–1855), who one Christmas Day supposedly told his congregation to apply themselves to the study of Greek literature, 'which not only elevates above the vulgar herd, but leads not infrequently to positions of considerable emolument'.[16] Gaisford's is the most concise statement available that *financial* capital can be accumulated through Greek. The distinction between lucre and *social* capital is further explored in the memoir of Charles Frederick Briggs, an American citizen, published in 1855. His father was a merchant, but

> had enlarged views for his son, and determined to give him what he had always felt the need of himself—a thorough education; that he might have a capital to start with, which no adverse circumstances could deprive him of. Bonds and stocks might prove worthless, banks might fail, and

> merchandise depreciate in value; but no changes in the market could affect Latin and Greek; and with a good stock of these commodities, the father had no fears for his son.[17]

In Burke, Bridges, Gerrald, Knighton, Gaisford and Briggs, the pearls of Greek and Latin bear values that go beyond intellectual life to embrace religion, aesthetics, class and money. Translation into the mother tongue is in turn implicated in a threat to the established political order and the consequent need for the subordination of the social swine. In class-ridden British society, knowledge of classical Greek itself bore also some mysterious *moral* value, shown in William Thackeray's novel *Pendennis* (1849–1850). As a child, the titular hero, Arthur Pendennis, or 'Pen', mistranslates a word in Greek. The crisis comes when his terrifying teacher, the Doctor, 'put him on to construe a Greek play. He did not know a word of it, though little Timmins, his form-fellow, was prompting him with all his might, Pen had made a sad blunder or two'. At this point the Doctor delivers a tirade:

> "Pendennis, sir," he said, "your idleness is incorrigible and your stupidity beyond example. You are a disgrace to your school, and to your family, and I have no doubt will prove so in after-life to your country … what a prodigious quantity of future crime and wickedness are you, unhappy boy, laying the seed! Miserable trifler! A boy who construes δε *and*, instead of δε *but*, at sixteen years of age is guilty not merely of folly, and ignorance, and dullness inconceivable, but of crime, of deadly crime, of filial ingratitude, which I tremble to contemplate. A boy, sir, who does not learn his Greek play cheats the parent who spends money for his education. A boy who cheats his parent is not very far from robbing or forging upon his neighbour. A man who forges on his neighbour pays the penalty of his crime at the gallows".[18]

Mismanagement of a Greek particle can lead, in satire, to capital punishment. Knowledge of the classical languages has historically meant a great deal more than it says on the tin.

Previous historical studies of the applications of Greek and Roman culture in British education and society have focussed primarily on men like Gaisford and the often-repeated tale of his forebears, the mostly Continentally trained Humanists active from the late 15th century, such as Thomas Linacre, William Grocyn and Thomas More. There has been enthusiasm for biographical (often hagiographical) studies of dead professors, a mere 'history of personalities'.[19] These have focussed on the custody of this particular intellectual property within academic institutions and discourse.[20] We are more interested in the instrumentality of Greek and Roman culture in political and social life than in Professors and Fellows within ancient colleges. We have another pantheon of heroes to propose in the real-life counterparts of Thomas Hardy's Jude Fawley, in *Jude the*

Obscure (1895), the stonemason who struggled against all odds to pursue his passion for ancient Greek.

We also have a different canon of books found on the shelves of workers' libraries, such as *A History of the Ancient Working People and The Ancient Lowly to the Adoption of Christianity by Constantine* (1887), usually abbreviated to *The Ancient Lowly*, by Cyrenus Osborne Ward, the work that introduced many thousands of people in the Labour Movement across the English-speaking world to ancient history, but from a working-class perspective. As Gareth Stedman Jones has put it, 'one of the uses of history has always been (in Western society at least) the creation of traditional mythologies attributing a historical sanctity to the present self-images of groups, classes and societies';[21] most historians of antiquity read before the late 19th century adopted the perspective and implicitly supported the interests of the ruling classes, but they did not all: Ward rewrote ancient Greece and Rome from the viewpoint of their workers. Himself raised dirt-poor to work on his parents' Illinois farm, he left home in 1848 when he was 17, earning his keep in manual trades and as a violinist. After becoming involved with organised labour in the Brooklyn Navy Yard, his political writings brought him to the attention of international socialists.[22] His volume I concentrates on ancient slavery, although it also assembles evidence for ancient trade unions. Volume II is perhaps the most trenchant expression in existence of the view that early Christianity was the religion of slaves and the Roman poor, but all too soon co-opted by the ruling classes to become the official religion of European imperialism.

Our book is therefore a response to several ways in which ancient Greek and Roman culture was historically entangled, in Britain until World War II, with the thorny issue of social class. It is a history of Classics, understood to mean the whole subject-area constituted by the texts, artefacts and archaeological remains produced by people who spoke Greek and Latin between the late Bronze Age and the Christian closure of pagan temples in the late 4th century CE. As we shall see in Chapter 2, the plural noun 'Classics', with or without a definite article, was first used with this meaning at the dawn of the 18th century. But *A People's History of Classics* is an account written from a perspective informed by awareness of the system by which Britons during this period were divided along lines determined by *class*. This noun (which, as we shall also see, comes from the same Latin root as 'Classics') began to be used in the socio-economic sense in precisely the same historical period.

Classical Reception, itself a relatively new field, has attended to several aspects of the British experience in the 18th, 19th and early 20th centuries, especially to *belles lettres*, fine art and Oxbridge curriculums.[23] There have now been several studies of ethnicity, slavery, imperialism and colonialism in relation to Classical Reception in Britain and her territories abroad.[24] Although a very few notable women classicists had earlier received biographical attention, the topic of gender and Reception in relation to Classical Philology in a wider historical perspective has only belatedly transpired, for example, in *Women Classical Scholars from the Renaissance to Jacqueline de Romilly* (2016, edited by Rosie Wyles and Edith Hall).[25] But Classical Reception, like most other academic disciplines, has hitherto neglected social class as a category of analysis. As the literary historian Stefan Collini has said, in the 'quartet of race, class and gender and sexual orientation, there is no doubt that class has been the least fashionable, despite the fact that all the evidence suggests that class remains the single most important determinant of life chances'.[26]

The neglect is not solely a matter of fashion, either. Sayer has shown in his penetrating philosophical enquiry, *The Moral Significance of Class*, that scholars and students, like everyone else, display embarrassment, awkwardness, defensiveness, evasiveness, nervous judgement of others or self-deprecation and other signs of unease when the topic of class is raised, even at the most abstract academic level.[27] Class position is arbitrary and produces social injustices, yet is associated with an extensive set of moral discourses expressing evaluations on behaviour, taste, industriousness, ethical standards and perceived deservingness. 'Class is morally problematic because of its arbitrary relationship to worth, virtues, and status, and this is why it is a highly sensitive subject ... We are shamed by class because it is shameful'.[28]

Another reason, besides unease with its moral implications, for the neglect of class-conscious research amongst scholars of Classical Reception is that many critics, especially in the USA, have historically denied that class is a legitimate category of analysis, attempting to argue that both class-conscious art and class-oriented criticism are reductive and partisan.[29] Our response to this is that any study of human society and culture which *avoids* class must be limited and partial. It is surely the absence of any available study of working-class instrumentalisation of ancient Greece and Rome in Britain that allows a prominent cultural historian to introduce a summation of 19th-century classical presences with the unnuanced claim that 'the classics were responsible for more humbug than almost anything else in the Victorian age'.[30] Chris Stray's *Classics Transformed: Schools, Universities, and Society in England, 1830–1960* (1998), albeit focussed on school and university curricula, is a notable exception; it looks at Classics from the 'top-down', elite perspective and has influenced us profoundly.[31] So have literary studies of African American and Caribbean writers by Emily Greenwood, Justine McConnell and Patrice Rankine, as well as Michele Ronnick's work on African American classicists during the struggle against slavery and the post-bellum period.[32] A few important studies have addressed the role played by Classics in social exclusion, notably Françoise Waquet's *Le latin, ou L'empire d'un signe* (1998), although her major focus is on the Renaissance and Early Modern periods and she does not engage with working-class perspectives.

Some exceptions include Hall's exploratory articles from 2008 onwards,[33] a pilot conference on the theme which she convened at the British Academy in 2010, and the previous publications and website produced by the AHRC-funded project *Classics and Class in Britain* on which she collaborated with Stead between 2013 and 2016.[34] Books have subsequently appeared on late 18th- and

19th-century educated British males' responses to two Latin poets, Stead's monograph *A Cockney Catullus* (2015), and Stephen Harrison's *Victorian Horace: Classics and Class* (2017). There is, however, no precedent for a substantial study with the single, over-riding aim of providing a systematically class-conscious avenue, with the emphasis on lived individual experience, into the history of Classics in Britain.[35]

Classics has long functioned to exclude working-class people from educational privileges. The time-consuming study of the Greek and Latin languages was adopted as the core of the education of the newly redefined British 'gentleman' in the early 18th century, and as the symbolic marker that he was fit for a profession, a marriage into the gentry, a career in prestigious educational institutions or government, or advancement in the civil/imperial service. Of the 61 boys born in 1798–1799 who studied Greek and Latin at Aberdeen Grammar School, of whom a small minority were scholarship boys from working-class homes, 2 grew up to inherit substantial estates, 2 became local civic dignitaries, 4 'planters' or farmers, 2 army officers, 2 naval officers, 7 schoolmasters (some in addition to other occupations such as 'bookseller and planter in America'), 10 surgeons, doctors or druggists, 1 an 'Employee of the British King' who died in Java, and 1 an insurance banker who became a diplomat, working as consul in Prussia and the Netherlands. One became an antiquary and newspaper owner, one a clergyman, one worked in an unknown position for North British Railway, another as purser of an East Indiaman. More than a third seem to have worked most of their adult lives or settled abroad, in China, Calcutta, Bengal, Madras, 'India', the West Indies, Australia, the USA (one even becoming a Congressman), Canada, Java and Sierra Leone. If these are added to those in naval or army service, the number who travelled professionally comes to more than two-thirds.[36] We shall return to the fascinating case of Aberdonian classical education in Chapter 11.

Classics was uniquely instrumental in the intellectual and cultural reproduction of class hierarchies in Georgian, Victorian and Edwardian society, which was itself partly a product of the rigid segregation of social classes in the educational system, as Matthew Arnold saw.[37] Yet did this mean that lower-class culture was ever a 'Classics-Free Zone'? Richard Altick and Jonathan Rose showed, in landmark studies,[38] that it is as easy to underestimate as to overestimate the levels of knowledge and education amongst the poorer sectors of society. Subsequent books on working-class intellectual culture have unfortunately not addressed the importance of Classics in the definition and self-definition of the proletariat in the 18th and 19th centuries,[39] probably because few scholars of literature in English today have much training or interest in the ancient world. Yet our work overlaps with theirs, as well as that of Altick and Rose, in the autobiographical materials we have examined and in the methods of reading we have applied.

Our volume excavates the cultural past at the precise intersection of classical culture on the one hand and socio-economic status and identity on the other. The study is intended as the chief conduit for the results of researches into diverse sources of information, both published and unpublished, in archives, museums and libraries across the United Kingdom and Ireland. In our first book, a collection of essays entitled *Greek and Roman Classics in the British Struggle for Social Reform* (2015), we and our guest contributors focussed on classical ideas and education in the personal development and activities of British social reformers in the 19th and first six decades of the 20th century, most of whom were originally from the lower echelons of the middle class. Such reformers often tumbled down the class system to end their lives deported, on the gallows, in prisons or paupers' graves, and they make appearances in this more substantial volume, especially in Chapter 23. But here we listened hardest, rather, to the voices of working-class people. These have been routinely excluded from previous histories of classical scholarship and pedagogy. Having identified many relevant archives and fields of evidence, as well as problems that need to be investigated in further detail, we acknowledge that our book is not remotely comprehensive. It is highly selective and reflects our own aesthetic and cultural interests. Some chapters survey a broad area of evidence, while others focus on one or two illuminating case-studies where there is a rich seam of evidence to be mined. But we publish it in the hope that it will prove seminal in this area of scholarly investigation and stimulate further research; a whole monograph or doctorate of path-breaking originality could be written on almost any of the topics explored in any chapter.

Our methodology is grounded in the principles of Cultural History. More than three decades ago, Robert Darnton predicted that both Intellectual History and the History of Ideas would inevitably yield to Cultural History, because its core strength is an essential concern for the experience of the historically silenced or 'inarticulate'.[40] In a path-breaking article published a year later in the *Journal of Interdisciplinary History* (1981), European Renaissance scholar William Bouwsma argued that Intellectual History must expand its horizons to incorporate not only canonical texts and their elite interpretation but a far wider social history of how humans make meaning for themselves in their own environment and in accordance with their specific experience.[41] And in his 2006 manifesto on appointment to the editorship of the *Journal of the History of Ideas*, Anthony Grafton advocated the new Cultural History which grasps, 'successfully, for previously unrecorded and unplumbed worlds of experience'.[42] We have been influenced by several scholars who have traced the relationship between certain kinds of what Pierre Bourdieu calls 'cultural capital' and the maintenance of class boundaries in Britain, France, Belgium, Switzerland, Germany, Sweden, Hungary, the USA and elsewhere;[43] taking our cue from the historian A.L. Morton's stated goal of 'explaining things in a simple way',[44] we have endeavoured, however, to avoid theoretical metalanguage that might alienate readers other than professional academics.[45] The approach is that of empirical cultural historicism, combined with a class-conscious perspective which starts from Pierre Bourdieu's premise that 'culture and education aren't simply hobbies or minor influences. They are hugely important in the affirmation of differences between groups and social classes and in the reproduction of those differences'.[46]

We cover multifarious individuals, groups, regions and activities. The diversity of the evidence is part of our contention that monolithic models of experience are unhelpful in intellectual history. The records of working-class experience which we feature here (memoirs, autobiographies, Trade Union collections, poetry, factory archives, playscripts, artefacts and documents in regional museums) have revealed a complex picture, but our principal propositions are twofold.

First, while there is no doubt that 'classical education' frequently functioned to emphasise class boundaries and social exclusion, British people with no or minimal formal education throughout the period between the accession of William and Mary in 1689 and the outbreak of World War II in 1939 found numerous avenues by which to access the culture of the ancient Greeks and Romans. Our book studies a selection of the more prominent avenues. These include inexpensive published series such as *Everyman*, recreational activities involving popular theatre and sport, workers' libraries and political activism, Nonconformist schools, the 'autodidact' tendency and employment in industries where classical content was prevalent (printing, theatre or pottery, for example).

Second, what less privileged people did with their often hard-won 'classical' intellectual property varied. Many used it as a springboard to social advancement, and in embracing the elite connotations of Classics, abandoned their identification with the working class and loyalty to the cause of its progression. Others furthered their careers and joined the establishment, with careers in prestigious schools, Higher Education, parliamentary politics or commerce, but retained a sense of obligation to their natal class expressed in philanthropic and charitable activities. Some were intensely vulnerable to propaganda using classical material devised to serve ruling-class interests (the use of the ancient British leader Caractacus in encouraging unemployed Welshmen to enlist in World War I, explored in Chapter 12, is an outstanding example). Others discovered an 'alternative canon' which helped them to cope with poverty, oppression and boredom (Epictetus, Marcus Aurelius), inspired them with revolutionary ideals and republican heroes (the Aeschylean Prometheus, Plutarch's Spartacus in his *Life of Crassus*) or provided them with models for their own radical poetry (for example, the two Chartist 'rhymers' we discuss in Chapter 13). Yet others waged a more subterranean class war in creating a tradition of cheeky, sometimes caustically parodic subversion of 'classical' literature and languages, in burlesque theatre, *poses plastiques*, fairground spectacles and insouciant sports journalism.

Since our research and analysis have been necessarily so multidisciplinary, indeed *trans*disciplinary,[47] we have striven to emphasise the precise research questions which have guided all our enquiries. Was there working-class access to 'Classics'? What happened to working-class people who gained access to classical culture and even languages? What motivated them? How did they use it, as groups or individuals?

'Classics' today often denotes any iconic, archetypal or ideal examples of a thing—vintage cars can be 'classics', as can pop songs, novels or recipes. But we understand the term to refer to the cultural output specifically of ancient Greece and Rome. This is what the term most often meant in the period we are primarily researching, and what it means in educational contexts today. We have chosen the term partly on account of its cultural scope. We don't just mean the *written texts* of the ancient Greeks and Romans, but their entire cultures; in this we follow the injunction of Gilbert Murray, that it is ancient Greece, not ancient Greek, that should be the primary object of the Hellenist's enquiries.[48] But the term also reminds us of the historic connection between socio-economic hierarchies ('class') and the disparity between the cultural and imaginative lives of people in different classes. It helps us ask how 'Classics' has been used to maintain class distinctions, but also whether Classics' elite connotations have been or must remain inevitable.

'Class' is an even more contested term. Everyone knows that it exists, but it is far less easy to identify and define than social stratifications based on gender, age or race.[49] Our determination to reveal the imprecision of the category 'popular culture',[50] which blurs and erases the true economic inequities from which such culture emerges, has led us to careful use of the term 'class' in the sociological sense of Anthony Giddens.[51] But we apply it specifically as a category which aids the investigation of the cultural uses of the ancient Greeks and Romans. That is, *we read the history of the uses and abuses of 'classical' culture from a perspective that is conscious of the social class of the agents involved.* But 'class' in the sociological sense means two different things, although they are often commensurate: 'objective class' is an economic category, while 'subjective class' defines the way individuals and groups are perceived by themselves and others. Everyone has an 'objective' class identity in that everyone has a position in the economic workings of society. Everyone acquires their subsistence from somewhere. Everyone plays a role in the way that goods and services are consumed and distributed. Objective 'class analysis' simply asks what the source of subsistence and the role are. All the people in our historical period of study derived their basic subsistence from one or more sources, just as everyone does today.

But matters are more complex than this. Since the industrial revolution, there have been so much social confusion and mobility that precise sub-categories of class (for example, 'upper proletariat', 'under-class', 'service sector' or 'lower middle/white collar') can become difficult to apply consistently. Paul Fussell's 1983 'classic' of class analysis, *Class, A Guide Through the American Status System*, proposes a nine-tier stratification of contemporary American society, ranging from the super-rich (who have amassed such large fortunes that their descendants need never work) through to no fewer than five discrete categories of low-class persons: in descending order, these are skilled blue-collar workers, workers in factories and the service industry, manual labourers, the destitute unemployed and homeless, and the 'out-of-sight' members of the population incarcerated in prisons and institutions. In *The Stamp of Class*, however, Ohio-born poet Gary Lenhart argues that class identities are much more fluid in the USA than in Europe,[52] and in the USA, even more than in the UK, the history of slavery means that categorisation by race is usually more visibly related to oppression than working occupation is. Yet, despite the fluidity and complexity of the sub-categories, there are still only nine basic ways to acquire money to survive: earn it, extract it legally from the labour of others, steal it, live off interest on capital or rent on property, inherit it, win or be given it with no strings attached, derive it from the state, derive it from charity or be supported by another individual (spouse, parent, lover, sponsor, patron, guardian).

During the period covered by this book, most British people fell into the first or last categories, in that they earned their livelihood from physical labour, or they were financially dependent on someone who did. This means that they were *objectively* 'working-class'. But it is as a subjective definition, rather than the socio-economic role, that most people understand the term 'class'. Class position is often 'subjectively' diagnosed or perceived from a whole cluster of identifying markers, ranging from style of speech and accent, hairstyle and clothing, to recreational tastes and educational attainments.[53] The 'subjective' markers of class, especially in the modern world and where there is social mobility, are *not* always co-extensive with 'objective' class position.

Our over-arching question is simple, but the evidence we use to answer it is diverse. The extent of the diversity was not planned, but we became conscious of the need for it soon after we began following our working-class subjects, readers, writers, members of circulating libraries, authors of memoirs, poems and polemics down intricate paths. There were many moments where we discovered, in an obscure provincial archive, an individual or group encounter with the ancient world which took our breath away. One was finding the lesson preparation of Isabelle Dawson, a primary school teacher in the tiny town of Buckie on the Moray Firth, who just before World War I was teaching her small charges the Greek alphabet alongside the three Rs and domestic science.[54] Our original literary emphasis, it became clear, needed to develop into one which could accommodate other sorts of documentary material. This was especially the case with working-class women, for whom far fewer institutional resources (the libraries of Mechanics' Institutes, for example) were generally available, and who were, even more than their middle- and upper-class female counterparts, regarded as utterly incapable of learning ancient languages.

The life stories of the working-class children, women and men we study often show that they were encountering classical material not only in their reading and writing lives, but in their domestic, civic and workplace environments, their media of entertainment and places of recreation, and, regardless of their political affiliations, in the maintenance of their class identity and political activities. As Asa Briggs put it in his preface to the second edition of *A Social History of England* in 1994, the cultural and social historian must switch 'from kitchen to drawing room or bedroom, or into the garden, from field to factory, from village to town and city, from warehouse and office to the corridors of Westminster and Whitehall', while seeking 'to read every cultural signpost'.[55] Our response to the breadth of our evidential brief was to break down our narrative into four sections, which are intended, like four differently placed cameras, to cumulatively create a panoramic view of the diverse opportunities working-class people had to access the Greeks and Romans. But they start from four different trajectories.

Part I, which this chapter opens, *Canons, media* and *genres*, applies a wide-angle lens to outline the contours of the 'Big Picture' which our book paints. It defines our chronological and regional scope and key terms. It introduces our readers to the research resources we have used. It defines the different 'canon' of ancient literature, myth and history which emerged amongst the working-class literary community in comparison with that of their social 'superiors', the genres (poetry, life-writing, visual art, popular theatre) in which they put that knowledge to use, and the sources of knowledge other than literary texts—especially environmental and recreational materials—on which the book draws.

Part II, *Communities*, then looks at the presence of Classics in the identity construction and psychological experience of substantial groups of working-class Britons, emphasising the religious and regional differences between them: Nonconformists (many of whom were based in the south-west of England and in East Anglia), members of workers' educational institutions and movements, especially 'Settlements', the Workers Educational Association, the Council of Labour Colleges and the Plebs League; these are followed by separate chapters on the lower-class inhabitants of Ireland, Scotland and Wales.

In part III, *Underdogs, underclasses, underworlds*, individual working-class subjects are put at the centre of the radar. Classical material does feature in poor people's expressions of class dissatisfaction and frustration, disaffection, anger, deprivation, psychological trauma (even diagnoses of insanity) and dispossession. The opening chapter discusses the role of Classics in democratic and Chartist activism. The next traces the prodigious professional rise of a handful of outstanding autodidacts who, from illiterate beginnings, acquired university chairs. Their classical education was instrumental in their meteoric rise up the academic ladder. But the next four chapters house some of the most original and vivid testimony in our book. They leave the 'respectable' working class far behind to enter a carefully chosen series of mendicant, homeless, revolutionary, dissident, sleazy and sometimes criminal underworlds, including prisons, madhouses, taverns, fairground entertainments, strength performances, bars and brothels where Classics—especially Greek—bore bizarre associations of the transcendent and occult.

Part IV, *Working identities*, discusses the role played by classical material in defining the labouring classes' multifarious experience of remunerative work. It discusses the proud and colourful use of figures from classical mythology and history in Trade Union banner art and in emblems of positive self-definition amongst craftspeople, some of which originated in medieval guilds and some of which had long been established as traditional nomenclature (e.g. amongst seamen and fire services). It examines the heightened literacy and political consciousness, leading to an interest in Classics amongst shoemakers, pottery workers and miners. It exposes the ironies of the intense relationship between mining and the ancient world, traceable to Georg Bauer's influential treatise *De Re metallica* (1546). Trained and professional Classics teachers and academics active in the socialist and communist movements from the end of the 19th century form the focus of Chapter 23, and the work of communist theatre practitioners in the 1930s brings the book to its conclusion. But the penultimate Chapter 24 centres on the army. The topic is the only World War I poem, David Jones' *In Parenthesis*, which used Classics at length, in detail, and with an admixture of colloquial diction in order to express the psychological trauma of the ordinary (non-Officer-class) English and Welsh British soldier.

Above all, our book strives to show that the inspirational works of the ancient Greeks and Romans have been contested across class lines. They have contributed to the self-definition of many lowly British people who challenged class hierarchies. Burke was concerned that the 'pearls' of intellectual culture would be besmirched if the swinish masses were allowed access to them, but Hobbes was more worried that these masses would be provoked by ancient examples into open rebellion. In *Leviathan* (1651), just before the dawn of the period covered by our book, Hobbes frets that classical literature inspires people to revolution:

> And by reading of these Greek, and Latine Authors, men from their childhood have gotten a habit (under a false shew of Liberty,) of favouring tumults, and of licentious controlling the actions of their Soveraigns; and again of controlling those controllers, with the effusion of so much blood; as I think I may truly say, there was never any thing so deerly bought, as these Western parts have bought the learning of the Greek and Latine tongue.[56]

We might put it the other way around, with Thomas Jefferson, who found the idea of the pursuit of happiness in Aristotle. In *Notes on the State of Virginia* (1782), he defined the one real goal of education as equipping people to defend their freedom; he argued that history, including ancient history, was the subject which made citizens so equipped.[57] To stay free requires also comparison of constitutions, fearlessness about change and critical, lateral and relativist thinking across time and different cultures. The ancient Mediterranean world offers an ideal context for the development of these forms of intellectual understanding and skills. Matthew Arnold, who had observed hundreds of schools in France and Germany, as well as in Britain as one of Her Majesty's Inspectors, criticised the excessive linguistic emphasis of contemporary Classics teaching in a talk he gave at Eton while advocating the importance of studying the entirety of Graeco-Roman civilisation. He said that a linguistic emphasis destroys the precious facility

> to conceive also that Graeco-Roman world, which is so mighty a factor in our own world, our own life … as a whole of which we can trace the sequence, and the sense, and the connection with ourselves.[58]

Our title pays tribute to A.L. Morton, whose evergreen *A People's History of England* (1938) was the first book to trace the fundamental outlines of English history, from pre-Roman times, from the perspective of its ordinary inhabitants.[59] Published for the Left Book Club by Lawrence and Wishart, it became the standard introduction to national history for members of workers' organisations, Trade Unions and socialist political parties. Morton in turn borrowed his title directly from the book which Charles Kingsley's imprisoned Chartist titular hero in *Alton Locke*, who was inspired by the real-life Classicist and Chartist Thomas Cooper (Figure 1.3), tries to write in gaol.[60] Morton wanted to record the past from the viewpoint of working people rather than monarchs and government ministers, but he also wanted to inspire his contemporaries to make a different future. He wrote in a new foreword to *A People's History of England* in 1964 that this had made it difficult for him 'to know where to stop'.[61] Although in other publications, both previous and forthcoming, we address much more recent developments,[62] in this volume our cut-off point has been World War II. Yet we, like Morton, have an interest in making a difference in the future. We are both children of university-educated fathers in middle-class professions and do not identify as working-class. But we are politically and emotionally committed to the provision of excellent educational opportunities to everybody in the world, as well as the entire British nation.

FIGURE 1.3 Thomas Cooper (1805–1892), from Cooper (1872), reproduced from copy in Hall's personal collection.

Currently, few of the 93% of British children and teenagers in state-sector secondary education today are offered any access even to Classical Civilisation and Ancient History, taught in translation, in their schools and 6th-form colleges; the ancient languages are now rarely available except in the private sector. From this perspective, *A People's History of Classics* is timely and topical: it brings new historical depth and nuance to public debates around the *future* of classical education in Britain. Our gallery of colourful individuals whose lives were enhanced by engagement with the Greeks and Romans, whatever the obstacles they needed to overcome in order to achieve that engagement, changes the parameters of this debate. Edith Hall's Gaisford Lecture at Oxford University in 2015, published at the time in the *Guardian Review* as 'Classics for the People', made precisely this argument.[63]

Our findings show that the experiences of classical antiquity by the historical British working class have been messy, complicated, fragmented and variegated. They have also been inspirational and depressing by turns. But we hope that they can help us think about the place of the ancient Greeks and Romans within the modern curriculum. Our book refutes wholesale the argument that classical education must be intrinsically elitist or reactionary; it has been the curriculum of empire, but it can be the curriculum of liberation.[64] We choose to emphasise the historical instrumentality of the 'legacy' of Greece and Rome in progressive and enlightened causes, both personal and political. Understanding the ancient world can enrich not only the imagination and socio-cultural literacy, but also citizenship skills and the power of argumentation and verbal expression. Our case-studies prove this irrefutably. As Neville Morley has put it, 'classical antiquity and its legacy still have power in our world, for good or ill'.[65] Our book, therefore, is not just about the past, but a rallying cry to modern Britain to support the case for the universal availability in schools of classical civilisation and ancient history.

Notes

1 Burke (1889) vol. III, 334–5.

2 Herzog (1998) 506. There may also be reverberations of the episode reported in Matthew 8.28–33 in which Jesus cast out devils by sending them into the bodies of some swine, which then hurled themselves into the water and drowned.

3 In modern Greek there is an idiom, 'he didn't put a breadcrumb (*margaritari*) in his mouth', meaning 'he didn't eat a thing', and in the Byzantine ecclesiastical tradition, the noun *margaritēs* occasionally means a crumb of communion bread. St. John Chrysostom, Archbishop of Constantinople from 397 CE, explains how to approach the distribution of Christ's body: 'do not have your hands stretched out, but make of your left hand a seat for the right, and hollowing your palm as about to receive a king, receive with great awe the Body of Christ so that no breadcrumb fall from your hand' (*Patrologia Graeca* 63.898, *Ecloga* 47). See Kahane and Kahane (1957).

4 See the witty and insightful discussion in Herzog (1998), especially 508–11.

5 Bridges (1771).

6 Anon (1762). This may in fact have been the work of Francis Grose, whom we shall meet again in Chapter 16. See G.F.R.B. (1885).

7 Bridges (1797) vol. II, 111.

8 Currie (1838) 127. On Pope's enthusiastic 18th-century female readership, see Thomas (1994).
9 Miller (1854) 28–9; see further below, pp. 114, 240.
10 See below, p. 296.
11 See Hall and Macintosh (2005) 224–7 and below, pp. 174, 275.
12 See Rawson (1889–1895) vol. II, 152; Bobrick (2001) 14–70.
13 Gerrald (1794) 202; see further Herzog (1998) 506.
14 Anon. (1802). See also below, pp. 294–9.
15 See Wallace (1987) 81. The suppressed first edition of *Swellfoot* was written in 1819 and published anonymously in 1820 (Shelley (1820a); see Behrendt (1989) 206, and, on *Queen Mab*, Fraistat (1994). A small circle of revolutionary artisan poets and publishers had already been trying to popularise Shelley amongst a lower-class readership from around 1815: see McCalman (1988) 81, 160, 211–21 and Scrivener (1993). Shelley's 1817 *A Proposal for Putting Reform to the Vote*, written under the pseudonym 'the Hermit of Marlow', had also played its part: see Cameron (1945).
16 Quoted in Tuckwell (1907) 24. Gaisford's remark may have been apocryphal (see Stray [2018] 76–80), but that does not detract from the ideological potency of such a sentiment circulating in the 19th-century context.
17 Briggs (2002 [1855]) 481.
18 Thackeray (1849–1850) vol I, 16–17.
19 Porter (2008) 471.
20 Clarke (1945); the indispensable Stray (1998a); Goldhill (2002); Tilley (1938); the canonical histories of classical scholarship by Sandys (1906–1908); von Wilmowitz-Moellendorff (1921), translated into English, with an introduction by Lloyd-Jones, as von Wilamowitz-Moellendorff (1982); Pfeiffer (1968).
21 Stedman Jones (1972) 112; see also Cartledge (1995) 76.
22 *The Ancient Lowly*, first published by Charles H. Kerr, America's oldest radical bookseller, was repeatedly re-published; the 1907 reprint helped to educate a whole generation of American and British socialists between the two Russian revolutions of 1905 and 1917. The archive holding Ward's papers in the New York Public Library contains his membership card in the International Workingman's Association, dated 1870 and signed by Karl Marx. Thanks to Sara Monoson for help on Ward.
23 See, e.g. the canonical studies and collections of Turner (1991), Jenkyns (1980) and (1991), Stray (1999) and Edwards (1999); more recently see, e.g. Eastlake (2019). The essays edited by Clarke (1989) on Hellenism and the British imagination are typical: they mostly address elite poetry, architecture, painting, public schools and cast-collecting.
24 Some include: Johnson (2019); White (2019); Goff (2014); Hall, Alston and McConnell (2011); Lambert (2011); Orrells, Bhambra and Roynon (2011); Hall and Vasunia (2010); Hardwick and Gillespie (2010); Goff and Simpson (2007).
25 On Jane Ellen Harrison see Peacock (1988) and Beard (2002); see also McManus (2017) and Prins (2017).
26 Milner (1999) 9.
27 Sayer (2005) 200–1. See also Driscoll (2009).
28 Sayer (2005) 211–12
29 See Konstan (1994) 47; Rose (1992); Hall (2018f).
30 Gilmour (1993) 42.
31 Stray (1998a); see also Stray (1998b). Some of Stray's arguments were anticipated in Wilkinson (1964), who was in turn influenced by Max Weber's analysis (1952) of the way that Chinese imperial administrators had traditionally been examined in arcane Chinese classical literary texts. See also Lawton (1975) 60–1; Larson (1999); Vasunia (2005).
32 Greenwood (2010); McConnell (2013); Rankine (2006); Ronnick (2004), (2005), (2006) and (2016).
33 Hall (2007b), (2008b), (2008c), (2008d), (2014), (2018a) and (2018b).

34 For the project website, designed by Stead, which contains much additional information and research results, see www.classicsandclass.info.
35 Although we have collaborated on every single topic and paragraph in the book, the first full drafts of Chapters 1, 2, 5, 6, 7, 10, 11, 12, 13, 14, 16, 17, 19, 21 and 24 were written by Hall, and of 3, 4, 8, 9, 11, 15, 18, 20, 22 and 25 by Stead. Chapter 23 was a joint composition from the start.
36 Aberdeen Grammar School (1807–1855).
37 Rapple (2017) 120–2.
38 Altick (1957); Rose (2001); see also Webb (1955).
39 E.g. Krishnamurthy (2009a).
40 Darnton (1980).
41 Bouwsma (1981).
42 Grafton (2006).
43 See especially Bourdieu's *Distinction: A Social Critique of the Judgement of Taste* (1984), originally published in French in 1979 and *Language and Symbolic Power* (English translation, 1992). See Abrams (1992); Aron (2006); Baumgarten (1997); Driscoll (2009); Furuland and Svedjedal (2006); Ragon (1974); Roberts (2002); Ronnick (2004); Treue (1978); Vicinus (1974); Krevens (2001); Lenhart (2006); and more recently Savage et al. (2015); Friedman and Laurison (2019).
44 Morton quoted in Cornforth (1978) 7.
45 See Hall (2019).
46 Quoted in Eakin (2001).
47 Dunbar (2010).
48 Murray (1889) 13.
49 Reid (1981) 5–6.
50 See the model proposed by Shiach (1989), which obscures the real class divisions underlying the exponential growth in cultural output and accessible 'popular' publications during this era, and draws on the Russian Formalist notion of 'the dominant', on which see Newton (1997) 6–10.
51 Giddens (1973), especially Chapters 3–5; see also Saunders (1990) 22–3.
52 Lenhart (2006) 4–5.
53 On the complexity of subjective signifiers of class produced by different media and genres, for differing consumers, see Marwick (1990), especially 10–16.
54 Anon. (1913). Chapter 11 below clarifies some reasons why Greek would have been on the agenda in this part of Scotland.
55 Briggs (1994) 10. The first edition was first published in 1983.
56 Hobbes (1651) 111.
57 Jefferson (1784 [1772]) 271–4.
58 Arnold (1882)186; see Rapple (2017) 144–6.
59 Morton (1964 [1938]).
60 Kingsley (1898 [1850]) vol. II, 195. See Crust (2016) 13, and, on Cooper, further pp. 287–9 below.
61 Morton (1964 [1938]) 12.
62 Hall, Holmes-Henderson and Corke-Webster (forthcoming); Stead (forthcoming).
63 Hall (2015e). The Gaisford lecture can be viewed at https://podcasts.ox.ac.uk/gaisford-2015-lecture-pearls-swine-past-future-greek. See also Hall (2014a).
64 For some radical English uses of classical ideas in the Early Modern period, see Nelson (2004); Cartledge (2016) 283–7.
65 Morley (2018) 130.

2

THE INVENTION OF CLASSICS AND THE EMERGENCE OF CLASS

What does 'Classics' mean?

Pagan Latin and (to a far lesser extent) Greek authors were read by English-speaking elites long before. But British Classics, under that title and as we know it today, was born as a discipline during the period between the Glorious Revolution and the mid-18th century. This was against the background of the Bill of Rights, the circumscription of the powers of the monarchy, the Whig and Anglican ascendancy and, in 1707, the Act of Union. This chapter traces the emergence of the label and of the closely related term *class* to designate a social, economic and political status. It enquires into the reasons why they emerged when they did, and explores some challenges made to the claim of the wealthier 'gentlemen' class, on account of the difficulty of the ancient languages and the costly leisure required to acquire them, to exclusive ownership of classical authors.[1]

Thomas Brown (Figure 2.1), a brilliant satirist, translator and a major influence on Swift, Addison and Steele, was also known to be a linguistic innovator.[2] His *Letters from the Dead to the Living*, which are informed by Lucian of Samosata's satirical *Dialogues of the Dead*, include one written by a fictional physician. 'Giuseppe Hanesio, High-German Doctor and Astrologer' records from the Underworld the many cures he had effected when he was alive. His patients had included Pope Innocent XI and the Sophy of Persia. He had also cured the Mughal emperor 'Aurung-Zebe' of *epilepsia fanatica*: 'by my *Cephalick Snuff* and *Tincture*, I made him as clear headed a Rake as ever got drunk with Classics at the University, or expounded *Horace* in *Will's* Coffee-House'.[3] The joke here is that the notorious religious intolerance of the fanatical Aurung-Zebe (Muhi-ud-Din Muhammad) had been deactivated by making him the opposite of clear-headed. He had been made as confused as rakish students reading classical authors at

DOI: 10.4324/9781315446608-3

FIGURE 2.1 Thomas Brown (1762–1704), from Caulfield (1819) v.1, reproduced by courtesy of The British Library.

the university, 'Classics' here apparently meaning, rather than ancient authors or texts, his fellow students and perhaps tutors of Greek and Latin themselves.

Brown had an axe to grind against university teachers of ancient languages. He was born into a relatively poor Shropshire household. His father, a farmer, died when he was eight. He was only educated because his county offered free schooling at that time. By scholarships he proceeded to Christ Church, only to develop an aversion to the then-Dean, Dr. John Fell, a disciplinarian. The story goes that Brown, who loved to drink, was about to be expelled, but Fell challenged him to translate Martial I.32. A literal translation of this poem would run, 'I do not love you, Sabidius, and I am unable to tell you why. All I can say is this: I do not love you'.[4] Brown is said to have responded,

> I do not love you, Dr Fell,
> But why I cannot tell;
> But this I know full well,
> I do not love you, Dr Fell.[5]

Brown, to whom the discussion will return later in this chapter, left Oxford without a degree. He eked out an income to support his libertine lifestyle, first as a schoolmaster in Kingston-upon-Thames and then as a Grub Street writer and translator. His own experience of rakishly getting drunk on or with 'Classics' at university surely lies behind that early instance of the term.

Less than 70 years previously, 'classics' could still mean 'war trumpets' or 'trumpets-calls', as the neuter noun *classicum*, plural *classica*, did in canonical ancient authors.[6] In 1635 King Charles I commissioned an epic poem on his predecessor Edward III's achievements from Thomas May, renowned translator of Lucan's *Civil War*. In one passage May draws a comparison with the impact made by Julius Caesar's army in France long ago,

> When dreadfull Classicks in all parts were heard,
> And threatning Eagles every where appear'd.[7]

By 'dreadfull Classicks' being heard in parts, May does not mean that Caesar subjected the Gauls to long recitations of ancient Greek and Latin literary works.

What have military trumpets to do with either class or Classics? When the Romans heard their Latin noun *classis*, from which was derived that word for trumpet, *classicum*, it contained a resonance that we do not hear when we say either Classics or class: deriving from the same root as the verb *clamare* ('call out'), a *classis* consisted of a group of people 'called out' or 'summoned' together by trumpets. It could be the men in a meeting, or in an army or the ships in a fleet. The word has always been associated with Servius Tullius, the sixth of the legendary kings of early Rome, who was thought to have held the first census in order to find out, for the purposes of military planning, what assets his people possessed (Livy I.42–.4). This explains the ancient association of the term class with an audible call to arms. Yet, by not long into the 18th century, the term was adopted in order to distinguish different strata within English society: in 1796 the radical democrat John Thelwall refers to the treatment of the different 'classes' by Servius Tullius when trying to arouse the British working class to imitate the French revolutionaries.[8] (Figure 2.2) The working poor of England began to be called members of 'the lower classes' rather than just 'the poor' or members of 'the lower orders'. The word 'poor' was too imprecise; the notion of hierarchical 'orders' too inflexible and too infused with medieval and feudal notions of birth-rank to accommodate the unprecedented new levels of social mobility.

The language of 'rank' lingered in John Locke's *Some Thoughts Concerning Education* (1693), written at the precise moment when 'Classics' was being invented as a subject label: 'that most to be taken Care of is the Gentleman's Calling. For if those of that rank are once set right, they will quickly bring the rest into order'.[9] A new definition of the 'Gentleman' can be seen at work here (see below, pp. 29–33), but alongside the old term 'rank', the term *class*, which (like its ancient prototype) implied a status with an economic basis rather than an inherited rank, was a result of the incipient erosion, during the early industrial revolution, of the transparent and relatively stable hierarchical ranking system which had earlier governed the English social structure.[10] The French

FIGURE 2.2 'Copenhagen House', A drawing by James Gillray of John Thelwall speaking at a Corresponding Society Meeting at Spa Fields in London (1795). Public Domain.

and German languages soon imitated the English one, often replacing the terms *état* and *Stand* with *classe* and *Klasse*. Nevertheless, for most of the 18th century the labouring and artisanal classes were often spoken of as a mass of 'commoners' or 'common people'. The term 'working classes', in the plural as a category including workers in industry, agriculture, craft, itinerant trade and domestic service, as well as unemployed people who could only hope to find work in those spheres, first appears at the time of the French Revolution.[11] By 1815 the now-familiar double-barrelled terms 'middle classes' and 'working classes' had become accepted parlance.[12] The more modern socio-economic usage emerged when writers such as Robert Owen began to employ the formulation 'working class/es' within widely read essays and journals in the second decade of the 19th century.[13] The plural *the Classics*, meanwhile, had been used in English by 1679, as we shall see, to designate the corpus of Greek and Latin literature.

It is to the legendary first census that there must also be traced the origins of the term Classics. In Servius' scheme, the men in the top of his six classes—the men with the most money and property—were called the *classici*. The 'Top Men' were 'Classics'. This is why the late 2nd-century CE Roman miscellanist Aulus Gellius, could, by metaphorical extension, call the Top Authors 'Classic Authors', *scriptores classici*. This was to distinguish them from inferior or metaphorically 'proletarian' authors, *scriptores proletarii* (*Noctes Attici* XIX.8.15). Gellius recalls Cornelius Fronto exhorting him and another author that, when they were in doubt whether a noun should be singular or plural, to do as follows:

> Ite ergo nunc et, quando forte erit otium, quaerite an 'quadrigam' et 'harenas' dixerit e cohorte illa dumtaxat antiquiore vel oratorum aliquis vel poetarum, id est classicus adsiduusque aliquis scriptor, non proletarius.
>
> So go now and investigate, when you happen to have spare time, whether any more antique orator or poet has used *quadriga* or *harenae*, provided that he is a writer of class and substance, not a proletarian one.

The metaphors are even more specific than that: *classicus adsiduusque*, here translated 'of class and substance', could equally well be translated 'of the taxpaying class', one specific meaning of the term *adsiduus*.

Every tradition of writing, art, music and sport—English Literature, Dutch painting, Jazz, motorcycles, horse races—now claims its own 'Classics', and in the case of English Literature, this custom began in the early 18th century not long after it was applied to texts in ancient Greek and Latin.[14] But the most venerated Classics amongst all others have always been the authors of Greece and Rome—the supposed *primi inter pares* or 'first amongst equals' when compared with all the cultural *Classici* produced in world history. In its earliest instances, there is an additional definite article *the* prefixed to the term Classics, enacting a final sub-division by which the most elite texts of all can be identified by the few refined individuals supposedly able to appreciate them. The unit at Harvard University which studies these Greek and Roman 'Hyper-Classics' still styles itself 'The Department of the Classics'.

The involvement, historically, of the study of Greece and Rome in the maintenance of socio-economic hierarchies is thus obvious in the very title Classics. Over the last three decades some scholars have considered abandoning it altogether, and replacing it with a label such as 'Study of the ancient Mediterranean' or 'Study of Greek and Roman antiquity' or even, in jest, 'Ancientry'.[15] Their motive has been to expand the study of the ancient communities where Greek and Latin were spoken to include all the other languages and peoples who shared this world, from Sumerians, Nubians, Phoenicians and Carthaginians to Gauls, Batavians and Etruscans. But surely the class connotation of the nomenclature *Classics* is ideologically just as objectionable as the ethnic one that privileges Greek and Latin over other ancient tongues.

The *Attic Nights* was a favourite Renaissance and Early Modern text, first printed in 1469.[16] By 1602, the adjective classic, variously spelt classick, classicke and classique, is found occasionally, if only in scholarly contexts, to describe a canonical author or text of any era: William Perkins writes in a theological work written in 1602, 'Neither Plinie (who writ after Paul) nor any other ancient classique author, doth make mention of Phrigia'.[17] He needs to distinguish between 'ancient' classic authors and more recent ones, and seems to include St. Paul's epistles amongst 'classical' works. Amongst scholarly writers, we find the term classic qualifying 'folio' in 1628,[18] and a 'word' in the Latin language in 1646.[19] By 1645, with the circulation in European circles of the Greek treatise *On the Sublime* attributed to Longinus (the first English translation, by John Hall, was published in 1652), Sir Dudley North fuses the idea of a top literary *class* derived from Aulus Gellius with the new interest in sublimity: 'Farre more sublime and better Authours have discovered as little order, and as much repetition; witnesse the Collections of Marcus Aurelius, St. Augustines Confessions, and some of a higher Classe'.[20] By 1694, the former Archbishop of Canterbury Willian Sancroft can be praised posthumously by another divine for having been 'an admirable Critic in all the Antient and Classic Knowledge, both among the Greeks and Romans', although here, too, the words 'Antient and Classic' probably include biblical literature.[21]

The inclusion of biblical literature and patristic writers in the category of 'classic' authors persisted in some quarters for decades. Anthony Blackwall, the author of an influential 1718 *An Introduction to the Classics; Containing a Short Discourse on their Excellencies and Directions how to Study them to Advantage*, felt impelled to correct any impression that he was disrespecting Christian texts with a long essay on the subject seven years later in 1725. Its title is *The Sacred Classics Defended and Illustrated; or, An Essay Humbly offer'd towards proving the Purity, Propriety, and true Eloquence of the Writers of the New Testament.* The title page further eleborates the arguments: in the first part, 'those Divine Writers are vindicated against the Charge of barbarous Language, false Greek, and Solecisms'. The second part shows

> that all the Excellencies of Style, and sublime Beauties of Language and genuine Eloquence to abound in the Sacred Writers of the New Testament, With an Account of their Style and Character, and a Representation of their Superority, in several instances, to the best Classics of Greece and Rome.

Naming a discipline

By late in the 17th century, the plural noun with a definite article, 'the Classics', begins, infrequently, to mean both texts written in antiquity by non-Christian ancient authors in Latin and ancient Greek, and the authors of these texts. The 17th-century examples, however, remain few. The earliest we have identified appears when a schoolmaster writes to an implied specialist audience of teachers. His book is a guide to Latin syntax published in 1679, authored by one Jonathan Bankes. The author's intention was to simplify the famous 16th-century Latin grammar of William Lyly: the full title is *Januae clavis* ['Key to the door'] *or, Lilly's syntax explained its elegancy from good authors cleared, its fundamentals compared with the Accidence, and the rules thereof more fitted to the capacity of children.* In the preface,

Bankes explains the system he has used for explaining the different types of verb: 'The Rules … are explain'd by adding the *Verbs* … whose variety is shewn, and whose difficulties are cleared by contracted sentences out of the *Classics*'.[22] So there it is, although of course 'the Classics' here means authors or books in classical Latin rather than both Latin and Greek.

By 1684, at least in educational contexts, 'the Classics' can mean ancient authors or texts *including* Greek ones as studied by well-to-do junior males. That year, a translation of Eutropius' *Breviarium historiae Romanae* was published, and its authorship credited to 'several young gentlemen privately educated in Hatton-Garden'.[23] Hatton Garden was a new residential development off Holborn, with splendid houses, favoured by the rich wishing to flee the squalor of the old city after it had succumbed to a bout of plague in 1665 and been ravaged by the Great Fire of 1666. The Eutropius translation, apparently the first into English, served as an advertisement for their school. It was prefaced by a poem entitled 'To the ingenious translators', and praising their efforts, by the Irish poet Nahum Tate (whose adaptations of Shakespearean plays were currently all the rage in London): 'Auspicious Youths, our Ages Hope, and Pride, / Exalted minds'. Tate praises their teacher while regretting his own less happy experience of reading ancient authors: he had been

> by Pedants led astray,
> Who at my setting out mistook the way.
> With Terms confounded (such their methods were)
> Those rules my Cloud, that should have been my Star:
> Yet groping forwards **through the Classicks** went,
> Nor wholly of my Labors may repent.

Later in the poem he recommends that they read not only Cicero but Demosthenes.[24]

The prose preface to this fascinating volume is by the Hatton Garden schoolmaster, Lewis Maidwell (1650–1715), one of Dryden's correspondents. It is dedicated to John Lowther, 2nd Baronet of Whitehaven in Cumbria, who spent some of the vast income he derived from the coal pits there on sending his two sons to the school. They were amongst the translators.[25] Its list of excellent things the boys may find in ancient authors includes material which shows they might expect to study Homer, Plutarch and Dionysius of Halicarnasssus, who is quoted, briefly, in Greek. Maidwell argues that England is lacking a system of education for boys which is making sufficient use of their intellectual potential: if more fathers took their sons' education seriously, 'the sleepy Genius of our Nation would rouse itself … Your nice assistance in Education well imitated, might adorn our Country within itself, and save many the trouble of dry-nursing their Youth abroad'. He specifies France and Italy.[26]

Yet the impact of French scholarship can be seen at work even in Mr Maidwell's school for proudly English boys. This translation was published the year after the

Delphin edition of Eutropius, the work of Madame Dacier.[27] The 25 Delphin volumes of Latin texts, with Latin commentary by 39 scholars, were commissioned for Louis, le Grand Dauphin, beginning in 1670. The editions were masterminded by the duc de Montausier, the dauphin's governor, and the Jesuit-trained scholar Pierre Daniel Huet, with a team including both Anne Dacier and her husband André. They transformed educational practice and intellectual life across Europe.[28] One of the authors published early in the series, in 1681, three years before Maidwell's students' Eutropius, had been Aulus Gellius himself.[29]

The impact of the Delphin series can be seen from a different, comic perspective, in 1712. Richard Steele published a satirical article in the *Spectator* containing what he claimed were letters he had recently received from two schoolboys. One of them, a 14-year-old, complains that his father, although wealthy, does not think that training in ancient authors will do his son any good, and will not buy him the (expensive) books he needs to further his studies of Latin authors: our teenager laments, 'All the Boys in the School, but I, have the Classick Authors in usum Delphini, gilt and letter'd on the Back'.[30] By 1712, acquisition of the famous French 'Delphin Classics' series had become indispensable to what was beginning to be called 'a classical education'.

They remained so until 1819, despite the launch of rival series,[31] when they were superseded by the new series of well over 100 leather-and-gilt volumes of *The Latin Writings after the system of the Delphin Classics, with Variorum Notes*, masterminded by the entrepeneurial Abraham J. Valpy, who hired editors including George Dyer (see below pp. 169–71). By this time, some regarded the Delphin editions as allowing boys to 'cheat' insofar as they contained easier Latin paraphrases in the margins. Valpy used texts from diverse sources, added his own critical apparatus, and combined information from the Delphin editions with updated matter from other series. In Hardy's *Jude the Obscure*, Jude Fawley's attempts to teach himself Classsics draw on Hardy's own experience as the son of a rural stonemason who struggled to further his classical education while apprenticed to an ecclesiastical architect.[32] In chapter 5, Jude is given a decrepit horse and a creaky cart to deliver bread near Marygreen. He sits with a dictionary on his knees, and a crumbling Delphin edition of a Latin author, Caesar, Virgil or Horace, which he could just about afford

> because they were superseded, and therefore cheap. But, bad for idle schoolboys, it did so happen that they were passably good for him. The hampered and lonely itinerant conscientiously covered up the marginal readings, and used them merely on points of construction, as he would have used a comrade or tutor who should have happened to be passing by.[33]

A key agent in shaping the early 18th-century fashion for the classical curriculum, when the Delphin Classics were cutting-edge, was Henry Felton, in his *A Dissertation on Reading the Classics, and Forming a Just Style*, written in 1709 and published four years later. Felton had been educated at Charterhouse and St.

Edmund Hall, Oxford. He wrote the work as domestic chaplain to the Duke of Rutland, and dedicated the work to his pupil, John, Lord Roos, later the third Duke. It embeds its recommendations for imitating the example of the classic writers not only in style but in the morality of the great men they portrayed and the distinctive new vocabulary surrounding the new 18th-century concept of the gentleman: civility and politeness.[34]

The book cites the rhetorical handbooks of Cicero, Quintilian, Longinus and Aristotle as its ancient forerunners, but places itself at a particular time and place in its advocacy of the Classics. It celebrates the Duke of Marlborough's successes in Belgium and France; it talks at length about the need for a new, politer, more civil style of speaking and writing than had prevailed in the Restoration period. It insists that all education needs to be subservient to the duties of the Christian religion, but also that 'humane' education can be immeasurably enriched by the study of the Classics:[35]

> Your Lordship will meet with great and wonderful Examples of an irregular and mistaken Virtue in the *Greeks* and *Romans*; with many Instances of Greatness of Mind, of unshaken Fidelity, Contempt of human Grandeur, a most passionate Love of their Country, Prodigality of Life, Disdain of Servitude, inviolable Truth, and the most publick disinterested Souls, that ever threw off all Regards in Comparison with their Country's Good; Your Lordship will discern the Flaws and Blemishes of their farest Actions, see the wrong Apprehensions they had of Virtue, and be able to point them right, and keep them within their proper Bounds. Under this Correction Your Lordship may extract a generous and noble Spirit from the Writings and Histories of the Ancients. And it would in a particular Manner recommend the *Classic Authors* to your Favour, and they will recommend themselves to Your Approbation.

Felton's pedagogical handbook was popular for the next 40 years, running into 5 editions and numerous reprints, playing a seminal role in the establishment of the Classics as the polite and refined curriculum for any aspiring gentleman.

A curriculum for gentlemen

By 1715, socio-economic class appears in discussions of the correct content of education for a gentleman, for example in *The Gentleman's Library, Containing Rules for Conduct in All Parts of Life*: the author answers the hypothetical objection that 'the refin'd Education' he is recommending 'is calculated but for One Class of People: That I have accommodated my precepts to the Rich alone, and neglected to sute them to the Children of the Plebean'. He answers that every father should 'consult his Fortune and Circumstances' and *Cut his Coat according to his Cloath*'.[36] The volume assumes a classically educated reader: its Latin and Greek quotations from a wide range of authors are often untranslated.

The modish new syllabus prompted many publishing ventures. John Pointer's new textbook *Miscellanea in Usum Juventutis Academicae* of 1718 provided everything a schoolmaster might need—instructions for 'Reading the Classick Authors', 'A Chronology of the Classick Authors', 'A Catalogue of the Best Classick Authors and their Best Editions', information on pagan mythology and Latin exercises. The maturing discipline in turn prompted the publication of a new genre of book designed to help the teacher in his tasks. These involved not only the grammatical, syntactical and rhetorical explication of the texts but also the classroom discussion of the myths, religion and geography to be found in them and occasionally even their aesthetic value and material objects and artworks which could illuminate them.[37] And, by 1736, we find the term 'class' in its modern, socio-economic sense being used alongside 'Classics'. It occurs in a polemic questioning the point of asking boys to spend such a large proportion of the hours available for education on acquiring proficiency in the ancient languages, when reading relevant material, such as newspapers, had a more obvious application to the aspiring businessman.[38]

> Teachers are "as capable of contributing to the Welfare or Prejudice of a State, as any of the several **Classes** of Men of which it is composed" … . Learning Latin, especially how to compose verses in Latin, inculcates no skills useful to business. Better to read newspapers instead: several famous writers "spell and write English perfectly (better than others who have read the **Classics**), tho' they are quite ignorant of Latin".

This adventure in lexical history leaves us with a question: *why* did Classics/the Classics acquire its new name, identity and function in this precise period of British history, when a new ruling order was being created?[39] One factor is that education was being discussed with a new self-consciousness. The thinkers influential in the 18th century were united in stressing the importance of education, whatever their views of what its contents should be, from Locke to Rousseau, Shaftesbury to Johnson. But British educators, while imitating the French, were also keen after the Glorious Revolution to *distinguish* the new Anglican gentlemanly classical curriculum from the Continental model, *especially* the French one. The French *querelle* between the ancients and the moderns was transformed to suit local English literature,[40] and the rise of the Classics and Dryden's translation of Virgil are inseparable from that cultural dispute. There was also a debate on whether boys should be educated at home or at school. The *Spectator*'s educational expert, Budgell, found Locke's preference for home-schooling unrealistic.[41] Swift strongly favoured school education.[42] Even the über-aristocrat Lord Chesterfield sent his son to Westminster for three years. But the most significant factor was socio-economic: the rise of a new Whiggish mercantile segment of the ruling class. This process, which was beginning to transform Britain, is often subsumed by historians under terms like 'emergence of the bourgeoisie': it entailed the appearance of the anonymous-exchange market and the evolution of what Jürgen Habermas defined as the 'bourgeois public sphere' (*bürgerliche Őffentlichheit*), accompanied by an explosion in printed communication and accelerating urbanisation.[43]

Most importantly, the Whiggish sons of tradesmen and the Tory sons of hereditary nobles were increasingly being schooled *together*.[44] Classics emerged to provide a curriculum which could bestow a shared concept of gentlemanliness upon them all. The 18th century saw exponential growth in private boarding schools, mostly small and run by Anglican priests, offering a classical curriculum aiming to provide the patina of gentlemanliness and access to Oxford and Cambridge.[45] In early 17th-century England, the sons of gentry had often been educated beside merchants' children at town grammar schools, but after the Restoration they were educated at home by tutors, or sent to one of the tiny group of richly endowed public schools.[46] Divisions had become very visible in education. A fresh tone and model of manliness was required for the new and heterogeneous audience after the Bill of Rights 1689.

A new species of gentry among the merchant sector bought land and wanted prestige and a high 'class'. In this context of the contestation of status and social mobility, substantial wealth had become attainable by a wider sector of the literate population and they wanted cultural capital and the status of gentlemen to match:

> In a society which has become more superciliously class-conscious than in earlier centuries, those already privileged to belong to this class, guard its frontiers with a fastidious sensitiveness to the subtleties of class distinctions; at the same time, an increasing number of new aspirants made attempts to climb into the privileged territory.[47]

And once they had made it, they usually began to exclude those who had not, to ensure themselves safe positions high up the social hierarchy.

The process whereby youths from landed and mercantile families are fused into a collective of gentlemen by reading Classics is literally enacted in the Reverend Thomas Spateman's three-part play for use in schools, *The School-Boy's Mask* (1742). This traces the careers of a group of men, born into aristocratic, professional and business backgrounds, from their schooldays to old age. The boys who don't read their Classics at school or in young adulthood (Rakish, Tinsel, Wild-Rogue, Fondler) become boorish louts who mix with prostitutes, acquire debts and die miserable early deaths in drunken squalor and poverty. The aristocrat who models himself on the heroes of Plutarch and Cornelius Nepos (Lord Grand-Clerck) founds a charitable infirmary and is rewarded with a dukedom. Bookish and Goodwill excel in Oxbridge classical studies and eventually become a Bishop and Lord Chancellor, respectively. Even their less talented friend, Rival, by working hard at his classical books and eschewing vice, lays the foundations of a successful career as a Doctor of Medicine.[48] The moral of the tale is brought out most explicitly by Lord Grandclerck, who says that classical education, the qualification of the true gentleman, needs to be difficult. The entrance to the 'delightful Land' of Learning is surrounded by thorns, 'to *keep off the great Vulgar, and the small;*' its fruits 'are too delicious to be gather'd by those who are not willing to be at some Labour to obtain them'.[49]

The concept of the gentleman was ambiguous. It might denote status, moral behaviour, or wealth (but only if invested in landed property); at other times the focus was refined manners and the good taste and 'polite' education becoming inseparable from education in the Classics.[50] In his 1742 novel *Joseph Andrews*, Henry Fielding directly asks whether a low-born man with a noble character and refined education was not as admirable as one who was genteel by birth: 'But suppose, for argument's sake, we should admit that he had no ancestors at all ... Would not this *autokopros* have been justly entitled to all the praise arising from his own virtues?'[51]

It emerges that it *was* only for the sake of argument that this possibility has been raised. Joseph is refined in conduct and principled, but can never, as an *autokopros*, become a gentleman. The term *autokopros* (never instanced in ancient Greek), invented by Fielding and glossed by him as 'sprung from a dunghill', links failure at gentlemanly status with a failure to know the ancient Greek language. Only someone who knew Greek could be familiar with the term he is imitating, *autochthōn*, the Athenians' own title glorifying the antiquity of their bloodline and its intimate relationship with the land they occupied. So only someone who trained in the gentlemanly classical curriculum could even understand why Joseph Andrews could never be a true gentleman after all.

In the 18th century, ideas about good breeding, honesty and good character were scrutinised in fiction as they shaped the revised concept of the 'Gentleman' as intimately bound up with education in the Classics, and thus different from the gentlemanly consummate courtier of the Renaissance.[52] Samuel Richardson's *Sir Charles Grandison* (1753) 'is a systematic attempt to devise every conceivable kind of situation in which an English gentleman may be called upon to display his gentlemanliness',[53] an aim which Richardson explicitly formulated in his preface. Fielding portrays depraved town gallants and brutal country 'gentlemen', but set against them a range of middle-class heroes—Parson Adams, Dr. Harrison, Squire Allworthy—whose moral characters, civility and kindness qualified them, even if they were not highborn, for the soubriquet of ideal gentlemen. Both Smollett's titular heroes Roderick Random and Peregrine Pickle desire to establish themselves as gentlemen, in novels where the author fulminates 'against the depravity vulgarity and sycophancy' of the born-and-bred upper classes of both Bath and London.[54]

From 1711 onwards, Addison, along with his collaborator Richard Steele, influenced the idea of the gentleman profoundly. Addison wanted *The Spectator* to proselytise for good breeding and for 'wit tempered with morality', 'effective among all the different sections of a rapidly growing middle class, as well as among the established upper class'.[55] He targetted the whole male reading public, including longstanding rivals and antagonists—men of the court, the town, the city and the country. These values were discussed and promulgated in public coffee houses and private clubs.[56] Simultaneously, the idea of *taste* emerges—a strange fusion of the aesthetic and the ethical, but tied to new forms of consumerism, including the book trade, the burgeoning entertainment industry,[57] the grand tour and the taste for the antique in architecture and internal décor. The 18th-century passion of the titled and rich for collecting classical or *al'antica* sculptures to grace their Palladian and neoclassical interiors, gardens, and alcoves was partly 'self-conscious expressions of refinement on the part of the owners, consistent with Lord Shaftesbury's idea of civic humanism: that to be truly virtuous one must display such refinement to spur like-minded individuals to honourable action'.[58] The visual arts of the ancient world were accessed in Britain through new compendia of prints, such as Domenico de Rossi's *Raccolta di statue antiche e moderne* (1704) or Jonathan Richardson's *An Account of Some of the Statues, Bas Reliefs, Drawings and Pictures in Italy* (1722), which served as a handbook for well-off grand tourists for centuries.[59]

People's Classics at the London Fairs

By the first decade of the 18th century, therefore, the study of ancient Roman and Greek authors had acquired the title by which we know it today, a set of desirable textbooks, and a status and role as the basis of the intellectual, cultural and moral education of the English (from 1707 the British) gentleman. This accompanied a new taste for the antique in other spheres than education. But the Classics were also being accessed differently, by city-dwellers of all social classes, in popular entertainments, some of which had transparently subversive overtones in terms of their celebration of working-class identity and self-fashioning. In particular, the working classes of London were given access to rowdy versions of canonical classical epic at their summer fairs.

The painted board at the centre of Hogarth's famous 'Southwark Fair' (painted in 1733 and engraved in 1734 or 1735) reads 'The Siege of Troy is here' (Figure 2.3). Hogarth had always been interested in the way that classical culture could be commodified. He opens his memoirs with the sad picture of his father, a classical scholar of repute, plunging his family into poverty after the failure of his project for a Latin dictionary.[60] Fairground theatre was a better business prospect. The show Hogarth portrays, performed amidst other colourful entertainments, was Elkanah Settle's 'droll', *The Siege of Troy*;[61] the woman just left of centre 'drumming up' business is either Mrs Mynn, the entrepreneurial show-woman who produced it, or her daughter Mrs Lee. In the droll, the Trojans, led by a plebeian cobbler named Bristle, survive the siege of Troy and hold a carousal. It was a favourite at the London Fairs from its première at Bartholomew Fair, probably in 1698, until at least 1734, when it was performed by two different companies—one of them using puppets—at Southwark Fair.

Settle had been a successful playwright. His productions had included a Restoration drama on a Herodotean theme, *Cambyses* (1666).[62] But he fell out of

FIGURE 2.3 'Southwark Fair' by William Hogarth (1733), from Hogarth (1833) 110, reproduced from copy in Hall's personal collection.

favour and shortage of funds drove him to accept the post of London 'City Poet', responsible for producing the pageants of the Lord Mayor's Show.[63] City pageants and fairground theatricals had much in common, besides their outdoor setting. The Lord Mayor's Show was traditionally held on October 29th. Contemporary sources speak of cartoonish images of faces stuck on windows, candle-lit balconies, and waves of soldiers, clowns and Company men in livery—vintners, brewers, butchers and apothecaries—jostling to take precedence in the procession, carrying symbols of their crafts.[64] Mumming and colourful costumes abounded: preparations for one of Settle's shows are described thus in 1705 by the satirist Thomas Brown:

> City-Poet instructing his Gods and Goddesses all the Morning, how to behave themselves in a Pageant, and welcome my Lord-Mayor. Cooks busie in raising Pye-crust Fortifications, which the Heroes of Cheap-side will storm most manfully next Day.[65]

Dead cats and joints of meat were hurled. Caged lions were displayed at the Tower and mad people at Bedlam. The mob could become riotous.[66] The atmosphere was similar to that of Bartholomew Fair, in the early 1700s still the largest fair. Its ancient function—to serve as a textile market—had largely been replaced, reports the eye-witness, by 'rioting and unlimited licence'. He describes 'the rumbling of Drums, mix'd with the intolerable Squalling of the Cat Calls and Penny Trumpets ... the Singeing of Pigs, and burnt Crackling of over Roasted Pork'.[67] From the upper floor of ale houses visitors enjoyed a view of the booths, and the actors 'strutting around their Balconies in their Tinsey Robes, and Golden Leather Buskins'; typical entertainments were rope-acrobats, sword-dancers, horse-vaulters, 'monstrous' freaks of nature (three-breasted women, three-legged cockerels) and performing dwarves.[68]

Fairground theatricals were a particular attraction since the two licensed theatres were closed during the fairs. As in Hogarth's picture, the booths offered a variety of entertainments. Mrs Mynn (or Mynns/Minns) ran a troupe of strolling players who certainly performed at the Cock-Pit in Epsom in 1708 and claimed to have performed 'at Windsor for the Entertainment of the Nobility'.[69] It is unknown when they first worked with Settle, but Theophilus Cibber states that he was

> the best contriver of machinery in England and for many years of the latter part of his life received an annual salary from Mrs Minns and her daughter Mrs Leigh, for writing Drolls for Bartholomew and Southwark Fairs, with proper decorations, which were generally so well contrived, that they exceeded those of their opponents in the same profession.[70]

The poet Dryden died on 12th May 1700. But he had lived to endure seeing Settle exploit the success of his own masterful translation of the *Aeneid* (1697), the publication of which had been nothing short of 'a national event'.[71] Settle's Trojan droll premièred in 1698 or 1699. There are two versions of the first printed edition of 1707. They claim respectively that its text represents the version of this 'Dramatick Performance', presented in Mrs. Mynn's Great Booth, 'over against the Hospital-Gate in the Rounds in Smithfield, during the Time of the Present Bartholomew-Fair' (i.e. in late August 1707) and 'in the Queens-Arms-Yard, near Marshallsea-Gate in Southwark, during the Time of the Fair' (i.e. in early September). (Figure 2.4.) But both texts have an identical preface 'To the Reader' informing us that *The Siege of Troy* 'made its first entry now Nine Years Since in Bartholomew Fair'. The current production is the third, and has had so much money and labour spent upon it that it is not inferior to any of the 'operas' performed in the Royal Theatres.[72]

The *Siege of Troy* has been called the 'most remarkable of the Bartholomew-Fair dramas which found their way into print'.[73] Its spectacular effects were agreed to have exceeded those of any other spectacle.[74] These effects, including the elephants, castles, temple and chariots, are carefully reconstructed from original sources in Sybil Rosenfeld's pathbreaking study *The Theatre of the London Fairs in the 18th Century*.[75] The script is fascinating in its subversive treatment of heroic epic and classical mythology. It enacts the Troy story as related in *Aeneid* II from the arrival at Troy of the wooden horse and the self-mutilated Sinon to the burning of the city and the Greeks' departure. The aristocratic and divine

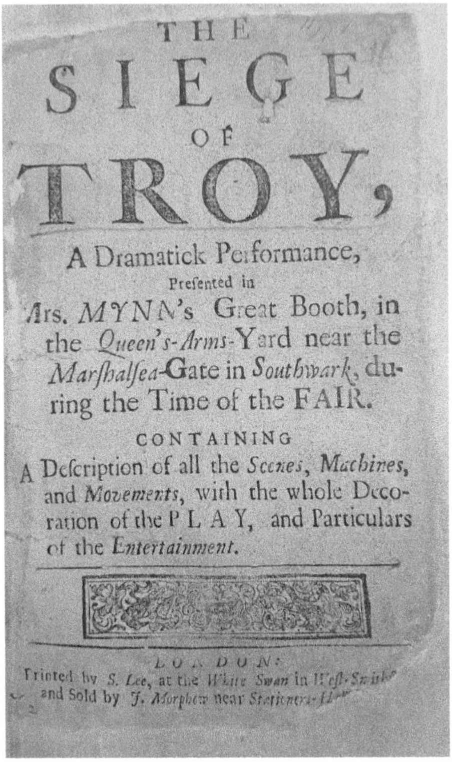
THE

SIEGE

OF

TROY,

A Dramatick Performance,

Presented in

Mrs. MYNN's Great Booth, in the *Queen's-Arms*-Yard near the *Marshalsea*-Gate in *Southwark*, during the Time of the FAIR.

CONTAINING

A Description of all the *Scenes*, *Machines*, and *Movements*, with the whole Decoration of the PLAY, and Particulars of the *Entertainment*.

LONDON:

Printed by *S. Lee*, at the *White Swan* in *West-Smith*

and Sold by *J. Morphew* near *Stationers-H*

FIGURE 2.4 Title page of Elkanah Settle's *The Siege of Troy* (1707), reproduced by courtesy of The British Library.

characters speak rhyming iambic couplets as they do in Dryden's *Aeneid* translation. Those from the Greek camp are Menelaus, Ulysses and Sinon; in Troy there are Paris, Helen, Cassandra and Venus. But a sense of how packed Mrs Mynn's booth platforms must have become, as indicated in Hogarth's depiction, is conveyed by the other 53 cast members listed under 'Actors' Names':

> A numerous Train of Trojan Mob, Spectators of the Wooden Horse and Actors through the Play … Three Persons drest in Gold for Statues in Diana's Temple. Nine Priests and Priestesses of Diana. Ten Persons richly drest, and Retinue of Paris and Helen. Twenty-two Officers, Guards and Trumpets, the Attendants of Menelaus. In the whole Fifty-three Persons drest, besides the Actors and Diana in the play.

The crucial element from the perspective of the droll's socio-political impact is that 'numerous Train of Trojan Mob', whose identity as 'Spectators of the Wooden Horse' is shared with the external audience of the droll. Some of that

Mob have sizeable speaking parts, and these characters, although nominally Trojan, come over as working-class city-dwellers indistinguishable from Settle's own public.

In 1614, Ben Jonson had laughed at the taste for introducing such a contemporary frame to classical mythical stories in the puppet-show in the final act of *Bartholomew Fair*, 'The ancient moderne history of Hero, and Leander, otherwise called The Touchstone of true Loue, with as true a tryall of friendship, betweene Damon, and Pythias, two faithfull friends o' the Bankside' (Act V scene 3).[76] Rosenfeld concludes that the 'populace could not be trusted to stand too much of the classical legend even though it was accompanied by scenic marvels; the comedians had to be brought on to amuse them with the rough and tumble life they knew'.[77] But another way of looking at the fusion of past and present in the world created by the droll is as a complex metatheatrical response, in a cross-class context, to the elite connotations of the classical material. There are two collectives responding to upper-class antique heroics, the Trojans within the play and the Londoners in the audience. The boundary between them is jeopardised.

In the second scene we are transported to 'Bristle, a cobler, and his wife'. These lower-class Trojans speak raucous prose. Mrs Bristle wants to go and see the wooden horse, but her husband Tom Bristle objects to her leaving the house:[78]

> *W:* Well, I am resolv'd I will go abroad, and see this sight, though the Devil stay at home and piss out the Fire.
>
> *Br:* Will you so! Then I'm resolv'd I'll give your Whores Hide such a lick of Styrup Leather, till I make your own Devilship spit it out.

Fortunately for Mrs Bristle, the Trojan Mob enters and she escapes domestic violence. In a magnificent spectacle, Paris and Helen now appear riding in a 'Triumphant Chariot', drawn by elephants painted on the flats. Ten more painted elephants support ten castles crowded with richly dressed attendants, with a vista of Troy beyond. Paris and Helen admire each other in rhyming couplets. A crazed Cassandra enters to condemn the adulterous pair, before Venus descends in a swan-drawn chariot and the attendants sing a celestial chorus.[79]

In Act II, Ulysses and Sinon persuade the Trojan mob, now led by Bristle who has appointed himself their Captain, to breach the Trojan Walls and drag in the horse. Cassandra is distraught, and performs miracles designed to 'preach bright Reason' to Paris. The next spectacular scene 'discovers the Temple of Diana' at Troy, complete with eleven golden statues of the Olympian gods, including Diana, and a heavenly vista. When Paris and Helen arrive, Cassandra waves her wand, and the statues' costumes miraculously turn black as the vista 'is changed to a scene of Hell'. But only the audience and Cassandra can discern the truth of this transformation: Paris and the Priest see nothing altered, and agree that she is insane.[80]

The vertiginous alternation between heroic and demotic is underlined by the next scene change to a street in Troy. The Greek army, streaming out of the

Trojan horse, disperses to begin its work of destruction; Captain Bristle and the Mob, unaware of the danger, enter for a night of revelry and fantasies of social levelling:[81]

> *Enter* Mob *drunk.*
> 1 *Mob.* Well, Captain, we have a tory rory Night on't.
> *Cap.* Ay Neighbour, the Noble Prince *Paris* has made all the Conduits in the Town piss Claret, and given such Feasting and Toping, and fidling and Roaring, till we are all Princes as great as himself.
> *All.* Ay, ay, all Princes, all Princes.

As they carouse, the siege ensues, the Grecians setting fire to houses and abducting maidens. Menelaus slays Paris; Helen commits suicide by hurling herself into the flames. But the members of the Trojan Mob led by Captain Tom Bristle survive. Menelaus pardons them:[82]

> … you've severely felt
> The Arm of vengeance, for your Princes Guilt;
> And do deserve our Pity.
> Here I have finisht my Revenge. Enjoy
> Your Lives and Liberties, go and rebuild your Troy.
> *Mob. Huzzah.*
> *Capt. Of the Mob* Hark ye, Friend, (*Speaking to a Grecian*) pray tell your King from me, he's a very civil Gentleman, and since he's so humbly Gracious, to bid us build our Town again, strike up Fiddles, we'll give him a Song and a Dance at parting.

The droll ends amidst revelry. Ulysses draws the moral that adulterous ladies endanger whole countries, a theme which has been reinforced by the extra-marital flirtations of Mrs Bristle.

The Siege of Troy is thus subversive on several levels. The blame for the Greek expedition against Troy is exclusively laid on the shoulders of Trojan royalty and the renegade Queen of Sparta. The royal culprits, Helen and Paris, both expire. The action ends with a Trojan working-class leader about to rebuild the city; this is radical enough in itself, but also repudiates the tradition of Troy's annihilation asserted by the canonical classical authorities Virgil and Homer. The aristocrats' rhyming couplets and elevated diction are deflated by juxtaposition with the indelicate dialogue of the Trojan commoners, who are given all the laughs. There is a further level of insouciance. Royal propaganda had associated William III with Aeneas, and his arrival on the sands of Torbay in 1688 with Aeneas' arrival in Latium; Dryden's publisher Jacob Tonson insisted on superimposing William's features on those of Aeneas when he reproduced in Dryden's *Aeneid* the engravings from John Ogilby's 1654 translation.[83] Settle omits Aeneas from his Trojan droll, thus avoiding offence to either Catholics or Anglicans amongst Mrs Mynn's customers. But in 1698, by refusing to use Troy to pay homage to the King, he threw into further relief his rejection of Aeneas as hero of the tale and preference for the plebeian cobbler. Moreover, the invention of the identifiably London/Trojan hybrid Bristle gives a makeover to the familiar story of Brutus the Trojan who had founded London as the 'New Troy'; the political message of a working class with a continuous identity and recreational culture (note 'The Siege of Troy **is here!**' in the present tense on Hogarth's billboard) needs to be understood in the context of seven decades of serial changes in constitution and kings.

Settle's rivals were aggravated by his ability to make money from the same material (and even stage properties) to different audiences. His generic versatility also challenged customary distinctions between 'high' and 'low' arts, especially when he had the temerity to publish, in addition to the text of the Opera, attractive souvenir volumes containing the script of the droll, adorned with a woodcut depicting Captain Bristle.[84] But, as we shall see in Chapter 17, worse was to come. *The Siege of Troy* was turned into an even 'lower' medium than a fairground droll—an itinerant puppet show.

Whose Classics?

The new identity and desirability of training in the Classical languages, as an obligatory accoutrement of the Gentleman, had also, by as early as 1700, inspired an altercation between those who despised reading the classical authors in translation and those who advocated it. In this debate, the arguments anticipated by three centuries those put forward today in discussions about the best way to give the nation's youth access to the ancient world. Thomas Brown, the first man to use 'Classics' without a definite article, and the author of the colourful description of the Lord Mayor's Show quoted above, was also probably the author of a wonderful piece of English prose published in 1700, the 'Preface' to an anonymous book, *Lucian's Charon: or A Survey of The Follies of Mankind. Translated from the Greek. With Notes, and A Prefatory Dialogue in Vindication of Translations* (Figure 2.5). The dialogue itself is one of Lucian's most elegant little dramas: Charon ascends to the world of the living and is taken on a whistle-stop tour of archaic civilisation by Hermes. The 1700 preface, however, is an original dialogue between two men, Eumenes and Philenor, on the theme of studying classical literature in translation. The arguments put forward by Philenor are diverse and cogent.

Philenor has published a translation, thus disappointing Eumenes. Philenor points out that translation of Greek masterpieces was good enough for the Romans, since Cicero, Ennius, Pacuvius and so on had all been translators. But Eumenes is having none of it:

> *For certainly Translations are the greatest obstructions of Learning immaginable: for to what purpose shou'd Men be at the expence of so much time and pains in*

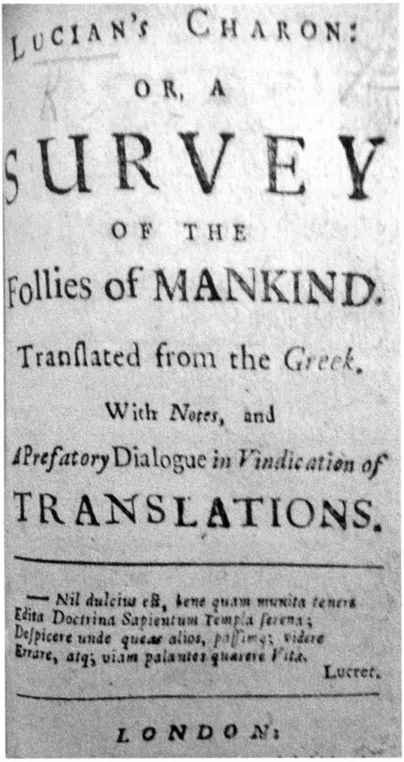

LUCIAN's CHARON:

OR, A

SURVEY

OF THE

Follies of MANKIND.

Tranſlated from the *Greek*.

With *Notes*, and

A Prefatory Dialogue *in Vindication of*

TRANSLATIONS.

— *Nil dulcius eſt, bene quam munita tenere*
Edita Doctrina Sapientum Templa ſerena;
Deſpicere unde queas alios, paſſimq; videre
Errare, atq; viam palantes quærere Vitæ.
Lucret.

LONDON:

FIGURE 2.5 Title page of *Lucian's Charon: or A Survey of The Follies of Mankind* (1700), reproduced by courtesy of The British Library.

> *studying Greek and Latine, when they may read the same Books in their Mother* Tongue?[85]

This is a curious case of putting the cart before the horse: we must not translate Greek and Latin into English *because it has cost so much effort to learn those ancient tongues.* Philenor sensibly responds that this does not represent an obstruction of learning. On the contrary, we '*shou'd think now that nothing in the World has a greater tendency to its advancement. Those rich Treasures of Knowledge & Learning among the Antients are no longer now lock'd up in unintelligible Words*'. Translating texts by the ancient Greeks and Romans into English

> "… has to our Country brought / All that they writ, and all they thought …" *Men may now* familiarly Converse *with the Wits of* Greece *and* Rome, *and that without the* laborious *and* ungrateful *Toil of Learning* Words & Syllables … *For now* Every Man *may hear* Plutarch *and* Tully, Homer *and* Virgil, Theocritus, Horace *and* Ovid, *and innumerable others, speaking in his* own

> Tongue *the wonderful works of* God *and Nature, the admirable Productions of Wit and Fancy, and what ever else may yield a grateful Satisfaction to noble and ingenious Minds.*

The patrician Eumenes plays the class card. If every man can read Plutarch and Cicero in his own native tongue, this will '*make Learning* common, cheap, *and* contemptible, *when every ordinary* Mechanick *shall be as well acquainted with these Authors as he that has spent* 10 *or* 12 *Years in the Universities?*' At the climax of his rant against reading ancient authors in translation, he cites the same proverbial pearls cast before swine that Edmund Burke was to invoke 90 years later, quoted at the opening of this book:

> *Those rich Treasures of* Knowledge *and* Learning *are now* unlock'd *indeed, and scattered abroad among the* Rabble; *and the mischief on't is, we do but* cast Pearls before Swine who will trample them under their Feet, and turn again and rent us: *for they have not* Capacities *to* understand *'em so as to* value *them, but just so much only as to make 'em* Conceited *and despise all the World as* illeterate *and* ignorant.[86]

Philenor points out that Eumenes looks upon

> Mechanicks *only as meer* Animals, *not considering that many who understand not* Greek *and* Latine *are yet more* truly wise *than your Learned* Criticks *and* Gramarians ... *A Man may be learned in the* Languages *and expert in all the* Sciences, *& yet be as great a* Fool *as others.*[87]

He quotes Montaigne to the effect when you observe the young men 'when they are newly come from the Universities, all that you will find they have got is, that their *Latine* and *Greek* has only made 'em greater and more conceited Coxcombs than when they went from home'.[88] And he triumphs when he argues that one of his aims has been to '*excite*' the desire of readers to improve their knowledge of the ancient language.[89] The pearls of ancient culture will not be besmirched by the swine forming the multitude. Whether consumed in fairgrounds or through mother-tongue translations, they just might edify and delight them instead.

Conclusion

By the end of the second decade of the 18th century, the battle-lines which still shape debates over Classics had been drawn up. Classics, along with the textbooks required to study it, had emerged as a product that could be purchased by any parent with the money to keep his son in education, rather than remunerative work, late into his teens. It did not matter whether the money was 'old' and related to land-ownership, or 'new' and related to colonial ventures or commerce, since the appearance of competence in Classics bestowed the status of a gentleman and a guarantee of his good taste and moral refinement. The length of time it took sometimes reluctant children and youths to acquire apparent competence in classical languages was central to its attraction, since proficiency in them obliquely drew attention to the financial prosperity, as well as the gentility and good taste of the family paying for the education. The issue of the usefulness of Classics to working life, especially business, was already raised; so was the fear—however faint—that enjoyment of Classics, if not controlled by an over-riding Christian faith, might have undesirable moral consequences.

But Britons who were not able or willing to bankroll their sons' classical educations were already fighting back. The Greeks and Romans could be approached by other routes that did not require those years glued to grammars and dictionaries. They could increasingly be read in mother-tongue translations, by great poets like Dryden and Pope, even though this was obviously derided as a vulgar and inferior mode of access to the Classics by those who had purchased the veneer of a higher social class offered by the linguistic training. The material covered in ancient authors could be enjoyed even by the completely illiterate in accessible entertainments such as fairground drolls. These also provided the opportunity to laugh at the elitist associations of classical education, as well as the elevated subject-matter and style of much classical literature, and thus wage a form of cultural class war in the most pleasurable of contexts.

Notes

1 Parts of this chapter adapt material also published in Hall (2018e) and Hall (forthcoming d).
2 Thompson (1917) 20–1.
3 Brown (1707) 20.
4 '*Non amo te, Sabidi, nec possum dicere quare*: /*Hoc tantum possum dicere, non amo te*'.
5 Brown (1709) 51.
6 See e.g. Livy 28.27.15, Caesar, *Civil War* 3.82; Virgil, *Aeneid* 7.637.
7 May (1635) book 7, n.p.
8 Thelwall (1796a) 43–4; see below pp. 276–7.
9 Locke (1913 [1693]) lxiii.
10 See the discussion of 'Class' as a keyword in Williams (1976) 60–8.
11 Krishnamurthy (2009b) 3; Wright (1988) 2–3.
12 See Briggs (1967).
13 Owen (1818).
14 An essay on girls' education in boarding schools suggests that they read 'English classicks': see Hawkins (1781) 45.
15 The witty suggestion of Quinn (2018).
16 Andreas (1469).
17 Perkins (1604) vi. 657. Perkins was incorrect; many ancient authors mention Phrygia.
18 Earle (1630) xxxiii.
19 Browne (1646) V.xiii.253.
20 North (1645) III.181.
21 'M.M.', in Sancroft (1694) xiii.
22 Bankes (1679) 'preface', n.p.
23 Maidwell (1684).
24 On Tate see further below p. 216.

25 The boys were named Christopher and James and, in 1684, were about 18 and 11, respectively. Christopher's gentlemanly classical education did not prevent him from succumbing to alcoholism and gambling debts; he was disinherited by his father in favour of James, who also fought a drink problem. See Beckett (1980a), (1980b) and (2004).
26 Maidwell (1684) n.p.
27 Dacier (1683). This book was also printed by a woman, who called herself on the title page 'widow of Antonius Cellier' (Apud viduam Antonii Cellier). Like the Daciers, Antoine Cellier was another Protestant who had converted, and his wife's name seems to have been either Anne or Florence. On Dacier see further Wyles (2016).
28 The adjectival 'Delphin' is derived from *dauphin*. Thirty-nine scholars contributed to the series, which was edited by Pierre Huet with assistance from several co-editors, including Jacques-Bénigne Bossuet and Anne Dacier. Each work was accompanied by a Latin commentary, *ordo verborum* and verbal index. The editors added many notes and appendixes. The original volumes each have an engraving of Arion and the Dolphin, and the appropriate inscription '*in usum serenissimi Delphini*' ('for the use of the most serene Dauphin'). See Volpilhac-Auger (1997) and (1999); Shelford (2007).
29 Proust (1681).
30 *The Spectator* no. 300, Wednesday March 19th, 1712.
31 See Hall (forthcoming d).
32 Millgate (2006).
33 Hardy (1994 [1895]) 22–3.
34 Felton (1713) xv, xx.
35 Felton (1713) 13–14, 9–10, 17, 18–19.
36 'Gentleman' (1715) 25.
37 E.g. Kennet (1713); Echard (1715); Dunster (1729) and several other important publications discussed in Hall (forthcoming d).
38 Stonehouse (1736) 4, 10. Our emphases.
39 On the economic, social and political aspects of this development, see the excellent study of Rosenheim (1998).
40 See Levine (1991) and (1999).
41 *Spectator* no. 313, Thursday, February 28, 1712.
42 See e.g. Gill (2016) 74–5.
43 Habermas (1989 [1962]); see Wahrman (1995) 6–7. The fashionable new curriculum prompted numerous new publishing ventures. British publishers began to produce series of textbooks intended to rival those expensive French Delphin editions. See further Hall (forthcoming d).
44 See the cogent and detailed study of Bründl (2003) 69–151.
45 Hans (2014 [1951]) 117–35; see also Miller (1997) 64–70 and Stray (1998b).
46 Monod (2009) 37.
47 Shroff (1983) 117.
48 Spateman (1742), especially 2, 7, 17, 19, 21.
49 Spateman (1742) 23.
50 For a fascinating study of the various definitions of masculinity from the 1740s, in the *Gentleman's Magazine*, see Williamson (2016).
51 Fielding (1742) volume I, 6–7.
52 Shroff (1983).
53 Shroff (1983) 11.
54 Shroff (1983) 12.
55 Shroff (1983) 38; see *The Spectator* no. 10, Monday, March 12th, 1711, where he defines his readership as 'Gentlemen', including 'all contemplative Tradesmen, titular Physicians, Fellows of the Royal Society, Templers that are not given to be contentious, and Statesmen that are out of business'.

56 Maurer (1998)15–18.
57 Maurer (1998) 16–17.
58 Coutu (2015) 3.
59 Coutu (2015) 8–9.
60 Hogarth (1833) 2.
61 See Hogarth (1833) 179 and 323, where the performers in the picture and their acts are identified. Hogarth himself called his picture simply 'The Fair' without specifying which one.
62 See Hall (forthcoming c).
63 Brown (1910) 28–9.
64 E.g. Brown (1705) 117–18.
65 Brown (1705) 117.
66 See Ashton (1882) volume 1, 246–9.
67 Quoted in Ashton (1882) volume 1, 188.
68 Ashton (1882) volume 1, 189–90.
69 See Rosenfeld (1960) 19.
70 Cibber (1753), volume 3, 352.
71 Walker (2003) xiv.
72 Settle (1707*a*) and (1707*b*).
73 Chambers (1862–1864) volume II, 265.
74 Victor (15141761) volume II, 74.
75 Rosenfeld (1960) 161–6.
76 Jonson (1641 [1614]) 73–5.
77 Rosenfeld (1960) 141.
78 Settle (1707b) 6.
79 Settle (1707b) 7–9.
80 Settle (1707b) 13–15.
81 Settle (1707b) 17.
82 Settle (1707b) 23.
83 Dryden (1697); Ogilby (1654).
84 For further images related to the droll, see Hall (2018e).
85 Anon. (1700a) 'Preface', 7.
86 Anon. (1700a) 'Preface', 10, and see above pp. 3–4 and 6–7.
87 Anon. (1700a) 'Preface', 11.
88 Anon. (1700a) 'Preface', 11.
89 Anon. (1700a) 'Preface', 14.

3

WORKING-CLASS READERS

Introduction

In his extraordinary autobiography, William Edwin Adams (1832–1906), a tramping plasterer's son who would become a self-educated radical journalist, referred to himself as a 'social atom—a small speck on the surface of society … just an ordinary person: no better, and I hope no worse, than the ordinary run of my neighbours'[1] (Figure 3.1). Adams epitomises the determined spirit of the 19th-century British working-class autodidact. He is also a wise and wry witness to the transition between two different experiences of working-class cultural life. During his lifetime, enormous social progress was made, including the dramatic expansion of the electorate,[2] national provision of basic education and the resulting benefits of an expanded literary marketplace.

This chapter examines the classical reading experiences of working-class people from the early 18th to the early 20th century in Britain. Personal reflections of working-class readers reveal that the transition witnessed by Adams was from hard-won experiences of classical literature, often in the original languages, characterised by extreme lack of materials, arbitrary educational provision, and prodigious perseverance and intellectual capacity on the part of the learners, towards smoother and more capacious routes of access to antiquity for considerably more of the working-class population, paved by democratising publishing practices and an emerging cultural infrastructure.

We begin with tales from the 18th century, sparse and sensational, which record the flowering of 'uncultivated genius' within the least fertile landscapes, attested by scant literary remains among the output of a print media run on a system of patronage. At the end we analyse the late 19th- and early 20th-century impact of mass cultural enterprises, fuelled by technological advancement (i.e. mechanised production) and propelled by the flourishing Labour Movement

DOI: 10.4324/9781315446608-4

FIGURE 3.1 Title page of William Edwin Adams' *Memoirs of a Social Atom* (1903), reproduced by courtesy of The British Library.

and commercial capitalism. Along the way we assess improvements made to the working-class reader's classical experience by the emergence of reading rooms, circulating libraries, city libraries and publishing ventures such as educational journals and magazines, self-improvement books, classical handbooks (e.g. grammars and reference works) and increasingly accessible and affordable translations.

The recent provision and population of online databases, especially Open University's *Reading Experience Database*, are increasingly enabling us to approach literature from 'the other side' of the reading process—from the perspective of the reader rather than the author.[3] This represents something of a revolution in literary history in three key ways. First, it challenges the myth still residually informing literary studies, which shapes a narrative about old dead white 'men of letters' in transhistorical dialogue, but is uninterested in the people who rescue them from oblivion—their readers.

Second, this approach facilitates challenges to the Western canon of texts deemed worth reading by the gate-keepers of culture. In the act of canonisation, the class-determined and class-determining phenomena of taste and literary merit find consensus among an elite. Such consensus-building can prop up reactionary values, under-represent certain cultures and endorse an ideal of cultural homogeneity. The historical role of classical authors within this canon can be uncomfortable for classicists to come to terms with. In this and subsequent chapters, we shall see how an alternative classical canon formed among working-class constituencies, according to a different set of criteria to those of the elite, although there was considerable intersection.

Thirdly, when the focus shifts from the author to the reader, we discover that the details of the identity of the reader and the location, reason for and nature of the reading experience reveal a picture of literature remote from the perception of classical literature as a 'high' literary endeavour. By accumulating evidence which reflects the material reality of reading practice—the act once deemed insignificant, passive and near-invisible—its significance in cultural dynamics is revealed. This poses new and harder questions about the creation and consumption of cultural artefacts including books. This chapter therefore uses evidence of actual reading experiences.

The 18th century

The evidence for 18th-century working-class readers of classical works is sparse. Labouring men and women rarely enjoyed sufficient education and leisure time to read classical authors either in the ancient languages or in English translation. Additionally, new books and journals were prohibitively expensive, free or public libraries from which a worker might borrow a book cost-free were non-existent and cheap lending libraries still rare. Circulating libraries existed in Britain from the 1720s onwards for readers who could afford to borrow books, but workers were excluded not only by the fee but by the mode of payment, often by subscription with a discounted upfront down-payment. Public libraries that loaned books without a fee were rarely available until after the 1850 Public Libraries Act.[4]

A few exceptional working-class people successfully accessed classical literature, however, even though the apparent anomaly they constitute reveals the effectiveness of the general exclusion of the poor from 'high' cultural activity. Chapter 4 will show that, following the astronomical rise in the 1730s of the Thresher Poet, Stephen Duck, a few workers deliberately became acquainted with the Classics to conform with and financially exploit contemporary literary tastes. Others taught themselves classical languages and literature in order to be of practical use in their community, whether in the role of the village cobbler, who often acted as unofficial adviser, or as a religious leader.[5]

The great age of literary translation from classical authors was, in Britain, the 18th century, but hot-off-the-press new translations were expensive. They took time to become the primary route to classical wisdom for working-class readers of English. Works in Latin, both scholarly treatises in neo-Latin and ancient Roman texts, were available second-hand at lower prices. Even tattered schoolbooks could be exchanged for money because their value was tangible. Picked up as bargains from stalls, discarded school-books often gave impoverished autodidacts their first contact with classical culture: learning Latin was a productive way to spend one's meagre leisure time, or—with luck—even working hours. Determined 18th-century autodidacts taught themselves Latin from standard textbooks including Thomas Ruddiman's *The Rudiments of the Latin Tongue* (1714),[6] Thomas Dyche's *Vocabularium Latiale, or Latin Vocabulary* (1709),[7] Richard Valpy's *Delectus sententiarum et historiarum* (1788) and Latin dictionaries—Adam Littleton's *Linguae Latinae Liber* (1678) or Robert Ainsworth's *Thesaurus Linguae Latinae Compendiarius* (1732).

Two years into his apprenticeship to a Buckingham tailor, Robert Hill (1699–1777), intrigued by Latin epitaphs in his church, acquired two beaten-up reference works that would change the course of his life: 'an imperfect Accidence and Grammar, and about three Quarters of a *Littleton's* Dictionary'.[8] According to Joseph Spence, a scholarly clergyman, academic and patron of under-privileged poets,[9] Hill devoured these dry tomes hungrily:

> From the first Moment of so great an Acquisition, he was reading whenever he could; and as they would scarce allow him any Time from his Work by Day, he used to procure Candles as privately as he could and indulge himself in the violent Passion he had for reading, for good Part of the Nights.[10]

Hill began running errands in his free time for pupils at the Buckingham Free School in exchange for explanation of the Latin grammatical rules he found difficult.[11] 'By such slow and laborious Means', Spence reports that Hill 'enabled himself to read a good Part of a *Latin* Testament which he had purchased, and a *Caesar*'s Commentaries that had been given him, before he was out of his Apprenticeship'.[12]

Once qualified, he was given a Horace and a Greek Testament by a gentlemanly employer and started learning Greek. In exchange for fishing lessons, another gentleman helped him with Greek grammar.[13] It took Hill seven years to learn Latin and twice that to learn Greek.[14] Later in life he enjoyed reading poetry, including Horace, Ovid and the *Iliad*, which, Spence relates, 'he had read over many Times' in Greek. When he first met Spence, he yearned to read the *Odyssey*, so his patron sent him away with the epic both in Greek and in Pope's English translation. Hill was apparently 'charmed with them both; but said, "He did not know how it was, but that it read finer to him in the latter, than in *Homer* himself"'.[15]

Hill remained poor throughout his life despite the financial assistance of Spence and his network of supporters of 'natural genius'. He worked as a schoolteacher, learned Hebrew and wrote *Christianity the True Religion: An Essay in Answer to the Blasphemy of a Deist* (1775). As a tradesman qualified to make an informed comparison between Pope's and Homer's texts, he was exceptional, but in his passion for Pope's translation, he was not. The shopkeeper Thomas Turner (1729–1793) noted in his diary for 22nd March 1756 that after his day's work he 'read part of Homer's "Odyssey", translated by Alexander Pope, which I like very well, the language being vastly good and the turn of thought and expression beautiful'.[16] Two days earlier he drew a moral lesson from book XIII.200–.16:

> I think the soliloquy which Ulysses makes when he finds the Phaeacians have, in his sleep, left him on shore with all his treasure, and on his native shore of Ithaca (though not known to him), contains a very good lesson of morality.[17]

Pope's version was crucial in providing access to Homer for the working classes, not because it was written for them, but because it was such a commercial success that it quickly filtered down to the bustling second-hand book market, frequented by readers of the lower social orders. As Penelope Wilson has noted, by 1790, Pope's *Iliad* had been through 27 editions, and the *Odyssey* 33.[18] Along with Dryden's translation of Virgil (1697), Pope's Homer stands on the summit of the British Parnassus of 'vernacular Classics', the slopes of which became crowded over the long 18th century with translations of the Greek and Roman poets.[19] For Wilson, the defining characteristic of these vernacular Classics was their 'commitment to the broadest possible spectrum of "literary" readers; collectively they ensured the continuing awareness and prestige of ancient texts in what was in many ways an aggressively modern world'.[20] In a comparable way to the collateral beneficence of the BBC's 'Third Programme', which aimed to deliver a high-brow cultural experience to a higher class of listener, but was in practice also accessed by culturally engaged but undernourished workers, these translations, printed in increasing numbers, reached constituencies that Homer and Virgil had never seen before, via market stalls and hawkers' baskets. And sometimes they took root and flourished.[21]

The early 19th-century market in second-hand classics

Pope's verse translations of Homer were even more widely read in the 19th century. Around 60 years after Hill compared Pope and Homer's Greek, James Carter (1792–1853), also a tailor, borrowed Pope's Homer from a friend. In 1819 or 1820, he read it at meal times and in the evenings after work. In his *Memoirs of a Working Man* (1845) he tells how he 'read them with much satisfaction', but 'greatly preferred the "Odyssey"; for the "Iliad" was too full of warlike descriptions for one of my pacific temper. I still retain this preference'.[22] Such evidence for working-class reading at the time is rare. It was in the late 1820s that major London presses began reprinting literary texts cheaply.[23] Previously, hard-up readers therefore relied on buying and sharing second-hand volumes.

The son of a Dissenting weaver, working in warehouses in Manchester, Samuel Bamford (1788–1872) became a renowned Chartist, as we shall see in

Chapter 5. But he was made to love poetry and ancient history by Pope's *Iliad*. Like Hill's discovery of Latin, Bamford's first contact with Classics was both by chance and incomplete: he picked up only the second volume of Pope's *Iliad*, which contained, he recalls in *Early Days* (1849), notes by Madame Dacier.[24] Like many contemporaries, Bamford treated Pope's translation as if it were Homer's composition:

> Homer I read with an absorbed attention which soon enabled me to commit nearly every line to memory. The perusal created in me a profound admiration of the old heathen heroes, and a strong desire to explore the whole of "The tale of Troy divine." To the deep melancholy of the concluding line I fully responded.
>
> Be this the song, slow moving tow'rd the shore,
> Hector is dead, and Ilion is no more!'[25]

At 20, Bamford could sometimes read while at work as janitor, porter and bookkeeper in a warehouse owned by Messrs Hole, Wilkinson and Gartside:

> As spring and autumn were our only really busy seasons, I had occasionally, during other parts of the year, considerable leisure, which, if I could procure a book that I considered at all worth the reading, was spent with such book at my desk, in the little recess of the packing room. Here, therefore, I had opportunities for reading many books of which I had only heard the names before, such as Robertson's history of Scotland, Goldsmith's history of England, Rollin's ancient history, Hume's [*sic*: read Gibbon's] decline and fall of the Roman Empire, Anachaises' [*sic*] travels in Greece; and many other works on travels, geography, and antiquities.[26]

Few working-class occupations permitted reading on the job. Fortunately, when Bamford's boss discovered that he hid reading material between the pages of the huge ledger, he did not reprimand him. He actively encouraged Bamford's literary pursuits.

The books Bamford recalls, if inaccurately, were pillars of 19th-century self-education.[27] Edward Gibbon's *The History of the Decline and Fall of the Roman Empire* itself achieved classic status as soon as its first volume was published in 1776. Charles Rollin's *The Ancient History of the Egyptians, Carthaginians, Assyrians, Babylonians, Medes and Persians, Macedonians and Grecians*, published in English translation between 1726 and 1737, was ubiquitous in bookshops, libraries, reading rooms and bookstalls.

By the book about 'Anachaises' Bamford means *Anacharsis' Travels in Greece*. Jean-Jacques Barthélemy (1716–1795), a French Jesuit scholar and numismatist, deciphered the Palmyrene and Phoenician alphabets.[28] First published in 1790–1791, William Beaumont's translation brought Anacharsis to British attention. French theatre, scholarship and translation were important in British engagement with classical antiquity. Many English translations benefitted from French scholarly notes, and French translations were a mediating presence between the ancient source and the English translation.[29] Barthélemy's four-volume *Voyage du jeune Anacharsis en Grèce* (1787) relates how the Scythian sage Anacharsis met distinguished Greeks including Solon and impressed all with his candid philosophical speech, drawing on Diogenes Laertius, *Vitae Philosophorum* I.101 and Herodotus IV.46, 76–7. Barthélemy's creative work, which also uses the Bible, Plutarch, Athenaeus, Aelian, Strabo and Cicero, is one of several French texts, on the cusp between historical and didactic fiction, which amalgamated ancient sources in a new narrative. The trend had been set by Archbishop François Fénelon's influential *Les Aventures de Télémaque* in 1699.[30]

A marginally better-known French travelogue featured the Persian king Cyrus the Elder. Its author was a Jacobite philosopher, Andrew Michael (Chevalier) Ramsay, who began life as the son of a Calvinist Ayrshire baker but followed his passion for French mysticism to Cambrai and the feet of Fénelon. Mary Stancliff, on the other hand, was the maid-servant of Gertrude Savile (the unmarried aunt of the politician Sir George Savile, eighth baronet).[31] On 21st February 1728, Gertrude notes in her diary that she rose at 10 o'clock. Mary (who had no doubt risen considerably earlier) read aloud to her from the English translation of Ramsay's new and popular *Travels of Cyrus* (1727).[32] Stancliff's example introduces the category of working-class classical reader whose duties included reading for their employer;[33] she must have acquired more than basic literacy to read out Ramsay's erudite story, informed by philosophy, theology, magi and Greek luminaries. In the tradition of identifying proto-Christian values in pagan lore, Ramsay proposes three states of humanity: the innocent, the fallen and the restored. Like Fénelon, Ramsay combined competing philosophical and scientific ideas in a mystical Christian context often drawn from ancient Greek sources.[34] But there are only four similar diary entries. We know only that Savile would listen to Stancliff read while she rested or knitted, and that the servant's performance was adequate: 'Mary read to me a little before dinner, (which she does tolerable); "Cyrus" a Romance. I wound silk'.[35]

Evidence of Ramsay's *Cyrus* in a worker's hands reappears a century later, when James Dawson Burn (c.1802–1882), an apprentice hatter, was given an old copy by a friend. In his *Autobiography of a Beggar Boy* (1856), Burn explains that the volume

> opened up to my enquiring mind a rich field of useful knowledge. The appendix to the work contained the *heathen mythology*: this part of the work completely fascinated me, and for a considerable time became my constant companion.[36]

Burn was raised by his mother, who earned a meagre wage carding wool for hats. He saw his youthful self as belonging to one of 'the various substrata of civilized society … who continually live as it were by chance'. He was, he reflects, 'born in poverty, nursed in sorrow, and reared in difficulties, hardships, and privations'.[37] As a boy, Burn had been taken begging and peddling in Northumberland and the Scottish Lowlands by his step-father, an alcoholic ex-soldier (hence the autobiography's title) who taught him to read but not write. In adolescence he worked in temporary occupations as a casual labourer and as servant to an eccentric Indian emigré named Mr Peters. At around 20 he became apprenticed to a Hexham hatter, and for 6 years can recall seeing nobody even read. When he was then given *Cyrus*, he became fascinated by the lengthy appendix, 'A Discourse upon the Theology *and* Mythology of the *ANCIENTS*'.[38]

In the early 1830s, Burn became involved in Glaswegian radical politics. An advocate of trade unionism and Chartism, he helped establish the Oddfellows, a charitable fraternity, about which he wrote his *Historical Sketch* (1846). But he never forgot his chance encounter with classical mythology:

> I had a continual craving to pry into the mysteries of literature; heretofore the glorious world of man's thought had been a sealed book to me, and I longed most ardently to hold communion with those master-minds who had scattered the beautiful flowers of their intelligence in the garden of humanity.[39]

The elegance of this prose is astonishing for a man who did not learn to write until adulthood.

Reference books were key to the classical self-education of the lower classes. One of the most famous was also derived from a French source: the English edition of the French Jesuit François Pomey's *The Pantheon*, repeatedly reprinted from 1694, although the 1698 translation, revised by schoolteacher and Gresham Professor Andrew Tooke, and often departing considerably from Pomey's text, swiftly became the edition of choice. First published in Latin in 1659, by 1810 the Pomey and subsequently Pomey/Tooke volume, which had gone through 32 editions in London, was printed for the first time in the US, where it remained in print until 1860. The striking illustrations accompany succinct descriptions of deities within a dialogue between a teacher, Mystagogus, and his inquisitive pupil Palæophilus. Although the *Pantheon*'s primary market was schools, it was appreciated by working-class self-educators seeking elucidation of references in their classical and classicising reading material.

After many hours winding yarn for a Leicester cardigan-jacket weaver, Tom Barclay, the Roman Catholic son of Irish immigrants (his father was a rag-and-bone man), revelled in his collection of 'second-hand, often tattered books', kept in a clothes-basket. He scoured market stalls for 'discarded school-books' which had 'copious notes telling of "filthy loves of gods and goddesses"'. 'What information', he reminisces,

> how strange, how intensely interesting. Jupiter, Juno, Mars, Apollo, Neptune, Vulcan, Pluto, Mercury, Venus, Minerva, Pan, Nymphs, Fauns, Satyrs, Dryads, Fates, Furies, Muses, Harpies. There we sat rapt, exchanging our health for what?–Listen. So and so (I forget his name) "whose fifty daughters Hercules deflowered (or debauched) in one night." There's stuff for big or little Christians to imbibe![40]

Barclay here alludes to the story of Thespius, who allowed Hercules to sleep with his fifty daughters in return for killing a lion (see [Apollodorus], *Bibliotheca* II.7.8). This episode from Hercules' story is not in the Pomey/Tooke *Pantheon*, but Barclay's language corresponds with the idiom typical of it and other classical handbooks. For all their professed distaste for heathen mores, they relished the amorous conquests of heroes and gods, using a quiver of paraphrastic rape terminology.[41] The Pomey/Tooke *Pantheon*, alongside Joseph Spence's illustrations of Roman poets in *Polymetis* (1747) and John Lemprière's *Classical Dictionary, Containing a Full Account of all the Proper Names mentioned in Ancient Authors* (1788) was a favourite of the so-called Cockney School of poets, including Leigh Hunt and John Keats.[42] They belonged to the middling classes; as the young sons of tradesmen and small business owners, they were often the intended readers of such books. But these texts, as we have seen, were used lower down the social scale, even though such uses often left no trace on the historical record. Barclay, moreover, despite having 'no Latin outside the ordinary of the Mass', enjoyed picking up Latin editions of the Roman poets Ovid, Juvenal and Catullus.[43] The notes in English conveyed juicy details about the amours of the heathen gods. In the 19th century, as this market became more standardised, several of the books discussed here were simplified and explicitly repackaged as schoolbooks.

Cheap serials, periodicals and mass-market editions

Barclay lived through the second half of the 19th century when access to educational resources improved markedly, providing a more guided route to classical culture. The formal infrastructure, with the Elementary Education Acts of 1870 and 1880, Board schools, and an increasingly standardised curriculum, raised the level of rudimentary education. He also experienced the rapid evolution of an *informal* infrastructure for self-education, consisting of public libraries, adult educational establishments, reading rooms, educative periodicals and other affordable improving publications. 'Many a studious youth', he reflects, 'has blessed another publisher, namely Cassell, for bringing out the *Popular Educator*'.[44]

This improved educational provision was experienced too by Adams, the 'Social Atom', with whom this chapter began. He placed the birth of the cheap popular education periodical in the 1840s. The key publications were Charles Knight's *Penny Magazine*, *Penny Cyclopaedia* and *Shilling Volume*, William and Robert Chambers' *Chambers Journal* and John Cassell's *Popular Educator* (Figure 3.2). These pioneers, all 'in the same ruinous business', as Cassell would

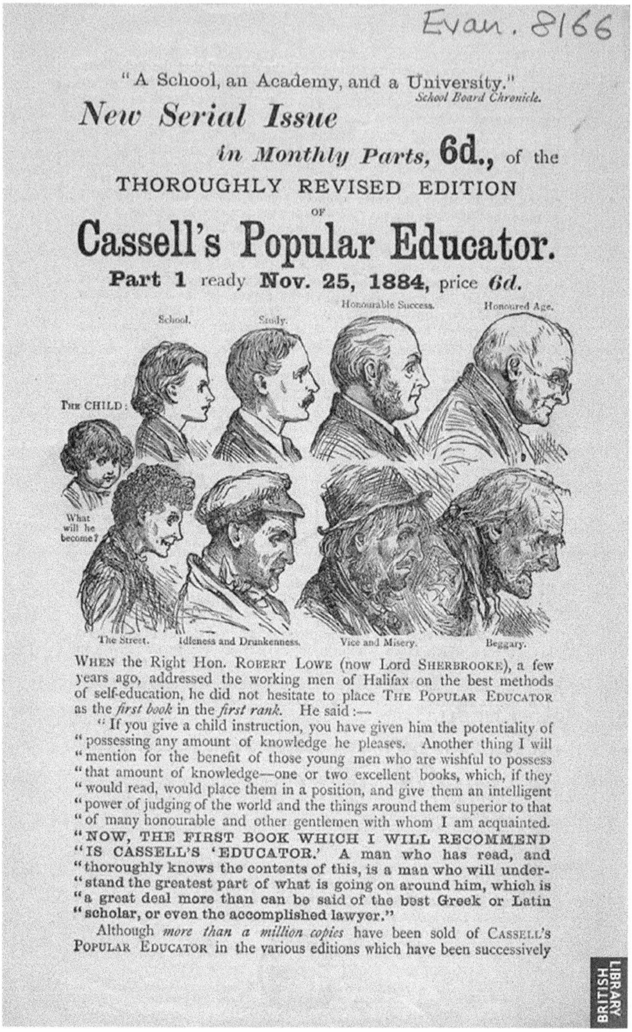

FIGURE 3.2 Advert for Cassell's *Popular Educator* (1884), reproduced by courtesy of The British Library.

put it, 'of giving the vulgar people more knowledge for a "*Penny*" than the lords used to have for a pound',[45] built on earlier enterprises in south-east Scotland and Lord Brougham's Society for the Diffusion of Useful Knowledge (on these see below, pp. 122–3 and 241–5). Cassell joked that 'the country is positively threatened with cooks, housemaids, nurses, footmen, grooms, mechanics, and peasants, that will have more information, intelligence, piety, and morality, than the kings, lords, clergy, and gentry, of the olden time![46]

As a teenaged apprentice printer to the owner of the *Cheltenham Journal*, Adams attended nightly classes and meetings. He founded a literary and debating society called the People's Institute, the first sign of his political awakening. 'If I did not at that time educate myself', Adams reflected on the 1840s and early 1850s, 'I at least did the next best thing—I tried to'.[47] He recalls how 'English grammar was picked up from [William] Cobbett; the lessons in Cassell's *Popular Educator* afforded some insight into Latin; French was studied from the same pages in conjunction with another youth',[48] although he believed that Tom Paine's works and lectures at the local Philosophical Institution had been more useful.[49]

Adams moved to London in the 1850s and wrote for the radical press. Under the pseudonym Caractacus he fulminated against slavery and demanded social reform in articles for Charles Bradlaugh's *National Reformer.* In 1864 he was the successful editor of the 'Pit-man's Bible' (the radical *Newcastle Weekly Chronicle*), and continued to educate himself. For Adams, 'Most of the self-educated people of my age and of later generations owe a deep debt of gratitude to John Cassell'.[50]

Adams was not exaggerating. John Cassell (1817–1865), who began life as a child labourer in a Manchester cotton mill and velveteen factory, was apprenticed at 16 to a joiner in Salford.[51] He became involved with the Temperance movement and lectured for the National Temperance Society, dressed in his joiner's apron. At 20, he walked away from the poverty of his childhood to London, married and opened a tea and coffee business. He ventured into the world of educational publishing, 'for the purpose', as he wrote in May 1851, 'of issuing a series of publications ... calculated to advance the moral and social well-being of the working classes'.[52] One of these was *The Working Man's Friend, and Family Instructor* (established 1850). From its inception it aimed to deliver 'what was wanted at the fireside of THE WORKING MAN, to improve his evening hour after his day of toil'.[53] Cassell had become a vociferous advocate for 'mutual instruction', which took place in what he called the 'operative academy':

> Oxford, Cambridge, Edinburgh, Glasgow, and similar places, are insignificant institutions, compared with our smithies, weaving, spinning, grinding, tailoring, carpentering, and shoe-making establishments. When boys or girls, men or women, go to any of these operative academies, they are not merely taught the art, trade, or mystery to which they are apprenticed, but there is a deeper and more important moral and intellectual education to which they are subjected.[54]

In 1852 Cassell launched his famous *Popular Educator*, which immediately became the staple reading of the working-class autodidact. The alumni of Cassell's 'school, academy and university' include not only Barclay and Adams, but the future Prime Minister David Lloyd George, and the workhouse boy who became Oxford Professor of Comparative Philology, Joseph Wright. We shall meet them both later.[55]

Thomas Burt (1837–1922), a Northumberland miner, began working life as a 'trapper boy' at Haswell Pit but lived to become Privy Councillor to King Edward VII and Father of the House of Commons. Burt considered Cassell's publication the 'chief handbook' in his self-instruction. He remembers sitting

> at the end of the table armed with the *Popular Educator* and a Latin dictionary, while with slate and pencil I translated as best I could the Latin lessons into English and the English into Latin. For variety and exercise I occasionally strolled into the fields and lanes, usually taking with me long lists of words, written out in shorthand, which I had taught myself from Pitman's *Phonographic Manual*. These Latin words, with their English meanings, I committed to memory.[56]

Cassell, however, cannot take credit for the lessons in his *Educator*; he was no classical scholar. The philological brains behind his entrepreneurial brawn belonged to the Reverend John Relly Beard. A devout Unitarian minister, Beard opened a school in Salford and later an important college for training Unitarian preachers. He was a crucial force behind the movement for popular education in Lancashire. His father was a Portsmouth small tradesman, with nine children, who were therefore brought up in a degree of poverty. At a time when other Unitarians feared that training ministers from the lowest classes would harm their cause, Beard never wavered in his zeal for universal educational to the highest level.

By the time he contributed the weekly lessons in Latin, Greek and English Literature to Cassell's *Popular Educator*, he had already produced *Latin Made Easy* (1848) and several accessible works on biblical subjects. He demonstrated the true extent of his political radicalism by publishing a biography of the leader of the Haiti slave rebellion, Toussaint L'Ouverture.[57] In his Greek lessons, released as a collected textbook edition entitled *Cassell's Lessons in Greek … Intended Especially for those who are Desirous of Learning Greek without the Assistance of a Master*, he describes the readership he assumes:

> Little more than some general acquaintance with grammar, and some general knowledge, shall I take for granted as possessed by my students. My purpose is to simplify the study of Greek so as to throw open to all who are earnest in the great work of self-culture. Nor need any industrious person of ordinary capacity despair of acquiring skill to read the New Testament; and if he pleases, and will persevere, he may go on to an intimate acquaintance with Xenophon, Demosthenes, Thucydides, Homer, and the other Greek classics.[58]

Although he did not did not learn Greek with Beard, Burt's classical education was extensive. With only two years' worth of formal schooling, at 17 he embarked on a serious course of self-study, which included Latin via the *Popular Educator*.

Fortunately, his father, also a collier at Seaton Delaval, had a collection of books that Thomas read.[59] 'It was greatly to his credit', mused Burt,

> that, with his [father's] scanty education and his narrow means, he had collected together so many good books. Yet, in truth, his books were few and insignificant enough. They greatly lacked variety, consisting almost entirely of sermons and theological works.[60]

One book that made a significant impact on Burt was Gibbon's *Decline and Fall*, which he purchased one volume at a time:

> My father, whom I always consulted about books, expressed grave doubts as to whether Gibbon was altogether safe and healthy for me. He had not himself read Gibbon's masterly work, except in extracts, but he knew something of the author's reputation for learning, and, alas! he must often have heard Gibbon classed with Voltaire, Hume, and others, and denounced from pulpits as an infidel … My heart however was set upon Gibbon … With youthful glee I read [the first volume] till a late hour. I slept but little that night; the book haunted my dreams. I awoke about four on the bright summer Sunday morning, and went into the fields to read till breakfast-time.

Gibbon was available to Burt on a pitman's wage because it had between 1853 and 1855 been published by another titan of cheap literature, Henry Bohn (1796–1884), in his 'Bohn's British Classics' series. Before Bohn, buying new books would have been unthinkable for a miner. His 'Libraries', including his famed 'Classical Library' of Greek and Roman classics, consisted of over 600 volumes; the *Gentleman's Magazine* opined in 1884 that it had 'established the habit in middle-class life, of purchasing books instead of obtaining them from a library'.[61] But Bohn's inexpensive volumes, as Burt's case shows, were not bought only by the middle classes.

> The stately, majestic march of Gibbon's periods had some attraction for me even then; but the *Decline and Fall*, it must be admitted, was hard reading for an unlettered collier lad. Yet I plodded on until I had finished the book which, besides its direct teachings, brought me many indirect advantages.[62]

Bohn's contribution to people's Classics goes deeper. He pioneered the provision of translated literature to the Victorian mass market, thus proving instrumental in the democratisation of reading. 'Bohn's Classical Library' (established in 1848), consisted of 79 titles,[63] which amounted to 116 volumes, each bound in durable dark blue cloth boards ingeniously treated to resemble leather, with gilt titles on the spine and embossed with a luxurious pattern. These volumes were enticingly cheap (between 3 and 5 shillings), but their uniformly ornate aesthetic made them desirable to collect.[64] Their popularity endured several decades. In 1924, Edward Bell (who had taken Bohn's over) was still claiming annual sales of over 100,000 volumes.[65] No library was complete without blocks of Bohn's dappled blue and gold on their shelves. One obituary relates how the British Library had to remove Bohn's books from the reading room because they quickly 'became so mutilated by students who were not content with reading them during the hours at which that institution was open'.[66] We do not know whether readers were smuggling them out, or tearing parts out. But they appealed widely and were abundantly useful.

The series was designed to provide what it termed 'literal translations' of Greek and Roman classics. The 1840s–1850s therefore saw a departure from the earlier model of fluent 'Englished' texts, or 'vernacular classics'. Some of those famous translations needed to be revised, augmented with prose translations or replaced altogether. The Classical Library, ran the advertising copy, would 'comprise faithful English translations of the principal Greek and Latin Classics':

> The versions will be strictly literal, that is, as true a reflection of expression, style, and thought, as the idioms of the languages will permit. Each work will be given without abridgment, but in the smallest practicable compass. The volumes will not be distended by diffuse notes and illustrations ... but brief suggestive notes, adapted to the real wants of the student, will be introduced wherever they are deemed essential ... Of existing translations, such as are satisfactory will be adopted; but the far greater number require correction, and will be carefully and competently revised.[67]

'Correction' sometimes meant bowdlerisation. Paul Selver (1888–1970) was the son of a Polish Jewish immigrant tailor. He grew up in New Cross, graduated from the University of London, and became a prolific writer and translator from Germanic and Slavonic languages. He recalled how his school friend Angus, son of a Lewisham Presbyterian minister, was disappointed by Ovid: 'Or rather, it wasn't so much the fault of Ovid as of Bohn, who had left all the tasty chunks in Latin'. Angus was not easily diverted from fornicating divinities. He began the long march towards satisfaction of his teenage curiosity: 'Angus was learning Latin, and hoped that in time he would be able to snap his fingers at the caitiff Bohn'.[68]

Bohn's policy was to print the 'untranslatable' in the original language, either in the body of the text or in a footnote.[69] But the man behind the translation of Ovid was Henry Thomas Riley (1816–1878), an excellent Latinist, who also wrote for the *Athenaeum* and the *Gentleman's Magazine*. He was the son of a South London ironmonger prosperous enough to send him to a boarding school in Ramsgate, from which he entered Charterhouse and Cambridge. He then embarked on a long career as a scholar, translator and editor.[70]

Yet Selver's advancement was precarious. He began school in Deptford, a deprived area of London, then mainly populated by dockworkers. 'There is quite an appreciable difference', explains Selver, 'between the son of a stevedore and the son, let's say, of a commodore'.[71] At his Board school in Gibraltar Street, he studied clay-modelling, basket-weaving and paper-folding rather than academic subjects:

> It is probable that while I was busy with such frolics as these, my upper-class counterpart, perhaps the scion of an earl, poor little devil, tethered in the kind of prep-school where they wore top hats on Sundays, was having his mind improved, with the aid of Latin deponent verbs and select chunks of Xenophon.[72]

Selver reminds us that the appeal of Latin was not universal: 'Latin, I didn't care much for, anyway. I couldn't imagine what value it had, except to brag about'.[73] When he did win a scholarship to a school that offered him more options (Whitaker Foundation School, 1900), on the advice of his father he chose German rather than Latin. But he proceeded on a scholarship to grammar school and could no longer avoid Classics. On entering 'Classical Fifth', he was impressed by how far he had come from Gilbraltar Street, now studying the Aeschylean *Prometheus Bound* and Horace's *Odes*:

> I discovered too that the boys of the Classical Fifth not only read Greek and Latin poetry, but actually wrote it. Witness the chestnut-covered work by Sidgwick on Greek verse composition, and the companion volume, scarlet as a pillar-box, in which Gepp, the darling of the Muse, led the pupil up the garden of Latin elegiacs. Hitherto I had felt no urge to pour out my feelings lyrically in the vernacular, yet now, it seemed, the wand of Sidgwick and Gepp would cause me to pen strophes in the dead tongues of Athens and Rome. I looked forward keenly to this Pentecostal process, which turned out to be, not so much fine frenzy as cold-blooded jigsaw.[74]

Selver had unwittingly stumbled into the most prized exercise in the Victorian, public-school, classical education—composition in Latin and Greek. The goal was 'the instant construction of inspired verse, the effortless composition, the immediate contact with perfection',[75] but Selver found it frigid and mechanical.

Selver's turn-of-the-century metropolitan experience may have been nationally atypical, and his world was a new one: the tenacity of a poor but intellectually curious lad was rewarded by an education that led to a university degree. In the South Wales iron town of Rhymney lived the young clerk who would become Deputy Secretary under four consecutive Prime Ministers: Thomas Jones (1870–1955). Opportunities for higher education were not in equivalent abundance,[76] and Jones remained pessimistic about the real possibilities for talented individuals to transcend working-class origins.[77] But the iron workers of Rhymney were enabled to engage with the Greek and Roman classics via the popular press. In 1858 the Rhymney Iron Company paid £3,000 to provide the town with a National School.[78] A library and reading room in Middle Rhymney, to house the Scientific Institution (established in 1850), was run by company officials and religious leaders. It opened with 126 members, workers paying 1 shilling and a quarter and everyone else 1 shilling and 6 pence.

Among the first library loans were translations of Plutarch's *Lives*, Josephus' *Jewish Wars*, *Chambers's Information for the People*, *Chambers's Miscellany of Useful and Entertaining Tracts*, *Chambers's Papers for the People* and *Chambers's Edinburgh Journal* (established 1832). The Chambers brothers, William and Robert, did much to improve the reading materials of the British poor as we shall see in Chapter 11.[79] These 'improving' periodicals promoted a familiarity, even fluency with world culture, including the literary and material remains of ancient Greece and Rome.[80]

In the mid-1850s, the library stocked 'Gibbon's Rome'—probably Bohn's British Classics edition. In the early 1900s the library was moved and subsidised by miners' subscriptions and the company. In 1905 a new institute was built; the stock of books rose to 3,000 with a weekly issue of 300. While his father read only the Bible and religious periodicals, Jones made full use of the Rhymney Workmen's Institute Library and booksellers, where he could buy for threepence one of the 209 paperback volumes issued weekly by Cassell's National Library:

> Two books from the shelves which fascinated me at some stage were a *Life of Napoleon* by E. Gifford and the *History of the Jews* by Josephus. But I relied mainly on the weekly volume of Cassell's *National Library* which introduced me to Shakespeare and all the chief poets; to Plutarch's *Lives* ... and to most of what was worth while in the whole realm of English literature and such classics as had undergone translation.[81]

Launched in 1886 by one of the 'titans of the reprint trade', Cassell and Co., *The National Library* was edited by the philanthropic UCL Professor of English, Henry Morley (1822–1894).[82] Jones could afford these slim volumes and found that he could smuggle them into the office at the ironworks. The manager was indulgent, even giving him Samuel Smiles' self-help books.[83]

By the age of 20, Jones' wages increased; he began to buy Cassell's sixpenny cloth boards and second-hand books, became a prize-winning Calvinist Methodist preacher, and inevitably decided to study for the ministry at University College of Wales, Aberystwyth. He graduated from Glasgow 11 years later, having lost his Christian faith. He went on to become one of the most powerful civil servants in London between 1916 and 1930. Affectionately known as 'T.J.', he became Deputy Secretary under David Lloyd George, and was considered indispensable by three subsequent Prime Ministers.

Cheap book production reached fever pitch around 1830 when the provision of reading material for the newly discovered 'mass reading public' was essayed by respectable London publishers.[84] While their trashier competitors were symbolised by the ubiquitous and infamous 'penny bloods' (later 'penny dreadfuls'), they specialised instead in improving—and at first predominantly religious—literature. The residual evangelical suspicions surrounding imaginative texts without an overtly Christian message faded; poetic and fictional non-copyright texts became a staple both of affordable periodicals and the mushrooming series of 'Classics', such as the sixpenny Plutarch's *Lives* issued monthly by Ward, Lock & Co. in 1885–1886, or 'classical libraries' (Figure 3.3).

Great literature thus began to arrive in the homes of the British middle and working classes.[85] Cheaper than Cassell's National Library were the thin wire-stapled, and intentionally ephemeral volumes of W.T. (William Thomas) Stead's 'Masterpiece Library'. Stead (1849–1912) brought out weekly pamphlets of Penny Poets and Penny Popular Novels.[86] The 'novels' were digests of classic novels, and the 'poets' reproduced selections from out-of-copyright English poets. They both, of course, sold for one penny. And sell they did: 11,500,000 copies in a year.[87] Stead was also a newspaper editor, publisher and social reformer, and he aimed at enhancing the cultural range of 'the New Reader, who is the product of the Education Act'.[88] His first issue was a Penny Poets version of Thomas Babington Macaulay's *Lays of Ancient Rome* (1895), which sold 200,000 copies in 4 months. As Lockwood has noted, the 'fairly austere classicism' of Macauley's *Lays* was a conscious choice by which Stead created the maximum 'clash' between the lofty content and its cheap medium, complete with advertisements for cocoa and tonics for various ailments.[89] But he also published versions of classical works specifically for children.[90]

The 'Books for the Bairns' series launched in March 1896 with *Aesop's Fables*. The son of an under-employed iron foundry worker and later an iron-moulder himself, Joseph Stamper (born in 1886) recalls reading Stead's pamphlets as a child in St. Helens, Lancashire. Stamper disliked school. 'Every day I came out with the feelings of a prisoner released after a long "stretch"'.[91] But he was enchanted by the tales from ancient Greece and Rome. He discovered them in Stead's 'Books for the Bairns', which

> had a pink cover and contained selections from the ancient classics: stories from Homer, the writings of Pliny the younger [i.e. the *Epistles*], Aesop's "Fables" [Books for the Bairns Nos. 1 and 26]. I took a strong fancy to Aesop, he was a Greek slave from Samos, in the sixth century BC, and workpeople were only just beginning to be called "wage slaves". I read all these; non-selective and Catholic [sic] my reading.[92]

Of 288 titles issued between March 1896 and June 1920, only 10 were overtly from classical sources: *Aesop's Fables* [1]; *Aesop's Fables Pt 2* [26]; *The Labours of Hercules* [27]; *The Story of Perseus and the Gorgon's Head* [30]; *Stories from Ancient Rome* [64] (Figure 3.4); *Some Fairy Tales of the Ancient Greeks* [99]; *The Quest of the Golden Fleece* [101]; *Stories of the Persian Kings* [152]; *Stories of the Greek Tyrants* [210]; and *The Quest of Orpheus* [235]. *Stories from ancient Rome* [64], issued in May 1901, was as usual lavishly illustrated, with prints on almost every page. The

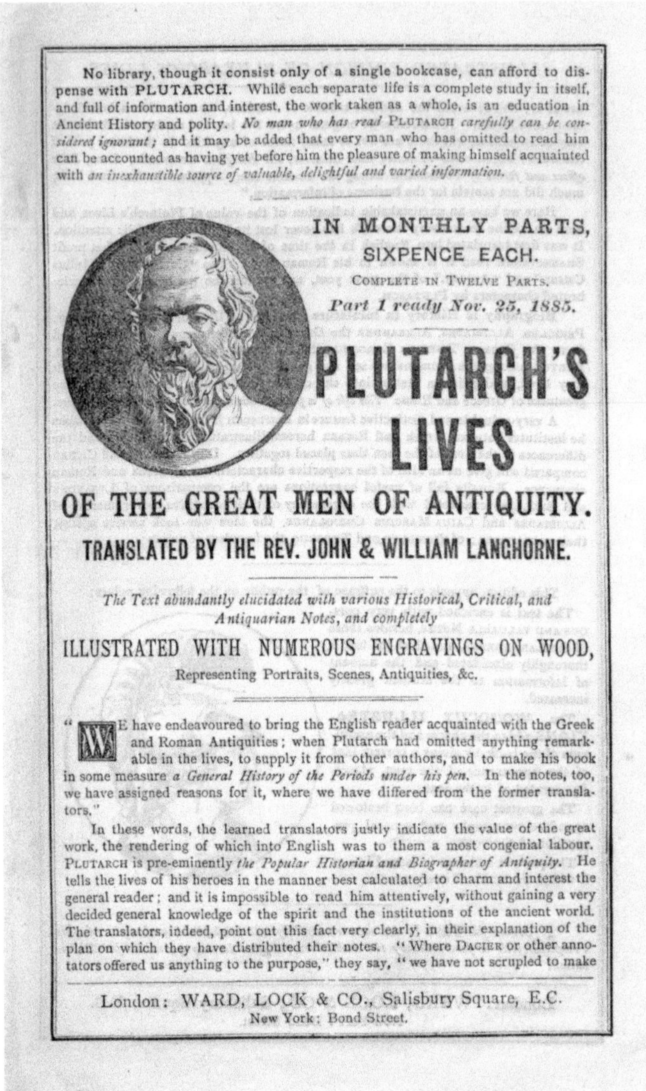

FIGURE 3.3 Sixpenny Plutarch's *Lives*, issued monthly by Ward, Lock & Co. in 1885–1886, or, classical libraries, reproduced from copy in Hall's personal collection.

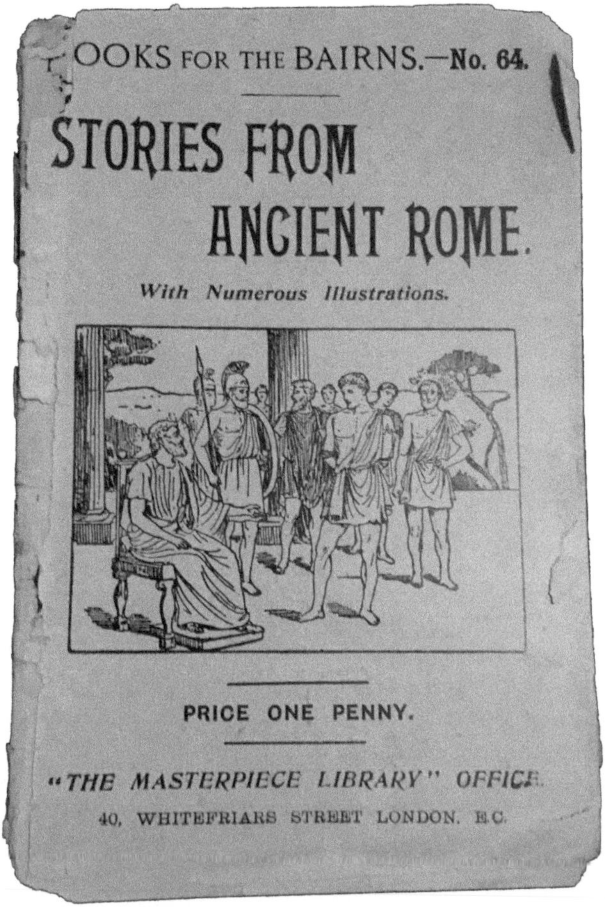

FIGURE 3.4 Cover of *Stories from Ancient Rome*, no. 64 of William Thomas Stead's 'Books for the Bairns' series, reproduced from copy in Stead's personal collection.

writing is divided into two thin columns, summarising tales from Virgil's *Aeneid* and Livy's *History of Rome from its Foundation* (*Ab Urbe Condita*).[93] The opening of 'The Story of Coriolanus' invites the child reader to make comparisons between contemporary and Roman Republican politics:

> The Patricians and Plebeians did not always get on well together. The Patricians, like some of the kings, wanted too much of their own way, and at last the Plebeians said they must have two officers, appointed by themselves, to look after their interests … The Tribunes were a little like our House of Commons, and the Patricians were something like the House of Lords'.[94]

Stead encouraged other cheap publishing endeavours, lauding the 1901 launch of Grant Richards' 'World's Classics' series:

> A publisher has arisen who has had the courage to attempt to bring out at 1s books fit to stand on any library shelf containing complete editions of the very best work to be found in the literature of the world.[95]

Before Richards was forced to sell his series to OUP, in 1906, he published Pope's *Odyssey* (1903) and Dryden's Virgil, including the *Aeneid*, *Georgics* and *Eclogues*.[96] The quality of these shilling books is remarkable. They are a rich, navy blue octodecimo with gilt titles and gilt patterned spines, somewhat resembling Bohn's duodecimo volumes. Cheap but expensive-looking, they were also portable. They could be read out of doors or on a train, but were small enough to shelve even in a cramped household.

Dent's Everyman's Library

While Richards' 'World's Classics; or, bound books for the million' was pioneering, and its afterlives at OUP (1906 to present) and George Allen (between 1907 and 1912) contributed significantly to educational publishing, the number of classical texts printed before 1939 is relatively small; the series is not named by working-class autodidacts.[97] Joseph Malaby Dent's Everyman's Library, however, launched in 1906, took cheap-reprint publishing and cross-class access to the Greek and Roman Classics to another level. (Figure 3.5.) The scale of this maverick publisher's achievement matches only his ambition. While other publishers were releasing one title at a time, Dent swamped the market with 50 new titles a year. This produced savings on materials, but also an intense workplan for the editors.

Everyman's Library printed 1,000 titles in its first 50 years. Forty-six titles are listed as 'classical' in genre; they include most standard works of Greek and philosophy, poetry and prose, from Marcus Aurelius' *Meditations* (the first classical text released), through the dramatic works of Aeschylus, Sophocles, Euripides and Aristophanes, to the epics of Homer and Virgil. The classical genre also includes Winifred Margaret Lambart Hutchinson's three-volume *The Muses' Pageant: Myths & Legends of Ancient Greece* (1912, 1914), a 'patchwork' narrative of Greek myths which aimed 'to give a bird's-eye view, so to speak, of the "realms of gold"',[98] and became one of the century's most widely read works on classical mythology. Hutchinson (born 1868), an associate of Newnham College, Cambridge, authored *Aeacus, a Judge of the Underworld* (1901) and *The Golden Porch* (1907, 'a book of Greek fairy tales' for children), *The Sunset of the Heroes: Last Adventures of the Takers of Troy* (1911), *Evergreen Stories* (1920), and *Orpheus with his Lute* (1909); she revised William Melmoth's eighteenth-century translation of Pliny's *Letters* (1921–1927). In 1909 she edited five books of Cicero's *On the Ends of Good and Evil* (1909).

FIGURE 3.5 Joseph Malaby Dent (1849–1926) by Alfred Reginald Thomson (1974), reproduced courtesy of Darlington Library.

The only ancient author in the 'oratory' genre is Demosthenes. The three-volume Plutarch's *Lives* were sold as 'biography', but his *Moralia* as 'classical'. Josephus (1 volume), Livy (6 volumes) and Tacitus (2 volumes) appear in the 'History' category, alongside the 12-volume Grote's *History of Greece* (1906), which had always been popular amongst working-class readers on account of its pioneering defence of Athenian democracy,[99] the 6-volume Gibbon's *Roman Empire* and Charles Merivale's 1-volume *History of Rome* (1912).

In 1904 Dent built his Temple Press, a book factory, in the new Garden City of Letchworth. The New York booksellers Messrs E. P. Dutton and Co. bought 2,000 copies of each volume as they were issued.[100] By his death in 1926, Dent had sold over 20 million Everyman books.[101] By 1975 more than 60 million copies (from a list of 1,239 volumes) had been purchased.[102] As Rose maintains, we cannot tell how many of these were bought by British working people, but they immediately became the standard texts for adult learners, including those many thousands engaged in Workers' Educational Association courses, which we will address in Chapter 9.[103]

Dent was the son of a Darlington painter-decorator. He wanted to run away with a travelling theatre, but after joining a Mutual Improvement Society caught the literature bug. Raised in a working-class family with 11 siblings and educated by Wesleyan Methodists, Dent was apprenticed to a printer, which led to the discovery that he had a talent for bookbinding. Against his parents' will, Dent used to sneak out to the old Barn Theatre in Darlington, where his three-penny coin bought him a gallery seat and transportation from the daily grind. Theatre broadened his cultural horizons:

> I still remember the first night I found myself there, fascinated by a play which I think must have been Sheridan Knowles's *Virginius*, for it had a Roman setting, and took me far away from things mundane into a world of imagination which has haunted me ever since.[104]

Knowles' Roman plays are discussed in detail in Chapter 7.

As often, it was the remunerative work in which the printer's apprentice Dent was engaged that brought him into contact with ancient literature.[105] Surrounded, however, like Barclay, Adams and Selver, by the emerging cultural and educational institutions of the later 19th century, Dent's path to the classical was less unusual than those of his predecessors. Inspired by preparing an essay on Boswell's *Life of Johnson* at the local Mutual Improvement Society, Dent realised the importance of literature. He often expressed his escapism through reading in classical imagery, his lifelong association with literature as a 'supreme happiness ... even though only as a door-keeper of the Temple'.[106]

Alfred Reginald Thomson's colourful portrait, painted in 1974, (Figure 3.5) well commemorates Dent's contribution to 20th-century literature.[107] The avuncular Dent sits holding a stack of Everyman books in his lap. Behind him is a map of the world representing his global achievement. The sales figures grew exponentially because of exports to America and the British Empire and the expansion in homegrown readerships through improved educational provision and population growth.[108] In the topmost corners are depicted readers of various nationalities, including a cowboy, an Eskimo, a London banker and what may be an African tribal woman, all with book in hand. To his left and right, either side of two studious children, are outdoor reading scenes; on Dent's right, an aristocratic couple read in the garden of their rural mansion; mirroring them, on his left, sit two working-class men, a pipe-smoking and aproned butcher or grocer and a moustachioed mechanic. All four hold the same editions of Everyman's library. Dent's pioneering series, providing high quality and well-produced literature at affordable prices, had trans-class appeal.

Dent progressed through the great literature of the world in translation, including—of course—the Greek and Roman Classics. He believed that the world could be improved if people read such authors, so the format had to be affordable. In 1906 he expressed his ambition that the series, edited by the industrious Ernest Rhys, would reach 1000 volumes. Rhys remembered the struggle to prepare the first 150 books back in 1905–1906, 'barricaded by huge piles of books at the British Museum'. Dent 'expected me to sweep all the books of the world into his net':

> The old Chief was really magnificent in the courage with which he planned that first year's campaign. He felt that no dribbling out of books in small batches would suffice to capture the big public. No–he must have it carried by great battalions, fifty volumes at one swoop ... Estimate what that meant for an editor who had no editor's staff: only one hard-working little woman, Marian Edwardes, who knew the ropes at the British Museum, and was a skilled transcriber, and two or three clerks, a clever boy among them–Frank Swinnerton, the future novelist.[109]

Fifty years after the first Everyman book was sold, Everyman fulfilled Dent's goal by printing their thousandth title, Aristotle's *Metaphysics*. It was through Dent's vision that the majority of the British reading public encountered the greatest poetry and prose composed by the ancient writers of Greece and Rome.

Altick has warned historians against equating accessibility with popularity.[110] Publishers reissued works repeatedly to get their full money's worth from the investment of time spent in the original preparation of an author's texts and plates. The amount of publishing of classical texts might suggest that, through cheap vernacular classics, everybody was reading the Greek and Roman texts, but just because the texts were now within the workers' reach does not necessarily mean that they bought them. Even sales figures do not equate with reading experiences, since there is a difference between buying a book and reading it. A cynical writer in the *Academy* observed in 1903 that the works of the 'Great Authors ... are regarded as part of the necessary furniture of the house—not the mind'.[111]

But there is some limited evidence of working-class reading of Everyman's Library. Born in 1892, Vero Walter Garratt worked in a factory, but his passion was for books:

> Every available evening I spent in the reference room [at Birmingham Central Library], searching for books which put me in company with the literary giants of the past. The *Iliad* and *Odyssey*, the advice of Epictetus, the principles of Longinus and the logic of the *Dialogues* of Plato I studied with particular relish for their wisdom seemed to be capable of modern application.[112]

By 17, Garratt's 'passion for reading had become so intense that a few hours during the evening seemed totally insufficient'.[113] He used to keep his 'pockets stuffed with a volume or two for the purpose of reading when I ought to have been working'. 'Chief among these first purchases', he explains, 'were the volumes from Everyman's Library'.[114]

> What a boon they were! A handy size for the pocket, they introduced me to Emerson's essays, Marcus Aurelius, Coleridge's *Biographia Literaria*, Carlyle, and to other writers. Now that the Library has grown to be the greatest treasure-house of knowledge in the world, the influence it has had in helping to raise the general standard of learning must be beyond calculation. In my formative years, "Everyman" was "Guide, Philosopher, and Friend," and I cherish an unfading gratitude to those who promoted this epic of publishing.

With the vast scale and uniformity of the Everyman series, classical texts share the field with other world literature titles. World literature's psychological impact as a package has diminished temporal and spatial borders, allowing Marcus Aurelius' *Meditations* (no. 9) to stand alongside Coleridge and Emerson. It is no longer an ordeal to access his thinking, as it had been for the uneducated classes for centuries.

Garratt is the most committed and ingenious workplace reader we have encountered. To protect his open book from view he would erect, on the shop floor of his factory's sheet-metal department, 'a screen by putting boxes of fittings (ostensibly for use) on the vital part of the bench, fixed a small mirror in line with the door of his [the foreman's] office'.[115] He propped up his Everyman's edition of Thomas Carlyle's 1836 *Sartor Resartus* (which itself has a workman intellectual, a philosophising tailor or *sartor* at its centre) and 'alternated spasms of sumptuous reading with arid efforts at soldering or riveting, which I accomplished with about half the attention I gave to the print'.[116] Garratt also worked out how to read up a storeroom ladder. This was made just about feasible by the reduced size and price of the cheap reprint series, which found their acme in Everyman's Library.

The readers discussed in this chapter would be considered, by Richard Hoggart, untypical members of the British working class. Working-class intellectuals, he wrote,

> are exceptional, in their nature untypical of working-class people; their very presence at Summer Schools, at meetings of learned societies and courses of lectures, is the result of a moving-away from the landscape which the majority of their fellows inhabit without much apparent strain. They would be exceptional in any class: they reveal less about their class than about themselves.[117]

From the mid-19th century, however, increasingly favourable conditions for such exceptional behaviour widened social engagement with cultural materials, such as classical texts, traditionally considered to be the preserve of the expensively educated elite. To what extent this 'massification' of culture was imposed on the working classes from above, and whether or not this was to the detrimental marginalisation of grass-roots cultural practice, are questions that merit further exploration.

Notes

1 Adams (1903) 1.xiii.
2 The electorate increased from approximately 214,000 in 1780 to approximately 8 million in 1885.
3 *Reading Experience Database*, see Digital Resources, Bibliography for access details.
4 On libraries before 1850 see Kelly (1966).
5 See Chapter 20.
6 Revised and reprinted until 1866.
7 Revised and reprinted until 1816.
8 Spence (1771) vol. II, 337.
9 Sambrook (2010).
10 Spence (1771) 2.337.
11 Spence (1771) 2. 338.
12 Spence (1771) 2. 338.
13 Spence (1771) 2. 338.
14 Spence (1771) 2. 345.
15 Spence, Joseph (1771) 2. 348.
16 Thomas Turner & David Vaisey ed. (1984) 317. For *RED UK* entry: www.open.ac.uk/Arts/reading/UK/record_details.php?id=6880 (accessed: 08 November 2018). See further Vaisey (2004) *ODNB*. On the technical reasons for the appeal of Pope's translation to the less educated English-speaking reader, see Mack (1988) 348–58.
17 Turner (1984) 317.
18 Wilson (2012) 31.
19 E.g. Banister (1791) [Pindar]; L'Estrange (1720) [Josephus, 1st ed. London 1702] and (1678) [Seneca]; Gifford (1802) [Juvenal]; Creech (1682) [Lucretius]; Langhornes (1770) [Plutarch].
20 Wilson (2012) 31.
21 On BBC's Third Programme see Whitehead (1989) and Wrigley (2015) 51–3.
22 Carter (1845) 208. For *RED UK* entry: www.open.ac.uk/Arts/reading/UK/record_details.php?id=7668 (accessed: 08 November 2018). On the James/Thomas name confusion see Ferguson (2016).
23 Altick (1957).
24 Bamford 1849) 192. On Dacier see above p. 28 and Wyles (2016).
25 Bamford (1849) 192.
26 Bamford (1849) 280–81.
27 Bamford's slip in remembering 'Hume' for 'Gibbon' should be understood as a momentary conflation of Gibbon's great work with David Hume's successful and innovative *History of England from the Invasion of Julius Caesar to the Revolution of 1688* (1754–1762). On Hume (1754–1762) and William Robertson's *The History of Scotland during the Reigns of Queen Mary and of King James VI* (1759), see Hicks (2012) 578–81. On Gibbon see also Hicks (2012) 583–7 with full bibliography.
28 See Aubagne (1996).
29 Wilson (2012) 31. See also Hall and Macintosh (2005), index, s.v. 'France, 'French' and Speck (1998) 94–6, 206–8.
30 See Hall (2008a) 26, 64, 107.
31 For a male domestic servant see Robert Dodsley (1704–1764), alias 'The Footman Poet', who became a publisher of many classical books.

32 Translated by Nathaniel Hooke in the same year of its original publication in French, Hooke (1727).
33 See on Charles Manby Smith, below pp. 309–11. In 1883, as a 13-year-old, Henry Hawker, the son of a coachman, read Homer out loud in English (Pope's translation) to his local vicar for 3 shillings a week: see below pp. 113–14.
34 Mandelbrote (2004) *ODNB*.
35 Savile & Savile (1997) 85. For *RED UK* entry: www.open.ac.uk/Arts/reading/UK/record_details.php?id=450 (accessed: 22 November 2018).
36 Burn (1856, 2nd ed.) 113.
37 Burn (1856, 2nd ed.) 2.
38 Burn (1856, 2nd ed.) 113.
39 Burn (1856, 2nd ed.) 113.
40 Barclay (1934) 19–20.
41 Barclay (1934) 14–16.
42 On 'cockney classics' and cockney culture more broadly see Stead (2015b), Dart (2012) and Cox (1998).
43 Barclay (1934) 20.
44 Barclay (1934) 16.
45 Cassell (1851) 2.193.
46 Cassell (1851) 2.193.
47 Adams (1903) 1.112.
48 Adams (1903) 1.112.
49 Adams (1903) 1.112–19.
50 Adams (1903) 1.113.
51 Mitchell (2004) *ODNB*.
52 Nowell-Smith (1958) 22.
53 Cassell (1851) 1.1.
54 Cassell (1851) 1.97–8.
55 For Lloyd-George see esp. pp. 254–67, and Joseph Wright esp. pp. 303–5.
56 Burt (1924) 121.
57 Beard (1853).
58 Beard (1856) 3.
59 Burt (1924) 113.
60 Burt (1924) 113–14.
61 Sylvanus Urban (1884) 413.
62 Burt (1924) 118–19.
63 Counting the series' *Dictionary of Latin Quotations* (1856) and Bohn's own *The Standard Library Atlas of Classical Geography* (1861).
64 For an overview of Bohn's Classical Library, and his expurgation policy in particular, see O'Sullivan (2009) 107–129.
65 Bell (1924) 75, qtd in O'Sullivan (2009) 112.
66 Anon. (1884a) 137. See also O'Sullivan (2009) 112.
67 Coxe (1847) unpaginated publicity material in front matter.
68 Grossek (1937) 139. Grossek is Selver's pseudonymn.
69 O'Sullivan (2009) 114.
70 Courtney (2004*a*) *ODNB*.
71 Grossek (1937) 33.
72 Grossek (1937) 26.
73 Grossek (1937) 53.
74 Grossek (1937) 243. On composition in Greek and Latin see Stray (1998a) 68–74; Sidgwick & Morice (1885) and Gepp (1871).
75 Stray (1998a) 68.
76 Lowe (2007).
77 Jones (1942) 3.

78 Jones (1970) 25.
79 Fyfe (2012).
80 Further study of the presence of Classics in the cheap and periodical press at this time would make for an excellent topic of research.
81 Jones (1970) 147–8.
82 Altick (1957) 10; on Morley, see Solly (1898) and below pp. 348.
83 Jones (1970) 97.
84 Altick (1957) 7.
85 Altick (1957) 11–12.
86 On Stead's 'Penny Poets' see Lockwood (2013). On his output as publisher 1890–1903 see Brake (2012).
87 Whyte (1925) 2. 229; Anon. (1896) 30.
88 Stead in Macaulay (1895) preface.
89 Lockwood (2013) 11.
90 Lockwood (2013) 8.
91 Stamper (1960) 100.
92 Stamper (1960) 162.
93 Table of Contents for 64: I. Æneas, the father of kings—II. The twins—III. Romulus, the founder of Rome—IV. The Horatii and Curatii—V. The geese of the capitol—VI. The story of Coriolanus—VII. Cæsar's ambition—VIII. Antony and Cleopatra.
94 *Stories from Ancient Rome*, 'Books for the Bairns' [64] 31.
95 Stead (1901) 545.
96 Pope (1903); Dryden (1903). Richards also published Gibbon's *Roman Empire*, Vol. I.
97 Aeschylus (117) trans. Lewis Campbell; Aristophanes (134) trans. J. Hookham Frere; Homer *Iliad* (18), *Odyssey* (36) trans. Pope; Sophocles (116) trans. Lewis Campbell; Virgil (37) trans. Dryden, and (227) trans. J. Rhoades; Gibbon (35, 44, 51, 55, 64, 69, 74). Other publishing series, which remain unrecorded in the working-class reading experiences, exist. Three of importance are: 1. William Blackwood and Sons' *Ancient Classics for English Readers* (1870–circa 1905). This series of small volumes, worthy of further study, was 'proposed to give … some such introduction to the great writers of Greece and Rome as may open to those who have not received a classical education—or in whose case it has been incomplete and fragmentary—a fair acquaintance with the contents of their writings, and the leading features of their style'. Anon. (1870) 45; 2. Frederick Warne's *Chandos Classics*, which published successfully the standard reprint Classics cheaply, including Pope's Homer, Dryden's Virgil, Gibbon's *Roman Empire*, Horace's *Collected Poems*. 3. James Loeb's *Classical Library*, a comparatively expensive and scholarly series of bilingual translations from Greek and Latin (founded 1911), familiar to all Anglophone students of Classics, has done much to facilitate the classical reading of those already someway acquainted with the classical languages. As good as they are at what they do, their reach beyond the educated elite has always been limited. They vary considerably between titles, according to the translator and date of publication, but almost all require (and perhaps have always required) a further level of translation to become readily legible to the general reader unacquainted with the somewhat specialised language of classical translation. For this reason they have been popular with verse, performance and otherwise experimental writers and translators, who have felt able to treat the Loeb's 'foreign' English as if it were the source text itself; see, e.g. Ted Hughes's use of the Loeb of Seneca in Stead (2013). Mirte Liebregts (Radboud University) has been working on the early history of the Loeb Classical Library, and may well uncover new work on this ubiquitous, influential and 'taken for granted' publishing enterprise.
98 Hutchinson (1912) 1.1.
99 Azoulay (2014) 205–6.

100 Dent (1938) 143.
101 Rose (2004).
102 Rose (2001) 135.
103 For an overview of Dent's Everyman Library see Rose (2001) 131–6 and Dent (1938) 123ff.
104 Dent (1938) 16.
105 See also the example of the cobbler's apprentice Samuel Drew, pp. 431–3. On the ragged Grecian see p. 311.
106 Dent (1938) 23.
107 The painting is part of the collection at Darlington Library.
108 The Elementary Education Acts between 1870 and 1893, especially the 1880 so-called 'Mundella Act'. Anthony Mundella MP, Vice-President of the Board of Education from 1880–1883, obliged all School Boards and School Attendance Committees to frame attendance bye-laws and made school attendance compulsory in England and Wales between the ages of five and ten and provided penalties for the illegal employment of children under fourteen.
109 Rhys (1940) 165.
110 Altick (1957) 17.
111 Anon. (1903) 319–20.
112 Garratt (1939) 93. For *RED UK* entry i.e.: www.open.ac.uk/Arts/reading/UK/record_details.php?id=31070, accessed: 09 November 2018.
113 Garratt (1939) 96.
114 Garratt (1939) 96.
115 Garratt (1939) 97.
116 Garratt (1939) 97.
117 Hoggart (1957) 4.

4

18TH-CENTURY WORKING-CLASS POETS

> Some tell us that Homer was a beggar, and we all know that Virgil was a keeper of sheep, and no doubt Sappho plied her distaff; so that is one of the greatest mistakes to suppose that the smith must leave his anvil, the shoemaker his last, the weaver his loom, the seamstress her needle, the laundress her furnace, the shepherd his crook, or the labourer his spade, pickaxe, or hammer, before either of them can relish the sweets or enjoy the transports of poetry.[1]

The anonymous author in the *Working Man's Friend* (1850), perhaps John Cassell himself, here reveals the 'remarkable fact' that 'the classics studied at our universities were not written by university men'. Although they were composed by people closer to the land and manufacture than most mid-Victorian gentlemen, we may question his assertions about the ancient poets' relation to labour.[2] But that would be to bypass his central point that ancient Greek and Roman classics need not belong to the educated elite alone. Artisanal trade and literature, even that of antiquity, were compatible. This was a powerful message to readers who felt trapped by their circumstances in an uncultured underworld of labour and subsistence living.

This chapter reaches back over a century before Cassell's *Working Man's Friend* to explore the rich classical engagement of labouring poets who left their humble jobs only if they could finance themselves by the pen. There are three types of classical presence in 18th-century working-class poetry. First, poets use classical materials to ridicule the upper classes to working-class readers or their sympathisers. Second, working-class poets draw upon classical civilisation to convey the extremity of workers' suffering, and the magnificence of their skills. Third, they sometimes invoke ancient pastoral themes and the notions of leisure and retirement so important to Roman poetry, especially Horace. After some remarks on the satirical approach, the discussion engages with all three types of classical

DOI: 10.4324/9781315446608-5

presence in the poetry of Stephen Duck, Mary Collier, Thomas Blacklock and Ann Yearsley, respectively.

Workers' satirical classicism

Working-class satire may rely on a level of education for its jokes to land, when class-conscious writers who have somehow amassed more cultural capital than their peers critique the reactionary establishment, as in these verses:

> Ye Muses who mount on Parnassian towers,
> Come trooping to Sheffield, and help me to sing
> The time when our sons have all got out their sours,
> And relate all the joys that our Saturdays bring.
>   But hard words and Greek-em
>   Let learned folks speak-em;
> It's epic and tragic, bombastic we'll write;
>   And loudly we'll sing O,
>   In plain English lingo,
> The stirring in Sheffield on Saturday night.[3]

The anonymous street poet who penned this 18th-century broadside invites the Grecian muses to industrial Sheffield, while distancing himself from 'learned folks' whose 'hard' poetry is customarily decked out with classical flourishes. He sets up the familiar 'them and us' dichotomy: 'they' are classically educated upper classes; 'we' are fun-loving workers (here Sheffield cutlers and their variously employed female counterparts), who speak 'in plain English lingo'.

The same dichotomy appears in a later 19th-century broadside poem by Samuel Laycock of Stalybridge (1826–1893), an out-of-work cotton mill worker. Written in Lancashire dialect, it was produced originally as a broadsheet (i.e. on a single side of usually cheaply printed paper and sold in large quantities for negligible sums). 'Quality Row' is a nosey, funny, door-to-door exploration of the residents of a particular street in his hometown:

> Th' next dur to this parson, at heawse number three,
> Ther's a young ladies' schoo' kept bi Miss Nancy Lee;
> Aw've a cousin 'at gooas, an' aw met her one neet,
> An' hoo is rarely polished! hoo is some an' breet!
> An' hoo does spread her fithers abeawt when hoo walks,
> An' screws up her meawth when hoo simpers an' talks!
> Hoo's goin' up to Lunnon hoo tells me next week,
> To translate th' word 'turnip' to Latin an' Greek.[4]

The poem offers a performer—originally Laycock himself—a rich opportunity for parodying a prim-and-proper teacher. Laycock venomously distinguishes her from the uneducated 'us' by her 'polish' and 'brightness', a comically over-employed anaphora of the relative pronoun 'hoo' (for 'who', 'whom' and thrice 'she'), and her resemblance to a strutting peacock. The extravagance and futility of her expensive journey to the capital to translate the mundane 'turnip' into a classical language reveals how detached Miss Lee at number three is from the reality facing Stalybridge during the 1860s Cotton Famine.

Robert Burns shared his dismay at the apparently ineffective classical education in a dialect epistle to his fellow farmer and 'Scotch Bard', John Lapriak (1727–1807):

> What's a' your jargon o' your Schools.
> Your Latin names for horns an' stools?
> If honest Nature made you *fools*,
> What sairs your Grammers?
> Ye'd better taen up *spades* and *shools*,
> Or *knappin-hammers*.
>
> A set o' dull, conceited Hashes,
> Confuse their brains in *Colledge-classes*!
> They *gang in* Stirks, and *come out* Asses,
> Plain truth to speak;
> An' syne they think to climb Parnassus
> By dint o' Greek![5]

The supposed transformative potential of a Classics education is reduced to the transformation of young cows into 'asses', dimwitted beasts of burden. Burns, like Laycock, observes the futility of knowing the ancient words for common things, here animals not turnips, but his real point is his own right to the ascent of Parnassus, by dint of his native wit and poetic competence rather than the rote-learned knowledge.

As Vicinus reminds us, 'Broadsides along with the unstamped press were the poor man's newspaper until the rise of the popular press in the 1850s'.[6] These broadside ballads of Yorkshire, Lancashire and rural Scotland show that poetic activity was not limited to the metropolitan world of 'book poetry', controlled by aristocratic subscription lists and/or commercial enterprise. While lavish tomes containing Dryden and Pope's 'Englished' classics were sold to the gentry for sums equivalent to many months' wages, old poetry books were circulating for a fraction of the price and extempore poetry was chanted in the street; rhyming songs were printed on thin paper and handed round crowds at public executions and sold by hawkers from baskets or directly by poets, sometimes one and the same.

To avoid imposing contemporary notions of 'the poet' on the past, we here examine ephemeral, anonymous rhyming broadsides alongside more formally ambitious and accomplished verses by named and published poets and introduce some casualties of canonisation. The subject of classical presences in working-class poetry is vast, unexplored and can here be only cursorily surveyed. It is ripe for further investigation.

In the 18th and long 19th centuries, readerships for poetry expanded commensurately with cheaper printed material resulting from technological innovations, improving literacy levels and the social advance of the poorer classes who increasingly enjoyed the means and leisure for cultural consumption. Poetry was accessible across classes since it was often short enough to be printed as a broadside or a short section in a newspaper or journal and read or heard quickly by those with restricted leisure time and/or reading ability.

Broadsides generally ignore Classics altogether or satirise them, projecting contemporary earthly hierarchies onto a 'lang syne' mythological plane inhabited by gods as well as mortals, thus absurdly emphasizing the class biases of the present. There is, however, another order of broadside classicism. This occurs in pseudo-panegyric, which extols mundane phenomena, thus cutting elevated ones down to size. In Dublin, in 1728, a poet named Miles Aston published *An Heroick Poem on the Powerful and Commanding Art of Brewing*. He asks what the Olympian gods would have made of contemporary Irish brewing practices.

> The heav'nly Guests, wou'd their *Ambrosia* scorn,
> Had They but known the virtue of this Corn.
> 'If Bacchus boast, the Invention of his Wine,
> Prest from the Clusters of the creeping Vine:
> Equal applause, attend the *Brewer*'s Pain,
> Distilling *Nectar* from the solid Grain.[7]

The poem's epigraph is Horace, *Epistles* I.5.19: *fecundi calices quem non fecere disertum?* ('Whom does not the flowing bowl make eloquent?') No translation was provided, which might suggest that an educated readership was assumed. Yet Latin legends and epigraphs were *de rigueur* in the verse genre this poem mimics. Moreover, the Latin source is charged by class politics; the freedman Horace's subsequent line asks, 'Whom does wine not liberate even in pinching poverty?'

The Latin epigraph to Aston's later poem, celebrating the weaving trade, reads *nec factas solum vestes, spectare iuvabat/ tum quoque, cum fierent: tantus decor adfuit arti* (Ovid *Met.* VI.17–18, 'And it was pleasant not just to see her [Arachne's] finished work, but to watch her while she worked—such grace and artistry').[8] Ovid stressed Arachne's humble origin as daughter of an obscure dyer named Idmon and a deceased plebeian mother (VI.7–8, 10). A contemporary poem, anonymously printed, celebrates the Journeymen Sheermen and Dyers by also invoking Arachne's example: 'The Tedious *Spinster* twines the *Distaff-Thread*, / And *Ariadne's* [*sic.* read *Arachne*] Care prepares the *Webb*'. A footnote declares, '*Ariadne* [*Arachne*] was Metamorphis'd into a Spider, suppos'd to be first Inventress of *Spinning* and *Weaving*'.[9]

Sadly, we know little about Aston, who wrote several other poems.[10] But the two other identifiable poets then employed in writing similar poems in Dublin were from working-class backgrounds. These were the bricklayers Henry Jones

(1721–1770), discussed further below p. 215, and Henry Nelson (floruit 1725–1729), author of *Cavalcade: A Poem on the Riding of the Franchises* (c. 1720). Nelson's trade and social status were intrinsic to his poetic identity. He refers to them in all his works. As William Christmas has noted, aside from the anomalous 'water-poet' John Taylor (1578–1653), no earlier author's original trade is known to have been thus advertised in print.[11] Nelson uses classical references to establish the appropriate tone for his genre as a lofty but accessible panegyric and to provide a humorous mythical aetiology for the recipient of his praise.[12]

On 1st August every third year, a mounted procession took place in Dublin. The 25 trade guilds demonstrated their work on large carnival floats. *Cavalcade* is a poetic catalogue of tradesmen, delivered like a live commentary on the procession. Nelson begins by invoking the Muses, and returns to them and other classical allusions, often absurdly, to propel him through his arduous literary feat.

> Next march the Smiths, Men bravely us'd to fire,
> Without whose aid all Arts must soon expire:
>
> Before them clad in Armour in his Pride
> A Brawny Vulcan doth in Triumph ride;
> Not like the limping God whom Poets feign
> In Bands of Wedlock join'd to Beauty's Queen:
> But like the God of War, prepar'd to charge.[13]

Vulcan, as the smith of Olympus, has forever been metal-workers' divine representative,[14] but Nelson comically dodges his lameness. The butcher's trade required more thought:

> Not great *Pelides* on the *Trojan* Plain
> E're slaughter'd more, each has his Thousand Slain.[15]

Rather than 'Achilles', Nelson calls this hero 'Pelides', which might have been confusing for some of his audience, although others would know the patronymic from Pope's *Iliad.* And likening a butcher to Achilles as prolific slaughterer is a masterstroke, enhanced by the following mock-heroic reference to widowed farm animals:

> Their pointed Steels have many Widows made,
> And sent vast Colonies to *Pluto*'s Shade.[16]

The saddlers, 'On sprightly beasts', with golden saddles, led by an imposing warhorse, are treated to a more obscure myth, that of Philyra, abducted by the Titan Saturn in equine form:

> Just such a Colour, Limbs, and such a Size
> Old *Saturn* took, when fearing Jealous Eyes

Of angry Spouse, who caught him in a Rape,
The Letcher gallop'd off and made his 'scape.[17]

The parallel is awkward, its self-conscious artificiality and mock learnedness driving its humour. Nelson was an entertaining mock-panegyrist. His classical learning feels at odds with his occupation, and it is this incongruity that engenders laughter. The erudition tests the boundaries of 'common' classical knowledge, sometimes becoming arcane, lending the poem a textured quality.

Stephen Duck on labour and leisure

In 1730, a Wiltshire agricultural labourer burst upon the London literary scene. For his extraordinary literary talents, Stephen Duck (c1705–1756) was celebrated by local aristocracy, crowned by a canny publisher 'The Thresher Poet' (Figure 4.1) and subsequently received the patronage of Queen Caroline. Many poets attempted to tread in Duck's footsteps and escape indigence by

FIGURE 4.1 Stephen Duck (1705–1756), from Duck (1764), reproduced by courtesy of the British Library.

verse, creating the 18th-century literary equivalent of the televised talent show. Aspirants were offered a chance in a million to achieve economic freedom on the whims of hereditary aristocrats or commercially appointed pundits.

These poets presented themselves to the educated poetry-reading public as working-class writers. They competed for readers' attention under the rules of the emergent capitalist economy and consumerism. Their humble origin was central to their branding; they were both exotically *other* and enticingly 'locally produced'. Who better to write a poetic treatise on agricultural labour in Virgilian style than an actual agricultural labourer, such as Robert Bloomfield (on whom see pp. 436–7)? Yet John W. Draper was surprised that Duck 'seems mainly to have modelled his poetic efforts neither on the ballad tradition of his own class nor on the religious-Sentimental tradition of his immediate social betters, but on the Neo-classical *formulae* of the aristocracy'.[18] A page earlier, Draper has characterised this aristocratic neoclassicism derisively: 'with its symmetrical couplets and sharp-cut rhetoric, the artistic progeny of the Latin classics half-learned at Oxford or Cambridge'.[19]

Why should Duck write what we might call 'classicising' verse? To engage the Augustan British reading public, he needed to respect the contemporary literary and commercial conventions of British poetry. However unfashionable now, such poetry comprises some of the most skilful versification and successful classical translation ever made in the English language. Williams argues that 'the court and the church and neo-classicism patronised and emasculated' Duck.[20] This expresses the still-dominant view that Duck's 'The Thresher's Labour' was good, but when 'he left the thresher's barn it was downhill all the way'.[21] Yet Christmas's reappraisal of Duck's Horatian imitations shows that this narrative of decline is unsatisfactory; omitting the remainder of Duck's *oeuvre* means ignoring how a working class poet might absorb literary convention to win 'a place at the table' where he could represent his class, while maintaining individuality by inhabiting classical texts through which he would speak.[22] Duck was the first labourer who succeeded through verse in improving his circumstances while demonstrating the arbitrariness of class division.

Duck's story is both inspirational and tragic. After negotiating a meteoric rise to fame, in 1750 he settled as the Pastor of Byfleet, Surrey, where just six years later he drowned himself. But he offers a profound example of working-class Classics. An agricultural labourer from the age of 14, he nevertheless read as widely as he could. He probably worked overtime to finance his reading habit, but some books were bestowed upon him by early supporters. The Oxford Professor of Poetry, Joseph Spence (see above, p. 48), took a special interest in Duck's 'natural genius', and his list of the books Duck had acquired by 1730 indicates an inquisitive mind. This self-educator's collection is, as usual, eclectic, but—notwithstanding some satire—inclines towards theology, history and poetry.

In addition to his Bible and a book on arithmetic, Duck possessed an edition of Milton's *Paradise Lost*, which he read through three times, it is said, as an educated man might read a classical text, slowly and with a dictionary: 'He studied *Paradise Lost*, as we study the Classicks'.[23] He revelled in *The Spectator*, which featured plenteous poetry in extracted form and criticism.[24] Duck's earliest classical favourite was Seneca, whom he read in L'Estrange's translation *Morals: Of a Happy Life, Benefits, Anger and Clemency* (1679), along with the same Tory-High-Anglican's edition of Josephus. His first taste of Homer came with Fénelon (see above p. 51). He knew Ovid, presumably through Dryden's translation, and Dryden's Virgil. Duck was familiar with around ten plays of Shakespeare; Spence also lists Epictetus, Samuel Butler's *Hudibras*, the classically infused satirist Tom Brown (on whom see above, p. 39), and tavern-keeper Ned Ward's *London Spy*.[25]

In 1730, after being brought to the attention of a wealthy landowner, Duck was encouraged to write down his existing poems, including his verse epistle 'Honour'd Sir', a formulaic but polished *recusatio* adorned with classical flourishes.[26] He also wrote a new poem about his working life, 'The Thresher's Labour', consisting of 143 heroic couplets. Both poems first appeared in *Poems on Several Subjects* (1730), which was pirated and released apparently without Duck's blessing.

'The Thresher's Tale' uses classical material to depict suffering. Lines 33–43 constitute the first known English verses detailing the process of agricultural labour, from a labourer's perspective:

> ... more quick we whirl them [threshalls] round,
> From the strong planks our Crab-tree Staves rebound,
> And echoing Barns return the rattling Sound.
> Now in the Air our knotty Weapons fly,
> And now with equal Force descend from high.
> Down one, one up, so well they keep the Time,
> The *Cyclops'* Hammers could not truer chime,
> Nor with more heavy Strokes could *Aetna* groan,
> When *Vulcan* forged the arms of *Thetis'* son.
> In briny streams our sweat descends apace,
> Drops from our locks, or trickles down our face.[27]

There is pride here as well as an articulation of the rigours of threshing work,[28] and it alludes to Dryden's translation of Virgil, *Georgics* IV.251–3:

> With lifted Arms they [the *Cyclops*] order ev'ry Blow,
> And chime their sounding Hammers in a Row;
> With labour'd Anvils *Aetna* groans below.[29]

Duck establishes the favourable comparison of the thresher's barn with Virgil's forge, but the *chiming* hammers and *groaning* Aetna create the direct allusion to Dryden. This sonorous section of Dryden's translation has informed Duck's description of the working threshers. Poetic allusion can be produced by sonic memory.

Duck describes the harvest-time torments of agricultural work. Six days a week, from dawn to dark, the reapers cut the crop under the scrutiny of harsh masters. Even asleep, the reapers endure the sun-drenched field and its 'perplexing thistles':

> Hard Fate! Our Labours ev'n in sleep don't cease;
> Scarce *Hercules* e'er felt such Toils as these.[30]

The comparison of the suffering reaper with Hercules heroises the individual whose subjectivity has been overlooked forever. Duck closes with a final mythological comparand to the labourer's plight, Sisyphus (see further below, pp. 85–9):

> Thus, as the Year's revolving course goes round,
> No respite from our Labour can be found.
> Like *Sisyphus*, our Work is never done;
> Continually rolls back the restless Stone.
> Now growing Labours still succeed the past,
> And growing always new, must always last.[31]

This 1730 volume also contained a Biblical narrative called 'Shunamite' (based on the Book of Kings) and 'On Poverty'. It was an instant hit, read by the Earl of Macclesfield in the presence of Queen Caroline at Windsor, and it transformed Duck's fortunes. In 1733 she made him a Yeoman of the Guard and in 1735 the Keeper of the Queen's Library in 'Merlin's Cave', a hermitage within the grounds of Richmond Lodge.[32]

Duck's first authorised collection, *Poems on Several Occasions*, appeared in 1736. Under the tuition of another supporter, Dr. Alured Clarke (1696–1742), Duck had augmented his 'natural genius' with scholarship. Duck had spent much of the intervening six years 'in endeavouring to learn a Language, of which I was then entirely ignorant', i.e. Latin.[33] This unlocked Horace, whose formal and aural qualities are difficult to appreciate in translation. Clarke also encouraged Duck to use handbooks including Chambers's *Dictionary*, Danet's *Dictionary of Antiquities* and Bailey's *Etymological Dictionary*.[34] He recommended that Duck should learn Pope's 'Essay on Criticism' by heart, perhaps an 'attempt to Neoclassicize' him,[35] and study Pope's Homer, in lieu of a 'satisfactory translation'.[36] But it seems unlikely that Duck, the seasoned self-educator, would allow his curriculum to be entirely shaped by another, and the educational norms of the time would have led him directly to Roman and Greek writers, anyway.

In *Poems on Several Occasions*, a long verse epistle entitled 'Every Man in his Own Way' addresses a friend of Duck by the Latin pseudonym 'Laelius'.[37] In an oblique defence of his right to be a man of letters, Duck challenges the contemporary chokehold of classicism:

> I know your judgement, sense, and taste require,
> A bard to sing with spirit, force, and fire;
> Compose such numbers as the Ancients writ.
> Are Ancients then the only Men of Wit?
> Is wit immutable? Is nothing so,
> But what was writ Two thousand years ago?

Yet Duck's six years of study established a connection to the Latin muse. In 'Penelope to Ulysses' he skilfully paraphrases Ovid's *Heroides* 1 into smooth couplets; he translates an Italian neo-Latin tribute to Milton, and imitates three of Horace's odes together with one by Claudian.[38] In his preface he writes:

> I confess myself guilty of a great Presumption in publishing Imitations of *Horace*, when many eminent Hands have done it much better before me: But when I was only endeavouring to understand him, I found it difficult to conquer a Temptation I had to imitate some of his Thoughts, which mightily pleas'd me.[39]

Duck was justified in being concerned about potential responses to his Horatian experiments. Learned readers might well have reacted as Samuel Johnson did in 1765 to the shoemaker James Woodhouse's poetry: 'A school-boy's exercise may be a pretty thing for a school-boy; but it is no treat for a man'.[40] Yet in this self-deprecation we may also hear a celebration of Duck's own classical attainment, a glee in his occupation of an elite preserve. His Horatian experiments express the joy of discovery. In 'Every Man in his own Way' he speaks of his compulsion to write as an itch: 'This itch of scribbling *clings about my heart*'.[41]

The poems by Horace and Claudian that Duck imitated revolve around a theme favoured in his Latin reading. Like many 18th-century gentlemen scribblers, he advocates Horace's idealised moderation and the simple life, but in writing from experience of agricultural labour, he lends a different ring to the 'golden mean' philosophy. In imitating *Odes* II.16, he praises, like Horace, *otium* ('ease', or freedom from business and the acquisition of fame and/or wealth), but also thrift, peace and contentedness. Money cannot buy peace of mind. He expands the original in the final two stanzas, stemming from II.16.35–7, 'you wear woolen clothes dyed twice over in African crimson'.[42] Duck has,

> THY Board tho' twenty Dishes grace?
> Thy Coat as many Yards of Lace?[43]

I envy not the purple Dye,
Nor all thy gaudy Pomp of Luxury.

Moreover, Duck alters the addressee of the original, whose name is Grosphus, to read 'Thee', which seems to represent the landlord class. This wealthy, well-dressed other is contrasted with the authorial 'I', identified throughout the book as Duck himself. The following, final stanza reads:

I share some Sparks of PHOEBUS' Fire,
To warm my Breast, if not inspire;
Too little Wealth to make me proud,
And Sense enough to scorn the envious Crowd.[44]

Duck omits both the pagan Parcae and the small estate bestowed on Horace, but accepts the *spiritum Graiae tenuem Camenae* ('slight puff of inspiration from the Graeco-Roman Muse'), simplifying it to 'sparks of Phoebus' fire'.[45] The next line indicates his own new social standing, still not high but with some money, even if 'too little to make him proud'. Duck, like Horace, had transcended the occupational restrictions of his native class. But he alters the 'ill-disposed common herd' (*malignum vulgus*) despised by Horace to the less class-specific 'envious crowd'.

Duck's imitation of *Odes* III.16 is addressed to his local patron, Reverend Stanley, Rector of Pewsey:

O STANLEY, Honour of my Muse!
I fear, and justly fear,
To steer the Course Ambition shews,
Or soar beyond my Sphere.
He's poor, who always after Wealth aspires;
He's rich, who always curbs his own Desires.
I more admire an humble Seat,
Than all the Pomps, which vex the Great;
And from their gilded Roofs retire,
On Isis' Banks to tune my Lyre.[46]

Duck would have known that Horace rose from relatively humble origins, describing his family in *Satires* I.6.6 as *ignoti* ('unknown') and himself as 'born of a freed-man father'. Horace in *Ode* III.16–17 claims to be horrified by his new-found fame and the anxiety that attends it; Duck fears becoming conspicuous in society, too, but his fear of soaring beyond his sphere is more class-based. Horace, the literary overlord of elevated 18th-century classicism,[47] paradoxically provides the formal Trojan horse within which Duck could cross the class divide and pioneer his status, new to Britain, as a working-class man of letters.[48]

Duck compliments Pope in his imitation of Ode II.10.17–20: 'If things are bad now, they will not always be so: at times Apollo wakens the slumbering Muse with his lyre; he does not always keep his bow taught').[49] Duck writes:

> Tho' POPE with Illness oft complains,
> POPE is not always rack'd with Pains;
> But, warm'd with PHOEBUS' Fire,
> Sometimes he wakes the sleeping String,
> Or bids the silent Muses sing,
> And charms us with his Lyre.

Duck plays on Apollo's dual identity as deity of music and prophecy, but also pestilence (as in *Iliad* I). The alteration of the original flatters his renowned but delicate contemporary by associating him with the god of poetry but also with illnesses. This avoids obsequiousness and projects confidence above his former station.

Duck's early poetry about his experience as labourer has always been preferred to his 'neo-classical' writings in Pope's shadow. But Duck's later, classically informed writing has been underestimated. Perhaps this is because a poet, originally a self-professed 'Country Clown',[50] in challenging class distinctions through cultivating Classics had become a 'culturally disruptive and influential force'.[51] The aesthetic distaste of post-Romantic critics for Augustan idioms of poetry was another factor in his fall from favour. His royal patron Caroline of Ansbach's death and his own suicide took their toll on Duck's reputation during his lifetime and after it.

Mary Collier

When Queen Caroline gave royal patronage to Duck, 'twenty artisans and labourers turned poets and starved', or so quipped Horace Walpole to Hannah More.[52] There was indeed a wave of labourer poets following Duck, when 'the status of labourer served as a form of symbolic capital in the literary marketplace' after Duck's propulsion to fame and (modest) fortune.[53] They achieved differing degrees of success. But, as a group, 'these poets faced stiff opposition from authors of the gentlemanly classes who often voiced their concerns in the periodical press'.[54] Many aspirant hearts were broken. The attraction of substituting pens for tools was still considered pervasive when Byron published his *English Bards and Scotch Reviewers* (1810):

> Oh! since increased refinement deigns to smile
> On Britain's sons, and bless our genial isle,
> Let poesy go forth, pervade the whole,
> Alike the rustic, and the mechanic soul!

Ye tuneful cobblers! still your notes prolong,
Compose at once a slipper and a song;
So shall the fair your handywork peruse,
Your sonnets sure shall please – perhaps your shoes.[55]

May Moorland weavers boast Pindaric skill,
And tailors' lays be longer than their bill![56]

Full collections of poetry were however published by the Spitalfields weaver, John Bancks (1709–1751); the footman, Robert Dodsley (1704–1764); and Robert Tatersal, a London Bricklayer (poetically active 1734–1735).[57] Bancks and Dodsley, after publishing relatively successful poetic miscellanies, carved out positions in the (again relatively) lucrative bookselling trade and 'represent important individual examples of plebeian social ascent achieved within a burgeoning literary economy, without the royal patronage Duck received'.[58] They exude classicism, imitate Horace, and deserve further inquiry.

A buoyant reply to Duck came from The Washerwoman Poet of Petersfield, Mary Collier (1688–1762), whose *The Woman's Labour: An Epistle to Mr Stephen Duck* was published in 1739. She criticises Duck's ungenerous portrayal of women in 'Thresher's Labour'. One hundred and seventy-nine years before the Old Age Pensions Act 1908, she writes that she is an invalided and poverty-stricken elderly woman confined, after a life spent scrubbing linen and brewing, to a garret in Alton.[59] She recalls that Duck's poems

> brought me to a strong propensity to call an Army of Amazons to vindicate the injured sex: therefore I answered him to please my own humour, little thinking to make it public; it lay by me for several years, and by now and then repeating a few lines to amuse myself, and entertain my company, it got Air.[60]

Like Duck's references to Sisyphus and Hercules, Collier's desire to invoke an 'Army of Amazons' betrays a cultural knowledge beyond that commonly associated with women who had received scarcely a year of formal education. Moreover, she responds, perhaps mockingly, to Duck's classical references. She repudiates his suggestion that men work harder at harvest time by stating that women, after working the hay, also go home to housework, cooking and needlework.[61]

Her first classical allusion is to Jupiter and Danae, probably inspired by Ovid's *Ars Amatoria* III, in which the poet requests the Amazon, Penthesilea, to contend in love affairs, alongside hordes of females, effectively against men:

Jove once descending from the clouds, did drop
In showers of gold on lovely *Danae*'s lap;

The sweet tongu'd poets, in those gen'rous days,
Unto our Shrine still offer'd up their lays:
But now, alas! that Golden Age is past,
We are the objects of your Scorn at last.

But women, regrets Collier, are today no longer respected:

And you, great Duck, upon whose happy brow
The muses seem to fix their garland now,
In your late Poem boldly did declare
Alcides' labours can't with yours compare;[62]

Hercules had made regular appearances in the first two books of the *Ars Amatoria*, which are addressed to men. This text was enormously popular, and translations had been frequently reissued in the early 18th century.[63] Sadly, there is a question mark over the authenticity of Collier's poem.[64] But the author, whoever s/he was, out-Ducks Duck's whimsical classical references, concluding,

While you to Sisyphus yourself compare,
With Danaus' daughters we may claim a share;
For while he labours hard against the hill,
Bottomless tubs of water they must fill.[65]

By alluding to a more obscure myth of female perpetual labour, that of the Danaids (also to be found in *Ars Amatoria* III), the author trumps Duck's Sisyphus.

Collier is scathing about the poor remuneration offered to women, concluding, as Christmas points out, with a picture of 'a propertyless group of rural labourers in conflict with the owners of the land which they work':[66]

So the industrious Bees do hourly strive
To bring their Loads of Honey to the Hive;
Their sordid Owners always reap the Gains,
And poorly recompense their Toil and Pains.[67]

Collier may allude to the contemporary debate about the economy of luxury provoked by Bernard Mandeville's *The Fable of the Bees*, consisting of a 1705 poem, 'The Grumbling Hive' and a prose commentary published together with it in 1714. The work is informed by numerous sources including Lucian, Cicero, Virgil, Seneca, Columella, Pliny, Aelian and especially Aristotle and Aesop.[68] Mandeville argued that luxury created employment and motored wealth acquisition, but E.P. Thompson argues that 'Collier shows us the underside of luxury, in the laundry and the kitchens'.[69] Duck had also expressed cautious criticism of the landlords exploiting the threshers' labour.[70]

Thomas Blacklock

The blind Scottish poet Thomas Blacklock (1721–1791) is connected to Duck by a mutual patron, Joseph Spence,[71] who presented him as another of his 'natural geniuses'. Blacklock (Figure 4.2) was born in Annan, Dumfriesshire, to English parents. His father, John, was a Cumberland bricklayer and Ann, his mother the daughter of a Cumbrian cattle dealer.[72] As a baby he contracted smallpox and lost his eyesight, which prevented him from bricklaying, but his aptitude for literature and poetry was noticed. His father and friends read to him from 'the works of *Allan Ramsay*, *Prior's* Poems, and the *Tatlers*, *Spectators*, and *Guardians*'.[73] He heard the best English poets, 'among whom, *Milton*, and *Spenser*, *Pope* and *Addison*, were his chief favourites ... Poetry he always heard not only with uncommon pleasure, but with a sort of congenial enthusiasm'; he began to imitate them.[74]

In 1740 his father was crushed to death while inspecting a faulty malt kiln. But Blacklock was assigned the assistance of Richard Hewitt, a boy from the village, who was educated alongside his charge. Blacklock moved to Edinburgh under the patronage of a physician, Dr. John Stevenson. Despite the disruptive 1745 Jacobite rebellion, Blacklock passed through grammar school and entered Edinburgh University, where he studied 'philosophy and then divinity, and continued his interest in languages including French, Greek, Latin, and Italian'.[75]

FIGURE 4.2 Thomas Blacklock (1721–1791), reproduced by courtesy of National Galleries of Scotland, © National Galleries of Scotland.

Blacklock came to Latin and Greek late and by ear alone, becoming able to read a Latin author comfortably only at 20.[76] According to Spence, Blacklock came to look upon Stevenson 'as his *Maecenas*'; the first poem in his collection, addressed to Stevenson, imitates Horace's *Ode* I.1.[77]

> Thou, whose goodness unconfin'd
> Extends its wish to human kind;
> By whose indulgence I aspire
> To strike the sweet Horatian lyre:
> There are who on th' Olympic plain
> Delight the chariot's speed to rein;
> Involv'd in glorious dust, to roll;
> To turn with glowing wheel the goal …

While Blacklock maintains his fluently rhyming tetrametric couplets, he reveals sensitivity to the Latin by flexibly leaning into and away from the original, at once knowing, skilful and deliberate. 'To turn with glowing wheel the goal' is a neat negotiation with Horace's 'metaque fervidis / evitata rotis' ('shunning [i.e. driving past, avoiding collision with] the turning post with glowing wheels').[78] In his 'Pastoral Song' (1746), inspired by Allan Ramsay's stage comedy *The Gentle Shepherd* (1724), Blacklock uses the trope of the lover's response to gazing upon their beloved popularised by Sappho 31 and Catullus 51.[79] 'Sandy the Gay', the 'blooming swain', fixes his eyes on Girzy, a bonnie maid with 'breasts like hills of snaw' in a loose robe, and is physically affected:

> He fix'd his look, he sigh'd, he quak'd,
> His colour went and came;
> Dark grew his een, his ears resound,
> His breast was all on flame.[80]

The polysensory description, inherited from antiquity, gave Blacklock, who had never gazed upon a lover, a range of sensations poetically articulated. Poor Sandy becomes infatuated with his landlady, for they are Girzy's flocks he tends. He resorts to suicide, bidding his 'harmless, sportive flocks' and 'faithful dog' adieu. The ballad's Scots diction, later to be purged completely,[81] is fused with classical allusiveness, revealing the literariness of Blacklock's experiential universe.

Catullus was not translated into English in book-length form until John Nott of Bristol's pioneering bilingual edition was printed by the radical bookseller Joseph Johnson in 1795.[82] In Blacklock's day, some Catullan poems circulated both in Latin and English imitation via periodicals and anthologies, and his fifth poem ('Vivamus mea Lesbia atque amemus') was popular. Blacklock's imitation is another smooth, clever and relatively plain rendition in iambic tetrameters:

> Tho' sour loquacious age reprove,
> Let us, my Lesbia, live for love:

> For, when the short-liv'd suns decline,
> They but retire more bright to shine:
> But we, when fleeting life is o'er,
> And light and love can bless no more;
> Are ravish'd from each dear delight,
> To sleep one long eternal night … .[83]

Blacklock may do nothing remarkable here, but it *is* remarkable that a bricklayer's blind son was translating Catullus in 1756.

Blacklock became an established figure on the Edinburgh literary scene, famously the first to acknowledge the genius of Burns. As Shuttleton argues, Blacklock straddles two traditions in Scottish literature often kept separate, the Scottish Enlightenment and the Scottish Vernacular Revival.[84] He was a member of David Hume's intellectual circle and Hume for a time acted as a patron. Yet, as a talented songwriter, Blacklock once considered a career as a street performer. Blacklock's experience of patronage was troubled. He coveted a lectureship in Edinburgh, but on his patrons' advice grudgingly trained as a Presbyterian minister, a career move that ended in disaster and a return to Edinburgh's literary scene when his Kirkcudbright congregation objected to his blindness.

By investigating Blacklock's irreverent, vernacular manuscript poems, Shuttleton has shown how his oeuvre was shaped and Anglicised by his patrons and supporters.[85] Yet Blacklock's social rise could not have happened without patronage. There were no other educational routes, no help with special needs, nor opportunities for upward mobility. Philanthropic patronage has been accused of corrupting and destroying the talent it aimed to nurture. But beneath the polite and sentimental surface of patronised poets we may frequently discover 'a more socially discontented and politically aware poet'.[86] Classical poetry is central to the 18th-century poet/patron dynamic, since the 'neoclassical' mode is both the zenith of dominant literary culture, and one capable of expressing subtle shades of dissent.

Ann Yearsley

The relationship between Ann Yearsley (1753–1806), or 'Lactilla' the Milkwoman of Clifton, and her patron, the bluestocking poet Hannah More, is well documented.[87] Yearsley (Figure 4.3) illustrates how worker-poets could challenge their upper-class readerships by creative engagements with classical material. Early in their relationship, More was struck, typically, by her under-educated protégée's 'natural genius'. She wrote to Elizabeth Montagu,

> All I see of her, raises my opinion of her genius … Confess, dear Madam, that you and I know many a head competently stored with Greek and Latin which cou'd not have produced better verses. I never met with an Ear more nicely tuned.[88]

FIGURE 4.3 Ann Yearsley by Joseph Grozer, after Sarah Shiells (1787) Reproduced by courtesy of National Portrait Gallery, London © National Portrait Gallery, London.

Yet More was not inclined to educate Yearsley: 'I am utterly against taking her out of her Station. Stephen [Duck] was an excellent Bard as a Thrasher, but as the Court Poet, and Rival of Pope, destestable'.[89]

Yearsley had hit rock bottom after the severe winter of 1783–1784.[90] Destitute, she lay with her husband, elderly mother and five children, starving in a barn, but was rescued by a local gentleman named Vaughan. In the autumn of 1784, Yearsley was again collecting hogwash and selling milk door-to-door. Yearsley came to More's attention because her cook was Yearsley's client. Despite her fear of disrupting her new charge's class position, More bestowed on her a carefully partial education in the form of James MacPherson's *Ossian* (1760), John Dryden's *Fables, Ancient and Modern* (1700) and 'the most decent of the *Metamorphoses*'.[91] Scottish epic and translated myth granted Yearsley amateur access to classical stories without risking of a professional or scholarly grasp of the original literature.

But Yearsley realised quickly that it was through the Classics, especially Virgil, that she should stake her claim to significance. When More asked, in

August 1784, who her favourite authors were, she replied, 'Among the Heathens … I have met with no such Composition as Virgil's Georgics'.[92] More was astonished: 'How I stared! besides, the choice was so *professional*'.[93] Yearsley had clearly read at least the Introduction to Dryden's translation, in which he states that the *Georgics* were 'the best poem of the best poet'.[94] Throughout her poetic *oeuvre*, the juxtaposition of her classical learning and her lack of education attracted and repelled her middle- and upper-class readers. Her poetry was socially and culturally transgressive, in a bold, incendiary manner fitting to her revolutionary epoch.

Yearsley campaigned against the slave trade on which her native Bristol's fortune was founded,[95] and spoke out against the most powerful.[96] Stepping beyond 'the ghetto of folk poetry',[97] and into the realm of polite and politically engaged letters was to breach decorum. Against her patron's wishes and protests, Yearsley demanded to be read on her own terms as a professional poet and one who disdained the pedantry of the reactionary elite.[98] More simply had nothing further to do with her.[99]

Rose observes that Yearsley 'could only find her independent voice by mastering classical literature, which she appropriated as the collective property of all classes'.[100] In place of the depoliticizing force of previous neoclassicism, Yearsley instrumentalised neoclassical tropes on behalf of the oppressed and was consequently criticised. In 'Addressed to Ignorance, Occasioned by a Gentleman's Desiring the Author Never to Assume a Knowledge of the Ancients', she reveals that her own self-definition has been shaped by canonical authors, yet she questions their right to receive the reverence long bestowed upon them by elite, and male, society. She shows off her knowledge of ancient figures, while insouciantly arguing that if Pythagoras's theory of reincarnation is to be believed, these august figures may all be engaged in lowly occupations now. She, conversely, may in a previous life have possessed a high status.[101] Rose calls the poem 'a high-wire burlesque', which 'transforms the great Greeks and Romans into Hogarthian lowlife' and in which Yearsley's levelling message is uncompromising: 'this is my culture as well'.[102]

She skilfully balances nonsense with witty pictures that display her learning. Diogenes, the Cynic philosopher who wore rags and slept rough, is reincarnated as 'an ambling old Beau'; the loquacious Nestor is now 'quite dumb'; the Spartan lawgiver Lycurgus is hanged as a thief 'by his own rule'. Democritus and Solon 'bear baskets of moss, / While Pliny sells woodcocks hard by'. Sly Ulysses is reincarnated as a fox; chaste Penelope has five lovers and the cuckold Menelaus is a 'doubly horn'd' Buck.[103] These allusions are accessible to people who have read their Classics in translation or adaptation. Lactilla, protected by the 'dark veil' of Ignorance, concludes,

> Heav'n knows what I was long ago;
> No matter, thus shielded, this age I defy,
> And the next cannot wound me, I know.[104]

Yearsley's *The Rural Lyre* was published in 1796. It includes three fictional verse epistles set in ancient Rome,[105] apparently from an unfinished project, which demonstrate her confidence in handling classical authors and culture.[106] But 1796 was a turbulent time (see Chapter 13). British working-class men were either dying in Caribbean and European wars or starving with their families at home. The book begins by addressing the Right Honourable Earl of Bristol and Bishop of Derry, Augustus Frederick Hervey (1730–1803), with a quotation from Vicesimus Knox:

> It is asserted that, "if *Alexander* and *Caesar* had been born in a cottage, they would have died in obscurity" … . If the "walls of a cottage" could have entombed forever such mighty spirits as those of Caesar and Alexander, how must the clown "dazzle", who emerges from the sequestered gloom with his wits about him!

The educator Knox supported revolution in Britain, denouncing William Pitt's assault on civil liberties and war against revolutionary France. He also supported women writers, including Yearsley, and endorsed their work in print.[107] It was thus with the radical left that Yearsley associated this volume.

The frontispiece is a sentimental engraving of the mournful goddess 'British Liberty', beside a monument to Brutus (the mythical Trojan founder of Britain). With one exposed breast, she leans a liberty-cap standard against her shoulder.[108] The Anglicised symbology of the French Revolution is unmistakeable. Waldron attempts to undermine Ferguson's reading of Yearsley as an early feminist and/or class warrior, instead understanding her as representative of 'a certain benevolent conservatism'.[109] But this interpretation is not supported by the major poem in this collection, 'Brutus', an epic 'fragment', in which native Britons, with divine intervention, peacefully capitulate to the Trojan invaders. Brutus (son of Ascanius), is led to Britain by Jove, on Venus's supplication. Liberty herself commands Brutus to 'let fall thy spear', since 'To yield is to deserve a throne'. She continues: 'My Britons are not slaves: / There lives no conqueror but the man who saves,' i.e. Jesus of Nazareth. When Brutus yields, making peace with an invading foreign power, it has desirable results in Yearsley's utopian vision: peace, plenty and liberty.[110]

Throughout the collection, Yearsley portrays the bitter plight of the poor under Pitt's war-hungry government. In 'Prayer and Resignation', she comes close to overt criticism of Pitt.[111] Whilst there were working-class pro-war 'Church and King' mobs during Pitt's ministry, the intensity of impressment and punitive taxation made him deeply unpopular among the poor; in October 1795 George III's carriage was bombarded by protesters calling for 'Bread', 'No War' and 'No Pitt'.[112] In her 'Elegy to Bristol', Yearsley details the shameful murder by the military of around 20 people protesting against the collection of bridge-tolls.[113] The turbulence of the times would soon produce a distinctive proletarian literary culture, but Yearsley, despite her humble origins, cannot be said to be writing proletarian literature. She was writing, successfully, in the dominant literary style of higher classes. As we see in other chapters, labouring-class literature reached its height in the Chartist movement, which had its own autobiographers, newspapers, novelists, visual artists, poets and dramatists, and established a literary culture whose echoes continue to reverberate today.[114]

Notes

1 Anon. (1850) 2.258.
2 The case for Virgil is more complicated, since the disparities in wealth under the late Roman Republic and early Empire were acute. The idea that Virgil ever kept sheep is absurd when we consider that Roman agricultural labour was founded on a slave economy, which classical writers write out of contemporary experience: see Fitzgerald (1996) 389–96, and Heitland (1921) 229. For Greek authors' erasure of the work of production see Hall (2011a) 26–7 and especially (2018f).
3 Anon. (1862) 86.
4 Laycock (1908) 60.
5 Burns (2001) 135, lines 61–72. See also Crawford (2009) 263, on Burns' preference for the 'vernacular life of the village' to mixing in Edinburgh University circles, where a copy of Cicero's speeches was bestowed upon him.
6 Vicinus (1974) 10.
7 Aston (1728) 1.
8 Aston (1734[?]) 1; On the scarcity of Roman poetry's focus on the life of the poor labourer see Fitzgerald (1996) 389–94.
9 Anon (1727) 1.
10 In addition to this celebration of the brewing trade, he also wrote *Virtue and Industry* (1727), *An Elegy on the Lamented Death of John Mullen* (1729), *An Heroick Poem on the Weaving Trade* (1734[?]) and *Hibernia out of Mourning* (1727).
11 Christmas (2001) 67. On John Taylor, the Thames waterman and royalist poet, see Capp (2004) *ODNB*.
12 N.B. the aetiology is sometimes derived from Biblical narratives, e.g. the inventor and thus 'patron saint' of tailoring (Nelson [1727] 1) is claimed to be none other than God himself, who first made clothes for Adam and Eve out of animal skins (*Genesis* 3.21).
13 Nelson (1725) 1.
14 Nelson (1725) 1. See Ravenhill-Johnson (2015), Hall (forthcoming f) and below, pp. 404-6.
15 Nelson (1725) 1.
16 Nelson (1725) 1. For a similar play on butchers as sacrificing Homeric hecatombs, see below, p. 147.
17 Nelson (1725) 1. See Apollonius Rhodius' *Argonautica* II.1233, Ovid, *Met.* VI.126, Virgil, *Georgics* III.92 and 549.
18 Draper (1926) vi.
19 Draper (1926) v.
20 Williams (1973) 134.
21 Duck and Collier (1989) vii.
22 Christmas (2001) 7; Christmas (2009) 27; 43–5.
23 Spence (1731) 11.
24 Spence (1731) 23. On this periodical, see especially above pp. 32–3.
25 Spence (1731) 9.
26 It was so learned and literary, in fact, that its recipient, a locally born 'young gentleman of Oxford' named Thomas Giffard, did not believe it to be Duck's own work. Batt (2015) I.428–.9.

27 Duck (1736) 12.
28 Goodridge (1995) 47.
29 Dryden (1697) 129.
30 Duck (1736) 25.
31 Duck (1736) 27.
32 Stephen (2004) *ODNB*.
33 Duck (1736) x.
34 Clarke (1847) 1.191. The publications correspond to: Chambers (1728); Danet (1700); and Bailey (1721).
35 Clarke (1847) 1.194; Davis (1926) 36; Pope (1711).
36 Clarke (1847) 1.198.
37 Gaius Laelius was the friend of Scipio Africanus and the subject of Cicero's treatise on friendship *de Amicitia*. The name, possibly given to Spence, is thus flattering, associating him with an ancient archetype of friendship. Laelius is also thought to be of relatively low social status. As *aedilis plebis* in 196 BCE he was certainly not a patrician.
38 'Penelope to Ulysses': Duck (1736) 119; 'Ad Joannem Miltonum': Duck (1736) 271; Horace *Odes* 2.10, 2.16 and 3.16 appear in sequence in Duck (1736) 272–7; and an imitation of Claudian 20.52 (*Felix qui* …) follows at Duck (1736) 288–92.
39 Duck (1736) xi.
40 Boswell et al. (1936) II.127: on Woodhouse see below pp. 421–5.
41 Duck (1741) 1 (line 6); see Juvenal *Satires* 7.51 (*cacoethes scribendi*).
42 Rudd (2004) 129.
43 Duck (1736) 280.
44 Duck (1736) 281.
45 Duck (1736) 281.
46 Duck (1736) 285 (lines 47–56).
47 On Horace and cultural capital see Harrison (2017), especially 1–3.
48 On the emergence of the working-class intellectual see Krishnamurthy (2009b) and, on Duck as pioneer, see Christmas (2009) 27 in same volume.
49 Christmas (2009) 21. Translation Rudd (2004) 115.
50 Duck (1750) 436.
51 Christmas (2009) 27.
52 Walpole (1961) 220.
53 Christmas (2001) 65.
54 Christmas (2001) 20.
55 For 'tuneful cobblers' see below, Chapter 20.
56 Byron (1810) 59.
57 See Christmas (2001) 95–7.
58 Christmas (2001) 110.
59 Collier (1762) v.
60 Collier (1762) iv.
61 Collier (1762) 9–11.
62 Collier (1762) 7.
63 See e.g. King (1708).
64 Her book carries the names of nine Petersfield residents, all attesting to her authenticity, which to a cynic would prove only that the booksellers knew that the text appeared spurious. The maiden name of Joseph Spence's mother was Mirabella Collier, but this may well be a coincidence.
65 Collier (1762) 16.
66 Christmas (2001) 127. For the bees and Virgil *Georgics*, via Dryden, see Milne (2001) 109–29 and Landry (1987) 115. For the Virgil's bees as idealised slave gang see Fitzgerald (1996) 394 n.19.
67 Collier (1762) 16.
68 See Farrell (1985), and, on the complicated publishing history, Kaye (1921).

69 Duck and Collier (1989) xiii.
70 Duck (1730) 18.
71 On whom see above, 48 and 79-80, and below, p. 424.
72 Smith (2004) *ODNB*.
73 Spence in Blacklock (1756) ii. Allan Ramsay (1686–1758) was a poet whose father was superintendent of the mines at Leadhills, Scotland. The poet Matthew Prior (1664–1721) was the son of a Dorset joiner whose talent was spotted when an aristocrat saw him reading Horace.
74 Spence in Blacklock (1756) iii.
75 Smith (2004).
76 Spence in Blacklock (1756) v.
77 Spence in Blacklock (1756) iv; 'Horace Ode 1. Imitated' (1756) lv.
78 Authors' translation.
79 Blacklock (1756) 84–9. On the sources of and attitudes accessible in the period towards the Catullan/Sapphic hybrid poem see Stead (2015b) 193–4.
80 Blacklock (1756) 86, lines 29–32.
81 See Shuttleton (2013) 30, who describes the Anglicisation of Blacklock's poetry by his patron David Hume and others.
82 Stead (2015a) 33–98.
83 Blacklock (1756) 60.
84 Shuttleton (2013) 21–2.
85 Shuttleton (2013) *passim*.
86 Shuttleton (2013) 41.
87 Andrews (2013) with bibliography; see also the biography of Waldron (1996) and, for an account of Yearsley's attitudes to nation, class and gender, Ferguson (1995) 45–9.
88 Hannah More to Elizabeth Montagu, 22nd October 1784 [Huntington Library MS MO 3988, p. 1, p. 4], quoted in Landry (1990) 18.
89 More to Montagu: 27th September 1784: MS MO 3988, p. 1, quoted in Landry (1990) 20 and Mahl and Koon (1977) 279.
90 Waldron (1996) 18.
91 Mahl & Koon (1977) 279.
92 More to Montagu, August 27th 1784: Huntington Library MS MO 3986, p. 3, quoted Landry (1990) 128.
93 More to Montagu, August 27th 1784: Huntington Library MS MO 3986, p. 3, quoted Landry (1990) 128.
94 Yearsley used her newly won capital to found a circulating library, 'Ann Yearsley's Public Library', which had a copy of Dryden's *Virgil*: see Yearsley (1793).
95 Yearsley (1788).
96 For 'social good' threatened by 'lamented war' see Yearsley (1796) 16.
97 Rose (2001/2010) 19.
98 Landry (1990) 18–9.
99 Rose (2001/2010) 19; Landry (1990) 18.
100 Rose (2001/2010) 19.
101 Yearsley 1787, 93–9; see Waldron 1996, 155–7. The poem has been discussed by Rose (2001/10) 19-20, Doody (1985) 130, Hall (2007b) 128–9 and Richardson (2015a).
102 Rose (2001/10) 19
103 Yearsley (1787) 95; 97 and 95.
104 Yearsley (1787) 99.
105 'The Consul C. Fannius to Fannius Didius' (47–59), 'Familiar Poem: From Nisa to Fulvia of the Vale' (60–4), and 'Familiar Poem: From C. Fannius to Plautus' (65–6). Her chief source for Roman history is most likely to have been Oliver Goldsmith's *The Roman History* (1769), which appears in her circulating library catalogue.
106 See 'Advertisement' in Yearsley (1796) ix.

107 Knox (1783/4) and multiple subsequent editions, and Knox (1789?) with multiple subsequent editions.
108 High up on the subscription list to Yearsley's volume was the famous Foxite campaigner the Duchess of Devonshire.
109 Waldron (2004) *ODNB*; Ferguson (1995) 45–9.
110 Yearsley (1796) 1–27.
111 Yearsley (1796) 128–35.
112 Rose (1911) 282–3.
113 Yearsley (1796) 100–9.
114 Goodridge (2006) 1.xv.

5

CLASSICS AND CLASS IN LIFE-WRITING

Introduction

In his 1931 memoirs, Ben Tillett, Trade Unionist and former MP, now over 70 years old, recalled working in the east London docks in the late 19th century (Figure 5.1). He had realised the need to acquire some conventional education when the harshness of life in the East End persuaded him to become an agitator and labour evangelist. But he felt ill-equipped; 'Before I could enter upon that stage of my career there were arrears of education to make up. I had much to learn, as well as something to forget'.[1] A native of Bristol, Tillett was labouring in a brickyard by the age of eight, followed by work as a fisherman, circus acrobat, cobbler and sailor. He moved to London and, in 1887, formed the Tea Operatives and General Labourers Union, later renamed the Dock, Wharf, Riverside and General Labourers' Union, while working at Tilbury docks. He earned fame as a union leader in the London Dock Strike of 1889, and in 1910 co-founded the National Transport Workers' Federation, later the TGWU. One paragraph of his memoirs starkly evokes the exhaustion induced by his work.

> As a docker I had tried to save money, and starved to buy books. I was struggling to learn Latin, and was even trying to study Greek, lending my head and aching body to the task after my day's work on the dock-side, or in the tea warehouse where I was employed—work which meant carrying tons on my back up and down flights of stairs.[2]

Despite failing to master Greek and Latin, the attempt at self-education revealed that he was talented as a wordsmith: he could have been a professional writer, he says, if he had been born 'under a luckier star, with fuller opportunities than I enjoyed in the way of leisure, and a more intensive cultivation of my native

DOI: 10.4324/9781315446608-6

FIGURE 5.1 Ben Tillett (1860–1943), from Tillett (1931), reproduced from copy in Hall's personal collection.

qualities'.[3] He returns to the theme later: 'If I have one grouch against the world rather than another, the lack of opportunity for acquiring education in my earlier days is that one big grouch'.[4]

The image of Tillett struggling against fatigue is haunting. Fortunately, in later life he possessed both leisure and writing skills to preserve his invaluable memories. Almost all the book is devoted to his political career and has nothing to do with antiquity. But the frustrating encounter with Classics as a young activist represents a psychological turning-point in the text. He sees through to the heart of the problem facing the labour movement—that people who have always had to sell their labour simply do not have the time and leisure to acquire the education that will allow them to be emancipated in class terms. At the same time, he identifies his own skill with language, which he was subsequently to use effectively both as an orator and as a writer in the cause of the working class. But the classical encounter occurs simultaneously with his recognition of his life's purpose as a socialist proselytiser. It is a transformative episode that marks the turning-point in his life.

One mode of reading autobiography is as a source of historical evidence. Despite A.J.P. Taylor's claim that 'written memoirs are a form of oral history set down to mislead historians', and 'useless except for atmosphere',[5] even the most crafted literary autobiography can be mined for certain kinds of historical information, in that the process of writing it often prompts otherwise buried memories,[6] or it offers an intelligible account of experience.[7] Some working-class writers offer lists of books they claim to have read in their earnest autodidactic endeavours which seem too extensive to be persuasive. Yet even where there are grounds for scepticism, autobiographers' claims about their reading provide titles that are informative about the kind of literature which authors, and the readership they anticipated, would find it plausible that it had been available and appealing. Certain works—Pope's Homer, Gibbon, Rollin, *Cassell's Popular Educator*, James Harris's *Hermes: or a Philosophical Enquiry Concerning Universal Grammar* (1751), the *Penny Magazine* and later *The Harmsworth Self-Educator* (1905–1907), recur in workers' accounts of the first serious books they encountered and have supplied some of the evidence we have cited in other chapters.[8]

But the primary purpose of studying autobiographies may not be to uncover factual truth. The realisation of the wishful fantasies informing much of what Heinrich Schliemann wrote about himself illuminates his psychological make-up, his aspirations, and the contents of his imagination.[9] Analysing the overall narrative arc has been customary since Georges Gusdorf's seminal *Conditions et limites de l'autobiographie* (1956) proposed that people narrating their lives to themselves, or to others, reconstruct series of events, which may have unfolded randomly, in a way that attempts to impose a unified structure upon them.[10] Among the more self-conscious working-class life writings from the late 18th century to the early 20th, a development can be traced from spiritual or confessional biography to a narrative with a clear rite-of-passage consisting of an educational opportunity or encounter with a mentor, leading to personal self-improvement; alternatively the initiatory moment may be a recognition that the individual has been excluded, with significant consequences, from education. By the 1880s, the dominant structure has become a public-facing story of how a disadvantaged individual developed into a career politician, academic or a servant of the labour movement, often tracing an arc which consists of continuous social ascent against odds. An outstanding example of the last category is the bestselling autobiography of Jack Lawson (1881–1965), *A Man's Life* (1932), which he dedicated to his fellow miners. It is discussed in detail below on pp. 469–70.

Other tools for the analysis of autobiographies can aid the recovery of working-class intellectual history. James Olney precipitated the poststructuralist obsession with fictions of the self by emphasising the metaphors which memoirists use in describing their remembered experience.[11] Rockwell Gray examined how the unity of an autobiographical narrative unravels under the pressure of its author's ambivalence and shifting sensibilities over time; more illuminating than imposed unity is the conflict between the subject's rival aims, principles, qualities and talents.[12] Others study the gap between the 'reality' of the individual as suggested in other sources and the crafted 'mask' or 'persona' created by their historical self-fashioning.[13]

A useful concept for analysing the intersection of Classics and class in such materials is transformation, which Carolyn Barros, in her study of five eminent Victorians' autobiographies, argues is central to life-writing.[14] The shape imposed on the narrative in autobiographies (and those of the working class are not exceptions) usually entails progress and change; the 'How I was once' and 'What I became' of the author. 'It is the internal transformation of the individual—and the exemplary character of this transformation—that furnishes a subject for a narrative discourse in which "I" is both subject and object'.[15] In *Grace Abounding to the Chief of Sinners* (1666), Bunyan traces his passage from sinner to exemplar of Christian virtue.[16] Rousseau's *Confessions* (1782–1789) relate the author's path from innocent but inquisitive and risk-addicted youth to the (misunderstood) Romantic social reformer he regarded himself to be in maturity;[17] this book fundamentally informed the entire tradition of radical autobiography, being studied by, for example, the docker Ben Tillett.[18] Even where the overall narrative arc may trace gradual teleological evolution or sustained execution of the individual's life project, there is usually a pivotal or transformative moment.

For Kettering textile worker John Leatherland, it was moving at the age of 21 from employment as a ribbon weaver, which required total attention, to a complex loom and then a velvet-factory. There he had just sufficient freedom from the machinery to organise a Mutual Instruction Society and read enough to become a part-time poet and lecturer on literature. His favourite books included Plutarch's *Lives* and Gibbon's *Decline and Fall.* He began publishing after he won first prize, financed by 'some gentlemen of Kettering', for an essay entitled 'Best Means of Improving the Condition of the Working Classes'.[19]

Prominent Methodist Joseph Barker, born into abject poverty into a family of spinners near Leeds in 1806, embarked on a programme of self-education, which included studying Greek, in order to read the New Testament in the original, as well as Latin. This enabled him to identify his life project as a preacher because he could now see religious subjects

> in a clearer and more satisfactory light. Mysteries that had hung around religion from the beginning, began, in part at least, to fade away. The light began to pour itself in something like its purity upon my mind.[20]

Although Cardinal Newman was born into a prosperous banking family, the turning-point in his autobiography, underlined by the doubleness of its occurrence, illuminates those in working-class equivalents. In 1864, he describes how his conversion to Roman Catholicism in 1845 was adumbrated by rediscovering his first school Latin verse-book, inscribed just before his tenth birthday: he had drawn a cross and a rosary on its first page.[21] Two pivotal incidents—the sketching child and the adult wavering before he took that momentous decision—are in this passage fused through the symbolism of the Latin text-book. An equivalent encounter to those narrated by Tillett, Lawson and Newman, specifically with classical authors, is not infrequent in the many working-class memoirs from the late 18th to the early 20th centuries. This chapter looks at the literary context from which these emerged, before teasing out the similarities and differences between a selection of eight of these pivotal encounters, and concluding with a few remarks on the reflection of literary expressions of such real-life experiences in the canonical 19th-century novel.

Contexts and evidence

Working-class memoirs include not only published books, but unpublished reminiscences, letters, diaries and personal journals. Annotated details about the majority of these were compiled in the pioneering three-volume *The Autobiography of the Working Class*, published by John Burnett, David Vincent and David Mayall in the 1980s. This collection has made it far easier to study them,[22] and we have learned much from three pre-existing specialist studies of their characteristics by Vincent, Nan Hackett and Regenia Gagnier.[23] Given the prominence of classical education in the definition of class since the late 17th century, the presence—or absence—of references to classical material in them is necessarily revealing. Many workers counted themselves fortunate to have had acquired basic literacy at Sunday School and one form of evidence is the deafening silence in many memoirs on any historical, cultural or philosophical topic at all, let alone on ancient civilisations; instead, many relentlessly describe the hunger and privation suffered by people who had worked as children in mills, mines and quarries. 'A vast amount of wheeling, dragging, hoisting, carrying, lifting, digging, tunneling, draining, trenching, hedging, embanking, blasting, breaking, scouring, sawing, felling, reaping, mowing, picking, sifting and threshing was done by sheer muscular effort, day in, day out'.[24] One might add labour in the domestic realm: minding infants, peeling vegetables, scrubbing floors, laundering and mending textiles, bed-making, carpet-beating and emptying chamber-pots; discussions of reading materials in the autobiographies by working-class women have proven especially difficult to locate.[25]

Thomas Jordan, a County Durham miner born in 1892, says that his schooling stopped abruptly in 1900 when he was eight. He could not learn 'higher mathematics, beyond simple arithmetic', and 'so I was doomed for the pits'.[26]An Airedale factory girl recalls how her natural aptitude for language and thirst for reading had been repeatedly frustrated by the need to earn money, from the time when she was first put to work in a brickyard just after her eighth birthday.[27] Pioneering Workers' Educationalist and Trade Unionist Edith Hall (no relation), in her memoir *Canary Girls and Stock Pots*, eloquently expresses her frustration at the limits of her education. Her eyes had been opened to the possibilities of using books for personal development only when she read Hardy's *Tess of the D'Urbervilles* and could relate to the heroine who was, for once, labouring-class.[28] Hardy had himself been writing from personal experience. As the son of a stonemason, and apprenticed to an architect's firm, he had been denied a public school and university education; like the hero of another novel, Jude Fawley of *Jude the*

Obscure, he had struggled to learn enough Greek to read the *Iliad* as a teenager.[29] But unlike Jude, Tess or Edith Hall, Hardy rose through the social ranks to become a prosperous pillar of the literary establishment.

Gustav Klaus' collection of a variety of short stories of the 1920s, supposedly based on real narratives and set in mining, factory and vagrant communities, for example, contains no mention of education whatsoever, with a single exception so conspicuous that it proves the rule. In R.M. Fox's *Casuals of the City*, Jack Smith, an interesting tramp, is described as

> a hoarse little cockney … He had a talent for public exhortation, varying from railings in Hyde Park to pill-selling and tie-selling in different market-places … His friends [i.e. other tramps] called him the Westminster Demosthenes.[30]

Yet some encounter with classical material does feature in a noticeable proportion of working-class life writing, often in an episode similar to Tillett's frustration when attempting a Docklands self-education, where the subject comes to a realisation about either their limited opportunities or their desire for self-improvement.

Although well-educated individuals had written accounts of their lives much earlier,[31] both the working-class prose memoir and the actual term *autobiography* seem first to have appeared in the 1790s.[32] In 1796, an article discussing Edward Gibbon's *Miscellaneous Works* approves of the emergence of individuals' secular accounts of their lives rather than the religious or spiritual spoken confession; the 'modern practice of self-examination, autobiography, and written instead of auricular confession, may be considered as an improvement in the republic of letters'.[33] Yet, by 1809, a disgruntled Isaac Disraeli prophesies

> an epidemical rage for auto-biography to break out, more wide in its influence and more pernicious in its tendency than the strange madness of the Abderites, so accurately described by Lucian … Symptoms of this dreadful malady (although somewhat less violent) have appeared amongst us before. London, like Abdera, will be peopled solely by "men of genius".[34]

The classical reference is deliberately arcane, pointing to chapter 1 of Lucian's *How to Write History* (*Quomodo Historia Conscribenda Sit*), in which the entire population of Abdera imagined they were nonpareil actors after witnessing the international star tragedian Archelaus perform in their city.[35]

By the 1820s, when modes for the literary expression of a self-consciousness about working-class identity was beginning to be developed in journalism produced by and for the working class,[36] memoirs of the non-famous had become a recognised genre.[37] They were also already criticised for offering mediocre non-entities the opportunity for self-publicity.[38] The phenomenon of the working-class memoir was noted, with disapproval, by James Lockhart, who in 1827 derides what he calls the new 'belief that England expects every driveller to do his Memorabilia':

> Our weakest mob-orators think it a hard case if they cannot spout to posterity. Cabin-boys and drummers are busy with their commentaries *de bello Gallico*; the John Gilpins of "the nineteenth century" are the historians of their own *anabaseis*, and thanks to "the march of the intellect", we are already rich in the autobiography of pickpockets.[39]

He snidely shows off his classical training by citing examples of ancient life-writing by Julius Caesar and Xenophon (the authors of *On the Gallic War* and the *Anabasis*, respectively), while juxtaposing them with cabin-boys, drummers and John Gilpin, the demotic hero of a comic ballad by William Cowper which he published under the pseudonym 'John Gilpin, Citizen of London'.[40] Lockhart blames these new working-class memoirs on 'the march of intellect', the slogan describing the rapid advances in workers' education and technological progress associated with the campaigns of Henry Brougham, especially the foundation of the Society for the Diffusion of Useful Knowledge (on which see below, pp. 244–5) and the educational initiatives of Robert Owen at his mill in New Lanark.

In the 1820s, the slogan had produced a wave of satirical cartoons depicting proletarians engaged, ludicrously, in intellectual pursuits.[41] In a comic attack on plebeian education by W.T. Moncrieff, a mother bewildered by the newfangled omnibus asks her son Billy to speak to the guard, since she is scarcely literate, but Billy has learned 'Latin, French and Greek'.[42] Moncrieff shows off his awful puns while complaining that even domestic servants now know their Classics:

> So much does intellect increase
> In manner systematic,—
> Our *kitchens* smell of classic *Greece*,
> Our *garrets* are all *attic*![43]

The growing agitation for reform is explicitly blamed on the 'March of Intellect' and the working class's demand that its voices be heard is lamented.

But not all middle-class readers agreed. In June of 1822, the *Scots Magazine* published an essay 'On Auto-Biography', announcing that 'if the humblest individual were to relate his own life, the narrative could not fail to be interesting'.[44] The requisites of this sub-genre of memoir were an impression of sincerity and an accumulation of minute and plausible detail.[45] Middle-class readers may have found this allowed them to satisfy their curiosity about their supposed social inferiors while simultaneously defusing the threat they posed. Working-class autobiographies are sometimes thought to 'tame' the authors, packaging them in a way designed to appeal to a voyeuristic bourgeois audience. On the other hand, it is easy to be patronising about the urge of people in traditionally silenced groups to narrate their own subjective experiences. The simple act of conscious recollection and narration can be political in itself, as analysts of more recent autobiographical texts have argued. Julia Swindells writes that autobiography has the potential to be the text of the oppressed and the culturally displaced, forging a right to speak both for and beyond the individual;[46] Linda Anderson sees the potential of autobiography as 'a way of testifying to oppression and empowering the subject through their cultural inscription and recognition'.[47]

The craze for working people's memoirs did not spring from a vacuum. Scholars have identified several popular 18th-century publishing genres which prepared the stage for the entrance of the proletarian 'authors of their own *anabaseis*'. An important contributing genre was the 18th-century novel, often artfully presented as a disguised true story, featuring an 'ordinary' protagonist—Defoe's *Robinson Crusoe* and Richardson's *Clarissa Harlowe*. By their moral strength and endurance, despite their flaws, such figures exemplified a non-elite version of the Christian hero.[48] Equally significant were bestselling translations of French and Spanish picaresque novels with roguish antiheroes such as LeSage's *Gil Blas* and Cervantes' *Don Quixote*, both of which enjoyed multiple reprints in the mid-18th century.[49] In *Tom Jones* (1749), Fielding produced a hero resembling both the Continental picaresque antihero and the British non-elite Christian lead who triumphs over serial adversity.

Fictive biographies of individuals who had sensational lives abroad or amidst criminal underclasses, much influenced by the picaresque idiom, were prevalent in the mid-18th century; Robert Goadby's *An Apology for the Life of Mr Bampfylde-Moore Carew Commonly called the King of the Beggars* (1768) includes what Carew, on his title page, calls a comparison, inspired by Plutarch, of the parallel lives of his subject and Henry Fielding's Tom Jones. A crucial plot device is Carew's knowledge of Greek and Latin, acquired at Tiverton School, to which his father, a respectable parson, had sent him. After he has been admitted to a gypsy community at the age of fifteen, this knowledge several times saves him from arrest, because it leads people to assume that he is a gentleman.[50] (Figure 5.2.) There is even one such picaresque *auto*biography, which must contain much fictional elaboration, by Thomas Pellow (1740). He was sent to Latin school in western Cornwall, where Latin had been associated with rebellion during the Reformation and a sense of its importance had survived in local communities. But his emphasis on his youthful struggles with Latin helps to explain how he survived after his uncle's ship, on which he was travelling at the age of 11, was taken by Barbary pirates and its entire crew sold into slavery. Pellow used his linguistic ability to learn Arabic, which enabled him to enter domestic service in an Ottoman palace rather than hard labour, live as a Muslim and work as a translator in the multilingual society of Morocco, where Latin-based languages (Spanish, French, Portuguese and Italian) were spoken alongside Dutch, English and several African tongues.[51]

By the late 18th century, accounts of celebrities' and dignitaries' lives had also become widespread, demonstrated by the huge collection of British biographies amassed by Sir William Musgrave and bestowed on the British Museum.[52]

FIGURE 5.2 'King of the Beggars', Bampfylde Moore Carew (1693–1759), from Caulfield (1819) v.3, reproduced by courtesy of The British Library.

Meanwhile, William Godwin was experimenting with romantic semi-fictional historical biography.[53] In an early example of déclassé memoir, Robert Scott, a middle-class man from Falkland in Fife, published a verse autobiography in 1801 explaining why he had abandoned ambitions to become a lawyer in favour of carpentry. He had been taught at his local school by a Catholic master, John Coldstream,

> ... to rehearse
> In English prose and Latin verse;
> Yea sometimes he would well define
> How I should scan a Latin line.[54]

Scott claims that it was a fear of the pressgangs marauding the streets of Edinburgh during the Seven Years' War (1756–1763) that had plunged him down the rungs of the class ladder and made him flee that city.

The likelihood of working-class people writing about their own lives increased proportionately with the amount of access they enjoyed to workers' libraries and other institutional support. The first workers' libraries were in Scotland in the

1750s at Leadhills and Wanlockhead (see below pp. 467–8); such institutions were raised to a fine art in South Wales in the later 19th century. Their catalogues show that ancient authors who wrote about their own lives, especially Xenophon, Caesar and Augustine, usually in translation, were often included, along with the Stoics whose writing might be classed as spiritual autobiography—Epictetus and Marcus Aurelius. In addition to these, Bunyan's works were universally available, as was Gibbon's *The History of the Decline and Fall of the Roman Empire* (1776–1788); the publication in 1796 of Gibbon's own autobiographical fragments, edited by Lord Sheffield, was an important publishing event which inspired many to follow Gibbon's example.[55] His was the first 'extended autobiography of a celebrated Englishman, intimate but not bearing on religious experience', and 'printed and widely disseminated within a few years of his death'.[56] An intention seems to have been 'to vindicate his decision to devote almost all his adult intellectual energies to a single written work',[57] a motive with which single-minded autodidacts and political activists could identify. By 1826, one publisher embarked on an ambitious multi-volume series of autobiographies penned by French and British literary and social celebrities of the 18th century.[58] As the 19th century developed, a few working-class memoirs, such as Hugh Miller's (see below), achieved canonical status and were frequently reprinted. They were found in workers' libraries and often referred to by other working-class life-writers.

Classical turning-points in eight workers' autobiographies

One important category of autobiographies by individuals born into the working class is constituted by those who succeeded in accessing a classical education, which directly precipitated them into a professional career. A very few—mostly Scotsmen—became distinguished scholars of Classics or comparative philology (see Chapter 14). Another Scotsman, Alexander Bain, eventually became one of Scotland's foremost philosophers, being appointed Regius Chair of Logic at the newly unified University of Aberdeen in 1860 (Figure 5.3). In London in the 1840s and 1850s, he had made friends with the Scottish philosopher and economist, John Stuart Mill, and the political radical and classical historian, George Grote;[59] he also lectured at Bedford College for Women.

His autobiography creates a picture of a man as proud of his contributions to working-class education as to academic philosophy: in 1850 he wrote a series of articles in Chambers' *Papers for the People*, commissioned by Chambers' literary manager, on ancient Greece. 'Education for the Citizen', and 'Every Day Life of the Greeks' (commented on by his friend Grote prior to publication), and 'The Religion of the Greeks' (which drew on Grote's early volumes).[60] Bain was as familiar with ancient philosophy as he was with modern, in 1872 taking it upon himself, following Grote's death, to finish and prepare for posthumous publication (with Croom Robertson) Grote's unfinished work on Aristotle, as well as editing Grote's shorter pieces.[61] A few years earlier he had reviewed Grote's *Plato and the Other Companions of Sokrates*.[62]

FIGURE 5.3 Alexander Bain (1818–1903), Photogravure by Synnberg Photo-gravure Co., 1898. Reproduced from copy in Hall's personal collection.

But the seeds of this impressive career were sown by two separate youthful encounters with Latin, without which Bain would have spent his life in humble occupations. In his autobiography he lovingly recalled the precise moment when he realised that he could succeed at Latin. After a basic education begun by his father, a handloom weaver,[63] Bain began his classical education at Gilcomston Church School between 1826 and 1829. He was required to study the *Rudiments of the Latin Tongue* by Thomas Ruddiman, and

> in the conjugations of the verbs, I soon hit on the device of shortening the labour by marking agreements and differences. Before leaving the school, I had the rudiments pretty well by heart, and had begun to translate short sentences for an easy collection.[64]

His discovery led him to embark on an astonishing self-education despite needing to leave school to work, first as an errand-boy to an auctioneer, and then as a weaver. The second important moment occurred when a kindly minister offered him Latin lessons free of charge so that he could learn enough to get admitted free to the Grammar School in Aberdeen for three months,[65] in which time (he tells us) he consolidated his Latin and learned ancient Greek.[66] Although he was disappointed not to win a full bursary for Marischal College—competing against classmates who had been consistently in grammar-school education for years—he obtained one for £10.

As a distinguished intellectual looking back, he is careful to describe in elaborate detail the extensive classical curriculum he studied at Marischal,[67] but stresses his continuing commitment to the class into which he was born by recalling that, all the while he was at college, he supplemented his bursary by teaching Mathematics at the Mechanics' Institute.[68] He also delivered a course there on philosophy and rhetoric, which included analysis of Demosthenes' *On the Crown*.[69] Bain was also a respected educationalist, twice wading into debates on the efficacy of classical education, to which he referred as the 'interminable Classical question'. Does learning Latin *and* Greek really prepare our youth for modern life? The question was hotly debated in 1879, as it had been a hundred years earlier by Tom Paine and others. Bain argued (successfully, he tells us) that the benefits in mental 'discipline' from learning Greek and Latin could be acquired just as well by learning just *one* of the two ancient languages.[70]

Bain identified the cause of his success as a combination of intellectual talent, hard work and the generosity of a local minister. He was also lucky, as can be seen from a comparison with the tragic tale told in autobiographical letters by another Aberdonian handloom weaver, William Thom, who wanted to be a poet. The letters—requests for patronage—were sent to a prosperous local man named Gordon of Knockespock, who reproduced excerpts from them in a pamphlet. Thom had been badly injured at the age of seven when a nobleman's carriage ran over him at the Aberdeen Race Course. He had been placed in a public factory at the age of 10, then served an apprenticeship of 4 years, before working for 17 years as a weaver for Gordon, Barron and Co. During his apprenticeship, he had picked up a little reading and writing. But Thom felt defensive about not having achieved the autodidact's holy grail of a classical language. He wrote that after his apprenticeship, he had 'set about studying Latin—went so far, but was fairly defeated through want of time, &c.—having the while to support my mother who was getting frail'.[71] In the early 1840s, he succeeded in having a poem published in the *Aberdeen Journal*, 'The Blind Boy's Pranks', about Cupid leaving Paphos and shooting arrows at a young man in Scotland; the poet named himself 'A Serf' and stated that he 'must weave fourteen hours of the four-and-twenty'. In another letter, he laments the difficulty of accessing books: 'I have few of my own, pick up a loan where it can be had; so of course my reading is without choice or system'. Thom did join the London literary scene for a spell, befriended by the progressive playwright Douglas Jerrold. But he died soon afterwards, in abject poverty, in Dundee.[72]

Thom's lament about his missing Latin is replicated in several other working-class autobiographers, where the pivotal encounter with Classics is constituted by an angry recognition that ignorance of Latin and/or Greek had led to an experience of exclusion. Sometimes, in hindsight, a writer realises that the experience propelled him onto a useful path. Timothy Claxton was the founder of the first Mechanics Institute in London (1817). He had been refused membership by the City Philosophical Society of London, where he had applied to attend courses on Natural Philosophy and Chemistry run by Mr John Tatum. These famous courses were attended, for example, by the young Michael Faraday, who was also working-class, but better at pleasing rich patrons. As Claxton recalled in his *Memoir of a Mechanic* (1839), in a paragraph beginning 'I have now arrived at what I consider the most important period of my life', he recounts how he had educated himself by attending lectures and private study of steam engines and Natural Philosophy, despite having been bewildered by the 'very names of the subjects to be treated, such as pneumatics, Hydrodynamics, Aerostation, etc.' because 'they were all Latin to me'.[73] Even access to science courses therefore required an understanding of the classical languages which he did not possess; it is not clear whether he was aware that the terms he was describing as 'all Latin' to him were actually Greek, or whether he is making the mistake deliberately to emphasise his rhetorical point. He knew why he had been rejected from the Society: it was because he had no friends at court and because 'I am a mechanic: that is the difficulty'. The rejection proved essential to his decision to spend his life using, as he put it, 'all my efforts to improve the class to which I belonged'.[74] After setting up the proudly named Mechanics Institute in London, Claxton subsequently moved to Massachusetts to work in a cotton factory. He then founded both the Boston Mechanics' Institute in 1826 and the Boston Mechanics' Lyceum in 1831.

Another working-class autobiographer, similarly deprived of Classics, was more embittered. The poet Samuel Bamford, born at around the same time as Claxton, believed that this deprivation had arrested his intellectual development and career. (Figure 5.4.) A poet and campaigner for universal suffrage in Middleston, near Manchester, he was acquitted when tried for treason in 1817. But he was convicted for his role in the demonstration that led to the Peterloo massacre in 1819, on a charge of 'assembling with unlawful banners at an unlawful meeting for the purpose of inciting discontent'. He spent a year in Lincoln Prison.

Bamford, whom we have met earlier in the context of workers' reading material (see above, pp. 49–50), identified the moment at which he was formally excluded from learning classical languages as the opposite of a turning-point—it was the event that determined that he would stay labouring-class forever. He worked as a floor-sweeper, farm labourer, sailor, warehouse man, handloom weaver and journalist. The decision to prevent him from learning Latin was taken by his father. Bamford had come top of the senior English class, and would normally have been expected to advance into the Latin class.

> But, alas! when called upon I could only inform the master, with blushes on my cheeks and tears in my eyes, that my father did not wish me to go into the Latin class at present, but desired that I might remain in the class to which I then belonged. My master, I can recollect, looked at me incredulously; studied, questioned me again, and, with an expression of disappointment, motioned that I should return to my place. This was a sore humiliation to me.[75]

FIGURE 5.4 Samuel Bamford (1788–1872) from Bamford (1844), reproduced from copy in Hall's personal collection.

Less intellectually able peers did begin Latin, so Bamford felt humiliated and lost the drive to improve himself academically at all:

> Henceforward I thought meanly of my position, and never glanced at my former comrades without a feeling which lowered the zest of my future school-life. This as it regarded my welfare was probably the most momentous and ill-advised step which my father could have determined upon. Had the threshold of the classics been once crossed by me, great must have been the difficulties indeed which would have prevented me from making the whole of that ancient lore my own. I was just at the right age, and in the right frame of mind, with faculties as it were newly come to life, and with an instructor who I have since had many reasons for supposing would have done all he could towards helping me forward into the upper schools; and, had I once got fairly introduced to the learning of the ancients I should not have stopped short on this side of the university I think.[76]

This incident created a wound in Bamford's psyche which never healed. His father had correctly seen that learning Latin took time to learn, which for boys who could never become 'doctors, or lawyers, or parsons', would be time 'thrown away'.[77] The episode uncannily foreshadows the father, a miner, in Tony Harrison's feature film *Prometheus*, who angrily says to his schoolboy son, reading a Greek tragedy, 'God knows why they feed yer all that crap'.[78]

A more complicated variation on the theme articulated by Bamford occurred in the case of Thomas Wood, an engineer born in Bingley in Yorkshire in 1822, son of a handloom weaver. Wood's grandfather did the opposite of Bamford's father. Wood was sent to a local grammar school because he could read quite well at six and his grandfather had a friendship with the local vicar.

> I was at this school till about eight learning Latin grammar and writing. I don't remember ever being required to learn the multiplication table, or working a sum of arithmetic at school, or hearing or seeing one worked. It was a Latin school.

Wood supposed that his totally illiterate grandfather had intuited at some level the grand opportunities that classical languages might confer: 'I suppose grandfather thought learning was a great thing without stopping to ask about the quality or applicability of it to the practical purposes of life'. This was unusually insightful of the old men, since other 'working folk derided the idea of their children learning Latin, or, indeed, anything at all if it cost anything or entailed any inconvenience'.[79] Wood did not have the opportunity to capitalise on his exceptional chance of studying Latin. He hastened the end of his schooling, as the eldest of eight children, by helping to wind bobbins for his father. This meant he skipped lessons and got into trouble at school. He left it at eight years old and started full-time work at the mill. But the care he takes to point out his thwarted academic potential throws light on his confidence, later in life, in his ability to write down his life for others to read.

The various painful turning-points narrated by Thom, Claxton, Bamford and Wood might have elicited a snort from Joseph Arch (1826–1919), the son of a Warwickshire shepherd,[80] who worked in the fields from the age of nine, and played a leading role in the formation of the National Union of Agricultural Labourers in 1872. He was twice elected MP for North West Norfolk. In his pugnacious autobiography *From Ploughtail to Parliament* (1898), Arch steers a course between (1) exposing elite fear of the working class becoming educated, (2) deriding the book learning of the elite and (3) reminding the reader that he had personally read a great deal. He explains that when he was young it was still widely understood that education for the working classes should be restricted to the religious doctrine of the catechism. He suggests the following motto for inscription on the door of his school: 'Much knowledge of the right sort is a dangerous thing for the poor'. This was because, 'The less book-learning the labourer's lad got stuffed into him, the better for him and the safer for those above him, was what those in authority believed and acted up to'.[81] Throughout his childhood, he tells us, he was exposed to two bodies of literature:

> Shakespeare and the Bible were the books I was brought up on, and I don't want any better. I have heard and read a good deal since then, but I have never come across anything to beat them.[82]

In the autobiography of Guy Aldred, also known as The Knickerbocker Rebel, a once notorious atheist campaigner for free speech, and much-published expert on the earlier radicals Tom Paine and Richard Carlile, learning classical languages is treated with derision.[83] But in his case, there is a palpable and acknowledged intellectual debt to studying classical authors in translation.[84] The son of a lieutenant in the navy and a factory girl, he described himself both as a communist and as an 'Anarchist Socialist Impossibilist'; he regarded parliamentarianism as a toxic 'legacy of Roman Imperialism' that could never solve 'the key problem of all human misery, the problem of class society'.[85] He was best known for his leading role in the campaign against the ban—enforced throughout the 1920s—of all forms of public speech and meetings on Glasgow Green. He always lived on the breadline. He does not describe his life's story as one of social rise, but of consistent active service of his fellow man.[86] (Figure 5.5.)

The account of his early life features two pivotal moments, both related to classical material. He recalled hating the Saturday classes in ancient Greek offered him by the Reverend George Martin;[87] he distrusted the reverence for classicism as much as for any other source of authority. But in his teens he had been a devout Anglican street-preacher. It was only in 1904 that his grandfather,

FIGURE 5.5 Guy Aldred (1886–1963), by unknown photographer (June 1906). Image from Aldred (1955–1963), reproduced by courtesy of British Library.

a fishing tackle manufacturer, the evening after his grandson's street pulpit had been stormed repeatedly by police, introduced him to atheism:

> That night, on my return home, my grandfather went to his secret cupboard and produced a collection of Atheist pamphlets ... My grandfather delighted in poetry and on the evening when he introduced me to the Atheist writings, he gave me a volume of Shelley and another of Byron. He told me the story of the Titan God, Prometheus. If I wished to serve mankind, he warned me, I must expect scorn and abuse. But, he continued, I must maintain my position with perfect sweetness. I must not permit persecution or neglect to make me bitter. He asked me to consider the lofty heroism, the enduring patience, the unselfish love, and the perfect sweetness in service, the tragic story of Prometheus inspired.[88]

Aldred attended a series of Wednesday lectures delivered by a man called Septimus Buss on 'The Religions of the World'. Lecture seven of the series introduced the audience to the pragmatic religion of ancient Rome.[89] The series nourished his growing atheism, further supported by his encounter with Stoicism when the Reverend Charles Voysey introduced him to teachings of Zeno of Citium. He consequently became convinced of what he describes as an anti-religious moral and humanist theism: 'The unconditional service of man defines conduct that must arise out of a life that is in absolute accord with the supreme harmony of the universe [or God]'.[90] Zeno's teachings effectively gave him a means by which he could shift his evangelistic energies from the Christian God to socialism. In his copious political writings, Aldred often turns to the heroes of ancient history, alongside Napoleon and Jesus, as historical exemplars. In an article on one of his pet topics of discussion, free love, entitled 'History for Prudists', he discussed the love affairs of Julius Caesar and Mark Antony. He concluded that when we survey the history of

> all creeds and races, and find record upon record of amours, the talk of "adultery" becomes drivel of the most appalling description. And if "adultery" is so evil how comes it that the most notorious adulterers rank as the greatest men of their time.[91]

A similarly discouraging early encounter with Classics, which nevertheless nourished a love of literature and learning in maturity, was recorded by Henry Hawker, the son of a Somerset coachman (1870–1918). He eventually became Stationmaster at Stonehouse, Gloucestershire, after 32 years of service to the Great Western Railway Company. But in his memoir he recalls that in 1883 he was hired for 3 shillings a week, at the age of 13, to read Homer out loud in English to his local vicar:

> Just before leaving school the Rev. Turner, curate of St. James (who lived in rooms above some offices in Hammett Street and was studying), came to

> the school and asked to hear some boys read, accordingly I, with two others, was brought before him and tested, we knew not what it was for, but I was asked to go on the following morning at eleven o'clock to his rooms, and found I was required to read "Homer," which presumably Mr. Turner was comparing with the original Greek, as he would occasionally stop me to make a correction, sometimes the error was mine, and sometimes his, this I did for two hours daily (on Saturdays three hours).[92]

Hawker admitted in his memoir to finding the process 'dry work in more senses than one',[93] but in later years he grew fond of literature. He proudly lists his favourite music and books, which included such vernacular classics of John Dryden's translations of Virgil, Thomas Babington Macaulay's *Lays of Ancient Rome* (based on Roman history drawn largely from Livy and stylistically enhanced by imitations of Homer's *Iliad*) and—revealingly—Alexander Pope's Homer. The early experience had been instrumental, no doubt, in his stated mature preference for 'the older writers'.[94]

The most independent-minded discussion of the advantages and disadvantages of a conventional Classics education, as opposed to enjoyment of those classics in translation, occurs in the celebrated autobiography of Cromarty stonemason and pioneering geologist Hugh Miller, *My Schools and Schoolmasters*.[95] He had literate uncles who made sure that while at Dame School he had access to fairy tales, bible stories and Pope's *Odyssey* and *Iliad*, which he adored.[96] The uncles, like Miller, were stonemasons, tradesmen whom he regards as of equal intelligence to shoemakers (he cites Bloomfield the poet, on whom see below pp. 436–7) but prouder. The mason

> is in general a blunt, manly, taciturn fellow, who, without much of the Radical or Chartist about him, especially if his wages be good and employment abundant, rarely touches his hat to a gentleman. His employment is less purely mechanical than many others … every stone he lays or hews demands the exercise of a certain amount of judgement for itself.[97]

The parish schoolmaster, identifying Miller's intellectual talent, transferred him into the Latin class. Miller found declining nouns a waste of time, and began 'to long for my English reading, with its nice amusing stories, and its picture-like descriptions'. He was, he assures us, brighter than his class-fellows, and used his intelligence to work out a way of learning the entire English-language cribs off by heart so that he could spend lesson-time reading Dryden's translations of Virgil and Ovid, which he smuggled into class, instead.[98] And that enjoyment of ancient masterpieces in translation informed his mature writing style, as in his rapturous description of the Liassic deposits of the Hill of Eathie, where its extraordinary layers, sandwiches, fossils, branches of pines and strangely patterned ferns are compared to rows of pages in books.

> Page after page, for tens of hundreds of feet together, repeat the same wonderful story. The great Alexandrian library, with its tomes of ancient literature, the accumulation of long ages, was but a meagre collection … compared with this marvellous library.[99]

When faced with a challenging river to ford in the course of his work, he was reminded of Julius Caesar and Horatius Cocles who 'could swim across rivers and seas in heavy armour'.[100] He also used the linguistic talent his pivotal encounter with Latin had confirmed to learn Gaelic, which he regarded as far more useful than classical languages.[101]

He keeps his insights into the long-term intellectual benefits of Classics until late in the volume. He kept up with some friends from school and met others through his work as a mason who had been taught at university.

> I sometimes could not avoid comparing them in my mind with working men of … the same original calibre. I did not always find the general superiority on the side of the scholar which the scholar himself usually took for granted.

He concedes that the scholars were better trained to frame arguments than working men, but insists that the workers were better at practical reasoning, better read in English literature, and better equipped to conduct business. But Miller is no radical. He reveals ambivalence about his birth class in laying the blame for the

> over-low estimate which the classical scholar so often forms of the intelligence of that class of the people to which our skilled mechanics belong' on pushy workers who force themselves on the notice of the classes above them.[102]

Fictionalised turning-points

In the 19th-century British novel, the trope of the exclusion of the working class from the classical cultural realm, especially from access to the ancient languages, became a standard feature of the genre, culminating in Thomas Hardy's tragic Jude Fawley in *Jude the Obscure* (1895), locked out forever from studying Classics at Christminster (a fictionalised Oxford).[103] The extent of the use of classical mythology by these writers, especially George Eliot, in relation to working-class characters, has attracted attention,[104] but the importance of their engagement with real-life narratives they encountered in newspapers and periodicals less so. So steeped were most of these writers in classical mythology that sometimes they read a contemporary event through a classical lens, before integrating both into a new fiction: Hardy's Tess in *Tess of the D'Urbervilles* (1891) shares features with both Clytemnestra and with Elizabeth Martha Browne, a Dorset servant whom Hardy witnessed being hanged in 1856 for murdering her adulterous husband with a hatchet.[105] And these novelists certainly read published working-class autobiographies, from which, along with their own life experiences, they absorbed the trope of the pivotal encounter with Classics.

Sometimes it is in a simple comparison of the sturdy, healthy physique of the stereotypical working-class man in comparison with the sickly classical scholar exemplified most famously by Edward Casaubon in Eliot's *Middlemarch*.[106] At other times, it marks an important moment of recognition about the class status of the novel's central figures or those with whom they interact. Dickens, notoriously conflicted about the desirability of classical education, probes the class system with a tragicomic scalpel in *David Copperfield* (1850). The envious Uriah sees David as a privileged young snob, but refuses to accept the offer of Latin lessons because he is 'far too umble. There are people enough to tread upon me in my lowly state, without my doing outrage to their feelings by possessing learning'.[107] Charles Kingsley's Chartist tailor in *Alton Locke* (also 1850) does eventually improve his social situation as well as come to a greater understanding of his historical moment by teaching himself classical languages and literature with help of a Scottish working-class intellectual who is a thinly disguised Thomas Carlyle.

Stephen Smith, the autodidactic stonemason's son in Thomas Hardy's early novel *A Pair of Blue Eyes* (1873), catastrophically betrays his humble origins to the man he would like to make his father-in-law, the Reverend Swancourt, by his unconventional pronunciation of an Horatian ode. Stephen has been taught his Latin (and Greek) exclusively by written correspondence with a fellow of an Oxford college. Swancourt, an intellectual snob, concludes to Stephen,

> you have a way of pronouncing your Latin which to me seems most peculiar. Not that the pronunciation of a dead language is of much importance; yet your accents and quantities have a grotesque sound to my ears. I thought first that you had acquired your way of breathing the vowels from some of the northern colleges; but it cannot be so with the quantities. What I was going to ask was, if your instructor in the classics could possibly have been an Oxford or Cambridge man?[108]

The moment that Stephen's true class origins are betrayed in this momentous encounter, the reader knows he will never win the hand of the Reverend's fair daughter. The trope of the narrative turning-point marked by the central figure's relationship with Classics in his youth has moved from 18th-century fiction to 19th-century autobiography and back to fiction again.

Notes

1 Tillett (1931) 76.
2 Tillett (1931) 94.
3 Tillett (1931) 81.

4 Tillett (1931) 271.
5 Quoted in Thompson (1988) 104.
6 Deutsch (1973) 15; see also Spacks (1976) 19.
7 Wallach (2006).
8 *The Harmsworth Self-Educator: A Golden Key to Success in Life* (1905–1907) was the brainchild of Arthur Henry Mee, a working-class Baptist from Nottinghamshire whose only education was at the Stapleford Board School until he was 14. The volume is dominated by the technological, domestic and commercial skills which will advance the careers of readers both female and male, and the message is reinforced by the frontispiece—Frederic Leighton's mural for the Royal Exchange depicting Phoenicians bartering with ancient Britons, 'The Birth of British Commerce'. But courses in both Latin and ancient Greek history are included (Mee [1906] 601–5, 753–5, 667–80, 772–5). He collaborated on this and his *History of the World* (1907), of which a substantial proportion is devoted to Greek and Roman history, with John Hammerton. Several other of his educational publications need urgent investigation by classical scholars.
9 Spacks (1976) 18; Calder (1972) 343.
10 Gusdorf (1980 [1956]) 37.
11 Olney (1972). For critical, structuralist and formalist theories of autobiography, see Nussbaum (1989) 4–10 and Anderson (2001).
12 Gray (1982).
13 Pascal (1960).
14 Barros (1998).
15 Starobinski (1980) 78.
16 Barros (1992) 1.
17 Barros (1992) 16.
18 Tillett (1931) 249.
19 Leatherland (1862) 9–13, 16. That he taught himself Greek is clear from p. 88. He subsequently became a somewhat half-hearted Chartist, but repudiated any radical tendencies entirely after reading Burke's *Reflections on the Revolution in France*: see pp. 20–1.
20 Barker (1880) 63.
21 Newman (1994) 24.
22 See especially the comments of Vincent (2016).
23 Vincent (1981), Hackett (1985), Gagnier (1991) 138–70.
24 Harrison (1971) 35.
25 On which see epsecialy Swindells (1985) 115–84.
26 Quoted in Burnett (1974) 91. N.b. Bamford may well have confused Gibbon with Hume because he also read Hume's.
27 Factory Girl (1853), especially 16–37.
28 Hall (1977) 39.
29 Seymour-Smith (1994) 39–40; see also Ebbatson (2010).
30 This story was first published in Fox (1930) 1–9 and is reproduced in Klaus (1993). Fox was a trade unionist and writer whose autobiography was entitled *Smoky Crusade* (1937).
31 Starr (1965); Delany (1969).
32 Schoenfield (2015) 95. On the late 18th- and early 19th-century emergence of the autobiography, and specifically the working-class autobiography, see also Yagoda (2009) 57–70.
33 *English Review* vol. 27, 501.
34 Disraeli (1809) 386.
35 Hall (2002) 36.
36 Rose (1994).
37 Hess (2005) 13.

38 Treadwell (2005) 3.
39 Lockhart (1827) 149; see Lee (2007) 1. On Lockhart's class-based commentary on the middle-class 'Cockney School' see Stead (2015a) and (2015b).
40 Cowper (1782).
41 See e.g. the 1828 etching 'The March of Intellect' by Henry Heath, in which a ragged dustman relaxes by reading a large book. V&A Museum no. E.87–1936. The joke persisted: see the satirical novel by Gideon (1845).
42 Moncrieff (1830) 12.
43 Moncrieff (1830) 16.
44 Anon. (1822) 742.
45 Schoenfield (2015) 96.
46 Swindells (1995) 7.
47 Anderson (2001) 104.
48 Beasley (1973) 161.
49 Beasley (1973) 160.
50 Goadby (1768) 50, 230, 293. See further below, pp. 308–9.
51 Pellow (1740).
52 Griffiths (1992); on 18th-century English biography in general, see Stauffer (1941).
53 Pérez Rodríguez (2003).
54 Scott (1801) 9.
55 Gibbon (1796).
56 Shumaker (1954) 27; see also Spacks (1976) 92–126.
57 Cartledge (1995) 134.
58 The first volume contained the *Life* of Theatre Impresario Colley Cibber, and the second, the *Lives* of David Hume, William Lilly and Voltaire: Autobiography (1826) vols. I, II.
59 Bain (1904) 104, 176, 217–18, 231–2.
60 See also Bain (1904) 212–13.
61 Grote (1880) and (1873). See Bain (1904) 310–11.
62 Bain (1865); Grote (1865).
63 Bain (1904) 4.
64 Bain (1904) 7–8.
65 Bain (1904) 29.
66 Bain (1904) 30–2.
67 This included, in addition to Latin and Greek languages and ancient history, Sophocles' *Oedipus Tyrannus*, Herodotus' *Histories*, Demosthenes, Aeschines, Aristophanes, Andrew Dalzel's *Collectanea Graeca Majora*, Thucydides, Virgil's *Aeneid* book VI and *Georgics*, the *Odes* and *Epistles* of Horace, Cicero's *de Officiis* and Livy.
68 Bain (1904) 43–51, 56, 63, 72.
69 Bain (1904) 65.
70 Bain (1904) 342–3.
71 Knockespock pamphlet in Thom (1841–1963) 1, 9–11.
72 Knokespock pamphlet and other notices in Thom (1841–1963). His poems were published as Thom (1880) and some are included in a popular collection of demotic north-eastern Scottish poetry edited by Walker (1894).
73 Claxton (1839) 34.
74 Claxton (1839) 34–5.
75 Bamford (1967 [1849]) 91.
76 Bamford (1967 [1849] 92.
77 Bamford (1967 [1849] 92–3.
78 Harrison (1998) 9.
79 Quoted in Burnett (1974) 312.
80 Arch (1986 [1898]) 5.
81 Arch (1986 [1898]) 25.
82 Arch (1986 [1898]) 9.

83 Aldred (1908) 28.
84 Aldred (1908) esp. 27–9, and in his journalism e.g. Aldred (1923).
85 Quoted in Aldred (1966) 6.
86 Aldred (1955–1963).
87 Aldred (1908) 28–9; Aldred (1955–1963) 66. On Martin see below pp. 319–21.
88 Aldred (1955–1963) 83.
89 Aldred (1955–1963) 42–3, 46–8.
90 Aldred (1908) 27.
91 Aldred (1923) 21.
92 Hawker (1919) 12.
93 Hawker (1919) 12.
94 Hawker (1919) 53 and 54–9.
95 Miller (1993 [1854]).
96 Milller (1993 [1854]] 27
97 Miller (1993 [1854]) 181.
98 Miller (1993 [1854]) 44–6.
99 Miller (1993 [1854]) 155.
100 Miller (1993 [1854]) 237.
101 Miller (1993 [1854]) 231–2.
102 Miller (1993 [1854]) 351.
103 Hall (2008b) 386.
104 See Hall and Macintosh (2005) 182, 197, 331–2, 421, 454; Jenkyns (1980), 115–17, 125–7; Hurst (2006) 170–83.
105 See www.bl.uk/collection-items/the-early-life-of-thomas-hardy.
106 Hale (2010). See Wright (1932) vol. I, 37 and Wilson (1925) 175–6: 'Why employers are always pictured as large bulky men I've never been able to understand, because comparing the average Labour leader with employers, I think Labour could give points to Capitalists on the question of adipose tissue. Even I could turn the scale one time at sixteen stone, although it was well distributed'.
107 Dickens (1850) 169; see Hall (2015f), especially 107–8.
108 Hardy (1877) 46.

6

WORKING-CLASS CLASSICS VIA THE VISUAL ENVIRONMENT

Cultural literacies

Since even rudimentary education for children under ten did not become compulsory until the Elementary Education Act 1880, the opportunities for studying ancient languages were inevitably limited to households above a certain level of income. Even personal study of antiquity in modern translations would have been beyond the reach of the sizeable proportion of the British population who, at least until the late 19th century, had difficulty reading a text of more than a few pages in extent.[1]

Statistics are hard to infer from the available evidence, but it is generally accepted that basic literacy grew significantly over the 18th and 19th centuries.[2] About 45% of men and just under a third of women in England and Wales could sign their name by 1714. By 1885, 89% of men and 87% of women could do so.[3] But literacy did not always increase steadily. The unnamed author of an 1838 article in *The Penny Magazine*, from Crowle in Lincolnshire,[4] acquired the help of the local vicar in examining signatures in the marriage registers from 1754 onwards.[5] The percentage of signers who could write climbed until 1818, when it suddenly collapsed back to the same level as the 1760s. The author cites the paucity of schools (the parish's only endowed school for the poor had been closed in 1818), the impact of the most recent enclosures, and the number of men leaving agriculture for manufacturing jobs. This increased the demand for child labour in the fields.[6]

The Crowle resident was probably correct about the local drop in literacy. He was the first of many to use the ability to sign one's name on an official document as an indicator. Yet the method is problematic: it neither implies nor precludes fluency in reading. Other problems associated with assessing historical literacy levels include the disparities between rural areas and towns, where literacy was

DOI: 10.4324/9781315446608-7

higher, and between different regions of the country. The Lowland Scots were more likely to be literate than Highlanders; some southern counties, despite their proximity to London, had high levels of illiteracy because agricultural labourers and employees in cottage industries worked long hours for low pay.[7]

Attempting to assess the extent of the readership of published books and periodicals is also methodologically problematic. Reading rooms and workers' libraries allowed many people to read the same publication: in 1829 it was estimated that one journal might be read by as many as 25 people.[8] The unstamped radical press, directed during the later 18th century towards artisans, soldiers, sailors and servants, was by its nature illegal and has often not survived.[9] There is a danger of under-estimating the extent to which readerships extended lower than the middle classes: as early as 1730 Montesquieu was struck to see that, in England, even a slater would have newspapers brought to him to read on the roofs of houses.[10] And that slater may well have read passages aloud to his less literate co-workers; Thomas Paine's *Common Sense* was consumed by literate and non-literate people alike, in written and oral form; it was read by public men, but its contents were repeated everywhere—clubs, schools and even from pulpits.[11]

A man named Tam Fleck kept the townsfolk of early 19th-century Peebles entranced with tales of the fall of Jerusalem. He owned a copy of Roger l'Estrange's 18th-century compressed translation of Josephus' *The Wars of the Jews*,[12] and would tour the households of Peebles reading that narrative 'as the current news'. Wherever possible, he ended on a cliff-hanger, taking care to break off in the same place at every house, so that all his listeners would be left in the same suspense. This had the effect of turning Josephus into a sort of soap opera.[13] He would take about a year to get through the whole Jewish War, at which point he would simply start again. Despite this, according to a listener, 'the novelty somehow never seemed to wear off':

> "Weel, Tam, what's the news the nicht?" would old Geordie Murray say, as Tam entered with his "Josephus" under his arm, and seated himself at the family fireside.
>
> "Bad news, bad news", replied Tam. "Titus has begun to besiege Jerusalem & it's gaun to be a terrible business" and then he opened his budget of intelligence, to which all paid the most reverential attention.[14]

This account suggests emotional investment in the narrative on the part of Tam's audience, literate or not. The famine that fell upon the besieged citizens of Jerusalem (described in several horrific passages in Josephus, principally *Jewish War* VI.199–.216) 'kept several families in a state of agony for a week', while the final fall of the city (VI.230–.442) elicited 'a perfect paroxysm of horror'.[15]

The way we think about literacy was changed by Richard Hoggart's *The Use of Literacy* (1957), which includes, under the heading of working-class literacy, activities quite other than the reading of continuous printed texts—the consumption of entertainments and culture via theatre, cinema, radio, television or pictures in magazines and advertisements. Peter Burke has explored a range of ways in which we can use visual culture as a historical source.[16] These scholars would have approved of Sian Lewis' reminder that the slaves of ancient Greece poured their masters' wine from vases decorated with mythical, ritual and domestic scenes; since vase-paintings were 'an open form of communication, available to every gaze', their meanings were construed in the minds of slaves as well as those of free people.[17] Similarly, the meanings of many hundreds of such vases on display in British collections have always been construed in the minds of viewers, whether literate or not.

In London in the second half of the 18th century, the windows and doors of second-hand booksellers were often festooned from pavement to roof with prints, ranging from tasteful reproductions of fine art and portraits of celebrities to political cartoons, caricatures and pornography. By the 1780s, prints sold individually outnumbered those published in journals, and shops specialising in a particular category, such as political caricature, began to open.[18] The labyrinthine streets to the south of the Strand in London were packed with such shops,[19] and since the area was poor and otherwise deprived, the print displays provided a free form of entertainment to the passer-by with a few minutes to spare. Since colleting prints began as an aristocratic pastime, there is some dispute as to how many working-class people these images reached, but contemporary memoirs and pictures imply crowds of every rank, including illiterates, vagrants and children thronging at the shop windows.[20] Plebeian self-improvement and radicalism were constant sources of subject-matter for humorous prints.[21] This was not just a metropolitan affair, either, since prints were produced and sold in Bath, Bristol, Dublin and Edinburgh.[22] Some contained phrases in Latin,[23] or jocular imitations of ancient Greek; a large category used ancient mythology, often in complex series; Charles James Fox' initiatives were routinely presented as different labours of Hercules.[24]

One print which makes fun of attempts to bring classical education to the lower classes is William Heath's 'A Classical Teacher: the Schoolmaster is abroad', published by Thomas McClean in London (1830). (Figure 6.1) It shows Henry Brougham, the Whig politician committed to extending education, who had masterminded the foundation of the Society of the Diffusion of Useful Knowledge.[25] The traditional Classics master is unimpressed by this socially aspirational candidate for a post, whose clothes do not fit and who confuses the names of Homer and Virgil with names of places outside London.

But Brougham was not easily discouraged, and the publications initiated by the Society offered visual alongside textual education. Charles Knight's cheap weekly *The Penny Magazine* (1832–1845), which was for several years a great success,[26] contained attractive wood-engravings reproduced by steam printing press. This made it extremely popular, especially amongst working-class families with children. It sold more than 200,000 copies in 1832.[27] On numerous occasions, the cover image depicted a famous work of ancient art such as the Portland Vase,[28] often with a suitable classical text printed after it in translation (Figure 6.2);[29] it was

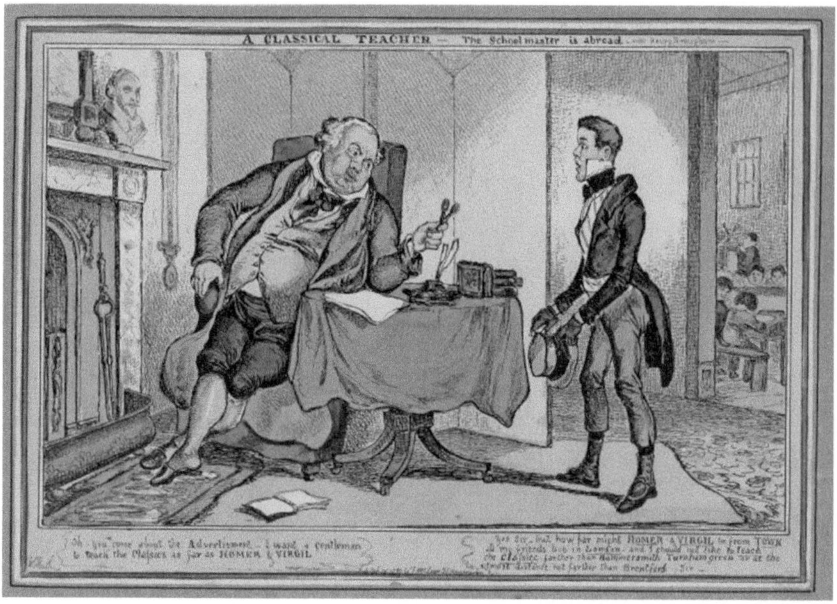

FIGURE 6.1 'A classical teacher—the schoolmaster is abroad—vide Henry Brougham' (1830), reproduced by courtesy of the British Museum © The Trustees of the British Museum.

inevitable that when the autodidactic efforts it encouraged were caricatured, the engraving features a Greek statue and an artisan looking at an advertisement for a reading room in which he can peruse 'All the Classics', as well as radical English authors (Figure 6.3).[30] Brougham may have been derided by the middle and upper classes, but he was held in high esteem by workers and radicals, including the Chartist autodidact Samuel Bamford.[31] In this he contrasted with other educationalists who produced digests of ancient authors for the workers, such as Seymour Tremenheere's potted extracts from Aristotle, Polybius and Cicero included in *The Political Experience of the Ancients: in its Bearing upon Modern Times* (1852); this omitted Plato on the ground that ideas in the *Republic* might foment socialist agitation.[32]

Pompeii everywhere

In terms of the visual consumption of ancient Rome, there has been no rival in Britain to the popularity of scenes of destruction of Pompeii, still a newly discovered wonder in the late 18th century. After Herculaneum began to be exhumed in 1738 by workmen digging trenches for the foundations of a palace for Charles Bourbon, King of Naples, Pompeii was also excavated. But the visualisation of the Vesuvius eruption fascinated Britons. By 1772, the Marylebone Gardens staged a spectacle entitled 'The Forge of Vulcan', in which a Vesuvius-inspired mountain

THE PENNY MAGAZINE

OF THE

Society for the Diffusion of Useful Knowledge.

31.] PUBLISHED EVERY SATURDAY.

BRITISH MUSEUM.—No. 6.

FIGURE 6.2 Cover of *The Penny Magazine*, no. 31, September 29th (1832), reproduced by courtesy of the British Library.

erupted, 'with lava rushing down the precipices'.[33] The English painter Joseph Wright, from Derby, visited Italy in the 1770s and, in 1775, made a preliminary gouache sketch, now in the Derby Museum and Art Gallery, of Vesuvius in the process of erupting. He painted the scene at least thirty further times.[34] Wright's moody, turbulent representations of the eruption, depicted in dark reds and black, were supplemented in the public imagination by the attractive engravings reconstructing the appearance of ancient Pompeii in William Gell's two-volume *Pompeiana: The Topography of Edifices and Ornaments of Pompeii* (1817–1818), which was republished in an updated edition in 1832 and inspired scenic designers in the countless theatrical and operatic accounts of the destruction of Pompeii during the 19th century. Londoners were treated to a cataclysmic visual experience of Pompeii's last hours when, in 1823, John Martin's apocalyptic painting 'The Destruction of Pompeii and Herculaneum' was displayed in the form of a diorama at the Egyptian Hall, Piccadilly.[35] Martin, who had been born into a one-room Northumberland cottage, and learned his craft painting heraldic devices as a coach-maker's apprentice, was derided by John Ruskin, but he was the most

FIGURE 6.3 'March of Mind' by Robert Cruikshank (1826), reproduced by courtesy of the British Museum © The Trustees of the British Museum.

popular painter of his day: railings were used in art galleries to keep admiring crowds at a distance.[36]

The Pompeii craze was given its biggest boost by Edward Bulwer's bestselling novel *The Last Days of Pompeii* (1834), which was reissued in many 19th-century reprints and editions, often with dramatic illustrations. The impresario John Buckstone speedily produced a playscript: *The Last Days of Pompeii, or, Seventeen Hundred Years Ago*, which ran for over 60 nights (a remarkable run in those days) at the Adelphi Theatre on the Strand; the following year three separate London spectacles, including one with added fireworks at Vauxhall Gardens, made Pompeii's fall widely available.[37] The almost wearisome plethora of Pompeii shows is reflected in its inclusion amongst the tattered playbills stuck to the wall in John Orlando Parry's painting 'A London Street Scene' (1835–1837),[38] and the title of Robert Reece's classical burlesque *The Very Last Days of Pompeii!* at the Vaudeville Theatre on the Strand (1872). The familiarity of Pompeii stage spectacles inevitably meant that it was made into an early silent movie, *Gli ultimi giorni di Pompei* (1913),[39] released almost immediately in British cinemas as *The Last Days of Pompeii*.

The built environment

Even travel abroad to view classical art was not invariably beyond the reach of at least skilled artisanal workers. Between June and October 1867, 3,000 working men from London, Sheffield, Coventry, Bradford and Newcastle-under-Lyme attended the Paris Exhibition, on special subsidised excursions funded by the Society of Arts and the Birmingham Chamber of Commerce.[40] At government level, the chief supporter was the radical MP and excavator of Assyrian antiquities Austen Henry Layard, who personally led the first batch of 200 workers around the wonders on display at the Louvre.[41] One of the delegates, a London cabinet-maker named Charles Hooper, recalled visits to other museums, galleries and lectures halls, including a tour of the fine art at Versailles.[42]

In the access to classical civilisation available to Britons, visual culture has often been paramount. The passion for ceramics informed by ancient art required workers who were knowledgeable about ancient vases and iconography, as we shall see in Chapter 21. Several important draughtsmen were also born into low social classes: James 'Athenian' Stuart, who with his wealthy friend Nicholas Revett published one of the most influential books in the history of architecture and aesthetics, *The Antiquities of Athens Measured and Delineated* (the first volume appeared in 1762), suffered a near-destitute boyhood in Ludgate after the death of his father, a Scottish sailor.[43] As the eldest son, to support his mother and siblings, he was apprenticed to a fan-maker on the Strand. One biographer believes that the decorative Grecian buildings he painted onto the fans directed his mind 'to the study of classical architecture'.[44] It was only by good luck and a massive autodidactic effort that Stuart learned Latin and Greek and travelled to Rome. There, after becoming an expert engraver as well as a connoisseur of fine art and architecture, with Revett he conceived the plan to visit Athens to draw its antiquities in person.

The taste for the antique encouraged by the work of Stuart and Revett can be seen even earlier in dozens of 18th-century stately homes usually built by nouveau-riche bankers, merchants or adventurers returned from the colonies. At least, they ordered them to be built, hired fashionable architects and interior decorators, and handed over the physical work to local labourers. As Brecht put it in the opening lines of his poem 'Questions from a Worker who Reads', composed in 1935:

> Who built seven-gated Thebes?
> In the books are stated the names of kings.
> Did the kings drag the boulders up?
> And Babylon, so many times destroyed—
> Who built it up so many times? Where are the houses
> In golden-gleaming Lima where the people who built it live?
> The night the Great Wall of China was completed, where did
> The masons go? Rome is great
> And full of triumphal arches. Who erected them?[45]

The 18th-century hyper-rich who adored antique art and architecture—rather than the construction workers who fulfilled their fantasies—have attracted myriad academic studies.[46] A taste for the antique allowed people of means to signal their class identity ostentatiously. The Neo-Palladian obsession distinguished those who favoured it from the associations of the Baroque, by this point seen as Francophile, unenlightened, decadent and feudal.

Neo-Palladianism means the imitation of the architectural principles of the 16th-century Paduan architect Andrea Palladio. In Britain the most important text for the dissemination of neo-Palladianism was Colen Campbell's *Vitruvius Britannicus*, the three volumes of which were published between 1715 and 1725—that is, at the same time as the emergence of an agreed classical curriculum, based in the ancient languages, for the teenaged sons of leisured gentlemen. Architectural and artistic books were mostly published by subscription, and the more luxuriant the format, the richer the subscribers needed to be. This 'Neo-Palladian bible' was supported by the upper echelons of society, including many peers of the realm. The original success of neo-Palladianism 'was a direct result of the extensive links within these highest social strata',[47] newer members of which were determined to associate themselves with hereditary aristocracy rather than trade, and to showcase what they wanted to be seen as their intellectual accomplishments. One of the grandest and earliest neo-Palladian structures was the water gardens, with their Doric 'Temple of Piety' and Ionic 'Temple of Fame', built at Studley Royal in West Yorkshire by the enterprising John Aislabie. Studley was designed by Colen Campbell himself, and the plans published in *Vitruvius Britannicus*.[48]

The men who disguised the mercantile origins of their wealth by creating the classicising fantasy at Stourhead in Wiltshire were Henry Hoare and his son, also called Henry. Henry Senior was himself the son of a successful Smithfield goldsmith, Richard Hoare, who founded the oldest surviving private bank in Britain, C. Hoare & Co. Henry Senior made an enormous fortune out of the South Sea Bubble crisis in 1719. His son Henry Junior (1705–1785) expressed his self-definition as a Hellenistic philosopher-king in the Arcadian landscape he commissioned at Stourhead, with its numerous Neo-Palladian buildings and allusions to ancient literature. He stated that it was 'the habit of looking into books and the pursuit of knowledge which distinguishes only the gentleman from the vulgar'.[49] Hoare dedicated the Stourhead Pantheon to Hercules, who chose to pursue virtue rather than pleasure, in order for Hoare to visually represent his own refined taste and commitment to moral rectitude. Indeed, by adopting Neo-Palladianism, like purchasing their sons a classical education, the new rich demonstrated to the powerful landed aristocracy that they were highly educated and cultured Enlightenment gentlemen whose children were entitled to intermarry with nobles.

The new money often came from colonial ventures. In a typical socio-economic pattern, Robert Clive himself, made newly but fabulously rich by India, bought the Claremont Estate in Surrey from the widow of the Duke of Newcastle, thus removing it from the possession of an old aristocratic family with a prominent profile in government. There he built his Palladian residence, designed by Capability Brown and Henry Holland. Similarly, Basildon

House, an outstanding Neo-Palladian architectural pile in Berkshire, obliterates any reference to the source of the money that built it: India. It was the creation of Francis Sykes, son of a modestly prosperous Yorkshire Yeoman (i.e. non-aristocratic) farmer. Sykes arrived in Calcutta at the age of 18 to work for the East India Company. He rose to become immensely powerful, in Bengal second only to Robert Clive. When he returned to England in 1769, he had amassed a gargantuan private fortune of half a million pounds. He was the archetypal 'nabob'. Sykes formally joined the aristocracy when he was made a baronet in 1781, although allegations of corruption dogged his attempts at a parliamentary career. His ascent of the class ladder found its ultimate expression in his self-fabrication at Basildon as a classically educated member of the land-owning gentry. Every detail, from the plant pots and statues in the extensive gardens to Doric facades and internal plasterwork, reinforces the classicising illusion.[50]

An ostentatious aficionado of the classical style was Sir Rowland Winn, 5th Baronet of Nostell. In one portrait he displays his wife Sabine Louise d'Hervert as one of his valuable possessions, likened by the integrated classical bust and picture-within-the-picture to a Grecian goddess. They stand in the fabulous library Winn had commissioned at the family seat, Nostell Priory in Yorkshire; its shelves, holding tomes including Greek and Latin classics, are adorned with busts of ancient poets and sages.[51] When Rowland succeeded his father in 1765, he began to turn Nostell into a sumptuous neoclassical stately home, hiring Robert Adam as architect and interior designer, Antonio Zucchi, Angelica Kauffman and Hugh Douglas Hamilton for the lavish figurative painting on classical themes, and Thomas Chippendale to make the furniture. How many workers they needed between them to complete the spectacular mansion is anybody's guess. Some of the internal paintwork delicately replicates frescoes uncovered at Pompeii and Herculaneum. But the façade featured the elaborate Corinthian-style columns which Adam had recently made famous in *Ruins of the Palace of the Emperor Diocletian at Spalatro in Dalmatia* (London, 1764): only the palace fit for a Roman Emperor was good enough for the 5th Baronet.[52]

The Winn family, originally textile merchants, had acquired their Baronetcy as a reward for Royalism on the restoration of the monarchy in 1660. They made money not only from textiles but from corn and the mining of coal, already a well-developed industry around Wakefield by the mid-18th century: there was a coal-mine in the area of Nostell as early as 1541.[53] When the neoclassical landscape of Nostell Priory was designed, scrupulous care was taken to conceal the path taken daily by the local miners on their way to the pits, distastefully close to the house, using gentle mounds and artfully placed vegetation.

The 5th Baronet's extravagant tastes brought his dynasty to the brink of bankruptcy by his death in 1785. Its fortunes were not restored until the estates were inherited by his capable grandson Charles in 1817—the product of a scandalous interclass elopement. Charles was born to Sir Rowland's daughter Esther and the Nostell Priory baker, John Williamson, after they had defected together to Manchester.

Some working-class people must have acquired familiarity with classical art and architecture through close association with such edifices, whether as builders, miners who laboured a stone's throw from their elegant windows, or women in domestic service. And classical revival architecture was not confined to country estates. Working-class people built and walked past countless municipal buildings such as the Doric Town Hall in Bexley Square, Salford, which was begun in 1825, with its personifications of Agriculture, Music, Lyres and Poetry, and Unity (a bundle of fasces or rods), War and Peace, all classical in costume and conception. It was designed by Richard Lane, who had studied neoclassical architecture in Paris with Achille Leclère, famous for his restoration of the Pantheon in Rome. For decades from its erection in 1837–1838, the entrance to Euston station was a spectacular Doric propylaeum, seventy-foot high, facing onto Drummond Street.[54] Across the Euston Road, St. Pancras Church, designed in 1818–1819 by William and Henry Inwood soon after the nation acquired the Parthenon sculptures from Elgin, boasts eight elegant caryatids inspired by the single one looted from the Athenian Erechtheion.[55]

Working-class archaeologists and museum visitors

Visual culture often proved a significant avenue for lower-class people to access classical civilisation because those whose occupations involved farming, care of horses, mining, digging, gamekeeping, fishing, dredging and other outdoor pursuits were more likely to come across ancient remains in their neighbourhoods. The horde of Roman ceramics which the pottery workers of Staffordshire were encouraged to feel somehow prefigured their own trade was dug up by construction workers demolishing the Farewell Nunnery in 1747.[56] In the mid-19th century, a hoard of 400 Roman silver denarii was discovered by brick-makers near Rossall Point in Lancashire; they were given to the Harris Museum at Preston (on which see further below p. 129–32).[57] The miners of north-eastern England prided themselves on their knowledge of Roman Britain; their interest is reflected in the banner of the Fenhall Drift Lodge (Lanchester) miners, which depicts a 20th-century miner and a Roman soldier as equally at home in underground caverns south of Hadrian's Wall.[58] The earliest, precious examples of ancient Greek script in Britain were discovered by builders: two bronze plaques were found during the construction of the railway station in York, which opened in 1841. They were dedicated to the gods in the 1st century CE by a man called Demetrius.[59] During the Crimean War, low-ranking British soldiers discovered ancient Greek artefacts when camped on the site of the ancient city of Tauric Chersonesos outside Sevastopol; drawings were reproduced in the *Illustrated London News*.[60]

The Museum of the Caerleon Antiquarian Association,[61] which opened in 1850, was built to house the Roman inscriptions and artefacts which labourers and farmers found locally.[62] Caerleon is the site of the Roman Isca Augusta, the base of the Second Augustan Legion. Encouraged by the society's founder, John Edward Lee (a landed proprietor), middle-class antiquarians including the vicar,

John Jones, received and sometimes grabbed Roman artefacts from the workers who dug their ditches and broke the stones for their roads. The famous Caerleon 'labyrinth mosaic' was discovered by grave-diggers at the parish church of St. Cadoc. Shards of Samian pottery were uncovered by builders digging a trench. A beautiful ivory tragic mask was found by a man digging a drain in the garden of Castle Villa, the residence of John Jenkins, manager and co-owner of the tin works in Ponthir.[63] Paradoxically, Caerleon had been the site of an important Chartist uprising. Jenkins had even attended Chartist meetings, in order to 'know his enemy'.[64]

Museums in Britain were visited by a wider class cross-section than their equivalents in France, Germany and Italy, where the admission of visitors to the princely galleries was closely monitored.[65] There was a sense that art and archaeology somehow belonged to the nation rather than exclusively to wealthy individuals, and free admission was customary.

> These were spaces where, in theory at least, people of all classes were offered the same experience, and permitted to see objects that in the past would have been the preserve of the few. At a time of wild disparities of educational provision, this was already a considerable, if grudging, concession.[66]

Lower-class visitors were drawn to museums out of curiosity; their memoirs often imply that what they saw nurtured an impulse towards self-education.

When Zacharias Conrad von Uffenbach toured the Ashmolean Museum in Oxford in 1710, he was shocked at the vulgarity of the visitors.[67] Ralph Thoresby, whose collection at the Museum Thoresbyanum, founded by his father in Leeds in the late 17th century, included Roman British finds, complained bitterly about visiting plebeian hordes.[68] A Prussian traveller was surprised in the 1780s that the visitors to the British Museum, founded in 1753, were 'various … some I believe, of the very lowest classes of the people, of both sexes, for as it is the property of the nation, everyone has the same right … to see it, that another has'.[69] Museum keepers expressed fears about the vulgar behaviour which they associated with the policy of free admission.[70] In 1815, the museum's Principal Librarian, Joseph Planta, complained to its trustees that 'our popular Visitors … in the fervour of independence, pride themselves in showing a disdain of order'.[71] Gustav Waagen was distressed by the chaotic and filthy masses crowding the National Gallery.[72]

The desire to display objects from classical antiquity, especially after the British Museum acquired Sir William Hamilton's classical collection in 1784, and the Parthenon sculptures from Lord Elgin in 1816, was a motor behind the 19th-century emergence of municipal museums.[73] A typical example is the Harris Museum in Preston. A combination of funds raised by the local people and a large bequest left in the will of lawyer Edmund Harris allowed the Preston Corporation to set up a library, museum and art gallery to honour the memory of Harris' father the Reverend Robert Harris (1764–1862). The longstanding Headmaster of Preston Grammar School, he was himself the upwardly mobile son of a 'goods carrier'. His success was owed to his talent for Classics, spotted in childhood.

The grand neoclassical building to house all three was designed by local architect James Hibbert and eventually opened in 1893. Besides finds illustrating local history from Roman Lancashire, the exhibits include plentiful British ceramics and hundreds of oil paintings, by (amongst others) George Frederick Watts and Lawrence Alma-Tadema. But the décor of the building itself was planned by Hibbert to edify his fellow Prestonians: it is a material monument to great artworks and authors of antiquity. The imposing pediment of the tympanum, supported by the six fluted Ionic columns of the imposing portico which faces into the market square, is filled by a sculpture, the work of Edwin Roscoe Mullins. It is partly inspired by those of the Parthenon and known locally as both 'The Age of Pericles' and 'The School of Athens'. Pericles sits helmeted in the centre of 12 other figures representing philosophers, poets, orators and artists. Around the lantern the epigraph reproduces a sentence from Pericles' 'Funeral Speech' in Thucydides. The sides of the building bear two inscriptions from Marcus Aurelius' *Meditations*.[74]

Inside, more columns and mosaic floors create a classical aesthetic, enhanced by the plaster casts of famous ancient and Renaissance sculptures—Assyrian (the Nimrud frieze of Ashurnasirpal), Greek (the Parthenon frieze and metopes, as well as the frieze from Apollo's temple at Bassae) and Florentine. Most jaw-dropping is the stained-glass window celebrating ancient Greek achievements in philosophy, science, art, literature, and riding horses bareback to the Parthenon (Figure 6.4). Commissioned in 1905, its creator was Henry Holiday, a colourful character who admired William Morris and campaigned for Irish independence, women's suffrage, socialism and dress reform.[75] He believed that homo sapiens was being destroyed by sartorial uniformity and that we should all wear different clothes. He personally liked to wear an outfit of medieval chain-mail.[76] But he was obsessed with Greek art, designing a frieze 'Apollo and the Muses' for Clifton Theatre,[77] and for years keeping a cast of Praxiteles' Hermes and an enormous model of the Acropolis he had constructed for himself in his studio.[78]

The lowest window panel portrays Sappho, Aeschylus, Sophocles, Euripides and Homer, with quotations in ancient Greek from Sappho and the *Iliad*. The middle panel, with its Greek inscription 'The Great Panathenaea', is a vivid rendition of some Parthenon horsemen. The top panel portrays philosophers, artists and scientists, including Aristotle and Pheidias. The mill-workers of Preston, in the mid-19th century far-famed for their mutinous strike actions, could learn a great deal about ancient Greece in a single afternoon at their museum.

By Edwardian times the same could be said by the crofters, masons and fisherfolk of Aberdeen, after more prosperous citizens added to their Museum and Art Gallery a new hall to display casts of ancient Greek statues and a reproduction of the entire Parthenon frieze. But the story of the far-reaching visual impact of ancient material culture on Aberdeen extends far further back in time, to 1820. It was then that an impoverished Scottish crofter-turned-stonemason,

FIGURE 6.4 Photograph of window in Harris Museum, Preston, designed by Henry Holiday. © Edith Hall.

Alexander MacDonald (1794–1860), moved to the city. There was a supply of beautiful raw local stone in the form of granite, which could be made into matte-surfaced mantelpieces, paving stones and funeral monuments. But Alexander was frustrated because neither he nor anyone else could work out how to give the gritty local stone a sheen and polish equivalent to that which could be given to marble.[79] In 1829 he read about an exhibition at the British Museum of ancient sculptures from Egypt, some of them from the Hellenistic period. They had been brought to Britain by the explorer Giovanni Belzoni, a former fairground strongman-entertainer.[80]

MacDonald travelled all the way to London to visit the exhibition and was astonished to see that the luminous statues made of granite—even those with rounded surfaces—were highly polished. The Egyptians and Ptolemies, mysteriously, had known how to do what no stonemason had done ever since. MacDonald set about trying to reproduce the lost art. But polishing by hand was far too laborious and time-consuming to be practicable. He did crack the problem of the rounded surfaces by using a wheel turned by two workers. But since everything had to be done by manual labour, it was too slow to be viable except for tiny pieces, and even they took days. The Ptolemies possessed enormous armies of slaves who could be kept at the lathe for entire lifetimes.[81]

The breakthrough came when MacDonald's neighbour, who ran a comb-making factory, let him use power from his new steam engine. With the aid of steam power, which drove the cutting and polishing machinery, monumental polished granite artefacts became feasible again. The granite industry of Aberdeen was now unstoppable. Polished, shiny granite gravestones became the rage, and ever bigger monuments and edifices were built, constructed out of granite exported from Aberdeen and exported all over the British Empire. In London alone, think of Waterloo Bridge, or the terraces of the Houses of Parliament, or the reddish granite of the fountains in Trafalgar Square. The visual impact of the Ptolemaic statues was therefore instrumental in altering the mode of granite production, the appearance of British imperial cities, and in due course the entire economy of north-eastern Scotland.[82]

The ancient inspiration behind MacDonald's granite was reflected in Alexander MacDonald's son and heir, also named Alexander, a man who became obsessed with the Greek-themed paintings of George Watts, Frederic Leighton and Lawrence Alma-Tadema. Alexander Junior spent some granite profits on his fine art collection, which he bequeathed to Aberdeen Art Gallery.[83] The gallery contains some of the most famous Victorian and Edwardian painted images of ancient Greek stories, including Alma-Tadema's tambourine-tapping brunette in *The Garden Altar* (1879), Waterhouse's *Danaides* (1906) and *Penelope and the Suitors* (1912). [84]

The people's Parthenon

Classics met the issue of social class in the gallery through another important Scottish philanthropist who, like Alexander MacDonald Senior, transcended his impoverished birth-rank and lack of formal schooling. George Reid grew up to become a famous painter, mostly of portraits but also of scenes of working life—fishermen and farm labourers. When the Aberdonians decided to add to their Museum and Art Gallery a new hall for casts of ancient Greek statues, Reid's own benefaction was a magnificent reproduction of the complete Parthenon frieze, which runs around the entire interior of the new sculpture court.[85] He was an intellectual leveller, who wanted to make the beautiful artworks of the ancient Greeks available to everyone in Aberdeen. The new gallery was opened at a splendid reception in April 1905. A specially commissioned train arrived from Euston containing 62 distinguished passengers. Among them was Thomas

Hardy, the poor boy from Dorset who had been apprenticed to a stonemason in his early teens, but had managed to learn some Greek and classical mythology in the evenings.[86] He was thrilled on this occasion to be awarded, at last, a university degree, conferred on him by Aberdeen University.[87]

George Reid's Aberdonian replica of the Parthenon frieze was one of hundreds of artefacts displayed nationally that reproduced part of the spoils which Thomas Bruce, the 7th Earl of Elgin, had amputated from their original sites on the Athenian Acropolis.[88] His own modest fortune derived from the labours of industrial workers in lime kilns, coal mines and iron foundries on his Broomhall estates. He had originally planned to house the sculptures at Broomhall; several architects drew plans for turning it into a grand Caledonian Parthenon. He commissioned expensive Doric columns which never got installed; instead they grace Perth Sheriff Court. But his rich wife left him, he ran out of money, and in 1816 persuaded the government to buy his booty. It is not well-known that there was substantial opposition to the payment of £35,000. Many Britons were outraged. Most of them did not have the vote, let alone a say in the Report of the Select Committee which recommended the purchase. There was a catastrophic harvest in 1816 and many were starving. The debates in the House of Commons were vigorous, one MP stressing in an allusion to Matthew 7:9 that many veterans had inadequate pensions: 'if we could not give them bread we ought not to indulge ourselves in the purchase of stones'. Lord Milton agreed: 'the want of subsistence was the cause of riot and disturbance in many parts of the country'.[89] The purchase was opposed by both John Christian Curwen, MP for Carlisle and the owner of coal mines, on the ground that times were unusually hard, and the more radical Whig MP for Coventry, Peter Moore, who said he would demand the money for his constituents, rather than give such a sum 'to look at broken legs, arms, and shoulders'.[90]

This cartoon by George Cruikshank is entitled 'The Elgin Marbles! or John Bull buying stones at the time his numerous family want bread' (Figure 6.5). Cruikshank depicts the Leader of the House of Commons, Lord Castlereagh, as a sinister salesman trying to entice John Bull, the archetypal sensible Briton, to buy some broken statues. Castlereagh says, 'Here's a Bargain for you Johnny! Only £35,000!! I have bought them on purpose for you! Never think of Bread when you can have Stones so wonderous Cheap!!' Bull, in patched clothes, is surrounded by his emaciated children. Mrs. Bull's baby is sucking a meatless bone. Other children shout 'Don't buy them Daddy! we don't want Stones. Give us Bread! Give us Bread! Give us Bread!'[91]

The Parthenon sculptures nevertheless furnished perhaps the most familiar visual images in Britain. The Society for the Diffusion of Useful Knowledge, in association with the British Museum, published a book containing detailed drawings of the sculptures in 1833.[92] Similar cast friezes are on display at the Fitzwilliam Museum in Cambridge and in Manchester City Art Gallery, to which the King donated the casts in 1831. One was rather mysteriously donated to Surbiton High School, which opened in 1884. Smaller pieces were acquired to

FIGURE 6.5 'The Elgin Marbles! or John Bull buying stones at the time his numerous family want bread' by George Cruikshank (1816), reproduced by courtesy of the British Museum © The Trustees of the British Museum.

grace the stairways and landings of Self-Improvement societies and subscription libraries across the land, for example at the Newcastle Literary and Philosophical Society.[93] Moreover, since Elgin gave permission to any artist, including the 'Cockney Raphael', Benjamin Robert Haydon,[94] and the radical Paisley modeller John Henning, designs imitating the Parthenon sculptures were much reproduced for private sale all over the European Continent.

Henning (1771–1851) was a working-class carpenter-turned-sculptor, the son of a Paisley carpenter and builder. He specialised in the reproduction of ancient Greek relief sculpture and cameo-style portraiture. As a teenager, Henning inherited the democratic politics of his father Samuel, who served as secretary of the Paisley Branch of the Society for the Friends of the People. This had assembled at the 1793 British Convention in Edinburgh to press for universal suffrage and parliamentary reform.[95] John Henning would later claim to have been on a list in 1794 of 185 people in Paisley who were to be imprisoned under the suspension of the Habeas Corpus Act.[96] Thankfully these arrests never took place, and when Henning moved to London he continued in the struggle for social reform by selling the radical Paisley-printed *Weavers Magazine*.[97]

In 1799 Henning realised that what he called his 'doll making', the creation of plaster-cast likenesses of the local 'great and good', was becoming more lucrative than his father's high-end house carpentry. To boost the value of these 'dolls' (often medallions with heads in profile), he experimented for a time with casting in vitreous enamel rather than plaster.[98] When in 1811 Elgin gave the now London-based Henning permission to draw and model from the Parthenon Sculptures, the President of the Royal Academy, Benjamin West, protested unsuccessfully: 'My Lord, to allow Mr. Henning to Draw from your Lordship's Marbles would be like sending a boy to the University before he had learned his letters'.[99]

Henning made and sold a number of cabinets containing beautifully crafted (and to scale—1:20) reproductions of the Parthenon and Bassae Friezes. Examples may be viewed in the British Museum and Paisley Museum.[100] In 1812, at the height of metropolitan Grecomania, he was commissioned by Princess Charlotte to cast her likeness in classical dress. When sitting for her Grecian portrait, the fashionable and popular 15-year-old princess even perused some of Henning's radical Scottish literature. She politely remarked: 'Mr Henning, I am not indulged with that kind of reading'.[101] The Princess's patronage established Henning's reputation. Josiah Wedgewood issued six of his medallions.[102]

Sadly for Henning, his career was plagued by competition from third parties who copied his work and reproduced it internationally.[103] Neither as rich nor as famous as he might have become, a 60-year-old Henning taught himself enough Latin, Greek and Hebrew to be able to discuss the merits and shortfalls of various translations of the Holy Scriptures with his friends—quite a feat for a man who left school at 13.[104] One of his eight children, John Henning Junior, followed in his father's footsteps, turning his stonemasonry skills towards the installation of classical reliefs on buildings.[105] He was, for example, commissioned to decorate the exterior of the Athenaeum Club in Pall Mall under his father's supervision and using his Parthenon marbles design. He also went on to produce the classical reliefs on Decimus Burton's triple screen at Hyde Park Corner and the reliefs for the front of the Manchester City Art Gallery.[106]

The Parthenon frieze was treated to a more class-conscious reading by Godfrey Sykes for the Sheffield Mechanics Institute. Sykes was a Yorkshireman, who left his apprenticeship to an engraver and enrolled at the newly opened Sheffield School of Art in 1843.[107] He was influenced by the neoclassical sculptor Alfred Stevens, who designed Greek revival buildings in the area. Sykes's other works include several paintings of people at work, in smithies, forges and steelworks. Perhaps it was his reputation for sympathetic portrayal of industrial work that led, in 1854, to his being commissioned to design a frieze by the Sheffield Mechanics Institute. It had opened in 1832, and had several hundred members, including one hundred women; its lecture hall could accommodate a thousand. Rather than simply reproducing the Parthenon frieze, Sykes adapted it to a Sheffield context, substituting more than 60 artisans, labourers, miners and steelworkers for Pheidias' procession of Athenian horsemen (Figure 6.6). Headed by Minerva/Athena and other gods, in Sykes's vision, the workers of Sheffield proudly wield their tools and push their trucks around the whole 13 painted panels, in oil on paper in trompe-l'oeil imitation of relief sculpture, extending

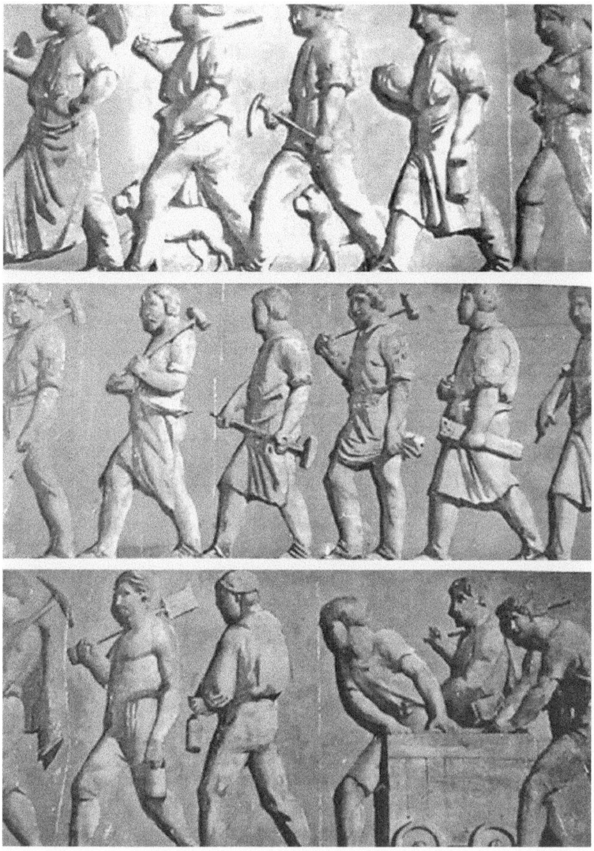

FIGURE 6.6 'Godfrey Sykes' Mechanics' Frieze'. Photograph reproduced courtesy of Sheffield Museums and Art Galleries.

to 60 feet, of the frieze.[108] The background is a bright (aquamarine) blue and the figures stand out in a deep gold. Sykes subsequently moved to London, and became supervisor of the decorative design of the Victoria and Albert Museum, but sadly died young at the age of only 41.

Classics and class in painting

But by the mid-19th century, at any rate, just one or two painters began to use classical material to think about class-related issues. We discuss here the handful of such images we have identified amongst the collection of more than 200,000 paintings in museums, universities, galleries, town halls, and other institutional buildings all over Britain on the website of Art UK.[109] A moving example is Henry Wallis' tragic *Stonebreaker* (1857) in Birmingham City Art Gallery. The painting was inspired by the chapter in Thomas Carlyle's satirical novel *Sartor*

Resartus (1836) entitled 'Helotage', the ancient Spartan system of state slavery. The exhibition catalogue when the picture was first put on display at the Royal Academy in London quoted the passage of Carlyle which laments the intellectual starvation of the worker who lives and dies without acquiring knowledge of anything but physical deprivation and toil.[110] Wallis' manual labourer seems asleep, but he has actually been forced by poverty to work until he dies. In the novel, Carlyle ironically proposes a revival of the ancient Spartan custom of murdering helots arbitrarily to keep them intimidated:

> now after the invention of fire-arms, and standing armies, how much easier were such a hunt! Perhaps in the most thickly peopled country, some three days annually might suffice to shoot all the able-bodied Paupers that had accumulated within the year. Let Governments think of this. The expense were trifling: nay the very carcasses would pay it. Have them salted and barrelled; could not you victual therewith, if not Army and Navy, yet richly such infirm Paupers, in workhouses and elsewhere, as enlightened Charity, dreading no evil of them, might see good to keep alive?[111]

George James Howard painted ancient Mediterranean farm labourers being brought water to quench their thirst. *Refreshing the Reapers* (c. 1870), now in Tullie House Gallery in Carlisle.[112] It is in the style of the 'Etruscan School' of painting, emotive landscapes of Etruria in central Italy. But Howard's picture imagines ancient Etruscan society in its beauty and sensual physicality. Another painting by Howard portrays peasant women reclining in the ruins of the Baths of Caracalla.[113] In both scenes it is the working people and their social community, rather than the landscape, which count.

Howard, who was friends with the socialists William Morris and Walter Crane, as well as Burne-Jones, was anything but lower-class himself. He was educated at Eton and Cambridge (where he was influenced by the lectures of Charles Kingsley) and inherited his title Earl of Carlisle, along with the 78,000-acred Howard Estate, in 1889. His aim in life, besides painting, was to make fine art available to everyone. Howard was a trustee and then chairman of the National Gallery, helped found the Tate Gallery, and was a member of the Society for the Protection of Ancient Buildings.[114]

His political views were, if not radical, then philanthropic and progressive. His wife was an ardent supporter of women's suffrage and the temperance movement, and ensured that the dreamy George, who would have been happy to paint all day, was kept up-to-date on political issues. As Liberal MP for East Cumberland 1879–1880 and 1881–1885, and subsequently in the House of Lords, he argued patiently for the provision of artworks in provincial museums, and for the opening of museums and art galleries on Sundays. On 19th May 1882 he argued in parliament that British people of all classes 'had a right to see the treasures of which they were joint owners on the only day it was convenient for them to go there'. Moreover, since 'Trade Unions had secured great advantages' in securing half-days and holidays for their members, they needed places to visit where they could enjoy high culture.[115] He also campaigned to keep children out of public houses, for the pension rights of policemen and for the employment of ex-servicemen in the nation's galleries.

Victor Rainbird's 'Greek Builders', probably painted around 1920, is now to be seen at the Old Low Light gallery in North Shields.[116] Rainbird was a working-class painter and stained glass artist from this borough of Newcastle-upon-Tyne, where the economy was based on fishing and coal. He lived his whole life in North Shields. A blue plaque on the exterior wall of 71, West Percy Street commemorates the years he lived in this small terraced house (1917–1933). Although under-appreciated in his own lifetime, Rainbird's reputation has been growing recently. In 2013 a new primary school in Newcastle was opened. Its name is Rainbird Primary School. In April 2018, a stage play by Peter Mortimer, *Rainbird: The Tragedy of an Artist*, was performed by the Cloud Nine Theatre Company at the Exchange Theatre, North Shields.[117]

Rainbird served in World War I at non-officer rank, in both the Northumberland Fusiliers and the Durham Light Infantry, and suffered psychological trauma. He then made his living from his paintings, but died of alcohol-related problems in 1936, aged only 47, and was buried in a pauper's grave. He was fascinated by scenes of work, and his favourite subject-matter was the fishermen and fishwives on the local wharves and sea-shores, as in 'Fish Market'. Like the visiting American artist Winslow Homer before him, Rainbird was a leading member of the Artists' Colony at the fishing village of Cullercoats. His only surviving work in stained glass commemorates six men, all from the Shetland island of Papa Stour, who died in World War I. It is in Papa Stour Kirk.[118]

Nothing is known of the genesis of 'Greek Builders'. But it is striking that when Rainbird, unusually for him, chose to depict a scene from the ancient world—indeed a beautiful temple with a columned portico—he focuses on the labourers rather than the classical edifice. Realistic, muscular but in no way 'classically' handsome or idealised, against a cloudy rather than sunlit sky, his serious-minded ancient Greek labourers are exerting themselves in physical tasks: digging, cutting down a tree, stone-working or carrying supplies.

It is female labour that is celebrated by Cliff Rowe, a British painter whose conscious mission was to put working people at the centre of the visual arts. A working-class boy from Wimbledon, he left school at 14 and managed to get into the Wimbledon Art School. Five years later he was working as a commercial illustrator, but the economic crisis and the growing threat of Fascism persuaded him to join the Communist Party. After 18 months in Russia absorbing Soviet innovations in design, he returned to England and set up the Artists' International Association.[119] This organisation, at its height with a membership of nearly a thousand, aided German refugees and sent medical assistance to the British International Brigade during the Spanish Civil War. Most of Rowe's paintings lend beauty and grandeur to scenes of people working in industry, for example 'Woman cleaning a loco boiler'.[120] But in 'Three Graces', the power of

FIGURE 6.7 'The Three Graces' by Clifford Hooper 'Cliff' Rowe (1904–1989), reproduced by courtesy of the People's History Museum, Manchester.

the image derives from Rowe's recasting of three women working at a factory conveyor belt in the unmistakable postures of the three Graces—the one in the centre with her back to the viewer (Figure 6.7).

This design concept goes all the way back to antiquity, and features in a famous mural at Pompeii and mosaic in the Shahba Museum, Syria. This arrangement of a beautiful trio of women is recurrent in Western art from at least as early as Botticelli's 'Primavera' (1486); its most famous instantiation is probably in Canova's neoclassical statue group of around 1816. But the very idea that such a vision of classical perfection could be located in an industrial setting embodied by low-income women in the roles of Grecian goddesses, calmly in control of the complicated machinery they are operating, illustrates the profundity of Rowe's revolutionary political aesthetic.

Conclusion

A large proportion of Britons in the period covered by this book could not read in English, let alone Latin and Greek. Yet there were innumerable ways for some of them, especially those living around London and other cities, to access classical culture via visual media. Print shops provided free displays of caricatures and cartoons rich in allusions to classical mythology. The publishers of inexpensive self-education journals offered lavish illustrations of classical artefacts to appeal to the less literate and to children. Spectacular shows furnished an education in the ancient Roman city of Pompeii, while art galleries and museums, usually free to visit, were frequented by a wide cross-section of the population. The fashion for classically styled buildings and decorations both on country estates and in civic centres introduced countless people who built them, cleaned them and walked past them to Greek and Roman architecture. Many museum exhibits were originally discovered by manual workers labouring outdoors.

Since draughtsmanship, painted decoration and modelling were trades often learned by apprentices from poor backgrounds, the visual understanding of some of the most important ancient sites, such as Pompeii and the Athenian Acropolis, was often provided by originally working-class men like John Martin, James Stuart and John Henning. And some working-class artists were inspired by ancient themes to create new artworks which explicitly comment on the relationship between Classics and class, by portraying labourers as classical heroes or reinventing the Parthenon frieze. In the next chapter, we shall see how the visual medium of theatre could also be used to turn classical material into commentary on the British class system.

Notes

1 The intellectual elite of course found new ways of disparaging the vastly expanded readership produced by late 19th-century legislation, and the more arcane aspects of early literary Modernism, which was rich in its own form of classicism, were part of their response, according to the brilliant study of Carey (1992).
2 The canonical study has long been and remains Vincent (1989). For a wider European perspective, see Blanning (2000) 165–6.
3 Stephens (1990) 553-6. For Scotland see Houston (1965) 163–5.
4 Anon. (1838).
5 The 'Hardwicke' Marriage Act 1754 had made the registration of all marriages, births and deaths in the parish register obligatory. (Separate registers were kept by Jews and Quakers). See also Hall and Macintosh (2005) chapter 5.
6 Cowan (2012) 49–50.
7 Stephens (1990) 558.
8 Anon. (1829); see Aspinall (1946) 30.
9 Barker (1998) 22–44. On radicalism in the army and the unstamped press, see Mansfield (2013).
10 Montesquieu (1826) 446.
11 Corner (1948) 114–15; Keane (1995) 110–11.
12 L'Estrange (1720). We are grateful to Jonathan Davies for drawing Tam Fleck to our attention.
13 McCleery (2005), based on a lecture originally delivered at the Museum of Edinburgh, Huntly House.
14 Chambers (1872) 25–6.
15 Chambers (1872) 26.
16 Burke (2001).
17 Lewis (1998-1999); Hall (2006) 196–206.
18 Hunt (2003) 6–7.
19 Inglis (2014) 157–8.
20 Hunt (2003) 12–13, with illustrations on 11; Moores (2015) 4; Dickinson (1986) 13–15.
21 Brewer (1986) 29–32.
22 Hunt (2003) 16.
23 Moores (2015) 5.
24 See, for example, 'Hercules reposing' by James Gillray, 7th May 1799. There are at least 100 satirical prints from between 1780 and 1832 where the central joke is an allusion to classical mythology in the *Catalogue of Political and Personal Satires* in the Department of Prints and Drawings in the British Museum.
25 For detailed discussions of all the publications of the SDUK including those on Classics and classical archaeology, see Cavenagh (1929) and Rauch (2001).

26 Gilbert (1922) 70.
27 See Bennet (1984).
28 'The British Museum: the Portland Vase', no. 31, 29th September (1832) 249–50.
29 In 1832 alone, see also 'Ancient paintings' no. 24, 18th August, 200; 'Zeuxis', no. 25, August 25th, 207–8; 'The British Museum: the Elgin Marbles', no. 28, 8th September, 228–9; 'The Warwick Vase', no. 29, 15th September, 233; 'Description of the shield of Achilles, no. 33, 22nd September, 241–2; 'Tivoli', no. 34, 13th October, 273.
30 'March of Mind' by Robert Cruikshank (1826). British Museum no. 1948,0214.982.
31 Gilbert (1922) 114.
32 See See Webb (1955) 97; Hall (2008c) 316.
33 Malcolm (1808) 405; see Altick (1978) 96.
34 See Nicolson (1968).
35 Daly (2015) 26; see Pendered (1923) 107 with plate.
36 See Pendered (1923) 19–41, 186–95; www.artfund.org/news/2016/08/03/curator-of-the-month-julie-milne-tyne-and-wear-archives-and-museums.
37 Daly (2012) 45–6.
38 Dellarosa (2018).
39 Directed by Mario Caserini and Eleuterio Rodolfi.
40 Anon. (1867); Strong (2014) 59 with further references in 183 n.1
41 Layard (1903) vol. II, 235.
42 Hooper (1867) 3, 12; see Strong (2014) 82–91.
43 Watkin (1982) 14–15.
44 Cust (1885-1900) 86.
45 Brecht (1976) 656–7; our translation.
46 See e.g. Ayres (1997), Cruickshank (2009) 367–84, 393–4, 402–3 and the huge bibliography in Kurtz (2000) 431–47.
47 Fry (2003) 180.
48 See Eyres (1985).
49 National Trust (1981) 36.
50 Hall (2010a) 13–14 with fig. 2.
51 See further Laing (2000) and the image on the National Trust Website at www.nationaltrustimages.org.uk/image/81285.
52 See further Nostell (1954) and Nostell (2001).
53 Brockwell (1915) 382–3.
54 See the beautiful illustrations in Smithson and Smithson (1968). The arch was depicted on the banner of the London Cabdrivers' Trade Union, founded in 1894. See the reproduction in Gorman (1973) 146.
55 For the Erechtheion's influence on the architecture of the church, see Lee (1955) 38–40, 43 and plate 3.
56 Knight (1984 [1847]) 24–5.
57 King (1981) 40 n.1.
58 See the frontispiece to this book.
59 See William Rhys Roberts (1913) 291 with references. He came across the plaque in York Museum while organising University Extension classes from Leeds University (on which see Draper [1923] 25), at which he was one of the first teachers of Classics after its foundation in 1904. His discussion concludes with the rousing statement that it is a pleasure 'to reflect that some of our best graduates in classics have been sons of men earning a weekly wage, and to hope that they may not be entirely lost to the ranks in which they were born, but may do something, by means of daily intercourse and reading circles and tutorial classes, to spread among their friends and neighbours a knowledge of those literatures and civilisations which have taken so strong a hold upon themselves'. He was a Welsh-speaking Greek scholar who was instrumental in the late 19th-century organisation of the colleges of the University

of Wales (see Roberts [1892]), published a comparison of Greek, Latin and Welsh prose rhythm (Roberts [1914]) and in 1916 gave a lecture at the British Academy entitled *Greek Civilization as a Study for the People* (Roberts [1916]).

60 *Illustrated London News* Jan 19th (1856) 80. See further Hall (2013a) 13–14 and Hall (2018c).

61 Now the National Roman Legion Museum and the Monmouthshire Antiquarian Association respectively.

62 Brewer (1987)

63 See Hall (2002) 16 with figure 4.

64 Kennerley (1975).

65 Waterfield (2015) 3.

66 Waterfield (2015) 37.

67 Quarrell and Quarrell (1928) 31.

68 Waterfield (2015) 23.

69 Moritz (1795) 68.

70 Waterfield (2015) 37.

71 Quoted in Wilson (2002) 67.

72 National Gallery (1850) iv.

73 Waterfield (2015) 3.

74 Hartwell & Pevsner (2009) 519–522.

75 See e.g. Holiday (1914) 292, 316–19, 383, 393–5, 402–12

76 Holiday (1914) 173.

77 Holiday (1914) 157–8 and plate opposite 114.

78 He was inspired by a long visit to Greece in 1885: see Holiday (1914) 299–305; his casts can be seen in the photograph opposite 314.

79 Hall (2018f) 203–4.

80 Mayes (2003).

81 See Hall (2018f) 204.

82 Donnelly (1979).

83 See Melville (2010) 5–7.

84 Carter (n.d.) and Melville (2010) 34.

85 Melville (2010) 24–31.

86 Seymour-Smith (1994) 39–40.

87 Ray (1995).

88 St. Clair (1998).

89 Both cited from Heringman (1998) 59–60.

90 'House of Commons' (1816).

91 For further discussion, see Heringman (1998).

92 British Museum (1833), of which the anonymous author was Sir Henry Ellis. On the SDUK, the brainchild of Henry Brougham, see especially Rauch (2001) 40–6.

93 Watson (1897) 93–4. The Society also acquired some Greek vases, an Egyptian mummy case in 1821 and 'slabs from Nineveh' (Watson [1897] 300, 94.) A local sculptor who had risen from extreme poverty named John Graham Lough exhibited his colossal statues of Milo and Samson in London, became famous after receiving attention from Lord Brougham, and subsequently bestowed Milo on the Society: Watson (101–4). See Watson 278, 345, 347, 348, 350, 352, 353, 356, 359, 362, 363, 364, 365, for lectures or lecture series delivered there on 'The Roman Wall' (1848–1849), 'Great Cities of the Ancient World' (1850–1), 'The Rise and Fall of the Roman Republic' (1853–1854), 'Trajan's Pillar' (1856–1857), 'Roman Coins' (1860–1861), 'Greek Art' (1864–1865), 'The Animals of Ancient Writers' and 'An Old Greek War' (1867–1868), Greek Language and 'The Roman Wall' in 1869–1870, 'The Roman Wall', in 1873–1874, 'The Discovery of the Temple of Diana: the Results of the Excavations at Ephesus' and 'Claudian: the last of the Roman Poets' (1874–1875), 'Justinian and his Times' (1878–1879), 'Discovery of Roman Remains

at Vinovium (Binchester' (1879–80), 'Life in the Greek Heroic Age' (1883–1884), 'Rome, Ancient and Modern' and 'Hesiod' (1885–1886), 'The Meaning of the Roman Empire' (1886–1887), 'Ancient Tragedies for English Audiences' and 'Ancient Comedies for English Audiences' (1886–1887), and 'Pompeii' (1892–1893).

94 Haydon (1960) vol. I, especially 16.

95 See British Convention (1893).

96 Letter from John Henning to his brother-in-law Joseph Thomson (1836), printed in Malden (1977) correspondence item number 28.

97 Malden (1977) [unpaginated] 3; Malden (2004) *ODNB*.

98 Malden (1977) [unpaginated] 5; Malden (2004) *ODNB*.

99 *The Mechanics' Magazine, Museum, Register, Journal and Gazette* (1836) October 3–April 2, 1836, vol. XXIV, p. 169.

100 There is also one of Henning's casts of the Bassae frieze (BM 530 and 522) housed at the Ure Museum of Greek Archaeology, University of Reading.

101 Pyke (1973) 66.

102 Malden (1977) [unpaginated] 8; Malden (2004) *ODNB*.

103 Malden (2004) *ODNB*.

104 For more on Henning and his reception of the classical, see Allan Hiscutt's PhD thesis on the subject, Hiscutt (2018).

105 Malden (1977) [unpaginated] 10.

106 Malden (1977) [unpaginated] 10.

107 See further Barringer (2005) 198–204.

108 Barringer (2005) 218–21 with figure 95–6.

109 I.e. https://artuk.org/. On one further painting, by Gilbert Daykin, see below pp. 463–5. We have not yet been able to conduct similar research into sculpture and statuary.

110 Hamlyn (1984).

111 See colour reproduction and further discussion in Barringer (2005) 95–7.

112 Viewable online at https://artuk.org/discover/artworks/refreshing-the-reapers-144497/search/actor:howard-george-james-18431911/page/1/view_as/grid.

113 Now held by the Department for Communities & Local Government, 2 Marsham Street, London.

114 Ridgway (2004) *ODNB*.

115 See https://api.parliament.uk/historic-hansard/commons/1882/may/19/opening-of-national-museums-c-on-sunday#column_1148.

116 Viewable online at https://artuk.org/discover/artists/view_as/grid/search/artists:rainbird-victor-noble-18871936, and reproduced as the cover of the paperback edition of this book.

117 Mortimer (2018).

118 https://papastour21century.wordpress.com/about-papa-stour/the-papa-stour-kirk/war-memorial-window-2.

119 Watkinson (1987) 14–20.

120 Now in the People's History Museum, Manchester.

7

STAGING CLASS STRUGGLE CLASSICALLY

Introduction

There are several class-conscious approaches to the relationship between Classics and enactment in theatre (and later cinema) during the period addressed in this book.[1] Most of this chapter examines a controversial tragedy about the Gracchi, drastically censored during the revolutionary period before and after the 1819 massacre at Peterloo.[2] The censor's stranglehold on spoken theatre from 1737 onwards illuminates the apparent lack of overtly class-conscious plays on classical themes in public theatricals. Other aspects of the theatrical politicisation of antiquity, including the amateur productions of plays and musicals about Caractacus during the World War I recruitment drive in Wales, and the revolutionary workers' theatre versions of Aristophanes' *Lysistrata* developed in the 1930s, are discussed in Chapters 12 and 25. Radical plays were sometimes imported from abroad, such as the American socialist Susan Glaspell's *Inheritors*, a tragedy based on Sophocles' *Antigone* performed at the Liverpool Repertory in 1926. It indicts the abuse of both Native Americans and Indians under the British Raj.[3] But this area is ripe for further research.

Classics in demotic theatre

David Mayer and others have investigated the popularity in Britain of the 'toga drama', on the theme of struggles between Romans and early Christians, in both popular theatre and early cinema between the 1880s and about 1920.[4] In a subsequent chapter of this book we briefly discuss the phenomenon of mid-19th-century 'classical burlesque', of which most actors and some of the spectators were lower-class, and a few of which (for example, those by the brothers William and Robert Brough) were critical of the establishment.[5] Despite a surge of recent academic interest in the genre in response to work by Hall and Macintosh,[6] many

DOI: 10.4324/9781315446608-8

important burlesque productions have yet to be investigated, especially those which were hits in the provinces as well as metropolitan theatres. An example is Francis Cowley Burnand's *Ixion, or the Man at the Wheel* (1863), an outstanding success in London, Liverpool and the USA.[7] The class politics of this piece, the success of which depended on a density of excellent puns, are far from radical. It begins with an amoral Ixion afflicted by gambling debts. He is driven by a revolutionary mob into exile on Olympus. But the people of ancient Thessaly are associated with Tom Paine and mocked as a 'Crowd of Red Republicans, Unread Republicans … appropriately crowned with mob caps'.[8] They come to an ineffectual end, struck motionless by Mercury when their humorous potential is exhausted; Ixion then redefines democratic agency as the mere ability of the masses to make any theatre performance a commercial success or failure.

Another context where class-conscious theatre performances might be expected is in the world of amateur dramatics, which are difficult to document, because so few permanent records have survived from before the digital age. But certain examples of left-wing amateur theatricals even before World War II are better attested than others. At a concert held by the Southwark branch of the Social Democratic Federation in 1886, the party leader recited passages from Aristophanes' *Birds*.[9] In Sheffield, The Little Theatre, part of Sheffield Educational Settlement, run by Arnold Freeman (1918–1955), a proponent of Rudolph Steiner's principles of Anthroposophy, staged several classical productions, including Aeschylus' *Oresteia* (1931), Euripides' *Trojan Women* (1932) and Sophocles *Antigone* (1936).[10] The People's Theatre in Newcastle-upon-Tyne was co-founded in the premises of the local branch of the British Socialist Party by professional footballer Colin Veitch (1881–1938) and his wife Edith. They had been involved in the Clarion movement. The productions between 1931 and 1946 included three plays by Euripides, Aristophanes' *Frogs* and even Menander's *Rape of the Locks*, all in Gilbert Murray's translations.[11]

Murray's translations, especially his *Medea*, were even performed in the South Wales coalfields.[12] Their multiple reprints and availability on the second-hand book market, along with the popularity of Murray's classic study *Euripides and his Age* (1913), inspired Adult Education groups across the country, for example a reading class run in Glasgow under the aegis of the YMCA in the 1920s.[13] In 1938, the Left Book Club Theatre Group performed Murray's translation of Euripides' *Trojan Women* in Plymouth.[14] But the records of most of the British workers' theatre productions, especially those organised by the Co-operative and Clarion movements from the 1880s onwards, which included ancient plays and plays on ancient historical themes, have been neglected.

Dramatic performance has always had a relationship with politics in Britain. At the height of the early 18th-century struggle over the ownership of classical cultural property, the *Odyssey* was treated to a class-conscious reading in a ballad opera staged at the Little Haymarket Theatre. In Chapter 2 we saw this struggle triangulated in the rival avenues of access to classical texts provided by private schools, by the refined translations of Dryden and Pope, and by demotic fairground entertainments. *Penelope*, by John Mottley and Thomas Cooke, in 1728 transposed the *Odyssey* to a working-class London tavern. The epic story is set in the Royal Oak Ale-House; the Sign hanging outside reads, '*This is the Royal Oak, the House of Pen, / With Entertainment good for Horse and Men*'.[15] The publican is Pen, wife of Ulysses; a sergeant in the grenadiers, he has been absent fighting for 19 years. Meanwhile, she has been besieged by suitors: a butcher, a tailor and a parish clerk.

The songs of ballad opera (folk tunes, urban popular ditties and famous refrains by composers like Handel), were known on the streets, and the audiences sang along. Cooke, although an innkeeper's son, was a classical scholar (indeed, the first translator of Hesiod into English[16]), and the opera is his barbed response to his long-time enemy Alexander Pope's translation of the *Odyssey*, issued in 1725–1726. But Mottley, as a Grub Street pamphleteer and the son of an absentee Jacobite soldier, was equipped to write about abandoned women and the seedier underside of London life.

The opera's demotic tone is set when Penelope tells the audience that she has not combed her 'matted locks' for a month, and put on only one clean smock in the last three. Her maid Doll suggests that she seek comfort in the bottle, but neither gin nor whisky can help. Penelope calls Doll a 'silly sow', and Doll recommends that she marry Cleaver the butcher, singing: 'He's tall and jolly, / Believe thy Dolly, / It wou'd be Folly, / To slight his Pain'. Penelope complains that all the suitors are but 'rakehells'; she will not choose one of them until she has finished weaving her cabbage-net. She despises, she says, the hotpots, stout, ale and punch with which they woo her.[17]

Doll is less restrained. She favours the butcher because he bribes her with tasty offal; she is less impressed with the tailor's silver thimble, and nonplussed by the parish clerk's Bible and offer of a reserved pew at church. (The man of God is himself sent up for his supercilious manner of speech and respect for the crown.) Doll and Cleaver are secretly in love and plotting; Cleaver will marry Penelope, thus acquiring her property, and keep Doll as his mistress. Cleaver is evil but engaging, and able wittily to send up the Homeric archetype. He is a butcher, and therefore asks, '*Shall I my Fame with whining Sorrows stain, / Whose Arms have Hecatombs of Oxen slain?*'[18] But the opera ends as satisfactorily as the *Odyssey*, and with less bloodshed.

Penelope is inherently subversive. It invites its audience to laugh at the elevated ancient text, pored over by the schoolboy sons of the well-to-do, through a class-conscious lens. It domesticates the ancient story by appropriating it to a déclassé context while telling it in vernacular language sung to melodies from the street. Such was the climate of hostility to the King and Walpole amongst literary men at this time that even John Gay's *Achilles* (Covent Garden 1733), another frivolous burlesque of a classical myth, was read politically by some of them.[19] But as a light-hearted entertainment, like the exceptionally popular later 18th-century burletta *Midas* by the Irish playwright Kane O'Hara, in which Olympian gods and goddesses spoke in the language of a 'Wapping landlady',[20] and the 19th-century classical burlesques which will be discussed further in Chapter 17, *Penelope* was unlikely to incite audiences to riot in protest against class hierarchies.

Censoring political theatre

Since the main case-study in this chapter concerns the drastic censoring of James Sheridan Knowles' play about the Gracchi because it was so sympathetic to the working class, a brief account of stage censorship in Britain is needed here to provide context. By 1728, theatre riots were breaking out when plays touched on sensitive political issues. This produced the legislation that effectively prevented spoken drama being used for radical purposes. Under the Licensing Act, passed on the 24th of June 1737, the Lord Chamberlain assumed the power to refuse a licence to any play acted 'for hire, gain, or reward', anywhere in Great Britain, 'as often as he shall think fit'. The Act provided the basis for the law surrounding theatrical censorship that survived, substantially unchanged, until the 1968 Theatre Act.[21] All theatres were 'under the immediate Directions of a Court Officer'. The main thrust of the legislation was political, having been drawn up by the first Prime Minister, Robert Walpole, in order to curb attacks on him in the theatre from the more radical sectors of the new urban middle class. Tension between Walpole and the theatres had mounted with such thinly veiled defences of the constitutional principles of the Glorious Revolution against their perceived betrayal as the Irish author Samuel Madden's oppositional (and partly Plutarch-derived) *Themistocles, the Lover of his Country* (1729), and plays on episodes from the Roman republic such as William Bond's *The Tuscan Treaty; or, Tarquin's Overthrow* (Covent Garden 1733) and William Duncombe's *Junius Brutus* (Drury Lane 1734).[22]

Other attacks had been made in comedy, where the ancient author most implicated was Aristophanes. Henry Fielding's *The Author's Farce* (based on *Frogs*), which premiered in 1730, exposed the problems Walpole's increasing scrutiny of the stage posed to dramatists.[23] The immediate effect of the Act was to reduce London theatres to just the two licensed playhouses, Covent Garden and Drury Lane, plus the King's Opera House, which did not perform new stage plays. It seems amazing that James Thomson's anti-Walpole *Agamemnon* (1738) escaped cutting except for six lines of the prologue. The Thomson play which was banned from the stage was one which drew heavily on Euripides, *Edward and Eleonora* (proscribed 1739). The next play using an ancient Greek source to be refused a licence was James Shirley's *Electra* (1762): it savagely denounced the then Prime Minister, John Stuart, third Earl of Bute, and his influence over the Royal Family, by equating him with Aegisthus.[24]

Staging the Gracchi brothers

It is one thing to use the stage to criticize the government from the perspective of the disgruntled middle classes, as Fielding and Thomson did. It is another to argue that the gaping economic inequality between social classes, and especially the grinding poverty of the working classes, need immediate correction. A significant play on a classical theme to address this issue was also the first British play about the Gracchi, the brothers Tiberius and Caius Gracchus, immortalised in Plutarch's *Parallel Lives*, who both attempted to redistribute land illegally appropriated by the Roman nobility amongst the Italian poor. The work of Irishman James Sheridan Knowles, *Caius Gracchus* was first produced in 1815, the year of Waterloo. It was revived during the tempestuous next decade, when class conflict reached explosive levels in the suppression of protestors, both agricultural and industrial workers, not only at Peterloo but in London, East Anglia, Yorkshire, Preston, Nottinghamshire, Derbyshire, Wales, Scotland and Ireland.[25]

Plutarch's account of the death of Caius Gracchus is inherently visual. Several classical scholars have argued that there must have been an ancient play on the theme informing the tradition long before Plutarch's seminal contribution.[26] Caius committed suicide in a sanctuary of Furina, but he was beheaded and his skull filled with molten lead. Yet the Gracchi arrived late in the theatres of Europe, at least relative to other heroes celebrated by Plutarch, such as Julius Caesar or Coriolanus. The sole opera about either Gracchus was the apolitical *Caio Gracco* by Leonardo Leo, performed at the palace of his patron, the Viceroy of Naples, in 1720.[27] The delay was a result of the way the Gracchi set off political alarm bells.

The most influential ancient view of the Gracchi was, for a long time, Augustine's seminal discussion in *City of God*, III.24. Augustine acknowledged some unfairness in the stranglehold of the nobility on public land. But the Gracchi's attempts at land reform, according to Augustine, echoing most previous Latin authors, were seditious and resulted in fearful destruction, unleashing the violence of the Civil War, with riots, mobs and bloody massacres.[28] Augustine's characterisation of the Gracchi's actions can be found everywhere in texts before the 18th century—from Machiavelli's argument that even if right they were ineffective, to British Restoration apologists for the absolute monarchy, who routinely cited Plutarch's *Life of Tiberius Gracchus* as evidence for the sedition and anarchy that arose with any sort of republican or democratic constitution.[29]

The Gracchi were not even widely adopted by Parliamentarians during the English Civil War,[30] although their first identifiable admirers had been reforming Protestants of the early 16th century. A picture of the Gracchi radically different from that derived from Augustine first emerged from the pen of Johann Eisermann, Rector of Marburg, the first Protestant University to be founded without papal permission. He paraphrases Plutarch when discussing the problem of tyranny in his work on the good ordering of a commonwealth, *De Re Publica Bene Instituenda, Parainesis* (1556), the first edition of which had been published in 1533. The English translation by William Bavande, published three years after the 1556 edition, was a foundational text for English Protestantism. Eisermann responds to details in Plutarch's *Life* of Tiberius Gracchus more sympathetically; for example, his account of the process by which Tiberius comes to identify with the cause of the Italian poor is presented in emotive detail, citing the lamentations of the poor and the children dying of hunger.[31]

Eisermann's sympathy with the Gracchi was connected with the date he began writing the book, in the 1520s, only a decade after the Peasants' Revolt had rocked central Europe and bitterly divided the Protestant leadership. Yet the same book answers the question why the Gracchi did not become *stage* heroes until so much later. For Eisermann, however much he admired Tiberius Gracchus, deplored the theatre and all its arts. To put the matter in a nutshell, until the 18th century, the only Renaissance and Early Modern circles who read Plutarch's Gracchi as politically positive exemplary heroes were the very circles whose systematic anti-theatricalism ensured that the Gracchi were never to mount the stage. The Gracchi only began to become acceptable, and then only on the radical wing of the European Enlightenment, in 18th-century France and Italy. The death of Caius Gracchus became popular in French painting in the years immediately before and after the revolution,[32] most famously in Topino-LeBrun's 'Death of Caius Gracchus' (1792, first exhibited 1798). The revolutionary agrarian reformer Babeuf would take the name Gracchus, in place of his baptismal names François-Noël Toussaint Nicaisse, as part of the 'de-Christianization' movement of autumn 1793.[33] He had previously preferred the pseudonym Camillus, in imitation of the Roman statesmen of the fifth–fourth centuries BCE, the Tribune of the People and so-called Second Founder of Rome. But by October 1794, he had penned a manifesto polemicizing against tyranny and pleading for the sovereignty of the people, in which he describes himself as 'Gracchus Babeuf, people's tribune, defender of the rights of man, of press freedom, and other freedoms'.[34] Partly inspired by the revolutionary French tragedy by Marie-Joseph Chénier, *Caius Gracchus* (1792), James Sheridan Knowles wrote his Anglo-Irish *Caius Gracchus* (1815). Knowles, as a man of the theatre and an Irish radical, was fully acquainted with the French stage repertoire.

The Gracchi, moreover, had been identified as exemplary heroes earlier in Ireland than in Britain (Ireland, although ruled from Britain, was not formally united with England, Scotland and Wales until 1800). Anglo-Irish writers, as well as Irish authors writing in English, had long used ancient Greek authors to express discontent with the situation in their country, especially rural poverty.[35] But the Gracchi seemed particularly relevant in Ireland. Since the ancestors of many Catholics had been dispossessed of their land with the creation of the 17th-century plantations, the Irish peasantry identified intuitively with the cause of the ancient Roman poor. By 1773, a caustic critic of Lord Townshend's administration signs himself *Caius Gracchus*.[36] In 1781, Dissenting poet Mark Akenside, from Newcastle-upon-Tyne, adopted directly from France the radical Gracchi as opponents of oppression in Ireland.[37]

Knowles' revolutionary Romans

The impact of the French revolution in Ireland differed from its impact in England. The Irish peasants, oppressed by English or Anglophile landowners, identified with the French revolutionaries. They took hope when the new French government in 1791 said that it would offer military help to any movement attempting to depose their own monarch, and in February 1793 declared war on Britain and Ireland. It was in this context that Knowles, always known to his friends as 'Paddy', found himself at the age of nine in the position of political exile.[38] He was to grow up to be described in 1847 as

> a writer full of individuality as of geniality, who has been popular without coarse conception, and received as a poet without making any extraordinary pretensions. The first and last cause of his well-deserved popularity as a dramatist, is the heartiness of his writings ... The *heart* which Mr Knowles puts into his work lays hold of the hearts of his public; and this is his secret ... In fine, counting Burns at the head of the Uneducated Poets ... we think that Mr Sheridan Knowles will keep his place in the annals of the British Theatre as King of Uneducated Dramatists.[39]

The playwright's father ran a small Dublin school. A radical Protestant, and cousin of the dramatist Richard Brinsley Sheridan, Knowles Senior advocated Catholic Emancipation. After publicly supporting a liberal newspaper whose editor was imprisoned for criticising the government, he had to leave Ireland for London, with no money and his small son, in a hurry. William Hazlitt, himself of Irish Protestant descent, befriended them. Hazlitt was a conduit through which French Enlightenment and Continental revolutionary thought was disseminated in Britain, and his influence on the little Knowles was profound.[40] Knowles at this time read classical literature in English as well as works in modern languages; this is demonstrated by his knowledge of famous 18th-century translations of the tragedians and Roman rhetoricians. He discusses these in the lectures he delivered in mid-life to self-improvement societies in provincial cities including Belfast, Liverpool, Newcastle-upon-Tyne and Barnsley.[41]

But in the 1790s, the future playwright and his radical father watched from England while, back in Ireland, the United Irishmen were founded. This organisation brought together forward-looking Catholics and Protestants, intending to establish a democratic republic along French lines. When the British began murdering the members of this organisation, the result was the 1798 rebellion which was brutally put down at the Battle of Vinegar Hill. The French sent reinforcements who landed at Mayo on the western coast, but the joint Franco-Irish rebel army was again defeated.

When he grew up, Knowles worked as an actor centred in Bath and Dublin until, after the birth of his first child, he opted for the safer income of a teacher. He had no university-level education himself but was widely read, and was hired to teach English Literature at Belfast Academical Institution. There he began to write stage plays. He moved soon afterwards to teach in Glasgow instead; until a sudden conversion to a Protestant faith in the 1840s, he divided his extra-curricular energies between theatre and radical politics. For a time he co-edited, with indefatigable journalist William Spencer Northhouse, the newspaper *Glasgow Free Press*, which campaigned for Catholic Emancipation, Abolition, Parliamentary Reform, Municipal Reform, Abolition of Capital Punishment except in cases of murder, Repeal of the Tests and Corporations Act and Free Trade. It briefly became the most popular paper in western Scotland when it agitated for higher wages to be paid to the handloom weavers.[42]

Knowles became an exceptionally popular dramatist, his *Virginius* (1820), *William Tell* (1825) and *The Hunchback* (1832) chiming perfectly in tune with the reformist spirit of the late Georgian period and remaining for years staples of the early and mid-Victorian low-to-middlebrow stage repertoire. The Robert Burns of the stage wrote *Caius Gracchus* for the Belfast Theatre. It was first performed there on 13th February 1815. According to a review in *The Belfast News-Letter*, it 'was throughout received with the rapturous plaudits of a crowded house'.[43] This is scarcely surprising; not only did it speak to the plight of the Irish poor, but it encouraged more British-identified members of the Belfast audience to draw connections between poverty in ancient Rome and modern Britain after the 1813 Corn Laws had kept the price of bread impossibly high. This had been followed at the end of the Napoleonic Wars by a drastic economic slump and widespread famine afflicting the North of both England and Ireland in 1814.

When Knowles' play opens, Caius has returned to Rome and tells the audience how stirred he is by the sufferings of the poor: 'they are bare and hungry, houseless and friendless, and my heart bleeds for them'.[44] The second scene is a noisy enactment of the trial of Spurius Vetteius, a friend of Caius' dead brother Tiberius and supporter of the people, for sedition. There are two factions on stage, senators and citizens, and class-based insults are traded; afterwards, Flaminius and Fannius plot to bring discredit to Caius in the Senate. The overall politics of the piece are most clearly expressed in the third scene of Act II, where the plebeians Titus and Marcus, who support Caius, have an altercation with two servants of men of the Senatorial class in the Campus Martius. There is mass civic tumult, the senators' men raise their weapons and the plebeian Titus delivers a stirring speech in the prose style which Knowles is imitating from some of Shakespeare's lower-class characters:

> Down with your staff, master, for I have another that may ruffle the gloss of your cloak for you. What! has anything surprised you? Do you wonder that the order which wins your battles in the field, should refuse your blows in the city? You despise us when you have no need of us; but if an ounce of power or peculation is to be gained through our means, oh! then you put on your sweet looks, and, bowing to the very belts of our greasy jackets, you exclaim, "Fair gentlemen!—kind fellow-citizens!—loving comrades!—sweet, worthy, gentle Romans!—grant us your voices!" Or, if the enemy is to be opposed, oh! *then* we are "men of mettle!"—(poor starved devils!)—"the defenders of our country!"—(that is, your cattle as you call us)—and so indeed we are. We bear your patricians on our backs to victory; we carry them proudly through the ranks of the barbarians! They come off safe—we get the knocks, the pricks, and the scratches. They obtain crowns and triumphs,—we cannot obtain—a dinner! They get

their actions recorded—we get ours forgotten! They receive new names and titles—we return to our old ones with which you honour us—"the rabble!—the herd!—the cattle!—the vermin!—the scum of Rome!"[45]

Quintus, one of the Senator's attendants, responds simply, 'These greasy citizens are uttering treason against our masters, the noble patricians'.

Caius is arraigned by the Senators on trumped-up charges, but is acquitted. He persists and puts his name forward as tribune:

Ye men of Rome, there is no favour
For justice!—Grudgingly her dues are granted!
Your great men boast no more the love of country!
They count their talents—measure their domains—
Number their slaves—make lists of knights and clients—
Enlarge their palaces—dress forth their banquets,
Awake their lyres and timbrels, and with their floods
Of ripe Falernian, drown the little left
Of Roman virtue![46]

The evil aristocrats in Act III scene 1 plot to use Drusus in order to attack Caius. Drusus, who has a naïve belief in the patricians' good motives, agrees to propose something so attractive to the people that he wins their favour, thus lessening Caius' grip on them. In the next scene, set in the Forum, Caius pleads with the people not to treat him like a king, but Drusus argues that Caius is not going far enough. There ensues a competition in benefits to be offered to the people. Drusus claims to be acting on the instructions of the Senate, but Caius caustically responds, like a proto Chartist, that if the members of the Senate love the people so much then they won't mind if they are all given the vote.

Caius can't persuade Drusus that he is being duped by the Senate. But Caius' colleagues can't persuade *him* that he must court the people to retain his influence with them. He loses the tribuneship. Opimius is elected Consul and announces that he is about to repeal all Caius' reformist laws. The Senate declares a state of emergency and identifies Caius as the enemy of the state. There is going to be a showdown. There are emotive scenes between Caius and Cornelia and Caius and his wife Licinia, clutching his little son. Both women try to prevent him from going out in public. They fail.

The final scene is set in the temple of Diana. The women pray while class war rages in the streets. They learn that many of Caius' plebeian supporters desert him. His aristocratic allies are killed by the Consul's forces, leaving him isolated and vulnerable. He arrives and commits suicide, but only after saying of the plebs,

May they remain the abject things they are,
Begging their daily pittance from the hands

Of tyrant lords that spurn them! May they crawl
Ever in bondage and in misery,
And never know the blessèd rights of freemen!
Here will I perish![47]

The implication is that the only real barrier to an egalitarian republic is the inability of the common people to rise manfully to the challenge. Knowles here shows himself sensitive to the nervousness felt even in radical Irish circles towards the bloodbath in which the French revolution had culminated during the Terror. Knowles was certainly acquainted with the tragedy of Chénier. But his play is more pessimistic about the possibility of reforms, even if it is even more convinced of their desirability.

In London, however, the play that made Knowles' name was his better-written *Virginius*, which continued to be revived for decades. The young actor who created the stirring role for the premiere of *Virginius*, on 17th May 1820 at Covent Garden, was William Charles Macready. This was also a history play, set in an earlier phase of Republican Rome, and based on the story of Virginius as related in Livy III.44. The tale had previously been dramatised as the Jacobean *Appius and Virginia* by John Webster and Thomas Heywood. Knowles' *Virginius* certainly had a political message, in that Appius Claudius abuses his political power by lusting after Virginia. But a play that rages against tyrants demanding sex with their inferiors is not political dynamite of the same order as a play that rages against poverty and hunger. Even this far less explosive play was first censored, however, under the terms of the 1737 Licensing Act.

Knowles' *Virginius* was only given permission for performance 'after the Lord Chamberlain, at the express command of the newly crowned George IV, had cut out some of the lines on tyranny'.[48] Censorship of the stage had always been erratic and inconsistent, and depended on the political atmosphere at the time and the temperaments of the Prime Minister, Lord Chamberlain and their officers. But George IV was detested, and his ostentatious coronation in 1821 heralded increasingly harsh censorship. At the time of the premiere of *Virginius*, and the London production of *Caius Gracchus* three years later, the Lord Chamberlain was the Duke of Montrose, a Scottish Tory 'determinedly antagonistic to plays on revolutionary themes'.[49] But the man who actually wielded the blue pencil from 1778 and until the end of December 1823 in the post of Examiner of Plays was a dour Methodist by name of John Larpent.[50] Having served in the Foreign Office and in George III's household as a Gentleman Usher and a Groom, Larpent delegated some of the play-reading to his much younger wife, Anna Margaretta, so we will never know who actually made the final decisions on Knowles' scripts.

Despite the enforced cuts to *Virginius*, the enthusiasm of its public reception inspired Knowles to return to his previous play *Caius Gracchus*, which had been performed in Edinburgh. (Figure 7.1.) George IV was becoming steadily more unpopular, perceived as corrupt, autocratic and dissolute. The political

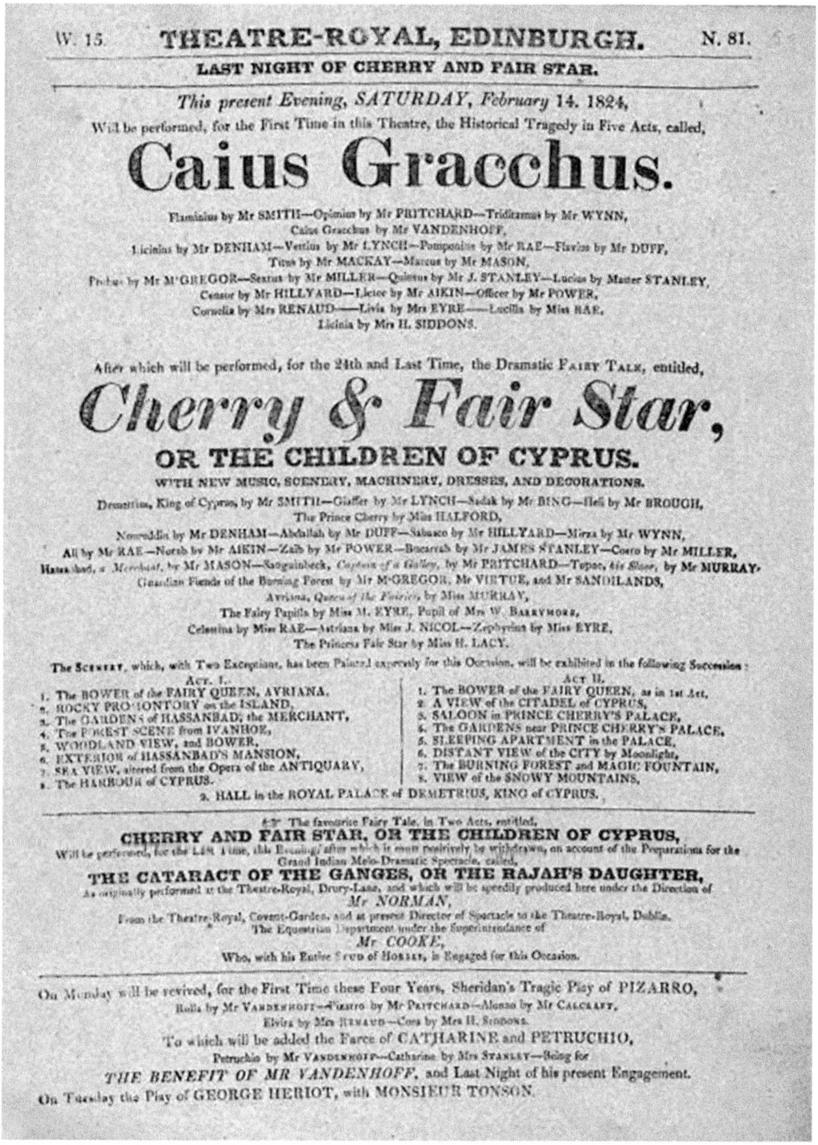

W. 15. THEATRE-ROYAL, EDINBURGH. N. 81.

LAST NIGHT OF CHERRY AND FAIR STAR.

This present Evening, SATURDAY, February 14. 1824,

Will be performed, for the First Time in this Theatre, the Historical Tragedy in Five Acts, called,

Caius Gracchus.

Flaminius by Mr SMITH—Opimius by Mr PRITCHARD—Triditanus by Mr WYNN,
Caius Gracchus by Mr VANDENHOFF,
Licinius by Mr DENHAM—Vettius by Mr LYNCH—Pomponius by Mr RAE—Flavius by Mr DUFF,
Titus by Mr MACKAY—Marcus by Mr MASON,
Probus by Mr M'GREGOR—Sextus by Mr MILLER—Quintus by Mr J. STANLEY—Lucius by Master STANLEY,
Censor by Mr HILLYARD—Lictor by Mr AIKIN—Officer by Mr POWER,
Cornelia by Mrs RENAUD——Livia by Mrs EYRE——Lucilla by Miss RAE,
Licinia by Mrs H. SIDDONS.

After which will be performed, for the 24th and Last Time, the Dramatic FAIRY TALE, entitled,

Cherry & Fair Star,

OR THE CHILDREN OF CYPRUS.

WITH NEW MUSIC, SCENERY, MACHINERY, DRESSES, AND DECORATIONS.

Demetrius, King of Cyprus, by Mr SMITH—Giaffer by Mr LYNCH—Sadak by Mr BING—Heli by Mr BROUGH,
The Prince Cherry by Miss HALFORD,
Noureddin by Mr DENHAM—Abdallah by Mr DUFF—Sabasco by Mr HILLYARD—Mirza by Mr WYNN,
Ali by Mr RAE—Norab by Mr AIKIN—Zaib by Mr POWER—Bucarrab by Mr JAMES STANLEY—Cosro by Mr MILLER,
Hassanbad, *a Merchant*, by Mr MASON—Sanguinbeck, *Captain of a Galley*, by Mr PRITCHARD—Topac, *his Slave*, by Mr MURRAY,
Guardian Fiends of the Burning Forest by Mr M'GREGOR, Mr VIRTUE, and Mr SANDILANDS,
Avriana, *Queen of the Fairies*, by Miss MURRAY,
The Fairy Papilla by Miss M. EYRE, Pupil of Mrs W. BARRYMORE,
Celestina by Miss RAE—Astriana by Miss J. NICOL—Zephyrina by Miss EYRE,
The Princess Fair Star by Miss H. LACY.

The SCENERY, which, with Two Exceptions, has been Painted expressly for this Occasion, will be exhibited in the following Succession:

ACT I.	ACT II.
1. The BOWER of the FAIRY QUEEN, AVRIANA,	1. The BOWER of the FAIRY QUEEN, as in 1st Act,
2. ROCKY PROMONTORY on the ISLAND,	2. A VIEW of the CITADEL of CYPRUS,
3. The GARDENS of HASSANBAD, the MERCHANT,	3. SALOON in PRINCE CHERRY'S PALACE,
4. The FOREST SCENE from IVANHOE,	4. The GARDENS near PRINCE CHERRY'S PALACE,
5. WOODLAND VIEW, and BOWER,	5. SLEEPING APARTMENT in the PALACE,
6. EXTERIOR of HASSANBAD'S MANSION,	6. DISTANT VIEW of the CITY by Moonlight,
7. SEA VIEW, altered from the Opera of the ANTIQUARY,	7. The BURNING FOREST and MAGIC FOUNTAIN,
8. The HARBOUR of CYPRUS.	8. VIEW of the SNOWY MOUNTAINS,

The favourite Fairy Tale, in Two Acts, entitled,

CHERRY AND FAIR STAR, OR THE CHILDREN OF CYPRUS,

THE CATARACT OF THE GANGES, OR THE RAJAH'S DAUGHTER,

As originally performed at the Theatre-Royal, Drury-Lane, and which will be speedily produced here under the Direction of
Mr NORMAN,
From the Theatre-Royal, Covent-Garden, and at present Director of Spectacle to the Theatre-Royal, Dublin.
The Equestrian Department under the Superintendance of
Mr COOKE,
Who, with his Entire Stud of HORSES, is Engaged for this Occasion.

On Monday will be revived, for the First Time these Four Years, Sheridan's Tragic Play of PIZARRO,
Rolla by Mr VANDENHOFF—Pizarro by Mr PRITCHARD—Alonzo by Mr CALCRAFT,
Elvira by Mrs RENAUD—Cora by Mrs H. SIDDONS.
To which will be added the Farce of CATHARINE and PETRUCHIO,
Petruchio by Mr VANDENHOFF—Catharine by Mrs STANLEY—Being for
THE BENEFIT OF MR VANDENHOFF, and Last Night of his present Engagement.
On Tuesday the Play of GEORGE HERIOT, with MONSIEUR TONSON.

FIGURE 7.1 Early 19th-century playbill, James Knowles' *Caius Gracchus*. Reproduced from original in Hall's personal collection.

tension meant that when in November 1823 *Caius Gracchus* was submitted to the Lord Chamberlain, who then operated from St. James' Palace, it inevitably ran into trouble. Via Larpent, who was in the last weeks of office before retirement, the Lord Chamberlain let it be known that he was 'shocked at its liberal sentiments'.[51] In a drastically censored version, when permission was 'at length obtained',[52] *Caius Gracchus* was produced at Drury Lane, starring Macready, on 18th November 1823 for seven nights. (Figure 7.2)

The physical manuscript submitted to the Lord Chamberlain has survived in the Larpent Collection of plays (now held in the Huntingdon Library, San Marino, California). So does a printed version of the original play, as performed in Belfast, which was published in 1823 in Glasgow, and to which Knowles restored many lines which had been cut for the Drury Lane production. This allows us a precious opportunity to study the processes by which a performance text deemed acceptable to the authorities was painfully achieved. Knowles (or more probably the Drury Lane manager, Alfred Bunn) had chopped out some of the most incendiary material before it was even offered to the Lord Chamberlain. Almost all of Titus' prose speech (quoted above, pp. 152–3) has been prudently omitted, so that it reads simply, 'Down with your staff, master, for I have another that may ruffle the gloss of your cloak for you!' From Opimius' speech (see

FIGURE 7.2 William Macready as Caius Gracchus. Early 19th-century theatrical print, reproduced from original in Hall's personal collection.

above, pp. 153), the Drury Lane rehearsal script has omitted the provocative line saying that the great men of Rome 'Number their slaves—make lists of knights and clients'. But the Censor also struck out the line saying that these men 'Enlarge their palaces—dress forth their banquets'. The most drastic deletion comes in a speech delivered by Caius himself, in Act III scene 1, claiming that Opimius does not succeed by 'flattering' the Roman populace but by offering them bribes which bring the worst out in their characters. In the Belfast production, reflected in the printed version, Caius said,

> Opimius then is not the people's flatterer.
> He'd make the people look below themselves.
> How would he rate them? As we rate our herds.
> How would he use them? As we use our herds.
> O may the people ever have such flatterers
> As guard them from the kindness of such friends![53]

The text submitted to the Lord Chamberlain wisely took out the two middle lines suggesting that Opimius respects the people no more than herds of cattle. But this did not go far enough for Larpent, who took his blue pencil to the last two lines as well.

Macready still managed to make Caius' tragedy seem politically mutinous enough to persuade his ambitious rival actor, Edmund Kean, not to appear on a stage with him for several years subsequently.[54] Macready endured poverty and humiliation as a child and his response was to become an ardent republican. His father, a prominent lessee of provincial theatres who originally came from Ireland, was imprisoned for debt, blighting the ambitions of his Rugby-educated middle-class son, who knew and loved his Classics. He was forced to leave school at the age of 15 to rescue his father's failing theatre in Manchester. Unable to attend Oxford University, as he had planned, the youth decided to stay on stage himself. But he loathed the monarchy with an unusual intensity and banned the phrase 'lower classes', insisting that they be called 'poorer classes'.[55] He remained socially insecure all his life, indeed once insulting Knowles, the shabby Irish playwright who helped make him famous but to whom he clearly felt superior in class terms. After the première of *Virginius*, Macready was the only untitled guest dining at an aristocrat's house. Knowles arrived to present a copy of the play, but Macready was embarrassed by his presence and hissed at him that he should not have come. Only later did he come to his senses and apologise.[56]

In 1823 Macready was still only 30 years old, and had not yet become the most famous actor-manager in Britain, known always to select roles which allowed him to impersonate 'the defender of the Hearth, Home, and the People against the brutality of tyrants', and to pour out 'the zeal and heat of his own political convictions'.[57] These included not only James Knowles's classical heroes but Thomas Talfourd's stirring republican adaptation of Euripides' *Ion* (1836).[58] Watching Macready playing Caius Gracchus, a Roman hero who dies attempting to defend the rights of the poor, must have been exciting. Conservative stage critics were already denouncing Macready in the early 1820s for habitually appearing in 'democratic, ranting, trashy plays'.[59]

Caius Gracchus was not a commercial success. Macready blamed what he saw as the execrable acting of Margaret Bunn, the wife of the Drury Lane manager, as Cornelia. But even he acknowledged that the contemporary taste for more emotionally appealing stage entertainment was not hospitable to the polemical gravity of *Caius Gracchus*: 'it was not in the nature of things that such a play should become really popular'.[60] It was not, to our knowledge, publicly revived. But because it had been performed by Macready, and because Knowles remained a respected writer for the rest of his life, it continued to be read and almost certainly performed in private theatricals.[61] *Virginius*, however, continued to be a smash hit and a key play in Macready's repertoire for another 30 years,[62] inevitably drawing readers to Knowles' other Roman history play, so famous that sculptures to remind the viewer of his Romans are carved conspicuously onto his tomb-building in the Glasgow Necropolis.

The effect of Knowles' play on the afterlife of Plutarch's Gracchi, moreover, remained conspicuous in the case of the Chartists,[63] and of Ireland, 'Gracchus' becoming thereafter almost a code-word for the cause of Irish Republicanism. Indeed, 'Gracchus' was the chosen pseudonym of John O'Callaghan, the Irish activist and poet, who in *THE EXTERMINATOR'S SONG* (1842) celebrated in the persona of 'Gracchus', in a dialogue poem, the call for total rent strikes by the peasants made by the agitator William Conner:

> 'Tis I am the poor man's scourge,
>   And where is the scourge like me?
> My land from all Papists I purge,
>   Who think that their votes should be free—
>   Who think that their votes should be free!
> From huts only fitted for brutes,
>   My agent the last penny wrings;
> And my serfs live on water and roots,
>   While I feast on the best of good things!
>   For I am the poor man's scourge!
>   For I am the poor man's scourge!
> [*Caius Gracchus* responds:]
> *Yes, you are the poor man's scourge!*
> *But of such the whole island we'll purge!*[64]

It took historical events as drastic as the massacre at Peterloo and famines in Britain and Ireland to make the Gracchi speak sympathetically from public stages to wide cross-class audiences. Yet, paradoxically, once they had found their place in the dynamic medium of live theatre, they found themselves being controlled again. Caius Gracchus and his plebeian supporters had their rhetorical wings stripped almost bare by the hard right in Britain, owing to the ideological power of the ultra-conservative Lord Chamberlain's office, in the democratic agitation of the 1820s. Plutarch's vision of the brothers who stood up for the People could just not stop being political dynamite.

Notes

1 The intersections between Classics and class in cinema, as in advertising, is an area which we have been unable to cover in any depth in the current study. See Hall (forthcoming f). Both would require particularly careful handling in order to discuss the idea of 'popular culture' from a rigorously class-conscious angle.
2 Some of the material on James Sheridan Knowles' *Caius Gracchus* adapts material from Hall's paragraphs in Hall and Wyles (2018).
3 Hall (2015a) 161–2.
4 Mayer (1994); Michelakis and Wyke (2013).
5 Richardson (2015b).
6 See e.g. Monrós Gaspar (2011); Richardson (2015b); Davies (2019); Hall (1999a), (1999b), (1999c), (2017a) and (forthcoming e); Hall and Macintosh (2005) 336–461.
7 See Filon (1907) 93–5; Allen (1991) 3–6.
8 Burnand (1863) 2; Hall and Macintosh (2005) 373, 376.
9 *Justice*, March 5th (1886) 4; see Samuel, MacColl and Cosgrove (1985) 13.
10 Roberts (1961).
11 Veitch (1950) 130, 142, 200–8.
12 Three photographs held at the Imperial War Museum show preparations for the 1941 production of *Medea* in the Settlement Hall in Trealaw by the Old Vic Travelling Theatre Company in association with the Council for the Encouragement of Music and the Arts: IWM catalogue nos. D 5668, D 5668 (actresses including Sybil Thorndike applying make-up) and D 5669.
13 See Willis (1928) 17.
14 *Trojan Women* (1938), listed in the APGRD Production Database, accessed at www.apgrd.ox.ac.uk/productions/production/5630.
15 Mottley and Cooke (1728) 16.
16 Cooke (1728).
17 Mottley and Cooke (1728) 19, 20, 22, 23; Hall (2008) 134–5.
18 Mottley and Cooke (1728) 30.
19 Loftis (1963) 111; Hall and Macintosh (2005) 105.
20 Anon. (1773b) 177; for a detailed discussion of *Midas* see Stead (2018a).
21 For the general history of stage censorship in Britain, see Fowell and Palmer (1913), Findlater (1967), and Johnston (1990). On the 1737 Act see Vince (1988)14–15, 25–6.
22 Hall and Macintosh (2005) 105.
23 Hall (2007a) 70–4.
24 Full detail of these 18th-century licensing fracas can be found in Hall and Macintosh (2005) chapters 4 and 6.
25 See the vivid account in Tilly (2005) 240–83.
26 E.g. Beness and Hillard (2001).
27 There were two operas about another member of the Gracchi dynasty, both entitled *Tito Sempronio Gracco*, performed in Naples in February 1702 (by Domenico Scarlatti) and 1725 (by Domenico Natale Sarri).
28 For a translation of the complete passage see Hall and Wyles (2008) 129 n.8.
29 Macchiavelli (1531) I. 37; Wilson (1684) 48.
30 Yet John Evelyn, the English translator of Lucretius book 1, gardener and diarist, did reveal the possibility that Caius Gracchus might be due for a reappraisal when he wrote in 1667, after the Restoration allowed him to restart his public career, that

Caius Gracchus was *rightly* criticised for retreating from public life after his brother's death. See Evelyn (1667) 23.

31 The translation by Bavande (1559) book 7, 144.

32 Already in 1787 Jean-Germain Drouais, a student of David, was drawing a design for a painting of the death of Caius Gracchus, which his death in 1788 prevented him from completing. For this theme in French revolutionary art, see Rubin (1976).

33 Parker (1937) 140–1.

34 Caute (1966) 124. See also Russell (2008) and Cartledge (2016) 291. Like Caius Gracchus, Gracchus Babeuf was killed for political reasons. He led the secret society Conspiracy of Equals and ended under the guillotine in 1797, accused of wanting to overthrow the government. He is often identified by historians as the first modern communist.

35 See Wyles (2007) and further, below, Chapter 10.

36 Published as Anon. (1773a) 155.

37 'An Epistle to Curio', lines 210–18 in Akenside (1781) 125.

38 According to his son, Richard Brinsley Knowles (1872) 1, Knowles' ancestry could be traced no further back than his grandfather, one John Knowles of Dublin, but his father 'cared very little for matters of this kind; and indeed he was one of the few radicals I have met who have not at heart a profound veneration for good birth'.

39 Chorley (1847).

40 R.B. Knowles (1872) 6–25. Hazlitt certainly discussed the Gracchi, and regarded interest in them as emblematic of a certain kind of literary radicalism: Hazlitt (1902–1906), vol. XVI, 20–1. He remained firm friends with Knowles in later years: Jones (1991) 307–8.

41 J.S. Knowles (1873a) and J.S. Knowles (1873b), especially 9–11.

42 R.B. Knowles (1872) 76–8.

43 Quoted in R.B. Knowles (1872) 64–5.

44 J.S. Knowles (1823) 4.

45 J.S. Knowles (1823) 19.

46 J.S. Knowles (1823) 19.

47 J.S. Knowles (1823) 57.

48 Archer (1890) 53. See further Conolly (1976) 109–10.

49 Stephens (1980) 18.

50 On whom see Johnston (1990) 46.

51 R.B. Knowles (1872) 69–70.

52 Archer (1890) 69.

53 J.S. Knowles (1823) 27.

54 Kean was himself illegitimate and from a lower-class background; according to Page (2003) he was popular with the poorer audience members in the pits of the theatres, but he took care not to offend the authorities.

55 Marston (1888) vol. I, 65.

56 Trewin (1955) 62.

57 Shattock (1958) 5.

58 See Hall (1997), revised version in Hall and Macintosh (2005) chapter 11.

59 Words from a review of Macready's performance of *Virginius* in *John Bull* of October 13th 1823, quoted by Archer (1890) 68.

60 Quoted by Archer (1890) 69.

61 See the Publisher's remarks in the 'Advertisement' to Knowles (1856), the published version of Knowles' complete plays: they have been induced 'to issue the present elegant and extremely cheap edition' because the plays have met with 'very marked favour … both as acting and as closet plays … from the general public'.

62 Archer (1890) 204.

63 Tanner (1962) 62.

64 Printed in Duffy (1845, ed.) 184–5.

PART II
Communities

8

DISSENTING CLASSICS

In the wake of the Restoration of the British monarchy, the four statutes of the Clarendon Code (1661–1665), along with the Corporation Act (1661) and the Test Acts (1673 and 1678), barred non-Anglicans from holding any civil, military, religious or educational positions of power. This excluded them, for example, from Parliament, the state-funded established Church, from graduation from Cambridge University and even admission to Oxford University. Non-Anglicans included not only Roman Catholics and the small Sephardic Jewish population, who built their first synagogue (Bevis Marks) in Aldgate in 1701, but also Presbyterians, Congregationalists, Baptists, Quakers and some smaller groupings including émigré Huguenots.[1] These Acts effectively used religious conviction to eliminate any challenge, from huge sectors of the population, to the restored monarchy and the institutions supporting it. Oxford graduates were still obliged to submit to the 39 Articles of the Church of England until the 1850s.

The Act of Uniformity forced around 2,500 Puritan priests out of the Anglican church, in the so-called Great Ejection. The crisis uprooted and further radicalised many of the best minds of their generation, helping to make the idea of a unified 'Dissenting' community concrete, and in turn stimulating the establishment of alternative educational institutions, at first often organised covertly.[2] This amounted to a revolution in British educational practice, and pagan Greek and Roman authors often loomed large on Dissenting curricula, at precisely the time when the discipline of 'Classics' was being created.

After the Glorious Revolution, the providers of educational programmes amongst Nonconformists and Dissenters found new ways around many of the disabilities placed upon them.[3] There were of course limits to the impact of the 'Toleration Act' (1689), since it fully protected only Trinitarian Protestant Nonconformists, excluding Unitarians, Catholics, deists and atheists and leaving Dissenters forced, if they wanted to hold civil office, to take communion

DOI: 10.4324/9781315446608-10

within the Established Church.[4] Yet it did legalise important Dissenting activities, including not only conducting rituals such as communion and baptism, but also the building of chapels, meeting houses, schools and colleges.[5]

The impact of most of the Dissenting academies and the schools which fed them has been overlooked. Penelope Wilson has called it 'a hidden educational tradition', which was 'largely independent of the grammar school and university model'.[6] In these institutions, many of Britain's greatest and most progressive thinkers, writers, politicians and educationalists were instructed. They were also the places where many Britons across the lower end of the class spectrum were offered a new form of liberal education, which was centred around the study of Greek, Hebrew and Latin, even if the curriculum also extended to the sciences, geography, history (both ancient and modern), mathematics and metaphysics.

There was wide variety in the academies and schools set up by Dissenters. The variety was not limited to terms and denominations, but extended to class-based and geographical constituencies, in England as well as Ireland, Scotland and Wales. Presbyterians and (from their emergence in the mid-18th century) Dissenting Methodists were numerous in the industrial and mining hamlets of the north of England, while the miners, farm labourers and seamen of the south west were often Baptists. East Anglia, home of the British textile and clothing industry, was home to many Congregationalists.

Dissenting communities as a whole consisted overwhelmingly of the working and lower-middle classes, so it was within these communities that the sons (and sometimes daughters) of labourers, miners, skilled and unskilled tradesmen, as well as merchants, teachers and—of course—religious leaders were educated. The experience could be empowering, but in the newly industrial era of the mid-18th century the culture of Protestant Dissent, and especially Methodism, had a complex relationship with the working classes. The alternative vision of Christianity emerged simultaneously with industrial capitalism. In *The Making of the English Working Class* (1968), E.P. Thompson famously argued that Dissenting religion in the period performed a double service as the religion of both the industrial bourgeoisie and wide sections of the proletariat. In a chapter entitled 'The transforming power of the cross'—a passionate indictment of Industrial-Age Methodism—he shows how the virtues inculcated by that religion (discipline, frugality, honesty and hard graft) were necessary ideological accompaniments to the evolving new mode of production.[7]

On the other hand, Christopher Hill stressed in *The World Turned Upside Down* (1972) that it was in the 18th-century Dissenting academies that the embers of the radical and sceptical enquiry, progressive in religious, scientific and political terms, were stoked.[8] These embers, doused by the Restoration, flared up in support of the French Revolution and the social progress which that event seemed to offer Britain in the 1790s, as we shall see in Chapter 13, only to be extinguished thereafter. The educational systems which Nonconformist protagonists put in place, both in the formal sphere of schools and academies, and informally in tutorials, evening classes and Sunday schools, often provided sustainable paths from poverty towards the acquisition of educational, cultural and economic capital, not to mention spiritual nourishment, where there might otherwise have been none.

In the schools of Dissenters, different books were used from those in the hands of public- and grammar-school boys. The growing trade in educational publishing through the later 18th and 19th centuries was driven by and supplied new editions of these books. The success of such publications, based on new pedagogical techniques, meant that they were stocked even in Anglican institutions' libraries.[9] In short, the education provided by Dissenting establishments was more energetic and relevant to the contemporary world than that delivered in the establishments from which the teachers and pupils had, by virtue of their faith, been excluded. Most of these schools and academies were also open institutions in the sense that, unlike their Anglican competitors, they enforced no requirement of doctrinal allegiance. Thus, Nonconformists of any denomination and level of piety were educated alongside one another, and even alongside children from Anglican families. They sometimes offered the highest quality and most affordable education locally, although they did not tend to last very long as institutions.[10]

This chapter introduces several individuals, some of whom are well known, others entirely obscure. For each one of them whose names we know, there were tens, sometimes hundreds, who sat in the same forms, thumbed the same dictionaries and fed on the same information, but are now forgotten. These men and women—and in this chapter they are nearly all men—were extraordinary, but they did not always seem so to their peers. The evidence is too vast and incomplete to make an exhaustive survey possible, and not all the classically influenced individuals featured here are working-class. The Nonconformists whose names are remembered are often lower-middle-class radicals, but they interacted at deep personal and institutional levels with the working poor whom they aimed to edify and educate and who are the primary focus of our book. The number of individuals discussed in other chapters who were introduced to classical civilisation and history only through the agency of Nonconformist educational initiatives is testimony to their importance at the very lowest level of the socio-economic scale.

Joseph Priestley

From a young age, Joseph Priestley (1733–1804) (Figure 8.1)—the bright son of a Dissenting Calvinist cloth-dresser—was shaping up for life as a Calvinist minister. After dame school and a spell at the local Grammar School at Batley, where he learned Latin and some Greek,[11] he attended a school kept by John Kirkby, the Independent (i.e. Congregationalist) minister of Heckmondwike Upper Chapel in rural West Yorkshire, between Leeds and Huddersfield. With Kirkby, Priestley studied Hebrew and learned the basics of Chaldaean and Syriac (the Aramaic vernaculars of some early Christian literature) and Arabic.[12] He also became convinced by his teacher's Independent faith, which barred him from

FIGURE 8.1 Joseph Priestley (1733–1804), reproduced by courtesy of the Wellcome Library. Stipple engraving by W. Holl after G. Stew. Reproduced by courtesy of the Wellcome Library.

continuing his studies in Oxford or Cambridge. More prosperous Dissenting families sometimes financed their children's studies in Scotland or a university in continental Europe, but Priestley's could not. Instead, in 1752, he was among the first students admitted to the new Daventry Academy, established by the former carpenter and son of a Particular (i.e. a Calvinist) Baptist lay preacher, Caleb Ashworth (d.1775). Ashworth was in turn the protégé of the celebrated Independent minister and writer, Philip Doddridge, at whose own academy at Northampton reading classical Latin texts was a daily affair.

As Doddridge relates in a letter to his former teacher, the Presbyterian Minister Samuel Clarke, tutor and students would read a Latin author for around half an hour a day: 'One or another of us reads the original, and we inquire into the most difficult passages'. Terence was especially focused on, since the demotic Latin of his plays would help the students towards their goal of 'talking Latin'.[13] Much time was devoted to learning Hebrew, but the Greek New Testament and some classical Greek literature were read too.[14]

On arrival at Daventry, Priestley was disappointed by the shortage of Greek tuition. Either Ashworth had deviated from his mentor's curriculum, or Priestley's expectations were too high. In any case, he and his room-mate, John Alexander of Birmingham, responded by reading 'every day ten folio pages in some Greek author, and generally a Greek play in the course of the week besides. By this means', he continues in his *Memoirs*, 'we became very well acquainted with that language, and with the most valuable authors in it'.[15] Priestley notes that he and Alexander continued their reading long after they left the academy (1755), 'communicating to each other by letter an account of what we read'.[16] This systematic literary diligence recurs in the lives of Dissenting men of letters, as we shall see below in the case of William Godwin. Priestley eventually concentrated on theological pursuits and questions of natural philosophy, but he reports that Alexander became, by the time of his untimely death in 1765, 'one of the best Greek scholars in this or any other country'.[17]

On leaving the academy, Priestly came up against discrimination. Unwilling as he was to become a schoolmaster, he was eventually forced to do so, applying to teach Classics and mathematics at various institutions. He was, however, rejected—as he himself relates in his memoirs—not because he was unqualified, but because he was 'not orthodox'.[18] During his time at Daventry, he had been drawn to Arianism (i.e. non-Trinitarianism), when before he had moved from his native Dissenting Calvinism to Independence (closer to Congregationalism). Such theological shifts were not uncommon in the period, when it was hard to disentangle politics from religious affiliation, and when both were in flux. Conversion or transition from one denomination to another happened often. Priestley's increasingly liberal religious thinking was in line with the general direction of movement towards Unitarianism and Deism. His family, however—shifting to a more conservative brand of evangelical Calvinism—bucked this trend, and eventually disowned him for his broad-minded theological views.[19]

He taught Greek and Latin at two small institutions before taking a post at the famous Warrington Academy. Here he introduced a rigorous classical education. This Presbyterian (Arianist) establishment, which ran only between 1756 and 1782, may not have prepared as many students for the Dissenting ministry as other academies,[20] but its contribution to Dissenting culture nationally, and to revolutionary politics in particular, was unparalleled.[21] Moreover, Priestley made an enormous contribution to British philosophical, religious, scientific and political discourse. A pioneering chemist, he discovered oxygen.[22]

John Aikin (1713–1780)

Before Priestley arrived, the Classics master was John Aikin (1713–1780), the son of a linen-draper from Kirkcudbright, Scotland, and another protégé (like Ashworth) of Philip Doddridge. The tight network of Dissenting Classics begins to reveal itself. Aikin was Doddridge's first pupil at his Northampton Academy, and later completed his education at King's College, Aberdeen. After briefly teaching for Doddridge, he settled in a school in Kibworth, where he would teach the radical Dissenting classicist, Gilbert Wakefield (to whom we shall return); Wakefield remembered that Aikin

> had an intimacy with the best authors of Greece and Rome, superior to what I have ever known in any Dissenting minister from my own experience. His taste for composition was correct and elegant: and his repetition of beautiful passages ... highly animated, and expressive of sensibility.[23]

Aikin married Jane Jennings, the daughter of the Dissenting minister at Kibworth, John Jennings, who had taught Philip Doddridge, and may be seen as the godfather of 19th-century Dissenting Classics, since Doddridge inherited his pedagogical techniques and developed them. The tiny village of Kibworth—a few hours' walk south east from the city of Leicester—was the epicentre of a particular blend of radical and Dissenting classical activity, which directly informed the social, political and cultural debates raging throughout Britain in the decades leading up to the French Revolution.

The Aikins' two children both became renowned literary figures. John received a classical education at Warrington Academy, and became a physician, writer and editor of numerous periodicals, including the *Monthly Magazine*, the *Athenaeum* and Dodsley's *Annual Register*;[24] Anna Laetitia (married name Barbauld, 1743–1825) became a poet, essayist and educationalist. She had convinced her father to teach her Latin and some Greek, which gave her access to the academy's library.[25] Besides classical texts, it held encyclopaedic works of ancient history, classical mythology and works in translation. In 1773 the following books were among those recommended for trainee ministers: Rollin's *Roman History*, Temple Stanyan's *History of Greece* (1701), Smith's *Thucydides*, Basil Kennet's *Antiquities of Rome* (1713) and Potter's *Antiquities of Greece*.[26] The library also housed:

Vertot's *Roman Revolution*
Hooke's Roman History
La Motte [Le Vayer]'s Animadversion[s] upon ... [ancient] Historians
Montesquieu's *Reflections on ... the Roman Empire*
Josephus' works
Malley's observations on the Romans
Mavor's *Universal History, Ancient and Modern*
Rollin's *Ancient History*
Spence on Pope's *Odyssey*
Erasmus's *Apophthegms of the Ancients*
D'Arnay's *Private Life of the Romans*
Rene Le Bossu's *Treatise on Epic Poetry*.[27]

George Dyer

Along with Joseph Priestley, William Godwin and George Dyer (Figure 8.2) (all classically trained liberal Nonconformists, predominantly Unitarians), Barbauld entered the radical London set that centred around the courageous revolutionary bookseller Joseph Johnson (1738–1809). It was under Priestley's influence that Johnson—raised as a Baptist—embraced Unitarianism, becoming the key publisher for the writers produced by the Warrington Academy. Dyer (1755–1841), the son of a Thames boatman, was himself educated under a scholarship at Christ's Hospital and then as a sizar (student whose place is financed but who is required to earn it by doing jobs) at Emmanuel College, Cambridge. When tutoring in Cambridge, Dyer, via a disciple of Priestley named William Frend (on whom see below, p. 297), embraced the Unitarianism that would drive, in an unostentatious manner, his reformist writings.[28] His political pamphlet *Complaints of the Poor People of England* (1793), which carried the legend *Fiat Justitia* ('Let there be Justice'), stimulated by Paine's *Rights of Man* (1791–1792), called for social change, drawing on Dyer's own experience of poverty and expressing fellow-feeling for the poor of Britain. It is written accessibly, with only one Latin quotation, for which a translation is provided.[29] But his lucid rhetoric, especially

FIGURE 8.2 'George Dyer, with his dog, Daphne' by Henry Hoppner Meyer. © The Fitzwilliam Museum, Cambridge.

the anaphora, rhetorical questions (hypophora) and cultivated indignation, owe as much to Cicero as to the pulpits of the Dissenting divines:

> I have seen the rich man pay with reluctance, what has been earned with hard labour; and insult, when he ought to have relieved. I have seen the poor man, after the toil of the day, return at night to behold nothing but want and wretchedness in a numerous family ... I have heard men plead for keeping slaves in the West-Indies, and treating them like beasts, by asking, Are they not as well off as many poor people in England?[30]

Dyer fulminates against the class stratification of society in all areas of British life, using transhistorical parallels and contrasts. Talented common soldiers' careers were capped at the non-commissioned rank of sergeant-major, and Dyer protests, 'How different was the policy of those nations, whose military glory has been the wonder of ages! I mean the ancient Spartans, the Athenians, the Romans, and our warlike ancestors the Saxons!'[31]

In the same breath, as he draws on ancient exempla, he looks to revolutionary America and France for contemporary inspiration:

> The *common* people (so we call the poor) in America and France, understand the nature of government. Why? In those countries government is formed by the people, and made to serve their interest. This was also the case of some of the States of ancient Greece, particularly Athens and Argos. ... The English government is formed by the rich and great, and to them it is favourable, but to the poor it is highly injurious. ... No men understand the secrets of government but those who plan them. These men are enriching themselves and their families, and leave the *common* people to toil and beggary.[32]

Following the ferocious clampdown on the freedom of speech which Charles James Fox dated precisely to the 1798 trials for seditious libel of classicist Gilbert Wakefield (see below) and his associates, including Johnson,[33] Dyer turned his primary attention to editing classical literature. His work on Abraham Valpy's multi-volume edition (1819–1830; see above p. 28) damaged his eyesight.

Always an eccentric character with a dreamy disposition, Dyer's poor eyesight added dangerously to his absent-mindedness. One day, he turned the wrong way from his friend Charles Lamb's lodgings in Oxford and walked fully clothed into the river.[34] Leigh Hunt relates that he once walked all the way home from a dinner in Hampstead before realising he had left one shoe underneath the dinner table.[35] He was teased by contemporaries for being bookish and poorly turned out. Lamb described him as 'busy as a moth over some rotten archive ... in a nook at Oriel',[36] and observed that Dyer's 'Nankeen Pantaloons ... were absolutely ingrained with the accumulated dirt of ages'.[37] Given his grubby eccentricity, he was a candidate for our Chapter 15, on 'ragged-trousered philologists'. But he was also, more significantly, a leading proponent of the Dissenting tradition and radical reform (and may have become more freshly attired after his marriage to Honour Mather in 1824). For Lamb, his classicism, piety, political views, social conscience and daydreaming were all of one inextricable piece:

> For with George Dyer, to be absent from the body is sometimes (not to speak profanely) to be present with the Lord. At the very time when, personally encountering thee, he passes on with no recognition – or, being stopped, starts like a thing surprised – at that moment, reader, he is on Mount Tabor, or Parnassus, or co-sphered with Plato, or, with Harrington, framing "immortal commonwealths" – devising some plan of amelioration to thy country, or thy species.[38]

Gilbert Wakefield

At Cambridge Dyer met a fellow student, a scholarship boy at Jesus College called Gilbert Wakefield (Figure 8.3) (1756–1801), whose life story blends serious distinction as a prolific and sometimes brilliant classical scholar with the experience

FIGURE 8.3 Gilbert Wakefield (1756–1801), reproduced by courtesy of National Portrait Gallery, London. © National Portrait Gallery, London.

of grim reprisals for his revolutionary views, and national infamy or celebrity, depending on political viewpoint. Unlike his rival as a Hellenist, Richard Porson (an originally working-class scholar discussed below, pp. 294–8), Wakefield's support of radical democracy in the 1790s landed him in prison. Porson was sympathetic to his plight, even though they exchanged acrimonious scholarly assaults on one another. Wakefield would have more than merited a place in Chapter 13, 'Seditious classicists'; he was powerfully associated in the public mind with the Dissenting movement, as a high-profile repudiator of Anglicanism, and as a famous critic of Anglican support of Pitt's regime. But he was also central to the culture of Dissent through the Classics.

The son of a poor but educated Nottinghamshire parish priest, Wakefield was himself educated at Free Schools and excelled as a classicist at Cambridge. He was ordained, but curacies in Stockport and Liverpool turned him into a prison reformer, Abolitionist and Unitarian. He resigned as curate, had therefore to vacate his Cambridge Fellowship and then married and accepted a post at Warrington Academy. He taught alongside Aikin and Priestley until its closure, which was partly due to his political activism.[39] He tried to make a living as a freelance tutor, and published both an edition of Virgil's *Georgics* (1788) and the first of his three-part *Silva Critica* (1789, 1793, 1795), in which he proposed 'the union of theological and classical learning; the illustration of the Scriptures by light borrowed from the philology of Greece and Rome'.[40]

He accepted the Welsh Unitarian Richard Price's invitation to teach Classics at his New College, one of a cluster of Dissenting academies in Hackney, East London. New College was regarded as the most politically radical among them; Tom Paine was invited to be after-dinner speaker only weeks after he was charged with sedition for *Rights of Man*.[41] Nevertheless, Wakefield fell out with Price. Increasingly maverick in his religious views, he refused to be identified as a regular Dissenter. He opposed public worship of any kind. Since he felt that classical literature contained 'the true rudiments of all other science' and was the subject on which 'the greatest stress should be laid, in a system of liberal education', he 'inculcated' this point 'with an earnestness which probably appeared somewhat dictatorial to the conductors of the institution'.[42]

Wakefield continued living amongst the Dissenters of Hackney and produced a stream of editions of classical works, including *Greek tragedies* (1794), *Horace* (1794), *Moschus* (1795) and his respected three-volume *Lucretius* (1796–1799). Other publications were a translation of the New Testament and an autobiography. His notoriety grew with controversial theological tracts and his first public attack on Prime Minister Pitt, along with praise for the French revolution in *The Spirit of Christianity* (1794). The Treasury Solicitor filed the latter as suspicious alongside John Thelwall's lectures on Roman history (see below pp. 276–7).[43] Wakefield's *Reply to Thomas Paine's "Age of Reason"* (1795) added fuel to the flames. But the crunch came when he replied to the Bishop of Landaff's treatise in support of Prime Minister Pitt's proposal for an income tax,[44] which he deplored as a means of raising funds for war with France.[45] In his *A Reply to*

Some Parts of the Bishop of Landaff's Address (1798) he drew on classical literature to explain the conflict between Pittite policy and Christian morality. Matthew Hiscock's analysis shows that the classical references go far further; they 'cumulatively construct and embody an implicit call to revolution in Britain that would, stated explicitly, have exposed Wakefield to a charge of treason',[46] rather than the lesser charge of seditious libel. The *Reply* was published in three different editions, the third after Wakefield had received a barrister's advice when prosecution proceedings had begun.

When Bishop Watson attempted to stir up patriotic zeal, asking, 'When Hannibal is at the gates, who but a poltroon would listen to the timid counsels of neutrality?' and claimed that he was confident that 'hundreds of thousands of loyal and honest men are as ready as I am, to hazard every thing in defence of the country',[47] Wakefield replied that he would rather tend his study in peace, quoting Virgil's *Georgics*, 'Non res Romanae, perituraque regna' (II.498). Not even 'Roman affairs, and kingdoms bound to fall' would move Wakefield from his books any more than Virgil's idealised rustic from his garden.

Wakefield uses Virgil's *Aeneid*, but also acerbically compares the Bishop with the warlike Ulysses of Euripides' satyr-drama *Cyclops* (perhaps later inspiring Shelley to take note of this text), and suggests that, far from feeling bellicose, most ordinary Britons would find excuses, like Euripides' satyrs, for refusing to fight the French: they had 'made boastful profession of their readiness to assist the hero in burning the eye of Polyphemus, but miserably failed in the performance of their engagement' when actually called upon:

> "Do but see," says one, (a *city light horseman*) "what a long way I am off! It is impossible for me to reach him." – "Oh; what a sudden lameness has seized my poor leg!" says another (a *supplementary militia man*): "Aye! and mine too!" says a third (a *voluntary cavalier*): "A most unaccountable spasm began to contract my feet, just as I was ready." – "And these eyes of mine," explains another (a *provincial associator*), "are full of ashes from some inexplicable cause or other." – "The truth is," said a fifth (a *life-and-fortune man*), "it is a generous compassion for our *bones* that suggests these excuses; but I am acquainted with a charm of Orpheus, a most admirable specific! which will teach the brand how to march at once of its own accord, and put out his eye!"[48]

Finally, Wakefield quotes the Whig Samuel Croxall's version of Aesop's fable of 'The Sensible Ass'.[49] An ass refuses to flee from his master's supposed enemy when he learns that the enemy, unlike his master, has no intention of making him carry any panniers on his back.[50] To ensure that the allegory does not go unnoticed, Wakefield also quotes Croxall's 'application' or moral:

> This fable shews us, how much in the wrong the poorer sort of people most commonly are, when they are under any concern about the revolutions of a

> government. All the alteration, which they can feel is, perhaps, in the name of the sovereign, or some such important trifle; but they cannot well be poorer, or made to work harder than they did before …[51]

Just in case the relevance of the fable might be overlooked, Wakefield has reminded the reader that

> within three miles of the house, where I am writing these pages, there is a much greater number of starving, miserable human beings, the hopeless victims of penury and distress, than on any equal portion of ground through the habitable globe.[52]

Wakefield was prosecuted, along with his publishers Joseph Johnson (see above p. 169), Jeremiah Jordan and the bookseller John Cuthell. All were convicted. In his celebrated state trial, in front of a crowded courtroom, Wakefied conducted his own defence, taking the opportunity 'to elaborate his views on the moral and political character of the government. He would be recognized if not acquitted'.[53] He was sentenced to two years in Dorchester gaol.[54] In prison he helped his poorer fellow prisoners, and conducted a substantial correspondence with Samuel Parr and with Fox, mostly on issues of classical scholarship,[55] translated Dio Chrysostom and worked on a study of Greek metre published just after his release, and shortly before his death, under the title *Notes Carceriae* (1801).

William Godwin

Two other radicals who passed through the Hackney Unitarian College, this time as students, were William Hazlitt (on whom see above, p. 151) and William Godwin (Figure 8.4). Godwin, son of an impoverished Dissenting minister who taught Classics to supplement his meagre income,[56] entered the academy in 1770 and graduated in 1778. He may have been unusually studious, but he was a model product of Hackney College, which beyond preparation of students for ministry explicitly aimed to offer the lay student at Hackney 'a galaxy of acquisitions' including:

> Habits of diligence
> Knowledge to enable him to establish his reputation in life
> A basis for innocent intellectual leisure activities
> A foundation for the best type of friendship
> An outlook likely to encourage temperance and refinement
> Ability to be useful to others and to the community
> Interests and hobbies for eventual old age and, above all,
> Religious knowledge.[57]

As can be seen in his austere but regular diary entries (1788–1836), there was almost no day in his life that he did not read some Greek or Latin author before

FIGURE 8.4 William Godwin: 'AUTHOR OF "THOUGHTS ON MAN"' by Daniel Maclise (1883), reproduced by courtesy of the Maclise Portrait Gallery. Reproduced courtesy of the Maclise Portrait-Gallery.

breakfast. He read around five chapters a day of Herodotus in Greek from 20th May 1832 to 27th April 1833.[58] He also read classical authors in modern translation, including Plato's *Republic* in English and Xenophon's *Anabasis* in French.[59] Godwin fed his interest in ancient Sparta with Rollin's *Ancient History* and Mitford's reactionary *History of Greece* (1784).[60] His habit of consistent, independent study lasted his whole life. His confidence in his intellectual powers and his unorthodox moral reasoning were developed during his Nonconformist upbringing and propelled him into an active part in political struggles. Like Wakefield, he came to renown (or notoriety) with the publication in 1793 of his *Enquiry Concerning Political Justice and Its Influence on General Virtue and Happiness.*

In the polarising social, cultural and political debate of the 1790s, and after his defence of Thomas Hardy, John Horne Tooke and John Thelwall during the Treason Trials (1794),[61] Godwin was associated with the revolutionary left. In order to remain engaged in the struggle and to ply his trade, Godwin assumed another name for his work on his new literary endeavour the 'Juvenile Library'.

Writing as 'Edward Baldwin', Godwin published numerous classical (among other Biblical,[62] historical and grammatical) works designed for the liberal education of children. His own version of Aesop, *Fables, Ancient and Modern* appeared in 1805; it articulated a radical new desideratum that a book for a child would also stimulate his reflective and *imaginative* capacities.[63] Godwin explains that he had tried to adapt the material to make it appropriate to the emotional and cognitive needs of the child:

> I have fancied myself taking the child upon my knee, and have expressed them in such language as I should have been likely to employ when I wished to amuse the child and make what I was talking of take hold upon his attention.[64]

Godwin's combined household with his second wife, Mary Jane Clairmont, contained no fewer than five children. It may not have been difficult to find one to put on his knee.

His *Fables* (1805), which drew on Aesop, Phaedrus and numerous earlier editions,[65] is not ideologically neutral. There are moments, especially in the editorial explication of the fables, where Godwin may be seen sowing the seeds of a liberal mindset. He includes an Aesopian fable, of which the previous reception history had been unanimously racist, entitled (by Godwin) 'Washing the Blackamoor White'.[66] This fable tells of how a foolish woman attempts to wash Nango, her black footman, white. When she confesses that she thinks Nango is 'a very handsome man', Godwin, in parenthesis, assures his young reader that black men could be handsome and well-mannered. Godwin was by no means immune to the everyday racism of the times, but his comment challenges conventional prejudice. More markedly subversive is the secret contempt felt towards the woman by her servants and washerwomen.

In 'The Wolf and the Mastiff', a starving wolf befriends a domesticated dog, telling it: 'We are animals originally of the same class, only with a little difference in our education'.[67] The dog agrees and offers to take the wolf back to his home where his master will feed and care for him too. But the wolf notices the mark of the collar on the dog's neck. 'Hunger shall never make me so slavish and base', the wolf concludes, 'as to prefer chains and blows with a belly-full, to my liberty'.[68]

Godwin followed the *Fables* with his version of Tooke's *Pantheon* (1806), *The History of Rome: From the Building of the City to the Ruin of the Republic* (1809) and *History of Greece* (1821). He also commissioned the children's version of the *Odyssey* from Charles Lamb which was to have a profound effect upon generations of young Britons across the class spectrum, inspired numerous imitations and is seen as a landmark in the history of publishing.[69] His *Pantheon* (1806) was used and endorsed by the English 'public school' (i.e. fee-paying and private) Charterhouse. The book was dedicated to 'Rev. Matthew Reine D.D., Master of Charter-House School' because Godwin's stepson was a pupil there. Reine's endorsement boosted sales substantially, secured fair reviews and ensured that it became the standard text by which all children at the time accessed the mythology of Greece and Rome, for Godwin had made his original more refined. He declares that Tooke's *Pantheon* 'contains in every page an elaborate calumny upon the Gods of the Greeks, and that in the coarsest thoughts and words that rancor could furnish'.[70] Godwin felt no need to 'inveigh against the amours of Jupiter'. 'The office of the writer of such a book as this', writes Godwin, 'is to prepare his young readers to admire and to enjoy the immortal productions of Homer, Horace and Virgil'. The primary use of the study of ancient mythology, identified in his preface, was 'to enable young persons to understand the system of the poets of former times, as well as the allusions so often to be found interspersed in writers of a more recent date'.[71]

He declares that his new *Pantheon*, sold for an affordable price, has been 'expressly written for the use of young persons of both sexes', revealing a wish for his book to have a life beyond the traditional, elite, male-dominated schoolroom. The book was found in the chest of books left behind after his death by John Keats, poet and inn-manager's son (1795–1821).[72] Keats probably first encountered Godwin's book in his school library at Enfield Academy,[73] run at the time by John Clarke (1757–1820), formerly a teacher in the Baptist Minister John Collett Ryland's (1723–1792) Northampton Dissenting academy, and colleague there of George Dyer.[74]

Godwin's children's books had a wider reach and deeper impact than the work for which he is now most well regarded, i.e. his novels and political philosophy.[75] Was his shift to the preparation of books for children a retreat from ideological struggle? Children's literature was no safe haven. A reviewer objected to the extent of the alterations of the originals in his *Fables*, and to the possible anti-Christian implications that could be drawn.[76] A report written by an anonymous government spy in 1813 concluded that there was 'a regular system through all his [Godwin's] publications to supersede all other elementary books, and to make his library the resort of preparatory schools, that in time the principles of democracy and Theophilanthropy may take place universally'.[77]

In retrospect, the concern shown for Godwin's small-scale, unprofitable and short-lived publishing venture (1805–1825) seems disproportionate to the threat posed.[78] But the report shows that it was believed that Godwin had targeted constituencies of poorer readers: 'In order to allure schools of a moderate and a lower class, he holds out the temptation of an allowance of threepence in every shilling for such books as are published by him'.[79] The language is loaded because the threat of revolution had been intensified by increasing literacy and organisation among working-class communities. Although meetings had been made difficult by the Gagging Acts (1795), the spread of revolutionary ideas through cheap print was harder to proscribe. The agent may have had some justification in concluding that Godwin's intention with the Juvenile Library was to monopolise early educational publishing, 'and thus by degrees to give an opportunity for every principle professed by the infidels and republicans of these days to be introduced to their notice'.[80] In case the report's recipient would need help in detecting the urgency of the threat, the agent continues: 'By such means did Voltaire and his brethren for twenty years before the Revolution in France spread infidelity and disloyalty through the remotest provinces of that country, and we know too well how they succeeded'.[81]

Godwin himself maintained that the Juvenile Library was filling a hole in English educational provision. He wanted to teach children to think for themselves, not simply to know things, 'to plant the seeds of dissent and intellectual autonomy in a new generation of readers'.[82] And his *Pantheon* (1806) was a particular concern of the government agent: 'It is an insidious and dangerous publication'. The preface, he maintains, 'professes to exalt the purity and show the superiority of Christianity over the heathen morality taught in the Grecian and Roman mythology', but then the work that follows 'improperly excites the curiosity of young persons ... and artfully hints the wisdom of the morality of the heathen world'.[83] The book went through eight editions by 1836 and was stocked and studied in schools nationwide and in India.[84]

In Baldwin's ancient histories, so the agent reports, 'every democratic sentiment is printed in italics that they may not fail to present themselves to a child's notice'.[85] The agent explains that in his *History of Rome* (1809),

> Instead of carrying it down to the destruction of the Empire it leaves off at the reign of Augustus, and in italics remarks that it is useless to write the History of the tyrants who governed for the remaining 400 years, for when it ceased to be a *Republic* it ceased to deserve the name of History.[86]

In practical terms, Godwin was interested in replacing both Oliver Goldsmith's and Rollin's influential histories.[87] His diary reveals that he also drew on the proto-communist and staunch republican Gabriel Bonnot de Mably's *Observations sur les romains* (1751).[88]

The training of Methodist preachers

If Godwin's Dissenting education influenced the classical education of thousands of early 19th-century children, the rhetorical training of large numbers of Methodists was based on classical oratory. Until the death in 1791 of John Wesley, the founder of Methodism, the movement often operated within the Church of England, even though it always reached out to the poorest communities of workers and prisoners who were otherwise neglected by the establishment.[89] But after his death, between 1797 and 1849, a series of splits led by such groups as the Methodist New Connexion, the Primitive Methodists and the Bible Christians decisively took Methodism out of the Church of England to become the largest Nonconformist Christian denomination in the country.

At Oxford, John Wesley, who himself read the classical languages fluently, had studied Ciceronian oratory and its presentation in neoclassical handbooks.[90]

But he was convinced that his non-ordained male and female preachers, many of whom had hardly any previous education, would benefit from hands-on training, often in the open air, in the principles of classical rhetoric. He enthusiastically supervised them himself. He instructed them to read for between six and eight hours a day,[91] and recommended they study not only scripture, but Greek, Hebrew, early Church fathers, secular history, science, logic, metaphysics, natural philosophy and mathematics.[92] He also insisted that the preachers learn, from the Dutch scholar and theologian Gerard Vossius' introduction to Aristotelian rhetoric, the fundamental classical oratorical precepts of deportment, appropriateness, sublimity, force, relevance, simplicity and brevity.[93] Wesley's 'extracurricular system of reading, writing, and speaking rules' constituted an 'empowerment of the populace' and offers 'a rich site for examining historical connections between literacy, rhetoric, and class equality'.[94] The curriculum of the miners' and preachers' children educated at Kingswood, the school he founded near Bristol, also included ancient Greek and, in their case, Latin.[95] He modelled their education after his own, claiming 'Whoever carefully goes through this course will be a better scholar than nine in ten of the graduates of Oxford or Cambridge'.[96]

Even the roughest preachers, uneducated as children, developed honed techniques in public speaking, through oral, practical training, but applied them in the simple language of working-class people. This fusion of classical method and contemporary verbal medium goes a long way towards explaining the staggering success of the first Methodist preachers, who were an important impetus behind the rise of Trade Union oratory later. The Duchess of Buckingham (1680–1743) was appalled, writing to the Methodist Countess of Huntingdon in 1742 to complain about these politically 'levelling' preachers,

> Their doctrines are most repulsive and strongly tinctured with impertinence and disrespect towards their Superiors, in perpetually endeavouring to level all ranks and do away with all distinction. It is monstrous to be told you have a heart as sinful as the common wretches that crawl on the earth.[97]

Lewis Edwards and Robert Roberts

The 19th century saw the gradual decline of Dissenting academies and their provision of an alternative Higher Education. When London University was founded in 1826 and enabled to award degrees in 1837, the academy, as a place for non-Anglicans to obtain an Oxford and Cambridge level education, became obsolete. The establishment of provincial universities, where Dissenters were admitted, and then the reform of Oxbridge in the 1850s, brought an end to almost two centuries of a religious educational tradition. The final academies were transformed into denominational training colleges for ministerial candidates already in possession of a degree.[98]

Non-Anglican faith schools, of all denominations, were less affected than academies by these educational reforms and continued to serve their communities. One such was the Calvinistic Methodist preparatory school at Bala, North Wales, run by Lewis Edwards (1809–1887). Edwards (Figure 8.5) was a Calvinistic Methodist preacher, who was instrumental in the shaping of modern Wales through his educational writing and practice; his son Thomas Charles Edwards continued his educational work, becoming the first Principal of the University College of Wales, Aberystwyth. Lewis was convinced of the benefits gained from teaching the Greek and Roman classics, and in 1852 published in *Y Traethodydd (The Essayist)* his own Welsh translation of a passage of Homer's *Iliad.* He wrote in his journal:

> It seems to us that the prime place in education should be given to the classics; not for the sake of the Latin and Greek languages in themselves, but for the sake of the books that have been written in them. These books are worth reading and understanding because of their merits, inasmuch as they are the products of all the best thinkers who were ever in the world before the days of Christ, apart from the writers of the Old Testament; furthermore this is the best preparation for anyone who wishes to devote the rest of his life to reading the work of the greatest thinkers who were subsequently in the world.[99]

FIGURE 8.5 Dr. Lewis Edwards, Bala. Reproduced by courtesy of Llyfrgell Genedlaethol Cymru—The National Library of Wales.

According to these principles, he educated many of the next generation of Methodist ministers, and other working-class young men from the North of Wales who were destined for other careers. One of his students was Robert Roberts (1834–1903), who became known as 'Y Sgolor Mawr' (the great scholar), but who, in a pattern by no means unknown amongst the most educated Methodists of the later 19th century, eventually transferred his allegiance to the Church of England. Roberts (the cousin, incidentally, of the Welsh philosopher Henry Jones (1852–1922) on whom see below, pp. 293–4), worked his way from extreme poverty and life as a farmer's drudge to become a cleric and celebrated academic.[100] He grew up in Hafod Bach, on a tenanted farm in the hills of North Wales, which he considered neither pretty, nor sublime, but 'ugly' and 'utterly uninteresting'.[101] Too poor to afford schoolbooks, he struggled through Lewis Edwards' Calvinistic Methodist College and, against odds, excelled in his studies.

After just two years at school he spent a further two tutoring privately before heading to the Church of England teacher training college at Caernarfon. Not long after qualifying Roberts grew tired of teaching: 'I've tried to earn my bread by teaching, but that bread is so bitter that it is uneatable'.[102] He longed to go to Oxford University to further his education, but his knowledge of Greek and Latin was insufficient for him to win a scholarship. Spurred on by stories of others who *had* made it to Oxford from the Welsh working class—notably Reverend Morris Williams (1809–1874)—Roberts decided to gamble with the last of his savings and go for the entrance exams anyway: 'I had three months to read, and at it I went like killing snakes. I read up my Horace, Virgil, etc., and prepared to go up at the next October examination, *coûte que coûte*'.[103]

He never did make it to Oxford. Instead, in 1857 he enrolled at St. Bees Theological College (also Anglican), where he beat his English public-school-educated contemporaries to the Greek Prize. His friend and chief competitor, a young man named Castley, told Roberts:

> It's no use your talking, old boy–you know Greek books better than I do: if I know two or three Greek books better than you do, it is just because I read them carefully at a good school and you did not. But you know Greek Testament far better than I do.[104]

Roberts' exceptional grasp of the classical languages accelerated his ascent of the socio-economic ladder nearly as forcefully as his working-class roots impeded it. In 1859 Roberts applied to become an ordained deacon, for which he had to sit an examination. In the interview with Bishop Thomas Short of St. Asaph, his Oxford-educated examiner opened a page of Xenophon's *Cyropaedia* at random and told him to translate, explaining: 'When I want to know if candidates know any Greek', said Short, 'I always try them with Xenophon, it's such Greek Greek'.[105] Roberts had not read a line of the *Cyropaedia*. But, as he reports, he 'happened to light on a plain passage and got through pretty creditably'.

Bishop Short apparently responded to his efforts, thus: 'That'll do … You don't seem quite to see the force of it, but never mind–let's try the Greek Testament'.[106]

Conclusion

For some Nonconformists, the only desirable feature of a classical education had always been sufficient training in Greek to allow access to the New Testament. William Leask (1812–1884) was a Congregationalist minister, who grew up 'miserably poor' on the Scottish Isle of Orkney.[107] After being converted to Christianity at 16, he spent his evenings studying Latin and Greek in Kirkwall in order to further his biblical studies. 'There was', he explains in his autobiography,

> a very able schoolmaster in the town, who so thoroughly devoted himself to the benefit of others, that after conducting a school of more than a hundred boys during the day he spent his evenings in teaching young men in business.[108]

Described by Leask as a 'good classical scholar', the teacher, Mr. Anfield, instructed his student in Latin and Mathematics. Through the evening classes Leask was reunited with his former schoolmaster, Mr Brake, who apparently resigned his position in the nearby village school (Tankerhill) in order to work on his Latin and learn Greek with Anfield.[109]

Leask made other friends in what he called his pursuit along 'the thorny path of knowledge under difficulties'. The group of avid autodidacts were known about town as 'The Seven Friends'. Their motto was: *Suaviter in modo fortiter in re*—a much quoted Latin saying which means 'gently in manner, forcefully in deed'.[110] It was not before Leask became a junior clerk, married 'a gentle and economical wife' and started his career as a Dissenting preacher, that he embarked on his study of the ancient Greek language. In his biography he expresses no interest in the Greek or Roman worlds or their literature. He wanted to learn ancient Greek solely so that he could read the New Testament in its original language:

> Every spare shilling was laid out in books. I purchased a Greek grammar and lexicon, and resolved to study that language … I persevered and succeeded; and I found myself amply rewarded for the labour by the pleasure I derived from first reading a verse in the Greek Testament correctly.[111]

Yet this chapter has shown that there was crucial cross-fertilisation between Classics, class and Nonconformist intellectual and pedagogical culture which went far beyond study of New Testament Greek.

The mistreatment of former Puritans at the Restoration helped to create new and alternative educational institutions where classical authors were favoured as encouraging free thought and informed argumentation, at precisely the time when the gentlemanly discipline of 'Classics' was being created in the mainstream

Anglican community. Those educated in Dissenting schools and academies, even those who were not themselves from working-class families, were inherently likely to espouse political views sympathetic to labourers and the poor and frequently became teachers or preachers engaged fulltime in their communities. Dissenters were often responsible for enlightened and progressive educational publishing ventures on classical as on other topics; some who were Dissenters, or allied with them, including the notorious Greek scholar Gilbert Wakefield, were adopted as symbols of freedom of thought and class-conscious revolutionary politics. Classical authors and especially classical rhetorical models were crucial in the development of the profoundly affective—and effective—Wesleyan tradition of preaching, and contributed significantly to the uplift of literacy and educational standards amongst the poor across England and Wales. Methodist Sunday Schools, as other chapters document, may have helped create a diligent and obedient proletariat, but they also helped to make it articulate, literate and able to organise.

Notes

1 Rupp (1986) 138–78.
2 See the biographies collected by the Nonconformist churchman Edmund Calamy (1713).
3 We use 'Nonconformism' and 'Dissenting' and their cognates interchangeably.
4 See Watts (1978) 260, 265–6, 482–3; Coffey (2013).
5 Spurr (1989).
6 On the position of classical languages and literature in the Dissenting academies see Wilson (forthcoming) part III, chapter 23.
7 Thompson (2013) 385–440.
8 Hill (1972) 238.
9 See Whitehouse (2015) 216.
10 Parker (1914) 48.
11 Schofield (2013) *ODNB*.
12 Schofield (2013) *ODNB*.
13 Letter from Philip Doddridge to Samuel Clarke (7th August 1729), Doddridge (1829) 489.
14 Doddridge (1829) 490.
15 Priestley (1970) 77.
16 Priestley (1970) 77.
17 Priestley (1970) 77.
18 Priestley (1970) 84.
19 Schofield (2004).
20 James and Inkster (2012) 43.
21 O'Brien (1989).
22 Priestley (1970).
23 Wakefield (1792) 206.
24 Jones (2004) *ODNB*; Brooks (2004) *ODNB*.
25 McCarthy (2016) *ODNB*; Tomalin (1992) 101.
26 Smith (1954) 176–80. The following titles were reprinted many times: Rollin (1731); Stanyan (1707); Smith (1753); Kennett (1696); Potter (1697).
27 Smith (1954) 180f. The following titles were reprinted many times: Vertot (1720); Hooke (1738-71); La Mothe le Vayer (1678); Montesquieu (1752); L'Estrange ([1702]

1720); Mably (1751); Mavor (1802-4); Rollin (1731); Spence (1726); Erasmus (1753); D'Arnay (1761); Bossu (1695).
28 Roe (2004) *ODNB* and Roe (1992) 17–35.
29 Dyer (1793) 1.
30 Dyer (1793) 2–3.
31 Dyer (1793) 117.
32 Dyer (1793) 5–7.
33 BM, Fox to Dennis O'Bryen, 29th July, 1798, Add. MSS, 47566, fol; see Prochaska (1973) 71.
34 Lamb (1833) 237.
35 Roe (1992) 17.
36 Lamb (1820) 365–9.
37 Lamb (1975) 1.262 and Lamb (1978) 2.26.
38 Lamb (1820) 365–9. The reference to Harrington signifies James Harrington, see p. 299.
39 Brodribb (1885-90) 452–3.
40 Aiken (1810) 440.
41 Inglis (2014) 299–301.
42 Aiken (1810) 440.
43 Hiscock (2010) 108.
44 Watson (1798).
45 Wakefield (1798) 8.
46 Hiscock (2010) 99.
47 Watson (1798) 24.
48 Wakefield (1798) 15–6.
49 Hiscock (2010) 115: the choice of Croxall's version itself marks Wakefield's 'political allegiance' since it had been 'overtly designed as a Whig challenge to the dominance of earlier Tory versions by Roger L'Estrange'.
50 Croxall ([1722] 1790) 128–9; on this version see further Lewis (1996) 89–91.
51 Wakefield (1798) 18–9.
52 Wakefield (1798) 18.
53 Prochaska (1973) 76.
54 Prochaska (1973) 80–1.
55 Clarke (1940) 81–7.
56 Philp (2012) *ODNB*.
57 Smith (1954) 173.
58 See *The Diary of William Godwin* (online) May 1832 to May 1833. N.B. This appears to equate to the whole of Herodotus. Godwin did not consider himself a natural linguist; see Godwin (1992) 57.
59 Godwin read H. Spens' 1763 translation of Plato, and (probably) either the translation of Xenophon's '*Dix Mille*' ('Ten Thousand', i.e. the *Anabasis*) by Athanase Auger (1788), or the earlier popular edition rendered by Nicolas Perrot d'Ablancourt (multiple editions from 1648). See *The Diary of William Godwin* (online) September 1791 and 1832–1833.
60 See *The Diary of William Godwin* (online) 15–6 September 1791; 20 April 1791; 3–18 June 1809.
61 Godwin (1794). On these trials see also below, pp. 276–7.
62 For a full bibliography of the Juvenile Library's output, see www.rc.umd.edu/editions/godwin_fables/editions.2014.godwin_fables.title_list.html.
63 Baldwin (1805/2014) 1. 3–4.
64 Baldwin (1805/2014) 1. 4.
65 On the history of which see Hall (2018a).
66 Baldwin (1805/2014) 2.84–91
67 Baldwin (1805/2014) 1.193.
68 Baldwin (1805/2014) 1.212.
69 Hall (2008a) 26–7; see further below, p. 358.

70 Baldwin (1806) vi.
71 Baldwin (1806) viii.
72 On Keats' use of Baldwin's *Pantheon* see Osler (1967).
73 This was not a Dissenting academy in the sense that it was a higher education institution and existed in order to prepare students for Nonconformist ministry, but the school is still often referred to as an academy due to its unorthodox Christian roots.
74 For Clarke see Tompson (2004) *ODNB*.
75 St Clair (1989a) 177.
76 *The Eclectic Review* vol. 2, April, 1806, 314.
77 MacCarthy (1872) 162: 'A Few Particulars Concerning Godwin's Juvenile Library Which Ought To Be Made Generally Known' in MacCarthy (1872) 161–4. All references have been taken from MacCarthy. The original report is document TS11/951/3494 in the Public Record Office, or 'Domestic, Geo. III., 1813. January to March. No. 217'.
78 The 'red scare' and subsequent surveillance of British communist artists and writers in the 20th century is an instructive parallel, for which see, e.g. Smith (2013).
79 MacCarthy (1872) 162
80 MacCarthy (1872) 164.
81 MacCarthy (1872) 163–4.
82 Barnett & Gustafson (2014) 29.
83 MacCarthy (1872) 162.
84 Clemit (2009) 93–5.
85 MacCarthy (1872) 162.
86 MacCarthy (1872) 162–3.
87 Goldsmith (1769) and (1774b); Rollin's *Ancient History* was first translated into English and published in different parts and formats London between 1726 and 1737; its 18th edition was published in 1859.
88 *The Diary of William Godwin* (online) shows sustained engagement with the Abbé de Malby from February 1796–1800 (see Digital Resources in bibliography).
89 Wesley (1831) vol. I, 9.
90 Burton (2001) 70.
91 Shepherd (1966) 22.
92 Wesley (1831) vol. X, 490–2.
93 Burton (2001) 77.
94 Burton (2001) 68.
95 Wesley (1831) vol. XIII, 283.
96 Wesley (1831) vol. XIII, 289.
97 Knight (1853) 18.
98 See www.qmulreligionandliterature.co.uk/research/the-dissenting-academies-project/dissenting-academies, and Rivers and Burden (forthcoming).
99 Edwards (1865) 136. This was originally published in Welsh: Davies (1995) 113. See also Davies (2009) 35–47.
100 Roberts (1991) xli.
101 Roberts (1991) 9.
102 Roberts (1991) xxvi.
103 Roberts (1991) 352.
104 Roberts (1991) 364.
105 Roberts (1991) 377.
106 Roberts (1991) 377.
107 Leask (1854) 27.
108 Leask (1854) 107.
109 Leask (1854) 107.
110 Leask (1854) 107–8.
111 Leask (1854) 145.

9

ADULT EDUCATION

E.P. Thompson insisted that we recognise that

> the first half of the 19th century, when the formal education of a great part of the people entailed little more than instruction in the Three R's, was by no means a period of intellectual atrophy. The towns, and even the villages, hummed with the energy of the autodidact. Given the elementary techniques of literacy, labourers, artisans, shopkeepers and clerks and schoolmasters, proceeded to instruct themselves, severally or in groups.[1]

The term 'autodidact' suggests lone mavericks and eccentrics, but in this period it often took the form of organised working-class education, of 'mutual improvement'. Advances in cheap and improving literature, as detailed in Chapter 3, spread and intensified the energy driving self-education, and the institutional infrastructure for group learning came into being: 'the working-class response to the lack of suitable educational facilities was to form their own'.[2] Educational support was increasingly provided in communities nationwide via grass-roots initiatives, private enterprise and the state. The numbers of autodidacts instructing themselves individually dwindled when educational state provision became universal at the close of the 19th century.

This chapter traces classical presences in the major adult education initiatives offering opportunities to the working classes in the 19th and early 20th centuries. These included, most importantly, Mutual Improvement Societies, Adult Schools, Mechanics Institutes, University Extension schemes, the Workers' Educational Association (WEA) and the Labour Colleges. The demand for workers' education was met sluggishly by state legislation. It was not until the Elementary Education Acts of 1870 and 1880 that more evenly distributed educational provision was achieved. Once compulsory education for children under

DOI: 10.4324/9781315446608-11

13 was standardised, poorer families enjoyed the greater cultural confidence that comes with literacy, while the wealthy continued to safeguard their social distinction via other means, such as costly private schools. Classics still had an important role. The classical bottleneck to social progress constituted by compulsory qualifications in Latin and Greek for entrance to many British universities remained in place for almost another century.[3]

In the 18th and earlier 19th centuries, some philanthropic individuals and groups established initiatives to ameliorate educational deficiencies, which meant teaching literacy and the Bible. Sunday schools proved popular because some children as young as 5 worked 6 days a week, 12 or 13 hours a day.[4] 'Ragged schools' were charitable organisations founded from the 1840s onwards to educate the children of industrial workers, predominantly in deprived areas of large cities.[5] 'Classics' as an educational discipline remained out of reach, since their curriculum rarely extended beyond basic literacy and numeracy to embrace cultural or historical subjects.

Adult Schools and Mutual Improvement Societies

Around 1800, 'Adult Schools' began to be initiated, usually by Methodists or Quakers.[6] Established explicitly to teach illiterate adults to read the Bible, Adult Schools quickly diversified, offering, for example, tuition in grammar, geography and arithmetic. They also encouraged reading groups, debating and mutual aid activities.[7] They became important hubs not only for the promotion of literacy, but also for learning how the teachings of the Bible and Christian fellowship might help solve society's problems without the need for theological theorising, or, in the words of the schools' motto, 'Love, not dogmas; life, not creeds'.[8] The People's College, founded at Sheffield in 1842 by a Nonconformist minister, lasted for 30 years, and seems to have functioned along lines identical to those of the Adult Schools. Students arrived to study in an unplastered garret at 6 o'clock in the morning, before their working day commenced, and there studied Latin, Greek, Logic and Civil Knowledge.[9]

The tradition of the Adult School persisted. Mostly Quaker-led, they were in the vanguard of adult education in Britain, but their emphasis was not usually, as it seems to have been in Sheffield, on ancient Greek and Rome. Elizabeth Blackburn (b.1902), the daughter of weavers in the Ribble and Hodder Valleys, Lancashire, recalled how she and her friend Polly laughed when they overheard her mother speaking about 'adult school', since their assumption was that children went to school while adults went to work.[10] But her mother was 'a great buyer of second-hand books' and a daily reader of the newspaper.[11] When the WEA started to run classes in her town, she signed up immediately. As Elizabeth recalls: 'For a long time I imagined that there was magic in the letters WEA because in the words of my mother "they opened the door of a wider world"'.[12] Blackburn's mother's attendance at both Quaker Adult School and WEA classes shows how confused attitudes to working-class educational establishments could be. While each different institution staked out a claim to a certain educational approach, denominational affiliation, or political allegiance, adult learners accepted whatever provision was on offer at a convenient time and place. This suggests their indifference to the factional allegiances that often colour historical studies of adult education.[13]

Informal reading and study groups with wider intellectual interests sprang up in workers' homes, places of work, or public houses, as did more formal groups, which were frequently held in Nonconformist chapels or meeting houses. Mutual Improvement Societies, sometimes tiny and financially precarious, were usually founded by Owenites (followers of Robert Owen (1771–1858), founder of the early British Co-operative Movement[14]), Chartists and other politically radical groups. Handloom weavers, who organised early and embraced Co-operative ideals, dominate the early history of mutual instruction.[15] Workers met to teach and learn from one another, but also to address the social problems affecting their community,[16] to organise themselves unofficially, 'to combat the evils of the Industrial Revolution'.[17] In 1847, Samuel Smiles, the author of *Self-Help* (1859), claimed that there was scarcely a town or village in the West Riding of Yorkshire without one or more Mutual Improvement Societies.[18] Material evidence is so scarce that we cannot easily discover what these numerous workers were teaching each other, but the centrality of Classics in Victorian education and culture suggests that translated Classics must have featured in the classes of Mutual Improvement groups.

In the early 1860s, Joseph Malaby Dent, the publisher of the influential Everyman's Library discussed in Chapter 3, attended chapel meetings in his free time as a printer's apprentice. He

> became interested in what was then called a Mutual Improvement Society, where I found the members studied a book one week and in the alternate week listened to and criticised a paper prepared by one of them.[19]

Dent himself studied for an essay on Samuel Johnson. After finishing Boswell's *Life*, he 'got up from the book feeling there was nothing worth living for so much as literature'. 'To write a book', it seemed to him, was 'the only way to gain Olympus, and I am very much of the same opinion to-day, but it must be literature'.[20] Those early literary encounters formed the mind of the man who went on to publish classical authors accessibly alongside other more modern classics from other regions of the world:

> I have ranged extensively over the field of English literature, and enjoyed many Russian novels in translation and read much of the Greek and Roman classics, also of course in translation; especially of late years have I read Plato, much to my profit, particularly the Socratian dialogues.[21]

As a boy, Philip Inman (1892–1979), who ran errands for a boot-seller and lived with his impoverished and widowed mother, could not afford the £4 annual admission fee to the Technical College in his native town of Knaresborough, Yorkshire. His luck changed, however, when he became apprenticed to a chemist at Taylor's Drug Store, where the owner took an interest in his studies, securing for him private tuition to help prepare him for exams. The tutor was one Professor Daniels, who taught him Latin, French and English. 'From then on every penny I could spare', recalled Inman, 'was spent on the cheap reprints of the classics then available'.[22]

The local Mutual Improvement Society 'opened out new interests and wider horizons' for Inman.[23] It was partially financed by the local Nonconformist church, in this instance Methodist. Inman recalls that the group met 'on Monday evening for lectures, debates and discussions on questions of a social or political, as well as of a religious character'.[24] He saw the Mutual Improvement Society as 'a great educator', where 'We learned to think on our feet, to express ourselves publicly and with tolerable coherence. We also learned that there is usually more than one side to every question'.[25] One of the reprints of the Classics Inman read must have contained Plato's *Apology*, because, at the brink of death from tuberculosis, he recalled the words of Plato's Socrates: 'To meet Orpheus and Homer, Musaeus and Hesiod', said Socrates, 'what would you give for that? I would give a hundred deaths if it is true'.[26] Baron Inman recovered and went on to excel as manager of numerous charitable organisations, as MP in Clement Attlee's government and as Chairman of the Board of Governors at the BBC, but never forgot that he was 'still the same errand-boy who used to drag round a bag of cobbler's repairs to the back doors of customers' houses'.[27]

Mechanics' Institutes

The Mechanics' Institutes originated in Glasgow in the free public lectures Dr. George Birkbeck gave on scientific subjects, beginning in around 1800,[28] in the context of a wave of popular science lecturing across the country.[29] The most famous was the London Mechanics' Institute (later Birkbeck College) set up by Francis Place, a tailor, in 1823, with help from Jeremy Bentham and Lord Brougham.[30] Place had read some ancient authors in translation as a youth, but his ignorance of the Latin and Greek languages made him rather ambivalent about their utility.[31] The hundreds of other institutes which mushroomed in the earlier 19th century, especially in Scotland, the Midlands and the north of England,[32] were designed to instruct workers with little prior education in the sciences and technical subjects.

Unlike the Mutual Improvement Societies, they tended to be established not by workers but by philanthropic landowners and businessmen, and not always with the cynical intention of discouraging political activism. But the general top-down nature of the provision made many workers suspicious of these institutes, some of which were undoubtedly intended to counter the appeal of the Mutual Improvement Societies—breeding grounds for radical dissent, both political and religious.[33] Many Institutes even banned political and religious discussion in the classes.[34] This patently did not work, but all the same the Institutes, of which by mid-century there were more than 600 in England alone, with 100,000 members,[35] had largely become the preserve of shopkeepers and clerical workers—the membership that survived Chartism was predominantly middle-class. The general pattern shows workers flooding back to the mutual model of education in their own often poorly funded but independent and well-organised improvement societies and reading groups.[36]

One such 'Evening Institute' was founded by the wife of a businessman in a weaving community in Lancashire. We know about this apparently small-scale enterprise because it was attended by the weaver, Elizabeth Blackburn, whom we met earlier (p. 187). The classes were taught by a 'University woman' named Miss Paget-Moffatt, whose passion for English Literature rubbed off on the teenaged Elizabeth, who had by this point begun work in the mill and was attending the Institute after work. 'The long hours of weaving provided an ideal opportunity for learning poetry', she reflected in one of her autobiographical pamphlets.[37]

Elizabeth was born into a family where adult education was the norm. Both parents were involved in WEA and Adult School activities. They appear, to judge by the newspapers they read, to have been socialists, with an interest in the Co-operative Movement.[38] Her introduction to Classics, however, came from a neighbour, probably a fellow weaver:

> Here and there you would find a man or woman in whom even a limited schooling had lit a spark for learning. It was in the home of such a neighbour, a man with six children, where I first met the Greek classics. I can see him now reading them with a baby on his knee, apparently quite oblivious to all the noise and activity of the family around him.[39]

The Evening Institute frequented by Blackburn appears to have been relatively small compared to the one, for example, in Birmingham, founded in 1826.[40] Even in the larger cities, some working-class autodidacts put the quality and convenience of educational provision before their own political or religious convictions. It is common to see the same individual cherry-picking educational opportunities from various sources.

In practice, the educational provision of the 'Mechanics' Institutes', supposedly vocational, was diverse. Further research is urgently needed in local archives into the courses they each offered. The Birmingham Institute offered lectures on Arts subjects. In 1834 a class was run called 'Introduction to the Latin Language', with a textbook written by a young member named Joshua Toulmin Smith, who later became a prominent political theorist and editor of Thomas Keightley's popular *History of Rome* (1836).[41] In 1836 Smith also wrote 'A Popular View of the Progress of Philosophy among the Ancients', almost certainly for delivery at the Institute.[42]

By the 1840s, the Institute failed, mainly because its membership was divided over supporting the Chartist movement and the use of violence. An important alumnus was George Jacob Holyoake (1817–1906), reformer and inventor of the term 'secularism'.[43] The son of a Birmingham whitesmith and button-maker, Holyoake had begun work at the age of eight in a local foundry. He started evening classes at the Birmingham Mechanics Institute in 1836, where he first came under the influence of the ideas of Robert Owen and joined the Chartist movement. Even if the membership fees and middle-class presence often discouraged the poorest workers, the very offer of education meant that Mechanics' Institutes were rarely free from radical ideas.[44]

The architecture and internal decor of the Institutes and their associated buildings (libraries and lecture halls) were frequently neoclassical, with grand columns and arches, as were their printed advertisements, syllabuses and other paraphernalia. (Figure 9.1) The flying god Mercury adorns a prize medal struck to commemorate the opening of the Birmingham Mechanics' Institute in January 1826. The medal bears the inscription 'Knowledge is Power'. The Institute's avowed purpose was 'the Promotion of Knowledge among the Working Classes by means of Elementary Schools, a Library and Lectures on the different branches of Art and Science'. Mercury sits in an industrial landscape, with tall factory chimneys smoking behind him in the distance and a variety of artisanal tools lovingly outlined on the lower right. The Birmingham working men's economic relationship with the British Empire, on the profits of which their own opportunities

FIGURE 9.1 19th Century Prize Medal for Birmingham Mechanics Institute. Reproduced by courtesy of Birmingham Museums and Art Gallery.

for self-improvement ultimately depended, is signalled by the inscriptions on the two coffers, 'Africa' and 'East Indies'. Coins are strewn at Mercury's feet near the 'East Indies' chest, on which he sits and nonchalantly rests his caduceus, a recognised symbol of trade and negotiation. These medals were won by junior members who excelled in study, and their distribution is said to have 'excited a valuable spirit of emulation'.[45]

Working Men's Colleges

The need for a liberal education for the mechanics who did not feel comfortable in the Institutes led to the emergence of Working Men's Colleges. The most successful of these was the Working Men's College in Camden, London, founded in 1854 by Christian socialists led by F.D. Maurice, and still in operation on Crowndale Road.[46] A handbill exists from the previous year, advertising a series of pilot courses to be delivered in the Hall of Association off Oxford Street, including one currently 'in development' in Latin, to be taught by J.F. MacLennan.[47] In 1860–1861, 34 men enrolled for the Latin course; the year after there were 23, of whom 6 were manual labourers.[48] In 1885 it was described as the parent of several other similar institutions in Greater London, including 'the University Settlements which are now springing up in the East End',[49] such as Toynbee Hall in Tower Hamlets.[50] Settlements were subsequently established in Liverpool, Gateshead, Bristol, Reading, Letchworth, South Wales, Plymouth, York, Harlech, Birmingham, Evesham and Surrey.[51]

The collegiate philosophy aimed to offer a sense of community as well as education, recreation, and 'a social centre, to which men would be bound by strong and lasting associations, such as attach others to the old Universities of Oxford and Cambridge'.[52] Most teachers were London University academics, who gave their services free of charge so that 'charges must be fixed which the poorest can pay, and which the least educated will be ready to pay'.[53] The curriculum was designed to offer something far more ambitious than vocational instruction. The 1885 prospectus defines the subjects taught as those 'with which it most concerns English citizens to be acquainted'.[54] As one lecturer defined it that year, the college taught many subjects with no vocational or business content, but which he saw as valuable solely 'as elements of a liberal education' which fitted men to be citizens.[55]

The Working Men's College became nationally famous under its Principal between 1883 and 1899, Sir John Lubbock. He made a speech there in 1887, one of a series entitled 'The Pleasures of Life', which quote exhaustively from ancient philosophers (Epictetus, Epicurus, Plato, Plutarch, Marcus Aurelius, Herodotus, Aristotle, Aesop, Xenophon and Cicero).[56] In 'The Choice of Books', he drew up a list of the 100 books it was most important for a working man to read.[57] It caused a stir, and was leapt upon by working-class readers all over the English-speaking world as a guide to a speedy self-education. Lubbock, who became the first Baron Avebury, came from a privileged banking family, and was educated at

Eton. He was a reform-minded Liberal MP for Maidstone and subsequently for London University. Although he had not attended university himself, he was a prodigious polymath, specialising in archaeology and biological sciences.[58]

In Lubbock's List, the proportion of classical authors is remarkable: Homer, Hesiod, Marcus Aurelius, Epictetus, Plutarch's *Lives*, Aristotle's *Ethics* and *Politics*, Augustine's *Confessions*, Plato's *Apology*, *Crito* and *Phaedo*, Demosthenes' *De Corona*, Xenophon's *Memorabilia* and *Anabasis*, Cicero's *De Officiis*, *De Amicitia*, and *De Senectute*, Virgil, Aeschylus' *Prometheus* and *Oresteia*, Sophocles' *Oedipus*, Euripides' *Medea*, Aristophanes' *Knights* and *Clouds*, Herodotus, Thucydides, Tacitus' *Germania* and Livy. In addition, two famous works on ancient history, Gibbon's *Decline and Fall* and Grote's *History of Greece*, make it onto the list as necessary reading for any educated person, along with the most popular novel then in existence set in antiquity, Bulwer-Lytton's *Last Days of Pompeii*.[59]

More than a quarter of all the books are classical authors, and, with the addition of books entirely addressed to classical antiquity, the proportion is about one third. The classical riches on the working-class self-educator's bookshelf after 1887 can in large measure be attributed to Lubbock's ideal curriculum. Old translations of items on the list were reprinted and marketed as one of 'Sir John Lubbock's Hundred Books', for example Lord Brougham's rendering of Demosthenes' *On the Crown* (1840), intended to convey 'to persons unacquainted with the original some notion of its innumerable and transcendent beauties'.[60] One son of a London policeman recalls his father reading his meticulous way through the entire list, which his son regarded as worthy and boring, not long after it was published.[61]

Thereafter, the Camden WMC's impressive array of courses included Greek literature by Arthur Sidgwick (1840–1920). Sidgwick is best known now for his books on Greek prose (still in print) and verse composition.[62] He was, however, a champion of university reform, campaigning for the admission of women to undergraduate degrees, and arguing that the university should cater for poor students and allow applications from students who knew neither ancient language.[63] His brother was also a scholar, and they both resigned their fellowships at Trinity College, Cambridge, in protest against the Anglican religious tests imposed on academics. Sidgwick was the most popular tutor at Corpus Christi College, Oxford (where he taught between 1897 and 1902) and later University Reader in Greek; his pupils included the future Regius Professor of Greek, Gilbert Murray.[64]

In an article in the *Oxford Magazine*, dated March 5th, 1920 and obscurely signed 'A.H.S', Sidgwick described teaching a 'little group of tired city clerks, telephone operators and mechanics in Camden Town'.[65] In his evening class at the WMC he taught Plato's *Republic* and Sophocles' *Oedipus Tyrannus* in Gilbert Murray's translation.[66] Sidgwick reports a question asked of him 'with a buoyant gesture' by the Head Master of the public school, who was about to teach a class on Theocritus: 'Can you conceive anything more delightful than a class in Theocritus, on such a day and in such a place?' Sidgwick reflects that the remark left him 'picturing the progress of the class and thinking of the way in which, for so many succeeding generations, the classics have been steeped with the peculiar atmosphere of the public schools':

> What proportion of Englishmen who have learnt Classics at school feel that Theocritus or Plato or Thucydides signify, above all, English playing-fields, English class-rooms, and the scent of English limes? Of course in such an atmosphere much evaporates—the restlessness of the Greek intellect and many other things. There is even absurdity in the way in which some story of perverted passion is pleasantly droned through a drowsy summer afternoon. But the whole complex, whatever differences it blurs, has its own unique character and value.[67]

But Sidgwick has another constituency in mind: could this experience 'be reproduced for my little group of tired city clerks, telephone operators, and mechanics in Camden Town? Did one want to reproduce it?'[68] He contrasts the keen curiosity and active engagement of the workers in his evening class with the slow passive 'absorption' of the domesticated classical education texts imbibed at public school:

> Delightful as may be the process of gradually absorbing classical learning permeated with the most English of English atmospheres, there is something to be said for the value of the sharp contact of comparatively mature minds with an unknown literature and civilisation. The excitement and zest of discovery is something for which it would not always be easy to find a parallel in the classical education of the average public-school boy.[69]

Sidgwick's teaching in translation, which provides that 'sharp contact with an unknown literature and civilisation', was experimental. He described the exercises in close reading:

> The reading of Professor Murray's translation was the basis. But at intervals a few lines would be taken—say a strophe of a chorus—and we gave them what was a rather close examination. First there was the Greek to be read aloud, followed by a very literal translation. Then the class would be shown the actual order of the words in the Greek, and it would be pointed out how words calling up certain images were juxtaposed and so forth. The class obtained in this way some idea of the character of an inflectional language and the uses to which it could be put. Differences in the character of the language would be illustrated by comparison with Professor Murray's translation.[70]

This innovative approach seems to have worked well, and Sidgwick hoped that others would follow his example: 'I can at least reiterate the hope that before long the question of introducing the study of Greek translations in WEA classes may be taken up with the seriousness which it deserves'.[71]

From University Extension to the Workers' Educational Association

The public to which Lubbock addressed his list had become much more accustomed to the idea of widespread provision of adult education in the 1870s, partly because British universities and their academics were beginning to change their attitudes to wider society. Several educational 'movements' with marginally different approaches arose. The existing activities of Mutual Improvement Societies and the Mechanics' Institutes were increasingly channelled into larger national projects, including the University Settlement Movement mentioned above, the University Extension Movement, and the WEA. There was significant overlap and collaboration between their activities.

The University Extension Movement (in which Sidgwick was an exceptionally active teacher, as were classicists at Newnham College and in the universities of Leeds, Durham and Belfast[72]) promoted extramural higher education nationwide. It was started at Cambridge in 1873 by a radical young scientist from Fife, James Stuart (whose first childhood Latin teacher 'was probably the worst teacher who ever existed'[73]) and spread to Oxford in 1878.[74] It was a popular, if relatively short-lived movement, although the terminology often clung to what universities now call 'outreach' activities, long after extension had been subsumed into Albert Mansbridge's brainchild, the WEA, conceived in discussion at Toynbee Hall and founded in 1903 as the Association to Promote the Higher Education of Working Men. It soon achieved branches in Reading, Rochdale, Ilford, Yorkshire and the Midlands, and received 'public recognition from the representatives of nearly all the Universities and a large number of labour organisations' at a meeting in the Examination Schools of Oxford University on 25th August 1908.[75] Mansbridge (Figure 9.2) was considered by some of his Oxford WEA tutors as a radical champion of the oppressed, to the extent that they jokingly referred to themselves as 'conspirators' and the 'Catiline Club'.[76] The revolutionary syndicalists of the Plebs League, however, felt it was a dilettante organisation attempting to distract workers from class warfare.

Mansbridge (1876–1952), a carpenter's son who had left school at 14 but benefitted from Extension classes at King's College London, believed the Mechanics' Institutes had failed because they 'were largely the result of philanthropic effort, set on foot by some local magnate ... rather than upon the initiative of the mechanics themselves'.[77] His solution, the 'tutorial class', was a development along the lines of the Mutual Improvement model, built on the ideal of people learning together rather than listening to an omniscient lecturer. As a former Co-operative Movement activist, Mansbridge knew the value of collaborative learning: 'Each student is a teacher, each teacher is a student'.[78] He had benefitted from the tutorial technique between 1891 and 1901 when he attended University

FIGURE 9.2 Albert Mansbridge by Howard Coster 1945, reproduced by courtesy of the National Portrait Gallery, London. © National Portrait Gallery, London.

Extension classes (including chemistry, economics and Greek) at Toynbee Hall,[79] as did other working-class intellectuals such as J.M. Dent and Ben Tillett.[80]

The emergence of the WEA was inseparable from the debate on University reform at Oxford, launched in 1906, which was perceived by many workers as trying to take over the administration of Ruskin College and defuse its students' politics. It had been founded as Ruskin Hall in Oxford in 1899 as the first residential college specifically for working-class men; they came to study for a year or two on scholarships funded by an American philanthropic couple named Walter and Amne Vrooman, and were taught science by another American, Charles Beard.[81] Some middle-class and public-school educated Oxford critics of the status quo, who wanted to see their university opened to a much wider social range and its wealth redistributed, involved themselves, not always tactfully, in Ruskin's affairs.[82] Every single one had studied or was teaching Classics at Oxford: R.H. Tawney, William Temple, Alfred Zimmern, Richard Livingstone, J.L. Myres and William Beveridge.[83] This may lie behind Barbara Goff's perception that 'classics was a persistent, if minor, part of activities' in the first two decades of the WEA's history.[84] She identifies 'a contrast between the modest presence of classics as a taught subject and the rhetorical force which reference to classics could wield in the various discourses of the WEA, such as its magazine *The Highway*'.[85] Goff argues that the humanist Hellenism of some of the leading lights of the WEA, absorbed from these Oxford dons, offered a quasi-spiritual substitute for organised religion.[86] But many working-class autodidacts still began their intellectual journeys as Nonconformist theological rebels. She is correct that WEA rhetoric probably overstates the importance or prominence of the Classics in its courses, and that this may reflect the agency of the Classics dons, whose subject was beginning to lose the battle to remain central to the university curriculum.[87]

As a distinct subject, Classics was marginalised by the WEA,[88] although it proved a useful symbol of 'high' culture when rhetorically characterising the culturally impoverished worker. And classical authors were taught 'indirectly' by WEA tutors by inclusion on non-Classics courses. Plato, for example, looms large in the WEA archive, frequently appearing in Philosophy and Social Sciences courses.[89] The Greek dramatists were often read in English translation (often Gilbert Murray's),[90] especially the tragedians, in Literature classes; Ancient History and Archaeology were commonly offered as part of courses nationwide.[91] Goff's most arresting example of indirect access to Classics is that of a self-styled 'Manchester Socialist', who at his first WEA class met the scholar and tutor R.H. Tawney, a classicist alumnus of Rugby and Balliol who had discovered socialism and volunteered at Toynbee Hall.[92] Tawney introduced him to Greek civilisation at the Oxford WEA. This experience constituted 'the new-birth of my intellectual life'.[93] The anonymous Mancunian had signed up to an economics class and came away with an obsession with the Greeks. The passion ignited in the Manchester socialist surely could not fail to infect others in his family and wider community when he went back home after his sojourn in Oxford. Workers often use words such as 'revelation' to express their joy on being introduced to the classical world.[94] The combination of a tutor's guidance and good, modern translations created a cultural confidence attested in a review of Livingstone's *A Defence of Classical Education* in the WEA organ *The Highway* in 1917:

> Most of us know enough about the Greeks to want to know a great deal more … Plato is used as a text book in some tutorial classes; and if few WEA members can read him in the original, many understand some of the problems he handles better perhaps than the general run of those who can.[95]

Mansbridge's personal encounter with ancient Greek led him to believe that classical authors offered the best instruments to develop 'a larger view of life'.[96] In 1923, Charles Knapp published an extract from a letter Mansbridge had written to him on the subject of 'On the Classics and the Workers' in the American journal *Classical Weekly*. In it Mansbridge explains that the WEA teachers who best succeeded 'in awakening an interest' or 'in satisfying the interest when it is awakened' had themselves been students of Classics.[97] Moreover, the evidence presented to the Governmental Educational Commission in which he had participated unanimously showed, he claimed, that 'whether for the purpose of high business or for the actual study and teaching of modern languages, that man was best who had had a preliminary classical training'.[98]

Mansbridge was intervening in the heated 1920s debate on adult education. Sciences, Mathematics, Economics, Politics and Modern Languages were now deemed to be of at least equal importance to Classics. Mansbridge was 'no shallow paternalist',[99] but he had been wooed by Oxbridge dons and absorbed some of their conservative values. His radical critics saw the (now state-funded) WEA as an extension of the existing instruments of capitalism constituted by the ancient universities. But the students were split on the question of the purpose and content of workers' education, and on Ruskin's relationships with the Trade Unions and above all Oxford University,[100] as shown in this cartoon (Figure 9.3).

FIGURE 9.3 'A Fool's Paradise', a cartoon in *Plebs Magazine* vol.VI, July 1914, no. 6, p. 126. Reproduced by courtesy of the British Library.

The militant faction founded the Plebs League and began to provide their own education in a breakaway Central Labour College, which found a permanent home in Earl's Court, London, in 1911. These men wanted an education in Marxist sociology and revolutionary economics. They repudiated Mansbridge's dream of a liberal education for all.[101] With union support, they produced a two-penny monthly journal entitled *Plebs*. It objected to the influence of Oxford dons shouting to the workers, 'Back to Plato! Back to Aristotle',[102] but—perhaps surprisingly—wrote Roman history into its name and first editorial:

> Enter the Plebs, not from above but from below, not to fight a sham battle among the shadows but the order and for the interest of our masters, but to fight a real battle in the full light and with a clear knowledge of the issue before us … if the education of the workers is to square with the ultimate object of the workers—social emancipation—then it is necessary that the control of such an educational institution must be in the hands of the workers … Inability to recognize the class cleavage clearly was the downfall of the Plebs of old Rome. Let the Plebs of the 20th century be not so deluded.[103]

The magazine also featured serialised articles on ancient history from an economic perspective, by prolific socialist historian and railway worker Will White Craik,[104] a 'Free Rendering from Ovid's "Metamorphoses"' (Book X, the story of Pygmalion),[105] and a report on the discovery of a Sumerian tablet with an account of the flood.[106]

The Plebs League was never large, but its influence was out of proportion to its size.[107] The words of this editorial, probably the work of *Plebs* editor George Sims, a carpenter from Bermondsey, Social Democratic Federation (SDF) member and former Ruskin student, reveal the influence of the Marxist-Syndicalist Daniel De Leon (1852–1914). He had delivered two extemporaneous lectures on Roman history to the comrades of the Greater New York Section of the Socialist Labor Party. In Manhattan Lyceum, New York, on Wednesday April 16th, 1902, his evening lectures opened with 'Plebs' Leaders and Labour Leaders' and closed with 'The Warning of the Gracchi'. The Party stenographically recorded them and circulated them as pamphlets, which were also printed by the Socialist Labour Party (UK) in Glasgow and Edinburgh (1908–1913).

De Leon was born in Curaçao (a Caribbean island, then Dutch-ruled) (Figure 9.4), the son of Dutch Jewish parents. He was educated at the Hildesheim classical gymnasium and then studied medicine at Leiden University. He emigrated to New York in the early 1870s. On arrival, he taught Latin, Greek and Mathematics in a school before enrolling at Columbia College as a Law student.[108] In his first Roman lecture, De Leon insisted that there was 'a ruling class and a ruled class' in ancient Rome'.[109] The 'class cleavage' along economic lines was obscured by the leader or 'Tribune' of the Plebs, who in reality worked

FIGURE 9.4 Daniel De Leon (1852–1914). Public Domain, reproduced courtesy of Library of Congress.

against the interests of the people he was supposed to represent.[110] He was the ancient equivalent of the modern

> Labour leader, picked out and placed to-day by the grace of the capitalist class in the legislative bodies of America, Canada, England or Australia … where his vanity may be gratified with the hollow honours of his prototype, the Plebs Leader, dumb appendage of the Roman Senate.[111]

Sims echoes these words in his editorial: 'Let the Plebs of the 20th century be not so deluded'. His term 'social emancipation' is also derived from De Leon, who prominently glossed the term 'Socialist Republic' as 'the emancipation of the working class'.[112] In his second Roman History lecture, 'The Warning of the Gracchi', De Leon proposed a new radical reading in which the Gracchi, on whom he quotes Plutarch extensively, are portrayed as making 'a series of blunders' in their reforms, which his contemporary working-class activists should avoid.[113] He emphasised the socio-economic chaos of their time, against the background of the slave revolt led by Ennus in Sicily, to which the Chartist Ernest Jones had drawn attention (see below pp. 396–7),[114] and which the (by no means radical) Prussian scholar Francis Lieber had discussed in connection with antebellum slave plantations while working at South Carolina College during the American Civil War.[115]

His major emphasis, however, is on the obfuscation of the class cleavage in the Roman world, where even 'the ragged Roman proletarian came to consider himself a limb of the ruling power, held together with the Roman landlord-plutocrat by a common bond of political superiority' over the rest of Italy.[116] The situation was beyond reform.[117] The only option 'in such emergencies' is revolution. 'We of to-day, in the Rome of to-day, should take warning'.[118] The 'Gracchian tactics' appear to De Leon 'as a bell-buoy to warn the Socialist Movement of this generation of sunken rocks in its course'.[119] Each 'blunder', especially the Sempronian Law, informs his ten 'Canons of the Proletarian Revolution', a rousing check-list for the creation of the Socialist Republic:[120] 'Rough-hewn in the quarry of 500 BC to 400 BC, the proletariat of Rome was 300 years later shaped into final shape in the smithy of the Gracchian tactics', a fate De Leon's followers must at all costs avoid.[121]

De Leon's British followers were no advocates of traditional classical education, yet their identification with the Roman poor helped them formulate strategies in their struggle. Their classical education did not stop there. Mark Starr's *A Worker Looks at History*, published by the Plebs League in 1918 (Figure 9.5), was written explicitly for Labour College Plebs classes; it details the influence of 'Greek thought' on the world and explains the slave economies of ancient Greece and Rome as well as the impact on Britain of the Roman invasion.[122] Starr (1894–1985), a miner in the South Wales coal fields and member of the Miners' Federation and the Independent Labour Party, began his higher education in WEA classes, before winning a scholarship in 1915 to attend the Central Labour College.[123] A year later he returned to the South Wales Coalfield, where he began to lecture in 'Social Science' for the Aberdare District Miners' Federation.[124]

A conscientious objector in World War I, after a spell in prison, Starr was sent to work the land in Northumberland, where he would meet Plebs League members in the North-East Coal Field. Along with many leading members, Starr joined the CPGB, and even visited the USSR for an Esperanto conference in 1926.[125] But when the Plebs' League was absorbed into the National Council of Labour Colleges in 1927, Starr emigrated to the US, where he became an instructor in Brookwood Labor College in Katonah, New York.[126]

In the 19th and early 20th centuries, adult working-class education flourished. While there were factious divisions between educationalist ideologues, working-class self-learners were often indifferent to them. L.C. Stone wrote in the WEA organ *Highway* (1925), that the 'average worker-student does not care twopence about the WEA and NCLC squabble'.[127] Many were nevertheless conscious and engaged political agents. Starr himself argued that when it comes to acquiring education, which was still a challenge for the working-class people, especially in rural areas, 'expediency and opportunism' are culpable only if 'based upon false fundamental principles'.[128]

FIGURE 9.5 Advertisement for Mark Starr's *A Worker Looks at History* in *Plebs Magazine* vol IX January 1918, no 12. Courtesy of British Library.

The presence of classical material in adult education therefore changes substantially during the period under investigation. In the 18th century, little education for the worker existed, and then in anomalous clusters surrounding a religious enterprise or the opportunities encountered by workers in specific trades. In the 19th century significant progress was made thanks to the availability of affordable learning materials and through the establishment of the educational initiatives we have discussed. During the same period, classical scholarship began to be displaced from the centre of formal Higher Education even as it became professionalised and increasingly specialised.[129] But this transformation hardly impacted on the working-class autodidact. At the dawn of the 20th century, adult learners experienced a classical Indian summer in the educational offerings made by university teachers via Extension activities and the WEA, briefly committed to the symbolic act of extending the once monumental but now crumbling franchise of a classical education to those who had previously been excluded from it by their class.

Notes

1 Thompson (1968) 711.
2 Radcliffe (1997) 153.
3 Compulsory Greek at Oxford and Cambridge ended after World War I in 1919, but the compulsory Latin 'O' Level was not abolished as an entrance requirement at Oxford until 1960 (see Forrest [2003]), and it remained an informal requirement imposed by some colleges long after that, even until the late 1970s.
4 The Factory Act (1833) prohibited the employment of children younger than 9 years of age and limited the hours that children between 9 and 13 could work. The Mines and Colliers Act (1842) raised the starting age of colliery workers to 10 years. These two Acts brought an end to the systematic employment of young children.
5 See Montague (1904).
6 On Adult Schools see Kelly (1992) 147–57 with full bibliography, and Rowntree and Binns (1903). The first Adult School opened in 1798, when William Singleton (Methodist) and Samuel Fox (Quaker) set up a school in Nottingham for Bible reading and instruction in writing and arithmetic: see Kelly (1992) 80.
7 Smith (2004).
8 Rowntree and Binns (1903).
9 Mansbridge (1920) 4 in the context of his discussion of Adult Schools as precursors of the WEA.
10 Blackburn (1980) 19.
11 Blackburn (1980) 19.
12 Blackburn (1980) 19.
13 E.g. Fieldhouse (1983). See also Rose (2001) 256–7.
14 Podmore (1905); Kumar (1990).
15 The Weavers in the Scottish Lowlands engaged deeply with Classics and merit further investigation. On the scholarship of Carlisle weavers, who were often politically radical, see Graham (1983) 11–16.
16 For Mutual Improvement Societies see Radcliffe (1997) with full bibliography.
17 Graham (1983) 1.
18 Radcliffe (1997) 142.
19 Dent (1938) 22.
20 Dent (1938) 22.
21 Dent (1938) 26.
22 Inman (1952) 35; on cheap reprint series see Chapter 3.
23 Inman (1952) 44.
24 Inman (1952) 44.
25 Inman (1952) 44.
26 Plato *Apology of Socrates* 41a.
27 Inman (1952) 210.
28 Lee (2016) *ODNB*; Kelly (1992) 118–20.
29 Kelly (1966) 17–20 with further bibliography.
30 Tylecote (1957) 18–21; on the early days of the London Mechanics' Institute see Flexner (2014).
31 Place (1972) 109, 241.
32 Tylecote (1957).
33 Rose (2001) 62–6. Not all institutes were 'top-down'; see Kelly (1992) 123.
34 Kelly (1992) 134.
35 Fieldhouse (1977) 1.
36 Kelly (1992) 112–46.
37 Blackburn (1980) 27.
38 They took the *Daily Citizen* and then the *Manchester Guardian*, as well as *Co-operative News* and *Women's Outlook* (magazine of the Co-operative Women's Guild) Blackburn (1980) 49.
39 Blackburn (1980) 49.

40 Kelly (1992) 112–46.
41 Smith and Matthew (2013) *ODNB* 94.
42 Smith and Matthew (2013) *ODNB* 94.
43 Grugel (1976).
44 For a full discussion of the Mechanics' Institutes and radical opposition to them, see Kelly (1992) 112–46.
45 Stephens (1964) paragraph 14.
46 See www.wmcollege.ac.uk/.
47 Harrison (1954) fig. opposite page 16.
48 Harrison (1954) 59, 61.
49 Lucas (1885) 161.
50 On which see Pimlott (1935).
51 Pimlott (1935) 281–2; Waugh (2009) 4–5, 7.
52 Lucas (1885) 162; see also Maurice (1968) 148-9; Price (1971) 118–19.
53 Lucas (1885) 162.
54 Lucas (1885) 162.
55 Lucas (1885) 183.
56 Lubbock (1887) 1, 8, 15, 28, 30, 32, 36, 40, 42, 44, 47, 56, 64, 95–6, 98.
57 Lubbock (1887) 65–88.
58 Hutchinson (1914).
59 Lubbock (1887) 65–88.
60 Brougham (1840) 12 and Brougham (1893).
61 Rolph (1980) 82–5, 95–6, 132.
62 Paul Selver, chapter 3, recalls learning Greek verse composition from Sidgwick's 'chestnut-covered' work, Grossek (1937) 243; Sidgwick and Morice (1883).
63 Howarth (2004).
64 Thanks are due to Anthony Ellis (Bern University) and Witold Szczyglowski, at the Library and Learning Resource Centre coordinator at the WMC, Camden, for helping to identify 'A.H.S' as Sidgwick.
65 Sidgwick (1920) 259.
66 Murray (1911).
67 Sidgwick (1920) 259.
68 Sidgwick (1920) 259.
69 Sidgwick (1920) 259.
70 Sidgwick (1920) 259–60.
71 Sidgwick (1920) 260.
72 See pp. 479–80; 142 n. 59; 471–3; and 224.
73 Stuart (1911) 70.
74 On Stuart and the beginnings of the movement, see Stuart (1911) 152–93 and Draper (1923) 6–20.
75 Mansbridge (1920) 12–13.
76 Jennings (2002) 40, with further bibliography 191 n. 4; Waugh (2009) 10, who remarks on the running theme of Roman civil strife within the different factions of the adult education movement.
77 Mansbridge (1940) 49–50. For further discussion of the WEA and its detractors, see Rose (2001) 256–97.
78 Mansbridge (1944) 28.
79 Pimlott (1935) 147–8; In 1895 Mansbridge studied Greek at King's College and Latin at Birkbeck; see Mansbridge (1940) 31. For classical studies at Oxford from 1897 see Mansbridge (1940) 39.
80 Pimlott (1935) 54–5, 86.
81 See Borning (1962) xviii–xix.
82 See Oxford (1909).
83 Jennings (2002) 39–42.

84 Goff (2016) 216.
85 Goff (2016) 216.
86 Goff (2016) 231.
87 Goff (2016) 233–4; Stray (1998a) 204.
88 Languages, including the 'learned' ones, were considered beyond their remit: see Goff (2016) 220.
89 Goff (2016) 223.
90 The availability of readable translations and accessible supporting scholarship was clearly a factor in the determination of what made it onto syllabuses.
91 Goff (2016) 225–6; for Roman archaeology courses in the Northern Coal Field see Stead (2018b) 144–6.
92 Wright (1987) 4–5; on Tawney's work at Toynbee Hall, which his father tolerated because his son was not going to get into the Civil Service after failing to get a first-class degree in Greats at Oxford, see Terrill (1973) 28–35. Tawney, whose academic posts were in Economics, was elected to the executive committee of the WEA in 1905 and was its president for nearly two decades (1928–1945).
93 Goff (2016) 228–9.
94 Goff (2016) 228–9.
95 Anon. (1917).
96 Knapp (1923) 24.
97 Knapp (1923) 24.
98 Knapp (1923) 24.
99 Rose (2001) 276.
100 The whole WEA/NCLC debacle has been summarised by Rose (2001) 256–97, and (more incisively) by Waugh (2009).
101 The crucial stress on the independent nature of the working-class education at the dawn of the 20th century was shared not only by radical leftists in Britain and the US, but also by the workers involved in the Public Education movement in revolutionary Russia. See Stead and Paulouskaya (2020, forthcoming).
102 *Plebs* (1909b) 21.
103 *Plebs* (1909a) 1, 3.
104 Craik (1910a), (1910b), (1910c), (1910d), (1910e).
105 Anon. (1914a).
106 Anon. (1914b).
107 Beers (2016) 168.
108 Coleman (1990) 6–8.
109 De Leon (1908) 5.
110 De Leon (1908) 8.
111 De Leon (1908) 9.
112 De Leon (1908) 1.
113 De Leon (1908) 35. The Gracchi had been important to the British labour movement since the late Georgian era. See above pp. 148–59 and Butler (2013) 301–18.
114 De Leon (1908) 33.
115 See Malamud (2018) 122–3; Lieber wrote *Plantations for Slave Labor: The Death of the Yeomanry* (1863).
116 De Leon (1908) 34.
117 De Leon (1908) 34–5.
118 De Leon (1908) 35.
119 De Leon (1908) 37.
120 De Leon (1908) 38–48.
121 De Leon (1908) 48.
122 On Greek thought see Starr (1918) 74–5, under the title: 'Previous Advances in Learning'; on Roman invasion see Starr (1918) 21–2.
123 Lewis (1993) 275.

124 Lewis (1993) 275–6.
125 Lewis (1993) 277.
126 Lewis (1993) 278.
127 Stone (1925) 30.
128 *Plebs* (Nov 1917) 221–2, quoted in Lewis (1993).
129 Stray (1998) 1–2.

10

CLASSICS AND CLASS IN IRELAND

Introduction

The relationship between the Irish and the Greco-Roman world has always been intense, as their literature in both Gaelic and English reveals. Competence in Latin was fostered across even some of the lowest classes by Roman Catholicism and the informal education that a proportion of the poorest Irish children received at informal 'hedge schools'. These were run by educated men disqualified from earning a professional salary under the Penal Laws, which from the 1690s outlawed teaching by Catholics, along with the right to own land or weapons, to vote or hold political office.[1] The widespread knowledge in Irish communities of Latin (sometimes even Greek) baffled the Protestant British governing classes, who associated classical expertise with social prestige. In 1797, the painter George Holmes was astounded to meet, 'in the uncultivated part of the country', some 'good Latin scholars' who could not speak a single word of English.[2] The bafflement aggravated the British fear of Irish insurgency, since ancient history was associated with the Republican ideology of French revolutionaries. When Irish radicals came to England during the Chartist unrest of the 1840s and 1850s, the classical expertise of even those from poor backgrounds often caused astonishment.[3]

Richard Lovell Edgeworth, a prosperous County Longford Anglo-Irishman, supported Catholic emancipation. He was far from the worst oppressor of his Catholic countrymen. Yet in 1808, he reported from Ireland to the Board of Education,

> I have been told that in some schools the Greek and Roman histories are forbidden. Such abridgements of these histories, as I have seen, are certainly

DOI: 10.4324/9781315446608-12

> improper; they inculcate democracy and a foolish sense of undefined liberty; this is particularly dangerous in Ireland.[4]

Some working-class Irish people were indeed incited to rebellious thoughts by classical authors. The 18th-century blind poet of Tipperary, Liam Dall Ó hlfearnáin, describes his utopian vision of British masters being driven from his land, and blackbirds singing even more sweetly 'Than the notes brought by scholars / Over the sea from Rome'.[5]

Pride in classical accomplishments shines through fine Gaelic poetry. This is a verse in a popular drinking-song by Eoghan Rua Ó Súilleabháin (Owen Roe O'Sullivan, 1748–1782), a labourer, teacher and poet often compared with Robert Burns, in an English translation first published in 1855:

> My name is Ó Súilleabháin, a most eminent teacher;
> My qualifications will ne'er be extinct;
> I'd write as good Latin as any in the nation;
> No doubt I'm experienced in arithmetic.[6]

In another poem, where he asks his friend Seamus, a blacksmith, to lend him a spade, we hear that Seamus is a wit, 'Greek-tinged and poetic'.[7] Eoghan is going to Galway to sell his labour for a daily wage of 'breakfast and sixpence'; if exhaustion prevents him from completing the day's work, he will soften the steward's ire by reciting poetry:

> Then calmly I will tell him of the adventure of death
> And of classical battles that left heroes weak.
> Of Samson and high deeds I will talk for a while,
> Of strong Alexander eager for enemies,
> Of the Caesars' dictatorship, powerful and wise,
> Or of Achilles who left many dead in the field,
> Or the fall of the Fenians with terrible slaughter.[8]

For Gaelic poets, Ireland's tragic history could compete with the wars and heroes of classical antiquity; Irish, moreover, was a suitable vehicle as an ancient tongue itself, older than English.[9] Ó Súilleabháin inspired Yeats' alter ego Red Hanrahan, the 'hedge schoolmaster, a tall, strong, red-haired young man', who always carries a copy of Virgil.[10] He is mentioned as a fiery poet in John Millington Synge's *The Playboy of the Western World*.[11] He is revived as Owen MacCarthy, the hard-drinking, womanising, red-headed, multi-lingual poet and schoolmaster, obsessed with Ovid and Virgil, in Thomas Flanagan's distinguished novel about the brutal suppression of the 1798 Irish rebellion, *The Year of the French* (1979).[12]

Yet the few references to Classics in a collection of English-language verses by poets, mostly Protestant weavers, from County Antrim and County Down, seem disrespectful. John Dickey remembers wandering through hedgerows looking for yellowhead flowers or wild beehives while avoiding going to school, 'deeply to explore/The rules of English, Greek or Latin lore'.[13] James Campbell (1758–1818) resorted to a traditional use of Aristotle in rhyme:

> I've oft laid down my shuttle
> To meet my friends and bottle,
> And like great Aristotle,
> I've made my brains to reel.[14]

Sarah Leech, a Protestant weaver from Donegal who called herself 'a peasant girl', published a collection of poems in 1828. (Figure 10.1) She both claims to admire the example of Sappho and undercuts the notion of classical authority by reminding readers that she is herself 'unskill'd in classic lore', having not studied at college, and knows nothing of 'authors sage ... / Like those who speak the Greek and Latin'. She caustically reassures them she will not be leaping off any local cliffs, as Sappho did, out of unrequited love for Phaon.[15]

But the weavers' insouciance towards classical authority is just one amongst multifarious ways in which ancient Greek and Roman culture has haunted English-language literature by Irish authors. The genealogy proceeds from even

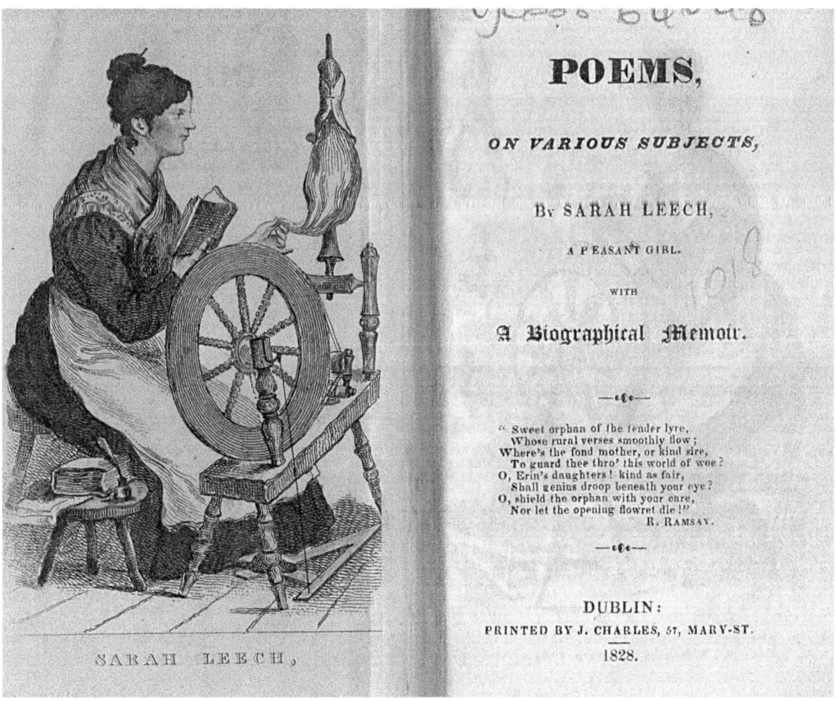

FIGURE 10.1 Frontispiece and title page of Sarah Leech's *Poems* (1828), reproduced from copy in Hall's personal collection.

earlier than Jonathan Swift's dazzling Lucianic satire in *Gulliver's Travels* (1726), via Oscar Wilde, George Bernard Shaw, James Joyce's *Ulysses* (1922), W.B. Yeats' 'Leda and the Swan' (1923) and Louis MacNeice to Seamus Heaney, Michael Longley and the dramatists Frank McGuinness and Marina Carr.[16] The earliest complete English-language translation (rather than adaptation) of Aristophanes, *The World's Idol; or, Plutus the God of Wealth*, is a politicised version by an educated Irishman designating himself as H.H.B., published in 1659. As Rosie Wyles has shown, *The World's Idol* was a landmark in the reception of Aristophanes because it rethought how drama might be used politically, even where theatrical activity had been curtailed. The author was probably the Catholic playwright Henry Burnell, central to the Kilkenny Catholic Confederacy, formed after the 1641 Irish rebellion; the introductory 'Discourse' makes a cryptic case against English colonial military interventions in Ireland and the ignorance which led the English to dismiss the common Irish people as 'barbarous' and in need of civilising. The pain of the dispossessed Irish consequent upon the 1652 Act for the Settlement of Ireland is palpable.[17]

Swift's Jacobite friend Sir Charles Wogan, like Ó Súilleabháin and Burnell, saw classical literature, adopted into either Gaelic or English works, as consonant with his defence of the Irish poor, victims of colonial oppression. After his arrest on a charge of High Treason, he escaped to France from Newgate Prison. Using a motif which became commonplace, he wrote to Swift that the Catholic Irish

> are reduced to the wretched condition of the Spartan helots. They are under a double slavery. They serve their inhuman lordlings, who are the more severe upon them, because they dare not yet look upon the country as their own; while all together are under the supercilious dominion and jealousy of another over-ruling power.[18]

The brutal floggings meted out to the Irish peasantry also attracted the attention of Dennis Taaffe, a Catholic priest and brilliant polemicist active in the Dublin political underground, who fulminated in 1798 that unenfranchised Irishmen 'are the helots, doomed to toil, torture, or death, at the pleasure of their task-masters'.[19]

These men belonged to the broad tradition of Irish classicism, explored in other chapters of our book,[20] as well as in one of the most important works in Classical Reception Studies, *Ireland and the Classical Tradition* (1976) by William Bedell Stanford, then Regius Professor of Greek at Trinity College Dublin. This tradition is not only a matter of ethnic, linguistic or national identity. The Irish labouring and mendicant poor, dominantly Catholic, were always subject to oppression resulting from their *class* position, however much it took racist expression, at the hands of their Anglo-Irish middle-class masters.[21] The near-total absence of autobiographies by Irish Catholics from the 19th century, in contrast with the plentifulness of those by Anglo-Irish subjects,[22] reflects the convergence of boundaries drawn by religion and class. Investigating the subjective experience of the Irish multitude is impeded by the near-absence of pre-1800 records, except for those concerning lawbreakers and recipients of Protestant charity.[23]

What is clear in Ireland's unique political context, however, is a bewildering *complexity* marking the intersection between identities grounded in a combination of class origin or affiliation, political views, language, religion and (in the case of the Scots Irish) original ethnic derivation. A vivid case is the troubled career of the distinguished painter James Barry, some of whose most famous works were allegorical studies of classical mythology ('The Birth of Pandora', 'Jupiter and Juno on Mount Ida' and 'Orpheus Instructing a Savage People'). He was born to a lower-middle-class Protestant father, who operated a cargo coaster out of the Port of Cork. But he enthusiastically adopted the faith of his Catholic mother, whose family had once owned lands but had become poor when they had been confiscated. He was saved from working as a sailor by Edmund Burke, no less, who spotted his talent, took him to England and subsidised his artistic education in Rome, although the two men were in frequent disagreement about politics and Barry's attitudes to authority. The tension between them is sardonically expressed in Barry's 1776 painting 'Portraits of Barry and Burke in the Characters of Ulysses and a Companion fleeing from the Cave of Polyphemus'.[24] Barry was appointed Professor of Painting at the Royal Academy in 1782. But his coarse speaking style, slovenly clothes (he was sometimes mistaken for a beggar),[25] support of Irish peasants, the French revolution, Abolition and Mary Wollstonecraft's feminism led to disputes which culminated in his expulsion from the Academy in 1799 and death in abject poverty seven years later.[26] His inability to embrace the British artistic and political establishments wholeheartedly was undoubtedly related to his confused religious and class identity.

The complexity can also be illustrated by the diverse uses to which people other than Catholic critics of English imperialism named above put the ancient Greeks and Romans. Some of the more colourful of these uses form the subject-matter of this chapter, concluding with the foundational working-class novel of literature in English, Robert Tressell's *The Ragged-Trousered Philanthropists* (1914), an extended meditation on working-class consciousness fundamentally informed by Plato's allegory of the cave.

Hedge school classicists

Interference from England began with the Norman invasion in 1169 and intensified in the 16th century when Ireland's importance grew on account of its position in relation to Atlantic trade routes. The Tudor subjugation was secured when Henry VIII announced that he was King of Ireland in 1541. Ireland was thereafter under the minority control of the Protestant landholders; after the rebellion of the United Irishmen, supported by French troops, was suppressed in 1798, the Acts of Union 1800 incorporated the island into the new United Kingdom of Great Britain and Ireland. More than a century of colonial persecution was to be inflicted upon the Catholic majority until the Irish Free

State was founded in 1922, leaving only the six counties constituting Northern Ireland within the United Kingdom, where they remain today. The picture of the Irish emanating from mainstream England throughout this history took classical expression in the Greek prose composition that won the prestigious Gaisford Prize at Oxford University just before Independence, in 1921. Christian Fordyce produced a pseudo-Herodotean account of the allegedly backward people of Ireland, on whom the rudiments of civilisation were imposed by British imperial administrators under their English monarch, *basileus*; these governors, 'satraps', are favourably likened to the provincial overlords of the Great King of Persia himself.[27]

Ireland is the only territory in our study where aspects of the knotty relationship between social class and Greco-Roman antiquity have previously been treated to a book-length study, Laurie O'Higgins' *The Irish Classical Self: Poets and Poor Scholars in the Eighteenth and Nineteenth Centuries* (2017). She argues that Irish people's sense of identity, crafted by learned Catholics who moved easily between their own island and Continental Europe, embraced traditional Irish saints and folklore but also 'an international past. Their story belonged with that of ancient Israel, the Scythians, the Greeks and Romans. It was part of a venerable and capacious human story'.[28] She reassesses the hedge schools, brought to widespread notice by Brian Friel's play *Translations* (1980), set in 1833, featuring the hedge school of Ballybeg, County Donegal, where Greek and Latin were spoken as well as Gaelic. It was believed that most hedge schools disappeared after many of their teachers died or emigrated during the terrible famine of 1845 to 1849.[29] After Irish Independence in 1922, hedge schools soon passed into nostalgic legend.[30] But they certainly existed, held in temporary structures beneath the shelter of a hedge or in barns.

Anecdotal evidence claimed that hedge school pupils had often learned chunks of Latin and even Greek poetry off by heart, and O'Higgins argues that this was no fantasy.[31] The Baron Coquebert de Monbret, a French diplomatic agent in Ireland between 1789 and 1791, had noticed schoolmasters in Galway earning less than £5 a year, 'who teach Latin and Greek very well to the young people'.[32] Thady O'Conolan (1780–1854) of Sligo, who insisted that he had studied Homer and Virgil as well as Philosophy and Mathematics at a hedge school, later converted to the Protestant faith and by 1807 was running a school with 50 pupils who could attend when they were not cutting turf. They read Homer and Virgil from single battered copies that were shared around; the younger children studied the popular chapbook *Seven Wise Masters of Greece*.[33] O'Conolan regarded Greek as the only language as beautiful as Irish.[34]

Classics books were smuggled in through Irish ports alongside devotional literature. Where there was even a semi-literate community, only one copy was needed, to be shared by loan or recitation. The 1685 ledger of Samuel Helsham, a Dublin bookseller, includes inexpensive Latin textbooks such as the *Sententiae Puerilies* (maxims for children).[35] The explosion in the size of the population in the 18th century led to the development of education as an industry, demonstrated by advertisements: John Fleming, Drogheda printer and bookseller, announced in 1772 that his stock included 'Classical, school and history books'.[36] The poet Antoine Ó'Raifteiri (Anthony Raftery, 1779–1835) studied classical languages at school and possessed a small English book about the ancient gods entitled *Pantheon*, probably the English edition of Pomey's *The Pantheon*, repeatedly reprinted since 1694.[37] Patrick O'Neill of Owning, County Kilkenny, ran his family's farm in 1780 from the age of 15, but constantly enlarged his private library with classical lexica, a Latin Horace, Martial and Ovid's *Heroides*, a Greek *Iliad* and Plutarch's *Lives* in translation.[38] Lower down the socio-economic ladder, hornbooks, chapbooks, broadsides and editions aimed at schools all included substantial classical material—elementary vocabularies, Aesop, extracts from Ovid or versions of Homer; *The Famous or Renowned History of Hector Prince of Troy* included an exciting illustration of the combat between Hector and Ajax in *Iliad* VII (Figure 10.2).[39] The writers of chapbooks were often themselves lower-class; the fee was less than a shilling a time.[40]

FIGURE 10.2 'Hector vs. Ajax', from Anon. (1700b) *The Famous or Renowned History of Hector Prince of Troy*, reproduced by courtesy of The British Library.

Catholic classical scholars and poets

O'Higgins perhaps underestimates possibilities enjoyed by Irish Catholics who could write, if they avoided signs of defiance, and professed gratitude to their Protestant patrons, to rise socially. The brilliant Enlightenment deist thinker John Toland came from destitution at Redcastle near Londonderry; rumour alleged he was the illegitimate son of a Catholic priest.[41] But his intellect was noticed. Once he renounced his Catholicism, he received generous patronage from Protestant families. After he had studied at both Glasgow and Edinburgh universities, English Dissenters financed for him a period at the University of Leiden and another in Oxford. At Oxford he talked to scholars, used the public library and wrote a dissertation on Atilius Regulus (published in 1722), declaring that the story of his death, reported by Livy and Diodorus, was fiction. His next book was his anti-Catholic polemic *Christianity not Mysterious* (1696), which required a philological grasp of New Testament Greek.[42] The book outraged many in Britain, but more in Ireland, where it was publicly burned and banned. Toland was reduced to penury.

He published more than a hundred books about republican authors such as Milton and James Harrington, the Whig principles of tolerance, reason and liberty and the evils committed by established religion. Some of his ideas were revolutionary. He was the first person to argue in Britain that Jews should be given citizenship and equal rights.[43] His profoundly original 1720 treatise *Hypatia* used the barbarous treatment of this ancient mathematician and philosopher by the Alexandrian Christians in the early 5th century CE to attack Catholicism, and argued that women had advanced intellects.[44] But in his anti-clerical and Whig convictions, Toland was an asset to the English intellectual classes who had adopted him and promoted his career.

Even one girl, poor, Catholic and endowed with a talent for classical languages, used them to facilitate her elevation into middle-class society. Constantia Grierson was born Constantia Crawley into an illiterate Irish-speaking family in Graguenamanagh, County Kilkenny.[45] Her father realised her intelligence and she was educated by the parish minister. She became an apprentice midwife, met the poet Laetitia Pilkington in about 1721 and thereafter moved in the same Dublin literary circles as Swift. Pilkington wrote in her *Memoirs* that Grierson had a command of Hebrew, Greek, Latin and French;[46] in their Introduction in *Poems by Eminent Ladies* Colman and Thornton describe her as 'a most excellent scholar, not only in *Greek* and *Roman* literature, but in history, divinity, philosophy, and mathematics'.[47] She married the Scottish publisher George Grierson, a devout member of the Church of Ireland, and edited classical authors for him, including Virgil, Terence and Cicero; she was working on Sallust when she died young.

The work that won most admiration was her three-volume edition of Tacitus published in 1730. Swift wrote to Alexander Pope praising her Latin and Greek scholarship and calling her edition of Tacitus 'fine'.[48] The Lancashire Dissenting classical scholar Edward Harwood described it as 'one of the best edited books ever delivered to the world. Mrs Grierson was a lady possessed of singular erudition'.[49] She also wrote English-language poems, replete with classical allusions, including one in which she mocks another woman for her inadequate knowledge of Latin.[50]

Grierson's Tacitus is a re-edition of Johannes Theodor Ryck's Leiden edition of 1687, but she has corrected errors and written an elegant Latin preface.[51] She presents herself as the loyal subject of the English crown, dedicating the work in unctuous terms to John Carteret, Lord Lieutenant of Ireland 1724–1730, who commissioned the work and has often inspected it during the printing process. She compares the suffering of the ancient Romans under the tyrannical rule of the emperors described by Tacitus with the blissful calm of life under English rule in 1730, in phrases with a Ciceronian ring:

> Felices nos qui in eis temporibus nati sumus, quibus talia nefanda et deflenda Facinora nullo modo nisi ab antiquis Scriptoribus, aut exterarum Gentium Calamitate cognoscere possumus.[52]
>
> Happy are we to be born in times when we can only learn about such evil and lamentable crimes from either ancient writers or the misfortune of foreign peoples!

A similarly obsequious tone marks a prologue she wrote for a play to be performed when Lord and Lady Carteret ('As fam'd a Pair adorns this Isle and Age') were in Ireland.[53]

If a Catholic wanted to rise socio-economically, it never harmed to be noisily grateful to have been colonised. Henry Jones was a Catholic apprentice bricklayer born near Drogheda, Co. Louth, in 1721. He composed a flattering poetic tribute to Lord Chesterfield when he arrived with his wife to assume the Lord-Lieutenancy of Ireland in 1745. It emphasised that HIBERNIA, unlike Jacobite-loving SCOTIA, was an obedient and loyal subject:

> No feuds intestine in *Her* Bosom jar
> No Breath rebellious wakes the Trump of War.
> Her martial Tribe a loyal Fervour feels,
> And Virtue's strength each Manly Bosom feels.[54]

The aristocrat swept the bricklayer off to London to embark on a writing career; before dying there in dissipated penury, Jones produced one successful play on English history. His largely sycophantic poems include an encomium of the Earl of Orrery's translation of Pliny's *Epistles* and one of William Pitt the Elder, likening his oratory in the early days of the Seven Years' War (1756–1763) to Cicero's against Catiline.[55]

Another protégée adopted by the Protestant Ascendancy was Ellen Taylor, the Catholic daughter of an 'indigent cottager' living 'in a poor hut on the commons',[56] who worked as a housemaid near Kilkenny. Her aesthetic sensibility was discovered when she was found weeping by a visiting gentleman as she gazed on a print in the drawing room she had just cleaned; it depicted a woman, perhaps Electra, in tears leaning on a classical urn.[57] The local well-to-do joined forces to publish a collection of her poems (1792); profits were to subsidise a permanent home for the informal school she ran for the poor.

The classically literate Irish Catholic child who made the biggest mark after the Acts of Union 1800 was Thomas 'Anacreon' Moore (1779–1852), an actor, singer and songwriter, well-known in Ireland as a prolific poet and for promoting Irish themes in literature,[58] but in cultural history most famous for being partially responsible, as Byron's literary executor, for burning his scandalous memoirs. Moore was able to graduate from Trinity College in 1795 (in 1793 it had at last allowed Catholics to enrol) and sought his fortune in London. His debut publication was *Odes of Anacreon, Translated into English Verse, with Notes* (1800); these are not authentic works by the archaic poet Anacreon, but the collection of late antique poems on erotic and wine-related themes known as the *Anacreontea* found in the same 10th-century manuscript as the *Palatine Anthology*. The *Anacreontea* had attracted the Anglo-Irish Protestant establishment in the 18th century, but this new, fluid translation was adorned with racy pictures and made an instant impact. It has been described 'as a formative presence at the genesis of British Romanticism'.[59] Moore also wrote a novel set in ancient Greece and Egypt, *The Epicurean* (1827), which is less interested in philosophy than the persecution of the Christians. Sadly, despite immense charm, cultivating an English accent, espousing conservative views and avoiding association with his radical fellow students at TCD, Moore was not always welcome in polite London drawing rooms, 'his plebeian origins as a Dublin grocer's son' being held against him.[60]

Anglo-Irish loyalists

Moore fulfilled, to an extent, his ambition of emulating the literary success enjoyed in London as well as Ireland by many of his Anglo-Irish Protestant countrymen, almost all of whom had been educated at either Kilkenny College (the oldest grammar school in Ireland, founded in 1538[61]), or TCD or both. Such authors had included, by Moore's time, Jonathan Swift and the playwrights Nahum Tate, George Farquhar, Oliver Goldsmith and William Congreve (who was born in England but raised in Ireland). The dramatist Thomas Southerne (1660–1746) was an early example.

The son of a Dublin brewer, Southerne served James II loyally in the army,[62] and was consequently careful to embrace the principles of the Glorious Revolution with enthusiasm.[63] He is best known for his influential 1695 stage adaptation of Aphra Behn's 1688 novel *Oroonoko*, but the progressive views on slavery and race it espoused did not extend to the white working classes. He wrote a play based on an episode from Livy XXIII (with insertions from books

XXV and XXVI), *The Fate of Capua* (performed at Lincoln's Inn Fields in 1700), in which the Capuans rebel in favour of Hannibal. Southerne emphasised that such mobs are uncouth, fickle and incapable of sensible decisions, basing his stage crowds on those in Shakespeare's *Coriolanus*. He completed Dryden's *Cleomenes, the Spartan Hero* (1692), and in 1719 found success with a similar drama, *The Spartan Dame*, drawing on another Plutarch biography, that of Agis.[64] Its politics are inherently conservative: 'As in *The Fate of Capua*, the Grecian mobs might have come from Eastcheap. The ignorant rabble quibbles much in the manner of Shakespeare's plebeians'.[65] Crites (III.1) says that 'they shake/Their brainless coxcombs, reading dirty palms/They snuffle out their fears'.[66]

The politics of Arthur Murphy (1727–1805) were even more reactionary. A Catholic native of County Roscommon originally from a lowly labouring background, he was sent by his widowed and impoverished mother to live with her sister in France. Before moving to London, he became an outstanding classical scholar at the famous English Jesuit College at St Omer.[67] A significant author, Murphy wrote biographies of Dr. Johnson, Fielding and Garrick and translated Latin prose, including Sallust and Cicero: his 1793 translation of Tacitus remained standard into the 20th century. But it also 'provided the occasion for his expression of anti-republicanism in response to the French revolution'.[68] In accordance with the 18th-century British taste for 'She-Tragedies',[69] he enjoyed hits with two vaguely anti-tyrannical tragedies featuring traumatised classical heroines. *Zenobia* (1768) draws on Tacitus' *Annals* XII–XIII and *The Grecian Daughter* (1772) dramatises a tale of filial piety from Valerius Maximus' *On Memorable Things Said and Done* (5.4).[70] But Murphy's last Tacitean classical play, *Arminius*, was an anti-Jacobin assault on any threat to the constitution, in which he revealed himself as violently anti-democratic, drawing on Quintilian, Lucan and Montesquieu along with Tacitus and other Roman historians in the process.[71] It was deemed unperformable.

Anglo-Irish radicals

The Anglo-Irish community produced radicals as well as conformists like Southerne anxious to pursue careers in England. In 1778 Thomas Campbell, a Church of Ireland clergyman dismayed by the ignorance of Irish affairs he encountered in England and by the dreadful policies that resulted, published a survey of rural life in Ireland aimed at changing opinion (James Boswell facetiously described it as 'entertaining'[72]). Campbell argued for reform of the penal code, and when describing the reaction of some Irish cottagers to their new landlord, followed Sir Charles Wogan in writing that they, 'like the *Helots*, were afraid of the lash of their accustomed masters'.[73] Helotage as metaphor for oppression of the Irish was also used by the noted Church of Ireland champion of Catholic emancipation, William Todd Jones, a man subsequently imprisoned for his political activities. In 1784 he complained that the way that the unemancipated Irish were treated meant that 'the ancient faith and ancient arms of Ireland ought to merge in the infamy of Grecian Helots'.[74] Eight years later, Jones said that the despotic power of the English settler 'over his Irish feudatory' was as bad as Spartan helotage.[75] He compared the licence that ancient Spartans had to kill helots with the outrageously lenient punishment received by a Protestant for killing a 'mere Irishman'. Irish writers frequently go beyond comparison or analogy to a subjective identification of the Irish with helots, in the most extreme instances using 'Helot' as a pseudonym, as in the *Letters of an Irish Helot* (1785) by the Presbyterian William Drennan, who was tried in 1794 for sedition.[76]

Jones and Drennan were both from Ulster and members of the United Irishmen, the early Irish republican movement, active between 1791 and 1798, which proposed an independent Ireland run by all religious denominations on an equal basis.[77] The focus of their activity and that of other local radicals was the Belfast Library and Society for Promoting Knowledge, which developed out of the Belfast Reading Society, founded on 13th May 1788 on the model of Benjamin Franklin's Library Company of Philadelphia.[78] Its founders were 'worthy plebeians who would do honour to any town, [of whom] not one among them was of higher rank than McCormick the gunsmith or Osborne the baker'.[79] There were similarly politicised initiatives in Dublin and Cork: the Cork National Reading Room was not just a meeting place and a library but a focus of political debate and Fenian agitation.[80] But there were higher literacy levels in Ulster.[81] There was a book club in Doagh, County Antrim, founded by local schoolteacher William Galt in 1768; in County Down the Newry Literary Society was founded in 1768, the Portaferry Literary society the same year, the Newtownards Society for Acquiring Knowledge in 1789 and the Ballnahinch Reading Club in 1790. Their collections always included popular classical authors such as Homer and Plutarch. But 'many of these northern societies were looked on with suspicion by the ruling class and the government, and some were to suffer accordingly'.[82] The libraries of the Doagh Book Club and the Newry Literary Society were destroyed after the 1798 rebellion.[83]

Originally a subscription society, for which the fee was kept to only one shilling a month,[84] the Belfast Library helped earn Belfast's reputation at that time as the 'Athens of the North'; the scientific and literary achievements of its people, facilitated by access to the sea for commerce and early industrial development, especially after Nicholas Grimshaw opened his water-powered spinning mill at Whitehouse in 1784. Education was advanced; a school opened in the High Street in 1760 by David Manson taught pupils of both sexes to read with teaching cards, books and grammars which revolutionised education across Ireland; there were two circulating libraries by 1775.

The earliest members of the Belfast Society almost all had radical tendencies and carried a motion as early as 1792 that Catholics must be admitted, which was noticed with dismay by the administrators at Dublin Castle and Westminster; women were also allowed membership.[85] Its second president wrote approvingly in 1793 that it did 'much honour to the sansculottes of Belfast ... sensible and reading mechanics'.[86] The library, which contained books on science, natural history, philosophy, the arts and all kinds of literature, including classical authors, acquired a museum and moved to Ann Street (in 1801 it moved again to the White Linen Hall), resolving to establish a Free School for the education of the sons of the poor. This was instrumental in the excellent provision of elementary education in 19th-century Belfast.[87] But the 1798 rebellion saw several of the Society's members arrested for the possession of seditious material, along with other United Irishmen across the country. Its charismatic librarian Thomas Russell, an expert classical scholar whose republicanism was fed by his interest in ancient history and literature, and who had been the one to suggest turning the reading group into a more public-facing educational institution,[88] was one of them.

Russell was home-schooled in Greek and Latin by his father, a classicist who had trained for the Church of Ireland at Kilkenny College until he was expelled for reading banned books. The youth, born at Betsborough, Dunnahane, Co. Cork, in 1787, was well-read; few, it was said, 'even with the advantage of a university education, could enter on the world better informed'.[89] He went to India to serve in the army but left after five years, disgusted by 'the unjust and rapacious conduct pursued by the authorities in the case of two native women'.[90] On his return, he met Wolfe Tone, a founding member of the United Irishmen, whose father was a Church of Ireland coach-maker but whose mother had been raised a Catholic. They spent the summer of 1790 together. Russell then acquired a position in the 64th regiment, quartered at Belfast.[91] He was a committed Christian, but objected to the regime's insistence that people charged with crimes were obliged to declare their religious denomination.[92]

He was impressed by the intellectual and political awareness of the northern Irish, observing that

> there does not exist a class of people in the same line of life, who possess the same enlarged ideas, or minds as well stored with knowledge, as the farmers and manufacturers of the province of Ulster.[93]

He admired their progressive views; they took responsibility for their poor not only by setting up accommodation and education for them but by attending to the city's paving, lighting and plumbing.[94] After attending a 1791 meeting of the Belfast Whig club held to celebrate Bastille Day, Russell abandoned the army and helped found the Belfast Society of Irishmen, leading its County Down militia. His friend and political ally, the physician Dr. James McDonnell, secured for him the post of librarian to the Belfast Society. Russell's 1796 polemic *Letter to the People of Ireland* proposes social, economic, political and constitutional reforms and support for the abolition of slavery; he was arrested at the library and held captive for six years in Dublin and Fort George in Scotland. His military skills meant that he was regarded as a particular threat, and he was unable to join in the 1798 uprising. He was exiled to Hamburg in 1802, but went instead to Paris, and thence to Ireland, where he participated in the doomed 1803 rebellion organised by Robert Emmett. This led to his arrest and execution, like Emmett, for High Treason. At the age of 32, he was first hanged, then beheaded.

Russell's roughly jotted diaries, which were never intended to be read by anyone else, reveal that his social ideas were informed by classical authors. He quotes Latin, argues about Horace at a dinner party with Tories and translations of Virgil with other Belfast radicals, and writes a whole essay criticising the Stoics, including Marcus Aurelius, for arguing that poverty is not an evil and for persecuting Christians.[95] He notes with approval that there are Catholic schools in the Cavan hills where children learn Latin, and that a reading society (probably the Doagh Book Club) had originated, as in Belfast, 'among the lower orders' and that most of the books were on history, philosophy and politics.[96] But it was as main contributor to the United Irishmen's newspaper, the *Northern Star*, that his classical learning was put to political use.

A target was fellow Irishman Edmund Burke's 1790 *Reflections on the Revolution in France*, in a satire worthy of the Swiftian tradition, by Russell and a radical barrister named William Sampson. It consisted of instalments of a review of a fictitious epic poem called *The Lion of Old England*. The apocryphal poem related the adventures of the English Lion, silenced by Burke's flattery. A flavour is conveyed by its discussion of the supposed Canto IV, on the Etonian Richard Howe, Commander of the Channel Fleet in the French Revolutionary Wars:

> We now find the Lion once more at sea with Lord Howe, in sight of the French fleet. The various ships which compose each line, are described in a very lively manner, also the personal qualities of each commander—we are sorry however to find too servile an imitation of the descriptions of Homer and Virgil.[97]

The satire parodies both patriotic British eulogies of leading men and the pompous classicism of literary journalism, larded with inept quotations from, for example, Plautus' *Captivi*.[98]

The epic's purported climax, published in *Northern Star* on October 31st, 1793, comes when Burke is appointed Prophet in the 'Temple of the Constitution' and in Canto XII delivers a panegyric of the Lion:

> Most noble and redoubted Lion bold,
> Know that the glories which you here behold,
> Beneath this temple's venerable dome,
> Are the proudest boasts of Greece or Rome—
> Even, as the spacious firmament on high,
> Is to the frail crust of a mutton pye.[99]

The verbose Prophet continues, hilariously, to compare the temple with the Roman amphitheatre [i.e. Colosseum] 'which has properly been denominated Amorphous, consisting of so many sides, curves, and angles, as to baffle all measurement' and to 'that inextricable labyrinth in Crete, in which it was impossible to expatiate without being lost'. The Island of the English Lion 'stands alone, like a bright gem on the bosom of the Ocean, which occasioned the poet of antiquity to say of its inhabitants, that, they were "*penitus toto divisos orbe Britannos*" ('Britons utterly separated from the whole world', Virgil, *Ecl.* 1.67). The orotund Prophet claims that Britain's origin is 'lost in the clouds of antiquity, which proves it divine'.[100]

The Latin professor, the Easter Rising and the working class

Russell was betrayed by Dr. James McDonnell, the man who had helped him gain the post of librarian. Drennan, their mutual friend, and author as we have seen of *Letters of an Irish Helot*, was outraged and may have been the author of the 'Epitaph for the Living', which accused McDonnell of being the turncoat 'Brutus of Belfast'.[101] But Russell's influence lived on. The Belfast Library he had administered was involved in the establishment of Belfast's own university, Queen's, in 1849, advising on its library provision.[102]

Like Russell, Robert Mitchell Henry (1873–1950), [Figure 10.3] Professor of Latin at Queen's, editor of Livy XXVII (on which see also Thomas Southerne, above), risked his life in the cause of Irish republicanism. In 1916, as a prominent

FIGURE 10.3 R.M. Henry (1873–1950) by unknown artist, reproduced courtesy of the McClay Library, Belfast.

Ulster public figure, he had much to lose. He was, nevertheless, involved in the struggle on the ground. On several dates between January and late March 1916, Henry wrote in his pocket diary that he was attending rifle practice.[103] These notices cease at the precise moment of the Easter Uprising in April 1916. The rifle practices he was attending were those of the local branch of the Irish Volunteers.

This organisation had come into being in Dublin on 25th November 1913, in response to the establishment in January 1913 of the Ulster Volunteers, the militia opposed to the introduction of Home Rule. While its membership overlapped with the constituencies that supported Sinn Féin—the Irish Citizens' Army and the Irish Republican Brotherhood—the Irish Volunteers (IV) was a separate initiative.[104] By the outbreak of World War I, there were at least 100,000 Irish Volunteers, which made the British authorities nervous. In July 1914, at Howth, the IV unloaded a shipment of 1,500 rifles, with 45,000 rounds of ammunition, purchased from Germany.

There were many Irish Volunteers in the northern counties and Belfast, although the atmosphere there was threatening to advocates of Irish independence. Henry's involvement is corroborated by his partisan eye-witness account of the training in which both the UV and IV members engaged in his most famous book, which was not on Latin literature, *The Evolution of Sinn Féin*.[105] In this, Henry occasionally inserts Latin phrases: in discussing how fast the early Anglo-Norman planters adopted Irish identity, he cites the old Latin saying, 'more Irish than the Irish themselves', *Ipsis hibernis Hiberniores*, sometimes attributed to Swift.[106] A tactic of the officers of the Royal Navy is likened to what Cicero calls Catiline's policy of putting out the fire by demolishing the house, *ruina exstinguere incendium* (*Pro Murena* 51).[107]

In a rare reference to a Greek author, Henry invokes Thucydides on 'ancient simplicity' (3.38.1) when describing the naive integrity that marked John Redmond and his proposed terms for the 1914 Home Rule Bill: 'with that simplicity of character, which, as the Greek historian says, "makes up a great part of good breeding", he promised without conditions'.[108] But the only words in ancient Greek in the book are kept for what is, in the arc of Henry's tragic narrative, the climax. The IV became infiltrated by violent advocates of immediate armed rebellion. Henry says they were affected simply by physical contact with weapons:

> The Volunteers were in the opinion of Sinn Féin a useful auxiliary in the task of developing the one quality from which alone ultimate success was to be expected, the self-reliance and moral resolution of the Irish people. But αὐτὸς γὰρ ἐφέλκεται ἄνδρα σίδηρος—the mere "sheen of arms" has an attraction superior to all arguments and all policies … the superior attractions of the Volunteers proved too strong for many young and ardent Sinn Féiners and induced them to put the means first and the end second.[109]

It was the availability of rifles, suggests Henry, that turned heads, when what was needed was cool deliberation.

The Greek means 'the iron itself draws a man on'. It is a quotation, minus the connective 'for', of a phrase from the *Odyssey*, αὐτὸς γὰρ ἐφέλκεται ἄνδρα σίδηρος, so famous that Juvenal quoted it with an obscene twist (*Sat.* 9.37). In the *Odyssey* it occurs twice (16.294, 19.13), in the mouth of Odysseus when he instructs Telemachus to hide the arms from the suitors. This saying is to be Telemachus' response if they should protest at his removal of access to the weapons. The context may have seemed as appropriate to Henry as the content: Odysseus' instruction is part of his detailed plan, entailing patience, caution and timeliness, which he says must be implemented before his loyal slaves and impetuous son may begin ridding the household of its unwanted occupants.

Henry deserves a biography which does justice to his copious documents in the McClay Library. At Easter 1916, he was in danger of being arrested himself. His longstanding commitment to the cause of an independent Ireland had won him few friends professionally. An expert in Latin, Greek and also Hebrew, he understood that a shared ancient language and a rich literature were indispensable to any culture's unity. His political views were mirrored in his regret that most of his compatriots had been deprived of their ancestral tongue. A searing passage in his history of Sinn Féin records, in his biting Tacitean tone, the impact of the 1800 Acts of Union and the imposition in 1831 of the 'National' Education System:[110] Henry mournfully observes that the task of 'educating' the nation out of its traditional language and culture was virtually complete by the end of the 19th century.

He supported Sinn Féin's cultural policies. In 1908, his diary includes references to attendance at meetings of the Gaelic Society. He was 'one of the staunchest allies' of William MacArthur,[111] another Belfast Protestant (Presbyterian) Gaelic enthusiast who, as a student at Queen's, campaigned for the introduction of Gaelic classes from 1903 and founded the College Gaelic Society in 1906. Henry spoke at its public meeting in the Great Hall in 1908, which resulted in the establishment of a new lectureship in Celtic in 1909.[112] Nor did his devotion to the cause of the working class ever vary: on 29th March of the same year, his diary records that he attended a lecture entitled 'Socialism' at the Literary Society.

The Latin Professor made an extraordinary contribution to the historiography of Sinn Féin and the background to the Easter Uprising in which he was prepared to risk his life. *The Evolution of Sinn Féin* is a short, intense and exquisitely written tragic history of Ireland culminating in the execution of Patrick Pearse, James Connolly and their 11 fellow leading rebels. Henry writes, his controlled anger palpable,

> At the same time arrests took place all over the country. Three thousand prisoners who had taken no part in the Rising were collected, many of them as innocent of any complicity in the affair as the Prime Minister. To have been at any time a member of the Irish Volunteers was sufficient cause for arrest and deportation. They were taken through the streets in

lorries and in furniture vans at the dead of night and shipped for unknown destinations.[113]

Whether any British official investigated Henry's links with the rebellion is not known; there is no direct trace in his papers. He decided to continue the fight through influencing public opinion by writing rather than fighting.[114]

After partition, to which he objected, Henry continued to exercise his political muscles in the twin causes of Classics and of the pan-Irish, especially the working class. His diaries for 1919 and 1920 record his attendances on numerous Trade Boards in Dublin and Belfast—those concerning the Tobacco, Confectionery, Box, Embroidery, Spinning, Shirtmaking and Rope Boards, as well as the Belfast Water Board and Co-operative Council. He supported Trade Unions and activities such as the Belfast Newsboys' Club. He was co-signatory of a letter in June 1925 asking potential donors to support the club,

> which it is proposed to conduct on civic and un-denominational lines … The value of the human material in the streets of Belfast is at once apparent, and if this little effort helps to make good citizens of some of them it will not have been made in vain.[115]

He was key to the foundation of the Belfast Workers' Educational Association in 1910. The minutes of the University Extension Committee amongst his papers show that there were 28 attendees for Course of Lectures on Civics by Professor John Laird, including 'The Ideal of Freedom', 'The Hope in Democracy' in 1920 and 56 for his own lectures on 'Roman Social Life Under the Early Empire'. He brought in lectures on Greek civilisation in 1922–1923: drafts of his talks on ancient women, labourers and slaves are all in the archive, including 'Working Class Life in the Early Roman Empire'. He contributed a long utopian socialist essay entitled 'The Ideal City' to *The Voice of Labour*, the 'Official Organ of the Irish Transport and General Workers' Union',[116] arguing for the importance of culture, education and recreation. As a result of his efforts, the senate of Queen's University created the post of lecturer and director of extramural studies in 1928.[117]

Henry was widowed without children soon after his first marriage and did not remarry again until an advanced age. He was, however, attached to his younger brothers, helping out the impecunious Paul Henry, a painter famous today. His landscapes of Achill Island and Connemara are associated with the Irish Free State's rural vision.[118] Paul remembered attending marches in 1898 on the Falls Road, marking the centenary of the 1798 uprising. No doubt his older brother had taken him.[119]

Robert Tressell's Platonic Cave of false ideology

This chapter has moved between regions of Ireland, but concludes with an exceptionally significant Irish author who, from his teens, never visited the land where he had been born just three years before Henry, in 1870; poor health and grinding poverty led him to a much earlier death and a pauper's grave, in 1911. In Robert Tressell's *The Ragged-Trousered Philanthropists* (Figure 10.4) the Irish tradition of political satire, informed by ancient literature and inaugurated by Jonathan Swift in the early 18th century, reached its most influential culmination prior to Independence. A short retrospective of Swift's satire is needed here, since Swift was overwhelmingly Tressell's favourite author.

Swift's usual satirical models were Lucian and Juvenal, but his relationship with Dr. Thomas Sheridan, pioneer in the performance of ancient plays,[120] and his personal library, reveal an intense interest in classical drama, especially the Roman comedy of Plautus.[121] Swift was a member of the Anglican Church, who was appointed Dean of St. Patrick's in Dublin; as a young man, he had been a member of the Whig party. He feared the restoration of the Catholic monarchy. But he feared Dissenters just as much, and his political views began to tend in a Tory direction. It is remarkable that later in life he became the most eloquent of spokesmen on the plight of the Irish poor, who regarded him as a heroic patriot.

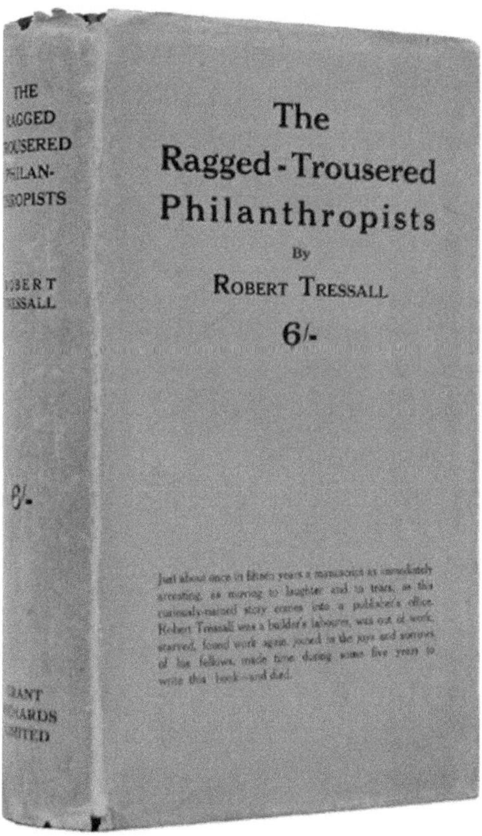

FIGURE 10.4 Cover of first edition of Tressell's *The Ragged-Trousered Philanthropists* (1914), reproduced from Hall's personal collection. Curiously, his name is given a slightly different spelling from that used in later editions.

There is no doubt about the raw class consciousness underlying Swift's masterpiece of sustained polemical irony, written during the crisis caused by series of disastrous harvests,[122] *A Modest Proposal for preventing the children of poor people in Ireland, from being a burden on their parents or country, and for making them beneficial to the publick* (1729). Its opening sentence describes 'the streets, the roads and cabbin-doors' of Ireland, 'crowded with beggars of the female sex, followed by three, four, or six children, all in rags, and importuning every passenger for an alms'.[123] He suggests that the problems of the poor in Ireland might be solved if they sold their children, who could be eaten by the rich. He is reliably informed that a one-year-old provides 'a most delicious nourishing and wholesome food, whether stewed, roasted, baked, or boiled; and I make no doubt that it will equally serve in a fricasie, or a ragoust'.[124] Swift targets the new rationalist economics of his era, but he also exposes callous treatment of the poor and British policies in Ireland. The chief classical model for *A Modest Proposal* was long assumed to have been Juvenal,[125] but the Carthaginian Church Father Tertullian's *Apologeticus*, a defence of Christianity composed around 197 CE, is more important.[126] Tertullian sends up the popular pagan allegation that Christians eat babies, pretending to argue that it is an excellent idea (2.5; 8.7 and 8.1–.2).

Swift's perhaps most outrageous use of a classical author was his libellous literary tour of the foul-smelling, corrupt Irish Parliament in *A Character, Panegyric, and Description of the Legion Club* (1736), which subverts Aeneas' visit to the Underworld in *Aeneid* VI. Yet of all ancient authors, it was Plato whom Swift most admired. He owned two editions of Plato, and chose the head of Socrates as the image on his personal seal.[127] The *Republic* is central to his political philosophy and use of allegory.[128] Although Socratic ideas permeate his work, especially when he is puncturing pompous Christian dogmas, it is in Book IV.8 of *Gulliver's Travels* that the influence of Platonic epistemology is best revealed. It is difficult for the Houyhnhnm master, a commonsensical spokesman of Socratic belief in the distinction between true knowledge and opinion, to comprehend

> the meaning of the word opinion, or how a point could be disputable; because reason taught us to affirm or deny only where we are certain, and beyond our knowledge we cannot do either.[129]

Nearly two centuries later, an Irish admirer of Plato and Swift named Robert Noonan wrote a satire dissecting the false opinions about reality which allowed the oppressive British class system to perpetuate itself. The central trope of *The Ragged-Trousered Philanthropists*, published posthumously in 1914 under the pseudonym Robert Tressell, is the famous Platonic allegory of the cave.[130]

The novel narrates a dark, cold winter in the lives of a group of Edwardian workmen renovating a mansion near Hastings known as 'The Cave', and their oppression by capitalist overlords. It analyses their sedation by alcohol and unthinking reproduction of false ideas required to perpetuate their oppression.

These ideas are disseminated by the Church, the Judiciary, Parliamentarians and the press, in particular by three newspapers known as *The Obscurer*, the *Weekly Chloroform* and the *Ananias* (the name of the disciple Jesus sent to cure Paul of blindness and offer him theological instruction).[131] Just one worker, a painter and decorator named Frank Owen, has studied socialism and Marxism, and 'has seen the light'—the truth about the economic system. He is as angry with his colleagues for their uncritical regurgitation of the lies they are fed as with their evil exploiters. Tressell uses the Platonic allegory of the Cave to explore the notion of false consciousness. The novel begins thus:

> The house was named "The Cave". It was a large old-fashioned three-storied building standing in about an acre of ground, and situated about a mile outside the town of Mugsborough. It stood back nearly two hundred yards from the main road and was reached by means of a by-road or lane, on each side of which was a hedge formed of hawthorn trees and blackberry bushes.[132]

Attention is soon drawn to the strange name of the house. One of the workers comments, when things have unexpected names, 'There's generally some sort of meaning to it, though'.[133] 'In the semi-darkness' of this Cave, 'the room appeared to be of even greater proportions than it really was'.[134]

Nobody acquainted with philosophy can fail to be reminded of *Republic* VII, where Socrates asks Glaucon to imagine a group of men living in an underground cave, approached by a long passage leading to the daylight. The men have been chained there from infancy, with their necks bound so they can only see in front of them. A fire burns at some distance behind and above them; between the men and the fire a wall resembling the screen set up by puppet masters. Other men carry objects which show above the wall—statues and model animals. The prisoners, naturally, infer that the shadows of these objects case upon the back wall of the cave which they must face are the only realities. But Socrates argues that if one of them were set free and led towards the fire, and then the sunlight, he would eventually accept that the sun is the real cause of everything in the visible world, and that the shadows down in the cave were unreal.

Plato's Socrates, of course, does not believe that the empirically discernible world lit by the sun is real, either: it is just a second-rate imitation of the real world of the ideal forms, which are invisible to the naked eye and only apprehensible by those trained in philosophy. But Noonan, in a brilliant transposition of the allegory, reminiscent of Swift's use of Plato, employs the Cave to expose how people living under an oppressive class system accept the ideology used to maintain it, which is in reality as false as the shadows the Platonic prisoners think are existent objects.[135]

The Ragged-Trousered Philanthropists was based on Noonan's own experiences as politically conscious underpaid painter/decorator and single father trying to survive in Hastings in the early 1900s.[136] His suspicion of religion and sensitivity to class hierarchies resulted from his Dublin childhood, when he must have felt as though he belonged fully to neither the Protestant Ascendancy nor the Catholic underclass. His father, who was old when Robert was born, was Samuel Croker, a retired Royal Ulster Constabulary officer who could read New Testament Greek.[137] Croker was a bigamist and may not have been married to Robert's mother, a poor Catholic named Mary Noonan. Croker died in 1875, but left money for his son to be educated (it is not known how or where he learned either his several languages—French, German, Dutch, Spanish, Italian, Gaelic, Latin and probably ancient Greek[138]—or his manual skills); his mother married a man named John O'Reilly who resented his stepchildren, and Robert ran away by the age of 16. He changed his name to Noonan, and by 1890 was working as a sign writer living in Liverpool. Charged with housebreaking and larceny, he served six months in Walton Gaol before emigrating to South Africa.[139] Eleven years later, he was back in England with a daughter but no wife, as a member of the International Independent Labour Party and of the Painters' Union.[140] He settled in Hastings, where unemployment was driving many to Poor Law relief, the workhouse and soup kitchens.[141]

From September 1903 to June 1904 he worked for Burton & Co. Building Contractors on the Val Mascal, a villa built in 1891 for the wealthy elite and owned by John Upson, who lived by private investment. It is the primary template for the Cave.[142] Noonan had conceived the idea for the book by 1907. His daughter and co-workers recalled that he retained an Irish accent, was a voracious reader and constantly copying extracts out. He often quoted Shakespeare, Fielding, Shelley, Byron, William Morris, Walter Crane and especially Swift. He scoured second-hand bookshops; according to a young workmate much influenced by him called William Gower, he organised an informal reading list/personal lending library for his workmates, which included Plutarch's *Lives*, Aristotle's *Poetics*, Pliny, Gibbon and of course Plato. He was close friends with one Father O'Callaghan, with whom he talked for hours.[143]

He took the pseudonym Tressell from the prop tables used by decorators, which appear in the novel (with that spelling, rather than trestle), where they support a coffin.[144] The title was inspired by the Republican journal which the youthful Wordsworth had planned to edit, *The Philanthropist*, and by the hypocritical use of this noun by exploitative civic 'benefactors';[145] Noonan originally intended calling the novel *The Ragged-Arsed Philanthropists*.[146] But he died of lung disease in Liverpool, intending to emigrate once again, in 1911; it was his daughter who succeeded in getting it published.

In Chapter I, Owen insists that the workers should have access to what

> we call civilisation—the accumulation of knowledge which has come down to us from our forefathers—is the fruit of thousands of years of human thought and toil. It is not the result of the labour of the ancestors of any separate class of people who exist today, and therefore it is by right the common heritage of all.[147]

His book collection sits beside his household fire, like the first signpost to true knowledge marked by the fire in Plato's cave;[148] there are extended sequences in the novel concerning a fire in the cave and also the installation of blinds to make it impossible to see daylight through the windows. The Platonic dimension is also revealed in the form, which, beginning with the 'Philosophical Discussion' at the 'Imperial Banquet' (recalling Plato's *Symposium*) in Chapter I, where the booze-loving labourer with the apt name of Philpot is described as 'philosophic', often takes the form of dialogue. Owen lays out propositions, leading his interlocutors on by question and answer to infer what he regards as the truths about the economic system. Sometimes he even uses diagrams drawn with decorating materials on the floor, like Socrates in Plato's *Meno*.[149] He is at his most Socratic in Chapter XV, where the men debate the existence of God:

> "If Gord didn't create the world, 'ow did it come 'ere?" demanded Slyme.
>
> "I know no more about that than you do," replied Owen. "That is—I know nothing. The only difference between us is that you THINK you know. You think you know that God made the universe; how long it took Him to do it; why He made it; how long it's been in existence and how it will finally pass away. You also imagine you know that we shall live after we're dead; where we shall go, and the kind of existence we shall have … But really you know no more of these things than any other human being does; that is, you know NOTHING."[150]

Over the last century, the novel has helped hundreds of thousands of Trade Unionists and workers to understand the workings of capitalism, as its frequent reprintings, dramatisations and film adaptations demonstrate. Len McCluskey, the General Secretary of Unite union, remembers his father saying that it was passed around the soldiers during World War II and helped the Labour Party to win their landslide victory in the 1945 election.[151] In 2009, after a BBC Radio 4 serialisation, it reached number 6 on the Amazon 'Movers and Shakers' list.[152] Through fusing Plato with the tradition of Irish political satire, Robert Noonan had put Classics to one of its most influential class-conscious uses in history.

This chapter has discussed Irish working-class Catholics who became classically skilled, some of whom supported Irish rebellion, such as Ó Súilleabháin and Ó'Raifteiri, and some of whom ardently opposed it, such as Toland, Grierson and Murphy. It includes classically educated working-class Catholic authors, like Moore, whose writings are informed by varying degrees of class consciousness, and Protestants unremittingly loyal to the English government. But two of the most radical Irish classicists campaigning in the interests of the Irish working classes were also Protestants—Thomas Russell and Robert Mitchell Henry, who were Church of Ireland and Nonconformist respectively; inspired by classical authors, they risked their lives in the uprisings of 1798 and 1916 on behalf of their poorest compatriots and the ideal of a free, united, non-sectarian Ireland. But the discussion has concluded with a novel by an expatriate Irishman who was both working- *and* middle-class, Catholic *and* Protestant. Perhaps it took Robert Noonan's hybrid identity to produce a work of such penetrating insight into the structures which have always kept down the working class, in Ireland and everywhere else.

Notes

1 O'Higgins (2017) 100.
2 Holmes (1801) 151; see further McManus (2004) 128–9.
3 See Ch. 13, pp. 284–7.
4 See Loeber and Stouthamer-Loeber (1999) 126 with O'Higgins (2017) 8 and no. 35. See also pp. 16 and 271.
5 Keefe (1977) 29.
6 Petrie (2002 [1903]) 158.
7 'Friend of my heart', translated in Keefe (1977) 32–3.
8 Translated in Keefe (1977) 33.
9 See the fascinating collection of material, with translations from Irish texts, in O'Higgins (2017) 53–98.
10 Yeats (1913) 1, 15. On Ó Súilleabháin's classical hedge school at Faha, see also McManus (2004) 87–8, 128.
11 Synge (1907) 19.
12 See Dillon (1979).
13 Hewitt (1974) 114.
14 Hewitt (1974) 24.
15 Leech (1828) 53, 55–6.
16 See e.g. Stanford (1976); Lamters (2000); McDonald and Walton (2002); Hall and Macintosh (2005), index s.v. 'Ireland'; Hall (2005b) Freeman (2001); Torrance and O'Rourke (forthcoming).
17 Wyles (2007).
18 Wogan (1789) 37. Wogan's original letter was undated, but written between the commencement of their correspondence in 1732 and Swift's death in 1745. See Hodkinson and Hall (2011) 89. On the adoption of the word 'helot' in the English language in reference to underclasses, see especially Cartledge (2004) 169.
19 Taaffe (1798) 10.
20 See e.g. pp. 147–54.
21 Beckett (1976) 64–5.
22 Grubgeld (2004) 3–4.
23 Carpenter (2018).
24 Lowe (1997) 62–4.
25 Webb (1878) 12.
26 Lowe (1997). Barrell (2017) seriously underestimates Barry's political radicalism.
27 Fordyce (1921).
28 O'Higgins (2017) 29.
29 O'Higgins (2017) 113–14.
30 See e.g. Corkery (1924) and Dowling (1935).
31 O'Higgins (2017) 36–51 and *passim*. See also the excellent study of hedge schools by McManus (2004).
32 Quoted from the manuscript diary of Charles-Etienne, Baron Coquebert de Monbret, in Ní Chinnéide (1978) 21; see further O'Higgins (2017) 121–2.
33 Owenson (1807) 131–50. See further below p. 416 and n. 49.
34 See Owenson (1807) 132, de Brún (2009) 14–39; O'Higgins (2017) 45–6.
35 Pollard (1989) 241, 243.
36 Finegan (1996) 45.

37 Gregory (1903) 26; see also Ó'Coigligh (1987) 37, 250 and O'Higgins (2017) 45. On Pomey's book, see above pp. 52–3.
38 Ó'Néill (2000) 262–7; O'Higgins (2017) 43.
39 Anon. (1700b). O'Higgins (2017) 44–5. Other outstandingly popular anonymous and undated (but 18th-century) chapbooks on classical themes, frequently reprinted and circulated across the British Isles and then all of Ireland, included the following: several editions of Aesop's *Fables*, *The History of the Seven Wise Masters of Rome* (the story of the sages summoned to help in the education of the young Diocletian), *The History of the Seven Wise Mistresses of Rome* (the education of Lucretia's daughter Sabrina by seven female sages), and *The Early History of England from the Invasion of Julius Caesar to the Norman Conquest*. Several copies of each of these are housed in the British Library.
40 Jones (1970) 15.
41 des Maizeaux (1726) v; see Daniel (1984) 5.
42 des Maizeaux (1726) vi–xiii.
43 Toland (1714).
44 *Hypatia* was first published as treatise no. 3 in Toland (1720). Its full subtitle is *Or the History of a most beautiful, most vertuous, most learned, and every way accomplish'd Lady; who was torn to pieces by the Clergy of Alexandria, to gratify the pride, emulation, and cruelty of their Archbishop, commonly, but undeservedly, stil'd St. Cyril.* On Toland see further Daniel (1984).
45 Tucker (1996) 20.
46 Pilkington (1748) volume I, 27.
47 Colman and Thornton (1755) 240.
48 Letter of 6th February 1730, in Swift (1963–1965) III, 369, 412.
49 Quoted in Todd (1984) 141.
50 Tucker (1996) 138–40. See also the references to Cicero (Tucker (1996) 133), Damon and Pytheas (135), Horace (136), and 'The speech of Cupid upon seeing himself painted by the Honourable Miss Carteret (now Countess of Dysert) on a Fan' (142–4). A manuscript published by Elias (1987) virtually redoubled the number of Grierson's poems known to have survived.
51 Grierson (1730) I, i–vi.
52 Grierson (1730) iii.
53 Tucker (1996) 141.4–5.
54 Jones (1745) 6.
55 Jones (1751); Jones (1758) 4.
56 Taylor (1792) 'Introduction', n.p.
57 Taylor (1792) 'Introduction', n.p.; see Carpenter (2018) 83.
58 Martin (1980) 16 and 17 fig. 7.
59 Moore (2013) 31–2, 30.
60 Jones (1991) 42.
61 Stanford (1976) 19–20.
62 Dodds (1933) 3.
63 See Root (1981).
64 Dodds (1933) 176–86.
65 Dodds (1933) 186.
66 Southerne (1721) 43.
67 On his obsession with Latin authors see Sherbo (1963) 5–6.
68 Spector (1979) 54–5.
69 Hall and Macintosh (2005) 64–98.
70 Foote (1811) 215–20, 222, 249. See also Hall and Macintosh (2005) 180–2.
71 Foote (1811) 304–5. Spector (1979) 161.
72 Boswell (1791) 609.
73 Campbell (1778) 317.
74 Jones (1784) 46.

75 Jones (1792) 12–13.
76 Cf. the early-19th-century anonymous work, *The Helot's Defence of Himself, O'Connell and Catholic Emancipation* (1834) and Hodkinson and Hall (2011).
77 See Curtin (1994).
78 Killen (1990) ix.
79 Mrs Martha McTier to Dr William Drennan, 28th October 1792, Public Record Office of Northern Ireland, Drennan Letters, no. 345. See Killen (1990) 7.
80 Cronin (1994) 140; see also Kennedy (2009).
81 See Whelan (1996).
82 Killen (1990) 9.
83 Brown (2016) 264.
84 Killen (1990) 9.
85 Killen (1990) 11–12, 20–1.
86 Caulfield (1894) 395.
87 Killen (1990) 19–20.
88 Clifford (1997) 37.
89 Madden (1846) vol. II, 144; see Clifford (1997) 11–12.
90 Madden (1846) vol. II, 145.
91 Tone (1826) vol. I, 34–8; see Clifford (1997) 9.
92 Clifford (1997) 37.
93 Russell (1796) 18.
94 Clifford (1997) 37.
95 Woods (1991) 60, 67, 159, 91–4.
96 Woods (1991) 141, 84.
97 Clifford (1997) 48.
98 Clifford (1997) 50.
99 Clifford (1997) 51.
100 Clifford (1997) 52.
101 Killen (1990) 47.
102 Killen (1990) 59.
103 See the entries in his diaries, Henry Collection (McClay GB 752 RMHP) for Thursday 13th Jan., March 3rd, 27th and 29th 1916. The contents of this collection, when I consulted them in May 2016, had not yet been fully itemised or numbered.
104 For an exciting eye-witness account of life during the Rising inside the IV by a Dublin sniper, see Shouldice (2015).
105 R.M. Henry (1920) 139–40.
106 R.M. Henry (1920) 106; see O'Faoláin (1947) 59; Wilson (1804) vol. I, 60.
107 R.M. Henry (1920) 152.
108 R.M. Henry (1920) 163.
109 R.M. Henry (1920) 142.
110 R.M. Henry (1920) 43–4.
111 Blaney (1996) 185.
112 Blaney (1996) 186.
113 R.M. Henry (1920) 219.
114 R.M. Henry (1920) 220–1.
115 Contained in M27 Box 3.
116 Henry (1924–5).
117 All this information is derived first-hand from his unsorted and unnumbered collection of papers.
118 See Paul Henry (1951) and Kennedy (1989–1890).
119 See the article 'Paul Henry' on the website *Achill 24.7*, p. 1. www.achill247.com/artists/paulhenry.html.
120 Hall and Macintosh (2005) 3, 110, 244–5.
121 Williams (1932) 72–7; Real and Vienken (1985) 373, 378; McMinn (2001) 38.

122 Damrosch (2013) 417; on the paradox of the Tory Swift as advocate for the victims of capitalism, see Morton (1952) 118–19.
123 Swift (1729) 3.
124 Swift (1729) 6.
125 Westgate and MacKendrick (1942).
126 Johnson (1958). Swift created abstracts of Tertullian's writings, of which he owned an edition: see Bensley (1930) and Williams (1932).
127 Samuel (1976) 440.
128 Burrow (1987).
129 Swift (1726) vol. II, 124; see also Burrow (1987) 495–6.
130 We seem to have come to this realisation simultaneously with Pierse (2018b) 175.
131 Tressell (2008 [1914]) 17.
132 Tresell (2008 [1914]) 7.
133 Tresell (2008 [1914]) 12.
134 Tressell (2008 [1914]) 114.
135 Noonan, who had read widely in ancient literature, will have been aware of the cave-quarries in Syracuse, a city to which Plato was a regular visitor. Plato was already a teenager when a large number of Athenian men had died a miserable death in these caverns in 413 BCE as a result of the Sicilian disaster, their suffering being recorded in agonising detail by Thucydides. See Stewart (1905) 252; Wright (1906) 138–9.
136 See Harker (2003).
137 Hernon (2015) 14–15.
138 Ball (1973) 67.
139 Hernon (2015) 16–20.
140 Hernon (2015) 26–36.
141 Hernon (2015) 42–3.
142 Hernon (2015) 72.
143 Hernon (2015) 71, 24, 83, 136, 140.
144 Tressell (2008 (1914)] 172.
145 See Tressell (2008 [1914]) 354: 'All through the winter, the wise, practical, philanthropic, fat persons whom the people of Mugsborough had elected to manage their affairs—or whom they permitted to manage them without being elected—continued to grapple, or to pretend to grapple, with the "problem" of unemployment and poverty.'
146 Hernon (2015) 209–10.
147 Tressell (2008 [1914]) 23.
148 Tressell (2008 [1914]) 73.
149 Tressell (2008 [1914]) 247–8.
150 Tressell (2008 [1914]) 140.
151 Hernon (2015) 'Preface' by Len McCluskey, General Secretary of Unite, 9–10 at p. 9.
152 Thorpe (2009).

11

SCOTTISH WORKING CLASSICS

The lad o' pairts

In 1765, the Scottish pedlar and chapman 'John Cheap', alias Dougal Graham (b.1724), first published his bestselling chapbook the *Entertaining Exploits of George Buchanan, who was commonly called 'The King's Fool'* (1765). This was a humorous, fictionalised account of a character based on the 16th-century Scottish poet, historian and administrator of the same name (1506–1582). Graham introduces 'George' as 'a Scotsman born', who 'tho' of mean parentage, made great progress in learning'.[1] He could outwit anyone, and specialised in outwitting Englishmen in high stations.

In one episode, George, having got the better of a certain bishop in a debate on religion, was taunted by a member of the same company of Englishmen, who said George alone possessed all the knowledge that was to be found in Scotland. George denied it: 'the shepherds in Scotland will argument with any Bishop in England, and exceed them mighty far in knowledge'.[2] Three clergymen were selected to travel to Scotland and dispute with shepherds. Clever George, who knew a quicker route, dressed himself as a shepherd:

> When he saw the clergymen coming, he conveyed his flock to the road side, where he fell a singing a Latin song: as so to begin the quarrel one of them asked him in French, "What o'clock it was?" To which he answered in Hebrew. "It is directly about the time of day it was yesterday at this time." Another asked him in Greek, "What countryman he was?" To which he answered in Flemish, "If you knew that you would be as wise as myself."

The clergymen, admitting defeat, 'went away shamefully, swearing, that the Scots had gone through all the nations in the world to learn their language, or the devil had taught them it'.[3]

DOI: 10.4324/9781315446608-13

This popular fiction, reprinted repeatedly and hawked across the British Isles in chapbooks for over a century,[4] reveals much about Scots' attitudes towards education. It shows how their education of the poor was measured favourably in comparison to England's.[5] But it also functions as a warning against falling unquestioningly for the same trick as the English clergymen in our assessment of Scottish working-class classicists.

Literary culture is of high antiquity in Scotland: the Dundee Burgh Library dates back to the fifteenth century and is the earliest town library in Britain.[6] The egalitarian tradition extends back to the Reformation, when Protestant reformers identified children's education as the instrument that could produce literate but godly citizens,[7] and attempted to bring in a national school system centrally administered by the Kirk. As John Knox put it in his *First Book of Discipline* (1560), the 'children of the poor' must be educated, and if

> they be found apt to letters and learning, then may they not (we mean neither the sons of the rich, nor yet the sons of the poor) be permitted to reject learning; but must be charged to continue their study.[8]

The existing parish school provision was expanded and further regulated, with the aim of providing universal education, and no fewer than four universities were founded in Scotland by the end of the 17th century; the Tounis College at Edinburgh, renamed King James' College in 1617, as the centre of the Scottish Enlightenment was by 1762 being called 'the Athens of Britain' for reasons other than its neoclassical architecture.[9]

In the 17th and 18th centuries, however, a huge number of unregulated 'adventure schools', to an extent comparable with the Irish hedge schools, came into operation to fulfil local needs.[10] Lord Brougham's 1818 report on education found 942 parish schools and 2,222 'ordinary' day schools, mostly adventure schools.[11] The teachers were usually kirk officers, who charged small fees in return for a curriculum that, at its best, added Latin and French classical literature in translation and sports to the inevitable Catechism.[12] It was with John Murdoch, who ran an adventure school in Alloway, that Robert Burns studied sufficient Latin, in addition to French, mathematics and books such as a biography of Hannibal, to become the world-renowned symbol of the clever, cultured Scot who transcended his labouring-class destiny.[13]

But opportunities for the poor were certainly not available nationwide nor to everybody. There was a high concentration of classical education around Aberdeen, as we shall see; Mr Roberts, a Church of Scotland preacher, was reading Flavius Eutropius with seven boys and even one girl in Rathven, Moray Parish, in 1842.[14] The edition may have been an old copy of Madame Dacier's for the Delphin series (see above p. 28). Girls had an even harder time than boys accessing intellectual culture, including Classics, though parish schools were open to them; about a third of registered pupils in 1851 were female, and they were sometimes offered Latin.[15] Parents wanted daughters educated in reading (but not writing) English, and they learned to sew, embroider, knit and cook.[16]

The Dundee Speculative Society was most unusual in admitting women to its debates in the 1770s and 1780s.[17] One woman was briefly a borrowing member of Wanlockhead Miners' Library, but working-class libraries 'were inclined to be prejudiced against women'.[18] The earlier established library nearby at Leadhills did not formally admit women until 1881.[19]

In the later 19th century, after the introduction of University Local Examinations, the number of girls taking classical languages remained tiny, but it was acknowledged that those who did tended to excel.[20] Professors at Edinburgh ran unofficial classes for women on many subjects, including Latin and Greek, and they proved popular amongst supporters of female suffrage.[21] Elizabeth Lipp of Fochabers, Morayshire, was the first girl from the north-east of Scotland to train as a certified teacher, at The Church of Scotland Normal School in Edinburgh in the 1870s, a beneficiary of the landmark Education (Scotland) Act of 1872. There she studied English, Geography, Nature Studies and Mathematics, as well as Latin (Caesar and Virgil were the set texts) and Alexander Adam's *Roman Antiquities* (1791).[22]

Lipp was an inn-keeper's daughter, but her six brothers all graduated from university as well, so careful with money and aspirational were their parents.[23] Lipp was lucky, however, to find employment as a teacher at a girls' school in Stornoway, in the Outer Hebrides, after achieving the coveted Certificate of Competency.[24] There is a recurrent trope of such a prodigiously clever girl, allowed by a broad-minded father to attend Greek or Latin classes, such as Jane Welsh (see below) or the schoolmistress celebrated in John Galt's 1834 story *The Mem* (i.e. schoolmistress), in which Miss Peerie 'excelled every young lady far and near in accomplishments. Greek and Latin were to her household words, and she would read Hebrew as easily as if it had been the A.B.C.'[25] But Welsh and Peerie were daughters of a doctor and a grammar school headmaster respectively: there are few signs of working-class equivalents.

Robert Burns' friend William Nicol, the son of a tailor who had died when he was a boy and who had been raised in penury in an Annan country village, learned enough Latin and Greek from a travelling tutor named John Orr to open a school of his own in his mother's house and eventually be appointed Classics master at Edinburgh High School in open competition.[26] But many remote rural regions were not even reached by itinerant tutors; few highlanders bettered their class position through education.[27] In new communities, established by captains of industry around mills and mines, a schoolhouse was often built alongside workers' cottages and a church, but attendance was not obligatory, and many workers fell through 'the educational gaps of … the parish system'.[28] Moreover, classical provision declined in Scottish parish schools in the 19th century. The Argyll Commission report (1865–1868) reported that the old-fashioned parish system of teaching Latin was holding children back from learning the three R's, and it was banished in many areas.[29] The tradition of the working-class boy who rose on merit can obfuscate the severe class inequality that made such a phenomenon exceptional, and in reality 'this function of the parish school was more limited than the democratic myth suggests'.[30]

That said, in some more populous regions of Scotland parishes were furnished, at first by the church and later the state, with excellent educational institutions. Combined with bursary schemes, these provided opportunities for promising working-class boys to be educated alongside their middle- and upper-class peers. Central to the popular narrative is the surprisingly widespread teaching of Latin (and to a lesser degree Greek) in parish schools.

The *Old Statistical Account* for the 1790s reveals how the educational system could work under optimal circumstances. One Kirkcudbrightshire schoolmaster, was able due to a particularly generous bequest, to offer free tuition in Latin and Greek.[31] The fortunate pupils were taught the learned languages 'with accompts and some practical parts of the mathematics; in short, every thing necessary to prepare the young student for the university, as well as to qualify the man of business for acting his part in any ordinary occupation'.[32] This distinctive feature of the Scottish system 'was possible', argues Robert Anderson, 'because university education itself started at a low level, requiring little more than a rudimentary knowledge of Latin, and because boys could go there at fourteen or even younger'.[33] The system created 'a pool of recruits' for the Scottish clergy, which the church supported with bursaries, enabling the 'lads o' pairts' from remote villages to gain university educations free of charge, and thus sometimes to leave their poverty behind them. In Chapter 22, on Classics in mining communities, we discuss one such parish, where working-class children could progress to higher social stations via fine educational and reading facilities.

The tradition of the learned working-class lad, despite operating in a twilight zone between historical reality and myth, also illuminates the ubiquity in this book of the engagement with Classics of Scottish people born into all walks of lower-class life across the nation: pedlars, gardeners, poets, carpenters, sailors, crofters, weavers, editors of radical newspapers, professors, philosophers, philanthropists, showmen, planters, prisoners, revolutionaries, circus performers, potters, granite workers, miners, MPs, stonemasons, barbers and gem engravers. A Scotswoman, Esther Easton, featured in the book's opening section; it concludes with the son of two Scottish socialists, the theatre-maker Ewan MacColl. The aim of the discussion here is to supplement the substantial presence of Scottish people in other chapters by focussing on four discrete dimensions of the Scottish working-class experience of ancient Greece and Rome, all of which affected British and indeed international life more extensively: the remarkable resources for studying and teaching the Classics that existed around Aberdeen, which furnished hundreds of educated men to work in the furthest outposts of the British Empire;[34] the cheap and popular publishing ventures of both George Miller in Dunbar and especially the Peebles-born brothers, William and Robert Chambers, whose educational publications found their way across the British empire; the use of classical myth in Thomas Carlyle's forceful denunciation of capitalism, which became a key text of the labour movement; and the novel about Spartacus by one of Scotland's best-loved writers, Lewis Grassic Gibbon.

Aberdeen and the north-east

At the time of the *Old Statistical Account*, fees for the parish schools were typically set according to a hierarchy of subjects. 'Reading' by itself might cost around 1s 6d per quarter, while 'Writing and Arithmetic' would cost commonly between 2 and 3s. 'Latin' was reserved for those willing and able to part with around 5s per quarter.[35] Here we can see exactly how classical education functioned as a tool of social division. The more costly Latin helped distinguish the middle classes from the masses, while the ability to read and speak English (not a given in Gaelic-speaking communities) enabled the poorest to access classical authors through translations in emergent cheap print media.[36] Despite regional variations, however, some working poor could enter the parish schools and even learn Latin, since there were systems in place for their fees to be covered. These had long been the responsibility of the kirk sessions—groups of parish elders—but in 1845 the obligation was transferred to the new Poor Law authorities, or parochial boards.[37] Some subsidised school places were provided by schools in exchange for supplements made to the schoolteacher's salary.[38] Such 'bequests' were usually named after the founding benefactor.[39]

The most celebrated was the 'Dick Bequest', established by James Dick (1743–1828), a shoemaker's son. He made a fortune trading in the West Indies and died leaving the vast sum of £113,787 for schoolmasters in the shires of Aberdeen, Banff and Moray. To secure a generously salaried position, teachers were required to pass a special Dick Bequest Examination, which ensured university-level standards of Latin and Greek provision; once in post they were regularly inspected.[40] The bequest strengthened the connection between north-eastern parish schools and the universities of Aberdeen, including Marischal and King's Colleges (united in 1860), both of which offered numerous bursaries. Boys competed for these by examinations in Latin translation into English and in Latin composition—writing 'versions'.[41]

There survives a detailed account of a class at the university in the 1860s. Alexander Shewan (1851–1941), the son of a Peterhead 'Master Mariner', graduated from Aberdeen University with a first-class degree in Classics in the 1860s. After serving in the Indian Civil Service, he retired in 1897 to St. Andrews, conducted research into Homer and compiled *Meminisse juvat: Being the Autobiography of a Class at King's College in the Sixties*.[42] Shewan's understanding of the class position of his peers is to be handled with care. He claims that many of the 137 students attended university only because they had won 'those precious bursaries'.[43] He says that northern Scottish schoolboys saw the annual competition for Aberdeen bursaries as equivalent to the ancient games at Olympia.[44] He praises the boys' training in the parish school, or (as he calls it) the *dura virum nutrix* ('tough nurse of men'). In the parish school, he explains, 'the laird's son and the ploughman's, the sons of the carpenter and of the Lord of Session met together'.[45] It is perhaps a consequence of the lofty company he kept in later life that Shewan speaks of his and his fellow students' 'humble origins'. Status is relative. He may, as a bursary boy, have felt inferior in class terms to his wealthier co-evals, but his life was lived at a comfortable distance from physical labour, skilled or unskilled.

Shewan was impressed that his Greek tutor was from plain Scottish farming stock. Professor William D. Geddes (1828–1900), who was indeed relatively low-born for a university professor, entered the University and King's College, Aberdeen, at the age of 15, graduated a few years later, taught at a local grammar school and was made Professor of Greek at his *alma mater* in 1855.[46] He had previously been educated at Elgin Academy, which was, like some other academies and 'burgh schools', expensive enough to remain 'the preserve of the middle classes. Not for the poor'.[47] Geddes may have been *relatively* low-class for a professor, and he walked 65 miles from his home to Aberdeen to attend his first bursary competition, but he was not therefore (as Shewan implies) from a family of poor labourers.

According to Shewan,

> no fewer than 48 (of the 80 about whose education he had information) received their early education in their native villages. Of most of us it may be said that "our lives in low estate began". Few were of wealthy houses.[48]

Of these, some may have been from middle-class families who sought to save money by entrusting their sons to the excellent local schoolmaster for their early education. Almost all, Shewan explains, completed preparation for the 'bursary contest' at one of Aberdeen's two grammar schools, although he personally attended a private school called the 'Gymnasium', on the humanist German model.[49] Like Horace, whom he quotes (*pauperum sanguis parentum*, 'blood [son] of poor parents' *Odes* 2.20.5–.6),[50] Shewan exaggerates his humble origins.

The Aberdeen bursary system constituted a significant formal educative route to the heights of classical scholarship for north-eastern boys of humble origins, but in the second half of the century, when Shewan attended, it was heavily trodden by middle-class boys. Shewan records that, of the 90 boys in his class, there were 4 sons of landed proprietors, 4 in government, municipal or railway service, 10 medical men, 4 professors, 4 lawyers, 15 ministers (2 of whom were also professors), 15 businessmen or shop owners, 3 schoolmasters and 25 farmers.[51] The numbers are not complete (90 out of 124), and the designation of 'farmer', for example, is ambiguous. All the same, these figures show that odds were stacked against the average son of a labourer.

The Dick Bequest and Aberdeen bursaries made the north-east of Scotland an oasis of classical education, but Shewan's account exaggerates how democratic and meritocratic it was, at least in the later 19th century. For most poor students, their social ascent ceased at the not-much-higher rank of schoolteacher or minister, usually after many gruelling years working as a pupil teacher and private tutor, which subsidised them through school and university respectively. In order to break into prestige professions, boys required additional and exceptional help from above. The arbitrary system of sponsorship and patronage continued to provide the sole framework in which real 'rag to riches' mobility could take place.[52]

Had the system been more egalitarian further back in time? Thomas Ruddiman was born in 1674 to a Catholic tenant farmer in Raggel in the parish of Boyndie near Aberdeen, and has been described as the archetypal 'Lad o' pairts'.[53] He shone in his Greek and Latin classes in the nearby Inverboyndie parish school.[54] At 16, he left home to compete for and win a bursary at what was then King's College, Aberdeen. His bursary enabled him to graduate; he later taught for a living. In 1699 he met by chance an eminent physician, Dr. Archibald Pitcairne, who helped place him in relatively lucrative positions in the Advocates' Library at Edinburgh and at Glasgow University.[55] Through his benefactor's intervention, the promising scholar was enabled to smash through his class ceiling and enter Edinburgh society as a scholar, printer and moderate Jacobite man of letters.

Ruddiman produced several editions of Roman texts, including, most notably, Livy and Virgil. But his most profound influence was exerted through what was to become the scourge of British schoolboys for generations, *The Rudiments of the Latin Tongue*. First issued in 1714, this primer became a publishing phenomenon. Repeatedly revised and reprinted throughout his life and until as late as 1886, it helped generations of schoolchildren and autodidacts alike take their first steps in Latin. Crucially, it was bilingual: it was in English and Latin throughout, whereas other grammars at the time and long after were often written entirely in Latin.[56] On visiting, in August 1773, the small town of Laurencekirk near Aberdeen, James Boswell, in his *Journal of a Tour to the Hebrides*, recorded that it was there that

> our great grammarian, Ruddiman, was once schoolmaster. We [he and Dr Johnson] respectfully remembered that excellent man and eminent scholar, by whose labours a knowledge of the Latin language will be preserved in Scotland, if it shall be preserved at all.[57]

In Chapter 5 we encountered Hugh Miller of Cromarty, just north of the Moray Firth. At parish school, he found Ruddiman's *Rudiments* 'by far the dullest book I had ever seen. It embodied no thought that I could perceive,—it certainly contained no narrative'.[58] He did not attend university and regarded the Aberdeen curriculum as intellectually limiting (see above pp. 114–15). But the contretemps with Ruddiman's *Rudiments* experienced by Alexander Bain (1818–1903) did lead to much greater things, as we saw in the same chapter (pp. 106–8). The Aberdonian son of a handloom weaver, Bain became a philosopher and Regius Chair of Logic at the newly united University of Aberdeen. He recalls being drilled in Ruddiman's *Rudiments* and 'found the memory work not at all congenial—but still I did it'.[59]

Like Ruddiman, Bain was aided by a chance meeting with an older and more economically secure man. In November 1835, he was in a bookshop owned by one member of his mechanics' class when the Reverend John Murray overheard their scholarly conversation.[60] Murray was the minister of North Parish, Aberdeen, and after a few meetings supported Bain in his effort to go to university, by helping to teach him Latin and preparing him for the bursary competition. As the competition drew closer, Bain was permitted to study for three months at the grammar school with no fee.[61]

Despite his progress, he did not win a full bursary, but his benefactors' support resulted in a 'vacant bursary' being found for the bright 18-year-old, which had 2 years left to run.[62] And that was how the Aberdeen weaver could become a Professor of Philosophy. In the 1860s, the Argyll Commission investigated the backgrounds of university students and found that over 20% of students came from working-class backgrounds.[63] Anderson notes that 'the figures showed that most working-class students were older than middle-class ones, and came after a period of work and self-education, not straight from school'.[64] Bain was one of these older students, if only by a few years, who were originally self-educated and fought hard to win and finance their university place. They still required a 'leg up' from individuals who knew how to play the system. But Bain never forgot his birth-class and, in 1850, as we have seen earlier, contributed articles on ancient society to an encyclopaedic multivolume series *Papers for the People*, published by the Chambers brothers (see above p. 106).

Reprint Classics

The Victorian passion for self-education literature had a significant forerunner in the figure of George Miller (1771–1835), son of a Dunbar merchant (Figure 11.1). His passion for books, and 'plebeian instruction',[65] drew him into a life as a printer and seller of the cheapest reading materials. Born into a family 'of the yeoman class', which had 'for generations ... been engaged on the land',[66] Miller was a philanthropist bent on social reform via mass self-education.[67] He was involved in the foundation of the Dunbar Mechanics Institute.[68] In his autobiographical writing, Miller recalls that he received a broad primary education, extending beyond the three R's and reciting the Catechism to English versions of Aesop's *Fables*.[69] He learned Latin in a local grammar school before becoming apprenticed to Alexander Smart, a Dunbar bookseller.[70]

In 1795, Miller invested in East Lothian's first printing press at Haddington, a town with a reputation for an educationally advanced population.[71] The region boasted a couple of libraries but, according to Miller, they were of no use to the public because the books were written in Hebrew, Greek and Latin.[72] The only way labourers, low-paid tradesmen and farm workers in the area could acquire affordable reading material was from bookstalls at the market and

FIGURE 11.1 George Miller (1771–1835) by Mungo Burton, reproduced by courtesy of John Muir House, East Lothian Council.

hawkers' baskets. The popular literature sold was considered by the pious and philanthropically minded middle classes to be sensational and poorly printed rubbish, including 'Lothian Toms, the John Cheaps, the Wise Willies, and other pernicious trash'.[73] But Miller felt that 'since the publication of my Cheap Tracts in 1802–1803 the complexion of the hawker's basket has undergone a very sensible alteration or material change to the better'.[74] His son James agreed: they had 'superseded the common trash of the hawker's basket'.[75]

Anne MacVicar Grant (1755–1838), author of *Popular Models, and Impressive Warnings for the Sons and Daughters of Industry* (1815), praised Miller's *Cheap Magazine* and its successor *The Monthly Monitor: or Philanthropic Museum*, writing that she would be 'deficient in zeal for the cause of plebeian instruction, were she to omit recommending' these magazines, 'works highly approved by the most competent judges, and so low priced, as to be within the reach of the lowest class'.[76] Alexander Somerville, author of *The Autobiography of a Working Man: By One Who Has Whistled at the Plough* (1848), described Miller as 'the father of cheap literature'. He was correct in his assertion that Miller 'lived before the age was ripe for him, and died, I fear, before he was fully appreciated'.[77] His relatively humble class background and (again relative) provinciality, when compared to the wealthy and Edinburgh-based Chambers brothers, played against him.

Miller's *Cheap Tracts*, which abound in classical references, were inexpensively printed pamphlets containing literature chosen for its instructional as well as its literary quality. In practice, this meant that they were short, sometimes abridged, versions or translations of well-regarded earlier prose writers. Many were later incorporated into Miller's fourpenny *Cheap Magazine; or, The Poor Man's Fireside Companion* (Figure 11.2), which circulated in Haddington for two years, 1813–1815.[78] It was an 'early example of a genre in which Scots led the way, the improving magazine aimed at artisans and tradesmen'.[79] Serialised articles

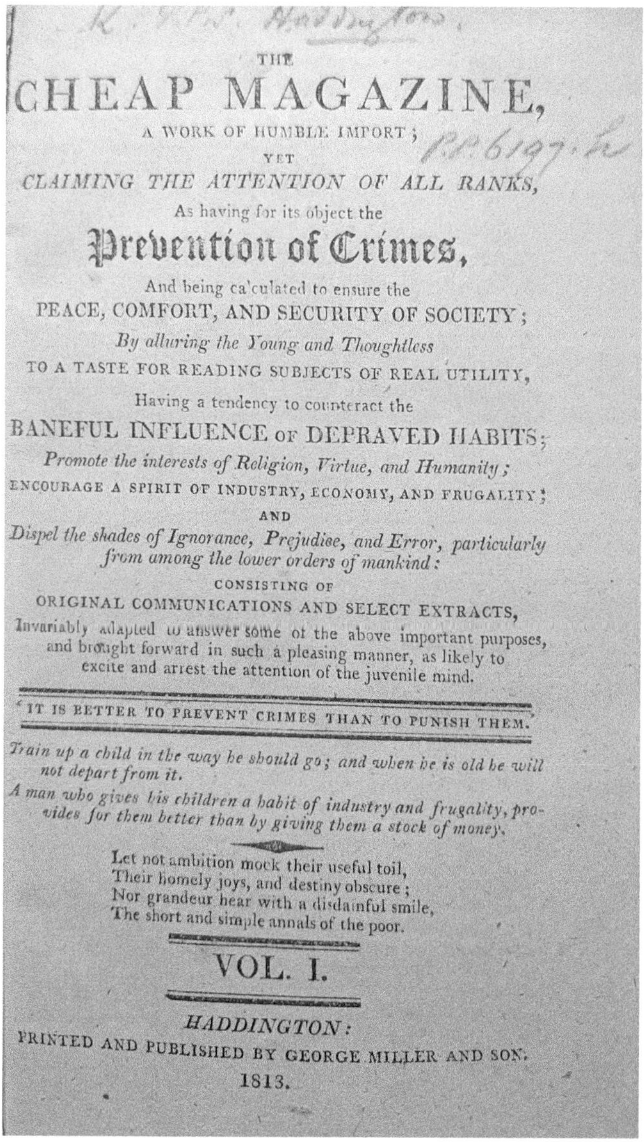

THE
CHEAP MAGAZINE,
A WORK OF HUMBLE IMPORT;
YET
CLAIMING THE ATTENTION OF ALL RANKS,
As having for its object the
Prevention of Crimes,
And being calculated to ensure the
PEACE, COMFORT, AND SECURITY OF SOCIETY;
By alluring the Young and Thoughtless
TO A TASTE FOR READING SUBJECTS OF REAL UTILITY,
Having a tendency to counteract the
BANEFUL INFLUENCE OF DEPRAVED HABITS;
Promote the interests of Religion, Virtue, and Humanity;
ENCOURAGE A SPIRIT OF INDUSTRY, ECONOMY, AND FRUGALITY;
AND
Dispel the shades of Ignorance, Prejudice, and Error, particularly from among the lower orders of mankind:
CONSISTING OF
ORIGINAL COMMUNICATIONS AND SELECT EXTRACTS,
Invariably adapted to answer some of the above important purposes, and brought forward in such a pleasing manner, as likely to excite and arrest the attention of the juvenile mind.

'IT IS BETTER TO PREVENT CRIMES THAN TO PUNISH THEM.'

Train up a child in the way he should go; and when he is old he will not depart from it.

A man who gives his children a habit of industry and frugality, provides for them better than by giving them a stock of money.

Let not ambition mock their useful toil,
Their homely joys, and destiny obscure;
Nor grandeur hear with a disdainful smile,
The short and simple annals of the poor.

VOL. I.

HADDINGTON:
PRINTED AND PUBLISHED BY GEORGE MILLER AND SON.
1813.

FIGURE 11.2 *Cheap Magazine; or, The Poor Man's Fireside Companion* (1813), reproduced by courtesy of The British Library.

under the headings 'Advice to Servants', 'Advice to a Young Tradesman' and 'A cottager's advice to his daughter' clarify the readership which Miller assumed. Classical literature and ancient history featured prominently, and the readership included a North Tyneside resident calling himself 'a friend to youth'[80] and a little girl of 11 named Jane Welsh, who grew up to marry Thomas Carlyle, but was then 'learning Latin like a boy'.[81]

'The Origins of Cock-fighting' discusses the practice in ancient Greece and Rome.[82] Achilles and Alexander the Great are cited as examples in 'An amiable portrait: John Howard'; Aesop and Terence receive short articles as having been born slaves (there are several articles advocating Abolition), as does Demosthenes for having persevered as an orator despite natural disadvantages; Vespasian is praised for rising to high estate on merit alone.[83] 'On the duties of schoolboys' opens with an exhortation from Quintilian.[84] 'Passion' discusses anger in relation to anecdotes about Alexander and Cleitus, Caesar and Pompey, Antigonus, Socrates and Alcibiades.[85] 'A Wise Saying' of the Spartan king Agesilaus encapsulates an improving moral,[86] and a long poem 'The Book of Nature; or, The Shepherd and the Philosopher' discusses Plato and Socrates.[87]

Miller did not only print and trade in new publications. He bought and sold diverse new and used texts in local auctions, often under the banner of BARGAIN or POPULAR BOOKS. His publicity material shows an awareness of the logistical issues facing the poor book buyer. These extended beyond their lack of money. He set up stalls in rural locations when the moon was full to assist the traveller arriving by foot from a distance.[88] The lists of his 'popular books' in the archives in the John Gray Centre in Haddington include, impressively, John Parkhurst's *A Greek and English Lexicon to the New Testament* (1813), James Moor's *Elements of the Greek Language* (probably the 1807 English-language edition), Rollin's *Ancient History*, Ovid's *Metamorphoses* translated by George Sandys (first published in full in 1626), Gibbon's *History of Rome* and James Banister's translations of Pindar's *Odes* (1791). Although there were 23 boys officially studying Latin in Haddington and Dunbar in 1842,[89] Miller's target market was the rural working-class self-educator.

In February 1832, the trailblazing publisher of popular periodicals, William Chambers, who had been raised in Peebles in the borders, wrote the inaugural editorial for his soon-to-be-famous weekly *Chambers's Edinburgh Journal*, often just called *Chambers's Magazine*.[90] When his younger brother Robert, a contributor, agreed to become joint editor, the magazine became a national institution. William defined his 'grand leading principle' as taking 'advantage of the universal appetite for instruction which at present exists'. His imagined reader is 'the poorest labourer in the country' or the schoolboy 'able to purchase with his pocket-money, something permanently useful—something calculated to influence his fate through life'.[91]

The Chambers brothers were far from working-class. Their father was a cloth manufacturer and merchant; their mother was born into the landed gentry.[92] Influenced by the Society for the Diffusion of Useful Knowledge (SDUK see pp. 122–3), William planned to improve the educational quality of reading material that the humbler orders could afford and enjoy:

> I intend to do a great deal for boys … . I was many years the worst scholar in the whole school … often did I think that mankind had entered into a conspiracy to torment boys with Latin. My distaste of this language drove me from the perusal of every kind of books, and I was near turning out an ignorant blockhead.[93]

Chambers' aversion to Latin, however, by no means extended to classical civilisation. In just the first few months, published topics included 'Ancient Pottery'; 'Grecian Monuments'; 'Grecian Philosophers and Christianity compared'; Romans; Pompeii and Herculaneum; Athens and Sparta; and 'A Roman City–Pompeii' (adapted from an SDUK publication in the series *Library of Entertaining Knowledge*[94]). Chiming with contemporary taste for antiquarianism and the Pompeii-mania, following the open-air excavations begun at Herculaneum in 1828, material culture and archaeology predominate, while Greek philosophy takes part in an instructive discussion on Christianity.[95]

As was common practice in periodicals of the time, the article on 'Ancient Pottery' is lifted verbatim from a previously printed source, the *Cabinet Cyclopaedia* masterminded by Dionysius Lardner, the Irish Professor of Natural Philosophy and Astronomy at University College, London. This 'cyclopaedia' was widely published from 1824 and, like Chambers' magazine, was associated with the Diffusion of Useful Knowledge and the self-improvement movement. Lardner's cyclopaedia contained a volume entitled 'History, Arts, Manufactures, Manners and Institutions of Greeks and Romans', which was written by the antiquary and clergyman, Thomas Dudley Fosbroke.[96] His *Encyclopedia of Antiquities and Elements of Archaeology, Classical and Medieval* (1825) is a monumental labour of love and eccentricity, ranging delightfully from ancient British road systems to courtship practices in the Classical Age.[97] The encyclopaedia writing of Fosbroke may strike us now as bizarre as it is learned, but it was certainly providing accessible and interesting information from the classical world and its cultural remains to readers of English. The classical knowledge is stripped of its potentially distancing scholarly trappings, i.e. of unknown languages, dense allusion, difficult terms and references to literature. As Alistair McCleery points out, the contents of the Chambers' journal represented 'a deliberate effort to raise the standards of reading beyond those of the other low-priced papers then available'.[98] The Chambers's selection of Fosbroke's work, however, shows that entertainment was perhaps as important a factor in a piece's selection as was its self-improvement value.

Thomas Carlyle

This Scotsman changed history (Figure 11.3). Keir Hardie, former collier, self-taught Latinist[99] and founder of the Independent Labour Party, believed that Carlyle's ideas had protected the British left from what he saw as the dangers

FIGURE 11.3 Thomas Carlyle (1795–1881), photographed on 31st July 1854. Public Domain image. Wikicommons.

of revolutionary dialectical materialism by stressing 'the spiritual side of man's being; showing how all material things are but useful in so far as they serve to aid in developing character'.[100] In 1906, when Labour MPs and the Liberals who had supported the 1903 Lib–Lab pact were polled, they named Carlyle, the Bible and Ruskin as the reading matter that had influenced them most.[101] The Dumfriesshire railway poet, Alexander Anderson, typically praised Carlyle (also from Dumfriesshire): 'One man, white-haired, with misty, flashing eyes/ Looms from the rest, in life's toil sublime,/And all that hath the power to make us wise'.[102] The docker Ben Tillett recalls being 'spellbound by the dark fury' of Carlyle's spirit.[103]

The book by Carlyle all of them read was *Past and Present* (1843), which Ralph Waldo Emerson called Carlyle's '*Iliad* of English woes'.[104] In its first two chapters, Carlyle's lament for the condition of the British working class is structured around two mythical figures. In chapter I, 'Midas', Carlyle argues that industrial capitalism, however bad for the workers who are banned from touching the enchanted fruit of the wealth they produce, is also bad for the rich Master Workers. They may touch the fruit but are impoverished morally.

> In the midst of plethoric plenty, the people perish; with gold walls, and full barns, no man feels himself safe or satisfied. Workers, Master Workers, Unworkers, all men, come to a pause; stand fixed, and cannot farther. Fatal paralysis spreading inwards, from the extremities, in St. Ives workhouses, in Stockport cellars, through all limbs, as if towards the heart itself. Have we actually got enchanted, then; accursed by some god?[105]

He concludes the extraordinary rhetoric of this chapter with a resume of the myth:

> Midas longed for gold, and insulted the Olympians. He got gold, so that whatsoever he touched became gold,—and he, with his long ears, was little the better for it. Midas had misjudged the celestial music-tones; Midas had insulted Apollo and the gods: the gods gave him his wish, and a pair of long ears, which also were a good appendage to it. What a truth in these old Fables![106]

Carlyle's class-oriented use of Midas proved influential, probably suggesting to George Eliot the climactic moment when Silas Marner the weaver, who works 16 hours a day, finds the toddler who will give his life love, joy and purpose: instead of the golden coins which had been stolen from him, he discovers 'a sleeping child—a round, fair thing with soft yellow rings all over its head'.[107] But Carlyle's use of the Sphinx, who gives her name to the title of chapter II, was to resonate even more profoundly.

Carlyle describes the Sphinx, whose face looks as seductive as a lovely woman's, but whose animal body contains 'a ferocity, fatality, which are infernal'.[108] Carlyle imagines her putting the 'riddle of Destiny' to the 27 million inhabitants of the country: how to live in true accordance with Nature, Truth and Eternal Justice: 'What is justice? that, on the whole, is the question of the Sphinx to us. The law of Fact is, that justice must and will be done. The sooner the better; for the Time grows stringent, frightfully pressing!'[109] Oedipus solved the riddle, but nevertheless suffered downfall. The Sphinx-riddle, Carlyle says, was first put by the 'poor Manchester operatives' who gathered at Peterloo:

> They put their huge inarticulate question, "What do you mean to do with us?" in a manner audible to every reflective soul in this kingdom; exciting deep pity in all good men, deep anxiety in all men whatever … All England heard the question: it is the first practical form of our Sphinx-riddle. England will answer it; or, on the whole, England will perish.[110]

We shall return to the influence of Carlyle subsequently, in Chapter 23.

Lewis Grassic Gibbon

A poor boy from a farm in Kincardineshire in north-east Scotland, Gibbon (whose real name was James Leslie Mitchell, 1901–1935), described by one of his biographers as the archetypal 'Lad o' pairts', became a convinced socialist during the Russian revolution as a reporter in Glasgow.[111] The hero of his famous novel *Spartacus* (1933) espouses identifiably Leninist principles[112] (Figure 11.4). After serving in the Royal Flying Corps, he embarked on a writing career, with the considerable input of his wife Rebecca, who also came from a poor Scottish rural background. She sat in the British Museum 'sifting through the main classical sources of the writings of Appian, Plutarch and Sallust'.[113] The novel draws extensively on Plutarch's *Life of Crassus* and uses specialist terminology relating to the Roman army, but there is also an unexpected engagement with Hesiod's myth of the Golden Age and the decline of the human race with the coming of technology.[114]

Gibbon's *Spartacus* does not draw explicit comparisons with British life in the early 1930s. But the consistent use of the term 'the Masters' to allude to the Romans would have made it impossible in the 1930s for readers not to draw their own transhistorical parallels. A leading character is Kleon, a maimed Greek slave-intellectual who plans that the revolt will produce a new utopian republic with

FIGURE 11.4 Lewis Grassic Gibbon (1901–1935) reproduced by courtesy of Arbuthnott Community Council.

its own constitution, the *Lex Servorum*, 'Slave Law'. He is reading Plato on the march and becomes chief advisor to Spartacus.[115] The slaves are international—Gauls and Germans, as well as Thracians, Greeks and Jews. Gibbon describes a scene of snowfall in Italy, to which men from different parts of the world, and accustomed to other climates, react quite differently: 'The Negroes thought it salt and licked their hands ... The Gaul and Teutone legions ceased their shivering ... they pelted the Eastern and African slaves ... the Northern men ... were remembering the long winter nights by the Baltic'.[116] Kleon describes how Spartacus grows in stature from 'a wild, brooding slave who sought no better future than freedom in a Thracian forest to a General, a statesman'.[117] Spartacus becomes a proto-socialist leader, who draws on the help of his philosopher colleague in their doomed attempt to win the war against their exploitative masters.

The continuing availability of enlightened humanistic education underlay the respect for the ancient world and its languages displayed by Gibbon's admirers, who included the Gaelic poet Sorley MacLean (the son of a tailor on the Isle of Skye and profoundly affected by classical literature in his early 20s[118]) and the controversial Marxist giant of Scottish poetry, Hugh MacDiarmid (i.e. Christopher Murray Grieve, 1892–1978). MacDiarmid, a postman's son, benefitted from a first-rate education at Langholm Academy in Dumfriesshire, the local library which was in the same building where he was brought up, and his teacher training in Edinburgh.[119] Despite his belief that Gaelic and Welsh poets needed to penetrate beyond the European Renaissance and 'undo that deplorable white-washing whereby Greek and Latin culture has prevented other European nations realizing their national genius in the way Greece and Rome themselves did',[120] his prolific socialist poetry is drenched with classical allusions and quotations in both Greek and Latin, all of which deserve further research.

The historiography of Scotland is hampered by fragmentation and proliferation of religious and political identities, nationalism and 'cultural sub-nationalism',[121] the turbulence of the 18th century, when the political class in Scotland split into factions under pressure from their English rulers, intent on 'bridling a troublesome, vexatious and unreliable neighbour'.[122] It is further complicated by the Victorian manufacture of an imagined past Highland community, the levels of emigration (far higher than from England or Wales) and the unparalleled contribution made by Scots to the administration of the British Empire.[123] In a Scottish national history that can be bewildering, the longstanding reputation for good working-class education is one of the few relatively stable factors and one which helps to explain how Scotland seems to have punched above its weight in British history proportionately to the size of its population. The contribution to the public understanding of classical antiquity and its political instrumentalisation made by the individuals in this chapter, by brain, pen and printing press, is incalculable. Besides the Aberdeen graduates and Carlyle, who studied at Edinburgh University, all were self-made lads o' pairts who, despite ending their formal education in their early or mid-teens, were inspired by the Greeks and Romans and handled them in the public arena confidently and competently.

Notes

1 Graham (1777) 3.
2 Graham (1777) 9.
3 Graham (1777) 10.
4 This cheap book was widely pirated and sold for over a century. The National Library of Scotland records 36 entries of editions printed between 1777 and 1880, Scally (2012) 2. 380.
5 Anderson (1995) 23, in agreement with Houston (1985), explains how Scotland's relatively democratic educational system does not look exceptional in a European context. It was England that lagged behind.
6 Harris (2011) 1107.
7 Todd (2002) 59–62.
8 McCrie (1812) 186.
9 Letter from Allan Ramsay to Sir Alexander Dick of 31st Jan. 1762 in Forbes (1897) 198. See Allan (2001) 398.
10 See Scotland (1969) 106–111, 262–5; Beale (1983) 183–4.
11 Smelser (1991) 235–6.
12 Wormald (1991) 183–5.
13 Hughes (1922) 17–18, 24, 199.
14 Gibson (1842).
15 Anderson (1995) 82; Moore (1984).
16 Scotland (1969) 108–9, 291; Anderson (1995) 8, 82, 171–2; Beale 1983) 185.
17 See Anon. (1774).
18 Crawford and James (1981) 19.
19 Crawford (1978) 3.
20 Scotland (1969) 263.
21 Scotland (1969) 353.
22 Hardie (1979) 15.
23 Hardie (1979) 9.
24 Hardie (1979) 74.
25 Galt (1978) 1.
26 Crawford (2009) 268; 272–5.
27 In 1801, a fifth of the Scottish population lived in highland regions: see Anderson (1995) 9–11.
28 Anderson (1995) 12–13.
29 For the Argyll report see Cruickshank (1967) 133–47.
30 Anderson (1995) 13.
31 *OSA* (1983) V.129.
32 *OSA* (1983) V.129.
33 Anderson (1995) 5.
34 See also above pp. 10 and 235.
35 *OSA*.
36 Houston (1985) 243.
37 Anderson (1995) 79.
38 Anderson (1995) 79–80.
39 Others included the 'Bell Bequest' at St. Andrews. The educationalist Andrew Bell (1753–1832), son of a wig-maker, who benefitted himself from a 'Glendie family bursary' and for a time worked for the East India Company, bequested on his death £50,000 to St. Andrew's University to found a new burgh school (present-day Madras College). His 'Bell Fund' also provided some bursaries. He left over £120,000 to support the education of the poor in Scotland and England, see Blackie (2004) *ODNB*.
40 Anderson (1995) 80.
41 Anderson (1995) 80.

42 Shewan (1905). *Meminisse iuvat* means 'it brings pleasure to remember'. Shewan published *Homeric Essays* in 1935.
43 Shewan (1905) 72.
44 Shewan (1905) 68.
45 Shewan (1905) 71.
46 Shewan (1905) 7 and 73.
47 Anderson (1995) 11–2.
48 Shewan (1905) 72.
49 Shewan (1905) 71.
50 Shewan (1905) 72.
51 Shewan (1905) 73.
52 Anderson (1995) 21–2.
53 Scotland (1969) 68–9.
54 Chalmers (1794) 5; Woolrich (2004) *ODNB*.
55 Chalmers (1794) 25; Woolrich (2004) *ODNB*.
56 It went through countless official and unofficial editions throughout the English-speaking world until the late 19th century. For example, a 20th edition was printed in Glasgow 1777; a 24th in 1782 (Glasgow); a 27th in 1817 (Baltimore). It soon became known as *Ruddiman's Rudiments* and was printed with appendices and exercises from other scholars. It was as *Ruddiman's Rudiments* that Chambers printed it in 1854, 1856 and 1887.
57 Boswell (1936) 52.
58 Miller (1869) 46.
59 Bain (1904) 7–8.
60 Bain (1904) 29.
61 Bain (1904) 31.
62 Bain (1904) 32.
63 Cruickshank (1967).
64 Anderson (1995) 153; see also Anderson (1983).
65 Miller (1833) 51.
66 Couper (1914) 21.
67 Couper (1914) 8.
68 Hogg (2009) 112.
69 Couper (1914) 30.
70 Couper (1914) 36–7.
71 Tyrrell (1969) 156–7.
72 Couper (1914) 77.
73 Miller (1833) 49.
74 Miller [G] (1833) 88.
75 Couper (1914) 89.
76 Grant (1815) 210. Articles discussing classical material in the *Monthly Monitor* include quotations from Pliny and a description of the ancient Phoenician trade in sea-purple in 'Origin of several important discoveries' (February 1815, vol. I, no. 2, 76–7); notice of a new 'Greek Literary Society' founded in Athens (February 1815, vol. I, no. 2, 108); 'On Happiness and Pleasure' (March 1815, vol. I, no. 3, 146–8); 'General rules for the attainment of knowledge (April 1815, vol. I, no. 4, 200–1); 'Paints in Greece' (April 1815, vol. I, no. 4, 230); Isaac Watts' poem 'The Hero's School of Morality' (May 1815, vol. I, no. 5, 298–9).
77 Somerville (1848) 93.
78 Timperley (1839) 845; Altick (1998) 320.
79 Harris (2011) 1120.
80 See the letter cited in Wood and Engholm (1907).
81 Welsh Carlyle (1889) 44–54.
82 *The Cheap Magazine*, February 1813, vol. I, no. 2, 80–3. The article was in turn excerpted and compressed from John Brand's *Observations on Popular Antiquities*,

published in 1777 by the radical bookseller Joseph Johnson (who is discussed elsewhere at pp. 88, 169 and 174). Brand's was the first major scholarly collection of British folklore customs and always explored the classical provenance of the customs he was investigating.

83 *The Cheap Magazine,* February 1813, vol. I, no. 2, 84, 'Aesop', 87 and in August, no. 8, 'Demosthenes, 375–6. 'Terentius Publius, or Terence' is in October 1814, vol. II, no. 10, 472 and 'Vespasian' in vol. II, no 12, 569.

84 The *Cheap Magazine,* June 1813, vol. I, no. 6, 273–7. This was extracted from the translation of the much-anthologised work of French ancient historian and educator Charles Rollin (1661–1741).

85 *The Cheap Magazine,* September 1813, vol. I, no. 9, 407–11.

86 *The Cheap Magazine,* October 1813, vol. I, no. 10, 460.

87 *The Cheap Magazine,* July 1814, vol. II, no. 7, 234–5.

88 Miller (1821).

89 Gibson (1842) 63. Twenty-three pupils studied Latin in the parochial schools, and three in an (unregulated) 'adventure school' in Cockburnspath.

90 The title was changed in 1854 to *Chambers's Journal of Popular Literature, Science, and Art,* and to *Chambers's Journal* in late 1897.

91 *Chambers' Magazine* (Saturday February 4, 1832) no. 1, 1.

92 Cooney (2014) *ODNB.*

93 *Chambers' Magazine* (Saturday February 4, 1832) no. 1, 1.

94 Clarke (1831–1832).

95 Anon. (1832a); Anon. (1832b); Anon. (1832c); [Discussion of ancient wines] Anon. (1832d); Anon. (1832e) [n.b. A three-part series on 'Pompeii and Herculaneum' (Nov 17–Dec 22) 1. 'Situation & discovery of Herculaneum and Pompeii, general character, forum, pantheon'; 2. 'Baths, theatres, amphitheatre'; and 3. 'Manuscripts, skeletons, paintings etc.']; Anon. (1832f); Anon. (1833a) [n.b. A two-part 'Popular information on History' feature on Romans (Jan 19–26). 1. 'The Monarchy and Republic'; 2. 'The Empire, its decline and fall']. Pompeii had been excavated since the mid-18th century.

96 Fosbroke (1833–1835).

97 Fosbroke (1825)

98 McCleery (2005) 13.

99 Levy (1987b) 151.

100 *Labour Leader,* January, 1893.

101 On Carlyle's huge influence across the British political spectrum, see Grose (1969) 42–9.

102 Anderson (1912) 23.

103 Tillett (1931) 77.

104 Emerson (1843) 96.

105 Carlyle (1843) 7.

106 Carlyle (1843) 8.

107 Eliot (1996 [1861]) 110.

108 Carlyle (1843) 9.

109 Carlyle (1843) 10, 17.

110 Carlyle (1843) 22. See also 49–50, where he compares himself with 'ill-boding Cassandras in Sieges of Troy': they are both figures warning their countries of imminent perdition, and who must do so, even if they are not believed, in the hope that 'the importunate events, if not diverted and prevented, will be rendered less hard'. He also suggests that the problems are surmountable and that it might yet be possible to reach the 'Happy Isles', whereupon he quotes Tennyson's 'Ulysses': 'There dwells the great Achilles whom we knew'.

111 Munro (1966) 60–6.

112 Malcolm (1984) 120.

113 Malcolm (1984) 116.

114 Young (1973) 71.
115 Gibbon (1996 [1933]) 14–15, 55, 59, 64–5, 117. See the interesting remarks of Munro (1966) 114–15.
116 Gibbon (1996 [1933]) 202.
117 Gibbon (1996 [1933]) 91.
118 Nicolson (1979) 26.
119 Kocmanová (1980) 61.
120 MacDiarmid (1970) 173.
121 Nairn (1981).
122 Shaw (1999) 1.
123 Morris and Morton (1994).

12

CARACTACUS AND LLOYD GEORGE'S RECRUITING DRIVE IN WALES

Noah was a Welshman, built his ark of wood;
Cutting down the Welsh oak, found it very good.
Solomon, a Welshman, got his tin from Wales.
Caractacus licked all the world because he drank Welsh ales.

[Part of a popular poem quoted in *The London Kelt* (1896) from an 1856 source[1]]

Introduction

An important component of the National Eisteddfod of 1894, held in Caernarfon, was an evening concert presided over by the 31-year-old David Lloyd George. Since 1890 he had been Member of Parliament for Carnarvon Boroughs. During the interval, Lloyd George delivered an address in Welsh, 'pointing out that the eisteddfod was a proof that Wales followed the muse and song when other countries in Europe had sunk into barbarity.[2] The climax of the concert was orchestral, 'the first performance of a new overture, *Caractacus*, composed by Mr J. H. Roberts', which was 'accorded a hearty reception'.[3]

If we fast-forward 22 years, to June 17th 1916, we discover another patriotic Caractacus-themed performance in Wales to which the discussion will return at the conclusion of this chapter: the notice under the title 'Brynamman' printed in *Herald of Wales and Monmouthshire Recorder* on that day (2):

> Private Gwyn Williams. Royal Welsh Fusiliers, of Llandeilo Road, Brynamman, has been killed in action. He was 23 years of age. A brother, Private Griff J. Williams, is serving in the Royal Welsh Fusiliers. Five performances of *Caractacus* were given by the Lower Brynamman Council School children at the schools last week, under the supervision

DOI: 10.4324/9781315446608-14

> of Mr. Willie Thomas, C.M., the choir being conducted by Mr. John. Morgan, A.L.C.M., C.M., both of the staff.

About a month later, another local newspaper, after reporting the death in action of a further Brynamman man, Priv. Morgan Morgans of the Gordon Highlanders, and the wounding of a third, Priv. Tom Parry, refers to the same school theatrical. The Brynamman branch of the British Red Cross Society, active as never before in the relief of wounded servicemen, had passed a vote of thanks to the committee and choristers responsible for *Caractacus* in gratitude for their donation of the proceeds.[4]

The recruitment drive in Wales had been extraordinarily successful. One historian describes it as 'incredible to this day that the Welsh responded in such large numbers to the call to arms'.[5] The 38th (Welsh) Division, popularly known as 'Lloyd George's army', had proved particularly attractive to the working-class men in both the Welsh-speaking North, where unemployment was an acute problem, and the industrialised South.[6]

Imperial ideology is a messy business. It is at its most complicated when an empire which has taken centuries to develop is still in the process of adding to its roll-call of ethnic, national and class identities both near the centre of metropolitan power and faraway across the planet. Such was the situation in which the British Empire found itself during its late 19th-century and Edwardian heyday. Historians of sport have noted the central role played by rugby 'in the popular incorporation of Welsh indigenous and British Imperial personas into the new definition of Welshness', a definition carefully crafted to transcend class identities, which emerged at this time.[7] But the classical figure in whom this tension was crystallised is the chieftain of the 1st century CE, known to the ancient Greeks and Romans as Caratacus or Caractacus, and to Welsh-speakers as Caradog.[8]

Caractacus between Britain and Wales

How can an ancient warrior to whom only a few paragraphs in classical historians are devoted be co-opted both as a forefather of Welsh ethnic identity (grounded in the living Welsh language and at times resistant to British rule) and as a heroic prototype of the British imperialist fearlessly imposing 'civilised' values on a worldwide empire, a prototype which appealed across the class spectrum? An important factor was the ideological project and impact of the 1898 cantata *Caractacus*, with music by Edward Elgar to a libretto by Harry Arbuthnot Acworth. The most significant response to this celebrated work was the wave of Caractacus plays, musicals and oratorios performed in the first decade and a half of the 20th century in Welsh schools. These fostered a fiery Welsh national identity committed to the British imperial project that David Lloyd George was to exploit in his 1914 recruitment drive. Caractacus furnished one of the most prominent filaments in the vivid tapestry of Welsh cultural and regional history experienced during the three decades between the appearance of Lloyd George on the political scene and the unprecedented casualties inflicted on Wales, especially miners and working-class Welshmen from the north of the country, by World War I.

Caractacus had been the subject of an important late 18th-century stage play by William Mason,[9] and throughout the Victorian period, Caractacus poems, paintings, statues and a few musical performances, usually with druidical overtones, sporadically appeared in both England and Wales, often in public, civic locations. An imposing statue by Irishman Constantine Panormo, 'The Liberation of Caractacus', was said to be 'expressive' and one of the most viewed of the artworks in the British section of the gallery at the Great Exhibition of 1851.[10] But Caractacus did not arrive at the epicentre of the British cultural radar again until the jingoistic celebrations of the late 1890s, when Queen Victoria's diamond jubilee (1897) foregrounded both the British imperial 'achievement' in India since the Government of India Act (1858) and the 'foundation' of 'Rhodesia' (1890). In this context, Edward Elgar's *Caractacus* premiered at the Leeds festival.[11] The libretto was by Elgar's Malvern friend and neighbour Harry Arbuthnot Acworth, a passionate advocate of the 'civilising' benefits brought to the Indians by the Raj, and retired President of Bombay. The piece, ideologically, is a transparent apologia for British global imperialism, but the location in the Malvern Hills places Caractacus' heroism in the liminal space between English and Welsh identities.[12]

The *Caractacus* of Elgar and Acworth, with its druids from around the Anglo–Welsh border, and its exploration of the relationship of a brave little country to a mighty imperial conqueror capable of clemency, swiftly attracted interest in Wales. At the 1902 Gwent Chair Eisteddfod in Rhymney, the test piece in the 'marching song' category in the Brass Band competition, won jointly by the Great Western and Cory Workman's bands, was a march from *Caractacus*.[13] The most famous Welsh composer of the day, Dr. Joseph Parry, was almost certainly prompted by the Elgar/Acworth cantata to write a four-part *Caractacus: A Choral Ballad*, which climaxed with a solo in F major for Claudius and full chorus, 'Free Prince Caradoc, the Briton brave!'[14] But it was a stage play in Welsh by Beriah Gwynfe Evans, performed at a school in Abergele in 1904, which inaugurated the Edwardian tradition of theatrical performances starring Caractacus. Evans saw Caractacus as fundamentally Welsh, rather than an incoming East Briton who took on leadership of the Silures, and required not only him but all the other Britons and even Romans to speak Welsh. This procedure, drawing on a long history of conflating the Welsh with the ancient Britons, decisively identified the Caractacus of ancient historians as the birthright of Welsh people in Wales.

Evans, born in Nant-y-glo, in 1848, began his career as a teacher who agitated for the use and teaching of Welsh in schools,[15] and in 1885 founded the Society for the Utilization of the Welsh Language.[16] A Congregationalist, he was intent upon dispelling the anti-theatrical prejudices which still prevented drama from being enjoyed in many parts of Wales, and shrewdly saw that patriotic readings of national history might be more acceptable than more frivolous content. He persuaded the organisers of the Llanberis Eisteddfod in 1879 to allow him to compete with his history play *Owain Glyndŵr*, and it won the prize, thus providing the first serious impetus to the dramatic movement in Wales and securing his lifelong membership of the Gorsedd. He has been described in M. Wynn Thomas's study of the forging of Welsh national identity between 1890 and 1914 as a 'vapid historical dramatist', but focussing on the aesthetic demerits of his plays is not useful where drama exerts the ideological influence of Evans' *Caractacus*.[17] The same play, along with a much later version of his *Owain Glyndŵr*, was later revived to be enacted in Caernarfon in the course of the celebrations of the investiture of the Prince of Wales in 1911.[18]

Evans subsequently became a journalist who has been described as 'omnipresent' on the Welsh cultural scene until his death in 1927. In 1892 he arrived in Caernarfon as managing editor of the Welsh National Press Co., which published *Y Genedl Gymreig* and *The North Wales Observer*. Here he developed his already strong relationship with Lloyd George, who was heavily involved with these newspapers: he later wrote a biography of his favourite politician, *The Life Romance of Lloyd George* (1915), published simultaneously in Welsh as *Rhamant Bywyd Lloyd George*.[19] His journalism, as a prominent member of the Cymru Fydd movement, was marked by a passionate commitment to Welsh nationalism and self-government but allied with a commitment to the British imperial mission.

Evans's *Caractacus*

As a prominent local journalist, in 1904 Evans was in a position to ensure that considerable publicity was devoted to the four pioneering performances of his new play *Caractacus* or *Caradog* by the pupils of Abergele County School, the last transferring from the school hall to the Public Hall in Colwyn Bay. After the performances, the Caernarfon paper *The Welsh Leader: A Weekly Record of Education and Local Government in Wales* published a special commemorative issue, almost certainly written by Evans himself, which was then reprinted as an entirely independent volume resplendent with photographs of the performance, (Figure 12.1 and Figure 12.2) taken by 'Mr T. Wills Jones of Rhyl', and a portrait of Evans as its frontispiece.[20] It includes an interview with the Head Master, Mr Jeremiah Williams M.A. He explained that he wanted to engage his pupils in a more challenging and interesting Christmas entertainment than the traditional concert or semi-performance of scenes from Shakespeare. He decided to be adventurous and actually stage a complete play connected with Welsh history, because his school was keen 'to foster an interest in Welsh History and Literature, and we are doing all that is possible to develop the school on Welsh National lines'.[21] Unsurprisingly, given the history of anti-theatricalism in Wales, he failed to find a suitable text until he met Beriah Evans, whose Welsh-Language drama *Llewelyn ein Llyw Olaf* had recently been performed at the Princes' Theatre in

FIGURE 12.1 Production photographs by Mr T. Wills Jones of Rhyl in *The Welsh Leader: A Weekly Record of Education and Local Government in Wales* (1904). Images reproduced from *The Welsh Historical Drama and How to Produce it: Being the Actual Experience of the Abergele County School Company in the Production of* "Caractacus", reproduced by courtesy of the British Library.

Llandudno. Evans had explained that 'he was writing a whole series of Welsh Historical Plays on characters from Caradog to Harri Tudor', and that *Caractacus*, which featured 'a Musical Scene with original music specially composed by Mr J.T. Rees, Mus. Bac. of Aberystwyth could be got read in a month's time'.[22]

The commemorative volume is designed to encourage other schools to follow suit by listing the advantages of patriotic theatricals for ordinary children. Besides those five spectacular photographs, it includes interviews with the music mistress in charge of training the chorus, choreographical diagrams and advice on the creation of costumes and scenery. The Head Master proudly remarks that his pupils have received invitations to perform the play at Liverpool, Porthmadog, Caernarfon, Bangor, Denbigh, Rhyl and Ruthin. The experience had increased his pupils' interest in the past history of Wales, but had also increased the standard of intelligence: 'There is a new zest, not only in historical, but in other studies. It is as though their outlook had been suddenly broadened, and their intelligent appreciation of facts quickened.' This improvement in knowledge base and cognitive skills had applied not only to the lucky performers, but to all the other pupils as well. Then Williams introduced a telling martial simile to explain the ideological potency of participation in patriotic theatricals at an impressionable age:

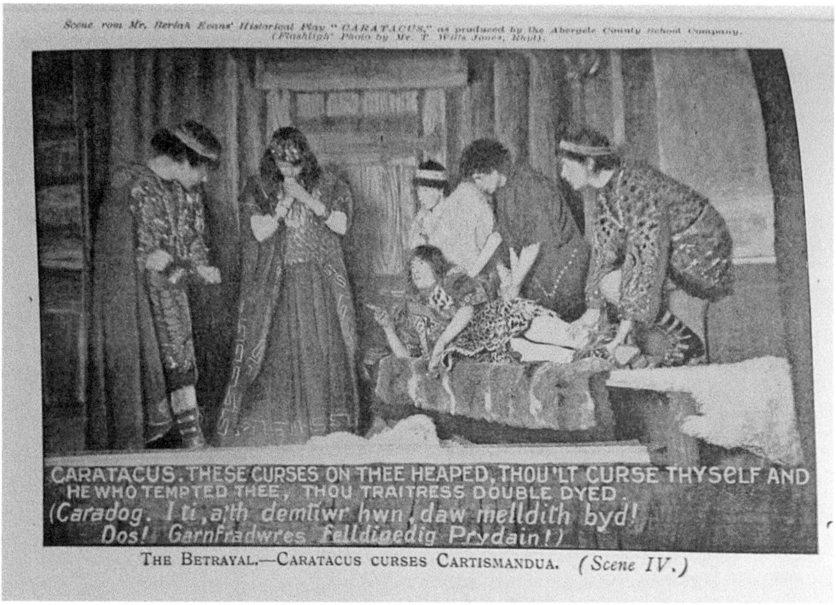

FIGURE 12.2 Production photographs by Mr T. Wills Jones of Rhyl in *The Welsh Leader A Weekly Record of Education and Local Government in Wales* (1904). Images reproduced from *The Welsh Historical Drama and How to Produce it: Being the Actual Experience of the Abergele County School Company in the Production of* "Caractacus", reproduced by courtesy of the British Library.

> Just as a new recruit enters his first campaign a raw lad and comes out a man, so our pupils, many of them, have suddenly sprung from being mere school children to the position of brightly intelligent youths and maidens … The lessons of patriotism, of loyalty, of truthfulness, of mutual duties and responsibilities, are insensibly but most effectively inculcated.[23]

Ten years later, this metaphorically recruited generation of children was to be asked by the British government, in which Lloyd George was the most eloquent advocate of war, to offer themselves up to the recruiting officer in reality.

Evans was convinced that the creation of a new tradition of Welsh historical drama held exceptional educational promise as well as being a useful instrument in the inculcation of patriotism. He was also aware that a country with no experience of fully staged amateur theatre might find the prospect of putting on a play intimidating. The Head Master insists that staging such a performance was far less difficult than he had anticipated: he believed that that nine out of ten County Schools in Wales, and 'scores' of local Literary and Dramatic Societies, would be up to the challenge. He had himself been invited to arrange a repeat performance before HRH Princess Louise (the King's eldest daughter).[24]

The play is complicated. Sub-plots include the scheme of Vellocatus, weapon bearer to King Venutius of the Brigantes, to seduce his master's wife and betray Britain to the Romans. There are two inter-cultural love affairs. Claudius' daughter Genwissa, who has been accompanying the Roman army on its British campaign, falls for Caradog's brother Afarwy, while Caradog's daughter Gwladys is destined to marry a Roman officer named Pudens.

But there is also substantial martial action and a suspenseful suggestion of semi-continuous fighting offstage between Britons and their Roman invaders. The Emperor Claudius himself appears on stage as early as in Scene I, set in an English forest, when he is persuaded against facing the Britons in immediate battle. Caradog appears in Scene II to regret that the Britons are in retreat. In Scene III, Gwladys saves the captured Roman ambassador Pudens, who works on behalf of the General Ostorius, from being tortured by Britons.

But in Scene IV, we arrive in Wales at 'Caradog's Camp in the Country of the Silures'. Here there is an important dialogue between Caradog and Pudens about the political situation. Amongst the British chiefs there are many who were once favourable to Roman involvement in their affairs, but they have all become followers of Caradog, determined to remain free of Rome and retain absolute sovereignty. After a long speech in which Caradog emphasises the strength of the British fastnesses in Snowdon and Anglesey, his loyal Britons sing a patriotic song with distinct echoes of 'Rule Britannia', of which this is an English translation:

> No! No! Britain answers no!
> Britain will not be enslaved! No! No!
> Britain's heroes will play their part!
> Britain stands on behalf of the weak!
> No! No! Britain answers No!
> Brave Britons never shall be slaves to anyone![25]

The most spectacular scene is V, in a 'Druidic circle in the centre of a forest', and, like Mason's *Caractacus*, it puts the goddess Andraste at the centre of the Britons' religion. A procession, dances and hymns precede the dramatic selection of Gwladys' daughter as willing sacrificial offering. She is rescued from the altar by Pudens.

Scene VI returns us to England, where Caradog is betrayed, albeit reluctantly by his cousin Aregwedd under the influence of the evil Vellocatus. And the final Scene VII opens on the crowded Field of Mars in Rome, where Claudius and Agrippina receive the captives and spoils from Britain. Caradog refuses to kneel before Claudius, delivers a paraphrase of his famous speech from Tacitus' *Annals* 12.37 and is freed, while the treacherous Vellocatus and Aregwedd are condemned.

Two years after the success of the Abergele school play, the Elgar/Acworth cantata itself arrived triumphantly at the centre of Welsh people's celebration of their national self-definition. In 1906, Caractacus provided the two highlights of the Royal National Eisteddfod, held as often at Caernarfon, in the enormous pavilion which had been built for the purpose in 1877. For the first time in Eisteddfod history, the programme included a spoken drama, Evans' Welsh-language *Caractacus* under a variant name, *Pendragon Prydain*. This title was presumably used to distinguish it from Elgar's *Caractacus*, an evening concert performance of which took place at the festival's climax. The cantata featured a specially convened 270-strong festival chorus consisting entirely of local townspeople, well-known Welsh soloists and the band of the Portsmouth Royal Marines Light Infantry. It 'gave very great satisfaction to the vast audience assembled'.[26]

A long article in the *North Wales Express* is sensitive to the ambiguity surrounding Caractacus' national affiliation. It addresses the potential problem that Elgar's *Caractacus* 'is an English work, of course', and notes that 'curiously … both the first Welsh drama to be connected with the Eisteddfod and the chief choral work this year treated of the same hero. But the writer concludes that Elgar's cantata was as welcome as Beriah Evans' drama by commenting that

> there was no Cymro in last evening's performance who did not feel that the music was instinct with that undefinable greatness associated in his mind with his country's glorious though pathetic past. Sir Edward Elgar has commenced his invasion of musical Wales.

He particularly applauds Elgar's version for its imaginative reference to a future 'potent Britain' which will rise 'in majesty' to sway 'Empires Caesar never knew'.[27]

Caractacus and the children of Wales

The triumph of the Caractacus story at the 1906 Eisteddfod in both spoken drama and sung cantata inspired a decade of amateur performances in schools and town halls across Wales. In addition to those by Joseph Parry, Elgar/Acworth and Evans, a fourth, more light-hearted work, combining speech and song with attractive dance sequences and comic interludes, had certainly become available by 1910. It seems swiftly to have become the most frequent choice for performance (it was shorter, in English, and made fewer demands on its performers than the long set-piece orations of Evans' more portentous work): its published version is entitled *Caractacus. A Juvenile Operetta for Boys and Girls and Infants*. The music was by George G. Lewis and Herbert Longhurst, and the libretto by H.E. Turner.[28] This opens with a scene in the Roman forum, with a chorus of slaves. Emperor Claudius and Empress Agrippina decide to invade Britain, and there is a procession of Roman soldiers. The action then moves to Britain, where there is an idyllic scene of village life including a maypole dance and games. Caractacus' wife Rotha and her mother Cartismandua are introduced, followed by Claudius and his aide-de-camp Bericus. There is a dance of British warriors, painted in woad and wielding axes and shields. Two strolling players arrive and provide comic relief, before the chorus of druids sings a psalm and the Arch-Druid prays. But suddenly there is a thunderstorm and the Romans attack. During the battle, Caractacus disappears and his wife Rotha desperately searches for him. Cartismandua has betrayed Caractacus. The scene then returns to Rome and the triumphal procession in which Caractacus and Rotha are led as captives before being dramatically released. The show ends with a final chorus in praise of the Fire God.

The collection of digitised newspapers held at the National Library of Wales yields up evidence of a substantial number of other provincial Caractacus performances and productions, and despite the predominance of the Lewis/Longhurst/Turner operetta when the work is actually specified, it is not otherwise always possible to identify which one—Elgar/Acworth, Parry, Evans or the operetta—was performed. It is possible that in practice there were new hybrid versions which transferred especially popular tunes or speeches from one version to another or rewrote them entirely. For example, in March 1909, the Kidwelly United Juvenile Choir performed an unspecified work described as 'the popular cantata "Caractacus"' to packed audiences, two nights running, in the Town Hall. There were costumes and scenery and the acting received commendation. In particular, some Kidwelly boys relished the opportunity to enact martial violence: 'Masters John Cydwel Davies and Harold Reynolds, as Roman soldiers, and Melvill White and Tudor Evans, as British soldiers, gave splendid representations of the martial ardour of those early days'.[29]

Perhaps prompted by a much-lauded rendition of the Elgar/Acworth cantata at the London National Eisteddfod of 1909,[30] or by the prominent position given to the story of Caractacus, as the opening episode of the ambitious National Pageant of Wales staged in Cardiff's Sophia Gardens in the summer of the same year,[31] the floodgates of Caractacus performances were flung wide open in 1910. The first documented staging of the Lewis/Longhurst/Turner operetta took place at the Judge's Hall, Trealaw in March 1910: it was sung by the Juvenile Choir of Salem, Llwynypia.[32] It was soon followed by a performance of the same work by the Pisgah Juvenile Choral Society at Bryndu School: 'All the little ones were tastefully dressed, and did their singing in a manner that showed a thorough training'. The proceeds were in aid of the Pisgah Baptist Church.[33] Not to be outdone, the Tabernacle Juvenile Choir of the Welsh Congregational Church Band of Hope performed the operetta during the same month, at the Tabernacle Chapel in Barry Docks. It was repeated at the Masonic Hall, Barry, when the proceeds were handed over to the Institute of the British and Foreign Sailors' Society (Barry Docks branch). 'Between the acts, Mr W. W. Marshall, port missionary to the British and Foreign Sailors' Society, proposed a vote of thanks to the choir, and those who assisted at the performance'.[34] 'Roman soldiers and juvenile Britons sang and drilled, recited, gesticulated, and even fought with true histrionic earnestness'.[35]

The next documented performance of the operetta followed in April. It took place in the Pembrokeshire Masonic Hall, and featured no fewer than 50 local people drawn from the teachers and pupils of the St. Catherine's Sunday School and Bible Class.[36] The hilarity of the strolling players Gip and Topsy 'evoked roars of laughter, and their witticisms and actions quite overcame the audience'.[37] In May 1910, the children of Milford Haven Parish Church Bible Class and adults of the Teachers' Operatic Society combined in the Masonic Hall at Haverford West to produce the operetta. The battle scene was highly commended as 'truly realistic. The glittering spears of the ill-trained Britons are poor defence against the short deadly swords of the Roman invaders, and many British fall dead on the plain'.[38] By popular demand, the production was revived later in the year, when the proceeds were donated to the St. Mary's Young Men's Institute.[39]

It is undeniable that there was strong feeling amongst the miners of the Rhondda during the Tonypandy riots of 1910 and 1911, especially after Winston Churchill, as Home Secretary, sent in the British army to support the police against the unrest. This must have meant the militarism of the Caractacus performances struck more ambivalent chords in some less Anglophile members of the audiences.[40] Yet 1911 undoubtedly marked the highest tide of the British Empire for Britons of all income brackets internationally. A year after passing his 'People's Budget', Lloyd George, as Chancellor of the Exchequer, had won the fervent support amongst the working classes of both Wales and England. He then masterminded both the newly crowned George V's 'Festival of Empire', when George and his wife Mary were crowned Emperor & Empress in a bizarre triumphalist pageant at Delhi, and the equally peculiar pseudo-druidical ceremony at Caernarfon Castle in which Crown Prince Edward was officially 'invested' as Prince of Wales.

The triumphant fusion of Welsh indigenous and British imperial identities at this time meant that Caractacus performances in Welsh schools continued to proliferate. In late October 1913, it was the turn of the Model School, Carmarthen, to essay the operetta at the Carmarthen Assembly Rooms, where the boys who played the parts of the Roman soldiers and the Britons were commended for the fine representation of the 'very good fight'.[41] In March 1914 the children of Ogmore Higher Elementary School performed the operetta twice, at the Ogmore Workmen's Hall, where the event was presided over by Alderman William Llewellyn. J.P., and at the Nantymoel Workmen's Hall. The children had been prepared for learning their parts by a lecture on the deeds of Caractacus on St. David's Day. The newspaper report comments on 'the educational effect' of this operetta, which was 'bound to be of immense value to the performers by giving them a clearer idea of life in Britain in the days of our ancestors, and life in Rome at the height of her glory and power'.[42]

The outbreak of war

By Empire Day 1914, nerves about the possibility of war were becoming more apparent. When the children of Swansea celebrated this event, several thousand marched in costume beneath bright sunshine on the Swansea Sands, singing 'Land of Hope and Glory', 'God Bless the Prince of Wales' and the National

Anthem as they saluted the Union Jack. At the Christ Church Infants' School in Rodney Street, children performed speeches and tableaux costumed as Britannia, Florence Nightingale with nurses, soldiers and John Bull's children, but the boys of Terrace Road School turned to ancient history. Their pageant enacted 'the taking of Caractacus to Rome' in full historical costumes.[43]

Britain declared war on Germany on August 4th 1914. Given his political views and experience as loyal servant of the British Empire, it comes as little surprise to find Elgar's librettist Acworth, on the Welsh border that month, delivering a 'stirring lecture' on the reasons for the necessity for fighting 'Prussia' (as he still called it): Prussia had 'throughout history proved herself to be of all States the most voracious, and of all States the least to be trusted. Greed and falsehood are writ large upon her action for many a hundred years past'.[44] And at national level, the politician who had worked hardest to convince Britons to go to war was the Welshman often himself described as a druid, bard, and reincarnation or scion of Caractacus, Lloyd George himself. Although scholars argue about the extent of his commitment to the 'moral argument' that Belgium needed to be defended against Germany, by 1911 he had become an interventionist who helped to plan the policies 'and ministerial changes that committed Britain to immediate participation in war and a continental strategy in 1914'.[45] For Lloyd George, as for most British political leaders, the important point was not Britain's possible obligations under international law to defend Belgium, but the imperative to avoid a defeat in France leading to a Europe dominated by Germany.

Once war was declared, the Caractacus performances in Wales became transparently connected with recruitment, morale and fund-raising for the war effort. The Trecastle section of a Brecon newspaper proudly reported in January 1915 that a local youth, Private John Evans, of the 3rd Battalion Welsh Regiment, had been seen marching at Cardiff; the journalist reports,

> Private Evans looked well in his uniform, and appeared fit to meet any number of Germans. I hear that the Recruiting Committee, appointed lately for Traianmawr parish, are doing excellent work. On Friday evening last a most successful concert was held at the old National School, Trecastle, in aid of the local Band of Hope and the Belgian Relief Fund. The room was crowded to its utmost capacity, and everyone thoroughly enjoyed the entertainment.

The programme's climax consisted, inevitably, of a play called *Caractacus*, followed by the singing of all four – Belgian, French, Russian and British – National Anthems.[46]

In the summer of 1915, Caractacus turns up specifically in the context of fund-raising for the war effort. The Pentrepoeth Girls' School, Morriston, had spent ten months 'engaged in knitting comforts—scarves, socks, helmets etc. for the soldiers and sailors'. They staged a special set of performances to raise 'funds to carry on the work'. They needed 'wool for making further comforts, which they intended sending to the children's fathers who were at the front. Mrs H.D. Williams read a letter which she had received from a soldier at the front showing how the men appreciated the comforts sent to them'. The programme consisted of tableaux representing 'Shakespeare's Birthday' and 'Empire Day' supplemented by 'A Ballad of the Ranks' and a 'Pageant of Famous Women'. But the main item on the programme was the 'playlet' entitled *Caractacus in Rome*.[47]

The children's choir of Gwaun Cae Gurwen performed a work entitled *Caractacus* early in 1916.[48] There were two performances of a 'cantata' called *Caractacus* by the Hermon Juvenile Choir in December 1917.[49] But after conscription was imposed in 1916, and the war staggered to its gloomy conclusion, the full extent of the slaughter began to sink into the national consciousness. Predictably, the craze for Caractacus theatricals waned. None is recorded in 1918, and just one 1919 performance of the operetta is recorded in Barry Port, by the Zion Choir in the Parish Hall, in May.[50] An awareness that the Caractacus tale had less relevance to everyday life in postwar Wales seems however to have bypassed the Breconshire poet Clifford King, who in 1917 claimed to be 'well known throughout Great Britain, India, Australasia and America by his poetical compositions' and 'Wales' greatest poet to-day and England's also'. Amongst honours conferred on him was the honorary Bardic title of 'Rhyd-y-Godor', by the late Archdruid of Wales, Clwydfardd.[51]

In 1920 King published his poems, which included earlier works such as a 'Coronation Ode' and an 'Ode on the Investiture of H.R.H. the Prince of Wales at Carnarvon'. But these were now supplemented by the 'Historical and Patriotic drama *Caractacus*'.[52] This had been conceived before the war ended, in 1917, and was dedicated to Lloyd George by his special and personal permission when he was still Prime Minister. King was emphatic that Caractacus was a native of Siluria in South Wales, and informs his reader that he has '(for alike patriotic, imperial and dramatic reasons—indeed, as a Silurian indigene personally) modified the historically-recorded speech of Caractacus before Claudius':[53]

> The torch I've lit shall ne'er extinguished be,
> But shall be handed on through centuries
> As Brythons each fall in life's fevered race.

The drama concludes with the British National Anthem followed by one verse of *Land of My Fathers, Hen Wlad Fy Nhadau*.[54]

For all King's regressive rhetoric, the story of Edwardian Welsh Caractacus performances has a tragic ending. The ancient Briton's legend was actively used as propaganda in the recruitment drive in Wales amongst the poorest, Welsh-speaking populations of the north and west of Wales. Their identity as men of 'gallant little Wales', most famously articulated in the verses quoted below, composed by two Talgarth residents, was explicitly used to foment identification with the suffering people of another 'gallant little' nation, Belgium. The entire poem, which continues to list previous battles in which Welsh soldiers have distinguished themselves by dying in the Crimean and Zulu wars, was printed in *The Brecon County Times Neath Gazette and General Advertiser* on 26th November 1914(2) with the explicitly stated 'hope that they may be used to stimulate recruiting':

> There were gallant little Welshmen long ago,
> Such as Caesar and his stalwart warriors found:
> They could then with steady courage meet the foe,
> And for home and freedom boldly stand their ground.
> Brave Caractacus for Britain fought his best,
> And Boadicea, too, the British warrior Queen;
> Their spirit lives, though they are long at rest,
> Our love of freedom living ever green.
>
> CHORUS.
>
> 'Tis defence and not defiance,
> 'Tis for freedom not for fame,
> 'Tis on right we place reliance,
> Crying better death than shame.
> When our Country calls us forward,
> When the enemy assails,
> There are loyal hearts to answer,
> In gallant little Wales!

Yet gallant little Welshmen suffered thousands of life-changing injuries and fatalities in the trenches. The miners were held to have suffered most, being recklessly courageous fighters.[55]

The ideological utility of school performances of plays and operettas featuring Caractacus is most painfully expressed in a third newspaper article reporting that staging we noted earlier, by the Banwen Council School scholars at Brynamman in June 1916, when the death toll of local men was mounting month by month. *The Amman Valley Chronicle and East Carmarthen News* for 15th June 1916 (5) is full of praise for the emotional impact of the show, enhanced especially by the acting of R.J. Jones as the Arch-Druid and Miss Sally Williams as Cartismundua, who with 'a withering gaze and hatred convulsing her whole body she thwarted those who had dared to wound her pride':

> Being under the shadows of the greatest war the world has ever seen it was very timely, and gave an opportunity to compare the old methods of warring with the advanced but more destructive methods of to-day. The interpretations were so realistic, and at times so absorbing, that we were unawares borne reminiscently to the Roman times. The audiences were fairly carried back to the actual period on which the work was based, and found themselves captives within that epoch until the end … . All the

> weapons and addresses were the handicraft of the children and were excellently done, and proved very suitable.

Small Welsh children across the class spectrum were still recreating ancient weapons as their elder brothers, inspired by the example of Caractacus, were dying in droves in the trenches of France.

Notes

1. *The London Kelt*, 29th February 1896, 11.
2. 'End of the Eisteddfod', *South Wales Daily News*, 14th July 1894, 5–6. The article is adorned with a portrait sketch of the firebrand young politician.
3. 'End of the Eisteddfod', *South Wales Daily News*, 14th July 1894, 6.
4. *The Amman Valley Chronicle and East Carmarthen News*, 13th July 1916, 3.
5. Llwyd (2008) xv.
6. Llwyd (2008) xvi–xvii.
7. Andrews (1991).
8. Another version of this chapter is also published as Hall (forthcoming g).
9. See Hall and Macintosh (2005) chapter 7.
10. *Illustrated London News*, 11th Oct. 1851, 'Supplement', no page number, with figure.
11. Elgar (1898).
12. McGuire (2007).
13. *The Pontypridd Chronicle and Workman's News*, 24th May 1902, 6.
14. *Weekly Mail*, 30th August 1902, 8. Joseph Parry, who had been sent down the Merthyr Tydfil mines at the age of eight, became a successful composer after emigrating to Pennsylvania in 1854. He returned to the UK in 1868, took degrees in Music and became a distinguished academic. His works include the evergreen song *Myfanwy* (1875) and the first Welsh opera, *Blodwen* (1878).
15. See Evans (1892).
16. Morgan (1981) 95–6. This was not the universal position of Welsh-speaking educationalists at this time, some of whom campaigned for bilingualism and some of whom were resigned to the eventual demise of Welsh altogether. See Hobsbawm (1992) 35–6.
17. Thomas (2016) 25. Evans (1904).
18. Thomas (2016) 25 is not aware of the previous performance history of Evans' *Owain Glyndŵr*.
19. Evans (1915); see Thomas (2016) 45–74.
20. Anon. (1904). The photographs opposite pages 4, 8, 12, 17 and 24 are respectively captioned 'THE RESCUE OF CLAUDIA BY PRINCE ARVIRAGUS'; 'PUDENS BRINGS OSTORIUS'S MESSAGE TO CARACTACUS'; 'THE SACRIFICE IN THE DRUIDIC TEMPLE'; 'THE BETRAYAL—CARACTACUS CURSES CARTISMANDUA' and 'CARACTACUS BEORE CAESAR—THE TRAITOR'S DOOM (FINAL SCENE)'.
21. Anon. (1904) 4.
22. Anon. (1904) 5.
23. Anon. (1904) 5–6.
24. Anon. (1904) 7.
25. Anon. (1904) 30.
26. Anon. (1906a) 627–8.
27. '"Caractacus". A Splendid Performance', *The North Wales Express*, 24th August 1906, 5: 'Mr O. M. Edwards, M.A., Lincoln College, Oxford, presided, and was warmly received. It goes without saying that he spoke in Welsh, and of Welsh. He said that it was worth their while to keep alive the Welsh language if a song had never been sung

it, or if it had no literature, because there was poetry in its words ... The Eisteddfod should make its influence fall upon other institutions--the elementary schools, and the secondary schools, and the university colleges, if he might venture to name them, and also upon the University itself, so that the dry bones might live ... They had learnt to look upon the Eisteddfod as an institution that reflected the life and progress of Wales. They expected something from the Carnarvon Eisteddfod. It had started with a. drama, and it was going to end with something that no other Eisteddfod had known'.

28 The earliest published version of the operetta we have been able to track is Turner, Longhurst and Lewis (1924).

29 'Kidwelly Notes', *The Carmarthen Weekly Reporter*, 12th March 1909, 3. See also *The Llanelly Mercury and South Wales Advertiser*, 4th March 1909, 4.

30 *The Cardiff Times*, 10th April 1909, 9.

31 See Edwards (2009) 9, 113–17 with the photographs of 'Caradoc' played by Mr Goodwin Preece, and the 'Silurian warriors and their wives', reproduced on pp. 116 and 117 respectively.

32 *Rhondda Leader Maesteg Garw and Ogmore Telegraph*, 19th March 1910, 1.

33 'Kenfig Hill', *The Glamorgan Gazette* 4th March 1910, 8.

34 *Barry Dock News*, 15th April 1910, 5.

35 *Barry Herald*, 18th March 1910, 3.

36 *The Pembroke County Guardian and Cardigan Reporter*, 22nd April 1910, 8.

37 *The Pembrokeshire Herald and General Advertiser*, 22nd April 1910, 3.

38 '"Caractacus". A splendid performance. Historical operetta at Haverford West', *Haverfordwest and Milford Haven Telegraph and General Weekly Reporter for the Counties of Pembroke Cardigan Carmarthen Glamorgan and the Rest of South Wales*, 1st June 1910, 2.

39 *Haverfordwest and Milford Haven Telegraph and General Weekly Reporter for the Counties of Pembroke Cardigan Carmarthen Glamorgan and the Rest of South Wales*, 28th September 1910, 3.

40 See Evans and Maddox (2010).

41 *The Carmarthen Weekly Reporter*, 7th November 1913, 5.

42 *The Glamorgan Gazette*, 3rd April 1914, 3.

43 *The Cambria Daily Leader*, 22nd May 1914, 1. Many Caractacuses must have appeared in pageants across Britain during these years: in the 1908 Cheltenham pageant as reported in 'Gloucestershire's History in Living Pictures', *Illustrated London News* no. 3612 for Saturday 11th July 1908, p. 43, the procession was led by a man dressed up as Caractacus.

44 Backhouse (2015): 'Newspapers reported on a stirring lecture given by Mr A. H. Acworth in August 1914. Such a talk was necessary as most people were quite unaware of the causes of the war. He gave the historical explanations for the tensions between the European empires, in particular where they boiled over in the Balkans'.

45 Gilbert (1985) 865.

46 *The Brecon County Times Neath Gazette and General Advertiser for the Counties of Brecon Carmarthen Radnor Monmouth Glamorgan Cardigan Montgomery Hereford*, 21st January 1915, 4.

47 *The Cambria Daily Leader*, 24th June 1915, 4.

48 *The Amman Valley Chronicle and East Carmarthen News*, 27th January 1916, 2.

49 *The Glamorgan Gazette*, 21st December 1917, 4.

50 *The Cambria Daily Leader*, 28th May 1919, 5.

51 'Hay's poet', *The Brecon Radnor Express Carmarthen and Swansea Valley Gazette and Brynmawr District Advertiser*, 14th June 1917, 2.

52 King (1920) vol. 3, 283–389.

53 King (1920) vol. 3, 289.

54 King (1920) vol. 3, 389.

55 See Llwyd (2008) xviii.

PART III

Underdogs, underclasses, underworlds

13

SEDITIOUS CLASSICISTS

Introduction

When Thomas Hobbes published *Leviathan* two years after the execution of Charles I, and three decades before 'Classics' began to emerge as the curriculum of choice for those who wanted to distinguish themselves from the working classes, he argued that reading Greek and Roman authors should be banned by any self-respecting monarch. Hobbes had studied the Athenian democracy in depth when he translated Thucydides (1628), and now argued that ancient political writings by authors such as Aristotle and Cicero foment revolution under the slogan of liberty, instilling in people a habit 'of favouring uproars, lawlessly controlling the actions of their sovereigns, and then controlling those controllers'.[1] He would have been little surprised at the inspiring role played by classical civilisation, especially Athenian democratic and Roman republican history, in efforts to emancipate the British working class.

This chapter looks at the different ways in which diverse British radicals—republican revolutionaries, advocates of constitutional reform, agitators for universal suffrage, workplace organisers and freethinkers—used or were motivated by the ancient Greeks and Romans between the American and French revolutions and the collapse of the Chartist movement. The first group is the democrats of the 1790s; 'democrats' was their own term of self-description. The label 'Jacobin', meaning one sub-category of French revolutionaries, was used indiscriminately by British conservatives to indict anybody critical of the establishment and to erase the considerable differences between different radicals' objectives and beliefs.[2] The second group is the late Georgian reformers whose militancy began at the end of the Napoleonic Wars and most of whom were imprisoned by the increasingly Draconian measures taken after Peterloo in 1819 to control the press and limit radical activities. The third is the Chartists whose activities reached a climax with the agitation of the 1830s to 1850s.

DOI: 10.4324/9781315446608-16

Late 18th-century democrats: Paine, Gerrald, Thelwall

The most influential British revolutionary of the 18th century was Tom Paine—soldier, stay-maker, excise officer, engineer, writer—who was born in Britain the year that censorship was imposed on British theatres (1737). He died in New York, impoverished, the year that Abraham Lincoln was born (1809). When working as a journalist in the United States, Paine's pamphlet *Common Sense* (1776), arguing for the superiority of representational government over monarchy, was instrumental in persuading colonists to fight against rule from England. His *Rights of Man* (1791–1792), which defended the French revolution against Edmund Burke's criticisms, was an 'early working-class best-seller' and inspired all the radicals to be discussed in this chapter.[3] But he was arrested in France for opposing the mass use of the death penalty, and wrote his critique of organised Christianity, *The Age of Reason* (published in three parts in 1794, 1795 and 1802), while detained in prison in Luxembourg. Paine has usually been held to be a kneejerk opponent of the study of antiquity, but this is incorrect.[4] He wrote that the majority of non-biblical 'ancient books are works of genius; of which kind are those ascribed to Homer, to Plato, to Aristotle, to Demosthenes, to Cicero, &c.' In fact, the *works* are so important that the name of the author does not particularly matter.[5] The thought of Aristotle, Socrates and Plato is indispensable, insists Paine, although saying that it is vital to remember that these men were not aristocrats: they are famous on merit.[6]

Paine was educated at Thetford School in Norfolk. Because his Quaker father distrusted the pagan and popish associations of the ancient languages, Tom learned neither. But he also knew that real competence in ancient Greek, at least, was acquired by far fewer members of the ruling class than liked to admit it. In a jibe at British parliamentarians' ignorance of the balance of trade, Paine said that Charles (later Earl) Grey, who was proud of his declamatory skills honed by a classical education at Eton and Cambridge, 'may as well talk Greek to them, as make motions about the state of the nation'.[7] Paine believed that learning Latin and Greek was too time-consuming to be useful in the education of most people, since there was so much other information they needed to absorb merely to make a living and function as citizens:

> Learning does not consist, as the schools now make it consist, in the knowledge of languages, but in the knowledge of things to which language gives names. The Greeks were a learned people; but learning with them, did not consist in speaking Greek, any more than in a Roman's speaking Latin.[8]

After all, the valuable information to be found in ancient authors could now be read in the mother tongue:

> As there is now nothing new to be learned from the dead languages, all the useful books being already translated, the languages are becoming useless,

> and the time expended in teaching them and learning them is wasted … . The best Greek linguist, that now exists, does not understand Greek so well as a Grecian plowman did, or a Grecian milkmaid.[9]

But knowing enough about etymology to ask what a word originally meant in Greek was advantageous: when considering the word blasphemy, used to accuse freethinking critics of doctrinaire Christianity, he recommends consulting 'any etymological dictionary of Greek'.[10]

Paine's irreverence towards classical antiquity scandalised some of his contemporaries and has ever since been misunderstood by scholars who only read his most famous writings. He pokes fun at the British parliament's hackneyed allusions, in references to the outbreak of the American war, to Julius Caesar having passed the Rubicon.[11] Paine saw Classics as inherently atavistic. He thought that it prevented living generations from conceiving a better future, and thinking how it might be achieved. He was puzzled that the civilisations of ancient Greece and Rome, in comparison with all other periods of history, were so lauded and emulated. He considered that this attitude prevented his contemporaries from seeing what they had themselves achieved: 'I have no notion', he affirmed, 'of yielding the palm of the United States to any Grecians or Romans that were ever born'; great progress had been made already, and in pouring praise on

> the wisdom, civil governments, and sense of honour of the states of Greece and Rome, mankind have lived to very little purpose, if, at this period of the world, they must go two or three thousand years back for actual lessons and examples. We do great injustice to ourselves by placing them in such a superior line.[12]

He also thought that excessive respect for the ancient aesthetic sensibility was daft: for Paine, the only things more beautiful than the Wearmouth iron bridge he had designed were women.[13]

But he was convinced that a grasp of human history, including the markedly political history and developed secular ethics of ancient Greece and Rome, were essential to modern democrats' understanding of the past. This enabled them to apprehend the extent of their own potential agency. In a dialogue modelled on Lucian, he resurrects the ghost of General Richard Montgomery to remind the reader of Plutarch's heroes:

> it is in a commonwealth only that you can expect to find every man a patriot or a hero—Aristides—Epaminondas—Pericles—Scipio—Camillus—and a thousand other illustrious Grecian and Roman heroes, would never have astonished the world with their names had they lived under royal government.[14]

'The Grecians and Romans were strongly possessed of the *spirit* of liberty but *not the principle*, for at the time that they were determined not to be slaves themselves, they employed their power to enslave the rest of mankind'.[15] Another encounter showing the influence of both Lucian and Swift with a dead general, Alexander the Great, which Paine wrote under the pseudonym 'Esop', satirises the powerful as pathetic parasites on society; in Hades, Alexander exhibits 'a most contemptible figure of the downfall of tyrant greatness'.[16]

Comparing ancient civilisations with the contemporary world could be beneficial in thinking through their different attitudes to war and empire:

> The principal and almost only remaining enemy, it now has to encounter, is prejudice; for it is evidently the interest of mankind to agree and make the best of life. The world has undergone its divisions of empire, the several boundaries of which are known and settled. The idea of conquering countries, like the Greeks and Romans, does not now exist; and experience has exploded the notion of going to war for the sake of profit. In short, the objects for war are exceedingly diminished, and there is now left scarcely any thing to quarrel about, but what arises from that demon of society, prejudice, and the consequent sullenness and untractableness of the temper.[17]

Ancient conquerors who enjoy praise caused damage:

> The Alexanders and Caesars of antiquity have left behind them their monuments of destruction, and are remembered with hatred; whilst those more exalted characters, who first taught society and science, are blest with the gratitude of every age and country. Of more use was *one* philosopher, though a heathen to the world, than all the heathen conquerors that ever existed.[18]

Like Confucius and Jesus, the Greek philosophers needed to be read, because they recommended benevolent moral systems.[19]

Paine never said that learning about the ancient world was anything but constructive. He thought that ancient Greeks and Romans provided useful comparands, provided that they were not held up as examples to emulate or invested with any special status or authority. They were just another set of humans, albeit very interesting ones, in another set of socio-economic circumstances. Paine was informed about ancient history and philosophy. In *Rights of Man* he quotes the rousing statement of Archimedes (whom, as an engineer, he much admired), saying that it can equally be applied to Reason and Liberty: if we had '*a place to stand upon, we might raise the world*'.[20] He appreciated Solon's recommendation that 'the least injury done to the meanest individual was considered as an insult to the whole Constitution'.[21] In his rhetoric against colonialism and tyranny, Paine's love of ancient literature provides him with images: what else was the status of colonial America to its British masters than Hector, cruelly tied to 'the chariot-wheels of Achilles'?[22] He recommends that comparison with antiquity was a fundamentally useful endeavour. He suggested that any revolutionary new republic should institute 'a society for enquiring into the ancient state of the world and the state of ancient history, so far as history is connected with systems of religion ancient and modern'.[23]

While Paine was in France, the London Corresponding Society, the largest radical organisation in Britain, was under attack. Joseph Gerrald, a West Indian of Irish descent, was one of two members, together with the secretary of the Society of the Friends of the People, arrested in Edinburgh in 1792 on a charge of Sedition. When Gerrald appeared in court in March 1794, he refused to answer the charges but advocated political reform, while dressed 'in French revolutionary style, with unpowdered hair, hanging loosely behind—his neck bare' in imitation of ancient Roman republicans.[24] He was sentenced to 14 years' transportation to Australia, where he met a tragic and premature death.[25] Shortly before he was deported, he wrote to thank Gilbert Wakefield, the most radical Greek scholar of the day, for his unwavering support during the trial, quoting the ancient Greek proverb 'ὀψὲ θεῶν ἀλέουσι μύλοι, ἀλέουσι δὲ λεπτά', meaning that the tyrants in power may not see their punishment coming, but that it will come in time.[26] In the same year, the assistant counsel for the defence, Felix Vaughan, defended Thomas Hardy, secretary of the London Corresponding Society, against the charge of treason. Twenty years earlier, Gerrald had performed the part of Oedipus in a Greek-language production at Stanmore School, 'with an unfaltering eloquence and moving pathos that excited general admiration'.[27]

For Gerrald and Vaughan were both classicists, former pupils of the charismatic headmaster, Dr. Samuel Parr, dubbed 'the Whig Dr Johnson', during his time at Stanmore School; they had followed him there when Parr's sympathy with John Wilkes' campaign to get the rotten boroughs abolished and the franchise extended cost him the headmastership of Harrow.[28] Parr's sympathy for the victims of repressive policies remained unwavering, and he had danced round the 'Tree of Liberty' following the fall of the Bastille. For British radicals, the French revolution was initially a beacon heralding democratic reform, lower taxes, lower food prices and the humbling of an arrogant ruling class.[29] But Parr, like Paine, stopped short of endorsing what he saw as 'the cruel execution of the unhappy prince' in France.[30] He had urged caution on the wayward Gerrald (whom he had reluctantly expelled from Stanmore for some 'extreme' indiscretion).[31] But that Gerrald remained a favourite to the end is demonstrated by Parr's efforts on his behalf, the financial support he offered him personally (which Gerrald failed to receive),[32] and finally by his commitment to the education of Gerrald's son following his father's death. Godwin was so affected by his friend Gerrald's fate after having visited him in prison that he rewrote the ending of his own Oedipal novel *Caleb Williams* (1794), because its pessimistic ending was too close to Gerrald's own end.[33]

The man responsible for popularising Godwin's ideas about human benevolence, and the capacity of reason to remake society, was orator, elocutionist, political writer and poet, John Thelwall (see above pp. 23–4). Thelwall was himself tried and acquitted on a charge of high treason in late 1794. Like Paine, he had left school in his early teens. But Thelwall did not become a public radical until his late 20s. The son of a London silk-merchant, he was apprenticed to a tailor, but unsuccessfully, since he was a dreamy youth and constantly reading. Then he was articled to an attorney in the Inner Temple, but became radicalised when required to serve writs on desperately poor people.[34] 'Lawyers', he later said, had 'spread more moral devastation through the world than the Goths and Vandals, who overthrew the Roman Empire'.[35] He became Literary Editor of the *Biographical and Imperial Magazine* and joined the London Corresponding Society. It took determined self-education (including in Latin), practising oratory at debating societies, the French revolution, a hatred for Edmund Burke and being befriended by John Horne Tooke, who stood trial alongside him, to turn Thelwall into a man perceived as a menace to the establishment.[36] He was over 30 when he emerged in the mid-1790s as the chief, strategist and orator of the LCS.[37]

Like Gerrald, Thelwall even looked like a Roman republican. At the time of the French revolution, some rebels threw away their wigs and powder and some cropped their hair close to their heads. During the scandal surrounding the sensational trial, both supporters and enemies of the alleged traitors produced popular songs and broadsides. One poem sympathetic to Thelwall commented on his appearance: 'Each Brutus, each Cato, were none of them fops/But all to a man wore republican crops'.[38] A new tax on hair powder introduced in 1795 meant that natural hair colour meant a man was either poor or sympathetic to the poor; informers even used the unpowdered hairstyle of a friend of Thelwall called Tom Poole, a Somerset tanner, as evidence of his revolutionary views.[39]

The infamous trials of the early 1790s prompted, in 1795, more Draconian new legislation against sedition and treason in both written and spoken form. This forbade the airing of political complaints in front of groups of more than 50 persons. In response, Thelwall took to the Classics, which he read in translation (for this, like Keats, he was derided by his reviewers) but in depth and extensively.[40] In *The Rights of Nature against the Usurpations of Establishments* (1796), directed against Burke, he imagines the aristocracy and its henchmen as tyrannical figures of Jupiter, brandishing thunderbolts to scare the British people, and as pouring forth toxic prose 'crowned with Corinthian capitals' and 'hung with antique trophies of renown', which must nevertheless perish: 'They are Augean stables that must be cleansed'.[41] He describes the deleterious effects of the 411 BCE coup at Athens and how principled democrats and Socrates sought to maintain the spirit of liberty.[42] He likens Burke's historiography of constitutions to the fanciful notions of Polybius (then a historian held in low regard).[43] He cites Dionysius of Halicarnassus, praising the original Roman Republic both for being founded by 'throngs of emigrants and refugees' and for choosing their governors by universal suffrage'.[44] He uses Tacitus and the helots of Sparta when discussing the horrors undergone by slaves in the West Indies.[45]

He went on a tour to lecture on Roman History, especially 'the abuses of monarchy and aristocracy in ancient Rome. This hoisted the banner of civic virtue once again while avoiding overt sedition',[46] although he sometimes used a direct comparison, for example between Burke and Appius Claudius, both ardent advocates of the rights of the aristocracy.[47] More often, the parallel was implied: he said that it was always the infighting between men at the top of the social tree, like Augustus and Mark Antony, which inflicted war on the rest of humanity.[48]

The censorship of public speech was stringent: 'Locke, Sydney, and Harrington are put to silence, and Barlow, Paine and Callendar it may be almost High Treason to consult', let alone discuss publicly. But 'Socrates and Plato, Tully and Demosthenes, may be eloquent in the same cause'.[49] Thelwall gave about 20 such lectures, before, in 1796, editing the 17th-century Republican Walter Moyle's *Essay on the Constitution and Government of the Roman State*, giving it the new and provocative title *Democracy Vindicated* (even though Moyle had been no democrat); Thelwall billed himself on the title page as a 'Lecturer in Classical History'.[50] His next series of lectures offered a far more radical view of the Roman Republic than had Moyle; they were idealistic and utopian in tone. The strength of the ancient Greek republics was that every single man participated in both labour and profit.[51] But all known societies—the polished Athenian, the austere Spartan, the voluptuous Roman and the Germanic barbarian—have divided their people into classes, to toil and fight.[52]

Thelwall took these lectures round the provinces, but his opponents ensured that he was received with hostility by crowds persuaded that he was an enemy of the people. At Yarmouth, his copies of Plutarch's *Lives* and Dionysius of Halicarnassus's *Roman Antiquities* were seized, torn to pieces or carried off as trophies.[53] He retired from politics in 1798, to re-emerge as a successful teacher of elocution later. He had saved enough money by 1818 to buy a journal, the *Champion*, which called (by then rather moderately) for parliamentary reform, but his political influence was effectively over before the beginning of the 19th century.

Thelwall was also a writer of poetry and prose narrative, three volumes of which were published as *The Peripatetic* in 1793, and more subsequently. In his later life, his radicalism was expressed on the level of sexualised poetry (his second marriage was to a teenager thirty-five years his junior) rather than of democratic agitation. Unpublished verses discovered by Judith Thompson in a manuscript of Thelwall's poetry in Derby Local Studies Library included not only steamy imitations of love poetry by Ovid, Anacreon and Catullus, but 'A Subject for Euripides' ('a transparently-oedipal, blank-verse gothic narrative about an older woman who miraculously keeps her youthful looks long past her prime'),[54] and 'Sappho', in which Thelwall deploys the female poet as a cross-dressed avatar of his younger self.[55]

Before and after Peterloo: Carlile, Hibbert, Wedderburn

After 1797 there was little discussion of parliamentary reform in the House of Commons, nor open public disorder, for more than a decade. It was in 1816, when the end of the Napoleonic Wars coincided with anti-government riots about food prices in Ely and Littleport, and at Spa Fields, Islington, that class conflict rose to the top of the national agenda. William Cobbett reported that numbers attending mass reform meetings multiplied at this time from 500 to 30,000.[56] March of the following year saw Richard Carlile, 'one of the most important British working-class reformers of the nineteenth century',[57] give up his attempt to earn a precarious living as a journeyman tin-plater and begin his journalistic career. His first articles were written under the pseudonym 'Plebeian' for *Sherwin's Weekly Political Register.*

Carlile was born in Devon in 1790 to a father who worked as a shoemaker and a soldier, and a mother who kept a small shop. He acquired a rudimentary education at a charity free school until he was 12, but in his early teens, when working for a local chemist, he read classical literature in translation and Paine's writings; he also taught himself Latin.[58] He switched to tin-plating, which he thought would be more remunerative, but at 21 and desperate for work, he moved with his young wife to London, where they lived in dire poverty. There were four reasons why he turned into a full-time radical in 1817: (1) the suppression of rebellious stockingers and day labourers in Derbyshire; (2) the politically motivated trials (and popular acquittals) of Thomas J. Wooler and the Spencean Dr. James Watson; (3) Carlile's reading of Constantin Volney's *Les Ruines ou Méditations sur les Révolutions des Empires* (1791), available in English since 1792 (and which also profoundly affected Shelley, especially in *Queen Mab*);[59] and (4), the examples of Robert Owen, Henry 'Orator' Hunt, Cobbett's *Political Register* and Robert Wedderburn, whom we shall meet again later in this section.[60]

After four months' imprisonment in 1817, Carlile ran a bookshop crammed with political and deist pamphlets and tried one revolutionary newspaper, *The Gracchus*. It was followed by *The Gorgon*, which was briefly an important organ of early trade unionism, the title chosen with an ironic reference to the way that the conservative press had often disparaged radicals by comparing them with the snake-haired villainess of mythology.[61] This newspaper advertised meetings of 'The Philanthropic Hercules', the loose federation of workers' unions formed in 1818 (see further pp. 446 and 467).[62] (Figure 13.1) On May 30th 1818, it ran an article on the abuse of charitable bequests which were supposed to fund schools, but were commandeered as personal profit by parish clergy and municipal corporations. In much of England 'there are erected what are termed Free Grammar Schools, for the instruction of poor children in Latin and Greek, gratis'. These were set up for praiseworthy motives. But they are neglected, teach few, and

> Latin and Greek, which used to be the most valued kind of learning, is now the most despised and useless. There can be no doubt but that the manner

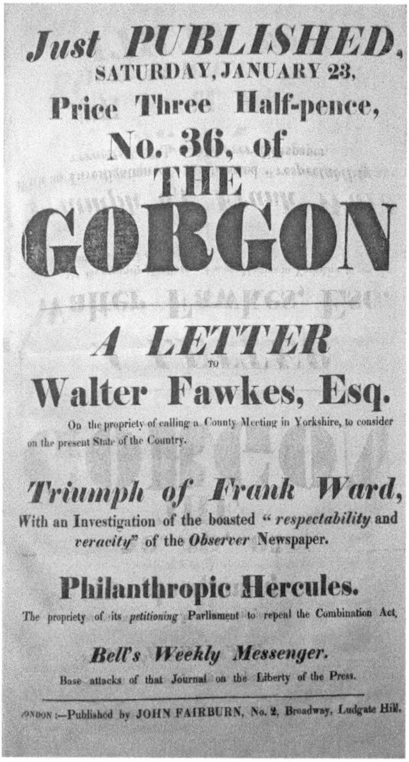

Just PUBLISHED,
SATURDAY, JANUARY 23,
Price Three Half-pence,
No. 36, of
THE
GORGON

A LETTER
TO
Walter Fawkes, Esq.
On the propriety of calling a County Meeting in Yorkshire, to consider on the present State of the Country.

Triumph of Frank Ward,
With an Investigation of the boasted "respectability and veracity" of the Observer Newspaper.

Philanthropic Hercules.
The propriety of its petitioning Parliament to repeal the Combination Act,

Bell's Weekly Messenger.
Base attacks of that Journal on the Liberty of the Press.

LONDON :—Published by JOHN FAIRBURN, No. 2, Broadway, Ludgate Hill.

FIGURE 13.1 Title page of *The Gorgon* no. 36 (1819), reproduced by courtesy of the British Library.

> in which these places are conducted at present, is contrary to the intentions of their authors.[63]

But Carlile himself knew the power of displaying a command of Latin, conducting an extensive discussion, including a five-line quotation in Latin, of Horace's *Satires* I, when defending Cobbett against criticisms.[64]

Carlile most outraged the authorities by illegally republishing works by Paine,[65] but he was at his most creative with classical material in *The Medusa*, the successor to *The Gorgon*, just before and after Peterloo in 1819. On 24th July, *The Medusa* prints a comparison of constitutional models dependent on Aristotle's *Politics*, which introduces the Resolutions passed at the meeting of the Radical Friends of Reform at Smithfield on 21st July. Then a parodic poem on 31st July teems with classical references. But on 16th August 1819, mounted yeomanry charged into a crowd of tens of thousands at St. Peter's Field, Manchester, who had amassed to hear Henry Hunt and other radicals address them. Eighteen people died of sabre wounds or trampling and crushing injuries. Carlile was present.

His first response in *The Medusa*, on 21st August, is a pseudo-Lucianic 'Dialogue in the Shades' between Paine and Pitt. But the idea of the classical underworld suggested a more adventurous trope. In order to report on the aftermath of the Peterloo 'murders', he uses the form of imaginary letters sent to Medusa by her sister Gorgons, using their authentic names Euryale and Stheno. They have access to both the murdered in the underworld and the courts where the events of that day were being processed judicially. The first letter, from Euryale to Medusa, was printed in the issue of 15th September:

> I have just left the banks of the Styx, where there several unadmitted shades deploring in the most heart-rending terms, the barbarity of the m____rs. As soon as the massacre at M________r became known to me, I obtained an indefinite leave of absence from Pluto and hastened to London ... You and I, who have seen nations rise and fall, have scarcely ever seen such hellish proceedings as have lately occurred in the B__t_sh Pandemonium, (i.e. M__ch____t).

On 26th September (279), the third Gorgon sister, Stheno, writes 'from the Styx' to Medusa as well: 'As soon as the late inhuman massacre became known to us here, we held a conclave for the purpose of advising those oppressed slaves in Britain'. She is outraged that the murderers are not to be prosecuted. Lamia (a notoriously bloodthirsty monster) has been advising that they should be assassinated. Stheno has dissuaded Lamia, but recommends instead, 'Let them meet, let them unite, let them ARM, and demand redress and justice, and a restitution of those rights which have been so long unjustly withheld from them'. Stheno's rallying cry is a response to the exoneration by the Prince Regent of the magistrates involved. He had thanked them via the Home Secretary, Lord Sidmouth. Robert Wedderburn had openly called for the abolition of the monarchy,[66] and Carlile wrote (in his own voice, not a Gorgon's), 'Unless the Prince calls his ministers to account and relieved his people, he would surely be deposed and make them all REPUBLICANS, despite all adherence to ancient and established institutions'.[67] There was a genuine danger of armed unrest, with rebellions in West Yorkshire and Lancashire in the autumn of 1819.

On 13th October (279–80), Euryale writes again to Medusa. She attended the Coroner's Inquest and was appalled at the peremptory treatment of the murders, before hastening to the Prince's bizarre palace at Brighton, the scene of debauchery. She describes the sleeping Prince, with his 'bloated features', in insulting terms. She encountered hanging over him the shade of Brutus, 'the illustrious patriot of the Ancients', who in a 'prophetic frenzy' recited a malediction, praying that the Prince die a terrifying death. A week later, Stheno, from the Styx, protests against the current crackdown on freethinking of any kind (18th October, 294). Confused by establishment figures calling the violence of Peterloo dictated by 'the Word of God', she had sent to the upper world for a copy, but the message went to the wrong country, and the Koran arrived instead of the Christian Bible. When she did get the 'Word of God' as read in England, she found it so full of 'murders, incests, &c.' that she was shocked. On 13th November (310–11) Euryale writes to Medusa of her concern that the British reformers are splitting into factions; she reiterates that armed force may be necessary (she cites the examples of the two Roman Brutuses and Wat Tyler). She concludes by saying that she hopes to be able to update her sister on the 'Mission of Brutus' shortly.

This confrontation between George IV (he became King in January 1820) and newspapers like *The Medusa* was ridiculed by caricature artist George Cruikshank in 'Coriolanus Addressing the Plebeians' (29th February 1820) (Figure 13.2). Cruikshank likens it to the face-off between the legendary early Roman statesman Caius Marcius Coriolanus, known to his readers from Plutarch via Shakespeare, and the plebeian class at Rome. Three of the Cato Street conspirators, who in February 1820 had planned to kill the Prime Minister and his cabinet, are arranged under the banner 'Blood and Thunder': Thomas Preston, Dr. James Watson and Arthur Thistlewood. Beside them are Carlile and Cobbett, who is holding Tom Paine's bones. Among the more moderate reformers lining up are the satirist William Hone and the creator of the caricature, Cruikshank himself. They sport the red cap of the Roman freedman.

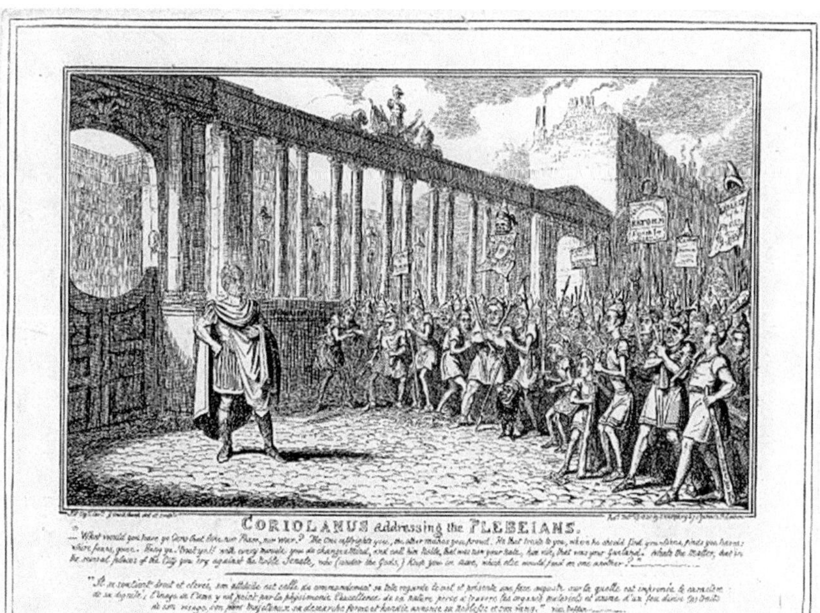

FIGURE 13.2 'Coriolanus Addressing the Plebeians' by George Cruikshank (29th February 1820), reproduced by courtesy of the British Museum. © The Trustees of the British Museum.

Carlile's Gorgons fulfil several subversive functions. By appropriating the Classics-laden rhetoric of the ruling class, he draws attention to cultural apartheid while undermining it. As a critic of Christianity, the mythical personae allow him to sidestep the pious bombast which the government was using against the radicals. By using the speech-within-a-speech form (Brutus quoted by Euryale) for expressing the desire for the Regent to die a horrible death, Carlile might have thought he could have defended himself personally against a charge of sedition. As immortals, the Gorgon sisters not only have long memories of the history of revolts against tyrants, but Stheno, at least, can move instantaneously between places to witness an inquest in Manchester and the (heavily guarded) bedchamber of the Regent. But the letters are also funny, and Carlile knew as well as anyone that collective laughter in the face of oppression can be politically effective.

Unsurprisingly, by the time the November issues came out, Carlile had already been convicted of blasphemy and seditious libel in one of the 75 prosecutions for those crimes brought in England in 1819 alone.[68] He was fined and incarcerated in Dorchester until 1825. He continued publishing the *Republican* from prison, but the *Medusa* ceased. The Prince Regent, who had once asked of a man, 'Is he a gentleman? Has he any Greek?'[69] was not assassinated, and the moment of greatest threat to the established order passed. After the Cato Street conspirators were hanged and beheaded or deported, new repressive legislation ('The Six Acts') meant that all British radicals found themselves in gaol. Carlile's wife Mary-Anne loyally moved into Dorset Prison with him, and in 1823 they had a daughter whom they named Hypatia after the ancient pagan intellectual. She died in infancy.[70]

The imprisoned Carlile acquired a large 'republican and infidel' following. His keenest supporters, in London, Salford, Stalybridge and Glasgow, founded 'zetetic' societies (from the ancient Greek verb *zētein*, to seek out or enquire after), which investigated the truth of existence by scientific and non-Christian methods.[71] The emphasis of his work fell increasingly on free thought once he began collaborating 'as Infidel missionary' with the Reverend Robert Taylor, an anti-clerical mystic who had been imprisoned for blasphemy after lecturing in London pubs on the immorality of the Church of England. Carlile promoted Taylor's published works, written in prison,[72] notably his *Syntagma* (1828) and *Diegesis* (1829). These argued that all religions were similar, based on solar and astral myths and sacrificed heroes, and that honorific titles such as 'Christ' and 'Lord' were merely the equivalents of epithets applied to Bacchus, Apollo, Adonis and Jupiter.[73]

In 1830, Carlile founded the Rotunda in Blackfriars Road, to nurture revolutionary sentiment against the 'aristocratical or clerical despotism, corruption and ignorance of the whole country'.[74] It became the recognised centre of London working-class radicalism, featuring spectacular 'infidel' dramas, in which Taylor showed that the gospels rewrote primordial Mithraic and Bacchic mysteries.[75] Carlile and Taylor were re-imprisoned, but the work at the Rotunda was continued by their Bolton-born disciple and sex equality activist, Eliza Sharples, who became Carlile's common-law wife. She led the mysteries in the persona of Isis, dressed in flowing gowns, with white thorn and laurel leaves underfoot.[76]

Carlile's intellectual mentor, on the other hand, was Julian Hibbert, whose death in 1834 shattered him. Hibbert was one of the most mysterious radicals on the post-Peterloo scenes, not least because, although highly educated and privately wealthy, he was tightly embedded within the working-class political community from which Carlile became distanced as his theological interests deepened.[77] In 1828 Hibbert published an edition of Plutarch's *On Superstition*, with other material including Theophrastus' character portrait of the 'Superstitious Man', which was adopted and much used by less erudite freethinkers. Hibbert humorously states that he regards 'no book so amusing as the Old Testament' and closes his preface 'by consigning all "Greek Scholars" to the special care of Beelzebub'.[78] He attaches dazzlingly erudite polemics on how religion is used to sedate what Burke called 'the swinish multitude', on all the individuals falsely accused of impiety from Xenophanes, Socrates and Aristotle via Julian the Apostate to the 19th century, and the many definitions of the word 'god'.[79] But Hibbert was active in radical politics as well. He was treasurer to the Victim Fund run by the agitators for the freedom of the unstamped press; the Chartist William Lovett recalled:

> He was a person of extreme liberal views both in politics and religion; indeed, he used frequently to say that he could wish to practise the good found among all religions, but had no faith in any of their creeds. He belonged, I believe, to an aristocratic family; had received an excellent education, and was, I understand, a capital Greek scholar. From my intimate knowledge of him I know that he possessed a kind and generous disposition, and that he was ever foremost in helping the downtrodden and oppressed without show or ostentation.[80]

Hibbert personally funded several of the legal defences of the radicals imprisoned after Peterloo, and had almost certainly furnished the arguments from Plutarch used by Robert Wedderburn, the mixed-race son of a Scottish planter in Jamaica by his African slave woman, when tried for blasphemy in May 1820.[81] (Figure 13.3)

A Unitarian preacher, and follower of Thomas Spence, Wedderburn had described Jesus Christ as a 'republican' and 'reformer' and compared him with Henry Hunt. Hunt was himself at the time in prison following Peterloo. A transcript of Wedderburn's trial including his speech, with learned notes, was simultaneously published. It is an uncompromising defence of freedom in discussion of scripture: 'Tyrannical and intolerant laws may exist and be enforced in times of darkness and ignorance, but they will be of little effect when once the human mind is emancipated from the trammels of superstition'.[82]

FIGURE 13.3 'Robert Wedderburn (1762–1835)', by Becky Brewis (2019) after engraving by unknown artist © Becky Brewis 2019.

The publication was edited by George Cannon, under the pseudonym Erasmus Perkins: a middle-class, educated radical, Cannon later became a notorious pornographer. With advice from Hibbert, he almost certainly wrote some of Wedderburn's plea—Wedderburn says that he had been unable to write it because his work as a tailor had wrecked his eyesight, and a court clerk read it out. Footnotes enhance the publication's air of erudition and authority. Amongst quotations from the Christian Fathers, and references to Roman myth, there is a discussion of the derivation of the two ancient Greek roots of the Greek word *blaspheme* (which Paine had also discussed; see above, p. 273), and a long note on the Delphic oracle. Plutarch is cited for arguing that it is better to deny the existence of a Supreme Being than to 'entertain degrading and dishonourable notions of him'.[83] Wedderburn's court appearance persuaded the jury to recommend 'mercy', resulting in a sentence of 'only' two years in Dorchester gaol.

Chartists: O'Brien, Jones, Cooper

Four years before Hibbert's untimely death, a fiery young Irishman named James 'Bronterre' O'Brien arrived in London. He was to play a key role in the first national working-class movement of Chartism. He was not only one of the greatest Chartist speakers, but perhaps the one most trusted by working people. The People's Charter demanded universal male suffrage, secret ballots, annual parliaments, pay for MPs and abolition of property qualifications to stand for election and equal electoral districts.[84] Bronterre, as he was known, probably on account of his thunderous oratory, was a middle-class man from County Longford. He had passed the TCD Classics exams with flying colours and, as an undergraduate, won prizes in both Classics and science.[85] Although he went to London to further his studies of law, he was already radicalised, becoming the editor of *The Poor Man's Guardian* in 1832 and campaigning for a free press.[86] In 1840 he was convicted of making a seditious speech in Manchester and spent 18 months in Lancaster Prison.

It was not until 1849 that he began publishing the 21 journal articles that became *The Rise, Progress and Phases of Human Slavery*,[87] an unjustifiably neglected book in which he brings his expert knowledge of Classics to bear on contemporary politics and economics (Figure 13.4). He argues that ancient slavery was in some circumstances ways less bad, because 'direct and avowed', than the condition of the Victorian working class, 'hypocritically masked under legal forms', which he defines as unjust agrarian, monetary and fiscal laws.[88] O'Brien's work remains important if only because Karl Marx, who arrived in London in 1849, told Engels he was 'an irrepressible Chartist at any price';[89] Marx's own theories were certainly influenced by O'Brien's theorisation of exchange in relation to the equivalence of ancient slaves and the 19th-century proletariat, the value of

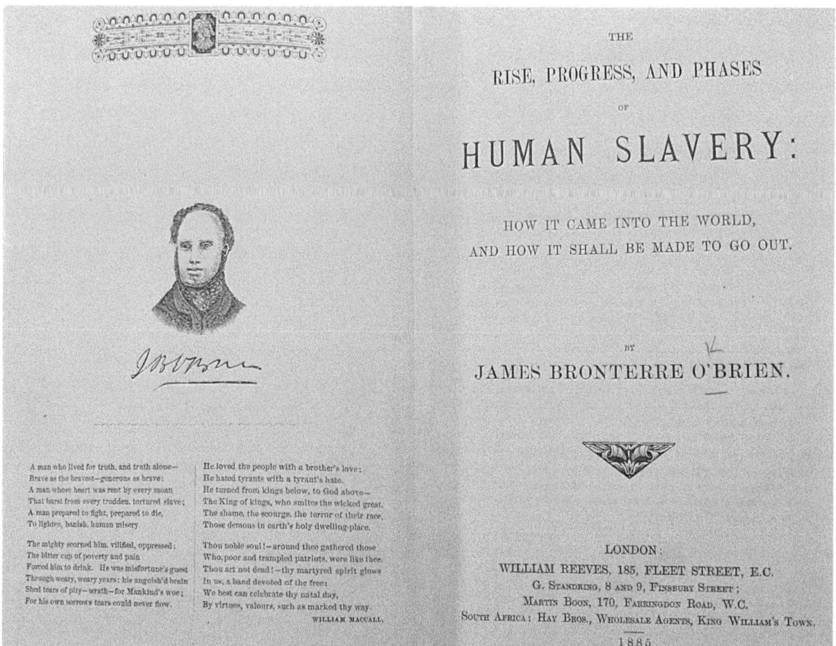

A man who lived for truth, and truth alone—
Brave as the bravest—generous as brave:
A man whose heart was rent by every moan
That burst from every trodden, tortured slave;
A man prepared to fight, prepared to die,
To lighten, banish, human misery.

The mighty scorned him, vilified, oppressed;
The bitter cup of poverty and pain
Forced him to drink. He was misfortune's guest
Through weary, weary years: his anguish'd brain
Shed tears of pity—wrath—for Mankind's woe;
For his own sorrows tears could never flow.

He loved the people with a brother's love;
He hated tyrants with a tyrant's hate.
He turned from kings below, to God above—
The King of kings, who smites the wicked great,
The shame, the scourge, the terror of their race,
Those demons in earth's holy dwelling-place.

Thou noble soul!—around thee gathered those
Who, poor and trampled patriots, were like thee.
Thou art not dead!—thy martyred spirit glows
In us, a band devoted of the free;
We best can celebrate thy natal day,
By virtues, valours, such as marked thy way.

WILLIAM MACCALL.

THE
RISE, PROGRESS, AND PHASES
OF
HUMAN SLAVERY:
HOW IT CAME INTO THE WORLD,
AND HOW IT SHALL BE MADE TO GO OUT.

BY
JAMES BRONTERRE O'BRIEN.

LONDON:
WILLIAM REEVES, 185, FLEET STREET, E.C.
G. STANDRING, 8 AND 9, FINSBURY STREET;
MARTIN BOON, 170, FARRINGDON ROAD, W.C.
SOUTH AFRICA: HAY BROS., WHOLESALE AGENTS, KING WILLIAM'S TOWN.
1885

FIGURE 13.4 Title page of James O'Brien's *The Rise, Progress and Phases of Human Slavery* (1885), reproduced by courtesy of the British Library. Reproduced by courtesy of the British Library.

labour, the concept of hidden bondage, and the workings of ideology which maintain class divisions.[90]

Bronterre's commitment to the working class never lessened. Even after the waning of Chartism, he opened the Eclectic Institute in Denmark Street, Soho, London, which served a useful purpose in the early stages of the Adult Education Movement, earning him the soubriquet 'Schoolmaster O'Brien' on account of his services to the self-education of working men.[91] An unrepentant admirer of the French revolution, in 1857 he acknowledged his own frustration in his Miltonic 'An elegy on the death of Robespierre', in which a group of workmen, after the parliamentary revolt of 9th Thermidor 1794, address the shade of Robespierre on how other 'godlike benefactors of our race' have been spurned and die miserably: Aristides, Socrates, and numerous Roman republicans.[92]

The other classicist Chartist well known to Marx was Ernest Jones, whom Engels regarded as the only educated Englishman in politics 'entirely on our side'.[93] Born in Berlin in 1819, the son of an army major and the daughter of a major Kent landowner, Jones received his excellent classical education at a prestigious school in Hannover and moved to London at 19. He came into a fortune through his marriage; it was going bankrupt in 1844 and his own precipitation into poverty that turned him into a passionate Chartist. His first collection of poetry, *Chartist Songs*, published in 1846, was popular amongst the working class.[94] He was arrested for seditious behaviour and unlawful assembly, enduring two years' imprisonment; in 1850 he said to a crowd in Manchester, 'I went into your prison a Chartist, but … have come out of it a Republican'.[95] After his release, Jones assisted on George Harney's socialist newspaper *Red Republican*. His long poem *The New World*, discussed below pp. 407, puts his classicist's grasp of ancient history to extended use. But his lectures often used arresting classical images, too: 'Everyone knows that Capital … is the offspring of Labour, and yet that Labour is the servant of Capital; nay! that the latter, reversing the legend of old Saturn, has been destroying its Creator'.[96] When arguing against private education, he stated that

> The schools of the rich, directly or indirectly, pervert the minds of the young—the great leverage of future oppression is planted in the brains of poor men's children. That is the "foot of space" whence the Class Archimedes hurls down liberty—this ought to be counteracted.[97]

Chartists from poorer backgrounds, aware of earlier radical uses of the ancient world, enjoyed rousing quotations from antiquity. When William Lovett and James Watson drew up their Declaration of the National Union of the Working Classes in 1831, one of the epigraphs was 'That Commonwealth is best ordered when the citizens are neither too rich nor too poor—THALES'.[98] Chartists often struggled to teach themselves the classical languages. Joseph Barker, born in Bramley, Leeds in 1806, was the son of a handloom weaver and at the age of 9 forced to go to work himself. But he would prop up books by his jenny gallows to read while he worked as a spinner, and at 16 started teaching himself Latin and Greek. He became a Chartist activist later.[99] Gilbert Collins was a Chartist bank clerk who taught himself Greek but could not afford the books from which to learn Arabic. The famous Chartist poet Thomas Cooper recalls that during the years 1836–1838, when he was working as a journalist in Lincoln, the two became friends partly because they 'had an equally strong attachment to the study of languages. Collins had learned Latin at school, and had taught himself Greek, and had translated for himself the entire *Iliad* and *Odyssey*. Of the Greek Testament, he had a more perfect knowledge than any one I ever knew'.[100] The pair decided to teach themselves Arabic. Another local friend, George Boole (a shoemaker's son who had learned Latin from a kindly local bookseller and went on to become the first Professor of Mathematics at Queen's College, Cork, later University College Cork) discovered their plan. He laughed at them, pointing out that they would need to acquire Richardson's Arabic dictionary,[101] which was quite out of their reach, costing at least 12 to 15 pounds.[102] Mortified, the pair 'felt ashamed of our thoughtlessness, and laid the project aside'.[103]

But Latin and Greek were more accessible through cheap second-hand textbooks. Although, as we shall see in Chapter 20, he had little formal education, Thomas Cooper, the self-styled Chartist Rhymer, had taught himself almost as much Classics as O'Brien or Jones. This is most apparent from his epic poem *The Purgatory of Suicides*, written in the early 1840s in Stafford Gaol, where he was imprisoned as a Chartist after being convicted of sedition.[104] *The Purgatory of Suicides* impressed not only its Chartist readership but Carlyle, Benjamin Disraeli and Kingsley.[105] The first six stanzas of *The Purgatory of Suicides* are, he says, a poetical embodiment of a speech he delivered in 1842 to the colliers on strike in the Staffordshire Potteries, as a result of which he was arrested for arson and violence.[106]

In book I, he is imprisoned and dreams of a voyage of death and meeting the souls of suicides; there is a sort of constitutional debate which draws on Herodotus Book III and Cicero's *Dream of Scipio*. Some of the ancient dead involved share characteristics with Chartists. They include Oedipus (who solved the riddle), the patriotic Athenian heroes Aegeus, Salaminian Ajax, Codrus, and the tragic national heroines Dido, Cleopatra, and Boadicea; others are less admirable (Nero and Appius).[107] In book IV, there is a dialogue between Sappho and Lucretius and an assembly of suicidal poets summoned by Lucan. Vicinus thinks that Cooper was indulging in shameless self-promotion by displaying his classical knowledge,[108] while Sanders suggests that the poem can 'be read as an attempt to democratize "elite" knowledge ... The fact that Cooper provides explanatory footnotes for a number of his protagonists increases the education value of the poem'.[109] But they overlook Cooper's creative dialogue between ancient India and Greece. The voice of India, in the mouth of the sage Calanus, transcends time and space, in a manner reminiscent of the choruses of Shelley's *Prometheus Unbound* and *Hellas*, to prophesy global liberation and universal suffrage.

Calanus is found in several ancient sources for Alexander the Great's activities in India, including Plutarch's *Life of Alexander* and Arrian's *Anabasis* 7.1.5–3.6. He was frequently praised by ancient philosophers and Christians including Ambrose for his self-control and bravery in the face of self-death.[110] In an essay entitled 'Every Good Man is Free', the Alexandrian Jewish scholar Philo (c. 20 BCE to 50 CE) had cited Calanus as an outstanding example of the true freedom enjoyed by every good man. Philo records that when Alexander tried to coerce him into leaving India and travelling with him, Calanus pointed that he would become a useless specimen of 'barbarian wisdom' for the Macedonian to display to the Greek world if he allowed himself to be forced to do anything against his will (Philo, 9.14.92–6). Cooper puts the idea of Calanus as a spokesman for true spiritual freedom to innovative political use.

Calanus is introduced in book II in order to provide a climax for a list of various *Greek* sages. Calanus tells the Greeks Empedocles and Cleombrotus of his utopian vision of the future—a spiritual allegory for the Chartists' vision of a levelled and democratic society:

> The time will come, O Hellene! when the sun
> Shall look upon a world no more o'errun
> With slaves to sensualism; when haggard Spite,
> And frowning Pride, and Envy pale shall sun
> Truth's glorious beams ...[111]

He says that the strong will end up seeking to break bread for weeping orphans, and

> Knowledge, the great Enfranchiser, is near!
> Yet, though their bonds the wide world's helots break,
> They seek not in their tyrants' blood to slake
> A thirst for vengeance ...[112]

That an ancient Indian sage should be selected to lecture ancient Greeks on the topics of feeding the destitute as well as enfranchising and educating the wide world's 'helots' reveals Cooper's intuition that British commercial interests in India were linked to the predicament of the working classes internationally. Cooper—an outstanding working-class intellectual—has read his ancient Greek sources on Alexander and Calanus significantly 'against the grain'.

The lowliness of Cooper's origins makes remarkable the detail of his knowledge of ancient history, as well as the topical appropriation to which he subjects that knowledge. Cooper was not only committed to universal male suffrage and agitation on behalf of the poor, but on an international level he was opposed to imperialism: one of his most inflammatory speeches, delivered at Hanley in the Potteries in August 1842, begins with a catalogue of 'conquerors, from Sesostris to Alexander, from Caesar to Napoleon, who had become famous in history for shedding the blood of millions'. He described 'how the conquerors of America had nearly exterminated the native races'. He excoriated 'British wrongdoing in Ireland'.[113] For the working-class activist Cooper, then, the ancient Brahmins of India, as filtered through ancient historiography and biography, represented a mystical fount of ancient knowledge of the post-imperial international utopia to be ushered in by the Charter. Cooper made Calanus, an ancient Indian, lecture an ancient Greek/Macedonian conqueror on social justice. Cooper had, of course, never been anywhere near India, however clear his understanding of the link between the class system in Britain and the oppression of indigenous peoples in her colonies.[114]

Cooper also lectured to working-class audiences at the City Chartist Hall in London, in which he popularised 'the magnificent themes of the Athenian democracy', and in late 1848 he spoke on the transition from 'legendary' to 'historical' Greece at the Hall of Science in City Road.[115] He uses ancient sources and is also familiar with the first volume of George Grote's *History of Greece*, which appeared in 1846. He was not the only Chartist routinely to use Athens and Rome as comparands on the lecture circuit. John Collins defended the Greek and Roman republics at a meeting of the Leeds Reform Association, because it was advocating household suffrage rather than universal male suffrage and the rest of the Charter's demands.[116] In Wales, Henry Vincent drew a dark picture of the invariable fall of proud empires which oppressed their poor, such as Rome, and his Monmouthshire audiences applauded loudly when he described the final victory of the northern barbarians who dashed 'the haughty usurper' down. Athens provided an even better example, because he could speak at length on her achievements, and St. Paul's visit, as well as describing how she became 'degraded' when she lost her love of liberty.[117]

Conclusion

The democrats of the 1790s, especially Tom Paine and John Thelwall, were immersed in and inspired by ancient philosophy and history read in translation. The radicals around the time of Peterloo, for whom free thought on religion was inseparable from agitation for social, political and economic reform, used Classics in diverse and creative ways to enliven their journalism, inform arguments at the trials, and explore religious questions that took them far beyond the limits of orthodox Anglican theology. Three of the most important Chartist intellectuals—Ernest Jones, Bronterre O'Brien and Thomas Cooper—were expert classicists, whether trained at distinguished educational institutions or self-taught, and whether this took expression in oratory, poetry or analysis of ancient slavery.

It took decades for the Chartists' demands to be met. Some urban working-class men were enfranchised by the Representation of the People Act 1867, but it was not until 1918 that universal male suffrage was finally achieved. With some exceptions, when working-class activism took off again in earnest in the last quarter of the 19th century, classical education was beginning to lose some of its social prestige, and most of the leaders of the labour movement were less concerned than the Georgian democrats and Chartists had been to acquire ancient languages or recruit the ancient Greeks and Romans to their cause. For some of those fascinating exceptions, see Chapter 23.

Notes

1 Hobbes (1651) 111, quoted in full above pp. 16 and 271.
2 Epstein and Karr (2007).
3 Murphy (1994) 9.
4 A similar position to ours was defended by Gummere (1965).
5 Paine (1796a) 51.
6 Paine (1795) 16–17.
7 Paine (1796c) 31n.
8 Paine (1794) 65.
9 Paine (1794) 67.
10 Paine (1797) 5.
11 Paine (1787).
12 Paine (1788) 26–7.
13 Quoted in Aldridge (1968) 379.
14 Paine (1776) 14.
15 Paine (1788) 26–7.
16 Paine (1817) 15–16.
17 Paine (1783) 48.
18 Paine (1783) 71.
19 Paine (1794) 10.
20 Paine (1792) 9.
21 Paine (1796b) 77n.
22 See Aldridge (1968) 371.
23 Paine (1824) 332.
24 Cockburn (1888) vol. I, 43–4.
25 See further Davis (2004).
26 Gerrald and Porcia (1812). 'The gods' mills grind belatedly but they grind small.
27 Derry (1966) 27.
28 See Hall and Macintosh (2005) 222–8 and 166–9.
29 Claeys (1995) xiii.
30 Cited in Derry (1966) 27.
31 So Johnstone (1828) volume 1. 453–4.
32 See letter to Mr Windham, 8th May 1795 cited in Johnstone (1821) volume 1, 451.
33 Hindle (1988) xxvii–viii.
34 Claeys (1995) xiii–xv.
35 Thelwall (1795) 29.
36 Claeys (1995) xvi–xvii.
37 Claeys (1995) xiii, xix.
38 The poem, by W.H. Green, was first published in *The Philanthropist* for 16th March 1795, reproduced in Eaton (1795, ed.) 5–6.
39 Sandford (1888) Vol. I, 131n.
40 Thompson (2015) 13.
41 Thelwall (1796a) 13, 15
42 Thelwall (1796a) 20–1.
43 Thelwall (1796a) 34.
44 Thelwall (1796a) 36, 43–4.
45 Thelwall (1796a) 61.

46 Claeys (1995) xxvii.
47 Claeys (1995) 340–1.
48 Claeys (1995) 93.
49 Thelwall (1796b) 7–8, 18–19. By Sydney he means Algernon Sidney, republican and member of the Long Parliament. Joel Barlow and James Callender were republicans working in America (Callender's first publications date from his earlier years in Scotland).
50 Moyle's essay as edited by Thelwall is included in Thelwall (1796a).
51 *The Tribune* I. 3:43, 46, 248, reproduced in Claeys (1995) 289–90, xlv.
52 Claeys (1995) 487
53 Claeys (1995) xxx.
54 Thompson (2009) 96.
55 Thompson (2009) 99.
56 Cobbett (1816) 353; see also Hunt (1820) vol. I, vi: 'The cause of reform languished until the year 1816'.
57 Wiener (1983) ix.
58 Wiener (1983) 4–6.
59 Volney (1792). Extracts in English had appeared even earlier (Volney [1791]). On the plight at this time of the stockingers of Derbyshire and Nottinghamshire, many of whom lost their homes and became beggars, see Stubley (2015) 115–21.
60 Wiener (1983) 16.
61 On Shelley's subversion of the conservative uses of Medusa at the same time, see Judson (2001).
62 See Fraser (1999) 14. There were earlier attempts in the 18th century at unionisation and forming links between unions in different trades, but the secrecy necessitated by the stringent laws against such activities makes them difficult to research: see Morton and Tate (1956) 17–20.
63 On 30th May, 1818, 12.
64 Carlile (1819) 4.
65 Cole (1943) 3.
66 Poole (2000) 154.
67 Poole (2000) 154.
68 Webb (1977) 109.
69 Castronovo (1987) 59; Larson (1999) 195 no. 43.
70 Wiener (1983) 84–5
71 Wiener (1983) 112–14.
72 Cole (1943) 23.
73 Wiener (1983) 132. The full titles are *Syntagma of the Evidence of the Christian Religion* (1828) and *The Diegesis: Being a Discovery of the Origin, Evidences, and Early History of Christianity, Never Yet Before or Elsewhere So Fully and Faithfully Set Forth* (1829).
74 Wiener (1983) 164.
75 Wiener (1983) 165–6.
76 Wiener (1983) 180–1. Cole (1943) 25.
77 Wiener (1983) 209.
78 Hibbert (1828) v, vi.
79 These appended essays are entitled 'On the Supposed Necessity of Deceiving the Vulgar', 'Of Persons Falsely Entitled Atheists' and 'Various Definitions of an Important Word'.
80 Lovett (1920) 90–1.
81 In prison Wedderburn was visited by William Wilberforce and wrote *The Horrors of Slavery* (1824), drawing on his own childhood memories, especially of his mother and grandmother being flogged. His importance as an early British-Caribbean mixed-race radical is now widely acknowledged. See McCalman (1986) and Hunt (2012).

82 Wedderburn (1820) 9.
83 Wedderburn (1820) 9.
84 Plummer (1971) 15.
85 Plummer (1971) 23.
86 Plummer (1971) 44.
87 Finally published in book form in 1885 and edited by a writer whose dedication 'To The People' is signed, simply, 'Spartacus'.
88 O'Brien (1885) 2, 25; Plummer (1971) 194–6.
89 Letter of 14th January 1858, in Marx and Engels (2010) 250.
90 Plummer (1971) 248–52. On Marx and classical antiquity, see p. 494 n. 33.
91 Plummer (1971) 253–8.
92 Bronterre (1859) 37, 39.
93 Murphy (1994) 30.
94 Saville (1952) 20.
95 Saville (1952) 113.
96 Saville (1952) 80.
97 Saville (1952) 113–14.
98 Lovett (1920 [1876]) 74.
99 J.F.C. Harrison (1957) 40–1.
100 Cooper (1872) 118.
101 Richardson (1777–1780).
102 Cooper (1872) 119.
103 Cooper (1872) 119.
104 See further Crust (2016).
105 Taylor (2003) 81.
106 Thomas Talfourd, a rare judge sympathetic to the Chartists whose radical version of a Greek tragedy, *Ion*, has been mentioned above, helped Cooper considerably. He gave him £100 when he realised that he should not have prosecuted him, since Cooper had played no part in the violence. See Cooper (1872) 339.
107 Cooper (1877) 24–7.
108 Vicinus (1974) 110.
109 Sanders (2017).
110 See Musurillo (1954) 237.
111 Cooper (1877) 67.
112 Cooper (1877) 68.
113 Cooper (1872) 187–90.
114 Hall (2010b) 42–3.
115 Gurney (2014).
116 *The Northern Star*, 23rd January (1841) 8.
117 *The Monmouthsire Merlin*, 12th May (1849) 4.

14

UNDERDOG PROFESSORS

Introduction

Until the Butler Education Act 1944, although it was most unusual for individuals born into low-income families to acquire sufficient education in the ancient languages for them to rise within the academic profession, it was not entirely unknown. It required extraordinary autodidactic efforts, like those of Joseph Wright, who eventually became Professor of Comparative Philology at Oxford University. It also usually required financial support, which only happened if a working-class boy's academic talent was spotted by an ambitious parent with the confidence to pursue middle-class contacts, a benevolent parish priest or a teacher at a Charity or Dame School, Dissenting teacher, or paternalistic wealthy local patrons on the lookout for prodigies amongst the impoverished families eking out a living on or near their estates. Their education was sometimes procured via scholarships at one of the old Charity or Bluecoat Schools; rich sponsors, especially Nonconformists, sometimes subsidised study at university.

A few working-class men became competent classicists before brilliant careers in, for example, academic philosophy. Henry Jones (1852–1922) was a village shoemaker's son from Denbighshire who rose through scholarships at Bangor Training College for Teachers and Glasgow University to hold chairs in philosophy at the universities of Bangor, St. Andrews and Glasgow and received a knighthood. Ever proud of his lowly roots and his Welshness, Jones was early inspired by the authors of ancient Greece and Rome. This is apparent above all in his *Essays on Literature and Education* (1924), a brilliant set of essays on popular authors in the English language and on the purpose of education. Scott's storytelling is compared to Homer's, Shakespeare's morality to Sophocles', the Brownings' debt to their education in Greek and Latin and to Euripides' erudition and Aeschylus is stressed.[1] When it came to revelling in the richness of

DOI: 10.4324/9781315446608-17

ancient literature, Jones was a classicist to the core. He opened his 1905 address to the subscribers of the Stirling and Glasgow Public Libraries, 'The Library as a Maker of Character', with an inspirational quotation from Benjamin Jowett's translation of the opening sequence of Plato's *Phaedrus*, when Socrates goes for a country walk with Phaedrus after meeting the young man with a book under his arm (230d): 'I am a lover of knowledge', said the ancient sage,

> and the men who dwell in the city are my teachers, and not the trees of the country; though, indeed, I do believe that you have found a spell with which to draw me out of the city, like a hungry cow before whom a bough or bunch of fruit is waved. For only hold up before me a book, and you may lead me all round Attica, and over the wide world.[2]

Welsh men destined to become Methodist preachers were also often trained rigorously in Greek, as we have seen above in the case of Lewis Edwards and his son Thomas (pp. 179–82). But a tiny handful of working-class men made their academic mark specifically on Classics or Comparative Philology. The obstacles which lay in the path of bookish youths from a humble background were considerable, and there were large variations in their attitudes in later life to other members of the social class from which they had emerged, escaped or had even betrayed, depending on their personal perspective. This chapter looks in detail at five such figures—three of whom were associated with the University of Edinburgh—in the 18th and 19th centuries, but there is undoubtedly far more work to be done in this area, especially on academics of the 20th century. By that time, careers in Classics were occasionally achieved even by women who were originally working-class, such as Kathleen Freeman at the University College Cardiff.[3]

Richard Porson

The most arresting example is Richard Porson (1759–1808), a weaver's son from rural Norfolk (Figure 14.1). His mother, a cobbler's daughter, was clever and literate and ensured he attended the village school regularly, followed at the age of nine by the Free School in the village of Happisborough. A local nobleman, impressed by the boy's classical prowess, paid for his education to be continued at Eton.[4] Porson did not enjoy the school, later saying that the only thing he remembered with pleasure was rat-hunting on winter evenings.[5] He seems also, however, to have performed enthusiastically in musical burlesques there; he could recall them word-for-word in later life, and used to sing raucous Vauxhall songs in elegant society, incurring opprobrium thereby.[6]

Several other patrons financed Porson's studies at Trinity College, Cambridge, where he was elected a Fellow; at some point during this earliest part of his career, he took a position as private tutor to a gentleman's son on the Isle of Wight, but was sacked 'having been found drunk in a ditch or a turnip field.'[7] In 1792, when it was decided that fellowships were no longer open to laymen, Porson declined

FIGURE 14.1 Richard Porson (1759–1808) Public Domain image digitised by Österreichische Nationalbibliothek—Austrian National Library.

to take holy orders and so lost his stipend. Unwillingness to take orders in fact took courage, since no great piety was required of the academic clergy at that time, and there was small chance of earning an adequate living outside schools or universities.[8] Porson was proud, principled and politically radical, supporting the French Revolution in its early days, advocating parliamentary reform, attending the House of Commons debates in 1792 on the Birmingham riots[9] and adamantly opposing Pitt's government.[10] Porson's reputation consequently suffered at the hands of conservative critics such as De Quincey, who alleged incorrectly that Porson read no poetry at all 'unless it were either political or obscene'.[11]

This working-class prodigy was responsible for what have been dismissed as 'ephemeral productions', but were, rather, clever uses of classical material to make political points.[12] In 1792 Porson published a satirical attack, later republished by Richard Carlile (on whom see Chapter 13, pp. 278–83), *A New Catechism for the Use of the Swinish Multitude, Necessary to be Had in all Sties*, (Figure 14.2) on Burke's *Reflections* on the French revolution. Burke had claimed that learning had been

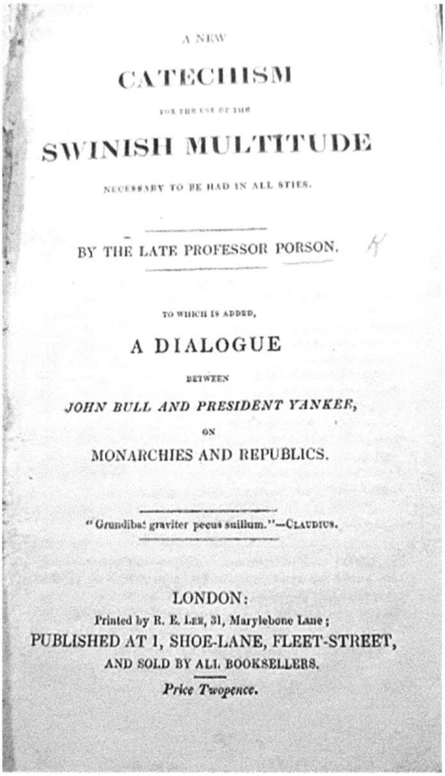

A NEW
CATECHISM
FOR THE USE OF THE
SWINISH MULTITUDE
NECESSARY TO BE HAD IN ALL STIES.

BY THE LATE PROFESSOR PORSON.

TO WHICH IS ADDED,
A DIALOGUE
BETWEEN
JOHN BULL AND PRESIDENT YANKEE,
ON
MONARCHIES AND REPUBLICS.

"Grundibat graviter pecus suillum."—CLAUDIUS.

LONDON:
Printed by R. E. LEE, 31, Marylebone Lane;
PUBLISHED AT 1, SHOE-LANE, FLEET-STREET,
AND SOLD BY ALL BOOKSELLERS.
Price Twopence.

FIGURE 14.2 Title page from Richard Porson's *A New Catechism for the Swinish Multitude* (1818), reproduced from copy in Hall's personal collection.

'trodden down under the hoofs of the swinish multitude': Porson's swine portray their suffering under the Hog Drivers. It is a witty piece. Any doubt that its target is Burke disappears with the second question, 'Did God make you a hog?', to which the prescribed answer is 'No; God made me man in his own image; the *Right Honourable* SUBLIME AND BEAUTIFUL made me a swine'.[13] To the question whether the resolutions made by the ruling class hog-drivers can be read by the hogs, the answer is no, because scarcely one in 20 hogs can read. The questioner says, 'They are written in *Hog Latin*, but that I took for granted you could understand', to which the hogs retort (remarkably, given that the author is a Classics Professor), 'Shameful aspersion on the hogs! The most inarticulate grunting of our tribe is sense and harmony compared to such jargon.'[14] But all is not lost, because the questioner notices that the pigs' spokesman talks sense, and asks 'whence had you your information?' The answer is 'From a learned pig', of which there are 'many; and the number daily increases.'[15] Porson is aware of the democrats' emphasis on working-class self-education. 'The allegory is obvious enough, and so are the Jacobinical sentiments'.[16]

Porson also wrote some 'Imitations of Horace' in *The Morning Chronicle* in 1794. One published on 12th August was an imitation of *Odes* 1.14, which he turned into an attack on Pitt, a 'cub that knows not stem from stern'.[17] The third, on 13th September, on *Ode* 1.34, uses Horace's problem that he had fought for the Republicans to comment on the contemporary clampdown on freedom of the press.[18] Porson prefaces his *Hymn of a New-Made Peer to* his Creator, savaging Pitt's additions to the peerage, with a quote from Athenaeus.[19] He became embroiled in the trial of William Frend, Fellow of Jesus College, Cambridge, who was accused of attacking the established church; in three raucous, uncompromising letters signed 'Mythologus', entitled 'Orgies of Bacchus', Porson defended the principle of freedom of speech on religious and political matters, through 'a learned though flippant account of the career of the god Bacchus, and the spread of his worship, written in terms that are clearly meant to suggest Christianity and its founder'.[20] He also undermined the credibility of the chief prosecutor in the Vice-Chancellor's court, Dr. Kipling, by wittily exposing Kipling's ropey grasp of Latin in a Latin poem and epistle published in *The Morning Chronicle*.[21] Porson was effectively using his own excellence at Classics to defend illegal political views against the mediocre scholarship of a defender of the establishment. No wonder that Porson's early biographers were so shocked by these texts that they assumed he was mentally unstable when he wrote them, advised that they be left unread, and even attempted to disguise one objectionable portion by translating it into Latin.[22] The ultra-conservative Denys Page ignored them completely in his 1959 lecture, on the bicentennial of Porson's birth, to the International Congress of Classical Studies.[23]

From 1792 onwards, Porson was supported by an annuity raised from friends' subscriptions. He is remembered for Porson's Law, applied to Greek tragic metrics, alongside the Porson Greek typeface based on his own handwriting, as well as his acclaimed textual work on Greek drama. Yet his lack of social niceties, foul mouth and capacity for alcohol were notorious. He regularly passed out in company and fell asleep under the table.[24] His antics shocked even Lord Byron who, in a letter of 1818, likened his behaviour to that of Silenus: 'Of all the disgusting brutes, sulky, abusive, and intolerable, Porson was the most bestial'; when he thought people were ignorant, he insulted them 'with the most vulgar terms of reprobation'. Byron elaborates this unlovely picture: 'He used to recite, or rather vomit, pages of all languages, and could hiccup Greek like a helot'.[25] Since Byron did not usually object to drunkenness, the language here—'vulgar' and 'helot'—implies snobbery based on social class. Porson probably had what we would now call a photographic memory, which was a source of misery to him as 'he could never forget anything, even that he wished not to remember'.[26] Such memories no doubt included those of his own lowly upbringing. His dislocation from his class roots may have contributed to his alcoholism, which killed him in 1808.

One witness, T.S. Hughes, remembers an encounter with Porson at Cambridge in 1807 in which Porson's conversation throws some more sympathetic light on the way his boorish conduct might have been born out of vestigial loyalty to the class into which he was born. Stories of the generosity or democratic fervour of ancient heroes out of Plutarch regularly reduced him to tears.[27] He told Hughes that he had become a misanthrope from an excess of sensibility, which his sympathetic defence of the poor pigs in his *Catechism* would support. One day a 'girl of the town' came into his chambers 'by mistake'. She 'showed so much cleverness and ability in a long conversation with him, that he declared she might with proper cultivation have become another Aspasia'.[28] He remained thoroughly indifferent to money and unimpressed by social status.[29]

Upwardly mobile Edinburgh professors

Porson once wrote a fractious letter complaining about the criticisms of his edition of *Hecuba* (1797) published in a review by a more contented working-class Greek prodigy, Andrew Dalzel (1742–1806).[30] Dalzel was a carpenter's son who rose to be a leading Edinburgh intellectual. He was born on the Newliston estate in Linlithgowshire; his father died when he was still small, but his talent for languages was spotted at parochial school.[31] Thence he progressed, helped by a friendly local Laird, to Edinburgh University. By 1779 he had succeeded to the Chair of Greek, which he held for over 30 years (Figure 14.3). In 1785

FIGURE 14.3 Andrew Dalzel (1742–1806), reproduced from C.N. Innes, *Memoir of Andrew Dalzel: Professor of Greek in the University of Edinburgh* (1861), reproduced from a copy in Hall's personal collection.

he received the additional appointment of University Librarian. Dalzel turned Greek Studies at the University around; it had dwindled to almost nothing under his predecessor. He soon had over a hundred students enrolled. He was proud of the standards of learning they achieved, contrasting them with those at Oxford and Cambridge, where 'dissipation, idleness, drinking, and gambling' predominated. 'The English Universities are huge masses of magnificence and form, but ill-calculated to promote the cause of science or of liberal inquiry.'[32]

Dalzel's *Analecta Graeca Minora* was used across Britain, in schools as well as universities, reprinted for decades and made his name popular throughout the world of Classics.[33] His lectures on the ancient Greeks were published after his death by his son John.[34] In the manuscript which was transcribed, Dalzel wrote trenchantly that the category 'the vulgar' was class-blind: it included 'not only the artisan and the peasant, but also such of the opulent as have made no use of the advantages of education'.[35]At Edinburgh University, where he studied Classics from the age of 12, Walter Scott recalls incurring the irritation of Dalzel by an essay placing Homer behind Ariosto in poetic merit.[36] But when it came to poetry in the English language, Dalzel abhorred the ignorance of many classically educated men; in his lectures he attempted to give his students 'a faint view of the beauties of English authors'.[37]

When Robert Burns arrived in Edinburgh, Dalzel wrote enthusiastically, 'We have got a poet in town just now, whom everybody is taking notice of—a ploughman from Ayrshire—a man of unquestionable genius.'[38] He praises many English-language works, including the *Epigoniad* of William Wilkie (see pp. 335–6), in which he says there are some 'sublime' passages, such as the death of Hercules in Book VII. Dalzel quoted more than a hundred lines from the *Epigoniad* in the final lecture of his series on epic.[39] A strength of the lectures is Dalzel's interest in what would now be called 'Classical Reception'; he repeatedly refers to the impact that the ancient Greeks had on previous generations of moderns—Thomas More's *Utopia*, Harrington's *Oceania* and Milton, whose love for the Greeks meant that he 'suffered himself to be transported, too far indeed, with a passion for popular government'.[40]

For Dalzel, unlike Porson, was no critic of the British ruling class. He was friends with Edmund Burke, and much admired him.[41] He was dismayed that there were radicals, whom he calls 'violent politicians', in the Edinburgh Royal Society who had voted against allowing Burke membership.[42] His letters suggest that the Edinburgh sedition trials (on which see pp. 275–7) passed him by altogether. His meticulously detailed *History of the University of Edinburgh* is almost eerily apolitical in its recitation of the names of staff and introduction of courses during the revolutions of the 17th century.[43] He even concluded his lecture course on ancient constitutional history with a eulogy of the British constitution, which avoided, he said, the vices of extreme monarchy, aristocracy and democracy alike.[44] But he wholeheartedly believed, and stressed in the first lecture that young men heard in his course on ancient Greece, that the point of a classical education was to learn

> to think and to act as men conscious of the dignity of your nature, and who scorn to be trampled on by tyrants, under whatever veil they may pretend to cover their authority. You will learn from the Greeks, that the service of rulers is due to the commonwealth, and that millions of human creatures were never designed by God and nature to be subservient to the lawless caprice of a despotic lord.[45]

Dalzel was an inspirational teacher, even getting his students to perform an English-language version of Theocritus' Idyll on the Women of Syracuse in class.[46] He was also exceptionally hardworking, teaching two two-hour classes daily. The first inculcated the Greek language through engagement with Lucian, Homer, Xenophon, Anacreon and the New Testament. The second class, which was itself divided into groups depending on level of linguistic attainment, focussed on Thucydides, Herodotus and Demosthenes, supplemented by more Homer, some tragedy and Theocritus. Dalzel also gave two lectures a week on 'the history, government, manners, the poetry and eloquence' of the ancient Greeks.

His student Lord Henry Cockburn recalled him as

> a general exciter of boys' minds … Mild, affectionate, simple, an absolute enthusiast about learning particularly classical, and especially Greek; with an innocence of soul and of manner which imparted an air of honest kindliness to whatever he said or did, and a slow, soft formal voice, he was a great favourite with all boys, and all good men. Never was a voyager, out in quest of new islands, more delighted in finding one, than he was in discovering any good quality in any humble youth.[47]

But the tenor of Dalzel's aesthetic views emerges from his censorious dismissal of the comedies of Aristophanes at the end of his lecture on comedy:

> they are so full of ribaldry and buffoonery, that I can scarcely recommend them to your perusal, unless on account of the Attic Greek in which they are written … . He was malignant and satirical, and at the same time had a gaiety of wit which recommended him to the mob. The comedies of Aristophanes, then, ought to be considered as abuses of this sort of composition.[48]

But the prim and conservative Dalzel remained sympathetic to the class into which he was born. Nobody was surprised when he hired as his assistant a poverty-stricken youth from Berwickshire, working as a gardener. In 1806, George Dunbar (1774–1851) succeeded Dalzel in the chair, a post which he was to hold for nearly half a century, but he remained fascinated by plants and was an enthusiastic member of the Caledonian Horticultural Society. Dunbar could never have entered the university without the kind financial support of a neighbouring landowner and, after graduation, he only survived as a classicist by working as tutor in the family of Lord Provost Fettes. Dunbar was retiring, and avoided public life and politics, but he was also hardworking and productive. His admirable *A Concise General History of the Early Grecian States* (1824) consists of 112 fluently written pages covering literature and philosophy, as well as history.[49] Its surprises include high praise of Aristotelian ethics (which were then out of fashion) and the hope that more people would study them.[50] He could be describing his own career when applauding the Athenian democracy, which 'possessed this advantage above all others, that it gave free access to every man, however mean his birth or moderate his fortune, to rise by the force of his talents to the highest situation in the state'.[51] He also published an impressive set of exercises in Greek syntax and idioms which he perfected by practising them out on his own students and publishing revised editions according to his direct pedagogical experience.[52] He believed passionately that study of Greek helped in the appreciation of literature in any language; like his predecessor and mentor Dalzel, he used poetry in English extensively in his teaching.[53]

Both Dalzel and Dunbar must have been keenly aware of Alexander Murray (1775–1813), the sickly son of an impoverished Galloway shepherd, whose childhood was spent in a room adjacent to the four moorland cattle which constituted his father's 'entire wealth',[54] yet who became Professor of Oriental Languages at their university. It was quickly apparent that Murray wasn't to follow in his father's footsteps; his eyesight was so poor that he couldn't see the flock he was charged to herd.[55] (Figure 14.4) After just a few months of formal schooling in rural Galloway, Murray embarked on his astounding programme of self-education in the late 1780s before his precocity was spotted by his parish Minister, and local patrons clubbed together to support his formal education at school; he responded by translating some lectures by German scholars on Roman authors, which he failed to get published, but in the course of visiting publishers in Dumfries in 1794, he received friendly advice from Robert Burns.[56] His tuition at Edinburgh University, which he attended from the age of 18, was paid for by the institution in consideration of his outstanding performance in the entrance examination. especially his command of Homer, Horace, the Hebrew psalms and French.[57] Lord Cockburn remembered him as a fellow-student, 'a little shivering creature, gentle, studious, timid, and reserved'.[58] By this time he already knew French, Latin, Hebrew, Greek and German, and had somehow picked up a smattering of Arabic, Abyssinian, Welsh and Anglo-Saxon. He was regarded as having an 'almost miraculous or supernatural genius for languages'.[59] After graduation, he entered the Church of Scotland and served in the parish of Urr.

As a youth he had written poetry, including 'a fictious and satirical narrative of the life of Homer', whom he 'represented as a beggar' and a 'Battle of the Flies', imitating Homer's *Battle of the Frogs and Mice.*[60] He read prolifically, including L'Estrange's Josephus, Plutarch's *Lives* and Robert Burns.[61] Murray supported himself in his teens and as an undergraduate by teaching children of

FIGURE 14.4 Portrait of Joseph Wright and other wool-sorters reproduced from Elizabeth Mary Wright, *The Life of Joseph Wright*. London: OUP. 1932, from copy in Hall's personal collection.

isolated communities, like his own, 'the three Rs' as a tutor, and teaching himself Hebrew, Greek, Latin and French.[62] He borrowed and bought (when cheap enough) whatever books he could lay his hands on. He received, for example, from a farmer in Glentrool, a copy of Plutarch's *Lives* and a bilingual edition (Greek and Latin) of Homer's *Iliad* from a lead miner at Palnure. He purchased a stout Latin Dictionary (1s 6d) from an old man in Minnigaff, and was gifted a Hebrew lexicon by a distant cousin.[63]

In his autobiographical writing, Murray reflected on a time when his 12-year-old self got hold of a copy of Thomas Salmon's *Geographical and Historical Grammar*. This book contained the Lord's Prayer in several languages. He recalled how much he had enjoyed and benefited from poring over those translations as a boy.[64] It is perhaps no wonder, considering the odd conglomeration of obscure and arcane texts at his disposal, that on growing up Murray should fix his attention on the acquisition and comparison of languages. By the end of his life it is reported that he knew most (if not all) of the European languages, ancient, modern and numerous Oriental languages. His reputation became international.

Despite his liberal views on religious tolerance and universal education,[65] when it came to class politics, like Dalzel, he was regarded by the conservative establishment as unimpeachably apolitical. In 1810 he was asked by the Marquis Wellesley, then Foreign Secretary, to translate a letter from the Ras of Abyssinia to the Prince Regent. On this account Wellesley's successor, Castlereagh himself, wrote a letter recommending that Murray be appointed to the Chair of Oriental Languages at Edinburgh in 1812.[66]

In the same year, Murray completed work on his magnum opus, *History of the European Languages: Researches into the Affinities of the Teutonic, Greek, Celtic, Slavonic, and Indian Nations*. He finished the book one year before his early death, and four years before the German philologist Franz Bopp (regarded as the founding father of Indo-European Studies) published his influential comparative grammar.[67] As early as 1808, Murray had provocatively written that 'Greek and Latin are only dialects of a language much more simple, regular, and ancient which forms the basis of almost all the tongues of Europe and ... of Sanskrit itself'.[68] But Murray's book did not see print before 1823, and so his pioneering contribution to Comparative Linguistics has been somewhat overlooked. But the scale of the two 19th-century monuments erected to his memory, one near his birthplace on the A712 between Newton Stewart and New Galloway, and the other in Edinburgh's Greyfriars Churchyard, reveals the respect that his outstanding intellectual gifts had won.[69]

Joseph Wright

The most prodigious British working-class classically trained scholar born in the 19th century was indisputably Joseph Wright. Born in Idle, Bradford, in 1855 to desperately poor parents, he spent some of his childhood in a Clayton workhouse. When his father, a weaver and iron quarryman, left his mother, Joseph started work as a donkey driver at the age of six at Woodend quarry, Windhill, near his home in Thackley. His job entailed leading a donkey-cart to and from the smithy for maintenance, from 7 a.m. until 5 p.m. When seven he started work indoors as a 'doffer' in the spinning department of Sir Titus Salt's mill at Saltaire, although he was under the legal age. Doffing means replacing full bobbins on the machines with empty ones, for which he was paid 3s. 6d. a week. He attended the factory school half-time, but had to leave it early all the time to make a full-time living, since his feckless father died leaving Joseph, his brothers and mother in dire straits. At the age of 13, unable to read or write, he moved to Stephen Wildman's mill at Bingley, where he was eventually promoted to wool-sorter, earning between £1 and 30s. a week (Figure 14.5). It was there, in 1870, that he determined to learn to read so he could follow the accounts of the Franco-Prussian war in the newspaper.[70]

He began with Bunyan's *The Pilgrim's Progress* and the Bible, and attended a night school for working lads run by John Murgatroyd, a Wesleyan schoolmaster. He also bought the fortnightly *Cassell's Popular Educator* and started teaching himself languages: French, German and Latin from Cassell's Latin Grammar.[71]

He attended lectures at the Mechanics Institute in Bradford and ran evening classes, charging local youths just 2d. a week. He saved £40 and spent it on a trip to Germany, where, after walking from Antwerp to Heidelberg University, he studied German and Maths for 11 weeks, until his money ran out.

On return he gave up mill work altogether, became a full-time teacher, taught himself Greek (which he found inspirational) and in 1882 passed the intermediate exam towards the London BA degree. Feeling intellectually equipped, he returned to Heidelberg, where Professor Hermann Osthoff encouraged him to specialise in philology. To finance his studies, he taught Maths until he achieved his PhD degree three years later. He had gone from illiteracy to a doctorate in 15 years by dogged effort. His thesis was entitled 'The qualitative and quantitative changes in the Indo-Germanic vowel system in Greek'. He then moved to the University of Leipzig, and worked for a Heidelberg publisher, overseeing the production of 30 scholarly books. The pioneering philologist Karl Brugmann then asked him to make an English translation of his *Grundriss der vergleichenden Grammatik der indo-germanischen Sprachen*, and it was published in 1888.

By bypassing the problem that he had no qualifications from Oxford and Cambridge, and coming back from Germany with a reputation for brilliance and association with the most cutting-edge philological methods, he was welcomed to the British academic community by Max Müller, the German who had held the Oxford Chair of Comparative Philology between 1868 and 1875. Wright made the leap into an academic post when, with Müller's support, he was appointed lecturer to the Association for the Higher Education of Women in 1888, teaching German, Historical Greek Grammar, Historical Latin Grammar and Greek Dialects at Oxford University. But his background and fascination with the speech of the north of England led him to specialise at this point in Germanic and Old English dialects, and he also lectured in German at the Taylor Institution. In 1901 Wright, the ragged boy from the Yorkshire quarry, was appointed Professor of Comparative Philology.

His great achievement was the six-volume *English Dialect Dictionary*, which preserves thousands of now-obsolete usages, and *The English Dialect Grammar* (1905). He was awarded Honorary Membership of the Royal Flemish Academy, the Utrecht Society, the Royal Society of Letters of Lund and the Modern Language Association of America. He continued to criticise Oxford University for the mediocrity of its research in comparison with the efforts expended on teaching privileged undergraduates. He told the Asquith commission on Oxford and Cambridge (1919–1922) that 'far too many of the administrative affairs of the University are in the hands of men whose minds have lost their elasticity'.[72]

According to his wife Elizabeth Mary Wright's biography, Wright insisted

> that it was owing to his plebeian ancestry that he brought with him to the field of science and letters that prodigious *vitality* of brain which enabled him to accomplish the intellectual feats which marked his progress.[73]

His work ethic and instinct for self-betterment came from his mother Sarah Ann, a committed lifelong Primitive Methodist, who, when shown the grand buildings of All Souls College at Oxford, retorted, 'Ee, but it 'ould mak a grand Co-op!'[74] As a young woman from a much more privileged background whom he met when she was studying at Lady Margaret Hall, his wife also recalled a rare occasion on which he had rebuked her. She had facetiously complained that doing philology, and consulting big dictionaries, required excessive 'manual labour.' Wright quietly pointed out that 'manual labour' meant physical *work*, for example with a wheelbarrow.[75] In adulthood he was always regarded as a prodigy and the subject of countless newspaper articles called 'From donkey-boy to Professor' or 'Mill-boy's rise to fame'.[76] But the really

> impressive thing about Joseph Wright was not only that he rose to this scholarly eminence from ragged illiteracy, but that he never allowed academic interests to obscure his origins, and enjoyed nothing better than to be able to use his native Yorkshire speech, which, like all dialects, he regarded as an authentic language, with every right to be taken seriously.[77]

Wright's meteoric rise is the exception that proves the rule. He was the Jude who did not remain obscure. He would never have risen from the workhouse and mill to the top branch of the academic tree without intelligence and moral qualities. But equally necessary were the availability of tuition at the Wesleyan night school and the Mechanics Institute, encouragement and patronage when it mattered, and the serendipity that a German scholar unrestricted by British academics' preconceptions about the proper *cursus honorum* for a professional scholar happened to hold the Oxford Comparative Philology chair at the right time.

All five 'underdog classicists' studied in this chapter enjoyed luck as well as good contacts. In the case of only one of them—Porson—did his class position at birth take him far left of the centre of the political spectrum. But all except Murray, who was silent on the topic, retained pride in their humble origins and were not afraid to say so. This is impressive, if only because it was not until the mid-20th century that university education in Classics was to become even a remote possibility for a wider cross-section of the population.

Notes

1 Jones (1924) 12, 91, 102, 182–3, 156–8, 168, 193–4.
2 Jones (1924) 212; Jowett (1892) 435.
3 She was the daughter of a travelling salesman: see further Irwin (2016).
4 Clarke (1937) 1–2, 6–7. Bamford (1967) xi remarks that, despite some attempts to rewrite the history of the endowed public schools in ways which suggest they did educate significant numbers of poorer pupils, the arrival of such a low-class boy as Porson at Eton was a truly exceptional event which more than proves the rule.
5 Quoted in Clarke (1937) 8.
6 Clarke (1937) 8–9; Page (1960) 15.
7 Quote in Clarke (1937) 12.

8 Clarke (1937) 31–3.
9 Letter from the Rev. Cleaver Banks to Samuel Parr, 20th May 1792, in Parr (1828) vol. VIII, 150.
10 Clarke (1937) 40–1.
11 De Quincey (1897) 417.
12 Clarke (1937) 46.
13 Porson (1818) 3.
14 Porson (1818) 5.
15 Porson (1818) 7.
16 Clarke (1937) 42.
17 Clarke (1937) 45.
18 Clarke (1937) 45.
19 *The Morning Chronicle*, 23rd February, 1795.
20 Clarke (1937) 49.
21 For 19th June and 18th July 1793.
22 They included Kidd (1815), Luard (1857), Watson (1861): see Clarke (1937) 49.
23 Page (1960).
24 Barker (1852) 14.
25 Byron (1839) 374. We are grateful to Jo Balmer for pointing out this text to us.
26 Page (1960) 13–14.
27 Rogers (1856) 121.
28 Watson (1861) 385.
29 Clarke (1937) 86–7.
30 Letter of 3rd September, 1803, in Luard (1857) 85–92. See also Dalzel (1862) vol. 1, 227–8.
31 Dalzel (1862) vol. 1, 1–5.
32 Dalzel (1862) vol. 1, 14.
33 Dalzel (1862) vol. 1, 208–9.
34 Dalzel (1821).
35 Dalzel (1821) vol. 1, vi.
36 Lockhart (1839) 57.
37 Dalzel (1821) vol. 1, ix.
38 Dalzel (1862) vol. 1, 71.
39 Dalzel (1821) vol. 2, 109–13.
40 Dalzel (1821) vol. 1, 7.
41 Dalzel (1862) vol. 1, 42–5, 51–2.
42 Dalzel (1862) vol. 1, 45.
43 Dalzel (1862) vol. 2.
44 Dalzel (1821) vol. 2, 465–85.
45 Dalzel (1821) vol. 1, 12.
46 Dalzel (1862) vol. 1, 19.
47 Cockburn (1856) 26–7.
48 Dalzel (1821) vol. 2, 146–7.
49 Dunbar (1824).
50 Dunbar (1824) 110–11
51 Dunbar (1824) p. 52
52 Dunbar (1822) iii.
53 Dunbar (1822) viii.
54 Hunter (2014) 9 (caption to the photograph of the ruins of the Murrays' tiny, isolated cottage).
55 Scot (1823) xli; Hunter (2014) 7.
56 Bayne (1885–1900) 346.
57 Murray (1812) 2; Bayne (1885–1900) 346.
58 Cockburn (1856) 276.

59 Murray (1812) 4.
60 Scot (1823) xxxiii–iv.
61 Scot (1823) xliv, xlvii.
62 Murray (1823) vol. I, xv.
63 Scot (1823) xlviii–lvii.
64 Hunter (2014) 12; see Salmon (1758).
65 Hunter (2014) 21.
66 Murray (1812) 29; Scot (1823) c.
67 Bopp (1816).
68 Scot (1823) lxxvii; Hunter (2014) 21–3.
69 Hunter (2014) 28–35 with several photographs.
70 On Wright's early life see Kellett (2004); Hall (2018b) 252–4.
71 Wright (1932) vol. II, 40.
72 Bodleian, Oxford; Asquith Commission papers, box 1, MS Γογ Oxon b 104, fol. 235.
73 Wright (1932) vol. I, 37.
74 Wright (1932) vol. 1, 5.
75 Wright (1932) vol. I, 131, 189.
76 Wright (1932) vol. 1, v.
77 Kellett (2004).

15

RAGGED-TROUSERED PHILOLOGISTS

The last chapter looked at the achievements of several working-class boys who overcame innumerable obstacles to become formidable classicists and occupy key positions in British intellectual life, if not always in its learned institutions. This chapter focuses on the experience of several equally extraordinary working-class boys who embarked on autodidactic quests, but whose journey *per ardua ad astra* ('through adversity to the stars') never quite got off the ground. Many others who failed to move upward socially via classical learning have disappeared from view. But those who were not ignored by the historical record, whether villains or countercultural heroes, deserve a place in any People's History of Classics. Investigating them takes us from Devon to North Wales, Scotland and the border country, before returning to Devon to meet the itinerant priest, the Reverend George Martin, and follow his Greek lessons and godly works in the metropolitan slums of Southwark.

Downwardly mobile Devonians

Social mobility was never a one-way street. Not even a grammar-school education guaranteed a middle-class occupation and comfortable living, as seen in the case of two alumni of Tiverton Grammar School. Established in 1604 by Peter Blundell (c.1520–1601), a wealthy clothier and philanthropist, the independent 'Blundell's School' is still in operation.[1] Its most notorious former pupil is Bampfylde-Moore Carew (1693–1759), the son of the rector of Bickleigh, Devon, a few miles from Tiverton. Destined for university and then the clergy, Carew built up 'a considerable knowledge of the Latin and Greek tongues' at the local grammar school.[2] But he soon became more interested in hunting than in his studies. The school 'had a fine cry of hounds',[3] and Carew became a proficient huntsman, which led him into trouble. After damaging considerable property

DOI: 10.4324/9781315446608-18

in a deer hunt, several of the Tiverton boys absconded from school, for fear of punishment, and joined a company of gypsies. 'Being thus initiated into the ancient society of gypsies, who take their name from Egypt, a place well known to abound in learning, and the inhabitants of which country travel about from place to place to communicate knowledge to mankind',[4] Carew gained a reputation for his wisdom, but also discovered a wonderful talent for disguise and deception.

His 'adventures' in tricking people out of their money were recorded in Robert Goadby's *An Apology for the Life of Mr Bampfylde-Moore Carew Commonly called the King of the Beggars* (1768). Carew's capacity for parting the unsuspecting from their money (sometimes multiple times from the same person in a single day) elevated him through the gypsy ranks; after the death of Clause Patch, he reigned as king of the gypsy tribe for more than 40 years. His classical education saved him on several occasions because he was assumed to be a gentleman.[5] His example, however extreme, complicates the commonplace narrative of linear progress through education.

The second Old Blundellian whose classical attainment brought scant reward was Charles Manby Smith. A journeyman printer, Smith was the son of a cabinet maker. Around 1815 he attended the Tiverton Grammar School, Devon, where he 'enjoyed the advantage of hic-haec-hoc-ing it for a couple of years'.[6] But after two years, his father went bankrupt; the family moved to Bristol, where Charles was bound apprentice to a printer. He quickly forgot his Greek, but made efforts to keep up his Latin, which

> grew by slow degrees into an accomplishment not common to my class … and I make the avowal for the benefit of all those to whom the cui-bono is a rule of action—that it never put a pound into my pocket.[7]

His Latin did, however, once win him a champagne luncheon. During his midday break from the printer's shop, he sat on a park bench to read 'a small duodecimo Sallust'. He had read ten pages, 'and was admiring the impudence of that redoubtable scoundrel Cataline [*sic*]', when he was tapped on the shoulder. A kindly old foreign man asked him if he could understand the Roman historian, to which he answered, 'I ought to—I've read him through half-a-dozen times'.[8] The man set him a riddle, '*Sum principium mundi; sum finis omnium rerum; sum tria juncta in uno; at tamen non sum Deus?*' ('I am the beginning of the world; I am the end of everything; I am three joined into one; but I am not God' [What am I?]). The answer is the letter 'm', with which ***m**undi* begins and *reru**m*** ends. Smith answered, '*Impransus sum*' ('I am unbreakfasted').[9]

Smith revels in displaying the extent of his Latin learning. His declaration '*impransus sum*' alludes, as the old man probably knew, to Plautus' *Amphitryon* (line 254), in which the slave Sosia reports on the lengthy military campaign of his master Amphitryon from which they were returning. He remembers one detail, because *illo die impransus fui* ('that day I had not eaten anything'). The word *impransus* occurs elsewhere in the works of Plautus and in Horace.[10] Using it might not have recalled that particular speech in the Roman play, had not Smith soon (on the same page) referred to the old man as 'my hospitable Amphitryon', which in turn characterises the unfed artisan as Sosia, Amphitryon's slave.

In his autobiography, entitled *The Working-man's Way in the World* (1854), Smith employs the familiar trope of apologising for the paucity of his scholarship:

> I make no claims to literary talent, and must crave the reader's indulgence for my want of literary tact … I am a working-man, in the plainest acceptation of the term, and one whose companionship, for more than thirty years, has been with working-men. My knowledge of the world is of the working-man's world, and my knowledge of books (the world of mind and of the past) has been derived from such books as a working-man could afford to buy or avail to borrow. So pardon, gentles all, and a plenary indulgence … for all the sins I may fall into, and all the *lapsus pennae* which must occur now and then to one but little accustomed to trail the quill.

This is an imitation of the faux-humble style of early working-class autobiographical writing (see above, Chapter 5). His self-demeaning performance is no more a 'slip of the pen' (*lapsus pennae*) than his incorporation of a Latin phrase or the assured affectation of referring to his pen as a quill. Written in the wake of the revolutionary turmoil of the late 1840s, Smith's opening is carefully weighted to obviate 'the popular question of the day', which he leaves 'to wiser heads' than his.[11] Or so he says. On the first page, he quotes the slogan which Thomas Attwood had cited when presenting the Chartists' petition to parliament in 1839 and which was popularised by Thomas Carlyle in *Past and Present* four years later.[12] On the other hand, Smith inveighs against communism and 'French' notions of socialism in a ten-page appendix.[13]

A socialist Smith may not have been, but a proud working-class classicist he assuredly was; he enjoyed illustrating plebeian occupations with mythical exempla. He depicts the local beer vendor with reference to Zeus' own wine-pourer, the beautiful son of Tros:

> As evening draws on, Pluto, the pewter Ganymede from the public-house in the lane below, makes his welcome appearance, bearing in each hand a bunch of pewter pint pots each containing half-a-pint of beer. He … vociferates, as he walks rapidly round, "Beer, gentlemen—gentlemen, beer!"[14]

In another book, *Curiosities of London Life* (1853), he describes the grim labour of 'tide-waitresses', women who sift the London mud for items to sell, snidely contrasting their dirty figures with that of the goddess of love:

> The "Venus rising from the sea", of the ancient Greek mythology, presents a very different picture to the imagination from that afforded by her

> modern antithesis, the tide-waitress of London descending into the bed of the Thames to forage for the means of subsistence among the mud and filth of the river.[15]

For at the age of 22, Smith, newly freed from his apprenticeship, had moved to London. It was as a journeyman compositor in a London printing house that he encountered a truly ragged-trousered classicist. A Greek volume, with Latin notes and scholia, arrived at the press where Smith worked. His fellow compositor, an old man with failing eyes and no Greek or Latin, gave up the job, which left the setting of the text to Smith. He made excellent money on it (12s a day), but could not work fast enough, so they advertised for a Greek compositor.

> When I heard that a Grecian was coming, I expected, as a matter of course, to see a first-class man, one of the gentlemen of the trade, and was not a little astonished to behold a wretched grey specimen of humanity, nearly forty years of age, fluttering in rags, and literally scaled with filth, with scarcely a shirt and but an apology for shoes, inducted into the next frame to mine as my coadjutor. He was a positive scarecrow, but his appearance was no index of his ability. He rained a perfect storm of Greek type into his empty case as he began distribution, and picked it up again when he commenced composing with proportionate rapidity.[16]

The ragged Grecian turned out to be a slower worker than Smith initially thought. He was a downwardly mobile alcoholic with a weakness for gin, which he sipped throughout the working day; he claimed payment for more work than he had done (a trick called 'writing horse').[17] There is no other source for the 'Cockney Grecian'.[18] Although Smith claims his own classical language skills never made him money, his own example and that of the ragged Grecian suggests that there was room (however limited) in the printing business for workers with knowledge of the ancient scripts.

Andrew Donaldson, The fanatic of Fife

Our next two 'ragged-trousered philologists' presented themselves in a state of sartorial disarray similar to the ragged Grecian's. Although neither of them was addicted to drink, they made such a colourful impression on the lives of others that evidence of their unexpected classical abilities has been passed down to us. Their scholarship seemed to run counter to the cultural expectations of their natal class and their outward demeanour and appearance. Most of the information about Andrew Donaldson, the mysterious Dunfermline teacher and casual labourer (1714–1793) was recorded in the *Edinburgh Portraits* of John Kay, an Edinburgh caricaturist whose bookshop in Edinburgh Donaldson frequented. Kay's two-volume *A Series of Original Portraits and Caricature Etchings* was first published in 1837–1838. When published posthumously by Hugh Paton, it included both a collection of portraits to 'gratify and amuse' the public and a graphic record.[19]

Born in the tiny Fife village of Auchtertool, Donaldson's career in the pulpit stalled through poverty. He was academically gifted and so took a post as Master in the Dunfermline Grammar School. Although well qualified to teach Greek and Hebrew

> it was not to be supposed, from the state of his mind, that his employment would be extensive, or that he was capable of pursuing any vocation with the necessary application and perseverance.[20]

In any case, he disliked teaching, remarking that he 'was sure Job never was a schoolmaster, otherwise we should not have heard so much of his patience'.[21] He resigned and took to living eccentrically:

> he deemed it unlawful to shave, on the ground that, as man was created perfect, any attempt at mutilation or amendment, was not only presumptuous but sinful. Following up this theory in practice, he increased the singularity of his appearance, by approximating still more closely to the dress and deportment of the ancient Prophets ... He adhered to the strictest simplicity of diet, and preferred sleeping on the floor.[22]

It was not his beard and long locks alone that made his appearance striking (Figure 15.1):

> His usual attire was a loose great-coat, reaching nearly to the ankle. In his hand he carried a staff of enormous length; and, as he seldom wore a hat or any other covering, his flowing locks, bald forehead, and strongly marked countenance, were amply displayed.[23]

Donaldson's sister married a respectable local carpet manufacturer, but he lived a single and singular life of unremitting poverty and semi-vagrancy. In 1793 he was buried in Dunfermline Parish Church, where his gravestone simply read, 'Here lies Andrew Donaldson, a sincere Christian, and good scholar'.

He had suffered episodes of delusional psychosis.

> Occasionally, when actuated by some strong mental paroxysm, he has been known to exchange his pilgrim's staff for an iron rod, with which he would walk about the streets of Dunfermline, declaring that he was sent to rule the nations, "with a rod of iron".[24]

Donaldson's literalist interpretation of the scriptures, especially when he brandished a weapon, could cause serious bodily harm to those with whom he felt righteously angry. He used his rod to beat a vagrant preacher because he would

FIGURE 15.1 Andrew Donaldson from the *Edinburgh Portraits* by John Kay (1877), reproduced by courtesy of the British Library.

accept a halfpenny fee for a sermon. He found this 'causeway preacher' guilty of making 'gain from godliness' and struck him while repeating the words 'Thou shalt dash them in pieces like a potter's vessel'.[25] For this crime, Donaldson was imprisoned.

Donaldson was an accomplished classicist, and eventually moved to Edinburgh to work as a private teacher of Greek and Hebrew, but struggled because he lacked interpersonal skills and application. His friends clubbed together to fund his frugal lifestyle, but his scriptural convictions precluded the taking of charity. He chose to abide by the aphorism of Paul the Apostle, 'if any is not willing to work, let him not eat' (Thessalonians 2.3:10). He therefore often nearly starved. Donaldson's biographer, who describes him as 'anchorite-like', alluding to his reclusive and devout lifestyle, blames his education for his idiosyncrasies.

> He was an ardent student; and it is supposed that too close application, particularly in acquiring a knowledge of the Greek and Hebrew languages,

> tended to impair the faculties of a mind which might otherwise have shone forth with more than ordinary lustre.[26]

Nowadays Donaldson would probably be diagnosed as being on the autistic spectrum. His aptitude for language learning may have resulted from his obsessive interest in the single activity of close reading. Intense scholarship was often seen as causing otherwise inexplicable mental maladies.

Richard Robert Jones: 'Dic of Aberdaron'

The phenomenal Welsh autodidact and itinerant linguist, Richard Roberts Jones, alias 'Dic of Aberdaron' (1780–1844) or 'Dirty Dick', was also an unconventional dresser. In perhaps the most poignant life story we have excavated, Dic was born to an impoverished carpenter and boatswain from Aberdaron, a coastal village in North Wales, whose small cargo boat shuttled between Wales and Liverpool. In his teenage years, Dic taught himself Latin, Hebrew and Greek, which he could write beautifully as well as read.[27] His father and elder brother used to beat him regularly for reading rather than working, but nothing could diminish the dreamy youth's passion for Classics.[28] He wrote several laborious works, including a Greek lexicon and a Hebrew Grammar. He is reported to have understood Biblical Aramaic, Arabic and Persian, and was completely fluent in Latin, French and Italian.[29]

Dic once visited Bangor School, where he was tested on his Greek, passed with flying colours, and given some classical books which he accepted with delight and gratitude.[30] Sadly, he spent much of his life as a homeless beggar in Liverpool, where he was a well-known character. His life improved slightly when the radical Merseyside poet William Roscoe gave him a small regular stipend. But Dic remained eccentric. Although his favourite author by far was Homer, he liked to sing the psalms in Hebrew, accompanying himself on a Welsh harp, and turned up at an Eisteddfod with an ancient Greek essay on types of stringed instrument.[31] Dic died as he had lived, a wandering bard and linguist—or 'a perfect child of nature' as one obituary called him.[32] He was buried in the churchyard of St. Asaph's Cathedral in Denbighshire.[33]

In a poem entitled 'Dic Aberdaron', R.S. Thomas wrote of his labourer's clothes, 'coarse trousers, torn / jacket, a mole-skin / cap',[34] basing his description on a painting in his house (Figure 15.2). We get a fuller idea of Dic's appearance from Roscoe, his biographer:

> At one time he chose to tie up his hair with a large piece of green ferret [ribbon], which gave him the most ludicrous appearance possible. Some time since, one of his friends gave him a light-horseman's jacket, of blue and silver, which he immediately put on, and continued to wear, and which, contrasted with his hair and beard, gave him the appearance of a Jewish

FIGURE 15.2 'Richard Roberts Jones' by unknown artist, reproduced by courtesy of The Welsh Library, University of Wales Bangor Information Services. © The Welsh Library, University of Wales Bangor Information Services 2019.

> warrior, as represented in old prints, and consequently attracted after him a crowd of children. In his present appearance, he strongly resembles some of the Beggars of Rembrandt.[35]

He also concealed inside his clothing his collection of books, both those that he was fond of reading and those that he was writing. He was thus a walking library, always pictured with books tucked under his arms and his cat, from whom he was never apart. He was fond of blowing a ram's horn, and at another time a French horn.[36] For a recluse, then, he was not shy of calling attention to himself, without directly soliciting passers-by; this enabled him to make his paltry living. People saw him as a prodigy and would offer him money and/or books in exchange for an audience, and translation or conversational services. He would answer in whatever language he was addressed. He found it nearly impossible to earn a living otherwise. An exception was three years of labour sieving ashes in the King's Dockyard at Dover, where he had an indulgent superintendent, was fed in the morning, occupied by an unchallenging task and paid just enough to survive and pay for books and Hebrew lessons with Rabbi Nathan after work.[37]

So who was Richard Roberts Jones? R.S. Thomas asks the same question in his poem. 'A / hedge-poet, a scholar by rushlight?' he guesses.[38] 'Scholar by rushlight' is evocative since the 'rush' was the cheapest kind of candle, used by only the poorest in British society. 'Scholar' catches well his single-minded pursuit of linguistic studies. His *magnum opus* was perhaps his trilingual Dictionary (Welsh, Greek and Hebrew) which took him more than ten years to compile (1821–1832). When it was complete, he went to a Bardic Eisteddfod held at Beaumaris, in order to gain assistance to publish his work. But he came away with no financial backing.[39]

We get flashes of Dic's complex neurology in Roscoe's description of his struggles in relationships and supporting himself. These qualities include his physical incapacity ('the inaptitude of his hands for any correct and continued labour')[40] which, combined with his poor eyesight, prevented him from holding down an occupation as a labourer; his paranoia ('Richard is very liable to misinterpret the intentions and conduct of his friends, especially when any restraint is attempted to be imposed upon him, and that he is by no means sparing in his complaints on such occasions');[41] his directness ('remarkable for his adherence to truth on all occasions');[42] his lack of social skills ('his ignorance of the customs and manners of society');[43] his struggle to focus and express himself clearly ('the difficulty of elucidating his meaning from collateral subjects') and his exceptional capacity for the acquisition of languages ('the faculty of which he possessed in an extraordinary degree').[44]

The picture that emerges is one of a remarkable autistic polyglot savant, a rare type that continues to puzzle scientists and medical practitioners to this day.[45] Brain and language scientists define a 'savant' as 'someone with an island of startling talent in a sea of inability'.[46] Roscoe hazarded his own interpretation of Dic's behaviour:

> The extreme degree of attention employed by the object of our present inquiry [Dic] on one particular subject [language acquisition] formed itself into a habit; that every thing which interfered with this pursuit was neglected or despised, till the other faculties of the mind became obscured and useless from the mere want of cultivation and exertion.[47]

Even Dic's subconscious mind was obsessed with ancient languages. He experienced vivid and portentous dreams and wrote them down. The Caernarfonshire artist, Ellis Owen Ellis ('Ellis Bryn-Coch'), who started painting whilst working as a carpenter's apprentice, intended to publish an *Illustrated Life of Richard Robert Jones (Aberdaron)*. The beautifully illustrated manuscript remains in the National Library of Wales (Aberystwyth). (Figure 15.3) Ellis drew one of Dic's dreams in which Homer's ghost appeared to him with a personification of the Greek language.[48]

FIGURE 15.3 'Homer's ghost appearing to Jones with the genius of the Greek'. Drawing vol. 51 from the *Illustrated Life of Richard Roberts Jones* by Ellis Owen Ellis, reproduced by courtesy of Llyfrgell Genedlaethol Cymru—The National Library of Wales. © Llyfrgell Genedlaethol Cymru—The National Library of Wales.

'Hawkie'

While Dic was tramping the road between Aberdaron and Liverpool, William Cameron (b.1784), or 'Hawkie',[49] was touring the Scottish borders and northern England (Figure 15.4). He walked with the aid of a 'stilt', or crutch, due to a leg injury. As with many autodidacts, a childhood injury protected him from hard labour, offering more opportunity to study. Hawkie's crutches, combined with a penetrating voice, made him instantly recognisable. Born in Plean, near Stirling, the son of an impoverished mashman,[50] he became a charismatic itinerant book pedlar, or a 'patterer'.[51] He claimed to have risen through ranks of beggars and chapmen to become the undisputed king of the Glasgow city speech criers. But the young invalid, destined to become the croaking 'Trongate Demosthenes', fought hard for his education.[52]

Hawkie's experience of school demonstrates how random provision of schooling could be in late 18th-century Scotland (see Chapter 11):

> At the age of four I was out to school; the teacher was an old decrepit man … writing and arithmetic were to him secrets as dark as death … At this

FIGURE 15.4 Cover of *Hawkie: The Autobiography of a Gangrel* (1888), reproduced by courtesy of the British Library.

> school I continued for four years, and was not four months advanced in learning, although I was as far advanced as my teacher.[53]

After finally learning to write in his next school, in Milton, Cameron was at 12 bound apprentice to a tailor in Stirling, but he abandoned the position soon. Fortunately, after his 13th birthday, he heard that his indenture had been lifted, so he could safely return to Stirling, where he joined the city's parish school of St. Ninian's. It was here that he began to study Latin in the daytime; in the evenings he learned arithmetic with one Robert McCallum.[54]

As an adult, Hawkie supplemented his begging by selling books in the city streets. He made a name for himself, in Glasgow especially, as a chapman, performing colourful passages from the chapbooks he was selling. He was a celebrity amidst the crowds of Old Trongate. In *Old Reminiscences of Glasgow and the West of Scotland* (1868), Peter Mackenzie reported that 'Hawkie was a most inveterate drinker of ardent spirits. This was his chief or greatest misfortune. Almost every penny he got went to the nearest whisky shop. He was never riotously or outrageously drunk upon the public streets'. He may have been continuously intoxicated, but he could still excel at his trade. One day he came up against a man called Jamie Blue—a fellow speech crier and chapman—who, according to Hawkie, had 'the reputation among the illiterate as a matchless scholar'.[55] They held a heated bookselling competition, which Hawkie describes in his autobiography:

> I urged the weakness of his ambition, and showed him the meanness of his conduct; but Pompey was no more determined for the Empire of Rome, than Jamie was to be "Head speech crier".[56]

Hawkie, orator and Latinist, implies he was the equivalent of Julius Caesar. He displayed such erudition as this, sold more books and won the contest hands down.

Reverend George Martin

Sources are few for the Reverend George Martin (1864–1946) (Figure 15.5), who always wore a ragged frock-coat, old workman's boots and ate only bread and butter. His classical activity is known from the pamphlet autobiography of the anarchist and Red Clydesider, Guy Aldred (whom we have met earlier, pp. 112–13), in the Special Collections of Glasgow's Mitchell Library.[57] Born into a wealthy Cornish family, Martin studied Classics at the same school as the gypsy king and journeyman printer with whom this chapter began, and at St. John's College, Cambridge, where he read Classics and Theology in preparation for Holy Orders. At the age of 35, after a decade of service as a rural vicar and for reasons unknown, the Cornish clergyman resigned the benefice of Caerhays (£700 p.a.) to work for around 18 shillings a week as a porter in London's Borough Market and attend to the working poor in Southwark. For his generosity, the press dubbed him a 'modern St. Anthony', a 'Priest without a Parish' and 'Saint George of Southwark'.[58] When a child in his community was taken ill, Martin alternated with the father keeping watch through the nights until the boy recovered.[59] When a fellow worker was disabled, Martin divided his earnings with the man's family until he could return to work.[60]

Aldred recalled how Martin had

> persuaded himself that a Christian priest must live the life of the people and if there are social depths, must sink to them with his people. He moved about a tough neighbourhood fearlessly, but was very gentle with all who erred and suffered.[61]

FIGURE 15.5 Reverend George Martin, 'The Saint of Southwark' by Becky Brewis (2019). © Becky Brewis 2019.

Aldred said that Martin fed 18 vagrants every day at Lockhart's Tea Rooms and gave away all his money:

> When not ministering to the people, he divided his life between the most severe introspection and classical studies … He loved scholarship and his society was a joy, for its quaintness, his classical digressions, and his broad human understanding … His love of Greek, and his interest in teaching it, amazed me for I was his victim.[62]

Aldred used to visit Martin's house on Saturdays to sit and read with him. 'He taught me Greek, in which I am not interested'.[63]

Aldred attributes Martin's benevolence and open-minded acceptance of people of all creeds or none to his classical education. Martin 'subscribed to the orthodox church theology with more than enthusiasm. But scholarship had broadened his moral sympathies and in his love of service he knew no distinction of person, creed or error'.[64] He was also brave if not dangerously reckless. He was arrested for threatening to blow up some (empty) spectators' stands which had been erected outside Southwark Cathedral for viewing Edward's VII's coronation procession; he saw these as symbolising 'the league between the Church and the more affluent classes, which is at present so great a barrier to a large proportion of the people from coming into the fold of the Church'.[65] He considered it an abomination that the Church should 'encourage the payment of large sums for such places [viewing stands] while so many of her members had not the necessities of life, and intended "to strike a blow for Christ"'.[66] A friend argued that instead of prison Martin might be best served by being sent to a home to recover his senses, but he refused the magistrate's offer: 'No; it is my duty to go back to the men from whom I come'.[67]

After several more adversarial encounters with the police while defending the poor,[68] Martin was knocked over by a lorry and treated in Guy's Hospital, just across the road from the tiny cubicle in which he lived. In an article entitled 'A Modern St Anthony: Hermit Priest Who Lives for Poor', The Reverend T.P. Stevens sang his praises:

> Everyone loves him, and while his ragged appearance might otherwise make him a butt of laughter, his personality is so strong that he is wonderfully respected. He has done untold good, living among the poorest of the poor and doing all his own work. He lives in rooms high up in the shadow of Guy's Hospital. He eats his bread and butter from a slab of slate, washes his own clothes, and hangs them to dry on the landing. To me he has always seemed saint-like – a mystic.[69]

When he died in an institution ward, he surprised everyone by leaving £22,000 to be given to the poor of Southwark as well as a legacy to St. John's College, Cambridge, to fund the training of indigent candidates for the priesthood.[70]

This chapter has observed five down-and-out classicists notorious for their ragged appearance. Three of them were devout Christians, two were drunkards, most of them spent their lives consorting with the poor and destitute and all were eccentric. Dic of Aberdaron and Hawkie were actually homeless: George Martin was exceptional among them, since he was by birth well-to-do, and a Cambridge graduate, but embraced the working classes and a career as a street philanthropist. The chapter's title, indeed, was suggested by Tressell's famous novel of working-class life we have discussed in a previous chapter, *The Ragged-Trousered Philanthropists* (see above pp. 226–30). And, in the next two chapters, our story will open out to discover classicists and classical presences in many other marginal, déclassé and shady corners of British society.

Notes

1 Youings (2008) *ODNB*.
2 Goadby (1768) 4.

3 Goadby (1768) 5.
4 Goadby (1768) 12.
5 See above pp. 104.
6 Smith (1854) 15. N.b. 'Hic-haec-hoc-ing it' refers to the practice of memorising Latin grammar, particularly the declension of the demonstrative pronoun 'hic' ('this').
7 Smith (1854) 15.
8 Smith (1854) 15.
9 Smith (1854) 38.
10 Plautus, *Rudens* 1, 2, 56; Horace, *Satires* II.2.7.
11 Smith (1854) 14.
12 *Hansard* (Commons) 14th June 1839; Carlyle (1843) chapters 3 and 12.
13 Smith (1854) 349–359.
14 Smith (1854) 287.
15 Smith (1853) 187.
16 Smith (1854) 182.
17 Smith (1854) 183.
18 Either Smith or his editor referred to the specialist Greek compositor as 'a cockney Grecian' in the page heading; Smith (1854) 182.
19 Kay (1877) 1. Vii. Most of the information about Donaldson is in Kay (1877) vol. II, 226–32.
20 Kay (1877) 2. 228.
21 Kay (1877) 2. 227.
22 Kay (1877) 2. 227.
23 Kay (1877) 2. 227.
24 Kay (1877) 2. 227–8.
25 Kay (1877) 2. 228.
26 Kay (1877) 2. 227.
27 Roscoe (1855) 4. His handwritten papers (in several scripts) may be read in the National Library of Wales archives in Aberystwyth.
28 Roscoe (1855) 4. There is also an account of Dic's treatment by his father in Dic's own hand at the foot of page 4 of the NLW edition of Roscoe (1822), in the 'G.V. Roberts Collection of Literary Papers and Letters', MS 18433C.
29 Roscoe (1855) 4–9. N.b. In May 1842, apparently at the request of a Liverpool Goldsmith, Mr Joseph Mayers, Dick translated Roscoe's memoir into Hebrew. This can be found in the back of the NLW edition of Roscoe (1822), in the 'G. V. Roberts Collection of Literary Papers and Letters' in MS 18433C. See also Anon. (1832g).
30 'Bangoriensis' (1844).
31 Anon. (1832g).
32 'Bangoriensis' (1844).
33 Anon. (1843).
34 Thomas (1987) 46, lines 5–7.
35 Roscoe (1855) 8.
36 Roscoe (1855) 7.
37 Roscoe (1855) 6.
38 Thomas (1987) 46, lines 8–10.
39 Roscoe (1855) 11. The manuscript dictionary is held at NLW.
40 Roscoe (1855) 7.
41 Roscoe (1855) 7.
42 Roscoe (1855) 8.
43 Roscoe (1855) 9.
44 Roscoe (1855) 3.
45 There are many parallels between Dic and Christopher Taylor (b.1962), who is the subject of a recent study by Smith, Tsimpli, Morgan, Woll (2010).
46 Smith, Tsimpli, Morgan, Woll (2010) 1.

47 Roscoe (1855) 10.
48 Ellis (1844) 9.
49 Hawkie was the name of the bovine protagonist in Cameron's own *The Prophecies of "Hawkie"*—a chapbook poking fun at a false prophet named Ross, who predicted a flood that would destroy Briggate and converted many on Glasgow's streets; Cameron (1823[?]). Cameron's visionary cow predicted a flood of whisky with hilarious results, see Urie (1908) 50–1.
50 'Mashman': a worker in a brewery or distillery who is responsible for mashing the malt (OED).
51 'The patterer would buy a quire, or if short of money a dozen, of eight-page chapbooks at wholesale prices, twopence a dozen, and then sold them at halfpenny each, so for someone who could tell a good tale it was a very profitable business.' Morris (2007) 176.
52 William Finlay in Cameron (1888) Appendix II, 119.
53 Cameron (1888) 11.
54 Cameron (1888) 12–3.
55 Cameron (1888) 98–9.
56 Cameron (1888) 98–9.
57 Aldred (1908) 28–9.
58 Aldred (1955-63) 66; e.g. Anon. (1948).
59 Anon. (1948).
60 Anon. (1948).
61 Aldred (1955-63) 66.
62 Aldred (1955-63) 66; (1908) 28–9.
63 Aldred (1908) 28.
64 Aldred (1955–1963) 66; Aldred (1908) 29.
65 *The Cornish Telegraph* Wed. 5th November 1902.
66 *Whitstable Times and Herne Bay Herald*, Sat. 5th July 1902.
67 *Lake's Falmouth Packet and Cornwall Advertiser*, Saturday 22nd November 1902.
68 Reported in *South London Press* Sat. 11th June 1904; *London Evening Standard* Mon. 21st November 1904; *Globe* Wed. 9th December 1903.
69 *Birmingham Daily Gazette* Fri. 27th July 1934, 7.
70 *Daily Mirror* 6th May 1947.

16

HINTERLAND GREEK

Introduction

The rarity of knowledge of ancient Greek and its strange alphabet gave the language a mystique in the popular imagination. In low-class circles, more often than Latin, Greek was associated with extreme, other-worldly intellectual prowess and arcane, even sinister arts. In the course of this chapter, we will find Greek being cited, used or abused in a variety of recherché contexts ranging from accusations of witchcraft, caricatures of menacing Jesuits, the dialects of the criminal underclass, the display of prodigiously intellectual dogs and pigs, the lives of notoriously uncouth Scotsmen, Welsh dream divination and downmarket pharmaceuticals and sex manuals. But the story, which will return at its conclusion to the Bible, begins with Greek's special status within Christianity.

Popish, Satanic and criminal Greek

When in the 16th century Jerome's Latin Vulgate, long the officially recognized Bible of the Catholic Church, began to be seriously rivalled by vernacular versions in English (et al.), the Greek New Testament attracted sustained attention. For the first complete English edition of the New Testament (1526), William Tyndale had used the Greek text as well as the Latin Vulgate. Erasmus' Greek New Testament, published a decade earlier in 1516, had proved seminal in the emergence of Renaissance Christian Humanism and the expertise in Greek for which educated Protestants like Tanneguy Le Fèvre, head of the Protestant Academy in Saumur, France, and his daughter Anne,[1] were later to become renowned; Martin Luther himself found numerous errors in the Vulgate Latin by comparing it in detail with the Greek.[2] It is now held that, as an Aramaic speaker, Jesus merely knew enough Greek (the international language of the eastern Roman

DOI: 10.4324/9781315446608-19

Empire) to communicate with Roman officials in it. But in the Renaissance and Early Modern period, it was widely believed that Jesus had spoken Greek as his first language. God himself, through Christ, was thus held to have communicated with the multitudes of the 1st century CE in Greek.[3]

On the other hand, especially after the Gunpowder Plot, knowledge of Greek was often perceived as suggesting ominous Jesuit connections. In the next chapter we shall see that, when in the early 18th century a Frenchman disguised as a native of Taiwan (then called Formosa, 'beautiful' in Latin) wanted to explain to Britons why he knew ancient Greek, he claimed that he had been taught it by a Jesuit missionary to the island.[4] Study of classical Greek authors as well as the New Testament was by that time being exported across the planet by the Society of Jesus. The best minds at the Jesuit school in Rome had in 1599 enshrined several Greek authors in their official plan for education, the *Ratio atque Institutio Studiorum*.[5] The men involved in the plot to blow up the House of Lords on 5th November 1605 included several from families who had protected Jesuit priests during the reign of Elizabeth I. Despite the attempts of Father Henry Garnet, the English Jesuit Superior, to dissuade Robert Catesby, the leader of the conspiracy, from committing any act of violence, the government was determined to incriminate the Jesuits. Garnet himself was executed. The Jesuits, with their expertise in Greek, were subsequently often blamed for any national disasters, including the 1666 Great Fire of London, the Popish Plot of 1678, and even the sinking of the Titanic in 1912.[6]

The mystical potency of Greek was certainly sometimes associated by Anglicans with 'papists'. William Perrye was an idle 13-year-old in Bilston colliery town who feigned Satanic possession in order to avoid school:

> Bilston was noted for the imposture of one William Perrye, a lad of thirteen, who practised a variety of grimaces and contortions, vomited rags and pins, &c., either from a habit of idleness, or to serve papist exorsists.[7]

The trigger for his fit was the Greek of the first verse of the Gospel of St. John, 'In the beginning was the word, and the word was with God, and the word was God'.[8] William claimed to have been bewitched by a poor old woman named Joan Cox. She was put on trial for witchcraft, and narrowly escaped conviction. The Bishop of Lichfield was summoned and unmasked the boy's imposture. The learned divine recited the *twelfth* verse of St. John, 'which the boy supposing the first, fell straightway into one of his agonies'.[9] But when the famous *first* verse, *en archēi ēn ho logos*, was read in Greek, Bilston Bill did not recognise it as his customary cue. In due course, he apologised.[10]

All Roman Catholics, regardless of what seems here to be connections between Greek and their practice of exorcism, were conversant with Latin. Latin's associations with popish rituals and superstition were only underscored by the Latin element in canting, the supposedly secret language of highwaymen. This was publicly exposed as early as 1610 by a writer under the pseudonym

'Martin Mark-all, Beadle of Bridewell'. At the end of his *Apologie*, he explains the origins of the *patois* used by the criminal underclass of his day, a mixture of Latin, English and Dutch. Bridewell Prison had been established in 1553 to control London's 'disorderly poor'. In a fascinating section offering a history of robber gangs of England, its Beadle, or governor, describes the day when, he claims, the *lingua franca* of highwaymen was invented.[11]

Tensions had grown between the two biggest robber gangs in the early 16th century. The dominant gang for several years was led by a tinker named Cock Lorrell, 'the most notorious knave that ever lived'. But a new 'regiment of thieves' sprang up in Derbyshire, led by one Giles Hather. This 100-strong gang called themselves 'the Egyptians'. Hather's woman, a whore named Kit Calot, was 'the Egyptians' Queen'. The Egyptians disguised themselves by donning black make-up. They made good money from fraudulent fortune-telling. The two 'Generals', Lorrell and Hather, decided to cooperate rather than compete with one another. They met as if they were establishing a new republic, 'to parle and intreat of matters that might tend to the establishing of this their new found government'.[12] This momentous diplomatic event took place in a famous cave in Derbyshire's Peak District, then known as 'The Devil's Arse-Peak' (prudish Victorians renamed it 'Peak Cavern'). The most important measure was

> to devise a certaine kinde of language, to the end their convenings, knaveries and villanies might not be so easily perceived and knone, in places where they come: and this their language they spunne out of three other tongues, viz. Latine, English, and Dutch.[13]

The speakers of the canting tongue, most of whom will have been illiterate, did not write it down. The Dutch element will have come from the intensive contact between the English and Dutch sailors, especially those who had escaped from the ships into which they had been pressganged in the port cities of northern Europe.[14] The priority of Latin was inevitable: it will have been the only language of which most members of the gangs (at least, everyone who had been to Catholic churches or through the courts of law) will have acquired at least a smattering. The lost Latinate language of the thieves and highwaymen of England was probably not 'devised' overnight in that cave in Derbyshire. But the fact that the 'Beadle of Bridewell' describes it in such detail suggests that he knew whereof he spoke.

Yet, by the time Classics emerged as a discipline at the dawn of the 18th century, it was not Latinate canting, but another underworld dialect, known as 'St. Giles's Greek', which was favoured by metropolitan Georgian felons. The enterprising Francis Grose (who may have penned the burlesque of the *Iliad* discussed above p. 3–4) treated it to a lexicographical investigation in his *Classical Dictionary of the Vulgar Tongue* (1785; much reprinted). (Figure 16.1) Grose was responding, no doubt, to the vogue for comprehensive dictionaries (Samuel Johnson's 1755 *A Dictionary of the English Language* is the most famous, but it had

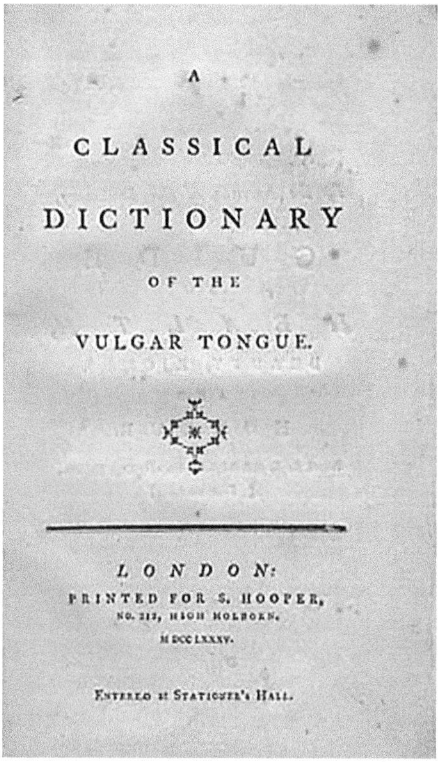

A

CLASSICAL

DICTIONARY

OF THE

VULGAR TONGUE.

LONDON:

PRINTED FOR S. HOOPER,

NO. 212, HIGH HOLBORN.

M DCC LXXXV.

ENTERED at STATIONER'S HALL.

FIGURE 16.1 Frontispiece to Francis Grose's *Classical Dictionary of the Vulgar Tongue* (1785) reproduced from copy in Edith Hall's personal collection.

followed hard on the heels of Lancashire-born schoolmaster Robert Ainsworth's *Thesaurus Linguae Latinae Compendarius* (1736) and Benjamin Martin's *Lingua Britannica Reformata* [1749]). Grose's subversive title parodied such scholarly works as Laurence Echard's *Classical Geographical Dictionary* (1715), Andrew Millar's *An Historical, Genealogical, and Classical Dictionary* (1743) and John Kersey's *New Classical English Dictionary* (1757). He expressed scorn for pedantic classicists 'who do not know a right angle from an acute one, or the polar circle from the tropics, and understand no other history but that of the intrigues between the eight parts of speech' while looking 'down with contempt' on everyone else.[15] Yet his biographer believes that he received a classical education in his boyhood; there is substantial knowledge of ancient authors on display in his *A Treatise on Ancient Armour and Weapons* (1786).[16] After an army career, Grose worked as an antiquarian and draughtsman; a warm-hearted man of ready wit, after visiting Scotland he became one of Robert Burns' closest friends.[17]

Grose explains in his preface that 'the Vulgar Tongue' consists of 'the Cant Language, called sometimes Pedlars' French, or St. Giles's Greek', plus burlesque or slang terms 'which, from long uninterrupted usage, are made classical by prescription'. He satirically explains what he means by 'the most classical authorities' for the latter category: 'soldiers on the long march; seamen at the capstern; ladies disposing of their fish, and the colloquies of a Gravesend boat'.[18] Grose had served at non-officer ranks amongst the rank and file of the army, having joined a foot regiment in Flanders as a volunteer at the age of 17. When serving in the Surrey Militia, he had met many robbers and highwaymen because he was charged with a clampdown on their activities. He took their lower-class speech seriously and created a scholarly lexicographical resource. He found some material in previous collections of slang, but also conducted primary research on nocturnal strolls amongst the London underworld with his servant Tom Cocking.[19]

Criminal cant was called 'St. Giles's Greek' because the parish of St. Giles (between Newgate Prison and the Tyburn gallows, now part of Camden) was notoriously the operating ground of thieves and pickpockets. 'Greek', being known by nobody except the elite, was a convenient term for the 'cant', a gibberish few understood.[20] These entries from the dictionary show that 'St. Giles's Greek' adopted a humorous approach to classical culture, Latin and learned etymologies: cobblers were called 'Crispins' after two early Christian saints. Blind men were called 'Cupids' and prostitutes 'Drury Lane Vestals'. *Ars Musica* meant 'a bum fiddle', a person always scratching their posterior (arse + a musical instrument); *Athanasian wench* means a promiscuous woman, who will sleep with anyone who offers, because the first words of the Athanasian creed are '*quicunque vult*', whosoever wants ... ; *Circumbendibus* means a story told with many digressions; the entry under *Fart* includes an obscene rhyming couplet in Latin; *Hicksius-doxius* means 'drunk', by making comical pseudo-Latin out of sounds suggestive of hiccups; *Myrmidons* means 'the constable's assistants' by association with Achilles' stalwart men-at-arms in the *Iliad*; *Trickum legis*—a hybrid Anglo-Latin comical phrase meaning 'legal quibble'; and *Squirrel* means a prostitute because it hides its backside with its tail. Here Grose cites a French authority who quoted a Latin proverb *meretrix corpore corpus alit*, 'a whore nourishes her body with her body'.[21]

Greeklessness, race, gender and class

In a collection of essays, Grose remarks that 'Greek is almost as rare among military people as money'.[22] The same could be said in the 18th century of many more middle- and upper-class men than would have cared to admit it. The result was that Greek acquired a totem-like status, and often appeared in rhetorical situations where exclusion from not only polite society but even fundamental rights as a human being were at stake; for example, when white people wanted to distinguish their intellectual abilities from those of black ones. An African American named Alexander Crummell travelled to Cambridge University and learned Greek during his theological studies at Queen's College (1851–1853), financed by Abolitionists. He later said that he had partly been motivated by a conversation he heard as a free but impoverished errand boy in Washington DC in 1833 or 1834, when pro-slavery thinkers were on the defensive. The Senator for South Carolina, John C. Calhoun, declared at a dinner party that only when he could 'find a Negro who knew the Greek syntax' could he be brought to 'believe that the Negro was a human being and should be treated as a man'.[23]

The author of a Cornwall/Devon newspaper article, written in 1852, sneers at what he sees as do-gooders with cranky views on education, the sort of 'educated man who believes that an ignorant servant, who cannot with both her eyes read "slut" visibly written on a dusty table, can … read a Greek *chorus* with her elbows'.[24] The rhetorical effect here comes from the manifest absurdity of imagining that a working-class female could achieve the educational standard symbolised by reading Greek lyric verse. The point depends on extreme class snobbery as well as misogyny: the serving girl's brain can never be developed (the body part mentioned is her elbows, symbol of manual labour). She is only by a syntactical hairsbreadth not dismissed as sexually depraved as well as educationally retarded.[25]

Of all forms of Greek, the words of the Greek tragic chorus seemed the most potent symbol of the elitist class connotations of the classical curriculum. For Victorians, the chorus symbolised esoteric intellectual matters, as people today talk about 'rocket science' or 'brain surgery'. In the polemics of educational reformers, such as those who established the College of Physical Science at Newcastle-upon-Tyne in 1871, the metres of the Greek chorus become the emblem of 'useless' education for its own sake. In 1871 a Yorkshire advocate of reformed, utilitarian and science-based education wrote an article in *The Huddersfield Chronicle and West Yorkshire Advertiser* entitled 'Useful versus Ornamental Learning': he said,

> Many men brought up in the strict traditions of academical learning will look with eyes of scorn upon the new College of Physical Science, just opened in Newcastle-upon-Tyne … How can a nation prosper, will old college Dons think, whose sons let their wits go wool-gathering after chemistry and natural philosophy, when they ought to be hard at work unravelling the intricacies of a Greek chorus, which sounds remarkably well in the sonorous rhythms of Eurypides [*sic*], but which is found to be a trifle vague, not to say idiotic, when translated. Verily will our Don think the old order changeth when hydraulics and hydrostatics are prized above choriambics and catalectic tetrameters.[26]

The new College grew out of the North of England Institute of Mining and Mechanical Engineers, a response to the horrendous mining catastrophes in the earlier 19th century. The first session, in 1871–1872, entailed 8 teaching staff, 173 students and the 4 subjects of Mathematics, Physics, Chemistry and Geology. But the antithesis between practical science which could save miners' lives and 'useless' classical scholarship was curiously subverted in the figure of John Herman Merivale, the College's first student, who became its first Professor of Mining.

He was warmly supported in his desire to alleviate mining conditions by his father, the Very Reverend Charles Merivale, Dean of Ely Cathedral, classical scholar, translator of Homer into English and author of *A History of the Romans under the Empire* (1850–1862). Merivale Senior also translated Keats' *Hyperion* into Latin verse (1863).

The Greek of freakish animals

The freakishness which labouring-class people associated with Greek comes over in a poem called 'The Fool's Song' by Thomas Holcroft, the revolutionary son of an itinerant pedlar. Holcroft was charged with treason in 1794. He considers all kinds of improbable situations with as much likelihood of coming about as a fair system of justice in Britain:

> When law and conscience are a-kin,
> And pigs are learnt by note to squeak;
> Your worship then shall stroke your chin,
> And teach an owl to whistle Greek.[27]

These are imagined prodigious fauna, but the provincial Englander's concept of the distance between real life and the ancient Greek language could be weirdly proven by performing animals. The British showed their intellectual superiority over the French in 1751 during a war between educated hounds.

When *Le Chien Savant* (or Learned French Dog, a small poodle-ish she-dog who could spell words in French and English) arrived in London, she was trumped by the *New* Chien Savant, or learned English Dog, a Border Collie.[28] The triumphant English Dog toured Staffordshire, Shrewsbury, Northamptonshire, Hereford, Monmouth and Gloucester, as well as the taverns of London. She could spell PYTHAGORAS and was advertised as a latter-day reincarnation of the Samian philosopher/mathematician himself.[29] Exhibited in a public house in Northampton in November 1753, this Learned Dog (for there were several other rival hounds touring the country during the 18th and earlier 19th centuries) had a range of talents. The local newspaper, the *Mercury*, recommended a visit to the exhibition heartily:

> Of all the extraordinary curiosities that have ever been exhibited to the inspection for the curious, none have met with such a general approbation and esteem as the learned English Dog, now at the Angel Inn in this town [which] actually reads, writes, and casts accounts; answers various questions in Ovid's *Metamorphoses*, geography, the Roman, English, and sacred history.[30]

This hound could tell the time, distinguish between colours and, at the climax of the show, display powers of Extra-Sensory Perception by reading spectators' thoughts.[31]

The erudite hound tradition may have been inspired by Scipio and Berganza, the canine conversationalists in Miguel de Cervantes' social satire *El Coloquio de los Perros* (*Conversation of the Dogs*), who understand the role played by displays of Latin and Greek in the Spanish class system. The last of Cervantes' *Exemplary Novels* (*Novelas ejemplares*, 1613), of which English translations were fashionable reading, the dialogue is overheard by a man in hospital with venereal disease. Scipio and Berganza are the hospital guard dogs. They agree that there are two ways of abusing Latin quotations. Berganza, who learned Latin tags when owned by schoolmasters, resents writers who insert 'little Scraps of Latin, making those believe, who do not understand it, that they are great Latinists, when they scarcely know how to decline a noun or conjugate a verb'.[32] Scipio, the more educated and cynical hound, sees humans who *do* know Latin as more harmful. Their conversations even with lower-class cobblers and tailors are flooded with Latin phrases, incomprehensible to their listeners and therefore creating opportunity for exploitation of the less educated.

Scipio woofs references to the myths of Ulysses and Sisyphus. He would rather bark about philosophy than abuses of Latin. Like Plato's Socrates, he becomes exasperated when his interlocutor relates anecdotes rather than producing definitions. Here is the dialogue after Berganza concedes that he does not know the Greek etymology of the word 'philosophy' and demands to know from whom Scipio learned Greek: Scipio responds, mysteriously,

> In good truth, you are very simple, Berganza, in making so great account of this, for these are things which every school-boy, even those in the lowest forms are acquainted with; and there are likewise some, who pretend to talk Greek, as well as Latin, who know nothing either.[33]

Scipio is in danger of exhibiting the very intellectual snobbery which he purports to criticise. But it is Berganza who concludes the discussion of Classics with a striking, problematic image. He compares people who deceive others into thinking they are refined by faking knowledge of Latin and Greek with people who use tinsel to cover up the holes in their breeches. But he also suggests that such intellectual imposters be exposed by the torture methods used by Portuguese slavers on 'the Negroes in Guinea', thus revealing that he is not himself free from 'human' indifference towards the plight of slaves.[34]

Most poignant of all, given Burke's insulting claim that putting scholarship anywhere near working-class people was to cast pearls before swine, were the Sapient Pigs which toured pubs in late Georgian England exhibiting their prodigious intellect. The most famous billed himself as Toby, the SAPIENT PIG, OR PHILOSOPHER OF THE SWINISH RACE. There was more than one such pig; Richard Porson, who was acutely aware that he had risen from a working-class background to become the most celebrated Greek scholar in the land (see pp. 294–9), wrote a Greek epigram for one in 1785 (prior to Burke's notorious diatribe), appending a humorous short article about him. It opens by calling the pig a 'gentleman', and hoping that said 'gentleman professing himself to be extremely learned, [he] will have no objection to find his merits set forth in a Greek quotation'. Porson then supplies the Greek, and an English translation which he claims he has procured from the *Chien Savant*, because 'it is possible that the pig's Greek may want rubbing up, owing to his having kept so much company with ladies'.[35]

The frontispiece to the autobiography *The Life and Adventures of Toby the Sapient Pig* implies that the learned swine's preferred reading was Plutarch (Figure 16.2). The poet Thomas Hood saw that no amount of learning could ultimately save a pig—or a lower-class human—from being sacrificed in the interests of the voracious ruling class. His 'Lament of Toby, the Learned Pig', woefully concludes with the poor porcine, despite being crammed with Classics at Brasenose College, Oxford, being fed and readied for slaughter:

> My Hebrew will all retrograde
> Now I'm put up to fatten,
> My Greek, it will all go to grease,
> The dogs will have my Latin![36]

Knowledge of ancient Greek authors was absolute proof of the *prodigious* intelligence of an animal. This is, in turn, telling evidence of the degree of difficulty—and therefore cultural prestige in financial and class terms—associated by the provincial inn-going public with such an arcane educational curriculum.

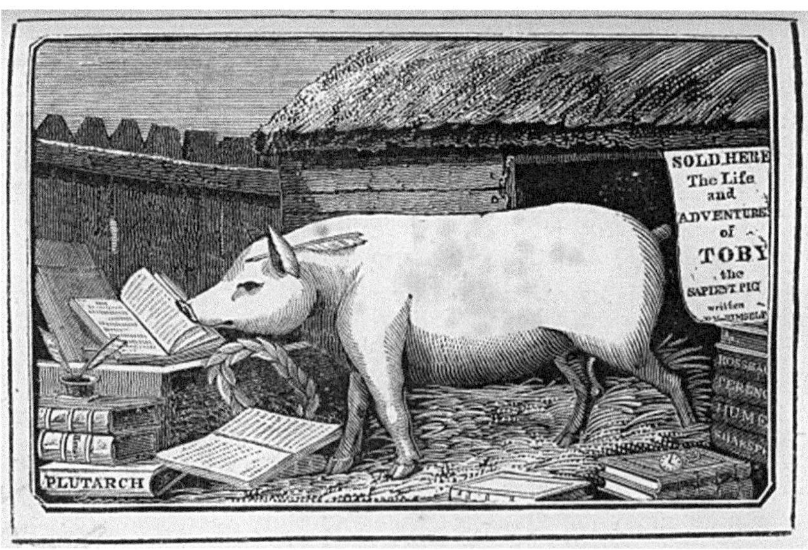

FIGURE 16.2 Frontispiece to autobiography *The Life and Adventures of Toby the Sapient Pig* (1817 edition) reproduced by permission of the British Library.

Ancient Greek authors sometimes pop up in other strange forms of plebeian entertainment involving fauna, especially in London. When Georgian showmen invited the public to view their exotic ostriches, they were sure to mention Xenophon.[37] 'The most astonishing and largest OSTRICH ever seen in Europe' was advertised as on display at the Pastry-Cook Mr Patterson's, no. 37 Haymarket. The advertisement informs the reader that 'Dr. YOUNG observes from Xenophon, that Cyrus had horses which overtake the goat and wild ass, but none could reach this creature'[38] (Figure 16.3). The reader is also told that a Satyr can currently be viewed, along with the rare Cassowary bird from New Guinea, at 'Gough's Menagerie', no. 99, Holborn Hill. Appearances in London were even made by the terrifying snake-like monster called the *basiliskos* mentioned in ancient texts including Heliodorus' *Ethiopian Tale* (III.8), Artemidorus' *Interpretation of Dreams* (IV.56—see further below p. 337) and Pliny's *Natural History* (VIII.78). There had been a 17th-century craze for the alleged discoveries of baby basilisks lurking in eggs, and examples, when dried, could reach a good

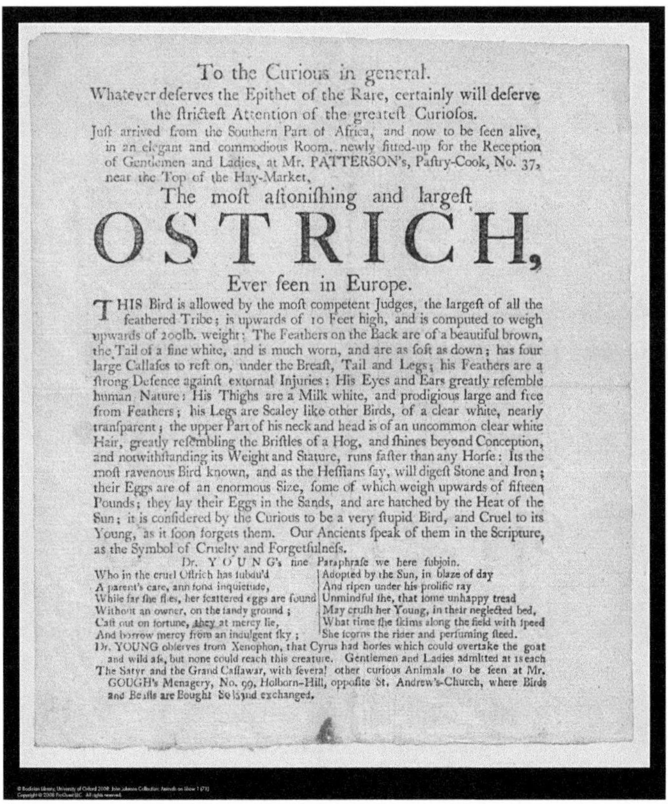

To the Curious in general.

Whatever deſerves the Epithet of the Rare, certainly will deſerve the ſtricteſt Attention of the greateſt Curioſos.

Juſt arrived from the Southern Part of Africa, and now to be ſeen alive, in an elegant and commodious Room, newly fitted-up for the Reception of Gentlemen and Ladies, at Mr. PATTERSON's, Paſtry-Cook, No. 37, near the Top of the Hay-Market,

The moſt aſtoniſhing and largeſt

OSTRICH,

Ever ſeen in Europe.

THIS Bird is allowed by the moſt competent Judges, the largeſt of all the feathered Tribe; is upwards of 10 Feet high, and is computed to weigh upwards of 200lb. weight: The Feathers on the Back are of a beautiful brown, the Tail of a fine white, and is much worn, and are as ſoft as down; has four large Callaſes to reſt on, under the Breaſt, Tail and Legs; his Feathers are a ſtrong Defence againſt external Injuries: His Eyes and Ears greatly reſemble human Nature: His Thighs are a Milk white, and prodigious large and free from Feathers; his Legs are Scaley like other Birds, of a clear white, nearly tranſparent; the upper Part of his neck and head is of an uncommon clear white Hair, greatly reſembling the Briſtles of a Hog, and ſhines beyond Conception, and notwithſtanding its Weight and Stature, runs faſter than any Horſe: Its the moſt ravenous Bird known, and as the Heſſians ſay, will digeſt Stone and Iron; their Eggs are of an enormous Size, ſome of which weigh upwards of fifteen Pounds; they lay their Eggs in the Sands, and are hatched by the Heat of the Sun; it is conſidered by the Curious to be a very ſtupid Bird, and Cruel to its Young, as it ſoon forgets them. Our Ancients ſpeak of them in the Scripture, as the Symbol of Cruelty and Forgetfulneſs.

Dr. YOUNG's fine Paraphraſe we here ſubjoin.

Who in the cruel Oſtrich has ſubdu'd
A parent's care, ann fond inquietude,
While far ſhe flies, her ſcattered eggs are found
Without an owner, on the ſandy ground;
Caſt out on fortune, they at mercy lie,
And borrow mercy from an indulgent ſky;
Adopted by the Sun, in blaze of day
And ripen under his prolific ray
Unmindful ſhe, that ſome unhappy tread
May cruſh her Young, in their neglected bed,
What time ſhe ſkims along the field with ſpeed
She ſcorns the rider and perfuming ſteed.

Dr. YOUNG obſerves from Xenophon, that Cyrus had horſes which could overtake the goat and wild aſs, but none could reach this creature. Gentlemen and Ladies admitted at 1s each

The Satyr and the Grand Caſſawar, with ſeveral other curious Animals to be ſeen at Mr. GOUGH's Menagery, No. 99, Holborn-Hill, oppoſite St. Andrew's-Church, where Birds and Beaſts are Bought Sold and exchanged.

FIGURE 16.3 'The most astonishing and largest OSTRICH ever seen in Europe'. Handbill in John Johnson Collection reproduced by permission of the Bodleian Library.

price across western Europe. A handbill in the British Library entitled 'A Brief Description of the Basilisk, or Cockatrice' shows that at least one fake basilisk was to be viewed in London. The handbill informs us that its owner, an impoverished Spaniard named James Salgado, had presented it to some gentlemen in London when begging for financial assistance.[39]

In April 1751 the *London Magazine* published an article supposedly exposing an April Fools' Day scam.[40] The story illustrates the kind of freak show, with an ancient Greek flavour, which snobbish readers thought credulous people of the lower classes could be tempted to pay to view. A few weeks earlier, a pamphlet had appeared announcing that 'the surprising CENTAUR, the greatest Wonder produced by Nature these 3000 Years' was to be exhibited on April 1st at the Golden Cross, Charing Cross[41] (Figure 16.4). The pamphlet described how the Centaur, whose name was Paul Ernest-Christian-Ludovic Manpferdt ('Manhorse'), had been born near a Jesuit College in Switzerland and had been

FIGURE 16.4 'The Surprizing Centaur' by Richard Bentley (1751), reproduced by Courtesy of the British Library. [i.e. Richard Bentley] 1751, *A True and Faithful Account of the Greatest Wonder Produced by Nature these 3000 Years, in the Person of Mr Jehan-Paul-Ernest Christian Lodovick Manpferdt; The Surprizing Centaur*. Reproduced by Courtesy of the British Library.

transported with difficulty to England. The Centaur has failings, said the pamphlet, especially dunging and urinating in any company, 'a propensity to all kinds of Indecency and Lewdness in his Talk', and drinking an 'immense quantity of Claret'.[42] The price of seeing the Centaur was to be five shillings for nobility and gentry and one shilling to everyone else. These extortionate sums are part of the joke; a shilling was more than most working people at the time could earn in a whole day.

Uncouth Caledonian Hellenists

Further north, in Scotland, where at least until the late 19th century the education system was kinder to low-class children (especially boys) than it was in England (see further Chapter 11), there was a curious phenomenon of notable Hellenists from lowly origins who retained a preference for a lifestyle too coarse to allow them to qualify as gentlemen. William Wilkie, the 'Scottish Homer' fluent in ancient Greek, composed a nine-book epic about Thebes while personally ploughing his few fields in order to plant potatoes. The son of a farmer who had fallen on hard times, Wilkie's aptitude for classical languages was spotted at Dalmeny Parish School. While he was at Edinburgh University he baffled leaders of the Scottish Enlightenment, Adam Smith and David Hume, and a friend named Henry Mackenzie recalled him as 'superior in genius to any man of his time, but rough and unpolished in his manners, and still less accommodating to the decorum of society in the ordinary habits of his life'.[43]

Wilkie was forced to leave university when his father died, leaving him with nothing but an unexpired lease of a farm in Midlothian, some livestock, and three dependent sisters. He was an outstanding agriculturalist who made advances in the cultivation of the potato. A biographer recalls that while he worked at his crops

> with the most laudable industry and perseverance, labouring much and frequently with his own hands, he did not neglect those studies which his classical education had placed within his reach. It was here and while labouring with scythe and sickle, ploughing and harrowing, that he conceived, and at intervals of leisure in part wrote, his poem of the *Epigoniad*.[44]

The epic, in rhyming couplets, is heavily influenced by Pope, steeped in first-hand knowledge of Homeric Greek and virtually unreadable. But in his eccentric Preface, Wilkie takes pains to stress that readers of any class can enjoy poetry set in ancient times:

> Neither is this knowledge of antient manners confined to the learned; the vulgar themselves, from the books of Moses, and other accounts of the first periods of the Jewish state, are sufficiently instructed in the customs of the earliest times, to be able to relish any work where they are justly

> represented. With what favour, for instance, has Mr Pope's translation of the *Iliad* been received by persons of all conditions.[45]

Although he became less indigent, being appointed to a Chair in Natural Philosophy at St. Andrews, Wilkie was inveterately mean with money. He said, to the end of his days, 'I have shaken hands with poverty up to the very elbow, and I wish never to see her face again'. He identified physically with the labouring class. His biographer reports that he slept in large piles of dirty blankets, and had an

> abhorrence of clean sheets … On one occasion, being pressed by Lady Lauderdale to stay all night at Hatton, he agreed, though with reluctance, and only on condition that her ladyship would indulge him in the luxury of a pair of foul sheets.

He cannot have smelled pleasant, either: 'He used tobacco to an immoderate excess, and was extremely slovenly in his dress'. Little wonder that Charles Townsend said that he had 'never met with a man who approached so near to the two extremes of a god and a brute as Dr Wilkie'.[46]

While Wilkie was composing his epic, the Professor of Greek at Glasgow, James Moor, was also horrifying polite society by his appalling manners. Born in Glasgow, Moor was the son of a Mathematics teacher. He matriculated in 1725, became a protégé of the Professor of Moral Philosophy, Francis Hutcheson, and graduated MA in 1732. He taught as a school teacher and a private tutor to the children of Scottish aristocrats, before becoming the University's librarian in 1742. He was appointed to the Chair of Greek four years later. An accomplished scholar, he collaborated with the University's printers, the Foulis brothers (themselves risen by hard work from a working-class childhood as the sons of a maltman) on their celebrated editions of Latin and especially Greek Classics.[47] But he was boorish in the extreme, living with his working-class wife in quarters regarded as unsavoury by colleagues. He spent much of his time in taverns and, when drunk, would engage in unseemly brawls; his Faculty had to discipline him for attacking a student with a candlestick. Moor died as he had often lived, insolvent. [48]

Arcane Greek lore

Earlier, we saw that pouring forth quotations in Greek might be construed as a sign of possession by a poor old woman believed to be a witch. The supernatural associations of Greek were combined with its aura of high erudition in the strange phenomenon whereby compounds of ancient Greek stems were used in the advertising of medicinal and cosmetic lotions and potions, simultaneously to associate them with precious wisdom and with an almost supernatural potency. 'We must walk through Holborn and the Strand with a Greek dictionary in hand', declares a journalist in 1851.[49] This marketing technique is parodied in the black-tinted hair oil with the brand name *Cyanochaitanthropopion* (Blue-Black-Hair-for-Humans) sold in Samuel Warren's 1841 novel about the adventures of an impoverished draper's assistant, *Ten Thousand A-Year*.[50] A similar sense of the special powers of Greek knowledge is attested by the popularity of the ancient Greek handbook of dream divination, Artemidorus' *Oneirocritica*, which was available in numerous Greek and Latin editions; it was translated into German in 1540, French in 1546, Italian in 1547, English by 1606[51] and even Welsh in 1698.[52] But the book which most clearly associated ancient Greek wisdom with arcane lore was the bestseller *Aristotle's Masterpiece* or *Compleat Masterpiece*, sometimes entitled *The Works of Aristotle, the Famous Philosopher*. Although not by Aristotle, this anonymous racy manual on sex, reproduction and midwifery, with lavish and exciting illustrations, was first published in 1684 and reproduced in hundreds of variant editions thereafter, both English and Welsh.[53]

A copy was bought in 1700 by John Cannon, an agricultural labourer, for a shilling. He wanted to 'pry into the Secrets of Nature especially of the female sex'. In order to verify 'Aristotle's' accounts, he bored holes in the wall of the family privy to spy on the maid.[54] Cannon did not find it in a catalogue put out by mainstream publishing houses. It was, writes Mary Fissell, 'part of a low culture of ephemeral productions, and sold in a variety of venues including "rubber goods shops", which also sold contraceptives, abortifacient pills, etc.' Her brilliant essay describes how this 'wildly popular sex manual ... taught and titillated through the early modern period and beyond' across the entire class spectrum.[55]

The reasons why the anonymous author invoked the authority of Aristotle are several. As the acknowledged expert in most scholarly fields—Dante's 'Master of Those who Know'—Aristotle possessed the cachet of the intellectual heavyweight.[56] But he was also seen as a sex guru. This perception was connected with a prurient 13th-century fiction which described Aristotle's affair with the courtesan Phyllis, who agreed to have sex with him if she could ride on his back as a dominatrix. The silly tale was made available in English by 1386, when John Gower told it in his collection of sex stories *Confessio Amantis*. But the immediate impulse to publish under Aristotle's name was the warm response which an authentic ancient Greek text attributed to him had received. An English translation of *The Problemes of Aristotle, with other Philosophers and Phisitions. Wherein are contained diuers questions, with their answers, touching the estate of mans bodie* had been published in 1595.

This book is easy to read; it was written by disciples of Aristotle, probably with the intention of publicising Peripatetic biology amongst a general ancient readership. The questions will have been normal in ancient Greek society, but may well have shocked Early Modern Christians. Why do some men wink after copulation? Why do some eunuchs desire women and excel at 'the act of Venerie'? Why do women love the men who deflower them? Why do fat men produce scanty semen?[57] Aristotle's name soon became a byword for knowledgeability—and knowingness—about sex.

Purchasers of *Aristotle's Masterpiece*, believing it to be, like the Peripatetic *Problems*, a translation of an authentic ancient Greek work, were tempted to part with their money by an almost invariable picture of a naked woman, often being inspected by a scholarly gentleman who might be assumed to be Aristotle, reproduced opposite the title page (Figure 16.5). One popular edition included bawdy poems designed to be read out to a woman being seduced and promising mutual gratification, which it explains (inaccurately) is required for conception.[58] But it also contains sensible information about care of the pregnant woman, the development of the unborn child, labour and parturition. This was one reason why it was so much consulted by women as well as men (Molly Bloom in James Joyce's *Ulysses* has her own copy[59]), but another is that, like John Cannon, adolescent girls were desperate to find out what to expect when they had sex with men. Mary Bertenshaw was 14 and working in a Manchester factory when her friend Gladys brought in *Aristotle's Masterpiece*. Mary describes it as 'a secret book'. They read it, laughing during their breaks until their boss discovered what they were doing. But Mary was grateful that she had read the book when her mother became pregnant.[60]

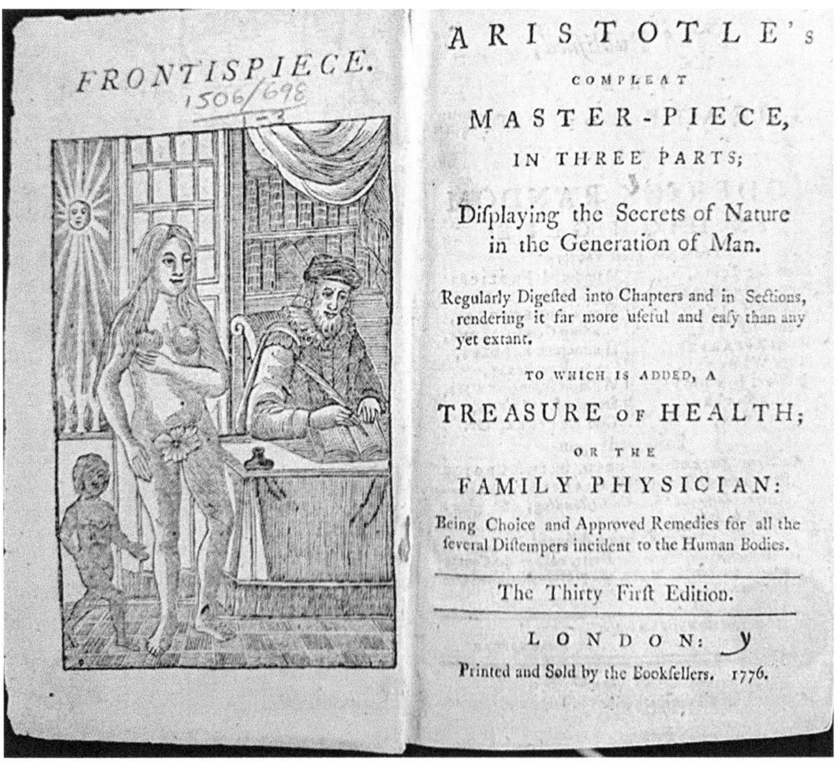
FRONTISPIECE.

ARISTOTLE's
COMPLEAT
MASTER-PIECE,
IN THREE PARTS;
Difplaying the Secrets of Nature in the Generation of Man.
Regularly Digefted into Chapters and in Sections, rendering it far more ufeful and eafy than any yet extant.
TO WHICH IS ADDED, A
TREASURE OF HEALTH;
OR THE
FAMILY PHYSICIAN:
Being Choice and Approved Remedies for all the feveral Diftempers incident to the Human Bodies.
The Thirty Firft Edition.
LONDON:
Printed and Sold by the Bookfellers. 1776.

FIGURE 16.5 Frontispiece from *Aristotle's Compleat Masterpiece* (1776) reproduced by courtesy of the British Library.

Finally, the ancient Greek savant's spurious manual lay behind one radical's questioning of Christian dogma, bringing this chapter full circle back to the issue of the Bible. Francis Place went on to play a leading role in the 1824 Repeal of the Combination Act, thus helping early Trade Unionism, and later in Moral-Force Chartism. But he was originally the illegitimate son of a man who ran a Drury Lane sponging-house, born in 1771. Before he was apprenticed to a maker of leather breeches in Temple Bar at the age of 14, Francis used to tour the bookstalls of London looking for exciting anatomical pictures in medical works, and read the *Masterpiece* while still at school. Aristotle, who did not believe in the direct involvement of any deity in human life, would have approved of one upshot of the *Masterpiece*'s physiology. Greek, however inauthentic, here did work that many of Place's contemporaries would have regarded as diabolical. For Place said that it was learning from its scientific description of the process of human conception that made him doubt forever the whole Biblical tradition of the Virgin Birth.[61]

Notes

1 Anne Dacier later converted: see above p. 28.
2 Wood (1969) 95–104. On Luther's insistence that reading the New Testament in the Latin vulgate rather than Greek would distort its meaning, see Goeman (2017).
3 Dr. Johnson is said to have used an Elizabethan folio edition of the Greek Bible, *Biblia Graeca Septuaginta* (1594) to strike down Thomas Osborne, 'because that notorious bookseller' had blamed a 'learned and diligent employee for a negligence': Jackson (1930) I, 167.
4 see Chapter 17 p. 342.
5 See Cueva, Byrne and Benda (2009).
6 Whitehead (2016); see also Edwards (1985) 83–114, 144–158.
7 Lawley (1860) 10.
8 Plot (1686) 280.
9 Plot (1686) 282.
10 Plot (1686) 282–4.
11 Mark-All (1610), the last three pages. There are no page numbers printed.
12 Mark-All (1610), third page from the end.
13 Mark-All (1610), third page from the end.
14 Linebaugh and Rediker (2000) 143–73.
15 Grose (1791) 40–1.
16 Farrant (2009) n.p.
17 Crawford (2009) 263, 316, 318, 320.
18 Grose (1785) iii, v–vi.
19 Stamper (2017) 154.
20 Grose (1785) s.v. GREEK.
21 See under these words as alphabetically lemmatised in Grose (1785); there are no page numbers in this part of the book.
22 Grose (1791) 7.
23 Crummell (1898) 10–11.
24 'Provincial medical and surgical association', *Trewman's Exeter Flying Post or Plymouth and Cornish Advertiser*, Thursday, August 26th, 1852; Issue 4522.
25 Knowledge of Greek as cancelling lack of entitlement based on class and gender was instanced prominently 20 years later in the USA, where it also features in a prodigy

narrative as signalling quasi-supernatural power. Tilton (1871), a biographical sketch of Victoria Woodhull, in 1872 the first woman to run for U.S. president, explains how she used the authority of Athenian statesman Demosthenes to legitimise her audacious move. Raised in a one-room wooden shack in Homer, Ohio, and the recipient of less than three years' education, she practised as a medium and grew up to be a freethinker, abolitionist and suffragist. She was often visited by the spirit of Demosthenes, who presented her with the text of a petition to Congress when she was asleep. He wrote on a scroll 'The Memorial of Victoria C. Woodhull', claiming under the Fourteenth Amendment the right of women as of all other 'citizens of the United States' to vote.

26 Anon. (1871); see further Hall (2013b) 292–3.
27 Holcroft (1784) 74.
28 The showman designing a *Harlequin Hercules* in Hawkesworth (1754) 14 (see below, p. 346) proposes hiring the Learned English Dog to impersonate Cerberus.
29 Bondeson (2011) 17–18.
30 Quoted in Everitt (1985) 182.
31 Bondeson (2011) 19.
32 Cervantes (1741) 33.
33 Cervantes (1741) 37
34 Cervantes (1741) 38.
35 'The Learned' Pig, reproduced in Porson (1815) 54–5, 54 and n.
36 Hood (1839) 540.
37 Hall (2016a) 455 and n.30.
38 John Johnson Collection of Handbills Animals on Show, no. I (7), Bodleian Library. See Xenophon, *Anabasis* 1.5.3.
39 Bondeson (2008) 180–1.
40 Anon. (1751a).
41 Anon. (1751b), title page. The author of the pamphlet was probably Richard Bentley.
42 Anon. (1751b) 19–20.
43 Quoted in Chambers (1835) 439.
44 Chambers (1835) 439.
45 Wilkie (1757) iv. On working-class knowledge of Josephus and of Pope's Homer, see esp. pp. 4–5 and 45.
46 Chambers (1835) 439.
47 On the Foulis brothers, see the library holdings and bibliography catalogued in Whitaker (1986) and Gaskell (1964), respectively.
48 Duncan (1831) 127–31.
49 Anon. (1851) 358.
50 Warren (1841) vol. II, 101–2; Strachan (2007) 222–5. The name is dependent on a formula used of the dark-haired god Poseidon and of Hector in Homer, e.g. at *Iliad* XX.144 and *Od.* IX.536.
51 Ryff (1540), Fontaine (1546), Lauro (1547), 'R.W.' (1606).
52 Jones (1698).
53 It is possible that the book was by the medical writer William Salmon; see Fissell (2015) no. 1.
54 Cannon (1743) 41.
55 Fissell (2015).
56 Hall (2017).
57 See the recent edition with translation by Mayhew (2011).
58 Fissell (2015).
59 Joyce (1922) 722; see also 226.
60 Bertenshaw (1991) 111, 113.
61 Place (1972) 45, 261.

17

CLASSICAL UNDERWORLDS

Introduction

John Strachan has lovingly documented the use of classicism in late Georgian brand-names, from Alexander Rowland's headache medicine 'Elixir of Cerelaeum' and dental product 'Odonto', to Samuel Jones' 'Patent Promethean' water-heating machine and 'Aetna' matches.[1] A London street ballad parodied the fashion, citing products which all really existed and were advertised on bill-boards throughout the city centre:

> O such a town, such a classical metropolis,
> Tradesmen common English scorn to write or speak.
> Bond Street's a forum—Cornhill is an Acropolis,
> For every thing's in Latin, now, but what's in Greek.
> Here is a Pantechnicon, and there is an Emporium.
> Your shoes "Antigropolos", your boots are "Pannus corium";
> "Fumi-porte chimney pots", "Eureka" shirts to cover throats,
> Idrotobolic hats, and patent Aquascutum overcoats.[2]

The aura surrounding the ancient cultures known as 'classical' did not signify gentlemanliness and civility everywhere. Alongside the gentry enjoying their Palladian mansions and expensive school curriculums there always existed more commercial, demotic, subterranean and secretive groups in British society who used imagery from the Greek and Roman worlds to communicate and self-identify: shopkeepers, salesmen, imposters, criminals, prostitutes, circus and fairground performers, showgirls, libertines, madmen and participants in recreational activities ranging from the merely vulgar to the illegal.

DOI: 10.4324/9781315446608-20

Showmen and Classics

Exotic Classics was central to the forged identity and publishing scam of a notorious fraudster, 'George Psalmanazar', who arrived in London in 1703. He was a penniless Frenchman who had never been to Asia, yet claimed that he was a nobleman from Formosa (Taiwan). He narrated Oriental tales in a mixture of beautiful Latin, broken English and snippets of Formosan. They were taken by many at face value. He became a celebrity. His bestseller *An Historical and Geographical Description of Formosa* (1704) includes lurid accounts of drug-taking, smoking, native cannibalism, polygamy and mass child sacrifice; although presented as serious ethnography in the Herodotean tradition, many of his more outrageous Formosan tales echo legends told by Homer and Ovid.[3] Psalmanazar describes how he, like all well-to-do Formosan children, learned Greek at one of the island's academies and Latin from a private tutor, who turned out to be a scheming Jesuit and responsible for Psalmanazar's abduction.[4]

By 1711, the London elite realised Psalmanazar was a fraud. The first issue of the *Spectator* published a fake advertisement for an upcoming play that poked fun at Psalmanazar's tendency to extol the virtues of cannibalism:

> *On the first of April will be performed at the Play-house in the Hay-market an opera call'd The Cruelty of Atreus. N.B. The Scene wherein Thyestes eats his own children is to be performed by the famous Mr. Psalmanazar lately arrived from Formosa: The whole Supper being set to Kettle-drums.*[5]

So Psalmanazar turned to lower-class audiences instead, with accounts of Far Eastern cannibals,[6] and displays in which he smoked enormous tobacco pipes, to which he said Formosan women were addicted, and took huge doses of laudanum.[7] In his *Memoirs*, posthumously published in 1765, Psalmanazar describes how he actually first encountered Latin when he was admitted to a Franciscan charity school. He claims to have been fully fluent in the language before he turned nine and soon became a scholarship boy at a Jesuit College where he learned ancient Greek and Latin, reading Ovid, Cicero, Horace and Homer.[8]

Psalmanazar's shows were a form of recreation routinely disparaged by the nobility and gentry, as were puppet-shows. This medium takes us back to Elkanah Settle's famous fairground droll commissioned by Mrs Mynn, *The Siege of Troy*, discussed in Chapter 2. In 1712 the Dublin puppeteer Martin Powell, the rage of London since his arrival with his equally talented son in 1710, staged Settle's droll—perhaps without paying Settle anything for the privilege—under the title *The False Triumph*. He blended his performance media in a conscious bid to attract more select audiences. The text was augmented with scenes including an epiphany of Jupiter, sung by Signior Punchanella, a famous castrato currently starring in the Italian Opera House.[9]

The appearance of an opera singer in a fairground droll based on Virgil's *Aeneid* but performed by puppets is symptomatic of the chaotic class-inflected struggle between entertainment media in London during the last decades of the 17th century and the first three of the 18th. Opera competed with spoken drama, and both increasingly featured the balletic interludes which were about to develop into a separate medium of musical theatre altogether. But certain hierarchies remained, if shakily, between types of entertainment. Despite their voguishness in the first half of the 18th century, even extending slowly to the more prosperous classes, puppet-show personnel were deprecated as 'Rogues and Vagrants' and suffered from a precarious status.[10] 'Serious' actors only resorted to working with puppet-shows if they could not get hired as live actors, even in the venue of the fairs.[11] In this period, for example in Hogarth's engraving, *A Just View of the British Stage* (1724),

> the puppet could serve as a visual emblem not just for the process of performance itself, but also for a broad spectrum of paratheatrical entertainment seen as invading and polluting a theater that had finally achieved a legitimacy to which Jonson had so painfully aspired over a century earlier.[12]

The scorn which puppet-shows incurred from the elite is expressed in Joseph Addison's 'Machinae Gesticulantes, anglicè A Puppet Show' (1698), a poem in epic Latin hexameters.[13] It is thus a highbrow and hyper-literate description of a performance medium which it not only explicitly describes as 'low' but also implies is 'infantile' in the technical sense—the puppets lack language altogther. The poem engages in complex literary allusion to Virgil, especially the *Georgics*, but in the year after Dryden's translation there are also explicit references to the *Aeneid* in the reference to the *bella, horrida bella* (51—'bristling' battles, see *Aeneid* VIII.86). Addison lambasts the vulgarity both of the medium of 'Gesticulating Machines' and their audiences. Nothing could more loudly proclaim the gulf dividing cultural circles of refinement from the boorish masses. Addison is unlikely to have known that by the 3rd century BCE there were popular puppet-shows enacting stories connected with the Trojan War.[14] His humour derives from negotiating the absurd discrepancy whereby the coarse puppet-show audience—the 'gaping throngs' from 'the grinning street'—are described with a mock-solemnity suited to Horace's *Ars Poetica* or a serious Roman epic, punctured in turn by the bathos of the idea that cash puts bottoms on seats differing in quality according to the amount paid: 'Nor reigns disorder; but precedence fit / Marshals the crowd, and as they pay they sit' (*Nec confusus honos; nummo subsellia cedunt / Diverso, et varii ad pretium stat copia scamni*, 9–10).

Yet the later 17th and 18th centuries have been described as the golden age of puppetry in London and in English provincial towns, performed in both fairgrounds and taverns,[15] and Powell was instrumental in making the medium somewhat more acceptable to the upper classes during Queen Anne's reign. He used jointed wooden marionettes moved by wires and standing about three feet tall. With these he presented 'witty plays, elegantly dressed and spectacularly staged';[16] his theatre began to attract the gentry and nobility of both sexes, and he tried, if unsuccessfully, to exclude prostitutes and keep his audience 'respectable'. His puppet-shows offered more sophisticated performance techniques than those of his rivals, using footlights and backcloths.[17] Their dialogue could be intricate and their plots fairly complicated. Their effects could be terrifying; the actor Tate Wilkinson was taken by his father to see one at Bartholomew Fair when he was small: 'I there saw a sea-fight, and a most terrible battle, which determined me never to see one again'.[18]

The False Triumph remained in the Powell family's repertoire for years. Powell Junior staged it in 1726 as a marionette 'operatic burlesque'. Another, more obscure puppet master named Mr Terwin also staged *The Siege of Troy*, under its original name, in Mermaid Court in 1734. But he had gone head-to-head with a revival the same year of the droll, featuring actors rather than puppets, produced by Mrs Mynn's daughter Mrs Lee in collaboration with one Mr Harper. They set up a booth on a new Southwark site at Axe and Bottle Yard and printed an advertisement boasting a famous cast and lavish visual attractions: 'in its decorations, machiner, and paintings [it] far exceeds anything of the like that ever was seen in the fairs before, the scenes and clothing being entirely new'. Lee and Harper, perhaps with an eye to Terwin's puppets, staked their prior rights to the famous entertainment, 'the only celebrated droll of that kind … first brought to perfection by the late famous Mrs Mynns', which 'can only be performed by her daughter Mrs Lee'.[19]

A fascinating text reveals the annoyance caused to some educated men by the claim made by entrepeneurial showpeople like Mynn, Lee, Settle and Powell to 'ownership' of classical antiquity. Thirteen years after Addison wrote that Latin hexameter satire on puppet-shows, he described a preposterous project for a new London entertainment incorporating all the fashionable spectacles available across the city.[20] He claims that in a coffee-shop he heard an aspiring impresario (informed by his perceptions of people like Mynn, Settle and Powell) propose a new scheme 'of an opera, Entitled, *The Expedition of Alexander the Great*'. This would include a ladder-dance, a posture-man, 'a moving picture', an erotic waxwork model of Statira, bear-baiting and dancing monkeys. The passion for stage prophetesses would be satisfied by opening the opera with Alexander consulting the priestess at the Delphic oracle. The comedian and booth manager William Penkethman 'is to personate King Porus upon an Elephant, and is to be encountered by Powell, representing Alexander the Great upon a Dromedary, which nevertheless Mr. Powell is desired to call by the Name of Bucephalus' (the name of Alexander's horse). The two kings are to celebrate the ratification of peace thus:

> Upon the Close of this great decisive Battel, when the two Kings are thoroughly reconciled, to shew the mutual Friendship and good Correspondence that reigns between them, they both of them go together

> to a Puppet-Show, in which the ingenious Mr. Powell junior, may have an Opportunity of displaying his whole Art of Machinery.[21]

Alexander the Great's favourite book was known to have been the *Iliad*.[22] Addison presumably wanted his readership here to imagine the operatic Porus and Alexander being entertained specifically by Settle's *Siege of Troy*, especially since the Powell family was at precisely this chronological point planning to transfer it to the puppet theatre.

Addison's showman further proposes that Alexander could be entertained by Penkethman's 'Heathen Gods', an automaton show (housed in the same building as Powell's puppets) about which we know from advertisements in *Spectator* 46 and subsequent issues:

> Mr. Penkethman's Wonderful Invention call'd the Pantheon: or, the Temple of the Heathen Gods. The Work of several Years, and great Expense, is now perfected; being a most surprising and magnificent Machine, consisting of 5 several curious Pictures, the Painting and contrivance whereof is beyond Expression Admirable. The Figures, which are above 100, and move their Heads, Legs, Arms, and Fingers, so exactly to what they perform, and setting one Foot before another, like living Creatures, that it justly deserves to be esteem'd the greatest Wonder of the Age. To be seen from 10 in the Morning till 10 at Night, in the Little Piazza, Covent Garden, in the same House where Punch's Opera is.

But Addison's climax is his allegation that this showman proposed to make the actors of *The Expedition of Alexander the Great* deliver their lines in ancient Greek:

> for that Alexander being a Greek, it was his Intention that the whole Opera should be acted in that Language, which was a Tongue he was sure would wonderfully please the Ladies, especially when it was a little raised and rounded by the Ionick Dialect, and could not but be wonderfully acceptable to the whole Audience, because there are fewer of them who understand Greek than Italian.[23]

The unintelligibility of ancient Greek would guarantee its success, just as the desire to listen to exotic sung Italian had fed the craze for Opera. And the ladies, who of course knew no Greek, would like its mellifluous sound.

The Oxford-educated Addison, an excellent classical scholar, believed (like most of his contemporaries) that the Macedonian dialect was not Ionic but Doric, and sounded uncouth to other Greeks: he is asking his reader to collude in condemning the equally uncouth showman's error. He revels in the absurdity of ordinary Londoners who frequent puppet-shows having any contact whatsoever with the ancient Greek tongue. The problem that no theatre performers knew the language was to be solved either by persuading 'some Gentlemen of the Universities to learn to sing, in order to qualify themselves for the Stage', or by bringing boatloads of Greeks from Smyrna (again, Addison invites his reader to spot the error in the idea that spoken Greek had not changed since classical antiquity); alternatively, it would only take 'a Fortnight's time' for opera stars to learn Greek. None of Addison's humour would work unless his readership was convinced that knowledge of that arcane tongue was only acquired through extensive and expensive study and was thus beyond the reach of most non-gentlemen, that is, of the working classes.

The Siege of Troy was far from the only classically-themed show available in the 18th and 19th centuries to audiences across the class spectrum; the *Oedipus* of Dryden and Lee was performed by strolling players in provincial barns.[24] Spectacular shows featuring the sacrifice of beautiful virgins, both the biblical daughter of Jephthah and Iphigenia, were to be seen on a Southwark bowling green, at Clerkenwell, Bartholomew Fair and Richmond.[25] The entrepeneurial hero of a satirical journal plans in detail a pantomime called *Harlequin Hercules*, adapting his labours to incorporate several current fashionable fairground freaks—exceptionally tall women as Amazons and a captured centaur.[26] William Godwin enjoyed a show with exactly this title in 1799 at Sadler's Wells on two separate evenings in 1799.[27]

Accessible versions of classical antiquity were provided by the travelling theatre companies who performed at race meetings, which attracted notoriously cross-class attendees, as well as provincial fairs. One of the most popular scripts in these companies' repertoires was a compact version of Nathaniel Lee's spectacular Restoration tragedy *The Rival Queens, or the Death of Alexander the Great* (1677), which for nearly two centuries was the medium through which many English and Scottish people knew about Alexander of Macedon.

Lee's Alexander eventually dies at Babylon, but only after five acts featuring the ghost of his father, drunken ravings, Indian dancers and an extended catfight between his two wives, the bloodthirsty Roxana and the devoted Statira. *The Rival Queens* crossed the class divide in a paraphrase, including north-eastern dialect forms, regularly performed by the troupe of Billy Purvis (1754–1853). Purvis was a working-class Scottish boy who had been an apprentice to a joiner but preferred the life of a professional clown and bagpiper. He toured the circuit of Northumberland fairs and racetracks, frequented by Geordie pitmen, with his booth theatre; the performances included a show called *The Greek Boy* and J.H. Payne's popular *Brutus, or, the Fall of Tarquin*, a hit in Hartlepool docks in 1849.[28] A painting survives which shows his travelling stage erected at Stagshawbank near Corbridge and Hexham, with flats and scenery depicting elephants and soldiers, suggestive of an Alexander the Great theme; the musician banging the drum may well be Purvis himself (Figure 17.1).[29] The same play, in another version, traversed the south-east of England when John Richardson adopted it into the repertoire of his travelling theatre, which from 1796 toured the fairs and race meetings around London.[30]

FIGURE 17.1 'A Border Fair' by John Ritchie, reproduced by permission of the Laing Art Gallery. Image reproduced by permission of the Laing Art Gallery.

Classical burlesque and *poses plastiques*

Richardson's show's greatest fame rested on its burlesques of serious dramas and operas, performed in the open air from his ingenious travelling theatre tent and vehicle. For the late Georgians and the Victorians, the distinctive genre of musical burlesque offered an exciting medium through which Richardson's audiences, Londoners, and the large proportion of the audiences at London theatres who travelled in from the provinces, could appreciate classical material. Charles Dickens, whose antipathy to the Greek and Roman Classics was connected both with his particular model of indigenous radicalism and with his conventional mid-19th-century taste for farce, sentimentality and melodrama, wrote to Bulwer-Lytton in 1867 that the public of their day could only be induced to go and see a Greek play in the form of burlesque.[31] Dickens was scarcely exaggerating: in 1865, for example, the London playhouses offered no fewer than five new classical burlesques: these featured Pirithous, the ancient mariner Glaucus, and Echo and Narcissus, along with the *Odyssey* and the Aeschylean *Prometheus Bound*.

Burlesques often opened at holiday times, when they reached large audiences: in the 1850s it was estimated that over 60,000 people visited the London theatres and places of amusement each Boxing Night alone.[32] The burlesque theatre transcended class barriers. Unlike virtually all other professionals, actors were recruited from across the class spectrum.[33] One censorious commentator describes the audience of burlesque as a mixture of 'vapid groundlings who take stalls, and, with vacant mind, "guffaw" over the poor antics they come to see' and the fashionable 'swell of our day'.[34] The Adelphi Theatre was associated with raucous burlesques known as 'Adelphi Screamers', and with the unruly fans of Mr Edward Wright, a drag actor specialising in transvestite roles such as Medea in Mark Lemon's *Medea; or a Libel on the Lady of Colchis* (1856).[35] The Grecian Saloon in Shepherdess Walk, off what is now the City Road, which could seat 700 members of the urban and suburban working and lower-middle classes, specialised in firework displays, cosmoramas, grotto scenes, statuary and colonnades.[36] It was home to John Wooler's *Jason and Medea* (1851), which was held to have been 'nicely got up, but very vulgar in dialogue'.[37]

Henry Morley, Professor of English Literature at University College, London, wrote in the early 1850s:

> There is a large half-intelligent population in London that by bold puffing can be got into a theatre. It numbers golden lads and lasses as well as chimney sweeps.[38]

Yet the audience also often included this worthy academic. An engraving by 'Phiz' captures the mixed constituents of the audience in the 1850s: in the stalls sit the middle classes, in the boxes the most affluent of families and in the gallery the standing hordes of the working classes.[39] At the end of the period of the popularity of classical burlesque, when it was replaced by a taste for light opera and Gilbert and Sullivan, the singer Emily Soldene recalled with pleasure that it had been her privilege 'to earn the applause of all ranks', from members of the royal family 'to the coster and his wife of Whitechapel'.[40] The clientele of Astley's Theatre in London were also heterogeneous. It had a large working-class audience, and yet middle-class families also took their children. In the unlikely event of any of the audience becoming bored during the action, they could raise their eyes to the ceiling (renovated in 1858), adorned with pictures of Neptune, Diana, Cybele, Apollo, Dawn and Venus, all riding chariots drawn by appropriate animals (peacocks for Venus, deer for Diana). The most famous of all the Astley circus performers, Andrew Ducrow, specialised in 'hippodramatic' enactments of Hercules' labours, of Alexander the Great taming Bucephalus, of the rape of the Sabine women and Roman gladiators in combat.[41]

A telling source for the variety of avenues by which the Londoner in the 1840s had access to classical mythology is the diary of Charles Rice, by day a lowly porter at the British Museum, guardian of celebrated Greco-Roman antiquities, but by night a tavern singer in the public houses of central London. On 19th February 1840, at the Adam & Eve in St. Pancras Road, he was engaged to put his knowledge of ancient sculpture to profitable use by delivering notices accompanying Mr Lufkeen's delineation of 'The Grecian Statues', a series of acrobatic poses based on classical statuary (a routine originally popularised by Ducrow), including 'Hercules wrestling with the Nemean Lion'.[42] Two years later, on 28th November 1842, a curious programme of entertainments was performed for the children of the Blue Coat School and the Deaf and Dumb Asylum at the Birmingham Royal Amphitheatre: a stunt using a centrifugal railway, laughing gas, and the Swiss Brothers' display of statue groups including 'Hercules', 'Ajax defying the Lightning' and 'A Roman soldier fastening his sandal'. [43] (Figure 17.2)

Yet this form of entertainment, in other contexts, frequently possessed pornographic associations. First popularised nationally by Emma Hamilton (formerly Amy Lyon and Emma Hart), classical 'attitudes' or 'poses plastiques' lent the eroticised display of the female form an illusion of propriety.[44] Hamilton was herself working-class, the daughter of a Cheshire blacksmith who died when she was a baby. She received no education and went into domestic service at the age of 12, before running away to London. Despite her Liverpudlian accent, which

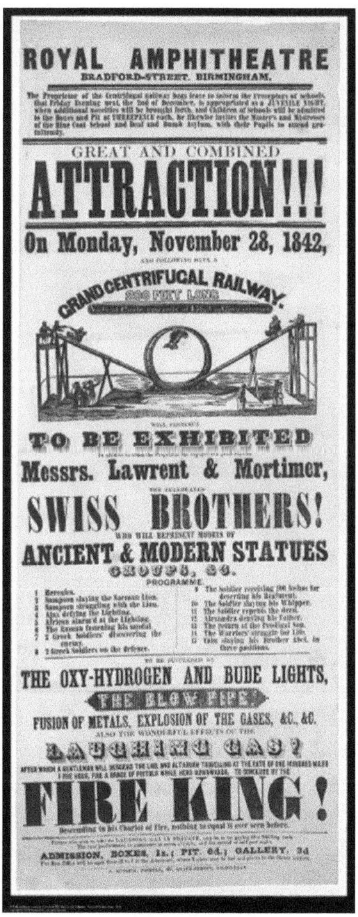

FIGURE 17.2 Early Victorian handbill advertising event at Birmingham Royal Amphitheatre reproduced from original in Edith Hall's personal collection.

she never lost, her beauty landed her a job impersonating Hygeia, the Goddess of Health and/or Hebe (Goddess of Youth) at the Temple of Health founded by the unconventional Scottish physician and sexologist James Graham. She also posed as a model for paintings of classical heroines by society artist George Romney.[45]

When she met and later married Sir William Hamilton, Emma launched herself into his world as an admirer of classical antiquity.[46] She researched classical statuary and the history of fine art on classical themes. She began to perform her 'mimoplastic' routines—alternating postures and dances, otherwise known as 'attitudes' or 'tableaux vivants'—in the roles of allegorical figures and heroines, many of them classical (Medea, Ariadne, a Bacchante, Circe, Flora, a Muse). She would emphasise her own allure with the aid of often revealing Grecian draperies, shawls and veils.[47] At first an aristocratic pastime, enjoyed by the same circles who secretively circulated accounts of the priapic objects discovered at Pompeii and Herculaneum,[48] 'attitudes' subsequently reached the lower echelons of society from which Emma had sprung.[49] From the 1830s onwards, well-developed female models in skin-tight 'fleshings' could be seen in the popular *poses plastiques*, in which they imitated naked classical statues for audiences said to include the 'worst sort' of person.[50]

In the same region of England as Emma's birthplace, in Great Charlotte Street, central Liverpool, the Royal Parthenon Assembly Rooms was founded in the early 1840s. It was renamed the Parthenon Music Saloon and later the Parthenon Music Hall in the 1850s. On 20th May 1850, a playbill advertises the week's programme of tableaux and songs, 'a truly CLASSIC exhibition, with 'a SUCCESSION OF NOVELTIES of a superior character'. The tableaux ranged over ancient history and myth, and were accompanied by vocal soloists. 'Brutus Ordering the Execution of his Son' was a dignified Roman history scene accompanied by a 'comic song' entitled 'Pity the Sorrows' sung by Mr Reed. But this was followed by tableaux entitled 'Diana Preparing for the Chase' and 'A Bacchanalian Procession, from the Borghese Vase'. Later in the programme the audience was promised three further classical tableaux, under the headings 'Greeks Surprised by the Enemy', 'the Amazons' Triumph' and 'the Grecian's Daughter'. The doors opened at half past six, and the performance commenced at seven. Entrance to the Parthenon was free; any profits were raised by selling food and drinks. In 1850, a Refreshment Token cost just three pennies.[51]

Such entertainments provided a narrative of eroticised female beauty in which proletarian sexual voyeurism was legitimised and lent an illusion of decorum by classical mythology. One of the more important directors of such events was the London impresario Renton Nicholson. Born on the Hackney Road and apprenticed at 12 years old to a pawnbroker, Nicholson had been a prisoner, gambler, tobacconist, publican, wine merchant and popular journalist. But he discovered his métier as the producer of entertainments in which an insouciant attitude to ancient Greece and Rome figured large. In 1841 he established the 'Judge and Jury Society' at a Covent Garden tavern. As 'Lord Chief Baron' he presided, in judge's regalia, over subversive mock trials based on celebrated cases of the day. Having made several court appearances for debt himself, Nicholson was familiar enough with judicial Latin to parody it effectively.[52]

The trials had a class-political angle: Nicholson liked cases involving the private lives of aristocrats, bestowing upon them new titles such as 'The Hon. Viscount Limpus versus the Hon. Priapus Pulverton'.[53] The female parts were acted by male transvestites, and Nicholson, who always acted the judge, entertained his cross-class audience by extemporising in streams of amateur Latin, especially when summarising what an observer denounced as the 'filthy particulars' of the cases.[54] He also held mock parliamentary debates and elections; he supported universal suffrage. Despite constant financial problems, he was reputed to be extremely generous to the poor and destitute. In 1860 he published his autobiography, *Rogue's Progress.* He is buried in Brompton cemetery.

His most famous shows were staged at the Coal Hole Tavern on the Strand. He hired working-class girls to enact scenes from classical myth which he accompanied with mock-learned 'lectures'.[55] A contemporary critic regarded Renton's *poses plastiques* as morally reprehensible, and was displeased that women were allowed to join the audience.[56] One of the most popular of his shows involved the lovers Cupid and Psyche as acted by half-naked young women in 1854. In this allegorical painting by Archibald S. Henning, the poses of 'Venus Arising from the Waves' and 'Andromeda Tied to her Rock' are illustrated in the bottom left and right-hand corners respectively (Figure 17.3). Other ancient figures shown at his public houses included Sappho, and Diana Preparing for the Chase.

FIGURE 17.3 'Venus Arising from the Waves' and 'Andromeda Tied to her Rock' flank portrait of Renton Nicholson, reproduced by permission of the Museum of London. Painting reproduced by permission of the Museum of London.

Classics and prostitution

Renton's showgirls often supplemented their income by sex work. One of the stranger tales of the collision of Classics and class in the later 19th century involves the symbolism of the mythical Minotaur being used in the campaign against on child prostitution. William Thomas Stead (whom we have encountered previously as a publisher, above pp. 61–4) deplored what he characterised as the voracious 'Minotaur' constituted by the appetite of rich men for girl prostitutes in their earliest teens. Educated at home and at Silcoates School in Wakefield, Stead was an exceptional Latinist. Profoundly religious, he channelled his fervour into reformist journalism and was appointed Chief Editor of the *Northern Echo* in Darlington at the age of only 22. 'I felt the sacredness of the power placed in my hands,' he later recalled, 'to be used on behalf of the poor, the outcast and the oppressed'.[57]

In 1883, Stead became editor of the gentleman's gossip journal *The Pall Mall Gazette*, and transformed it into a vehicle for sensational, political exposés.[58] The most famous was the 1885 series of four articles investigating the traffic in young girls in the underworld of London, *The Maiden Tribute of Modern Babylon: The Report of our Secret Commission*. Stead invented modern journalism by organising a complicated undercover investigation and writing in a lurid, sensationalist style, using a comparison with a famous mythical monster who committed atrocities.

The first article in the series consists of a detailed account of the Minotaur story, with long quotations from Ovid's *Metamorphoses* VIII, emphasising the death of innocent girls cast to a beast who was himself 'the foul product of an unnatural lust'. But then Stead turns to the 'maze of London brotheldom', and the Minotaur to which thousands of impoverished girl-children are sacrificed every month, because the

> maw of the London Minotaur is insatiable, and none that go into the secret recesses of his lair return again ... And if we must cast maidens–not seven, but seven times seven–nightly into the jaws of vice, let us at least see to it that they assent to their own immolation, and are not unwilling sacrifices procured by force and fraud.[59]

Stead's campaign was successful, and precipitated the raising of the age of consent, by the Criminal Law Amendment Act 1885, from just 13 to 16. He suffered for his efforts, however: he had staged the purchase of a girl as part of his detective work. He served a three months' prison sentence for abducting her.[60] His career never fully recovered. He turned to Spiritualism, and died as a passenger on the *Titanic* on 15th April 1912.[61]

Classics, boxing and Devon Wrestling

Dressing up beautiful young women in ancient Greek ceremonial robes became popular with the emergence of the fashion for reviving ancient Greek athletics competitions. In Britain this began with the 'Olympic Games' mounted in 1847 in Much Wenlock, a small town in Shropshire on the Welsh border, and culminated internationally in the 1896 Olympic Games at Athens. Pierre de Coubertin, founder of the International Olympic Committee, had even visited the Wenlock games. It was there that the idea of victory ceremonies was planted in his mind, so impressed was he by the 'quotations from Greek authors inscribed on the flags and banderoles' and the laurel wreaths.[62] The Dumfriesshire railway worker-poet Alexander Anderson wrote an ode for the Kirkconnel Athletic Games on 24th August 1889, recited by Miss Campbell of Knockenrig, described in the first stanza as wearing 'the graceful, snowy raiment of the Greek,/Her hand within a golden band was strung'.[63] But when sensation-addicted men of any class were bored with women, whether wives, showgirls, prostitutes or Olympic priestesses, a boxing match was a reliable recreational choice. The Georgian craze for bare-knuckle fighting was shared by labourers and royalty. Unlicensed and officially illegal, attracting huge amounts of gamblers' money, boxing escaped the authorities because a few patrons included the richest in the land. The 'Fancy' (boxing fraternity), wrote Pierce Egan, was a community in which all social hierarchies were temporarily abolished: 'a union of all ranks, from the brilliant of the highest class in the circle of Corinthians, down to the Dusty Bob gradation on society, and even a shade or two below that'.[64]

Egan (1772–1849) was the author of *Boxiana*, the foundation text of sports journalism in Britain. His background was Irish and obscure, but he began working life as a London printer's compositor. The first part of the first edition of *Boxiana, or, Sketches of Ancient and Modern Pugilism*, written in lively, slang-laden prose, appeared in 1812. Its detailed accounts of bloody matches offered the sporting public literary pleasure of a totally new kind. Since his sketches involved colourful biographies of the champion boxers, Egan was dubbed by the Irish poet Thomas Moore 'the Plutarch of the ring'.[65]

Boxing's brutality was celebrated as a manifestation of hyper-masculinity which transcended social class and even colour: some of the most famous boxers were Jewish or of African ancestry, like the East-Ender 'The Hebrew' (Daniel Mendoza) or the American 'Black Ajax' (Tom Molineaux). But *Boxiana* praises the divine boxer Pollux, Spartan brother of Castor, who won his seat on Olympus through his pugilist skills. Egan quotes Horace, supplying but also translating the Latin, mindful of his cross-class readership or perhaps that even many supposedly well-educated gentlemen had never really mastered the ancient tongue. His list of ancient boxers continues with Eryx the Sicilian vanquished by Hercules, Dares and Entellus, and Amycus visited by the Argonauts.[66]

Egan contrasts ancient boxing in weighted gloves and bare-knuckle fighting, discusses Greek and Latin boxing vocabulary, cites Virgil and Plutarch and compares contemporary prize fighters with Hercules, Ulysses, Coriolanus and Mars. He celebrates the inauguration of the national Pugilistic Society, which he claims to be the equal of the 'Royal Society, the Antiquarian Society, the Geological Society, the Mathematical Society, the Dilettanti Society' and the Society of

Arts. In his fantasy realm, men of all classes can be equals. He concludes this flight of egalitarian Fancy with a heady citation from Terence:

> Men of rank associating together learn to prize the native and acquired powers of human nature. They thus learn to value other distinctions, besides those of fortune and rank; and, by duly estimating them in persons of far inferior stations in life, they imbibe the principles of humanity and fellow feeling for our common nature. The lesson taught them in early life, by Terence, while at Oxford or Cambridge, Westminster and Eton, is here brought into actual practice:
>
> *Homo sum, humani nil a me alienum puto.*
>
> I am a man, and consider nothing belonging to man as foreign to me.[67]

Sadly, such cosmopolitan humanism was not what was experienced by Tom Molineaux, the American freedman and heavyweight boxer billed as 'The Black Ajax'.

Born into slavery on a plantation in South Carolina, he had won his freedom in a prize fight. After victories in America he had been invited to England by another ex-slave boxer, Bill Richmond. Also known as 'The Black Terror', Richmond ran a famous boxing academy in London.[68] The Greek hero Ajax was not a boxer, but a champion wrestler; in the *Iliad* (XXIII.709–.39), at the funeral games for Patroclus, he is matched against Odysseus. But the injuries they reciprocally inflict will have sounded to a Regency audience like those suffered by boxers: 'You could hear their backbones crack under the violent assault of their bold hands, and their sweat flowed down in streams, and their ribs and shoulders were covered with red. bloody weals'. The Homeric bout is declared a draw because the fighting has become increasingly brutal; while Ajax is physically stronger, Odysseus is his superior strategically. This makes the ultimate defeat of the Black Ajax at the hands of English heavyweight champion Tom Cribb, a former Bristol docker, all the more poignant.

On 10th December 1810, near East Grinstead, in front of a cross-class audience laying enormous bets, which included the roughest of itinerants as well as a few aristocrats and some pupils from Westminster School, the 26-year-old Black Ajax faced the most celebrated boxer in Britain. By the end of the match, they were both said to be half-dead, so bloody that their skin colour could not be distinguished.[69] The gigantic Cribb, now the proprietor of the Union Arms in Panton Street, London, had been persuaded to come out of retirement to defend the honour, it was felt, not only of Britain versus the apostate United States, but of all white men against their black brethren. Britons felt outraged at the ease with which the Black Ajax had that summer demolished two famous English pugilists, The Bristol Terror and Tom Tough.

On what was dubbed the 'Campus Martius' (Field of Mars) that stormy winter's day, Black Ajax was, according to Egan, robbed of the victory on account of the bias of the crowd, after 34 exhausting rounds.[70] Molineaux's career never recovered. He got drunk before the rematch and lost in 19 minutes. After Richmond abandoned him, he died of alcoholism in Ireland just eight years later.

Every bit as savage as bare-knuckle boxing was the ancient sport of Devon Wrestling, One of the last champions was Abraham Cann, who was nicknamed the Devon Hercules. In this painting by Henry Caunter (c. 1846), Cann is evoked as the last great exponent of the dying art of wrestling according to the brutal Devon rules. (Figure 17.4) These allowed shin-kicking in shoes soaked in bull's blood and then baked to achieve maximum hardness. The bouts, arranged at taverns, were notoriously rowdy and attracted cross-class audiences including both gentlemen who provided the prize money and labouring men.

Cann was the son of a central Devon farmer and malt-producer, who taught all his five sons how to wrestle and shin-kick, Devon-style.[71] The portrait of Cann, by including the Farnese Hercules in the picture, standing on a base which depicts a classical wrestling match, implicitly equates the ancient local custom with the sporting feats of ancient Greco-Roman heroes. Since it was rescued from the Baths of Caracalla in 1546, the Farnese Hercules has been one of the most widely recognised of all ancient statues.[72] It got its name from its

FIGURE 17.4 Abraham Cann (1794–1864) by unknown artist, c.1850, reproduced by courtesy of Exeter City Museums & Art Gallery.

collector, Cardinal Alessandro Farnese, but reproductions soon started to appear in the gardens, courtyards and dining rooms of the rich all over Europe, and the image was familiar to a cross-class audience through its use in advertisements for products ranging from bread to soap powder.[73] But there is also a specific reference to Cann's greatest victory when he won the title 'Champion of the West of England' in 1826. He defeated an enormous Cornish publican named James Polkinghorne by executing a full-body 'throw' to the astonishment of all onlookers. This invited a comparison with Hercules' victory over the previously invincible giant wrestler Antaeus, who was rejuvenated by his mother Earth every time he hit the floor.[74] So Hercules held him off the ground for as long as it took for his energy to dissipate completely.

Classicist criminals and lunatics

A few classicists have unambiguously joined the underclass in being convicted of violent crimes and/or confined in asylums. Eugene Aram (1704–1759) was a self-taught philologist from Ramsgill, Yorkshire, who, despite his humble origins (his father worked as a gardener for a clergyman) and scanty education, became a philologist of a high order.[75] (Figure 17.5) He compiled extensive evidence for the Indo-European roots of the Celtic languages almost a century before J.C. Prichard's *Eastern Origin of the Celtic Nations* (1831). Throughout his life, Aram taught himself Latin, Greek, Hebrew, Arabic and Chaldee. One of his major feats

FIGURE 17.5 'Eugene Aram (1704–1759)' by Becky Brewis (2019). © Becky Brewis 2019.

as a philologist was to dispute the then accepted notion that Latin was derived from Greek.[76]

But Aram was also a murderer, a thief and reportedly lived incestuously with his daughter.[77] In 1744, when he had been working as a schoolmaster in Netherdale, he was arrested in connection to the disappearance of his close friend Daniel Clarke. Although the local authorities found Clarke's possessions in Aram's garden, they had insufficient evidence to convict the teacher of his murder. Newly freed, Aram quickly abandoned his wife and began a new life in London, where he continued his philological research and taught Latin at a school in Piccadilly. In 1759, however, Clarke's body was found in a cave. Aram admitted his crime and attempted suicide by slitting his arm above the elbow. He failed in the attempt and was hanged without delay from the gallows in York before his corpse was suspended in chains in Knaresborough forest, where his friend's body had been discovered.[78] The dark philologist's infamy lived on in Thomas Hood's ballad *The Dream of Eugene Aram*, a novel by Edward Bulwer-Lytton called *Eugene Aram*, a play by W.G. Wills of the same name, and sundry allusions to his exploits in 20th-century poetry and fiction.[79]

The other murderous classicist was born exactly a century later, in Ireland. The Reverend John Selby Watson, a graduate of TCD and headmaster of Stockwell Grammar School, was in 1872 sentenced to death, despite his plea of insanity, for battering his wife to death with the butt of his pistol; his sentence was subsequently reduced to life imprisonment.[80] Watson had acquired mild fame as a prodigiously prolific classical translator; he had translated Quintilian, Xenophon, Lucretius, Cicero, Sallust, Florus, Velleius Paterculus, Justin, Cornelius Nepos and Eutropius for Bohn's Classical Library. He lived out his last 12 years in Parkhurst Prison, where he died after falling out of his hammock.[81]

Classical studies are sometimes associated with damage to mental health. At least two of the 'Ragged-Trousered Philologists' discussed in Chapter 15, Richard Jones and Andrew Donaldson, suffered from psychological disorders. The Norwich-based poet (and coincidentally student of Professor Dalzel), Frank Sayers, was reported by his friend William Taylor in the early 1829s to have suffered a breakdown while at university due to an excess of classical studies, no sunlight and no exercise.[82] At around the same time, one patient straitjacketed at Dr. Edward Fox's Brislington asylum was a red-faced lawyer whose principal symptom was jabbering passages from Virgil.[83] In 1840, at Bethlehem, St. George's Field, Southwark, Professor Edward Peithman was (probably without due cause) committed for lunacy after harassing Prince Albert with his eccentric schemes for educational reform; his diagnosis was much discussed because his ability to read Latin and Greek seemed at odds with his 'uncouth' appearance and 'indecent propensities'.[84] A sign of Georgina Weldon's incipient derangement during her affair with the composer Charles Gounod, whose most famous work at the time was *Sapho* [sic], was that she renamed the destitute girls in the orphanage she ran 'Sapho-Katie' and 'Sapho-Baucis'.[85]

One of the earliest adaptations of a classical text for young children, Charles Lamb's *The Adventures of Ulysses*, commissioned by William Godwin, is associated with both lunacy and alcoholism. At this time Charles was drawing strength from his unorthodox religious convictions in order to keep control both of his own drinking and of his sister Mary's sanity; after stabbing their mother (who had neglected her as a child) to death in 1796, Mary had only been allowed out of the asylum because her brother had promised to oversee her. Mary's input into Charles's writing during these years was immense; much of the first children's version of the *Odyssey* may therefore have been written by a childless manic depressive who had murdered her own mother.[86]

But the most famous lunatic classicist by far was Edward Oxford, who allegedly tried to assassinate the young Queen Victoria in 1840. His supposed madness was cured after he learned languages including Latin and Greek in the State Criminal Lunatic Asylum at Bethlehem and in Broadmoor. Oxford was born in Birmingham in 1822, became a barman as a teenager and by 1840 was working in the *Hog in the Pound* pub just off Oxford Street, London.[87] On 10th June he fired two shots from separate pistols at the pregnant young monarch as her carriage was driven out of Buckingham Palace. Although no bullets were ever found, he was tried for treason at the Old Bailey. His family gave evidence that he was insane. He was a model student in the asylum, becoming an excellent scholar of languages including the classical ones;[88] doctors remarked on his intelligence and regarded him as hardworking and sane.[89] Three years later he was released on condition that he emigrated forever to a colony, and he sailed for Australia. He lived in Melbourne, writing a book under the name of John Freeman, entitled *Lights and Shadows of Melbourne Life* (1888). This is an amusing and class-conscious piece of social analysis, which includes a comparison of a travelling winkle-seller to ancient ascetic philosophers, and a discussion of a wealthy snobbish female under the soubriquet 'Volumnia'.[90] It thus bears several traces not of an Oxford classical education, but of Oxford's classical education in the asylum.

Notes

1 Strachan (2007) 30–5.
2 Quoted in Anon. (1851) 359; see Strachan (2007) 97.
3 The entire text is conveniently reproduced in Earnshaw (2017).
4 Psalmanazar (1704), especially 5, 290.
5 16th March, 1711. this drama is suggestive Seneca's Thyestes.
6 Accounts of this sort reached the ears of the Irish satirist Jonathan Swift, who credited Psalmanazar with inspiring his famous *Modest Proposal* for serving poor Irish children as food, on which see above p. 226.
7 Earnshaw (2017) 32; Keevak (2004) and Lynch (2005).
8 Psalmanazar (1764) 62–70.
9 Speaight (1952) 42.
10 Shershow (1995) 115–16.
11 Bentley (1941–68) vol. II, 413 and 480.

12 Shershow (1995) 121 with fig
13 The Latin poem was published in Addison (1719). The English translation used here is the excellent Anon. (1813). There is a sophisticated analysis of the literary strategies deployed in the poem in Haan (2005) 71–87.
14 See the five-act *Nauplius* mentioned by Heron of Alexandria in his technical treatise *On Automata* ch. 22.3–6 par. 264 in the Teubner edition of Schmidt (1899) with Hall (2005a) 65 n. 38.
15 On post-Restoration puppet show history see Malcolmson (1973), Burke (1985) and Shershow (1995).
16 Speaight (1952) 41.
17 Novelty in the spectacle department was a key attraction of the most successful puppet shows: Richard Steele, deriding the new custom of sending youths off to the Continent to visit classical sites, claims that such lads spend their time 'as Children do at Puppet-Shows, and with much the same Advantage, in staring and gaping at an amazing Variety of strange things' (*Spectator* 364, for 28th April 1712).
18 Wilkinson (1790) vol. I, 19.
19 Advertisement in B.L. (1731–1831).
20 *Spectator* 31, for 4th April 1711.
21 *Spectator* 31, for 4th April 1711.
22 Plutarch, *Life of Alexander* 8.2.
23 *Spectator* 31, for 4th April 1711.
24 Hall and Macintosh (2005) 1–2 with figure 1.1.
25 Hall and Macintosh (2005) 32.
26 Hawkesworth (1754) 14–18.
27 Entries for 12th April and 1st July 1799 in Godwin's manuscript diary, published online by the Bodleian Library at http://godwindiary.bodleian.ox.ac.uk/diary/1799.html.
28 Robson (1849); Mayer (1971) 27–34. See the bills reproduced in Harker (2018) 57, 60. On Payne's *Brutus*, see below, pp. 393.
29 See Harker (2018) 100.
30 Rosenfeld (1977); Hall and Macintosh (2005) 339. See the 1816 etching by Thomas Rowlandson in the Wellcome Collection at https://wellcomecollection.org/works/urr25d86.
31 Letter of 25th Oct. 1867, cited in van Amerongen (1926) 72. See Hall and Macintosh (2005) 351 and, on Dickens and the Classics more generally, Hall (2015f).
32 Ritchie (1857) 17
33 Tracy C. D avis (1991) 3.
34 Percy Fitzgerald (1870) 150.
35 Ritchie (1857) 205.
36 Pearsall (1973) 27.
37 Wooler (1851); Blanchard (1891) i. 86.
38 Morley (1866) 23.
39 The engraving is reproduced in Pearsall (1973) 67.
40 Soldene (1897) 299.
41 East (1971).
42 Senelick (1997), 44–5.
43 Advertisement in author's own possession.
44 Smith (1996) 49–50.
45 This account is dependent on the excellent biography by Fraser (1986).
46 Faxon (2004).
47 Fraser (1986) 114–18.
48 See Cruickshank (2009) 370–3.
49 A tension discussed well by Stevens (2013).
50 See Holmström (1967); Altick (1978) 345–9; George Taylor (1989) 47.

51 Broadbent (1908) 346–9.
52 Bradley (1965) xi, 250–1, 291.
53 Stuart and Park (1895) 8–10.
54 Ritchie (1857) 80.
55 Bradley (1965) 298–9
56 Ritchie (1857) 80.
57 He wrote this in his personal journal, quoted in Scott (1952) 102–3.
58 See Jones (1988).
59 The articles were published on July 6th, July 7th, 8th and 10th, respectively, and are conveniently reproduced as Stead (1885).
60 Mussell (2012) 24–6.
61 See Jones (1988) 79–87.
62 MacAloon (1981) 149; see Stallings (1996).
63 Cuthbertson (n.d.) 68–9.
64 Quoted in Reid (1971) 17.
65 Strachan and O'Malley-Younger (2010) 3, 15.
66 Egan (1829) vol. II, 2–3.
67 Egan (1829) vol. II, 26; Terence, *Self-Tormentor* line 77.
68 Williams (2015).
69 Egan (1828–1829), vol. I, 405–8.
70 Cone (1982).
71 Boase (1885–1900).
72 It is now in the Naples Archaeological Museum.
73 For Classics in Victorian and Edwardian advertising, see Hall (forthcoming f).
74 Egan (1832) 326–8; there were several broadside ballads in circulation about the match, including 'A New Song on the Wrestling Match between Cann & Polkinghorne', printed by G. Rowe of Fleet Street, a copy of which is held in the British Library.
75 Watson (1913) 7–11.
76 See his proposal for a lexicon based on principles of comparative philology in Fryer (1842) 71–88.
77 For the speculations about Aram's habits, see Scatcherd (1875).
78 Anon. (1840).
79 See Tyson (1981).
80 Courtney (2004b).
81 Courtney (2004b).
82 Sayers (1823) xxxi–iii; on Dalzel see above, pp. 298–301.
83 Wise (2012) 33.
84 Wise (2012) 84–5.
85 Wise (2012) 336.
86 Hall (2008*a*) 26–7.
87 *Proceedings of the Central Criminal Court*, 6th July 1840, 476, online record at www.oldbaileyonline.org/images.jsp?doc=184007060064.
88 Sinclair (2000) 69–70.
89 Broadmoor Hospital case file in the Berkshire Record Office D/H14/D2/2/1/96. A76.
90 Freeman (1888) 224, 92.

18

CLASS AND THE CLASSICAL BODY

The overwhelming majority of beauty and strength performers in the long 19th century, including dancers, actresses, strongmen, contortionists, strongwomen, wrestlers, boxers, novelty performers, artists' models and posers of all kinds, came from working-class families.[1] Reliable biographical material, even if they became international sensations, is slim. In order to succeed in their chosen profession, performers who stretched the limits of contemporary conceptions of the body, needed to allure members of the middle and upper classes. Until the 1930s, this called for a new narrative, obscuring mundane origins, and, the greatest trick, rising above the chosen profession and the class position it betrayed. Their industry was the entertainment industry, their tools were their bodies, their lives were dependent on the paying public or wealthy patrons, and they appear in this chapter because they frequently used reference to the classical world to authorise, legitimate and broaden the appeal of their artform.

To convert their physical and often erotic capital into economic and social capital they draped their performance in the garb of respectability, which was either the lavish suits and dresses of the upper classes, or the fabric drapings, leather straps and bared flesh which people identified with Greco-Roman antiquity. The story of the relationship between the classical and the modern body in the late 18th to early 20th century is complex. To examine the performance of its protagonists is to witness an often perplexing dance, in which every step or flex of muscle risked confounding fair with foul and foul with fair. It is on this thin line, or perhaps 'high-wire', suspended above hazards including obscenity charges, scandal and oblivion, that the best strength and beauty performers deftly trod.

The smooth marble forms from Greek and Roman statuary could create aspirations for hygiene and physical health as well as for aesthetic and moral ideals. By desexualising the naked form (or by appearing to do so), performance which engaged with classical images perceived as incomparably noble could, and did,

DOI: 10.4324/9781315446608-21

enable discourse about the body without descending to unchristian corporeal knowledge. This was essentially analogous to the role of the fig leaf. But such performance was simultaneously exploited as a means by which sexual imagery, which tapped into our deepest 'heathen' desires, could be commodified and brought to market.

There are countless contradictions and conundrums associated with the performance of classical forms for modern audiences,[2] and they have been skilfully addressed by Anne Carden-Coyne and Joan Tumblety with regard, respectively, to Australian and French physical culture.[3] But categorising bodily performance nationally is almost impossible, since it was a global phenomenon. The lives of modern Herculeses and Venuses were international and fast-moving. Strong men and women, fighters, and all manner of posing novelty actors toured incessantly, both around their home nations and abroad. Their acts were uniquely transcultural because language was no barrier. Beauty, strength and erotic appeal tend to operate universally. The familiar imagery of the classical Mediterranean world, exported for hundreds of years by European colonialism, but now in a period when commercialised 'mass' culture was rising steeply, also played an important part in the global marketing of these performances.

The popular and international consumption of the erotic classicising performance operated in four distinct but interconnected traditions, all pioneered by men and women from economically disadvantaged backgrounds, who captivated British audiences and inspired them to view the human form through a classical lens. First, Emma Hamilton (1765–1815), a blacksmith's daughter from Cheshire, led the way in public appreciation for classical poses in her 'Attitudes', which she devised in Naples in the late 1780s.[4] Second, the early 20th-century craze for 'Greek dance' in sheer muslin draperies, whose performers offered a veiled promise of sexual availability by abandoning their shoes and corsets, was inseparable from the name of Isadora Duncan (1878–1927). She first developed her taste for ancient Greece in London, and her performances in Britain caused a sensation;[5] she was once referred to as 'the Schliemann of ancient choreography' for her reconstruction, restoration and 'rebirth' of ancient Greek dances.[6] Duncan and her siblings grew up in a low-income single-parent family and were required to make money from giving dance lessons to local children in Oakland, California, from an early age.[7] Third, the pioneer of equestrian circus performance was Andrew Ducrow from the Netherlands (1793–1842), the son of a Belgian circus performer and heavy athlete, Peter Ducrow, known as the 'Flemish Hercules', who had himself found great success on tour in Britain.[8] Ducrow Junior devised wildly acrobatic classical re-enactment, often done at high speed on the backs of horses (see above pp. 348–9).[9] Finally, Eugen Sandow (1867–1925) is widely considered to be the father of modern bodybuilding. Of obscure Prussian origins, in his youth Sandow plied the disreputable trades of artists' model and prize-fighter, but later became an internationally renowned strongman and *poseur*, establishing the global phenomenon of 'Physical Culture' on classical foundations, and we shall return to him later.[10]

Vulcana, La Milo and the Miniature Lady Hercules

Vulcana (Figure 18.1), with support from her trainer, publicist, stage 'brother' and common-law husband 'Atlas', alias William Hedley Roberts (1864–1946), wove these four traditions together. There is no evidence to suggest that Vulcana was especially elegant in her movements, but in the emerging mass entertainment industry, she still followed Hamilton and Duncan by elevating her artform as belonging less to the world of gritty corporality consisting of muscle, sawdust and animal sexual attraction than to ethereal realms of marble, beauty and the sublime. By referring to the classical world, via name, costume and poses, she pitched herself and her performance in that large and profitable sweet spot of mainstream culture between the unappealing poles of crass triviality and elitist prudery. To achieve and maintain success in the bawdy but conservative 19th- and early 20th-century music hall, a strongwoman act like Vulcana's could not afford to risk displays of excessive eroticism or brute strength, although both were more than welcome in moderation. The façade of Greekness tended to reassure audiences that what they were watching was more or less 'serious art', and therefore culturally and morally valid, as well as being 'just good fun'.

Like Sandow, Vulcana learned to market herself (with Roberts's guidance) as a figure of beautiful perfection *and* strength, rather than simply appearing either excessively strong or naturally beautiful, both of which extremes could all too easily slide into vulgarity or austerity. For women, it was even more important than it was for men to perform their miraculous feats of strength without

FIGURE 18.1 Vulcana in pose similar to 'Dying Gaul', reproduced by courtesy of Jane Hunt. Courtesy ofVulcana's great granddaughter, Jane Hunt—vulcanaonline.com.

showing the signs of exertion which would risk appearing either proletarian or unfeminine. The male Sandow, who at all times affected the gentleman, had been known to perspire in an unnaturally hot auditorium, but never simply because he was bent pressing a horse.[11] This was to ensure he passed as a gentleman, but for a strength athlete to pass as a lady was far more difficult. According to the heteronormative standards of the time, a female with developed musculature was quite as transgressive and challenging to morality as the muscle man's appeal to Wildean aesthetes.[12]

Roberts wrote all Vulcana's advertisements and press endorsements, including this effusive notice of 1904:

> All Ladies should see Vulcana … the only known woman of absolutely Correct Measurements, who is able to demonstrate to modern times the beautiful proportions of the female form divine as depicted by the Ancients.[13]

At the turn of the 20th century, many Britons, especially in Nonconformist communities, would have deplored any female flaunting her all-but-naked body on stage. It is in anticipation of the kinds of accusations that were levelled at the more risqué purveyors of 'living statues' that Roberts has emphasised the scientific ('correct', 'measurements') and classical ('divine', 'ancients') aspects of Vulcana's performance. The publicity calls explicitly to 'All Ladies', in an attempt to appeal to a potentially lucrative female audience: Sandow did succeed in attracting 'a considerable sprinkling of the fair sex' to his performances.[14]

Vulcana's biography is sparse and inconsistent. Her real name was Miriam Katherine Williams (1874–1946). Born in Bristol but bred in Glamorgan, Williams worked alongside Roberts ('Atlas'). Both on and off the stage they pretended to be siblings, although they were essentially husband and wife. Roberts was married when they met, and a divorce was not an option. When Atlas and Vulcana were not travelling, the whole extended family with children born to both women lived contentedly, it appears, together.[15] We learn from the few newspaper interviews Vulcana gave that she and Atlas were the children of an Aberdare churchman. This is likely to be fiction created by Roberts in order to provide a more respectable and relatable journey to stardom: 'My father was a clergyman … a Welsh Baptist of a very pronounced order. But he was an ardent athlete, and I suppose we inherited our athletic tastes from him'.[16] Roberts' real father, when he was not pretending to be Vulcana's brother, was James Roberts, a Welsh ironmonger and tinplate worker.[17] There are conflicting accounts of where Williams spent the 1890s. One has her living with her father, a Baptist priest, in Aberdare, South Wales, and possibly even working in a tannery in Abergavenny.[18] But this account is unlikely because it is based on a source that proves Vulcana to be the daughter of the well-known Baptist minister and poet, Robert Ellis Williams (1848–1911), alias 'Twrfab', of which we might expect Atlas to have made much in his hyperbolic marketing materials.[19] The tannery in Abergaveny would also be too far from her home in Aberdare to be a credible workplace. It is difficult to disentangle fiction and reality, but we can be sure that both Vulcana and Atlas were born into families with, at best, a modest working-class income; their performances were designed to enable them to break away from their origins, to make money and to see the world.

Roberts set up a gymnasium in Abergavenny in the 1880s. He said in an interview that he had previously been in 'the shipping trade, and lost £1,000 in it. I thought there might be a chance of recovering myself on the stage'.[20] It is true that he had worked in a shop on Cardiff docks,[21] but to say that he lost £1,000 makes him sound like a shipping tycoon. Again, Roberts has found a way to appeal to the respectable classes by claiming to have been one of them, whilst engaging his working-class fans by sharing their penury. There is a cross-class appeal in the notion of making, or winning back a fortune by performing feats of strength. At around this time Atlas started performing with his elder sister, Hannah Almira Roberts, as 'Atlas and Atalanta'. Atalanta was soon to step aside for the beautiful and talented teenager Vulcana, who began training with her brother.

From the beginning Roberts committed to the classical brand. In publicity shots, both Vulcana and Atlas wear gladiator sandals and pose in front of neo-classical architectural features (Figure 18.2). In a photograph titled 'Vulcana, the Society Athlete' she wears a 'Grecian' costume and shows off her powerful legs (Figure 18.3). These branding tricks were all learned from Eugen Sandow. In the early 1900s Vulcana even put her own stamp on the 'Dying Gaul', a pose identified explicitly with Sandow (Figure 18.1, above). To imitate it was a major statement because it is hard to display muscle definition while reclining, as if injured and dying. This was one of Sandow's greatest assets, because he was not in fact a large man. Vulcana was also the first woman to adopt Sandow's 'Tomb of Hercules' act. Two horses and a handler mounted a large board which was balanced on her shoulders and thighs, as she braced herself in a supine position on her hands (behind her) and feet.

From 1890 Vulcana and Atlas performed in music halls, fairs, vaudeville shows and circuses across Britain, the Continent and the Empire. The music halls in industrial cities were their bread and butter. It was a crowded market-place and they were constantly adapting their act to distinguish themselves from the competition. In the same interview quoted above, Roberts claims that Williams was the pioneer of the classical pose:

> It was Vulcana who set the example some years ago of classical posing, and she still continues this form of work, though her methods are not the same as those adopted by La Milo, [Yvette] De Laabé ["Electric Queen"], and others seen in Hull.

It is simply not true that Vulcana invented, or even 'set the example of', classical posing. It had been popularised, as mentioned above, by Emma Hamilton in the

FIGURE 18.2 Atlas and Vulcana, reproduced by courtesy of Jane Hunt. Courtesy of Jane Hunt—vulcanaonline.com.

1780s, and there had been imitators ever since. It was important, however, for Vulcana to distinguish her act from competitors. The Australian 'La Milo' and French Madame Yvette de Laabé were the best 'living statues' in the world, but their performance was currently mired by scandal. Both young women were striking famous poses, from classical, Renaissance and more modern classicising sculptures and paintings, covered in 'enamel' paint.[22]

Around the time of the interview, between 1906 and 1908, tensions had been rising in certain northern English communities against the profanity of 'Living Statues'. In 1907, Yvette de Laabé's performance in the Hull Hippodrome was closed down by the police.[23] Madame de Laabé, who argued that she was not nude because there was a 'fine covering' beneath the enamel, gave the following response:

> We people on the Continent look on things differently from you English. We look at living representations of statuary as only artistic. We think the human form is artistic in the highest sense of the word. I cannot understand it, but, if the police say it must not be, I go.[24]

FIGURE 18.3 Vulcana, the Society Athlete, reproduced by courtesy of Jane Hunt. Courtesy of Jane Hunt—vulcanaonline.com.

But it was not only the English who had a problem with 'living sculptures'. In 1908, 'The Correctional Tribunal of Paris' sentenced 'to a month's imprisonment and a fine of £8 the manager of a restaurant in Montmartre, who had organized dinners, during which displays of living statuary were given. The women were each sentenced to a fine of £2'.[25]

Neither de Laabé nor 'La Milo' could have lifted half what Vulcana could lift. They were not heavy athletes, but former chorus girls, who preferred a more natural femininity than did the self-sculpted Vulcana. 'The Modern Milo', or Pansy Montague (b.1885) (Figure 18.4), was named after the famous 'Venus de Milo' statue in the Louvre, which her body shape matched particularly well and which became her trademark performance piece. With clever lighting and well-handled black velvet she embodied the famous amputee.[26] Although she could not have lifted Vulcana's bar-bell, part of the wonder of Montague's act was its blatant physicality, and this was perhaps why Sandow championed her as a model of the female physique and featured her in his magazine.[27] Viewers marvelled at her stillness, how it was almost impossible to tell if it was a statue or not, unless she smiled (as she sometimes did). Her hair and body, pasted with some form of

FIGURE 18.4 'La Milo', the "Human Statue", *Sandow Magazine*, 1907. Courtesy of the British Library.

paint, made her look like a statue, rather than a person posing.[28] Like de Laabé's, Montague's repertoire included a mixture of classical and classicising artworks. These included paintings by Diego Velázquez ('Rokeby Venus' [c.1650]) and John William Godward [*The Tambourine Girl*, 1906), several famous statues (the Venus de Medici, Bertram Mackennal's *Circe* [c.1902–1904], Hiram Powers' *Greek Slave* [1847], Antonio Canova's libation-pouring *Hebe*, Edgar George Papworth Junior's *Maidenhood* [1860], Harriet Hosmer's *Oenone* [1854–1855] and Nelson Illingworth's *Bacchante*) and representations which have not been identified of Electra, Psyche, Diana, Andromeda and Sappho.

According to her publicity,

> La Milo claims most nearly to approach in figure the ideal of classical sculpture. She is at present giving representations at the London Pavilion of

> some of the best-known statues. La Milo ... is an Australian, the daughter of an English army officer, and art, not commerce, is admitted to be the motive of her stage career.[29]

We do not know if she actually was the daughter of an 'English army officer', but she began her career as a chorus girl in Melbourne in around 1898, which is not the standard occupation of the daughters of the officer classes. Her class position, like the other performers discussed in this chapter, is obscure and her biography is unreliable. We do, however, know that she made the princely sum of around £5,000 a year for the four she was in Britain.[30]

Her act was described as a 'fac-simile of Ancient and Modern Statuary and Sculpture'.[31] The newspapers tended to follow the legitimising publicity, at first. If you are not ashamed to take your wife to see classical sculptures, the story ran, you should not be ashamed to see La Milo. Montague's act was even sold as educational, since it was introducing the audience to mythological figures and other women from classical antiquity.[32] She arrived in Britain in 1906 and toured the British Isles causing a 'living statue' mania wherever she went. In 1907 the Archbishop of Canterbury and the Bishop of London called for there to be a ban on 'living statues'.[33]

The journalist William T. Stead, whom we have met above publishing popular classics books and campaigning against child prostitution (pp. 61–4 and 352), considered Montague's act to be an oasis of beauty in the cultural desert of the Music Hall,[34] always a place where 'posh' people felt uncomfortable. Neither its comic turns nor the rowdy conduct of his fellow audience members was to his taste, but La Milo was:

> As to the suggestion of indecency that is a fraud, and I fear that those who sell tickets on the strength of it are open to an accusation of obtaining money on false pretences. La Milo is indecent as statues are indecent, no more, no less.

Stead juxtaposed the beauties of her classical act with the 'uglinesses' of their surroundings:

> The contrast to the Venus of Milo was a sandwichman carrying a contents bill of the *Tribune*, which announced "A French Attack upon C. –B." "Maidenhood" was set off by a bowed-down old crone, who limped to a seat on the left of the statue, and so forth.[35]

Stead's observation shows that, however prurient their motive, workers were accessing the myths these statues and paintings enact in their own cultural domain. It also shows how brilliantly Montague's act succeeded, as only Sandow had before her, in providing a product that appealed equally to distinct social groups, represented respectively by Stead and the 'old crone' at the London Pavilion.

And what of the audience's reaction? Stead revels in his snobbery. Even mortals 'who grin over coarse allusions', he wrote,

> are capable of responding to something higher. Until then I had regarded them as something like the fishes in the mammoth cave in America, whose optic nerve has perished from long sojourn in the regions of eternal night. They seemed to have lost all consciousness either of morality, or beauty, or intelligence. But these fishes of the Pavilion have not gone totally blind. It was sufficient to display a picture instinct with a soul of beauty to elicit an immediate, although it might be but a transitory, response.[36]

Classical art, then, is a potential palliative to cultural poverty. But those 'fishes of the Pavilion', and many more Stoll theatres and fun palaces besides, swam out *en masse* to witness the 22-year-old Pansy Montague ride through the streets of Coventry in 1907 as Lady Godiva (Figure 18.5).[37]

Vulcana and the Atlas girls neither drew such crowds, nor made such astonishing amounts of money as La Milo. But they were bringing the classical into realms where people like W.T. Stead considered it alien. Vulcana also made a mystery of her background and early years, and harnessed the legitimacy of the classical idiom to elevate her transgressive talents into a product both desirable and acceptable to contemporary tastes and morality (Figure 18.6). In Figure 18.6, although we cannot pick Vulcana out individually, the women in the background of the cartoon represent the old guard of living statues. The cartoonist's depiction of a one-tonne bar-bell, cleverly and a little crudely reduces the

FIGURE 18.5 La Milo in Lady Godiva procession, Coventry, 1907, by unknown artist, reproduced by courtesy of National Portrait Gallery, Canberra, Australia. © National Portrait Gallery, Canberra, Australia.

performance of Vulcana's equivalents to a crude and old-fashioned type of show. All those performers who wore fleshings were condemned to history with the arrival of the Australian classical beauty, whose resemblance to ancient statuary was undeniable.

La Milo's act was, however, not difficult to imitate for any woman with a particular body shape and a pretty face. The same could not be said for Vulcana's weightlifting abilities. On 29th May 1913, Vulcana performed at Haggar's Theatre, Llanelli, in Wales. She had put out an open call, saying she would present '£50 to any woman … who can lift her Bar-bell, lifted by her Nightly at Haggar's'.[38] Questions were sometimes raised about the weights being lifted on Vulcana's stage, but here was an occasion when Vulcana could silence her detractors.

The challenge was met by none other than 'Athelda the Great', or the 'Miniature Lady Hercules', born in Manchester around 1880 under the name of Frances Rheinlander. Typically, little else is known of her early life, family or class status. Her name implies that she was from a family of German immigrants who came to Manchester in large numbers in the 19th century, and found their new home economically challenging. The 'Society for the Relief of Really

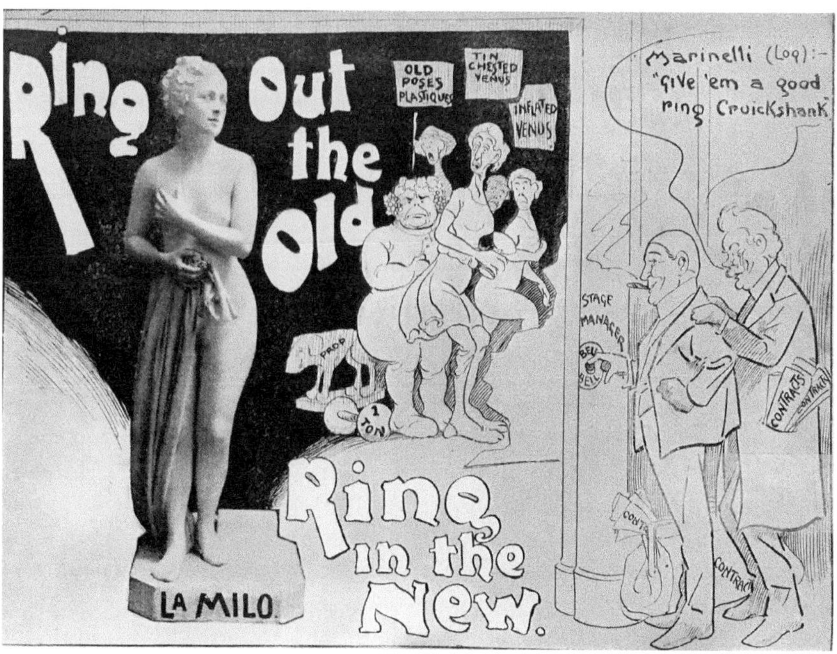

FIGURE 18.6 *The Performer*, December 27th, 1906, a cartoon of La Milo, reproduced by courtesy of the British Library. Cartoon of La Milo (in photographic form) compared to 'old guard' of living statues. Cruickshank (fellow performing artist, lighting sketcher) and Marinelli (agent) look on. Reproduced by courtesy of the British Library.

Deserving Distressed Foreigners', founded in 1847, gave aid to the large German minority.[39] Given Athelda's occupation, we can be confident that she was not born with a silver spoon in her mouth.

Rheinlander, 170 cm tall and weighing only 60–75 kg herself, could lift 25 kg with her little finger. Her act predominately consisted of lifting weights and people in front of music hall audiences. She was not as widely promoted as Vulcana but had a long and celebrated career. In 1916 Athelda created and toured a fusion of variety acts, consisting of several women in classical poses, who also sang and performed acrobatics,[40] about which we know sadly little. Back in 1913, Athelda, it was reported in the *Llanelly Mercury*, attempted to lift Vulcana's enormous bar-bell for 25 minutes without success.[41] She later complained of foul play and invited Vulcana for a rematch. But here the evidence trail goes cold.[42]

Sandow, Hercules and gladiators

Attitudes towards male and female posers and bodybuilders were different, but neither was free from scandal. Eugen Sandow's use of the classical idiom has attracted attention elsewhere;[43] here we ask why he was able to convert his act into a field of scientific study, of which he was made a 'Professor', i.e. Physical Culture, and how the ancient world featured in this achievement. Sandow was the first man in the modern world to sculpt his own physique following classical statuary, which attracted him aesthetically, as his template.

As a boy, so the story goes, Sandow marvelled at the beauty of the statues, when on holiday with his father, and was inspired by the representations of the male body.[44] Whether or not this story is true, it is the foundation myth of all physical culture. Since classical statues resided in the houses of the very rich and in the cities of the Grand Tour, most ordinary people did not see the statues in statuary form. They knew them from their reproductions in print, photo, plaster cast or figurine. Sandow's inspiration was supposed to come straight from antiquity, via the city of Rome.

For Sandow, as for many others, marble statues provided a model for physical perfection, simultaneously highlighting one's own physical defects and providing a goal to strive towards. The examples of Sandow and his imitators in the Music Halls before the war showed that it was possible to become a Hercules, for example, or a Discobolus. Magazines and books offered 'before-and-after' photographs of ordinary people. The scrawniest youth could, the fitness books promised, become a Greek statue by training for just a few minutes a day.

This came at a historical moment of acute physical self-consciousness. In Manchester in September 1918, Prime Minister Lloyd George advocated increased state control over the health and fitness of the people: 'I solemnly warn my fellow-countrymen that you cannot maintain an A1 Empire with a C3 population. Unless this lesson is learned the war is in vain'.[45] The fitness of the people was of national concern. There was a crisis of British masculinity. The mettle of the nations of Europe had been tragically tested in the Great War, in which the pride of the British nation had fallen in a new and newly mechanical kind of warfare (see further below, pp. 496–7). There was a sense that the cream of manhood had been killed, leaving behind only those who returned shell-shocked or had been unfit for military service. The roots of this crisis lay further back. The Boer Wars, and other conflicts in the empire, had begun to show that British masculinity was not capable of upholding the empire in the face of new war technologies,[46] especially tanks, poison gas and explosives. The response, bizarrely, was to seek a new model for virility in classical antiquity.

As Carden-Coyne puts it, 'In response to the physical, psychic and cultural trauma of war, bodybuilding sought to heal the pain of the immediate past through the creation of a new civilised future, only now based upon a dialogue between modernism and classicism'.[47] But even a modern Hercules cannot defend himself against bullets, explosives and gas. Bodybuilding in the classical idiom 'mythologised the corporeality of the war experience'.[48] Physical culture helped the nation to heal by encouraging individuals to pump iron. One of the loudest voices in the promotion of physical fitness was Sandow's. His system was already popular, since he had been successfully touring the music halls and theatres of Britain throughout the 1890s (Figure 18.7).

Before Sandow, even the strongest 19th-century prize-fighters did not have the defined musculature of Greek statuary. Many believed that these statues were inaccurate, idealised images which were in reality impossible to develop.

FIGURE 18.7 Eugen Sandow, by Benjamin J. Falk Public Domain image reproduced by courtesy of Library of Congress.

Fashionable men still regarded muscles as a marker of low social standing, developed by physical labour and heavy lifting. Before Sandow's popularisation of a more scientific approach (isolating individual muscles and working them carefully in front of a mirror), the techniques and basic apparatus for sculpting the physique towards the 'Greek' ideal did not exist, but his performances were always discussed in terms of classical statuary.

Sandow was popular across the classes up and down the British Isles, not to mention in America and the furthest reaches of the empire. On tour his performance would draw large crowds to music halls, theatres, town halls and Mechanics' Institutes. An excellent publicist, his presence often caused a stir in the local press. In the 1890s, Sandow's physique was incessantly likened to classical marble sculpture,[49] a comparison he fostered in his promotional material, the titles of his poses and feats and by dusting his skin with pale chalk before performances.

Sandow's specialism was posing, but his classically themed strength acts were impressive. 'Another feat', Sandow explains in his best-selling *Strength and How to obtain it* (1897), 'is performed lying prone on the ground. From this position I lift with one hand a Roman chariot, rising upright with it and afterwards lying down again. This brings the whole of the muscles into play'.[50] He continues, to describe his

> Roman horse exercise. Sitting on a horse and so bending my back as to throw my head over the animal's tail I raise at arms' length heavy weights from the ground. Next I pick up two men, one after another, raising them over my head and seating them in the saddle.[51]

His identification with Hercules and use of 'Roman' props acted as a high-cultural anchor, earning his thrilling circus spectacles a modicum of respect. They also put his 'respectable' and aspirational audience at ease; those who could afford them and needed the assurance (like W.T. Stead) could rest back into their expensive seats assured that they were enjoying a cultural activity rather than voyeuristic trash. Every aspect of the show—the classical music, the names and classical provenance of the pose sequences—was designed to raise his performance from its big-top origins and engage people across the classes. In this it was successful. With Sandow's new respectable formula, the stage-show act of the brutish strongman was reinvented to defy the social divisions of class, occupation and sex by attracting a surprisingly broad demographic: 'for even the highest price seats were well filled, and the popular parts of the place were crowded to overflowing. There was a considerable sprinkling of the fair sex in the audience'.[52]

Class and cultural consumption

There are countless forms of classicism, and as many ways to subvert them. A photo of Sandow wearing nothing but strappy sandals leaning on a column can bear different meanings to different groups of people. The use of a classical setting in a photo of someone posing nude served a similar purpose as the leaf (not always from a fig tree) which frequently covered Sandow's pubic region in photos, thus saving the blushes, and perhaps also the swooning gasps, of polite society.[53] But, as Brauer has argued, in Sandow's photographs the leaf functions less as a covering than it does as a phallic substitute; its shape and angle conjure that which it purports to conceal.[54] The idea that the classical paraphernalia (columns, elaborate sandals, leaves) actually serves to legitimate anything, is to fall for the same trick. The Roman sandal emphasises the model's bodily nakedness, the column establishes a dreamscape outside of contemporary reality, beyond the realm of modern morality and customs. And the tin, or 'post-production' leaves are there to tease and titillate the viewer.

At a period when Oscar Wilde was convicted for 'gross indecency with men' and the aesthete and 'invert' was considered a serious threat to the British public, men admiring Sandow's homoerotic nude could do so without fear of persecution. The illicit was flaunting itself in plain sight, but Sandow's credibility, even though his own homosexual relationship with the Dutch musician Martinus Sieveking was an open secret,[55] had attained such lofty heights that the eminently touchable gentleman Professor of Physical Culture, whatever his origin, had become untouchable, and he had set a precedent for others like Atlas and Vulcana to follow.

The classical is but one ingredient in this complex spell. In his magazines, for example, Sandow interspersed his 'living statues' (i.e. photos of his students from all over the world) with pictures of Greek and Roman statuary.[56] Brauer has persuasively argued that this had a 'virilizing' effect,[57] but the juxtaposition of the present-day humans and statuary does more than virilise. It creates a context in which heroism and gentility are evoked in equal measure. Being granted access to those hallowed pages was felt to be edifying, and to justify those hours spent flexing in the mirror. It enabled men from across the British Empire, of different countries, ethnicities, class origins and economic brackets to be considered on a level playing field as muscular heroes, bare-chested and stripped down to their universal, timeless selves. The factory worker, the doctor, the miner, the London cabby, the military officer posted abroad—each was raised to the classical ideal, simply by having a photo taken while tensing and posting it to Sandow.

> Sandow's body culture was then able to circulate as a multifarious sign straddling the nexus between the aspirational and the erogenous, the edifying and the homoerotic, the permissive and the perverse and, more specifically, between homophilic exhibitionism and homoerotic voyeurism.[58]

Its provision of a means by which 'healthily' masculine and heteronormative attention could be paid by men to other men's near-naked bodies also facilitated a burgeoning trade in homoerotic images, and to a degree helped to depathologise homosocial and homosexual encounters within an openly homophobic society.[59]

It is unlikely that this was Sandow's overarching goal.[60] The eroticism of physical culture was Sandow's stock-in-trade and imitated by countless enthusiasts of both sexes. He seems to have been genuinely committed to the idea of people being able to transform themselves not only physically but socially too. The economic rise of Britain throughout the Victorian period, accompanied by working-class agitation and demands for the vote and employment reform, also lay behind the new technologies and industries which were transforming the world at the time of Sandow's eminence. The surplus wealth extracted both from the empire and from home-exploited labour lay behind the increased leisure which created the demand for more and cheaper entertainment, including affordable books, cinema, and for the private cultivation of the body and the self which Sandow incarnates.

But this greater wealth was built on the suffering of the working poor. As Sandow himself reminds us, children brought up at the time in poverty were largely malnourished and under-exercised, and therefore rarely fulfilled their physical potential. The children of the rich, as Sandow remarks in *Life is Movement* (1919), had 'ponies or their bicycles to ride, their tennis-courts, and everything conducive to healthy physical growth'. By 1919 he believed that 'real social reform', through 'the socialization of health' and not wealth, was already in the wings:

> It was with the utmost pleasure that I read Lord Leverhulme's statement that in the North of England at least "though the children of comparatively well-to-do parents had advantages in health over middle-class children, children of poor parents living in suburban areas were now healthier than either". Such a pronouncement in any local district augurs what is possible if we take national and scientific measures to save the children of the nation.[61]

Sandow's message was that in the realm of physical fitness and strength, irrespective of their socio-economic position, people could succeed by their efforts alone. He exemplified the meritocratic principle that anyone could achieve national respect and social distinction.

The Scarborough Hercules and the Venus of the Pavilion

Despite his best efforts, (Figure 18.8) Thomas Inch (1881–1963) was no classical sculpture. Posing as a Roman gladiator in this postcard is as close as he got to 'living statues'. Far bigger and stronger than Sandow, Inch steadily took over his public role as the face of physical culture, launching a hugely popular mail order muscle course in 1903. His image of fitness was considerably less homoerotic, less confusing in visual message and focused on promoting health for the working man. The passing on of the baton was free from neither scandal nor mythologising, however:

> Attending one of the German's [Sandow's] famous shows, Inch sat in the audience and watched Sandow perform one of his trademark acts: ripping a pack of cards in half and throwing the split deck into the audience. Inch caught one half of the pack, proceeded to nonchalantly split that in half,

FIGURE 18.8 'Thomas Inch posed as a Roman gladiator', postcard (unknown origin), reproduced by courtesy of Ellis McKenzie—sandowplus.co.uk.

> and, much to the annoyance of Sandow, triumphantly threw it back onto the stage.[62]

Inch's book *Scientific Weightlifting* (1905) sold over 40,000 copies and was the first of several on how to achieve and maintain strength and other forms of physical and mental health. His scientific approach to bodybuilding also featured classical imagery. On the cover of *Inch on Fitness* (1923) stands coiled the *Discobolus* after Myron (Figure 18.9). The book is full of classically infused line drawings by R.C. Clarke. Early on, Inch also reveals that he has a Latin motto:

> With *multum in parvo* as my motto I have endeavoured to arrange physical culture in tabloid form, as it were, so that the busy man may keep himself fit by expending ten minutes daily on physical culture methods.
>
> Can you spare ten minutes?
>
> Is this too big a price to pay for attainment of, at any rate, a percentage of the glorious strength and staminal power enjoyed, as a rule, by the athlete in training?[63]

FIGURE 18.9 Front cover of *Inch on Fitness* (1923), reproduced by courtesy of the British Library. The statue appears to be the *Discobolo di Mirone* (Vatican Museum) or a replica.

Inch caters specifically for the labouring man: '"A change is as good as a rest"; and even the manual labourer will find that physical culture is quite a hobby and restful—it will assist him in his work and in his play'.[64] He is conscious of the working man's limits on time, energy after work and space in the home, advocating short spells of exercise that you can do in any room in the house. He also recommended taking exercise in the fresh air, sensitive to the 'vitiated atmosphere' in which much labour was conducted, surely thinking of his readers who worked down the mines or in countless other industrial factories and workshops where the air was frequently dangerous to breathe.[65]

The approach of our final physical performer, Olga Desmond (1890–1964), the Polish-German beauty who astonished Russian audiences in 1908 by performing stark naked, (Figure 18.10) was very different. Her controversial performance was even discussed in 1909 in the Prussian State Parliament.[66] As Dickinson has shown, Desmond exploited her glamour and notoriety to the full, opening or attempting to open various dance, beauty and physical culture institutions, and bringing to market beauty and hygiene products, including a breast-enhancement

FIGURE 18.10 Olga Desmond as living statue, c. 1908 when Desmond appeared in St. Petersburg (Russian postcard, source unknown, public domain).

cream and an anti-freckle formula.[67] Like La Milo, she performed in the London Pavilion in 1906, which is where she captured the attention of the British public.[68] For nine months she appeared as 'Venus' in a group of living statues called the Seldoms. After abandoning clothes altogether, Desmond countered accusations that she was enslaving the public by their own erotic urges by explaining that her high ticket prices excluded the men and women of the street, who might not have sufficient critical or artistic faculties to appreciate her act as 'high art'.[69] She came from an enormous and apparently chaotic family, with 13 brothers and sisters. Their strict mother was not averse to calling the police on her wayward daughter.[70] During and shortly after World War I she starred in several films, but after World War II, she worked as a cleaner in East Berlin.[71]

The classical was not the only idiom of performance at this time. The 'Oriental' was a fashionable aesthetic throughout Europe, prevalent among performers who wanted to dance seductively without clothes. It provided a legitimate means by which their living statues could move. The 'Grecian' aesthetic was, rather, a site for stasis, poise, balance and grandeur, while the 'oriental' was exotic, flowing, rhythmical and wild.[72]

The class-coding of activities and cultural products is a mysterious process, but those suggestive of 'low' class occupations such as sex work and manual labour, are often seen as 'low-brow'. Activities which stretch or overstretch contemporary mores, as did erotic dancing, nude posing and weightlifting, were also seen as thrilling and entertaining. It is their flirtation with the borders of the forbidden, the edge of control, that made them so. The classical frame, connoting calm, control and rationality, can frame the forbidden and uncontrolled, 'low' form of entertainment, making it palatable for a broad cross-section of the consumer base.

Around the turn of the 20th century, the classical idiom also connoted enlightenment and progressive modernity in opposition to old-fashioned Christian views.[73] The strength and beauty performances discussed in this chapter never achieved total acceptance in polite society, either as a spectacle or as a career, but their popularity and (sometimes) barely credible attempts to bestow respectability on them by applying a classical veneer, with or without fig leaves, allowed for the thrilling spectacle of beautified bodies, tensed or in repose, to enter the constantly shifting and hungry commercial marketplace.

Notes

1 Notable exceptions include Clara Ward, alias 'Princess de Chimay', a US heiress who married a Belgian prince in 1890: see Huxley (2013) 221.
2 Several of these are presented in Stead (forthoming), 'Sandow, the modern Hercules: Twelve Labours of the class-conscious historian of British classics', which takes Eugen Sandow as its guide.
3 Carden-Coyne (1999) 138–49; Tumblety (2012); on the queer Sandow, see Brauer (2017) 35–67.
4 See further above, pp. 349–50. On Hamilton's 'Attitudes' see also Contogouris (2018) chapter 3; Lada-Richards (2010) 32–3; Lada-Richards (2003) esp. 21–33; Touchette (2000) 123–46; Reynolds (2003) 30; Sewter (1951) 115
5 See Hall (2013a) 201–3.
6 Svetlov (1904) 5.
7 On Duncan see Naerebout (2010) 49–56; Albright (2010) 57–76; Smith (2010) especially. 83–9; Dickinson (2017) esp. 27–9.
8 On Peter Ducrow, a celebrity in his own right, see Webster (2000a).
9 On Ducrow as pantomime see Lada-Richards (2003) 21–33; see also Hall (2008b) 393.
10 On Sandow and Classics see Stead (forthcoming), Wyke (1996) 355–79; Squire (2011) 16–9; Hall (2013) 225–7; See also Chapman (1994).
11 A bent bress is a one-armed lift which leaves the lifted weight above the lifter's head with a straight arm.
12 For a discussion of Wilde and Sandow see Brauer (2017).
13 *The Entracte and Limelight: Theatrical and Musical Critic and Advertiser*, for Friday, 8th June 1906 (no. 1,928). The magazine reprints Atlas' copy.
14 Anon. (1890) 3.
15 Hunt (2016). In 1901 'Miriam K Williams' is clearly in the census at Bristol living as a 'visitor' with the Roberts family, the head of which (William H. Roberts) has as occupation 'Professional athlete/Worker', National Archives.
16 *Hull Daily Mail* Thursday 20 August 1908, 3.
17 1871 Wales census, Aberystwyth, Monmouthshire, Wales, National Archives.

18 Currently (April 2019) on *Wikipedia*, citing Hunt (2004).
19 1891 Wales Census, Aberdare, National Archives. It ought to be noted that the Aberdare birth account is that inherited by the family of Vulcana and Atlas (and relayed to Stead in an email exchange with Jane Hunt), and that the 1901 Bristol census record could equally be erroneous.
20 *Hull Daily Mail* for Thursday 20th August 1908, 3.
21 Roberts is listed in the 1891 Wales Census with the occupation 'Storekeeper (ships)' in Cardiff, National Archives.
22 Huxley (2013) 222.
23 Mellor (1970) records that Church authorities in Huddersfield attempted to suppress La Milo's show in 1907, which had the effect of filling the city's Hippodrome to capacity.
24 Reported by 'Dr. Bickersteth' in the *Yorkshire Evening Post*, Saturday 4th May 1907, 'Living Statuary Doomed'.
25 *Nottingham Evening Post* for Wednesday 2nd December 1908, 3, but widely reported in the British press.
26 Callaway (2000) 70; Huxley (2013) 222; Daley (2003) 89–92.
27 She appears on the front page (3rd May 1906) and there is a three-page feature on her at Anon. (1906b) 560–3.
28 Huxley (2013) 222.
29 See base of Fig 18.4, a magazine spread featuring La Milo, 1907 from the British Library.
30 The equivalent of around £1.5 million in 2010, Huxley (2013) 227.
31 Callaway (2000) 67.
32 Programme dated 22nd July 1905, Tivoli Theatre, Sydney, quoted.in Callaway (2000) 68.
33 Reported widely in the press, e.g. *Mid Sussex Times* for Tuesday 30th April 1907, p 7.
34 Stead (1906) 257.
35 Stead (1906) 257.
36 Stead (1906) 257.
37 *Nottingham Evening Post* reported a 30,000 strong crowd (7th Wednesday August 1907, 7).
38 A flyer printed at the Mercury offices, Llanelly, reproduced by Jane Hunt (Williams' great grand-daughter) on a blog entitled *Vulcana: Victorian Wonder Woman*—http://vulcanaonline.com.
39 Coates (1992) 26–8.
40 Advertised widely in the press, e.g. *The Era* Wednesday 22nd November 1916, 24.
41 Webster (2000b) 29.
42 This section owes much to David Chapman (2010), a wonderful pictorial history of muscular women.
43 Stead (forthcoming), see note 2 above.
44 Sandow & Adam (1894) 24–5.
45 Lloyd-George (1918) 9–10. A1 and C3 referred to the highest and lowest military service grades used by the army up to mid-1917. As the Prime Minister explains, A1 meant fully fit for military service. C3 meant fit only for limited home service.
46 Much scholarship has been written on World War I and the impact of mechanised warfare on British masculinity, beginning with Leed (1979). On the Boer War as precedent and a more gradual erosion of Victorian masculinity, see, e.g. Cranfield (2012) and Zweiniger-Bargielowska (2010) 76. See also Meyer (2009a and b) on WW1 and masculinity and Chapter 24 below, *passim*, on the speed of technological change in warfare.
47 Carden-Coyne (1999) 141.
48 Carden-Coyne (1999) 141.
49 His sculptural form is commented on widely in the press, e.g. *Preston Herald*, Saturday 5th December 1896, which suggests: 'Art students may learn much from him, and

points which have given rise to speculation in the marble works of long dead masters may easily be set at rest by Sandow's demonstrations'.

50 Sandow and Adam (1897) 154.
51 Sandow and Adam (1897) 154.
52 Anon. (1890) 3.
53 On the 'classicized body' and the legitimation of homoeroticism see Wyke (1997) 364–73. On Sandow and classical legitimacy see Squire (2011) 17–18. For more dynamic poses in performance, a leopard-skin loincloth was preferred to the leaf.
54 Brauer (2017) 40–1.
55 Chapman (1994) 51.
56 Brauer (2017) 55.
57 Brauer (2017) 55.
58 Brauer (2017) 59.
59 Tumblety (2012) 43–4.
60 Brauer (2017) 55–7.
61 Sandow (1919) 100.
62 Klein (1993) 36.
63 Inch (1923) 12.
64 Inch (1923) 20.
65 Inch (1923) 19.
66 Runge (2009) 175; Dickinson (2017) 53.
67 Runge (2009) 67; Dickinson (2017) 53.
68 Dickinson (2017) 53.
69 Dickinson (2017) 104–5.
70 Runge (2009) 7–8.
71 Runge (2009) 151.
72 Dickinson (2017) 37–43.
73 Dickinson (2017) 31.

PART IV

Working identities

19

GODS AND HEROES OF THE PROLETARIAT

Introduction: Iconic females

A few ancient female figures manifested themselves in working-class self-imagining and images of the working class. *Shafts: A Paper for Women and the Working Classes* ran between 1892 and 1899. Its emblem was an Amazon archer, shooting shafts of knowledge at women, the poor and unfranchised: its slogan was 'Light Comes to Those Who Dare to Think'.[1] A complex synthesis of feminism, socialism and more occult Theosophical lore, the London-based journal argued for access to birth control and universal suffrage. Its editor was Margaret Shurmer Sibthorp, born in Scotland in 1851. She became a founding member of the League of Isis, which campaigned for all women's rights to a healthy sex life, birth control, and medical care in and after pregnancy.[2]

Another martial female of ancient mythology, Athena/Minerva, was prominent in craft-people's iconography as patron of handiwork, and in self-educators' imaginations as the symbol of wisdom and acquisition of learning.[3] The 'General Library' on Leadenhall Street in London took its name from her and portrayed her, complete with a terrifying Gorgon on her shield, on the cover of its 1795 catalogue.[4] She made a typical appearance in 1825 on the membership tokens of the Liverpool Mechanics' Institutes alongside Mercury (representing trade and communications) and Vulcan.[5] As goddess of strategic forethought she was also to be seen, from the 1820s onwards, in London streets on the metal plaques called 'fire insurance marks' of the Guardian Fire and Life Assurance Company, which aided the company's firefighters to identify insured properties.[6]

More militantly, the republican and freethinker Richard Carlile named one of his newspapers the *Gorgon* because it equipped those who read it to turn their capitalist oppressors metaphorically into stone (see Chapter 13); the same idea lay behind the title of the short-lived *Medusa; or, Penny Politician* (1819–1820), so

DOI: 10.4324/9781315446608-23

radical that it rejected all Tory and Whig economics alike. Ceres, meanwhile, was a popular image in taverns and public houses frequented by the lowest classes from medieval times,[7] and is often depicted at corn exchanges, as well as on the 1908 extension to the Clyde Port Authority building in Glasgow.[8]

Cartoonist James Gillray, when revelling in the damage caused by Mary Anne Clarke, the working-class ex-mistress of Frederick, Duke of York, likened her to Pandora, opening her box.[9] (Figure 19.1) She publicly blackmailed the King's son by threatening to leak 'everything which has come under my knowledge during

FIGURE 19.1 Mary Anne Clarke as Pandora (1809) by James Gillray, reproduced by permission of the British Museum.

our intimacy, with all his letters'.[10] Despite her sex and class, when called to testify for two hours before Parliament, she gave a bravura performance; William Wilberforce recorded in his diary that, 'elegantly dressed, consummately impudent, and very clever', she 'clearly got the better in the tussle'.[11] But it was the Theban poet Pindar's famous line 'Water is Best', and the Greek gods, Aphrodite and Eros, whom Elizabeth Ann Lewis, the Blackburn Temperance Campaigner, celebrated in the painting she commissioned in 1915 from Horace van Ruith for the Blackburn Art Gallery (Figure 19.2). The daughter of a farm labourer, Lewis devoted her life to improving the condition of the poor of Blackburn, then recognised as the most drink-blighted town in the world.[12]

Most of the figures from antiquity with whom the working classes identified, or were identified with by others, were, however, male—martyrs, rebels, slaves and labourers, both human and divine. They were largely distinct from the heroes and gods instrumentalised by those higher up the social scale—Alexander,

FIGURE 19.2 'Water is Best', Horace van Ruith, painting reproduced courtesy of Blackburn Museum and Art Gallery.

Aeneas, Augustus, Jove and Juno, Apollo, Venus and Mars. The proletariat's gods and heroes are related to the distinct cultural canon we have earlier explored in relation to working-class readers and authors. This chapter asks which heroes from antiquity were admired and held up as exemplars by workers and which they were asked to identify with in their working lives. It also shows how certain figures, especially Hercules and Atlas, were violently contested, being used to symbolise both ruling-class or imperial dominion and the physical power of the proletariat, especially when organised into trade or labour unions.

Aesop the agitator

The gods and heroes of the British working class overlapped with those used by opponents of slavery. Thomas Clarkson's *An Essay on the Slavery and Commerce of the Human Species, Particularly the African* (1786), which began life as a Latin prose composition at Cambridge University, discussed ancient authors who themselves belonged to the slave class. It listed the fable composers Aesop and Phaedrus and the Stoic philosopher Epictetus,[13] all of whom also formed part of the unofficial syllabus of the home-grown British working class. Simple, illustrated versions of Aesop, including chap books,[14] were widely familiar, since they were used to teach literacy to both children and adults. Some editions of Aesop interpreted the fables in ways that furthered conservative or elitist agendas.[15] But they also proved magnetically attractive to radicals and revolutionaries of a more egalitarian kind, as we have noted already in the chapter on working-class readers above (Chapter 3).

Sometimes this directly affected the way the *Fables* were retold. Thomas Bewick, whose illustrations to Aesop are acknowledged as masterpieces of miniature design, was one of eight children of a Northumberland tenant farmer; his favourite among the few books at home was Croxall's 1722 edition of Aesop's *Fables*, with its beautiful illustrations by the 18th-century printmaker Elisha Kirkall. He remained troubled by the lack of access to beauty and culture suffered by the poor throughout his life; his last project was 'to improve the taste and morals of the lower classes, particularly in the country, by a series of blocks on a large scale, to supersede the wretched, sometimes immoral, daubs with which the walls of cottages were frequently clothed'.[16] Bewick hated Latin grammar but drew constantly, especially animals, which encouraged his interest in ancient fables. Despite poverty, in 1770 he bought himself a 17th-century edition of Phaedrus. But from his teens he mixed with various Newcastle-upon-Tyne radicals, including Thomas Spence, the notorious author of *The Real Rights of Man*.[17]

There are traces of Bewick's radical tendencies to be found in his engravings. For example, in the intricate tail-piece from his famous *General History of Quadrupeds* (1790), the crack in the wall surrounding the lush woodland hints towards the perceived fragility of land enclosure, against which radicals such as Spence railed. The sign above the crack reads 'steel traps and gins', serving to deter trespassers as well as indicate (like the bird house) the bloody desire to obliterate freedom.[18] The classical bust and urn symbolise opulence and governance, in contrast with the ragged dress of the beggar boy, who leads two blind fiddlers on their footloose course. The lower-class ancient Greek world of Aesop resembles the rural environment depicted in *The General History*, and Bewick returned to Aesop's fables repeatedly throughout his working life, from his apprenticeship to the Newcastle bookseller Thomas Saint onwards. In 1775 he illustrated a version of Aesop by the writer and publisher Robert Dodsley (published 1776), adapting the designs from Croxall/Kirkall originals. From 1812 to 1818, and in collaboration with his brother and multiple apprentices, he illustrated Brooke Boothby's Aesop of 1809.

A more explicitly political Aesop was illustrated by Walter Crane, the visionary graphic designer and chromolithographer, ardent socialist, Marxist, Trade Union supporter and friend of William Morris. Crane developed a widely intelligible artistic vocabulary that merged public and private and retained a moral basis while avoiding overtly religious symbols and complicity with images of capitalism.[19] Crane was apprenticed to the radical wood-engraver, William James Linton. Enthused by the Paris Commune of 1871, Crane became the artist of the cause, designing posters, Trade Union banners, cartoons and newspaper headings, adapting the emblematic figures of his paintings to socialist themes. *The Triumph of Labour*, drawn for May Day 1891,[20] is a Renaissance-style triumphal procession rendered in the gritty texture of wood-engraving and filled with sturdy workers, bullock carts, and banners.

Crane's *Baby's Own Aesop*, brought out in 1887, uses short, rhymed limerick stanza versions. In the preface, he tells us that he has produced the text of the tales from a manuscript kindly lent to him by Linton, but Crane does say 'I have added a touch here and there'.[21] Since Linton was as radical in his own Chartist way as Crane, it is impossible to tell who is responsible for the character of the morals, embedded within the frame of the picture and text: 'King Log and King Stork', for example, demonstrates simply 'DON'T HAVE KINGS'; 'The Farmer's Treasure' shows that 'PRODUCTIVE LABOUR IS THE ONLY SOURCE OF WEALTH'. 'The Cock and the Pearl' becomes an exhortation to feed the hungry poor: 'IF HE ASK BREAD, WILL YE GIVE HIM A STONE?'

The volume was scrutinised by Trade Union organisers and workers' reading groups. Although the motif had appeared in working-class art before, notably on the blacksmith James Sharples' dazzling banner for the Amalgamated Society of Engineers in 1851,[22] it was almost certainly through Crane that illustrations of one of the most profound of Aesop's fables, 'The Bundle of Twigs', came to prominence on several banners of the 1890s. The fable said that a father, worn out by the quarrels between his sons, asked them each in turn to break a tightly bound bundle of twigs. Each son failed. Then he asked them to break a single twig, a feat which they easily accomplished.[23] The moral the father drew in Crane's volume was that 'STRENGTH LIES IN UNITY'; the political relevance is again underscored by Crane in the detail of the red freedman's cap (Figure 19.3). This had been adopted by French republicans because they knew that when slaves were manumitted in ancient Rome, they were given a red 'Phrygian' cap (*pileus* or *pilleus*) to wear: *servos ad pileum vocare* ('to call slaves to the cap') was a summons to liberty, by which slaves were called upon to take up arms with a promise of emancipation (Livy XXIV.32). In ancient art, for example on coins minted during the reign of Antoninus Pius (138–161 CE), the personified Libertas sometimes wore or carried the cap.[24]

Before the wholly separate image of the originally Roman fasces was pirated by fascists in the twentieth century, artistic representations of twig bundles were inspiring and wholesome. When 19th-century workers without legal rights banded together against their employers and state legislation to form Trade Unions, Aesop was one of the few ancient authors most of them had met, since his fables were by then commonly used to teach elementary literacy. Integrating an illustration of the fable into a banner was visual shorthand for 'Unity is Strength'. Men trying to break bundles of twigs therefore appeared on, for example, the Watford branches of the Workers' Union (this magnificent banner is reproduced on the back cover of John Gorman's seminal study *Banner Bright* [1973]), the Ashton & Haydon Miners' Union, the Pendlebury, Pendleton and Kersley Good Intent Lodge (1890), the Amalgamated Society of Engineers,

FIGURE 19.3 'The Bundle of Sticks', reproduced from Walter Crane's *Baby's Own Aesop*. Public Domain image.

FIGURE 19.4 Banner of the National Union of Public Employees. Reproduced by courtesy of the People's History Museum, Manchester.

Machinists, Millwrights, Smiths and Pattern Makers,[25] and the East Ham branch of the National Union of Public Employees (Figure 19.4). Whatever the original political message of the ancient fables, Crane's work meant that Aesop indisputably became a figure whom the oppressed underclasses of late-Victorian Britain recognised as a political forebear.

Ancient ancestors

Identification with the inhabitants of Britain in Roman times was encouraged by the civic pageants. These began in the late 19th century but were turned into a craze after 1905, when in Sherborne, Dorset, 800 people participated in a show. It chronicled episodes in local history and was watched by 30,000. The numbers involved in pageants suggest that they 'cannot simply be seen as "topdown" efforts by upper-middle-class instigators to impose culture on the uneducated masses'.[26] Pleas for participants often needed to be made in newspapers, and roles were sought after keenly by women across the class system.[27] Most pageants affirmed nationalist and imperial values, but some assumed a more challenging political hue. When advocate of agricultural workers' rights Constance Smedley led 1,300 performers in 'A Pageant of Progress' in Stroud in 1911, with the intention of 'uncovering the hideous conditions round us', it was seen by the local wealthy to 'teem with political propaganda', indeed to be 'socialistic'.[28]

In Wales and the West Country, the star of the opening ancient history episode was usually Caractacus (who, as we have seen in Chapter 12, was the subject of numerous indoor stage performances at this time). In East Anglia, at

FIGURE 19.5 'The Forum at Aquae Sulis, with Façade of Roman Baths and Temple', reproduced from a copy of *Bath Historical Pageant: Book of Words* (1909) in Hall's personal collection.

the 1907 Pageant of Bury St. Edmund's, Boudicca was portrayed as a terrifying warrior in a horse-drawn chariot, defiant against the tyrannical Roman governor Faustinus, played with relish by the Mayor.[29] In Bath, a special sequence was devised in 'The Forum at Aquae Sulis, with Façade of Roman Baths and Temple'; (Figure 19.5) a procession by the Twentieth Legion and elaborate rituals accompanied the dedication of the temple of Sulis in the 2nd century CE.[30]

Part I scene 2 of the 1911 Pageant of London was 'Roman London: The Triumph of Carausius'. This tried to make the best of the occupation of ancient Britain by an empire centred in Italy. In Carausius, it focussed on the 3rd-century commander from Belgic Gaul who, according to Aurelius Victor, Eutropius and Orosius,[31] seceded from Rome and declared himself independent Emperor of Britain and northern Gaul (Imperium Britanniarum). The London Pageant was set by the Thames and used galleys to present him as a great naval commander, a worthy forefather of the Edwardian Britons with their global maritime empire. It invites the audience to draw the parallel:

> Carausius is no pageant-emperor—
> Nor as the symbol of past victory,
> But as the emblem of great things to be.[32]

The northern pageants focussed, rather, on the Emperor Hadrian. The Carlisle Pageant of 1928 portrayed Hadrian deciding to fix the northern boundary of the

Roman Empire, and sending off a legion to build his eponymous wall.[33] Finally, a remarkable amateur film survives of the Historical Pageant of Newcastle and the North, held between 20th and 25th July 1931 on common land in Leazes Park, with 6,000 performers, a 500-strong chorus, an orchestra of 100 and a covered auditorium housing 4,000 spectators. The first episode features Queen Amelduna of the Ottadeni greeting the Sixth Legion, led by Emperor Hadrian, who this time commands the building of the Roman bridge.at Newcastle-upon-Tyne.[34]

Plutarch for the proletariat

In a short story by Chartist Thomas Cooper, the hero is a young Nottingham lace worker interested in history. He knows all about Julius Caesar and Cicero and can't understand why his supposed social superiors make such trivial conversation.[35] Plays featuring male heroes from ancient history associated with the overthrow of tyrants and the inauguration or defence of liberty were popular across all social classes. Brutus, the founder of the Roman republic according to Livy I, Dionysius of Halicarnassus' *Roman Antiquities* IV and Cicero's *de Re publica*, had been adopted as hero of the peasants' revolt in Switzerland as early as 1526,[36] and became a darling of the French Enlightenment. He had been the subject of a famous play by Voltaire and became the protagonist of *Brutus: or, The Fall of Tarquin*, an exceptionally popular tragedy by John Howard Payne, an immigrant from New York City. It premiered at Drury Lane in December 1818, at a time when the British monarchy was at its most unpopular for centuries. Frequently revived, *Brutus* toured the provinces (here is a poster advertising a performance at Bridgenorth in Shropshire, Figure 19.6); its text was much reprinted.[37]

Plutarch's *Lives* was available in translation on the shelves of workers' libraries; the book was the source of the classical heroes with whom the working classes most unambiguously identified. We have already seen how the attempt of the Gracchi to redistribute land amongst the Italian poor inspired an important Georgian tragedy by James Sheridan Knowles, and several Irish rebels (Chapter 7). *Gracchus* was the title of another newspaper published by Richard Carlile (see above pp. 278–83) in the wake of Peterloo. The Gracchi also featured in one of the collections of Plutarch's biographies rewritten for children of between the ages of 10 and 14 by the socialist freethinker Frederick Gould. *The Children's Plutarch* (1906) had engravings by the then ubiquitous Walter Crane.[38]

Gould had taught in board schools in underprivileged London districts from his mid-20s to his mid-40s, and developed a programme for teaching secular ethics with the help of classical instead of Christian literature: in his subsequent volume, *Pages for Young Socialists*, published by the National Labour Press with a preface by Keir Hardie and also illustrated by Crane, Gould uses several other classical sources to inspire his intended audience, including Herodotus on Thermopylae, Xenophon's idealised marriage in his *Oeconomicus* and the caricature of Trimalchio in Petronius' *Satyrika*.[39] The entries in the index to *The Children's Plutarch* consist entirely of individual principles and virtues: Courage,

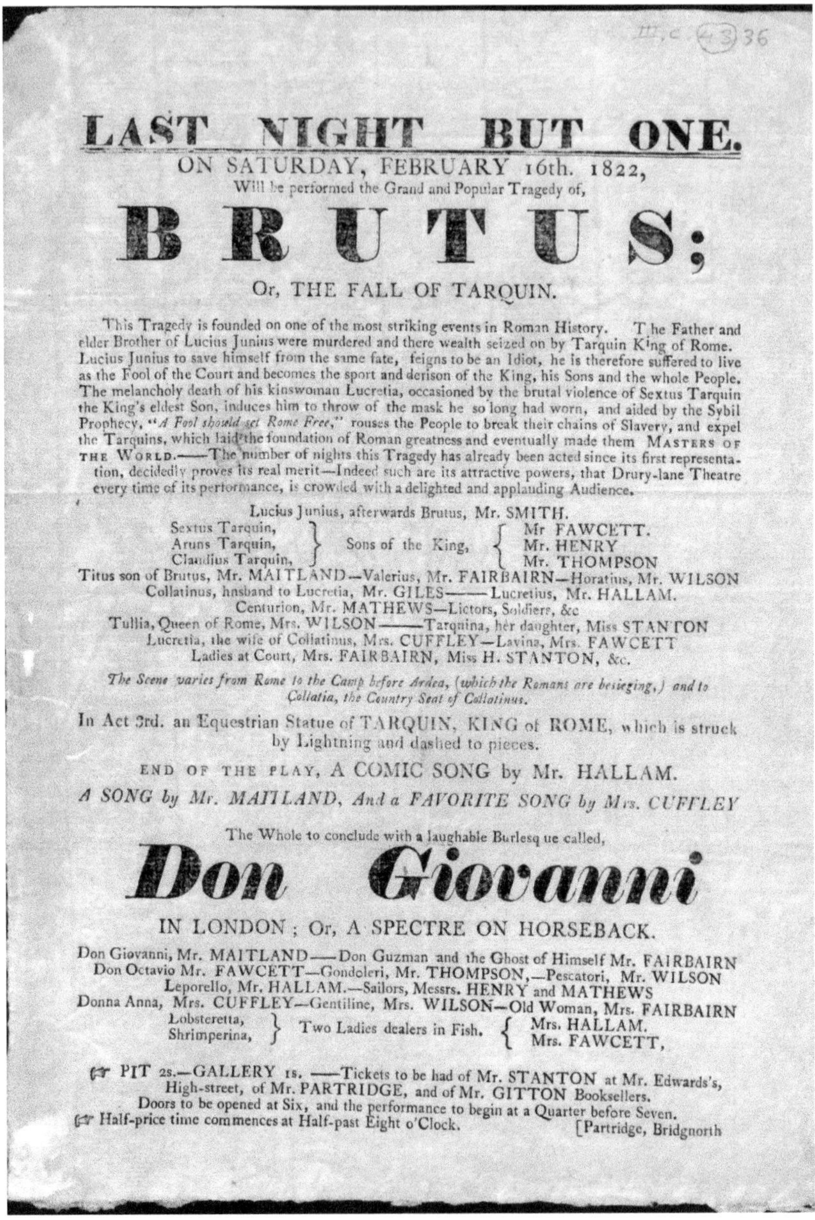

LAST NIGHT BUT ONE.

ON SATURDAY, FEBRUARY 16th. 1822,

Will be performed the Grand and Popular Tragedy of,

BRUTUS;

Or, THE FALL OF TARQUIN.

This Tragedy is founded on one of the most striking events in Roman History. The Father and elder Brother of Lucius Junius were murdered and there wealth seized on by Tarquin King of Rome. Lucius Junius to save himself from the same fate, feigns to be an Idiot, he is therefore suffered to live as the Fool of the Court and becomes the sport and derison of the King, his Sons and the whole People. The melancholy death of his kinswoman Lucretia, occasioned by the brutal violence of Sextus Tarquin the King's eldest Son, induces him to throw of the mask he so long had worn, and aided by the Sybil Prophecy, "*A Fool should set Rome Free,*" rouses the People to break their chains of Slavery, and expel the Tarquins, which laid the foundation of Roman greatness and eventually made them MASTERS OF THE WORLD.——The number of nights this Tragedy has already been acted since its first representation, decidedly proves its real merit—Indeed such are its attractive powers, that Drury-lane Theatre every time of its performance, is crowded with a delighted and applauding Audience.

Lucius Junius, afterwards Brutus, Mr. SMITH.

Sextus Tarquin, Aruns Tarquin, Claudius Tarquin, } Sons of the King, { Mr FAWCETT. Mr. HENRY Mr. THOMPSON

Titus son of Brutus, Mr. MAITLAND—Valerius, Mr. FAIRBAIRN—Horatius, Mr. WILSON
Collatinus, husband to Lucretia, Mr. GILES——Lucretius, Mr. HALLAM.
Centurion, Mr. MATHEWS—Lictors, Soldiers, &c
Tullia, Queen of Rome, Mrs. WILSON——Tarquina, her daughter, Miss STANTON
Lucretia, the wife of Collatinus, Mrs. CUFFLEY—Lavina, Mrs. FAWCETT
Ladies at Court, Mrs. FAIRBAIRN, Miss H. STANTON, &c.

The Scene varies from Rome to the Camp before Ardea, (which the Romans are besieging,) and to Collatia, the Country Seat of Collatinus.

In Act 3rd. an Equestrian Statue of TARQUIN, KING of ROME, which is struck by Lightning and dashed to pieces.

END OF THE PLAY, A COMIC SONG by Mr. HALLAM.

A SONG by Mr. MAITLAND, And a FAVORITE SONG by Mrs. CUFFLEY

The Whole to conclude with a laughable Burlesque called,

Don Giovanni

IN LONDON; Or, A SPECTRE ON HORSEBACK.

Don Giovanni, Mr. MAITLAND——Don Guzman and the Ghost of Himself Mr. FAIRBAIRN
Don Octavio Mr. FAWCETT—Gondoleri, Mr. THOMPSON,—Pescatori, Mr. WILSON
Leporello, Mr. HALLAM.—Sailors, Messrs. HENRY and MATHEWS
Donna Anna, Mrs. CUFFLEY—Gentiline, Mrs. WILSON—Old Woman, Mrs. FAIRBAIRN

Lobsteretta, Shrimperina, } Two Ladies dealers in Fish. { Mrs. HALLAM. Mrs. FAWCETT,

☞ PIT 2s.—GALLERY 1s. ——Tickets to be had of Mr. STANTON at Mr. Edwards's, High-street, of Mr. PARTRIDGE, and of Mr. GITTON Booksellers.
Doors to be opened at Six, and the performance to begin at a Quarter before Seven.
☞ Half-price time commences at Half-past Eight o'Clock. [Partridge, Bridgnorth

FIGURE 19.6 Handbill for John Howard Payne's *Brutus: or, The Fall of Tarquin* (1822), reproduced from Hall's personal collection.

Conscience, Freedom, Generosity and Kindness, etc. Forty-two of Plutarch's *Lives* are retold, and the political undertext is most obvious in those dealing with ancient heroes who despised financial greed (Solon, the Gracchi) and those who coveted it (Crassus).

As reforming Athenian statesman of the 7th–6th centuries BCE, Solon had helped define republican ideas in British literature ever since the late 16th century, when Plutarch first became available in English translation. Yet Solon could also be recruited in more conservative causes. At the peak of the conflict over the Corn Laws, a spokesman for the agriculturalists who wanted to maintain protection of British food producers, a resident of Sheffield (which, as an industrial city, was a centre of anti-Corn Law agitation), published a protectionist allegory under the pseudonym Solon. It is a mock-Aesopic fable, entitled 'The Old Sow and Her Litter of Pigs', followed by an epistle addressed to an opponent which insists that the working class has 'never had it so good'.[40] But, as Frederick Gould was aware, Solon's reputation as the legislator who had taken important steps in the foundation of Athenian democracy was confirmed by the discovery and publication of the Aristotelian *Constitution of the Athenians* in the late 19th century.[41] This is why progressive Cardiff University classicist Kathleen Freeman chose to publish her first substantial monograph on Solon in 1926,[42] and a Queen's Counsel, proposing a radical overhaul of the entire legal system in Britain, entitled his treatise *Solon: or, The Price of Justice* in 1931.[43] Solon was seen as meriting the title 'Herald of a New Age, Solon the Liberator'; he had given 'to the people who sat in misery and despair fresh hope and self-respect, and fresh opportunity of honourable self-directed industry'.[44]

As leader of the most famous slave revolt, recorded in Plutarch's *Life of Crassus*, Spartacus became the workers' favourite ancient historical figure. He had emerged as the Abolitionists' favourite hero in the French Enlightenment, when he was praised as a symbol of emancipation by Voltaire, Diderot and above all in the Abbé Guillaume Raynal's seminal 1770 *Histoire de Deux Indes*, which ran through 38 French and 18 English editions and was judged by British Abolitionists to be 'one of the primordial agents in promoting antislavery ideas in England during the 1770s'.[45] The Abbé had faith in the capability of black people to find their own rebel leader, provided only that the response of the colonial superpowers was not comparable with that of the Roman Senate in 71 BCE: 'Where is this great man to be found, whom nature perhaps owes to the honour of the human species? Where is the new Spartacus who will not find Crassus?'[46] The first truly British Spartacus was the hero of the short novel *Spartacus: A Roman Story* (1822), written by a young woman who was later to become an ardent abolitionist, Susanna Strickland;[47] this Spartacus is a Christlike Thracian shepherd, whose every thought was 'turned on forming some plan for the emancipation of himself and his comrades'.[48] Spartacus was soon, however, to supplement his political role as leader of the archetypal slave uprising with the new role of proletarian martyr. One cause was the international shockwaves created by the 1789 revolution in France, where the sharp controversy over slavery in the revolutionary assemblies had resulted in the temporary French Abolition of 1794, overturned by Napoleon in 1802.[49]

British supporters of the French Revolution, such as Tom Paine, inevitably supported Abolition; when John Flaxman contemplated designing a monument entitled 'Liberty', the iconography of the French Revolution collided with the Abolition issue in his conception of Liberty bestowing the red cap of liberty on a kneeling slave.[50] But Flaxman's kneeling slave is most reminiscent of the man in perhaps the most famous of all images from the Abolition movement, the seal designed in Josiah Wedgwood's factory in Stoke, with the enchained slave asking, 'Am I not a man and a brother?' The seal became widely available as a cameo.[51] Some impoverished white Britons, for example in late 18th-century Bristol, resented what they perceived as the special case being made by Abolitionists for slaves as opposed to other coerced labourers, especially those press-ganged into naval service.[52] But intimate connections existed between the anti-slavery movement and agitators for other forms of social emancipation—women's rights, the colonised Irish, electoral and factory reform.[53]

Spartacus is already leader of the universal proletariat in *The New World*, a remarkable poem criticising American slavery written in 1848–1850 by Marx and Engels' associate, the Chartist Ernest Jones, when in prison convicted of sedition. In the opening section Jones focuses on North America, conveying the doubleness of the British radical's view of that new nation after the abolition of slavery in the British colonies. Jones' poem shows how the strained applications of ancient mythology in the political imagery of this period reflect the complexity of the relationship between the Abolitionist movement and campaigns for other types of reform.[54] Since the American War of Independence, the new republic had offered an inspirational example to British radicals and republicans, and Jones configures not the old but the new country, after independence had been secured, as a young Hercules who even as an infant could slay the British monarchy and religious intolerance.

> Young Nation-Hercules! whose infant-grasp
> Kingcraft and churchcraft slew, the twinborn asp!
> What glorious visions for thy manhood rise,
> When thy full stature swells upon our eyes![55]

Yet in Jones' picture, the virtue of the new country is compromised by its practice of slavery, which it has not outlawed despite the example set by the British Abolition:

> Ah! that the wisdom here so dearly bought
> Would sanctify thy wild, luxuriant thought,
> And righteously efface the stripes of slaves
> From that proud flag where heaven's high splendour waves![56]

This Hercules, grown from revolutionary babyhood to corrupt adulthood, plays no further part in Jones' vision. What Jones sees as the millennia-long persecution and domination of Africa comes to symbolise the oppression of the working people of the entire world, the victims of capitalist classes at home and imperialism abroad; this procedure entails, remarkably for a Briton writing at this time, drawing a connection between British exploitation of colonial India and Britain's implication in the history of the slave trade.[57]

Jones, the imprisoned Chartist, presents himself allegorically as an African, soon to take over first Europe and then the rest of the planet. He turns now to Spartacus, supplemented (since Jones had received an excellent training in Classics at a German gymnasium) by the much less familiar Ennus (or Eunus). This rebellious slave had led a Sicilian slave revolt in the 2nd century BCE.[58] Africa's example, configured by Jones as a resurrection of the *historical* ancient slave rebels Ennus and Spartacus, can fire the dream of universal liberty dreamt by the new 'chained men' of Britain—the Chartist prisoners:

> Deep in the burning south a cloud appears,
> The smouldering wrath of full four thousand years,
> Whatever name caprice of history gave,
> Moor, Afric, Ethiop, Negro, still meant slave!
> But from the gathering evil springs redress,
> And sin is punished by its own excess... ./.../
> Near and more near, and fiercer and more fierce,
> East, West, and South, the sable legions pierce;
> On! to the site, where ancient Rome once rose,
> And modern towns in meaner dust repose.
> Up, Ennus! tip! and Spartacus! awake!
> Now, if you still can feel, your vengeance slake!

Ennus and Spartacus, whose example has liberated the world's slaves, can now help—in the imagination at least—to usher in universal suffrage.

Spartacus' slave revolt receives equally politicised notice, accompanied by a dramatic illustration of gladiators in combat (Figure 19.7) in Osborne Ward's *The Ancient Lowly* (on which see above, p. 8).[59] Raffaello Giovagnoli's long novel *Spartaco* (1874), which used its hero more as a symbol of Garibaldi's unification of Italy than of proletarian labour, was not translated into English, yet by 1913 could be seen by early cinema audiences in Britain in the silent movie directed by Giovanni Enrico Vidali (1913). In the film, the unification of Italy will have passed most British cinemagoers by, while the importance of Spartacus in Russian and subsequently German socialist movements inevitably attracted attention. Spartacus was celebrated by a readership of youthful Welsh workers, three years after the movie was first shown, in 'The Revolt of Spartacus', the rousing lead article in the *Young Worker* for August 1921 (Figure 19.8).

FIGURE 19.7 Illustration from Osborne Ward's *The Ancient Lowly* (1907 edition), reproduced from Hall's personal collection.

The author was T. Islwyn Nicholas, a Welsh-speaking founder member of the Communist Party of Great Britain, who worked tirelessly with young miners in South Wales.

In Scotland, a lively version of Spartacus' life, with an emotive picture of the mass crucifixion on the Appian Way, was included in John S. Clarke's *Young Workers' Book of Rebels* (1918), a Scottish textbook produced for teaching at the Proletarian Schools.[60] Thirty branches of these flourished in Scotland between the Russian revolution and the 1930s, with a few offshoots in England. Clarke (1885–1959) was one of 14 children born into a circus family living a nomadic gypsy life. He performed as a bareback rider and a lion tamer, but was stirred by socialism and joined the Socialist Labour Party, itself inspired by the writings of Daniel De Leon (on whom see above, pp. 199–200). Clarke edited the *Socialist* and the *Reform Journal*, spending much of World War I hiding from the police as a conscientious objector. He was later to become an important Labour Party author; his *Marxism and History* (1928), which contains a long analysis of the Roman Empire, was influential in socialist circles. He was elected MP for Maryhill in 1929. Perhaps the Scottish author of the most important British novel about Spartacus, Lewis Grassic Gibbon (on whom see above, pp. 248–9), learned about the rebel gladiator at Proletarian School, although one scholar thinks that his *Spartacus* (1933) was inspired even before that by the heroic martyrdom of the German Spartacists, Karl Liebknecht and Rosa Luxemburg, for whom he had written panegyric poems.[61]

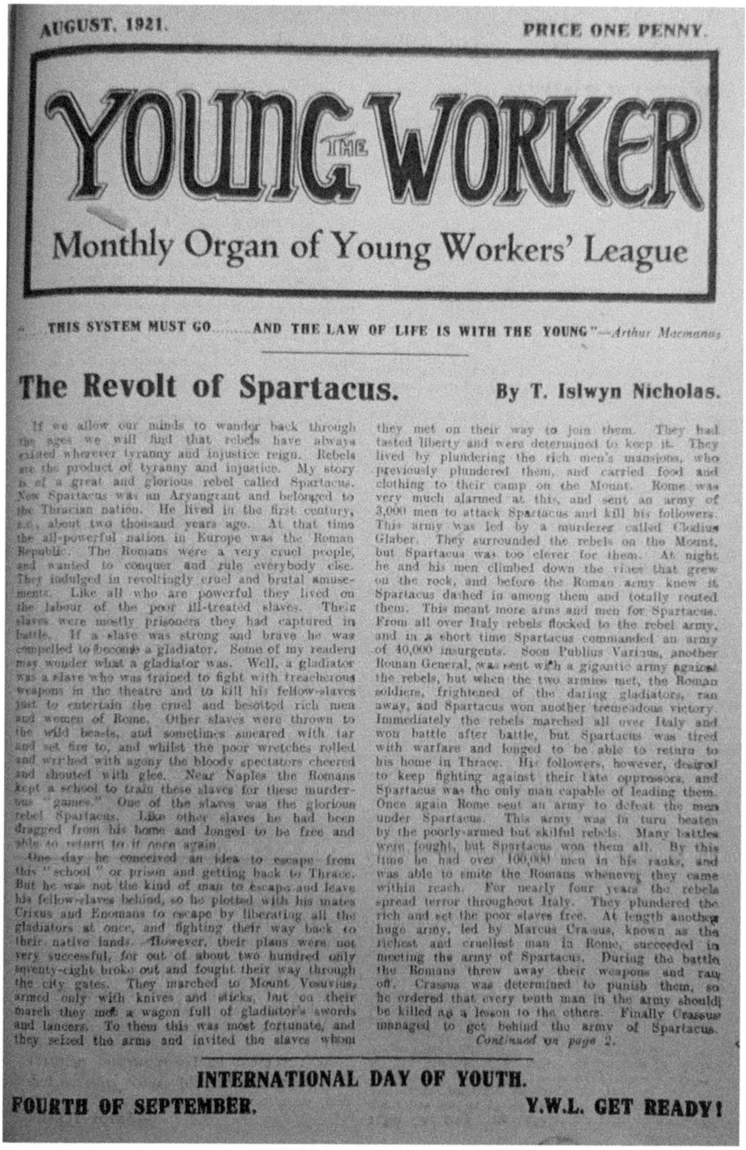

AUGUST, 1921. PRICE ONE PENNY.

THE YOUNG WORKER

Monthly Organ of Young Workers' League

" ... THIS SYSTEM MUST GO ... AND THE LAW OF LIFE IS WITH THE YOUNG" —*Arthur Macmanus*

The Revolt of Spartacus.

By T. Islwyn Nicholas.

If we allow our minds to wander back through the ages we will find that rebels have always existed wherever tyranny and injustice reign. Rebels are the product of tyranny and injustice. My story is of a great and glorious rebel called Spartacus. Now Spartacus was an Aryangrant and belonged to the Thracian nation. He lived in the first century, B.C., about two thousand years ago. At that time the all-powerful nation in Europe was the Roman Republic. The Romans were a very cruel people, and wanted to conquer and rule everybody else. They indulged in revoltingly cruel and brutal amusements. Like all who are powerful they lived on the labour of the poor ill-treated slaves. Their slaves were mostly prisoners they had captured in battle. If a slave was strong and brave he was compelled to become a gladiator. Some of my readers may wonder what a gladiator was. Well, a gladiator was a slave who was trained to fight with treacherous weapons in the theatre and to kill his fellow-slaves just to entertain the cruel and besotted rich men and women of Rome. Other slaves were thrown to the wild beasts, and sometimes smeared with tar and set fire to, and whilst the poor wretches rolled and writhed with agony the bloody spectators cheered and shouted with glee. Near Naples the Romans kept a school to train these slaves for these murderous "games." One of the slaves was the glorious rebel Spartacus. Like other slaves he had been dragged from his home and longed to be free and able to return to it once again.

One day he conceived an idea to escape from this "school" or prison and getting back to Thrace. But he was not the kind of man to escape and leave his fellow-slaves behind, so he plotted with his mates Crixus and Enomans to escape by liberating all the gladiators at once, and fighting their way back to their native lands. However, their plans were not very successful, for out of about two hundred only seventy-eight broke out and fought their way through the city gates. They marched to Mount Vesuvius, armed only with knives and sticks, but on their march they met a wagon full of gladiator's swords and lancers. To them this was most fortunate, and they seized the arms and invited the slaves whom they met on their way to join them. They had tasted liberty and were determined to keep it. They lived by plundering the rich men's mansions, who previously plundered them, and carried food and clothing to their camp on the Mount. Rome was very much alarmed at this, and sent an army of 3,000 men to attack Spartacus and kill his followers. This army was led by a murderer called Clodius Glaber. They surrounded the rebels on the Mount, but Spartacus was too clever for them. At night he and his men climbed down the vines that grew on the rock, and before the Roman army knew it Spartacus dashed in among them and totally routed them. This meant more arms and men for Spartacus. From all over Italy rebels flocked to the rebel army, and in a short time Spartacus commanded an army of 40,000 insurgents. Soon Publius Varinus, another Roman General, was sent with a gigantic army against the rebels, but when the two armies met, the Roman soldiers, frightened of the daring gladiators, ran away, and Spartacus won another tremendous victory. Immediately the rebels marched all over Italy and won battle after battle, but Spartacus was tired with warfare and longed to be able to return to his home in Thrace. His followers, however, desired to keep fighting against their late oppressors, and Spartacus was the only man capable of leading them. Once again Rome sent an army to defeat the men under Spartacus. This army was in turn beaten by the poorly-armed but skilful rebels. Many battles were fought, but Spartacus won them all. By this time he had over 100,000 men in his ranks, and was able to smite the Romans whenever they came within reach. For nearly four years the rebels spread terror throughout Italy. They plundered the rich and set the poor slaves free. At length another huge army, led by Marcus Crassus, known as the richest and cruellest man in Rome, succeeded in meeting the army of Spartacus. During the battle the Romans threw away their weapons and ran off. Crassus was determined to punish them, so he ordered that every tenth man in the army should be killed as a lesson to the others. Finally Crassus managed to get behind the army of Spartacus.

Continued on page 2.

INTERNATIONAL DAY OF YOUTH.

FOURTH OF SEPTEMBER. Y.W.L. GET READY!

FIGURE 19.8 Cover of *Young Worker* (August 1921), reproduced from Hall's personal collection.

Gibbon used the name Kleon for one of his most important characters, which was an intriguing choice, since the demagogue of that name was rarely adopted as a hero by working-class or leftist writers, despite his unwavering support of the lowest-class Athenians. This was because the sources, Thucydides and Aristophanes, are so contemptuous about him.[62] The Irish Chartist Feargus

O'Connor embraced the abusive word 'demagogue', once producing gales of laughter by saying, 'I am a demagogue; if the fools understood Greek, they would have known it was a term of honour, rather than reproach'.[63] But even he avoided using Kleon's name, and it was useful to reactionary English journalists wishing to decry another eloquent Irish republican, Daniel O'Connell.[64] Much the same can be said for Thersites, the ordinary soldier who tries to prompt a mutiny in *Iliad* II.211–.77, even though by 1898 Dublin Professor J.P. Mahaffy, who was no socialist, suggested that he 'seems drawn with special spite and venom, as a satire on the first critics that rose up among the people, and questioned the divine right of kings to do wrong'.[65] Tom Paine, predictably, was compared with Thersites by his bitterest enemies, including the snobbish Professor John Wilde, who also equated him with 'a fishwoman at Billingsgate', and C. Servilius Glaucia as described by Cicero in his *Brutus*, 'by far the vilest man alive, but experienced and shrewd and most of all laughable'.[66]

A slave-hero who may have reached a wider working-class audience even than Spartacus was the entirely fictional Diomed of Owen Hall's *A Greek Slave* (1898), one of the great hits of the late Victorian and early 20th-century British stage (Figure 19.9). This musical comedy, set in ancient Rome, ran for what was in those days a staggering 349 nights. It was performed in many provincial towns, for example at Swansea Grand Theatre in October 1899.[67] It even transferred to Broadway. Hall was an educated middle-class Anglo-Irish Jew. He set the drama at the time of the Saturnalia, a festival which involved social role-inversion in which masters and slaves temporarily exchanged places. His operetta's plot is in the spirit of Plautine comedy, in which slaves often outwit their masters. But after singing his rousing number 'Freedom',[68] Diomed actually *marries* his bourgeois master's daughter, reflecting the increasing class-consciousness of the audiences which flocked to see him win his liberty at the same time as his true love.[69]

Promethean heat

The Titan god Prometheus made a similar shift to Spartacus, from Abolitionists' hero to symbol of the proletariat. The suffering philanthropist, chained and tortured by Zeus' eagle for eternity, in the 18th century ousted the intellectual Prometheus, derived ultimately from Hesiod, who had bestowed the light of human reason on matters obscured by religion and superstition, and been a point of identification for the European Enlightenment.[70] The Abolitionist configuration of the hero in some ways harked back to the Prometheus of the Renaissance and Early Modern period, whose suffering on the rock was felt to anticipate Christ's passion on the cross.[71] But between them and the Abolitionists also lay the Romantic Prometheus of Herder and Goethe, the poet-demiurge, whose gift of fire as inspiration could remake the world anew—an aesthetic and psychological revolutionary.[72]

Aeschylus had not become available in any modern language, including English, until the 1770s, when the complete 1777 translation of Aeschylus by the Norfolk

FIGURE 19.9 C. Haydon Coffin as Diomed in *A Greek Slave*, reproduced from *Souvenir of a Greek Slave* (1898) in Hall's personal collection.

Abolitionist Robert Potter had made a huge impact.[73] This was followed by the edition of the Greek text of Aeschylus by Richard Porson (see above pp. 294–9), published in 1795 with interleaved engravings by Tommaso Piroli of illustrations by John Flaxman. Flaxman was closely associated with Josiah Wedgwood (who also produced the famous 'Am I not a man and a brother?' cameo).[74] These engravings were published separately during the same year. *Prometheus Bound* could now be easily read in English, and its effect in performance helpfully visualised. But the mythical reference was multivalent. Promethean liberation meant different things to different people: Byron used Prometheus to stand for home-grown Irish rebels rather than Africans in 'The Irish Avatar' (1821).

In 1807, a volume entitled *Poems on the Abolition of the Slave Trade* by three British authors was published in order to celebrate the passing of the 1807 Slave Trade bill. The cover is adorned with an engraved medallion depicting Hercules setting Prometheus free from his chains and the first poem, by devout Glaswegian James Grahame, is entitled 'Prometheus Delivered'.[75] The other poets were James Montgomery, an orphan and failed baker's apprentice who became a radical journalist in Sheffield (he had been imprisoned on charges of sedition in the 1790s), and Elizabeth Benger, a feminist eccentric and aspiring dramatist, whose enthusiasm for Abolition and prison reform is evident in her novel *The Heart and the Fancy* (1813). But the politics of Grahame (1765–1811) outdid them in extremity. His relatives felt the need to suppress his *Fragments of a Tour through the Universe*, which attacked not only the oppression of workers, but the press-gang, war and the monarchy.[76]

'Promethean' politics took on a particular resonance in an era which was seeing the emergence of international socialism. The Titan's popularity amongst radicals became assured with the publication of Shelley's *Prometheus Unbound* in 1820, by which time this poet was beginning to attract the attention of the working classes as well as liberals higher up the social scale.[77] Thomas Talfourd, a judge sympathetic to the Chartists, talked about the 'Promethean' heat of the class struggle palpable after the Peterloo massacre of 1819;[78] the man who invented the term 'communism', a 19th-century Christian socialist and Chartist named John Goodwyn Barmby, in January 1842 published the first issue of his call for socialism and entitled it *The Promethean; or Communitarian Apostle* (Figure 19.10). Its epigraph was six lines delivered by the Chorus of Spirits in Act IV of Shelley's *Prometheus Unbound*:

> And our singing shall build
> In the void's loose field
> A world for the Spirit of Wisdom to wield;
> We will take our plan
> From the new world of man,
> And our work shall be called the Promethean.[79]

The first page of the first issue consists of Goodwyn Barmby's manifesto, 'The outlines of Communism',[80] but the remainder is replete with material which turns the author's classical training to socialist use. One article is an address to the 'Author-Class', which discusses ancient poets including Homer, Anacreon, Horace and Ovid, as well as moderns from Milton onwards;[81] a poem celebrates the power of women to transform the world through a complex allegorical encomium to Aphrodite and the Graces;[82] further essays discuss the origins of slavery in Greek and Roman antiquity, of drama in the classical theatre of 5th-century Athens and divine inspiration in the Delphic oracle.[83]

The second issue includes a long article on the ancient Greek, Roman and Algonquin calendars in order to argue that the French revolutionary one, said to be closest to that of ancient Greece, should be adopted by communists.[84] In the third issue, along with a discussion of ancient and Early Modern models of utopia, Goodwyn Barmby officially declares the support of his paper and the association which publishes it for the People's Charter,[85] as well as advertising another publication, *The Educational Circular and Communist Apostle* and a series of

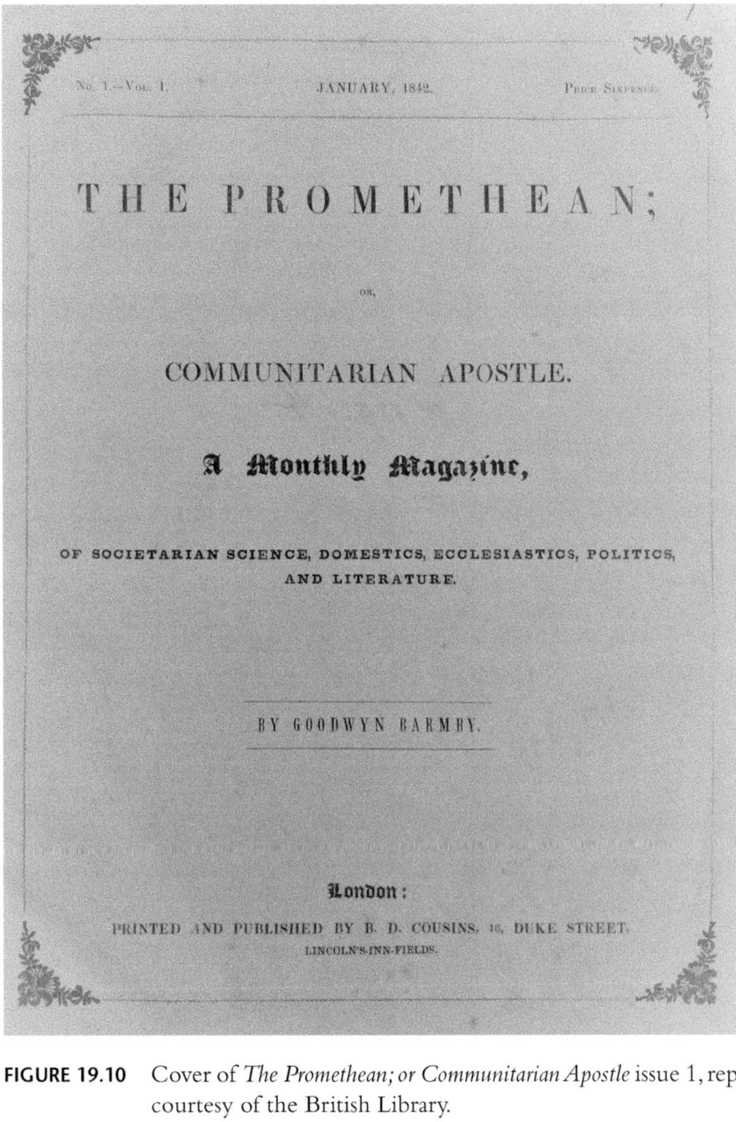

No. 1.—Vol. 1. JANUARY, 1842. Price Sixpence.

THE PROMETHEAN;

OR,

COMMUNITARIAN APOSTLE.

A Monthly Magazine,

OF SOCIETARIAN SCIENCE, DOMESTICS, ECCLESIASTICS, POLITICS, AND LITERATURE.

BY GOODWYN BARMBY.

London:

PRINTED AND PUBLISHED BY B. D. COUSINS, 18, DUKE STREET, LINCOLN'S-INN-FIELDS.

FIGURE 19.10 Cover of *The Promethean; or Communitarian Apostle* issue 1, reproduced by courtesy of the British Library.

'Lectures on Communism' to be delivered at the Workingman's Hall in Circus-Street, Greenwich.[86] Sadly, *The Promethean*, with its heady mix of feminism, Owenite socialism, slightly embarrassed admiration for the French Revolution, Chartist fervour, eccentric Christian spirituality and large dollops of classical information, lasted for less than a year.

But a fin-de-siècle spirit of Prometheus was later to fire up the UK Ethical Movement, a humanist organisation linked to socialist activism. In the late 1890s, the American Stanton Coit purchased a disused Methodist chapel on Queensway in Bayswater, renamed it The Ethical Church and commissioned Walter Crane to create the equivalent of an altarpiece. The painting is now in the Russell-Cotes Gallery in Bournemouth, but an old photograph exists of the painting *in situ*.[87] Crane's design, which depicts a pagan Athenian torch-bearing relay race, such as those run at the festivals of Prometheus and Hephaestus, is now clearest in the reproduction of his original line drawing.[88] The race at the Prometheia, which Pausanias describes (I.30.2), had recently attracted scholarly attention on both sides of the Atlantic.[89] Crane's recreation is the visual counterpart to a statement he made in his essay, 'The Socialist Ideal as a New Inspiration in Art':[90]

> From the tragic vicissitudes of history, of race-conflict, of conquest and domination of warlike tribes and the institution of slavery, the foundation and influence of the great ancient states and empires, and their inevitable decay and fall, and the new order springing from their ruins; the tragic tale of wars and pestilence and famine, of flood and of fire and of earthquake, and yet onward still through all these perils and disasters we may see humanity marching beneath the banner of social justice to fulfil its destiny; the hero spirits still passing the torch of enlightenment and freedom from hand to hand, and as one sinks into the silence another advances towards the full flush of the new morning.[91]

These ancient Athenian worshippers of Prometheus, complete with their liberty caps, are here adopted as the ancestors of all who have ever fought the fight for social justice, enlightenment and freedom.[92] Crane's picture was reproduced as the frontispiece to another book for young socialists published by the author of *The Children's Plutarch*, Frederick Gould (on whom see above, pp. 393–5), entitled *Bright Lamps of History and Daily Life*. The first story is an account of the race in ancient Athens, complete with a hymn to Prometheus and Vulcan combined.[93] But the torch was not destined to be handed on, at least in that Bayswater building. Since 1954 it has been Our Lady Queen of Heaven Catholic Church, and Crane's painting was replaced by a copy of Rubens's 'Descent from the Cross' in Antwerp Cathedral.

Classical labourers

The close connection between Prometheus and Hephaestus/Vulcan in ancient Athenian cults was replicated in the parallel appearances they made in industrial iconography, along with Prometheus' fellow Titan, Atlas.[94] Vulcan is sometimes attended by his fellow forge workers, the gigantic Cyclopes. The blackened, deafened Titanic foundrymen at the Cyclops Steel and Iron Manufactory on Saville Street, Sheffield, set up by Charles Cammell from Hull, were described in *The Official Illustrated Guide to the Great Northern Railway* (1861):

> After passing through an almost interminable succession of buildings occupied by swarthy workmen, engaged in their Titanic operations, we arrive

> at a series of very large buildings of more recent construction, consisting of rolling-mills, tilts, forges, and grinding wheels; and here the mighty power of machinery in its most gigantic proportions will astonish the beholder … The men engaged on these premises are models of herculean hardihood, so much does muscular exercise, even of the rudest and most severe character, develop the bodily frame. The hearing of these men is, however, frequently affected by their employment; nor can we wonder at this, for the clang of the machinery and tools is something prodigious.[95]

Along with the Titans and Hercules, Vulcan was favoured by industrialists as name and ornament. Charles Tayleur's Vulcan Works was founded in 1830 between Liverpool and Manchester to manufacture locomotives. A bronze relief panel depicted Vulcan on Henry Hoole's Green Lane metalworks in Sheffield.[96] Vulcan came to signify the city of Sheffield itself, at least after the town council commissioned Mario Raggi's 1897 bronze statue of Vulcan, complete with anvil, hammer and thunderbolts, to top their town hall. Art representing workmen of all kinds was often informed by ancient depictions of Hephaestus, especially since the Romans' Vulcan was often portrayed wearing the liberty cap, and no doubt some workers meditated on what they shared with their ancient avatar.

Vulcan made occasional appearances on Trade Union banners, including the early 19th-century banner of the Regular Carpenters of the City of Dublin.[97] Patent chimney sweeping machines brand-named 'Vulcan', manufactured in Derbyshire, were specifically marketed as 'the only efficient supporters of the law against climbing boys', referring to the Chimney Sweeps Act 1834 which had forbidden boys under the age of ten to be apprenticed to this trade.[98] But Vulcan was rarely adopted as a revolutionary hero, perhaps because in myth he is either quietist (he avoids open confrontation with the other, patrician Olympians in the Homeric epics), or actually a class traitor (in the Aeschylean *Prometheus Bound* he obeys Zeus's orders to chain the philanthropic Prometheus to the rock). Vulcan was used, rather, by non-proletarian employers, businessmen and cultural media to represent heavy industry. A cartoon published in *Punch* on 23rd September 1893 depicts Vulcan as a miner, opposed to Mars who represents British soldiers (Figure 19.11). The editor of this issue of *Punch*, Sir Francis Burnand, had been a famous writer of classical burlesques (see above, pp. 146).

A months-long conflict had been waged in the coalfields about severe pay cuts. Not only the police force but the army were sent to mining communities to quell protestors. Several had been killed by soldiers, who, at Doncaster, opened fire into the crowd. But the situation was complicated because the miners were themselves divided. Some districts (e.g. County Durham) had agreed to submit to arbitration, while others (especially in Yorkshire, Lancashire and Derbyshire) were opposed to it. In some coalfields, non-striking miners who had agreed to arbitration were protected by the militiamen and formed bonds with them.[99]

In the cartoon, the chaotic alliances and divisions are simplified by using classical allegory.[100] Mars signifies the alliance of the military with the less militant

FIGURE 19.11 Mars presents Vulcan an arbitration award. Public Domain image, *Punch* (1893).

miners who were prepared to enter arbitration. Vulcan represents the militant miners who were resolutely opposed to wage cuts and could not agree to arbitration. The conciliatory Mars says to the defiant Vulcan, 'LOOK HERE, BROTHER VULCAN!—WHEN EVEN I HAVE KNOCKED UNDER TO 'ARBITRATION', SURELY YOU MIGHT TRY IT?' The two gods meet beside a mine shaft. The areas around mines all over England and Wales had been turned into battlefields where different elements of the working class fought throughout the long summer of conflict. The cartoon is accompanied by Burnand's poem 'A LESSON FOR LABOUR'. Although sympathetic to the poverty of the miners, it implies that they, rather than the government, are responsible for the escalation of violence and patronisingly advises the militant wing to come to heel.[101]

We have already seen that Hercules could be used both to represent the slave-owning United States and, as liberator of Prometheus, the progress of the Abolitionist cause in Britain. Of all the labouring classical heroes associated with the working classes, Hercules' role is most conflicted and ambivalent. In 'Labour and Capital', a lecture he toured with in 1867, Ernest Jones still identified workers with Antaeus, the giant who wrestled with Hercules:

> Back to the land! it is the only safeguard against the assaults of capital. The Hercules, monopoly, wrestles with the Antaeus, Labour. When he lifts him from the ground his strength is gone—soon as he touches earth he is strong again.[102]

For Hercules' pedigree as symbol of the ruling class was long. In their excellent study *The Many-Headed Hydra*, Linebaugh and Rediker explore the centrality, from the 16th century onwards, of Hercules and his labours, especially his defeat of the many-headed hydra of Lerna, to the iconography of the divine right of European Kings and their colonial enterprises.[103] The hydra's many heads came to symbolise the plurality of places where rebellion could break out amongst slaves and labourers, only to be decapitated by the might of the Herculean ruling class.[104] Thomas Carlyle ironically alluded to this standard ruling-class trope in his description of Peterloo in *Past and Present*: 'Certain hundreds of drilled soldiers sufficed to suppress this million-headed hydra and tread it down, without the smallest appeasement or hope of such, into its subterranean settlements again, there to reconsider itself', but he also compared Cromwell's struggle with the monarchy to Hercules' combat with the hydra.[105] It was such a class-conscious reversal of the roles of Hercules and the hydra which 'Nicholas' the fisherman effected in a polemic which compares the oppressive forces in his city—the Dublin Corporation, excisemen, judges and magistrates—to the many heads of the Lernaean hydra. Published in 1784 under the name of 'An Advocate for Justice', his treatise is entitled *Oppression Unmasked, Being a Narrative of the Proceedings in a Case between a Great Corporation and a Little Fishmonger, Relative to some Customs for Fish, demanded by the former as legal, but refused by the latter, as Exactions and Extortions.*

Although the author laments Nicholas' lack of a 'liberal education', classical signposts enhance the harangue. It opens with an epigram from Virgil's *Aeneid* and closes with the Aesopic fable discussed above (pp. 389–90), showing that twig-bundles are unbreakable, the moral of which is 'Unity is Strength'. The tale is transplanted from Dublin to Utopia, which shares features with ancient Rome and Athens. The fisherman, Nicholas, sells his catches at a fish-market in the 'metropolis'. But in Utopia, he becomes subject to ever-increasing tolls payable 'to the Praetorian Body (answering to the Corporation of the City of Dublin) … appointed by the Praetor'. Nicholas gets legal counsel, tells the 'Forum' that the new tools were illegal, and embarks on a decades-long battle with the authorities. He is imprisoned twice, pays hefty fines, is arraigned before what he calls the Utopian 'Areopagus' for non-payment of rent for his fish-stall, is later re-arrested and persecuted by a magistrate 'attended with a posse of lictors' who destroy his stall and stock and near-fatally beat up his attendant. The polemic ends with an appeal for financial help with the imminent legal showdown. Nicholas intends to defend 'the public against the *oppressions* and *impositions* of TYRANNY ... Aided by the generous and spirited Hibernians, he may crush that hydra, that would devour the very entrails of mankind'.[106]

But it was not until the French Revolution, five years later, that the labouring Hercules emphatically changed political sides in favour of workers. At the Festival of Unity and Indivisibility of the Republic (Versailles, August 1793), the revolutionary public was amazed by the colossus in the form of Hercules, wielding his club on their behalf while strangling the serpent of deviant Federalism, with the hydra—enemy of revolutionary unity—writhing at his feet.[107] Thomas Spence was thinking of Hercules as well as the biblical David when, in 1794, he called in his paper *Pigs' Meat; or, Lessons for the Swinish Multitude* for the contemporary equivalent of mythical giants—aristocrats, landlords, etc.—to be destroyed: 'The extirpation of these should employ the philanthropic giant-killers, the deliverers of mankind'.[108] This almost certainly inspired the Union of Journeymen, formed in 1818 by its Chairman, shipwright John Gast, on 2nd December of that year, to extend the movement to other categories of worker and assume the name 'The Philanthropic Hercules'.[109]

Hercules' role as patron of trade unions reached its climax in the late 19th century when he appeared on the central panel of the Dockers' banner (Export Branch), strangling the snake which the caption beneath suggests 'Destitution, Prostitution, and Exploitation' (Figure 19.12). Ben Tillett led a famous dockworkers' strike in 1889, when the banner was adopted. Hercules' pose is modelled upon Frederic Leighton's sculpture 'Athlete struggling with a python', exhibited in 1877,[110] which Walter Crane had imitated for the illustration to the fable 'The Man and the Snake' in his *Baby's Own Aesop*:[111] the dockers' Hercules unambivalently represents the physical strength and political defiance of the working-class man, while the evil serpent of capitalism symbolises the middle and upper classes.[112] Similar Herculean figures were to be seen on other banners. An Edwardian May-Day banner in the People's History Museum depicts a red-capped female personification of Socialism strangling the snake of Capitalism with the help of several sturdy labourers. The Hercules-miner on the banner of Kellingley Colliery, the last deep-pit coal mine in Britain, was still carried in sad but proud procession the day the colliery closed on 18th December 2015.[113]

Other mythical labourers occur slightly less frequently in representations by and of the working class. In a poem prophesying the imminent triumph of the proletariat entitled 'Atlas' by Irish-born Victor Daley, who later emigrated first to England and then Australia, Atlas is identified as the exploitative parasite who can afford not to work because he has imposed his burden on the proletarian Hercules. Hercules now does all the world's labour for him: the spirit of Liberty comes to Hercules and works to saw through his chains 'With rasp and file of Knowledge, / And acid keen of Thought'.[114] But there was a left-wing identification with Atlas as well. Alexander Anderson was a Dumfriesshire surfaceman

FIGURE 19.12 Dockers' Union Banner, image reproduced courtesy of the People's History Museum, Manchester.

(i.e. navvy) with the Glasgow and South Western Railway Company, famous for his poems celebrating work on the railways (Figure 19.13). His 320-line epic 'A Song of Labour' (1873), published in a volume sponsored by *The Dundee Advertiser*,[115] is 'respectfully dedicated to my fellow-workers with pick and shovel everywhere'. In trochees which replicate the sound of machinery, it concludes with its self-description, 'Labour's mightiest Epic rolling through the world's heart of toil'. Despite being born into a one-room cottage, the son of a quarry worker, Anderson was a committed autodidact;[116] the poem bristles with references to the classical figures he associated with workers in heavy industry, beginning with Atlas:

> Then, my Brothers, sing to Labour, as the sun-brown'd giant stands
> Like an Atlas with the world shaking in his mighty hands;
> Brawny arm'd, and broad, and swarthy, keeping in with shout and groan,
> In the arch of life the keystone that the world may thunder on;
> Ever toiling, ever sweating, ever knowing that today
> Is the footstool for the coming years to reach a higher sway.[117]

FIGURE 19.13 Photograph from Alexander Anderson's *Surfaceman's Later Poems* (1912), edited and with a biographical sketch by Alexander Brown.

Next come Briareus, Laocoöns, Titans, Enceladus, Cyclopes and, of course, Prometheus. No wonder the *Sheffield Telegraph* called Anderson the '*Homer of the Iron Horse*'.[118] The left-wing view of Atlas in a poem by Sid Chaplin (discussed below pp. 465–7) is different again.

But Atlas could be deployed to define class struggle from the opposite political perspective. *Punch* magazine sympathetically depicted Stanley Baldwin, Conservative Prime Minister of Britain during the General Strike of May 1926, as being envious of Atlas. Atlas can concentrate on holding up the sky, whereas Baldwin is under constant pressure to find new funds to 'appease' the miners.[119] The cartoon exemplifies the almost universal vilification of these strikers, especially the miners, in the mainstream press. The owners of the mines wanted to cut the miners' pay and increase their working hours. To delay the crisis, Baldwin had responded by offering to subsidise the miners' pay for nine months and set up a Royal Commission. This cartoon marks what was seen by the middle class as a capitulation by Baldwin. But it was not; in March the Commission recommended, among other things, the reduction of miners' wages by 13.5%. In May the nine-day strike was broken by middle-class volunteers, including many 'blackleg' university students, especially at Oxford, who regarded it as a great lark to spend a few days driving buses, delivering groceries and working in factories.[120] Some of them sported fancy dress, including classical Greek costumes.[121]

Finally, the Underworld tortures of Sisyphus and Ixion occasionally appear in discussions of the plight of the working class. Stephen Duck's 'The Thresher's Labour' (1730) concludes with an explicit parallel between agricultural work and Sisyphus' punishment, as we saw in an earlier chapter (pp. 85–6). Perhaps Duck's poem was known to James Phillips Kay, later Kay-Shuttleworth (1804–1877), one of the most important reformers of Victorian education. In his treatise *The Moral and Physical Condition of the Working Classes Employed in the Cotton Manufacture in Manchester* (1832), for which the catalyst was the appearance of cholera in Britain, he wrote that the work of the mill artisan 'resembles the torment of Sisyphus', and that its monotony destroys the mind (22). Ixion was temporarily transformed into the leader of a revolt of the slaves working under a 'sordid and avaricious' flour-mill owner in Edward Fitzball's spectacular play at the Adelphi Theatre, *Black Vulture: or, The Wheel of Death*. Ixion stabs his master and curses him for transporting slaves from far away and forcing them 'to toil in thine accursed mill till the limbs trembled, and the straining eyeballs almost burst from their sockets', beating them just to add 'a grain of gold dust to thy still unsated coffers'.[122] The rebel Ixion is chained to the Wheel of Death, but sells his soul to the Black Vulture, and becomes a worse oppressor than his master had been, thus expressing Fitzball's underlying 'fear of social upheaval'.[123]

Nautical Neptunes

Probably the most visually recognisable ancient mythical figure of all is Neptune, endlessly reproduced since the Renaissance in the art of seagoing European peoples, the Dutch, French and the Italian, as well as the British.[124] But it was the national personification of Britain, Britannia (first revived for modernity in imitation of ancient Roman coins by Charles II) who in 1794 put aside her spear and began herself to carry Neptune's trident.

Neptune was early adopted as a symbol of British canal-building, which aimed to link inland industrial centres to the sea. In 1729, the statue of Neptune which dominates Durham marketplace was donated by local entrepreneur George Bowes, who supported a plan to build a canal which would link the River Wear to the Tyne, thus turning Durham into an inland port. Thomas Telford's astonishing staircase lock at Banavie, north of Fort William, the longest in Britain, took 19 years to build (1803–1822) and was called 'Neptune's Staircase'. Fisherfolk also knew all about Neptune, whose figure, sculpted by George Burn, stands on dolphins between two traditionally dressed Victorian fishwives atop the Fish Market (now a nightclub) on the Quayside of Newcastle-upon-Tyne, completed in 1880.

Sailors and dockyard workers have always been familiar with Neptune, and have even dressed up as the sea-god, often with his wife Amphitrite and other marine mythical beings—Oceanus, Triton, Nereids—in attendance. Sailors have performed the 'Order of Neptune' ritual when their ships crossed the equator since the late 16th century; some scholars have claimed that the idea was inferred from propitiation of sea divinities and monsters in the *Odyssey*.[125] The core of the ritual consisted of the arrival of Father Neptune, who would demand payment from any raw recruit who had never crossed the equator before. If the seaman refused, he would be shaved and either dunked in the sea from the yardarm or soused from a barrel.

A vivid account describes events on the Victorian Antarctic whale-ship, the Balaena from Dundee, when it crossed the equator on 25th October 1892:

> At twelve o'clock Neptune climbed over our bows and stood on the focsle-head, just as if he had come up from the bottom of the sea. He was followed by her Majesty; as she had a delicate tendency to embonpoint, it took some hauling ... to get her on deck.[126]

Neptune was played by a cockney Londoner, Able Seaman Charles Campbell, with a wig of ship's rope strands

> like the stiff ringlets of an Assyrian king. His crown was made of new tin, and glittered splendidly in the blazing sunlight; and his trident. Mrs Neptune was also a very imposing figure, and with a slight alteration of dress would have done well in the part of Mrs Gamp. Her towsy locks escaped from beneath a tin crown in beautiful confusion... she modestly tried to conceal a stubbly chin and ferocious moustache.[127]

The ancient gods processed around the main-deck to bagpipe accompaniment, before sitting in state on a special throne to dispense mock sentences to the crew (Figure 19.14). All in turn were summoned, interrogated and sentenced to lathering, ducking and shaving in a great pool, where other members of the crew disported themselves at the Sea-God's attendants, clad in seal-skins. Even Geordie, the second mate, 'a great, good natured, fair-haired Hercules, well liked by the crew', came forward blindfolded for sentencing. 'All hands being initiated into the rights and privileges of the subjects of King Neptune, the ceremony was over'.[128]

During the dockworkers' strike of 1889, a carnivalesque procession took place. An illustration from a collage published on the front cover of the *Illustrated London News* for 7th September shows two dockers dressed as Neptune and a helmeted warrior goddess, presumably Britannia; on the right one of the seated figures may be Hercules, a hero with whom dock workers, as sellers of their own muscle power, often identified.[129] The generally peaceful and festive nature of

FIGURE 19.14 Drawing reproduced from W.G. Burn Murdoch's *From Edinburgh to the Antarctic* (1894).

the public processions did much to engage public support.[130] Neptune was subsequently a regular feature of local parades in southern English seaside towns, including Eastbourne Carnival on 15th June 1933 (Figure 19.15).

But it was in the Royal Navy that the richest seam of identification with classical figures was to be found. Classical names were sometimes bestowed on ships from Elizabethan times, but the proportion of ships named after ancient Greco-Roman figures grew exponentially in the second half of the 18th century. The naval tradition holds that the man responsible was John Montagu, 4th Earl of Sandwich (1718–1792), who held the post of First Lord of the Admiralty three times between 1748 and 1792 and initiated extensive shipbuilding programmes. He was reputed to thumb through classical dictionaries picking out attractive names for new ships.[131] Certainly, of the 33 British warships involved at Trafalgar in 1805, 16 had classical names (Neptune, Agamemnon, Ajax, Orion, Minotaur, Spartiate, Mars, Bellerophon, Colossus, Achille, Polyphemus, Euryalus, Naiad, Phoebe, Sirius and Britannia); the ship art of some others (e.g. Thunderer) was classically informed. Each ship had a large, beautifully painted figurehead or, as

FIGURE 19.15 Father Neptune lights a cigarette for Miss Eastbourne, carnival by Edward George Malindine (1933), reproduced by courtesy of the National Science and Media Museum. Photograph by Edward George Malindine, part of the *Daily Herald Collection* at the National Media Museum, Bradford. Reproduced by courtesy of the National Science and Media Museum.

the shape of ships changed in the 19th century, other external artwork. In about 1890 the smaller internal decorations known as ships' badges assumed increasing importance, becoming an official feature in 1918.

Ship art illustrated the mythical or historical individual, battle or place after which it was named, and where several ships have over the centuries inherited the same name, the iconographic traditions can often be traced back certainly to the 18th and in some cases all the way to the 16th century.[132] The Royal Navy's museum at Portsmouth holds collections of ship art, including many antique unofficial badges. They gave individual sailors attached to a vessel a sense of identity. Some are straightforward portraits of famous ancient individuals with their easily recognisable accoutrements (HMS Cleopatra's badge showed her in profile in an Egyptian head-dress; Achilles, Ajax and Euryalus wore helmets; Terpsichore danced with a tambourine; Colossus has the spokes of the sun issuing from a massive head; Penelope wore a veil).[133] But some use symbolism likely to have excited discussion and explanation (HMS Argus' badge depicted a peacock; HMS Despatch the caduceus of Hermes).[134] The most sophisticated imply that sailors needed knowledge of whole mythical narratives to decode the image. For Actaeon there is substituted a stag being torn apart by hounds, for Theseus, the Minotaur and a sword, and for Ulysses, a ram and a stake.[135]

To understand why Agamemnon is represented by a manly arm holding a spear ready to be cast requires knowing that Agamemnon is the preeminent spear-thrower on the Greek side in the *Iliad*, as even Achilles acknowledges during the funeral games for Patroclus (23.890–1).[136] (Figure 19.16a) Ariadne is represented by a wreath of Dionysus' vine and a crown of stars, the constellation known as the Corona Borealis into which the god transformed his former lover (Ovid *Met.* VIII.152–.82).[137] Other badges which might encourage mariners to look up at the stars as well as retell classical myths include those of HMS Orion (a giant hunter) and HMS Venus, which simply uses the astrological symbol for this planet.[138] The hero of HMS Bellerophon flies astride the winged Pegasus, his bow strung and aimed downwards at the (unseen) Chimaera, which the viewer has to supply from his knowledge of mythology.[139] (Figure 19.1b). Dido is symbolised simply by flames, requiring an explanation of how and why she died.[140]

Many working-class people knew a good deal about Athena, Aesop, Brutus, the Gracchi, Solon, Caractacus, Boadicea, Spartacus, Prometheus, Vulcan, Hercules' labours, Atlas, the Cyclopes and Neptune. But the most impressive understanding of ancient myth and history amongst the British working class seems to have been possessed by the crews who manned the fleet of the Royal Navy, the largest organisation and bureaucracy in the British world, which employed tens of thousands of people, in the 18th century, in wartime at least, many more than any British city except London.[141] More than a third of them were Irish, and, until the Napoleonic Wars, a significant proportion had been violently press-ganged into service.[142]

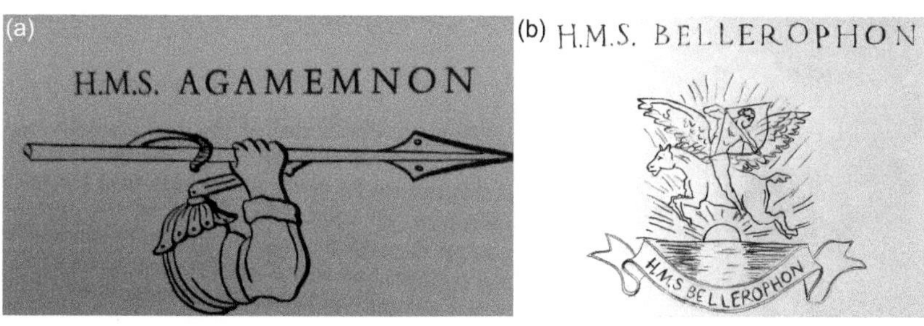

FIGURE 19.16 a and b Naval badges: H.M.S. Agamemnon and Bellerophon, © Edith Hall.

Notes

1 See Stead and Hall (2015) figure 12.1.
2 See further Youngkin (2007).
3 See, for example, William Humphrys' engraving 'Minerva Directing Study to the Attainment of Universal Knowledge', much reproduced in inexpensive late Georgian encyclopedias and on the cover of Stead and Hall (2015).
4 Minerva (1795).
5 Designed by John Ottley; British Museum MG.1053. See above p. 191.
6 See e.g. Museum of London object nos. NN10529, 33.104/9d-e and NN16045c.
7 See the oil painting on a wooden panel, from a tavern interior, now in Hertford Museum: https://artuk.org/discover/artworks/ceres-15680/view_as/grid/search/works:ceres/page/1
8 See www.theglasgowstory.com/image/?inum=TGSA05157.
9 1809 satirical print, British Museum ref. no.1851,0901.1268.
10 Clarke (1809) 10.
11 Wilberforce and Wilberforce (1843) 360.
12 Shiman (1992) 104–5.
13 Clarkson (1786) 27-30. Hall (2011a) 4–7.
14 See e.g. Aesop (1780), a rare copy of which is held in the British Library (ref. 315. aaa.6.(8)). On chapbooks see also above, p. 323, nn. 49 and 51.
15 See Hall (2018a).
16 Jardine (1843) 36.
17 Robinson (1887) 34–5.
18 Bewick (1791).
19 See Gorman (1973) 15, 42; Smith and Hyde (1989) 13–25.
20 Reproduced in Crane (1896).
21 Crane (1887) n.p.
22 See Müller-Straten, Christian (1977); Barringer (2005) 173–5 with figure 76.
23 This fable is no. 53 in the canonical numeration of Perry (1952).
24 See e.g. British Museum Coins and Medals Catalogue no. RE4p325.1948. For a depiction of ex-slaves wearing the cap in Roman funerary art, see Petersen (2006), 210–11 with fig. 133.
25 Beautifully reproduced in colour in Bentley (1968) 206. This banner also includes a Roman soldier and Grecian females representing the arts of War and Peace, respectively.
26 Thomas (2017) 380. See also Ryan (2007); Yoshino (2011).
27 Thomas (2017) 380; see 'Women Eager for Pageant', *Sunderland Daily Echo and Shipping Gazette*, 6 June 1938, 2.
28 Smedley (1929) 204.
29 Information derived from www.historicalpageants.ac.uk/featured-pageants/pageant-bury-st-edmunds-1907/.
30 Bath (1909) 17.
31 Aurelius Victor, *Book of Caesars* 39.20-21; Eutropius, *Abridgement of Roman History* 21; Orosius, *Seven Books of History Against the Pagans* 7.25.2–.4
32 Davey (1906) 6.
33 Anon. (1928) 18–24.
34 www.yorkshirefilmarchive.com/film/historical-pageant-newcastle-and-north-1931, from 3.00 minutes to 5.07.
35 Cooper (1845) 60–83.
36 In Heinrich Bullinger's drama *Lucretia und Brutus* (1533): see Raath and de Freitas (2005).
37 Payne (1818).
38 Gould (1906).

39 Gould (1913). Gould's secular ethical books for children and young adults are studied in more detail in Hall (forthcoming b).
40 Solon (1834). See also Çelikkol (2011) 101–2.
41 Kenyon (1891).
42 Freeman (1926).
43 Harvey (1931).
44 Woodhouse (1938) 208.
45 Sandiford (1988), 51.
46 Raynal (1780) 466.
47 Hunnings (2007).
48 Strickland (1822) 6.
49 For a succinct overview of the slave trade in the French colonies, see Geggus (2001).
50 Hall (2011a) 18 and figure 1.8.
51 Oldfield (1992).
52 Dresser (2007) 79.
53 A connection stressed in Walvin (1986).
54 On the ambivalent equation drawn by the Chartists between the British working class and black slaves, see Mays (2001).
55 Jones (1857) 5.
56 Jones (1857) 6.
57 Hall (2010b), 44–9. He had long taken an interest in Indian affairs. His poem, which he had written in prison, was a commentary on the rise and fall of civilisations, set against an Indian background. He republished it in the autumn of 1857 'as a prophecy of the Indian Mutiny' (Saville [1952] 65).
58 For the ancient sources on the slave revolt led by Eunus at Enna, in central Sicily, see Diodorus Siculus 34/35.2.1–48 and Strabo 6.2.6. There is today a large bronze statue of Eunus ('Euno') breaking his chains beneath the walls of the Castello di Lombardia in Enna.
59 Ward (1887) 332.
60 Clarke (1918) 16–22. Thanks to Dr Natalia Tsoumpra for helping us to track a copy down.
61 Malcolm (1984) 115–6. Prometheus was a central figure in Russian revolutionary and subsequently Soviet classical historiography and creative arts. see Rubinsohn (1987).
62 Hall (2018d).
63 Epstein (1982) 90–3; Gurney (2014) 578.
64 *The Times*, Saturday, 12th April (1873) 6.
65 Mahaffy (1898) 13. There is an excellent, lively account of Mahaffy's contradictory views and personality by Stanford and McDowell (1971).
66 Wilde (1793) 70–2. Wilde, himself from a relatively lowly background as the son of a tobacconist, is outraged that Paine's intellect and style of communication have found an admirer in the eminent schoolmaster, Dr. Samuel Parr.
67 See www.classicsandclass.info/product/114/.
68 Jones (1898) 10–16.
69 Hall (1898).
70 See Ziolkowski (2000) 112–13.
71 This comparison was brought to its most fulsome expression in Edgar Quinet's dramatic poem *Prométhée* (1838), where Prometheus is liberated by two Archangels and converts to Christianity.
72 Hall (2016b) 517–18.
73 Hall and Macintosh (2005) 209–10.
74 See above pp. 396 and below 448.
75 See Hall (2011b).

76 The only known existing copy is held in the rare-book collection of the Newberry Library, Chicago. See Bayne (2004).
77 Shelley (1820b).
78 Quoted from the *Reading Mercury* of 1819 by Brain (1904) 84–5; see Hall (1997) 288.
79 Shelley (1820b) 96.
80 Goodwyn Barmby (1842a) 1–2.
81 Goodwyn Barmby (1842a) 7–9.
82 Goodwyn Barmby (1842a) 9.
83 Goodwyn Barmby (1842a) 9–11, 18–20, 23.
84 Goodwyn Barmby (1842b) 30–2.
85 Goodwyn Barnby (1842c) 38–9, 48.
86 Goodwyn Barmby (1842c) 52.
87 See https://artuk.org/discover/artworks/still-the-race-of-hero-spirits-pass-the-torch-from-hand-to-hand-58750/view_as/grid/search/makers:walter-crane-18451915/page/1 and https://conwayhall.org.uk/the-ethical-church-queensway-bayswater/.
88 Crane (1911) 223.
89 Barnett (1898); Gulick (1899).
90 'The Socialist Ideal as a New Inspiration in Art', reproduced in Crane (1911) 82–101 was written for *The International Review*, when it appeared under the editorship of Dr. Rudolph Broda, as the English edition of *Documents du Progrès*.
91 Crane (1911) 99.
92 There is a strange amalgam of a Promethean torch-bearer and a flying Mercury on the 1930 banner of the Dublin Electrical Trades Union (although of course Dublin was no longer part of Britain): Loftus (1978) no. 81, reproduced there as fig. 33 on p. 56.
93 Gould (1932).
94 On Hephaestus as 'working-class' god in ancient art and literature, see Hall (2018i).
95 Measom (1861) 320.
96 See the photograph by Albert Coe, 'Detail on the entrance to Green Lane Works, Green Lane, originally the premises of Henry Hoole and Thomas Nicholson', ref. no. v03570 on the website www.picturesheffield.com/.
97 Loftus (1978) no. 3, illustrated as figure 6 on page 7.
98 Anon. (1849).
99 Neville (1976).
100 'A Lesson for "Labour"', *Punch* 105, 23rd September 1893.
101 See also the war cartoon by Frank Brangwyn, published in 1915 by the *Daily Chronicle*, viewable online at www.loc.gov/item/2003675364/. *Punch* used other ancient figures to represent the British working class, including Briareus and Procrustes and the Titans who fought the upper-class Olympian gods. He resents the current activities of the Titans called Bad-Temper and Blunder, who have 'corrupted our morals, / And taught us "Boycotting," and "Strikes," and "Lock-outs," and all sorts of mad quarrels.'
102 Saville (1952) 230.
103 Linebaugh and Rediker (2000).
104 Linebaugh and Rediker (2000) 61.
105 Carlyle (1843) 19, 25.
106 Nicholas the Fisherman (1794) 7–8, 13, 14, 30.
107 Hunt (1983) 104; Blanshard (2005) xi–xviii.
108 Spence (1794) 72.
109 Prothero (2013) 101.
110 Ravenhill-Johnson (2014) 174. Leighton's athlete is now in the Tate Gallery and can be viewed on its website: www.tate.org.uk/art/artworks/leighton-an-athlete-wrestling-with-a-python-n01754.
111 See further James (2015) 149 with references.

112 Ravenhill-Johnson (2013) 174. On the toned physique as a sign of moral superiority and its cultural colonisation by the British upper classes, see James in Ravenhill-Johnson (2013). There is an excellent colour reproduction of the banner in Gorman (1973) 130.
113 Henderson (2015).
114 Daley (1911) 80–3.
115 Anderson (1873) 1–10.
116 Cuthbertson (n.d.) 14–25, 29–30, 35–6, 97–103. Anderson was influenced by *Cassell's Popular Educator*, and taught himself French, German, Spanish and Italian. Upwardly mobile, in 1880 he left railway work, having been appointed Assistant Librarian at the Edinburgh University Library, which was followed by the post of Secretary to the Philosophical Institution. He did not retain any loyalty to his natal class and moved politically to the right. There is also a strong presence of Classics in his poems 'Two Brown Eyes' and 'A Night Vision in the Colosseum at Rome' (Anderson (1912) 154–5, 201–5). The image reproduced here is taken from Anderson (1912) opposite xxiv.
117 Anderson (1873) 1.
118 Cuthbertson (n.d.) 49.
119 'The Pocket Atlas' by Bernard Patridge, *Punch*, 21st April 1926.
120 Hyman (1966) 3–4.
121 Saltzmann (1994) 109.
122 BL Add. Ms. 42904, Lord Chamberlain's Plays, vol. XL.
123 Vernon (1977) 120.
124 See e.g. Bass (2011); Freedman (1995).
125 Beck (1973) 117; Lydenberg (1977); Richardson (1977) 155.
126 Murdoch (1894) 101.
127 Murdoch (1894) 102.
128 Murdoch (1894) 107.
129 See also Tillett (1931) 154.
130 Fraser (1999) 77–8.
131 Gardiner (1968) 171; Coleman (2001) 18.
132 Weightman (1957) 319, 2.
133 Weightman (1957) 122, 27, 204, 38, 414, 128, 334.
134 Weightman (1957) 63, 165.
135 Weightman (1957) 28, 415, 438.
136 Weightman (1957) 13.
137 Weightman (1957) 65.
138 Weightman (1957) 319.
139 Weightman (1957) 85.
140 Weightman (1957) 177.
141 Kinkel (2018) 12, 21.
142 Estimates for pressed sailors in the 1770s used to be place at around 50%, but Dancy (2015) 14, after reviewing muster books of 1793 to 1801 from Portsmouth, Chatham and Plymouth, argues that by this decade, at any rate, the figure was only 16%.

20
SHOEMAKER CLASSICS

Mechanisation virtually wiped out the profession of the shoemaker, and thus the phenomenon of the 'learned cobbler'.[1] By the late 1850s the closing machine, which took over the skilled task of sewing the sole to the upper shoe, had become widespread. Anti-machine shoemakers demonstrated and struck work in Stafford, Nottingham and Kendal in 1858–1859.[2] The loss of the traditional 'gentle craft', conducted jovially by the wizened sons of Crispin, the Roman patron saint of shoemakers persecuted for his Christianity under Diocletian, was felt deeply in communities that coalesced around the cobbler's shop. The Baptist minister and hymn-writer, William Edward Winks (1842–1926), wrote a book entitled *The Lives of Illustrious Shoemakers* (1882). Due to the use of machinery in the shoemaking process, 'the old-fashioned Shoemaker, with his leathern apron and hands redolent of wax, has almost disappeared'. Furthermore,

> There can be no doubt that the Cobbler, sitting at his stall and working with awl and hammer and last, will never again be the conspicuous figure in social life that he was wont to be in times gone by.[3]

Winks' title echoes Plutarch's *Lives of Illustrious Men*, as had the 1768 biography of a classically trained beggar we met previously (p. 104): 'Both in ancient times and modern', Winks explains,

> in the Old World and in the New, a rare interest has been felt in Shoemakers, as a class, on account of their remarkable intelligence and the large number of eminent men who have risen from their ranks.[4]

He knew that Plato's Socrates used shoemaker exempla frequently, leading Callicles to protest, 'By the gods! You simply don't let up on your continual

DOI: 10.4324/9781315446608-24

talk of shoemakers and cleaners, cooks and doctors, as if our discussion were about them!' (*Gorgias* 491a). Callicles' objection to shoemakers is because they work for their living and are not leisure-class. But Xenophon informs us that Socrates would debate with teenaged aristocratic youths, who avoided the rowdy market-place, in leather-works just outside it (*Memorabilia* IV.2.1). Simon the Shoemaker was a significant Socratic disciple who composed no fewer than 33 'leathern' dialogues (Diogenes Laertius II.122), supposedly written from notes he had made on shoe-leather.[5] His house and a cup inscribed with his name have been excavated and are indeed just beyond the agora boundary-stone.[6] Another shoemaker, Philiscus, listened attentively to Aristotle's *Protrepticus* when Crates of Thebes, the teacher of the Stoic Zeno, read it out to him.[7]

Pre-mechanical shoemaking was a sedentary trade, neither exhausting nor noisy. Its practitioners, who were often open-minded Nonconformists, could listen or converse while they worked, just as Philiscus could listen to Crates. Apprentices and errand boys were sometimes charged with reading journals aloud; poems could be memorised, recited or composed. Cobblers were proverbially good conversationalists and often considered to be the village's sages; where several worked together in an urban garret, ideas and information could be discussed. Cobblers' customers came from every social class, made wide-ranging conversations and helped produce the stereotype of the British cobbler as a working-class radical intellectual,[8] even if in practice some, such as William Gifford, embraced conservative politics.

Pliny, Apelles and James Woodhouse

According to Pliny the Elder, a lowly shoemaker once pointed out that the famous painter, Apelles, had inaccurately rendered a sandal.[9] Apelles corrected his work. But when the shoemaker continued to criticise him, Apelles shut him down: 'Sutor, ne ultra crepidam' ('Shoemaker, don't extend yourself beyond sandals'). Classically educated writers across the English-speaking globe often quoted these words to police boundaries of expertise, usually in order to expose another's ignorance.[10] But ambitious workers including shoemakers deleted the negative '*ne*', and used the slogan to promote progressive individualism: 'Sutor ultra crepidam', 'Shoemaker: more than sandals!'

The first to use it was the 'Poetical Shoemaker' James Woodhouse (Figure 20.1), baptised in 1735 at Rowley Regis, a few miles west of Birmingham. The eldest son of yeoman farmers, Woodhouse was educated until the age of seven or eight, probably in the local free school.[11] Woodhouse dedicated early poems to his first patron, the poet and landscape gardener William Shenstone (1714–1763), who lent him English translations of the Classics in the 1760s.[12] Pliny's doctored adage first occurs as the epigraph to 'Epistle to Shenstone, In the Shades', written in 1784 and printed in his 1803 collection *Norbury Park*, 'Sutor ultra crepidam'.[13] It is a bold start to a bold essay demonstrating that

FIGURE 20.1 'Mr [James] Woodhouse the Poetical Cobbler', 1765, reproduced courtesy of the Wellcome Collection. Etching, 1765, reproduced courtesy of the Wellcome Collection.

beauty is not the preserve of the rich, classically educated and powerful, heralding Woodhouse's later radicalism:

> Know, boasting Bard! a Rustic may be found,
> Who never trod on Learning's labour'd ground—
> Ne'er studied Nature's charms, in classic school,
> Yet tries her beauties, not by line and rule,
> But inbred taste and feeling, which decide,
> With more precision than pedantic pride.[14]

Woodhouse, apparently responding to a critical fellow poet, pitches his inborn taste and feeling against classical pedantry. The learned languages are not required to describe a fish's scales, the plume of birds, or other-worldly insects:[15]

> No vegetable's cloth'd in leaves of Greek;
> No insects, birds, or beasts, in Hebrew speak …

The list of things unnecessary to 'beauty, music, love and language', grows:

> Nor needs he skill Horatian verse to scan,
> Or [sic] old Homer's epic plan—
> To fathom Plato's philosophic sense,
> Or try the powr's of Tully's eloquence.[16]

This is a *recusatio*—a description of what an author claims *not* to be doing which takes the form of doing it. Woodhouse is confident in talking about ancient authors he cannot read in the original; after all, Plato had become widely available in the English edition of Madame Dacier's famous abridgement, frequently reprinted since 1701, while translations of Homer, Cicero and Horace abounded. Indeed, William Popple's *Ars Poetica* (1753) was sold by Robert Dodsley (1704–1764), Woodhouse's next patron, who kept a successful booksellers at Tully's Head, London. Woodhouse, also a working-class poet, had originally been apprenticed to a weaver, but set up the bookshop after publishing *A Muse in Livery, or, The Footman's Miscellany* (1732), written while working as footman to 'a person of quality at Whitehall' (John, Viscount Lonsdale).[17]

In 1764, Woodhouse's *Poems on Sundry Occasions* by a 'journeyman shoemaker' was printed by subscription, and an expanded edition was printed two years later. Both contain the rhapsodic encomium that won over Shenstone, 'An Elegy to William Shenstone Esq, of the Lessowes': 'Arcadian shades!/Where dwells Apollo'; classical references proliferate: daffodils line the stream's bank, and, 'like Narcissus, fondly pine away'.[18] Fragments of Arcadian poetry are poetically strewn around the garden, in English, Latin and Greek:

> To read them ALL would be my humble pride;
> But only part is granted, part denyed:
> I feel no GRECIAN, feel no ROMAN fire;
> I only share the BRITISH muse's lyre;
> And that stern penury dares almost deny;
> For manual toils alone my wants supply:
> The awl and pen by turns possess my hand,
> And worldly cares, e'en now, the muse's hour demand.

Woodhouse's assured handling of classical mythology culminates in his address to Shenstone, as his Maecenas (Virgil's, Propertius' and Horace's patron).[19]

In 'The Lessowes, a poem', a virtuosic marathon of rhyming sycophancy, Woodhouse returns to these classical inscriptions. Shenstone has translated one from Horace for him, and now, Woodhouse claims, he can forget the dreariness of a worker's life and inhabit the garden of poetry, as Horace tended his beloved country estate.[20] The imagined act of Horatian translation is at the centre of this idyllic 18th-century portrait of class division: educational imbalance distinguished master from grateful servant, who now understands that a 'good life' does not require great wealth after all.[21]

Other patrons were Elizabeth Montagu (whom, as Vanessa/Scintilla, he repaid with vitriolic satire in his *The Life and Lucubrations of Crispinus Scriblerus* (1814), first published after both their deaths) and the promoter of men of 'natural genius', Joseph Spence.[22] By around 1780, Woodhouse was running his own bookseller's shop and learned to despise Montagu.[23] But in a poem about Hannah, his wife (née Fletcher), whom he consistently addresses as 'Daphne', Woodhouse praises her beauty, laments her psychological sensitivity and compares her toil with Ixion's:

Ixion like, her fate she moans,
Whose wheel rolls ceaseless round;
While hollow sighs, and doleful groans,
Fill all the dark profound.

For oft she sighs, and oft she weeps,
And hangs her pensive head;
While blood her furrow'd fingers steeps,
And stains the passing thread.[24]

This is a capricious translation of a worker's suffering into a cultural language that their master-class readers must understand.[25] But there is more to Woodhouse's poems than might have occurred to readers of superior class.[26] In comparison to being bound eternally to a fiery wheel, Daphne's pricked finger seems negligible. Yet there is something disturbing about being asked to find humour in the image of Daphne's bleeding fingers,[27] which also implies that labouring women's misery is eternal, the task forever 'undone'.[28]

Woodhouse developed into an evangelical Methodist and defiant class rebel,[29] and elsewhere reveals a commitment to social justice, of which such ambiguities might be early manifestations. Christmas suggests that a passage attacking the Prince Regent in *Crispinus Scriblerus* indicates Woodhouse's 'social-levelling notions, tinged with an antimonarchical strain'.[30] The volume carries three epigraphs. In the first, he crowns himself 'Unpension'd Poet-Laureat of the Poor'. In the third he quotes Samuel Johnson's pithy epigram about Heraclitus, in turn inspired by Diogenes Laertius' account of his intolerance of stupidity (IX.1–3, 16):

Begone, ye blockheads! Heraclitus cries,
And leave my labours to the truly wise.

Woodhouse encountered these lines in Johnson's own epigraph to the much reprinted 208th and final edition of *The Rambler* in 1752.[31] Johnson's defiant epigraph would have attracted the now cantankerous Woodhouse by marshalling an establishment figure and the allusion to Greek philosophy in his cause. He turns the weapons of the establishment back on themselves.

But his second epigraph reuses the subverted exemplum from Pliny, proudly establishing him as 'Sutor Ultra Crepidam'. As Van-Hagen argues, each epigraph makes a separate 'claim to singularity: poet-satirist, (ex-)shoemaker and philosopher'.[32] Woodhouse, like Stephen Duck before him, had transitioned from obscurity to the public sphere as a working-class intellectual. But he posed a more serious threat because he struggled against the system of patronage, positioning himself explicitly as a representative of the poor with access to the public, an exemplar of meritocratic success.

'Small profits do great things'

Another ambitious son of Crispin was James Lackington (1746–1815) (Figure 20.2). Born in Wellington, Somerset, to a journeyman shoemaker and a local weaver, Lackington was from the start an entrepreneurial soul. His father was a drunkard and his family so poor that he left home at the age of ten to become a street pie-merchant, after observing the deficient sales techniques of an

FIGURE 20.2 Frontispiece of James Lackington's *Memoirs* (1791).

elderly pie hawker, whom he put out of business.[33] Four years later he took up his father's trade, becoming apprentice to a shoemaker in nearby Taunton. In 1768 he moved to Bristol, where he met his cobbling partner John Jones. What money they did not spend on women went on buying second-hand books. In 1773, they relocated to London. Following the death of his wife, Nancy, his grandfather died in the same year, leaving a legacy of £10 with which they opened their first bookshop in East London. They sold books they had collected over the years, supplemented by newly purchased second-hand stock bought with an interest-free loan of £5 from local Methodists. Within a year they were in profit and moved to central London. The 30-year-old Lackington spotted a different retail method by purchasing vast amounts of books to sell as cheaply as would still turn a profit and only accepting cash rather than offering credit. The doors of his 'chariot' (or carriage) proclaimed, 'Small profits do great things'. This opened up reading to a new, poorer demographic. Lackington was proud to be 'instrumental in diffusing that general desire for READING, now so prevalent among the inferior orders of society'.[34]

He became hooked on books in his early 20s, when living in Bristol. He first learned to read as an apprentice, 'in order to participate in the spontaneous debates on religious doctrine' arising in the workshop after the master's two boys converted to Methodism. He paid the master's youngest son three-halfpence a week for spelling lessons, which were given in the dark after bedtime.[35] His classical reading was largely of ancient philosophers in translation: 'I was taught to bear the unavoidable evils attending humanity, and to supply all my wants by contracting or restraining my desires'.[36] This directly affected his lifestyle:

> The account of Epicurus living in his garden, at the expense of about a halfpenny per day, and that when he added a little cheese to his bread on particular occasions, he considered it as a luxury, filled me with raptures. From that moment I began to live on bread and tea, and for a considerable time did not partake of any other viands.[37]

By cutting expenses he could purchase more books, to purge his mind and make it 'more susceptible of intellectual pleasures'.[38] The texts that helped him were 'Plato on the Immortality of the Soul [*Phaedo*], Plutarch's Morals [*Moralia*], Seneca's Morals, Epicurus's Morals, the Morals of Confucius the Chinese Philosopher, and a few others'. He then explains that he 'received more real benefit from reading and studying them and Epictetus, than from all other books that I had read before, or have ever read since that time'.[39] This catalogue of old moralists, especially Stoics and Epicureans, is not unusual for working-class intellectuals in communities where the dominant Anglican moral code was challenged by Dissenters. Lackington was attracted by ancient celebrations of abstemiousness and frugality. At a structural level, this played according to the rules of capitalism, helping to suppress competition and desire for great wealth among the lower classes.

Lackington reports that 'A friend once taught me the adage, (be not offended 'tis the only scrap of Latin I shall give you) "Ne Sutor ultra crepidam". But the event has proved it otherwise'.[40] The frontispiece to his memoir, which consists of a deep-browed portrait captioned 'J. Lackington, who a few years since, began Business with five Pounds, now sells one Hundred Thousand Volumes Annually', bears the legend: 'Sutor Ultra Crepidam Feliciter ausus' (See Figure 20.2). This inverts the meaning of the original by dropping the 'ne', and adding two words, 'feliciter ausus', meaning 'The shoemaker who successfully dared [to rise] above the sandal'.

Lackington's shop, or 'Temple of the Muses', (Figure 20.3) was situated on Finsbury Square (now in EC2, in the London Borough of Islington). In 1810 the impressively domed and flag-topped building's façade boasted that it was 'the cheapest booksellers in the world'.[41] With a store front over 40m long, it became one of the capital's major tourist attractions, but it was also a key site in the democratisation of literature, with 'lounging rooms' in which people could read for free, as well as buy the cheap shabbier books on the higher levels. As a schoolboy, John Keats used to visit it and it was there that he met his publishers, John Taylor and James Augustus Hessey, who worked there under Lackington.[42] The name and décor presented the Temple of the Muses as a classical shrine to learning. Books could be paid for with minted tokens, bearing its eccentric

FIGURE 20.3 James Lackington's 'Temple of the Muses', drawn by Thomas Shepherd and engraved by W. Wallis, reproduced from Stead's personal collection.

FIGURE 20.4 James Lackington's trading token, Courtesy of Bell House Educational charity, Dulwich.

owner's portrait on one side and a classical figure on the other (on this one [Figure 20.4] it is Fama, or Fame), to encourage further spending. Lackington retired to Budleigh Salterton, Devon, where he built 'Ash Villa'; having first heard John Wesley speak in the early 1770s, he spent £2,000 on building the Temple Methodist Church in 1812, a repayment with considerable interest of the loan of £5 in 1774.[43]

The ultracrepidarian translator of Juvenal

Lackington was no revolutionary, but his subversion of the classical motto, like Woodhouse's, reflects the defiant spirit of early 19th-century Britain. Only a few years later, the motto was mobilised against a former shoemaker named William Gifford (1756–1826) (Figure 20.5). Now a famous literary critic and editor of the Tory literary journal, *The Quarterly Review*, in an 1819 open letter from the radical Whig writer of Dissenting background, William Hazlitt, Gifford was dubbed an 'ultracrepidarian critic'. The letter begins

> Sir, You have an ugly trick of saying what is not true of any one you do not like; and it will be the object of this letter to cure you if it. You say what you please of others: it is time you were told what you are.

FIGURE 20.5 William Gifford (1756–1826) by John Hoppner (1810), reproduced courtesy of the National Portrait Gallery, London. © National Portrait Gallery, London.

Hazlitt calls Gifford 'a little person, but a considerable cat's-paw', because he has become the willing instrument of the Tory right.[44] He is the 'Government critic' and thus the supporter of the interests of the landed gentry and the Anglican clergy—in modern terms, a class traitor.

Leigh Hunt had long been an outspoken enemy of Gifford, rejecting him from his *Feast of Poets* (1814). He released a poem called *Ultra-Crepidarius: A Satire on William Gifford* (1823). The middle-class Hunt avoids stressing Gifford's earlier lowliness: 'Nothing can be more foreign from my purpose than to treat it with contempt for its own sake … What are called low origins and high origins are equally, to me, matters of indifference'.[45] Hunt attacks him for 'treating the community from which [he] sprung with scorn, and helping to deliver them into the hands of their taskmasters',[46] along with his misogyny and party politics. In *The Baviad* (1810), Gifford lampoons the disability of the much-loved 'Della Cruscan' poet Mary Robinson, who suffered from rheumatism in her final years:

> See Robinson forget her state, and move
> On crutches towards the grave, to "Light o' Love".[47]

Robinson had given up her stage career when the Prince Regent had pestered her amorously. Long after she turned her coat from Radical Whig to Tory, like Wordsworth, Hunt defended her on egalitarian grounds.[48]

The 'ultracrepidating' Gifford seized the most rigorous classical education available, and rose to a position from which he sniped at almost everything that moved. The son of a sporadically employed seaman, plumber, house-painter and glazier, Gifford was born in Ashburton, Devon. Until he reached the age of seven, Gifford's father was absent, having fled to sea after inciting a riot in a Methodist chapel, but his mother managed to send him to school, where he learned to read. Gifford's father died of drink;[49] and he was orphaned at 12 when his mother followed her husband to the grave the following year.

Gifford's godfather sent him to drive the plough. After a day, he swore never to return to it. He was not cut out for farm work, being small and having been injured in the chest as a child. He was tried out in a store-house, then found a place on a Torbay fishing boat, before working as a ship-boy on a coaster. Fortunately, family friends discovered his plight, returned him to his native village and (importantly) to school.[50] He wanted to become a teacher, and at 15 was more than qualified, but instead he was apprenticed to a Presbyterian shoemaker. He loved algebra, but lacked writing materials; this developed his memory, since at work he used a blunted awl to make only the most essential notes from concealed books on a thin scrap of leather.[51]

His master confiscated the algebra books he subsidised by reciting poems he composed. But a surgeon named William Cookesley showed an interest in the cobbler's talented apprentice. He drew up a subscription to buy out Gifford's remaining apprenticeship for six pounds and send him back to school.[52] In two years and two months he was declared 'fit for university'; his schoolmaster, Mr Smerdon, once Gifford had shown an aptitude for Latin and Greek, set him to translation:

> I do not know a single school-book, of which I did not render some portion into English verse. Among others, JUVENAL engaged my attention, or rather my master's, and I translated the tenth satire for a holyday task. Mr Smerdon was much pleased with this, (I was not undelighted with it myself;) and as I was now fond of the author, he easily persuaded me to proceed with him, and I translated in succession the third, the fourth, the twelfth, and I think the eighth satires.[53]

Cookesley helped him find a subsidised position at Exeter College, Oxford, and he also did some tutoring. In 1781 a subscription was put out for his verse translation of the satires of Juvenal and Persius, which made his name when published in 1802. It became the primary route of access to Roman satire for English readers for over a century. Its commercial edition was published in 1803, a second edition following in 1804 and its popularity exploded when it was printed alongside a prose version in Bohn's Classical Library (1852). It was repackaged once more in Joseph Malaby Dent and Ernest Rhys' Everyman edition (1902). A shoemaker who leapt across class boundaries but despised his class, Gifford might have been surprised that his vibrant, learned and accessible translations opened up Roman satire to generations of non-classically educated readers.

Dissenting shoemakers

James Lackington's social ascent was aided by Methodism: Samuel Bradburn (1751–1816), who worked as a cobbler's apprentice, converted to Methodism and became a celebrated, sensationally charismatic preacher. He was ordained in 1792 and made President of the Methodist Conference (1799–1800). Yet he was fond of 'company' and 'the ways of the world', i.e. women, booze and gambling. From 1802 to 1803 he was suspended from ministry for drunkenness.[54] He had been raised by an Anglican father, a former gardener tricked into the army by an unscrupulous recruiting officer. His devoted Welsh wife followed him to Flanders and in 1748, where Samuel was born 3 years later, 1 of 13 children.

He spent his first twelve years on the Rock of Gibraltar, where he received a fortnight's schooling. His father withdrew him because the fees were raised from a penny a week: 'The education of one of the greatest modern pulpit orators cost only twopence!'[55] Sometimes he felt keenly his want of education:

> I have read and written much this month, but sadly feel the want of a friend to direct my studies. All with whom I have any intimacy, know nothing of my meaning when I speak of my ignorance. They praise my sermons, and consider me a prodigy of learning; and yet what do I know? a little Latin, a little philosophy, history, divinity, and a little of many things, all of which serves to convince me of my own ignorance![56]

Where did he learn that Latin? He probably taught himself when apprenticed to the shoemaker Peter Haslam in Chester, from about the age of 13 to 21, enthused by his religious awakening.

Blanshard, Bradburn's biographer, explains that his subject had 'often been designated the "Demosthenes of Methodism"'; since Demosthenes had become a 'generic term in oratorical science', he approved of the title. But Blanshard thought that the 'Cicero of Methodism' might have been an improvement.[57] For although Bradburn possessed the 'majestic dignity' of Demosthenes, he lacked the Athenian's moroseness. Full of the 'sarcastic pleasantry' reported in Plutarch's *Life of Cicero* (5, 38, 41), Bradburn, Blanshard reports, exercised his oratorical duty full of smiles and jest, like the Roman, but unlike Cicero, he avoided tears when orating.[58]

Samuel Drew (1765–1833) (Figure 20.6) was the son of a Cornish farmer in St. Austell and sometime 'streamer for tin'.[59] He was put to work in the fields at seven. Taught to read by his self-educated mother, like his father a Wesleyan Methodist, he also proved a tireless self-educator, whose metaphysical writings later earned

FIGURE 20.6 Samuel Drew (1765–1833) Methodist preacher and metaphysician, reproduced by courtesy of National Galleries of Scotland. © National Galleries of Scotland.

him the soubriquet 'The English Plato'. At 10 he was apprenticed to a leather-worker; by 22 he was running his own cobbler's shop.[60] He inspired other workmen; his sister, who was married to a shoemaker, witnessed one of her husband's co-workers, 'emulous of Mr Drew's fame', quizzing a visiting gentleman on Greek and mathematics, which he had been 'puzzling himself about' on his own.[61] Drew had become known as a sharp-witted debater and a fount of knowledge. His master's specialism was saddling and he also offered leather bookbinding services. The shop was frequented by the local middle classes, who had horses and furnished Drew with a supply of books. He listened to disputes between local Calvinists and Arminians, and kept his reading up-to-date;[62] this cobbler's shop was, as often, a site of knowledge exchange conducive to autodidacticism.

According to his sister, he once hunted for Plato's *Phaedo* across Cornwall, but was disappointed by its contents. His search brought him to a bookseller's in Truro, where 'the singular incongruity between his unclassical appearance and the book for which he inquired' attracted the attention of some military officers.

> One of them, who thought him a fair subject for a joke, said, "Mr. —— [the bookseller] has not got Plato, my man; but here (presenting him with a child's Primer) is a book he thinks likely to be more serviceable to you; and, as you do not seem to be overstocked with cash, I'll make you a present of it".[63]

In his shabby clothing, Drew appeared too low-class to have an interest in classical philosophy. Yet he was destined to write a book that was long considered definitive: *An Original Essay on the Immateriality and Immortality on the Human Soul*, which was widely lauded and reprinted many times on both sides of the Atlantic, already reaching five English editions by his death in 1833. He remained a modest man, however, conscious of his lack of classical languages, and afraid of debating with university-trained academics who might flummox him with the Greek, Latin or French derivation of their terms.[64]

A third Dissenter among the shoemaker classicists was William Carey (1761–1834), who grew up in Paulerspury, ten miles south of Northampton. His father, originally a weaver, became a parish clerk and schoolmaster in 1767, which provided the young Carey with access to books. At the age of 12, we are told, he picked up a copy of Thomas Dyche's *Vocabularium Latiale: or, a Latin Vocabulary* (1709) and memorised it.[65] This achievement did not go unnoticed by his family, but grammar school or college was too costly, and the local schools, including his father's, could offer no classical training.

At 14 he became bound apprentice to Clarke Nichols, a shoemaker in the hamlet of Piddington, where a copy of the New Testament came into his possession. Some say he embarked upon teaching himself Greek under the guidance of a local vicar; others maintain that his instructor was a classically educated man from Kidderminster, who had fallen on hard times and become a weaver.[66] Social mobility is a two-way street. After a year, Carey's indentures were cancelled on account of the death of his master, and he moved to the workshop of a Mr Old as a journeyman shoemaker. He is said to have been so intent on learning his Latin, Greek and Hebrew that he could not produce a pair of boots that matched each other.[67]

In 1783 Carey was baptised by the theologian John Ryland (1753–1825), son of the renowned Dissenting educationalist John Collett Ryland. He began to preach to a Baptist congregation and was frequently visited in his shop by the shepherd turned Evangelical preacher and Biblical scholar, Reverend Thomas Scott (1747–1821). After years bent over his last and reading the scriptures in their original languages, in 1785 Carey became the pastor of a Baptist church at Moulton and a local schoolmaster. But poverty meant he could not give up awl-work: 'Once a fortnight Carey might be seen walking eight or ten miles to Northampton, with his wallet full of shoes on his shoulder, and then returning home with a fresh supply of leather'.[68] It was after moving to Calcutta as a missionary that he was able to capitalise fully on his linguistic talents, being appointed Professor of Sanskrit, Marathi and Bengali at the East India Company's Fort William College, where he translated the New and Old Testaments into six Indian languages and compiled three dictionaries.[69]

A Chartist cobbler

We have previously encountered Thomas Cooper as a 'seditious classicist' who turned Leicester into a Chartist stronghold (pp. 287–9), but his first employment was as a cobbler's apprentice. Born in Leicester, the illegitimate son of a dyer, and raised by his widowed mother in Gainsborough, Lincolnshire, Cooper showed early signs of intellect, reciting from 'Aesop's fables' at the age of three.[70] He won a Bluecoat scholarship to a local school,[71] and in 1816 began teaching the younger children at a boys' day school, in exchange for a more advanced syllabus.[72] Here he encountered books including 'Mavor's British Plutarch, and the abridgment of Goldsmith's Histories of England, Greece and Rome'.[73] His activist awakening happened when he overheard conversations at a brush-makers, who 'were the most determined politicians'; they lent him the radical weekly *The News* and criticised Castlereagh, and the Prince Regent 'until I hated the Liverpool Ministry, and its master, bitterly, and believed that the sufferings of the poor were chiefly attributable to them'.[74]

On 10th June 1820, at 15, he joined an old school friend as an apprentice in a cobblers' garret. His master, Joseph Clarke, introduced him to Shakespeare, Byron, Burns and Bloomfield.[75] He made something of a name for himself as a reciter of poetry, but he wanted to become a writer himself, and began a regime of self-education. He was inspired by a life of Samuel Lee (1783–1852), Regius Professor of Hebrew at Cambridge.[76] It was published in the *Imperial Magazine*, a popular educational journal edited by none other than Samuel Drew.[77] Lee, Cooper reflected,

> had been apprenticed to a carpenter at eleven years old, had bought Ruddiman's Latin Rudiments on an old book-stall for a trifle, and learnt the whole book by heart; and had stepped on, from Corderius's Colloquies to Caesar, and from Caesar to Virgil, and so on; and had learnt to read Greek, Hebrew, and Syriac, all from self-tuition, by the time he was five or six and twenty.[78]

Cooper secured cheap access to a supply of books via a kindly stationer, who allowed him to borrow, for a paltry sum, from a circulating library she ran from her shop.[79] Cooper began—in imitation of Lee—with Ruddiman's *Rudiments*, memorizing most of the book, as he says, 'notes and all'. Every Sunday evening he practised his Hebrew letters, copying from Israel Lyons' small Hebrew Grammar (much reprinted, but the first edition was dated 1735), which he found on a stall. 'I got hold of a Greek Grammar ... but did not master it earnestly, because I thought it better to keep close to the Latin for some time'.[80] 'Historical reading', he explains, 'or the grammar of some language, or translation, was my first employment on week-day mornings, whether I rose at three or four, until seven o'clock, when I sat down to the stall'.[81] In the winter, he would read standing up, wrapped up in his mother's old red cloak, 'and frequently kept my feet moving to secure warmth, or prevent myself from falling asleep'.[82] They could not afford to light the fire before his mother was up.

His confidence and competence as a Latinist improved steadily over the next two or three years, when he also recited declensions and conjugations at work.

> In the spring of 1826, after getting through Valpy's Delectus, and a part of Stewart's "Cornelius Nepos", and also a part of Justin, but somewhat clumsily, with the help of Ainsworth's Dictionary, I commenced Caesar, and sped on well, so that by the time I had reached the third book, "De Bello Gallico", I found myself able to read page after page, with scarcely more than a glance, now and then, at the dictionary.[83]

Cooper gives us a rare thing indeed, the Latin reading record of a self-educating worker and his thrill on achieving fluency:

> It was about five in the morning, the sun shone brightly; and as I lifted my eyes from the classic page of the great conqueror of the Gauls and Helvetians, and they fell on the mouldering pile called the "Old Hall"—part of which had been a stronghold of John of Gaunt, and of one of the barons in the reign of Stephen—I said to myself, "I have made a greater conquest, without the aid of a living teacher, than the proudest warrior ever made—for I have conquered and entered into the possession of a new mind". And that seems to me the truest expression, when you find you can read a language you could not read before.

After Caesar, Cooper fell in love with Virgil's *Aeneid.*

In 1828 Cooper opened a school in Lincoln, which was 'eagerly patronised by the poor',[84] who revered his prodigious learning. After a year he had 'an average attendance of eighty, and had to think of engaging an assistant'.[85] He made quill pens for his pupils every morning and spent a good deal of money on furnishing the classroom with 'pictures of every imaginable kind', and filled the corners 'with plaster figures and busts'.[86] His pupils' parents were not interested in their children being taught Latin, but he did it anyway. 'Soon, I had copies of declensions and conjugations written out on sheets of paper, with lists of the prepositions, and so on; and gave them to a good number of the boys to commit to memory'.[87] Every morning began with a chorus of Latin accidence.

Some of the boys made good progress with their Latin, even reading some Cornelius Nepos with their teacher, 'But the great body of them were never able to construe a Latin sentence. They had no taste for it themselves; and they had no stimulus at home'.[88] This information provides an important counterweight to this chapter's tales of marvellous self-education. The vast majority of the working poor would not have dared, like Lackington, Woodhouse, Gifford, Bradburn, Drew, Carey and Cooper, to set their sights higher than the working life into which they were born. And so what? Perhaps Cooper's pupils' parents were right when they complained, 'What's the use of his larning Latin? It will nivver be no use to him'.[89]

This chapter has been strangely centrifugal. Its protagonists left the trade behind and rose to more prominent and occasionally more lucrative positions. These cobblers often became men of letters—poets, theologians, scholars, teachers, translators, literary editors or booksellers. We have been handling the stories of exceptional shoemakers who made their way out of obscurity via

FIGURE 20.7 Robert Bloomfield (1766–1823), CCA.34.16(17) Reproduced by kind permission of the Syndics of Cambridge University Library.

routes—patronage, Nonconformism networks or Chartist conviction—in which classical learning is present in vivid variety. While celebrating their achievements, we need to attend to the structures that supported them, and heed the warning of Robert Bloomfield (Figure 20.7), a famous Suffolk cobbler-turned-poet. He was so astonished when he heard his popular classic *The Farmer's Boy* was translated into Latin by a local vicar that he wrote another poem, in which he darkly warns his protagonist against ever despising his humble origins:

> Hey, Giles! in what new garb art dress'd?
> For Lads like you methinks a bold one;
> I'm glad to see thee so caress'd;
> But, hark ye!—don't despise your old one.
> Thou'rt not the first by many a Boy
> Who've found abroad good friends to own'em;
> Then, in such Coats have shown their joy,
> E'en their own Fathers have not known'em.[90]

Notes

1 We follow the popular custom of using the terms 'shoemaker' and 'cobbler' interchangeably, although 'cobbler' sometimes denotes those who mend rather than make shoes. In practice, most were trained and accustomed to do both.
2 Wright (1922) 224.
3 Winks (1882) iv.
4 Winks (1882) iii.
5 See Sellars (2003) for other ancient references.
6 See Thompson (1960) and Camp (1992) 145–7.
7 Stobaeus (*Flor.* 4.32.21) via quotation from a lost work by the Hellenistic Cynic philosopher Teles of Megara. See Hall (2019).
8 On Political Shoemakers see Hobsbawm (1980).
9 *Naturalis Historia* 35.85.
10 E.g. Anon [Honestus] (1788) 528–30, to make fun of political dissent among mechanics in the alehouse; Beddoes (1800) 28, to challenge reactionary critics.
11 Woodhouse (1896) 1.1, 1.9.
12 Williams (1939) 648.
13 Woodhouse (1803) 96.
14 Woodhouse (1803) 96.
15 Woodhouse (1803) 99.
16 Woodhouse (1803) 100.
17 For an excellent biographical account and introduction to Woodhouse's poetry see Van-Hagen (2009). As bookseller, Dodsley's classical works included Christopher Pitt's edition of Virgil's *Aeneid* (1740), William Melmoth's *The Letters of Pliny* (1746), and translations of Callimachus (1744) and Sallust (1744). He also published Joseph Spence's influential *Polymetis* (1747).
18 Woodhouse (1766) 5–6.
19 Woodhouse (1766) 12.
20 Woodhouse (1766) 70–2.
21 On the British reception of Horace, see Harrison (2017).
22 Van-Hagen (2009) 387. For more on Spence see pp. 48, 79–80, 87–8.
23 For more on patronage and the 'politics of benefaction' see Rizzo (1990).

24 Woodhouse (1764) 31 ['Spring', lines 94–104].
25 c.f. Stephen Duck's Sisyphus and Mary Collier's Danaids, discussed on pp. 84–6 and 000 respectively; and Sid Chaplin's Atlas, p. 466.
26 Landry (1990) 14–16.
27 See Mary Collier's domestic injuries on p. 85.
28 Woodhouse (1764) 31 ['Spring', lines 105–8].
29 Van-Hagen (2009) 385.
30 Christmas (2001) 206. Woodhouse (1896) 2.61.
31 Woodhouse and Van-Hagen (2005) 2. Johnson (1958) 255.
32 Van-Hagen (2009) 398.
33 Lackington (1792) 65.
34 Lackington (1792) 350–1. His *Memoirs*, which remained in print until the 1830s, was published first in 1791, but we quote from the 1792 version.
35 Lackington (1792) 98.
36 Lackington (1792) 176.
37 Lackington (1792) 177–8.
38 Lackington (1792) 178.
39 Lackington (1792) 175–6.
40 Lackington (1792) 289.
41 Knight (1865) 282.
42 Roe (2012) 17–8.
43 In 1806 he also spent £3,000 on a Temple Methodist Church in Taunton, and made other donations to Methodist causes during his retirement in the South West of England.
44 'A letter to William Gifford' (1819), Hazlitt (1932) 9.13.
45 Hunt (1823) v.
46 Hunt (1823) v.
47 Gifford (1810) 10, lines 25–6.
48 Lessenich (2012) 274–5.
49 Gifford (1803) vii. His *Satires of Juvenal* were published first in 1802, but we quote from the more widely accessible 1803 version, which also contains his autobiographical introduction.
50 Gifford (1803) xi.
51 Gifford (1803) xiv.
52 Gifford (1803) xviii–xx.
53 Gifford (1803) xxi.
54 Blanshard (1870) 2, 8, 249–251 (suspension).
55 Blanshard (1870) 4.
56 Cork, March 31st (1779) quoted in Blanshard (1870) 75–6.
57 Blanshard (1870) 203.
58 Blanshard (1870) 203–4.
59 Drew (1834) 18.
60 Drew (1834) 63–5; he was occasionally involved in smuggling. In December 1784 he nearly drowned while unloading contraband in adverse conditions.
61 Drew (1834) 160.
62 Drew (1834) 83.
63 Drew (1834) 118–9.
64 Drew (1834) 366.
65 Winks (1882) 132. Dyche's *Latin Vocabulary* was first printed in 1709 and its 6th and final edition was printed in 1816. It is basically a primer with a vocabulary of the most common Latin words.
66 Winks (1882) 134.
67 Winks (1882) 131.
68 Winks (1882) 137.

69 Stanley (2004) *ODNB*.
70 Cooper (1872) 5; Winks (1882) 166.
71 Cooper (1872) 13.
72 Cooper (1872) 33.
73 Cooper (1872) 33; Mavor (1800); Goldsmith (1764), (1769), (1774a), (1774b).
74 Cooper (1872) 36.
75 Cooper (1872) 42–3; Winks (1882) 169–70.
76 Cooper (1872) 55.
77 Anon (1819) columns 177–189.
78 Cooper (1872) 55; Anon (1819) columns 179. The French-born Swiss scholar Mathurin Cordier, alias 'Corderius', published his *Colloquiorum scholasticorum libri quatuor* ('Four Books of Scholastic Conversations' (for children) in 1568. They were reprinted and read across Europe for three centuries. Cordier was born into Normandy's peasantry and lived to become director of the famous School of Theology at Lausanne. The *Colloquies* were printed in a bilingual edition, translated by Charles Hoole, in London from 1657. It became an important resource for English children to learn spoken Latin: Cordier (1568); Hoole (1657).
79 Cooper (1872) 52.
80 Cooper (1872) 58.
81 Cooper (1872) 59.
82 Cooper (1872) 60–1.
83 Cooper (1872) 59–60; Stewart (1818); Ainsworth (1758).
84 Cooper (1872) 72.
85 Cooper (1872) 73.
86 Cooper (1872) 74.
87 Cooper (1872) 75.
88 Cooper (1872) 76.
89 Cooper (1872) 76.
90 Bloomfield (1827) vol. II, 390: Clubbe (1801); Hall (2008b) 390.

21

POTTERY WORKERS

Introduction

Charles Shaw's *When I was a Child, by 'An Old Potter'* (1903) is a searing eye-witness account of child labour in the north Staffordshire potteries, where classically themed ceramics were always a major category of output. One of eight children of a Tunstall pottery painter, and born in 1832, at the age of 7 Charles began working 14-hour days in the factory of Enoch Wood & Sons in Burslem, subsequently moving to Samuel Alcock's pottery. His memoir contains horrifying descriptions of the hunger, brutality, dangerous working conditions and degradation suffered by the workforce, as well as first-hand accounts of the Chartist riots.[1]

Shaw was no classical scholar. He enjoyed Rollin's *Ancient History*, which he came across at Sunday school; Rollin, he wrote, 'opened a new world, but I never supposed that world had anything to do with the one in which I was then living. It might have been a world whose development took place on some other planet'.[2] He acquired most of his education as an adult in the Tunstall Young Men's Mutual Improvement Society. He became a Methodist minister, and studied further at Owens College, Manchester.

Shaw laments that the pottery industry has a disfigured nature: the

> lovely, peaceful, and fruitful valley is now choked with smoke and disfigured by mining and smelting refuse. If Cyclops with his red-handed and red-faced followers had migrated upwards from the dim regions below and settled on the surface amid baleful blazes and shadows, a greater transformation could not have taken place.[3]

The classical figures painted by his father lingered powerfully in his imagination. He described a ruthless local magistrate as one who 'ruled as the Jove of the

DOI: 10.4324/9781315446608-25

pottery district'.[4] The first Jove on which he will ever have laid eyes was probably this angry, thunderbolt-wielding figurine, produced by his first employer, Enoch Wood & Sons (Figure 21.1). This chapter asks how much the many thousands of working-class Britons like Charles Shaw working in the pottery industry learned from their workplaces about the ancient Greeks, Romans and Etruscans whose artefacts informed theirs. The popularity of classical designs remained steady, whereas alternative crazes waxed and waned; for example, for Italian Renaissance maiolica or Chinoiserie. Even companies which specialised in utilitarian ceramics such as chimney pipes and sanitary ware, the Stiff family's company in Lambeth, often had a sideline in classical tableware.[5]

Pottery was a significant industry in Britain during the period covered by this book, yet historians were long misled by its exclusion from Arnold Toynbee's seminal study *The Industrial Revolution* (1884).[6] He focussed on the Manchester cotton industry and the iron and hardware works of Birmingham. It was not until the mid-20th century that historians began to understand the contribution to the industrial revolution made by the technologies, machinery and workforce management of pottery producers.[7] This applied to several large pottery factories of the six towns which amalgamated to form Stoke-on-Trent in 1910, above

FIGURE 21.1 Enoch Wood and Sons porcelain Jove, photograph in Hall's personal collection.

all to Josiah Wedgwood's pioneering purpose-built factory, Etruria, and to the Herculaneum factory at Toxteth in Liverpool, which manufactured stoneware with an applied jasper dip in direct imitation of the classical designs produced by Wedgwood.[8] But other significant potteries, usually located to exploit the local availability of suitable clay, were swift to introduce new technologies, in Wales, Scotland and Ireland as well as England.[9] Such was the consumer demand for classically decorated ceramics.

A rival enterprise to Wedgwood's was Rockingham Works in Swinton, Yorkshire, founded in 1778, which produced 'Brameld' earthenware with white neoclassical figures in relief.[10] The Bishops Waltham Clay Company in Hampshire (founded 1862) used the region's fine red clay to produce beautiful imitation Athenian terra-cotta items.[11] The Aylesford Terra-Cotta Works, established in Kent in 1850, made elaborate neoclassical vases from the native clay until 1906.[12] Classical iconography abounded on the elaborate 'Limoges-style' later 19th-century ewers and pitchers produced by Royal Worcester.[13] The Blashfield Terra-Cotta Company at Stamford (1858–1875) provided neoclassical decorations for several buildings, for example Dulwich College, but also made classical vases.[14]

The many significant potteries in Wales included the Cambrian Pottery at Swansea, which, as we shall see below, aimed to produce reproductions of ancient pottery cheaply enough to be enjoyed by the working classes. In Scotland, the industry started in about 1748 and continued until World War II. It was centred in Glasgow. J. and M.P. Bell & Co. of Stafford Street made excellent earthenware and Parian; their exhibits at the 1862 Exhibition show several imitation red-figure amphoras.[15] Bo'ness and Kirkcaldy also had important potteries, as did Greenock and Alloa.[16] The Castle Espie works in County Down, Ireland, used local red clay to make neoclassical terra-cotta items, including a lovely vase with three Graces.[17] At Belleeck Pottery in County Fermanagh, Ireland, from 1863 onwards the workers made vases with classical maritime images and Parian Ware.[18]

In earlier chapters, we have noted how the taste for 'Classics' and the antique entered other spheres of British life—architecture, education, translating and publishing enterprises—at the dawn of the 18th century. The passion for the classical arose rather later in ceramic design, even though the pioneering Restoration potter John Dwight, who experimented with stoneware at his Fulham workshop and probably produced the earliest porcelain in England, occasionally attempted classical figures as well as innumerable busts of contemporary royalty, coffee-pots, mugs and noggins. His workshop's 'Meleager' (around 1680) is a 12-inch-high statuette of a nude youth with a hunting horn and boar's head, cunningly made of brown stoneware salt-glazed to resemble bronze, now in the British Museum.[19] Figures by Dwight representing Flora and Minerva, Jupiter, Mars, Neptune and Saturn are also recorded.[20] But his workmanship was of a level his contemporaries could not attain. The classical knowledge and technical skill needed to produce the 'Meleager' (of which the name of the actual sculptor remains unknown) were not generally available.

Another reason why classical ceramics were slow to become fashionable was the absence of materials suited to detailed modelling, a problem that was not solved until biscuit porcelain was introduced and Wedgwood's jasper—a fine stoneware usually unglazed and coloured to form a hard body—was perfected in the 1770s.[21] It was not until the adoption of hard white unglazed Parian at the Copeland Factory in 1842 that authentic-looking reproductions of intricately carved ancient statues in marble (thus the product name 'Parian', since much ancient marble came from the island of Paros) became possible.[22] But technological progress was in itself less significant than the ideological shift which took place in about 1763, when the end of the Seven Years War with France produced a revision in the associations of porcelain. It had been intimately tied in the British mind to the old absolutist continental regimes, but could now begin to be embraced by a far wider class base.[23] At exactly this point, Pierre François Hugues, the son of a bankrupt cloth-merchant from Nancy (the adoption of the spurious title 'Baron d'Hancarville' was a personal vanity) introduced William Hamilton to collections of classical antiquities in Naples, all then conventionally labelled 'Etruscan': many were finds from the excavations at Herculaneum and Pompeii. British classically themed ceramic art was effectively created when the images were circulated to individuals, including Wedgwood, which d'Hancarville and Hamilton eventually published as *Collection of Etruscan, Greek and Roman Antiquities from The Cabinet Of The Honble. Wm. Hamilton* (1766–1767).[24] The plates inspired the shapes and decorative art on the vases created by Wedgwood and his rivals, and their bas reliefs, friezes and designs on tableware. Once Hamilton sold them to the British Museum in 1772, they fed the new public appetite for replica ceramics which Wedgwood's workers and those in other factories across Britain laboured to satisfy.

In the new political context, classically designed porcelain suddenly seemed to embody a purer, simpler, more ideologically progressive ethos than the rococo and baroque porcelainwares of the old European courts.[25] Wedgwood expressed this himself in a 1769 letter to his partner Thomas Bentley, where he wondered whether they would be able to establish a good export business to France: 'I say we will fashn. [*sic*] our Porcelain after their own hearts & captivate them with the Elegance and simplicity of the Ancients'. But he doubts whether this can be successful, since he has observed how the French like their ceramics '*cover'd over with ornament*'.[26] The fresh, authentic feel of Wedgwood's 'Etruscan' wares to those who saw them in the late 18th century is conveyed in the 1792 discussion by the German antiquarian Carl August Bőttiger of the provenance of the so-called Etruscan vases excavated in Italy. Bőttiger describes a friend's visit to the Wedgwood showrooms in Soho: he felt as though he had been

> transported to a room in ancient Herculaneum at Portici, or into the cabinet of the Cardinal Borgia at Veletri. Catching sight of the most recent vases, flower-pots, coloured bowls and tripods made by Wedgwood and his assistants after the genuine Hamilton antiques, one sees a perfect imitation

not only in form and profile, but also in the intention to imitate the paintings through the re-invention of the Etrurian encaustic technique.[27]

The rise of the Staffordshire potteries

Bőttiger's reference to Wedgwood's 'assistants' prompts the question, how much did the many workers in the British ceramics industry know about ancient art? The industry was always concentrated in the Staffordshire potteries. By the 1880s, more than 50,000 people were employed in or dependent on the manufacture of ceramics there.[28] Women and girls had always worked in potteries, especially as printers who transferred the outline designs to the clay, but Wedgwood discovered that they were often talented painters who could acquire manual skills fast and proficiently while being paid much less than their male counterparts. By 1870, half the British pottery workforce was female,[29] a situation which made artistic portrayals of women pottery workers mildly fashionable, either in contemporary garb within neoclassical friezes, or in scenes where ancient 'Etruscan' women are depicted painting or carrying vases known from collections in museums.[30]

In 1910, the six towns constituting the Potteries (Stoke, Hanley, Burslem, Tunstall, Longton and Fenton) were amalgamated into the conurbation of Stoke-upon-Trent. The three biggest firms were Copeland, Minton and Wedgwood, but there were hundreds of smaller potteries, some of which produced classically themed wares. The Hill Top Pottery in Burslem, owned successively by Ralph Wood and Samuel Alcock, made delicate creamware and Parian goods. In Fenton there was the Minerva Works.[31] Tunstall had the Phoenix Works. In Hanley, the Old Hall Works produced Parian ware with elaborate classical mouldings,[32] and the Hope Street Works of the Dudson family made jasperware with white classical draped figures in the Wedgwood style.[33] Hanley was until 1880 also home to the Castle Field Pottery, which made black-ground and gold-printed imitation Athenian earthenware vases.[34]

In Stoke itself, the famous Spode Pottery was taken over by W.T. Copeland, which manufactured many neoclassical designs reproducing the shapes of and paintings on Athenian red-figure vases; for example, one showing three female figures on a vase displayed at the 1851 Exhibition;[35] the detail on the central figure's costume and head-dress is spectacular. Minton & Co. made colourful tiles with classical imagery and employed the doyen of *pâte-sur-pâte* neoclassicism, Frenchman Marc Louis Solon, whose stunning vase portraying the romantic hero Paris with Erotes was displayed at the 1871 Exhibition.[36] Similar neoclassical *pâte-sur-pâte* was made at the Trent Potteries, whereas the specialities at the Wharf Street Works were busts and figures tinted to resemble ivory, including 'Clytie', 'Apollo' and 'Penelope', which sold well in the USA.[37]

But the workers who made all these elegant products, and walked daily past municipal buildings designed in a variety of grand Doric and neoclassical idioms,[38] did not live luxurious lives themselves. The culture surrounding the industry was idiosyncratic; accounts even as late as the Edwardian era speak of a strong dialect, vocabulary impenetrable to outsiders, endurance feats, distance-walking races, al-fresco swimming, outdoor games called 'Prison Bar' and 'Burn Ball' and strange songs that all locals knew off-by-heart.[39] Drinking sprees, especially but not exclusively at fair-times, went on for three or more days. A journalist from Ireland who visited in 1809 reported that, on an ordinary summer Monday,

> I was surprized to find such crowds of people in a state of idleness, men, women, and boys: many of whom, even boys not exceeding 15 or 16, in a state of gross intoxication … I had formerly been a strong advocate for high wages to the working classes of the community, in hopes they might tend to increase their comforts and elevate their vices to some higher attainment of intellectual knowledge … The instance mentioned in a late commercial report, of the work people employed at the cotton factory at Rothsay [*sic*] in the Isle of Bute, purchasing a library, and employing their leisure hours in reading, forms a pleasing contrast.[40]

Violent sports including boxing and the baiting of unfortunate animals were popular. The grim housing, squalor and pollution of the potteries was notorious, as documented not only in Charles Shaw's memoir, and the fiction of local author Arnold Bennett,[41] but also in numerous government and workers' movement reports on the state of education, sanitation and healthcare from the late 18th century onwards.[42] Until well into the 20th century there was a grave problem with contamination from the toxic materials and chemicals involved in the production of ceramics, leading to an abnormally high level of early death, especially from lead poisoning.[43] The son of a Burslem potter born in 1915 recalls from his childhood the outside toilets of the pottery workers, and the impenetrable smoke that necessitated the far more frequent washing of curtains and interior upholstery than in the agricultural villages.[44]

The story of child labour in the industry is grim. At Etruria, children were treated better than anywhere else, but in 1816, nearly a third were under 18 and worked a 9- or 10-hour day. At other potteries they often did 13 hours. Even by the time of the 1840–1841 Report on the Employment and Education of Children, juveniles, often as young as 5, formed an eighth of the workforce.[45] Boys were usually employed as mould-runners, which meant dashing from one building to another, all day, in all weathers, to put newly made wares near a stove for hardening and then returning with an empty mould. Smaller children were put to being 'jigger turners', who worked raw clay to the necessary putty-like consistency. Girls were being used as 'paintresses' from the age of 8 even in 1862.[46] And the plight of the child chimney-sweeps used in the maintenance of all those ovens was as acute as anywhere in Britain.[47]

The grievances of the pottery workers were that they were not paid unless the pieces they had made were taken 'good from oven' and that deep job insecurity resulted from the journeyman system, where skilled men were hired on a single-day basis, and from annual bouts of hiring and firing. The predicament of the pottery workers led to a high level of political consciousness and unrest even in the 18th century, but it was the aftermath of Peterloo in 1819 which gave the union movement its first impetus. The area between the Potteries and Manchester was known to house the early union organisation called the 'Philanthropic Hercules', taking its example from the symbolic uses of Hercules as a symbol of the labouring man amongst French revolutionaries.[48] By 1818 this Hercules had issued a handbill in the last days of the Manchester spinners' strike, calling for the formation of a Philanthropic Society to which all trades would affiliate. After the Peterloo massacre a mass meeting was held at Hanley, chaired by pottery owner William Ridgway, an example of the alliance between the industrial working and middle classes against the aristocracy.[49]

The Journeyman Potters' Union was formed in 1824, with a smaller one for the pottery printers; the Potters Union, with 54 Lodges, had emerged by 1836, when there was a strike, lockout and widespread Chartist activism.[50] In the riots of 1842, miners and potters inspired by the 'Chartist rhymer' Thomas Cooper, also discussed in Chapters 13 and 20, took joint action.[51] Of the 20,000 participants nearly 700 prisoners, including 12-year-old boys and girls, were arrested and incarcerated in Stafford Gaols. The 1860s proved a turning-point, especially after the extension of the Factory Acts to cover potworks in 1864; regulation from central government agencies then began to change life in Staffordshire. A few measures were taken to reduce the effect of the black smoke.[52] Things improved again by 1921, when the bottle kilns had been replaced by cleaner gas-fired tunnel ovens.[53]

Josiah Wedgwood

The picture of uniformly drunken, mutinous and diseased pottery workers fails, however, to accommodate the evidence that they were better educated than their equivalents in many other industries. Literacy levels were relatively high: it is astonishing that, even by 1816, the 13 children under 13 at Etruria could almost all read and write.[54] Drama and variety shows were popular: in Hanley itinerant actors used to perform behind the Sea Lion Inn, and Chartist theatrical performances as well as lectures were attended in the People's Hall, even before surprisingly numerous theatres and hippodromes were built in the potteries from the mid-19th century.[55] Entertainments on classical themes could certainly be seen: a poster advertising performances at the Royal Pottery Theatre in Hanley during the 1850s includes forthcoming performances of T.C. King's drama, *Damon and Pytheas*.[56] And it is impossible that the men, women and children involved in the production, transportation and display of pottery did not pick up knowledge about the classical prototypes of these luxury wares. Once printing from copper-plates was introduced in the mid-18th century, the patterns were transferred from the plates (which had required enormous skill to etch) by cheap and unskilled labour. Women and children were often used to colour in between the lines transferred from the etching.[57] They must have been familiar with every minute detail. In reconstructing the workers' experience, most of the best evidence comes from Etruria, which has amassed a large archive of documentation, not least Wedgwood's own papers and correspondence. The oven books, for example, contain records created by the workers who fired the pots, and there are some fascinating small anonymous drawings of different classical shapes of vases, each carefully drawn to serve as an aide-memoire.[58]

Josiah himself was born into a family of potters in Burslem in 1730. As one of 13 children, when after his father's death the family fell on hard times, at 10 years old, he started full-time work throwing clay. His experience of poverty informed his own reformist political views. The hardships he underwent contrast with the privileged upper middle-class childhood and young adulthood of the Scottish architect Robert Adam, who received a serious classical education at the Royal High School and then the University in Edinburgh, followed by the Grand Tour. But it was these two men who were chiefly responsible for the wholesale revival of classical forms in Britain. Wedgwood was largely self-educated and relied on others to translate Latin and Greek for him.[59] But he was fond of French Enlightenment authors and fashionable writers in the English language, especially James Thomson, a Scottish poet whose radical tragedy *Agamemnon* had done much to invigorate British interest in the ancient theatre, as well as the poems of his friend Erasmus Darwin.[60]

Once Wedgwood had leased a small cottage with two kilns in 1759, in partnership with his cousin, he began to experiment with ceramic chemistry. Their business began to thrive. He then studied intensively the new art discovered at Pompeii and Herculaneum, as well as the history of ancient vases.[61] A letter of October 1767 shows the excitement he had experienced when first looking at images of what he called 'the Antiquitys', and the 'colours of the Earthen vases, the paintings, the substances used by the Ancient Potters, with their methods of working, burning &c.'[62] A year later, he is personally trying to create 'two or three sorts of faithfull copys from Etruscan Vases & am quite surpris'd both at the beauty of their forms, & the difficulty of making them'.[63]

The Arts of Etruria

Wedgwood's London shop opened in 1768, under his partner Bentley's management, and 'Etruria' was built in North Staffordshire. Over the years it hired thousands of workers to produce the medallions, miniature sculptures, vases and cameos that made the firm so successful. Wedgwood chose the name because, as we have seen, all ancient Greek and Italian vases were often subsumed under the name 'Etruscan': the very first six vases manufactured there, on 13th June 1769, bore the motto 'Artes Etruriae Renascuntur', 'The Arts of Etruria are Reborn'. Wedgwood threw these pots while Bentley turned the wheel. The shape and the illustration, depicting three semi-naked Greek heroic male figures, were all drawn from an image in the first volume of Hamilton's *Antiquities*. The pots were black, ten inches high, made of basalt and painted in the 'encaustic' enamelled manner with red figures then known as the 'Etruscan' style.[64]

On employing John Flaxman and John Voyez, a superb modeller of busts, the association of Wedgwood's name with classical shapes and imagery was consolidated.[65] Another important collaborator was James Tassie (1735–1799), a Scottish gem engraver and modeller, born into poverty in Glasgow and apprenticed to a stonemason. He was inspired to change direction after visiting central Glasgow during a fair and seeing the painting collection of the printers Robert and Andrew Foulis (see above p. 336), of whom a relation of his own, a Glasgow barber, was a good friend.[66] Still supporting himself by his masonry work, with the encouragement of a Dublin medallion-maker, Tassie developed a method of imitating ancient engraved gems in a hard enamel.[67] This required taking impressions of hundreds of examples in museums and private collections. He was the greatest expert on this category of ancient artefact in Europe,[68] and specialised in white enamel cameos of classical gods and heroes inspired by ancient artefacts.[69] Tassie provided numerous casts for reproduction by Wedgwood from 1769, and they constantly exchanged designs. Independently of each other they both made fine reproductions of the Portland Vase.[70]

Etruria set an example to the pottery industry internationally. Wedgwood based his factory organisation on the principle of the division of labour, requiring specialisation in each of his workers and single processes conducted in separate workshops. New types of ceramic product required the mastery of difficult new techniques in cutting, pressing and casting. The expanding size of the market demanded increases in the volume and variety of goods.[71] In the enamel works he opened in Greek Street, London, the same system was adopted: designs moved from the painting room to the kiln room, then the account room and finally the ware room to be stored. His workers were similarly separated: The 'fine figure Painters are another ord[e]r of beings' compared with the common 'flower painters', he wrote,[72] and they were kept separate, better paid, and required to develop their single skill to consummate level: 'We are preparing some hands to work at red & black [ware] … constantly & then we shall make them good'.[73] In June 1790, there were 278 men, women and children employed at Etruria, of whom only 5 were 'Odd Men', general workers of the lowest status assigned to no specific task.[74]

Wedgwood retrained his workers tirelessly. In 1773 Tsarina Catherine sent him her famous order for a 952-piece dinner service painted with 'the most embelished views, the most beautiful Landskips, with Gothique Ruins, Grecian Temples, & the most Elegant Buildings'; Wedgwood was worried that many of his workforce would not be up to the task—'hands who have never attempted anything beyond Huts and Windmills, upon Dutch Tile at three half-pence a doz!' But, as he wrote to Bentley, if they could 'succeed in this, tell me no more of your Alexanders, no more of your Prometheus's neither, for surely it is more to make Artists than mere men'.[75] Both the Macedonian monarch Alexander and the demiurge Prometheus, who had modelled the first humans out of clay, were the subjects of artworks made at Etruria by the very people Wedgwood was determined to make into artists himself. His visionary approach and encyclopaedic knowledge attracted requests for employment, for example from one Jos Mayer:

> ETRURIA, on Accot of the Proprietor, as well as the delightful, salubrious situation, and beauty of the place, is thereby render'd to me the most eligible … [I would like to work in] a place that derives its beauty, elegance, and granduer [*sic*], from the embellishments, and decorations of so good a judge, and so great a Connoisseur of the Fine Arts, as Mr Wedgwood is universally and justly allow'd to be.[76]

Despite his obsequiously flowery prose, poor Mayer did not secure a position.

One reason that pottery workers were keen to work for Wedgwood was that he invited them to participate in his vision that they were collectively engineering the renascence of the lost art of classical pottery, to make the Arts of Etruria live once again in Staffordshire. This was in the Enlightenment tradition by which workers in all kinds of trades identified classical ancestors or were compared with classical experts by admirers. The achievements of the late 17th-century potter John Dwight were summarised in 1677 by the Keeper of the Ashmolean Museum in Oxford thus:

> In short, he has so advanced the Art Plastick that 'tis dubious whether any man since Prometheus have excelled him, not excepting the famous Damophilus and Gorgasus of Pliny.
>
> (Nat. Hist. *lib. xxxv. c. 12*)[77]

Other factories in the potteries encouraged their workers to participate in similar flights of fancy, and to keep up with the news of finds in Mediterranean excavations. A Samuel Alcock vase was designed to imitate one found at Cumae in 1855 after an article publicising it was published in the *Illustrated London News* (Figure 21.2a and Figure 21.2b), as the information on the vase's base proudly informs the reader.

The 'renascence' trend spread across the nation. When Samuel Worthington opened his new pottery factory in Toxteth near Liverpool in 1796, he recruited about 60 skilled pottery workers from Staffordshire, and shipped them up by canal to their new homes. He chose to name the factory and the settlement for workers adjacent to it 'Herculaneum', in imitation of Wedgwood's 'Etruria' and in homage to William Hamilton's seminal collection.[78] An early commission was for the dinner and dessert services of the Liverpool Corporation for use at the Town Hall; these had the Liverpool coat-of-arms, complete with resplendent figures of Neptune and Triton printed on the rim of every item.[79] The stamp of Bell's Pottery in Glasgow depicted a classically delineated

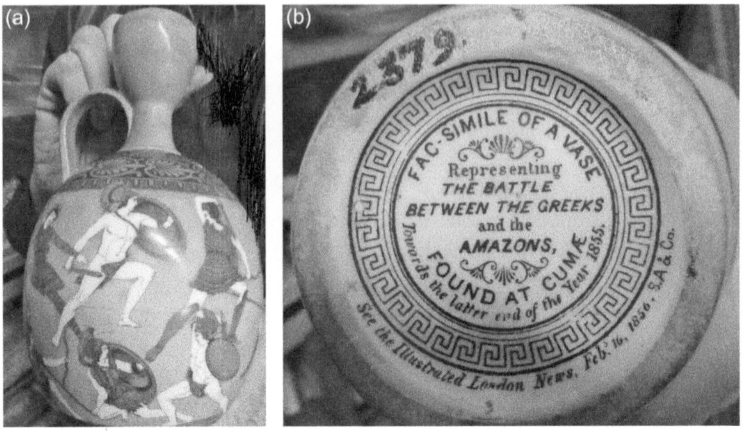

FIGURE 21.2 A and B Vase by Samuel Alcock, designed to imitate one found at Cumae in 1855, © Edith Hall.

Amazon on horseback. Ransome's Patent Stone Works in Greenwich had a single trade mark—a winged genius grinding an arrow copied from an antique Roman gem.[80] The principal painter at Dillwyn's Swansea works was William Young, who presented himself as an ancient Roman painter by using the signature 'YOUNG PINXIT'.[81] Instruction manuals for the novice potter conventionally ask the reader to remember that their art 'originated in the minds of great Assyrian, Persian and Egyptian modellers some 3000 years BC'.[82] When it comes to drapery, it is the ancient Greek and Roman sculptors who 'handed down to posterity the finest draped studies … such as the Venus de Milo'.[83]

Another attraction of employment at Etruria which throws light on the workers' expertise in ancient culture and art is Wedgwood's apprenticeship scheme, the plan for which he described in 1773 as 'a regular drawing, & modeling school to train up Artists for ourselves'. The idea was to 'pick up some likely boys of about 12 years old & take them apprentice 'till they are twenty or twenty one & set them to drawing'. He dreamed of imitating the proud ancient vase-painters who signed their works and made others in the workshop use their name, too: Exekias, Nikosthenes, Douris. The highly trained apprentices would paint the vases and make Wedgwood and Bentley famous for eternity: 'The Paintings upon these vases are from W & B school—so it may be s[ai]d 1000 years hence'.[84] At first he brought well-known artists to Etruria to work alongside low-paid employees, but the imported celebrities did not relish his factory regime. Instead he purchased their designs and implemented them personally in his workshops, where discussions of the necessary modifications were made: his workers, for example, were to bestow modest dresses and fig leaves on pagan, naked and libidinous classical figures to render them acceptable to the consumer base.[85]

Wedgwood's products drew on motifs copied, adapted, mingled or eclectically 'cut-and-pasted' from a vast variety of ancient artefacts—gems, intaglios, ivories, coins, bas-reliefs, frescoes, friezes, statues and sarcophagi as well as vases—and introduced figures copied from medieval, Renaissance or Palladian artefacts and monuments alongside antique ones: occasionally, the source is much more recent, for example female figures of the nymphs decorating the (thoroughly emasculated) statue of Priapus on a pale blue jasperware medallion of the 1780s. While Priapus' head is copied from an ancient gem, the source for the nymphs is a design by Angelica Kauffman.[86] Working on the frontline of design for Wedgwood entailed an intensive education in the visual culture of antiquity based on his huge collection of books, manuscripts, drawings and prints by everyone from the Italian antiquarian Antonio Francesco Gori to Johann Winckelmann and Thomas Dempster, the Aberdonian expert on Etruria.[87]

By 1790 he had effected a transformation in the ethos of his labour force that must have fostered a self-conscious professional identity and considerable pride in being the agents responsible for the renaissance of the arts of ancient Etruria. Many of them were female and a quarter of them were now highly skilled former apprentices—'Wedgwood's contribution to the tradition of the skilled artisan of the nineteenth century'.[88] He imposed strict rules about punctuality, attendance, cleanliness, tidiness and abstinence from alcohol. For his occasional absences, he devised a system of delegating authority to a supervisor in each of the workshops, an innovation in workplace administration that was to have far-reaching implications in 19th-century factories. Some workers were terrified of him; those who openly rebelled were soon silenced or replaced. He smashed any products he deemed sub-standard: a figurine of Achilles proved particularly troublesome, as he wrote to Bentley in 1779: 'We cannot master Achilles. I have had him demolished … more than once'; 'I have broke some which were to have been sent to you'.[89] It would be fascinating to know exactly what was wrong with the figurines of Achilles he had smashed. But the narrative suggests intense altercations involving knowledge of both classical aesthetics and ancient mythology.

Another clue to the expertise of his employees lies in the serious problem Etruria faced with industrial espionage and emigration. Spies from rival potteries infiltrated the factory in order to steal plans for new designs; financial incentives attracted his excellent workforce to potteries abroad. In 1773 Wedgwood became so concerned about losses that he published an appeal to his workers, using an argument that implies he knew that they took pride in being part of his whole enterprise and in their unusually high levels of skill: he asks them to remember that emigrants would be

> ruining a trade, which had taken the united efforts of some thousands of people, for more than an age, to bring to the perfection it has now attained, a perfection nowhere else to be found—an object exciting at once the envy and emulation of all Europe.[90]

His letters contain other indications that he discussed the products with his workers. He enjoyed being closely involved with them, in October 1769 writing: 'I have been an Etruscan, & dined at the works every day, except Monday, this week. I have been turning models & preparing to make such *Machines* of the *Men* as cannot err'.[91] A few weeks later he says that he is spending all his time in the workshops, 'I now give myself almost entirely to Vasemaking & find myself to improve in that Art & Mysterie very fast'.[92] He is concerned about whether to call them 'urns' or 'vases', and decides that urns are monumental and need covers but no handles; vases, meanwhile, 'are such as might be used for libations, & other sacrificial, festive & culinary uses, such as Ewers, open vessels &c.'[93] He records his impatience waiting for the first 'Etruscan' vases he tried to make himself to be brought from the kiln by a replacement fireman, because his usual 'old fireman is ill'.[94] He laughs about having to do the job of 'warehouseman' at the London shop himself when two of the regular employees were out and Lord Bessborough came in to view the Etruscan vases.[95] He is aggravated by a man called Boot, who is supposed to be making terra-cotta figures of sphinxes, lions and tritons, but whose behaviour is regrettably 'loose and wild'; fortunately, Boot later settled down and made the tritons and sphinxes at least 'very well.[96] But Wedgwood is delighted with one new employee: 'I hired an ingenious Boy last night for Etruria as a Modeler. He has modelled at nights in his way for three years past, has never had the least instructions, which circumstances considered he does things amazingly & will be a valuable acquisition'.[97] Even in 1769, Wedgwood was still personally putting the Etruscan vases, in new styles with which he was experimenting, 'into the oven' himself.[98]

Education via decoration

Diverse routes into the ancient world are exemplified on products from other potteries as well. Scenes from the *Aeneid* were reproduced in a combination of painting and printing on pieces produced at the Bow Porcelain Factory in London as early as the 1750s; one example in the Victoria and Albert Museum, London, depicts Aeneas, Anchises and Ascanius fleeing from Troy, with Creusa sorrowing in the background.[99] The heyday of Enoch Wood's pearlware figurines, which included Neptune with bright green dolphin and trident, a bearded Demosthenes in full oratorical flow and a colourful, recumbent Antony and Cleopatra two-piece set, ran from around 1785 to 1820. Bell's Pottery in Glasgow made elegant pitchers depicting three black-figure vases (one design was called 'Athens'), an Amazonomachy, or Sappho, surrounded by books and ancient Greek ceramics herself.[100] The workers at this factory enjoyed their own library, which included books on ancient Greece and Rome.[101] One rare design from Copeland and Garrett (so between 1833 and 1847, when the firm worked under this name) embellished a dinner service in white, each plate painted with 22 replicas of known ancient Greek jugs, vases and bowls—oenochoe, hydria, pelike, krossos, stamnos, pyxis, krater and karkhesion, whether geometric, black-figure or red-figure. It resembles nothing more than a page from a textbook on ancient ceramics (Figure 21.3).

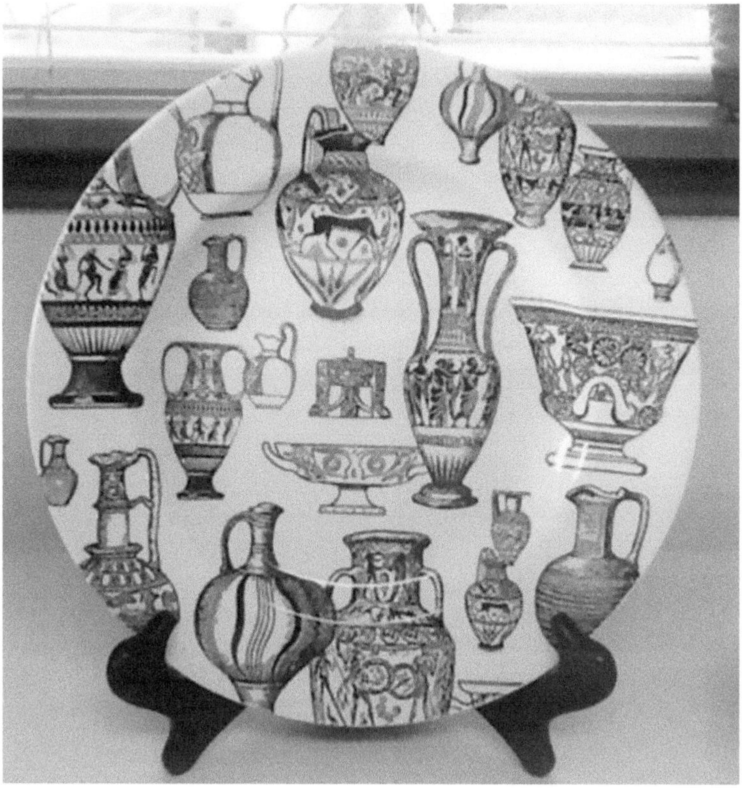

FIGURE 21.3 Decorative plate by Copeland and Garrett, © Edith Hall.

Brightly coloured porcelainware, from tea services to replica ancient urns and pitchers, were produced at Samuel Alcock's Burslem works in the mid-19th century, in which ancient Greek figures are picked out in brilliant jewel-like colours against backgrounds of deep blue, turquoise, brown, pink, orange, black or red, often with a key-pattern border. Favourite scenes are Greeks fighting Amazons, processions of musicians or victorious warriors, hunts, chariot-rides, sacrificial rituals and weddings complete with fluttering Erotes. In the late 19th century pictorial wall tiles became important after the introduction of cast-iron grates in fireplaces. Beautiful octagonal 'mosaic' tiles with classical heads were already produced by Maw & Co. in Shropshire in the early 1860s.[102] The series 'Classical figures with musical instruments', produced by Minton Ltd. (designed by John Moyr Smith) offered the workers involved in their mass production and their consumers an education in ancient Greek furniture and costumes as well as in different types of cithara, drum, cymbal and aulos.[103]

Pottery workers' ability to study ancient art formally, rather than by absorbing information during working hours, was slow to emerge. Public art lessons in the

Potteries first became available after the benefits they would bring locally, especially the provision of highly skilled labour, had been identified in a pamphlet written by the Reverend Benjamin Vale.[104] The Potteries Mechanics' Institute was established eight years later and its first premises were in Frederick Street, Shelton. But uptake was slow. The situation improved after the 1836 Select Committee of the House of Commons on Art and Manufacturers drew attention to the need for instruction in art amongst the working class.[105] Such instruction was only available from private masters, who generally taught the children of the wealthy in their homes. The Government School of Design was then established at Somerset House in London under the Board of Trade, but similar schools were also established in industrial centres such as Manchester, York, Birmingham, Sheffield, Nottingham, Glasgow and Norwich.

The workers in the Potteries themselves then began to agitate for a local school of design, and in 1845 the Hanley Mechanics' Institute applied to the Somerset House authorities for assistance. They responded by sending John Murdoch down from London to set up branch schools in both Hanley and Stoke.[106] The schools were managed by a committee of master potters and businessmen, with Herbert Minton acting as treasurer. A series of lectures delivered there by Edward Villiers Rippingille (1798–1859), an art journalist and water colourist, attracted wide public attention. But when John Robinson, who had trained in Nottingham, replaced Murdoch, the workers were not impressed with his plan to deliver a set of freestanding theoretical lectures with the highbrow title *The Aesthetic Theory of Ornamental Art* at the Mechanics' Institute in 1851. This initiative was abandoned after the first one because of the low turnout.[107]

But working-class art education in practical skills had the potential to grow. The first art classes in Longton began in 1852 at the Athenaeum and Mechanics' Institution, and the Burslem School of Design in 1853–1858 in the Burslem Wesleyan Schoolroom.[108] Extremely popular and affordable practical classes (43 takers and many more turned away) were briefly given in a local inn (in the evenings so that the workers could attend them), in drawing, landscape and perspective as well as figurative and ornamental design.[109] But once again the initiative failed. The failure was blamed on the insalubrious venue and the failure of bosses, workers and the art experts brought in to teach them, to agree on the purpose of the classes:[110]

> the manufacturers looked upon the working man as a sort of machine to produce marketable patterns, and the working man considered that by going to school a number of quarters, he should obtain the power of designing which would enable him to increase his wages; but a school of design had nothing to do with patterns, but was intended to make everybody recognise the great principle … of adding beauty to utility.

Nevertheless, the Minton Memorial Institute in Stoke opened in 1858 and included a museum to illustrate the history of pottery, a free library and a studio for teaching art.[111] Fenton followed in 1889 with Fenton Art School in the Athenaeum (which had failed as a Literary Institution)[112] and in 1899 the Sutherland Institute opened at Longton.

The most important art education establishment to be founded was surely the Wedgwood Institute itself, in 1869. This was in response to the continuing need for a Burslem School of Design as well as for a memorial to Josiah Wedgwood. Arnold Bennett himself was to study there in 1885. The architectural designs by George Benjamin Nichols of West Bromwich were chosen by competition, but the actual decorations were by Robert Edgar and John Lockwood Kipling (father of the famous author Rudyard). Kipling had risen from the rank of modeller at Hope's Factory, Fountain Square, Burslem (and we have met him earlier as the voice decrying the failure of the earlier Burslem art classes). His life had been transformed by winning a National Scholarship to South Kensington and some experience overseas in the Empire as Curator of the Central Museum, Lahore. The modellers of the decorations were also upwardly mobile Burslem men.[113] There are 12 'zodiac panels' with female personifications of the months, imitating draped figures on the Parthenon frieze. But there are also 2 sets of 'process' panels, with animated classical working figures depicting all the various processes of pottery manufacture, described in an article the designers published in 1864.[114] The Institute contained a free library and a school, and was opened by William Ewart Gladstone, then Chancellor of the Exchequer, in 1863.

Cheap reproductions

Could pottery workers ever afford to buy the goods they created? In the case of the Cambrian Pottery in Swansea, they were permitted to take home 'seconds' rather than having to watch them being smashed. Lewis Llewelyn Dillwyn was the Swansea industrialist responsible for a famous line of inexpensive ceramics imitating ancient Greek models, produced in his factory, the Cambrian Pottery, in the mid-19th century. At the time he employed no fewer than 162 workers, including at least 16 women. Using moulds, the potters and painters produced pottery in most of the canonical Greek shapes and decorated them with figures from Greek mythology including Odysseus, Amazons, Poseidon, Eros, Hector, Zeus, Hera and Helios driving his horses.[115]

Dillwyn had joined the management of his father's company in 1831. His wife Bessie created the designs after studying vases in the British Museum. Their ambition was to fuse ancient art with the local clay of the family estate at Penllergaer near Swansea, which, when fired, produced a fine red colour similar to the terra-cotta hue of ancient black- and red-figure vases. The pots were not only made by members of the local working class, but also aimed at a much less wealthy class of consumer than, for example, Wedgwood pottery. Dillwyn ware was far cheaper to produce because it was moulded rather than thrown on a wheel. An advertisement in *Art Journal* claimed the pots 'promise much towards carrying into the more humble homesteads of England forms of beauty in combination with useful ends, and in placing in the hands of all, ornaments of a high character at a cheap rate'. In fact, they cost between 2 shillings and 3 shillings and sixpence—just about affordable as an occasional luxury even by the local miners, who earned around £50 annually. The brand soon failed. Perhaps no miner could see the point. People who could afford porcelain assumed that cases made from 'flower-pot' clay would be coarse and rustic; others were suspicious of merchandise which looked so refined yet was available at such an affordable price. But Dillwyn ware continued and continues to be viewed in museums from Swansea to Bethnal Green.[116]

Finally, from the early 19th century onwards, pedlars selling inexpensive miniature plaster reproductions of famous busts and statues became a common sight on the streets of British cities, especially near museums and galleries. Better quality plaster figures had been available for decades at London shops, including the one run by John Flaxman's father (also named John) at the sign of the Golden Head, New Street, Covent Garden, London.[117] A broadside catalogue of around 1803 advertising the 'FIGURES BUSTS &c. IN PLASTER OF PARIS' available at Robert Shout's store in High Holborn lists more than 300 items, many of which are classical.[118] But street pedlars brought the products to a wider public; from towards the end of the Napoleonic wars, this business was dominated by Italian immigrants. Gangs of beggar boys would be recruited from the province of Lucca in Tuscany by adult figure-makers, who would take them all over northern Europe to make and vend their wares.[119] The youth working on London streets who is depicted in John Smith of Covent Garden's lively etching 'Very Fine. Very Cheap' (1815) is therefore, most likely, Italian.[120]

Conclusion

During the heyday of the taste for classically themed ceramics, the voices of people who worked in potteries are almost silent to us. Compared with, for example, miners and weavers, pottery workers seem rarely to have penned memoirs or diaries, and very few have survived until the early 20th century. But other sources, if read and viewed and thought about carefully, cumulatively build up a picture of skilled workers familiar with a large variety of ancient artefacts and with books visually reproducing and discussing them. At least in the Etruria and Herculaneum factories, pottery workers were encouraged to see themselves as participants in the rebirth of the ancient Mediterranean ceramic arts. They were trained in painstaking reproduction of details not only from ancient vases but from ancient gems, intaglios, ivories, coins, bas-reliefs, frescoes, friezes, statues and sarcophagi. They were familiar with the stories of a substantial number of ancient mythical and historical figures, and the different aesthetic conventions of classical Athenian, Hellenistic and Roman art. Some of them were able to study ancient art in their free time at institutions of adult education and had access to well-stocked workers' libraries. Some may even have taken products for domestic use, or purchased an inexpensive Dillwyn plate or a plaster reproduction Farnese

Hercules from a street pedlar in Holborn. Recovering the history of intellectual, artistic and cultural encounters experienced by virtually silent communities and individuals is methodologically challenging, but that does not mean we should avoid attempting it altogether.

Notes

1 Another version of this chapter is also published as Hall (forthcoming h).
2 Shaw (1903) 218.
3 Shaw (1903) 29.
4 Shaw (1903) 41.
5 See the advertising notices at www.gracesguide.co.uk/James_Stiff_and_Sons, within the excellent online resource *Grace's Guide to Industrial History*. There is a fascinating photograph of workers at the Stiff family's Lambeth works in Jewitt (1972 [1878]) 199 (plate 101).
6 See Jowett (1884).
7 See e.g. Archer and Shepley (1995).
8 Hyland (2005) 65–70 with figures.
9 Thomas (1936).
10 Jewitt (1972 [1878]) 235 with plate 113.
11 Jewitt (1972 [1878]) 153 and 155 plate 82.
12 Jewitt (1972 [1878]) 147 with figure 30.
13 Jewitt (1972 [1878]) 249 with plate 115.
14 Frank (1972).
15 Jewitt (1972 [1878]) 185 with figure 42.
16 Fleming (1923).
17 Jewitt (1972 [1878]) 160 and figure 36.
18 Jewitt (1972 [1878]) 148–9 and figure 32.
19 Museum no. 1874,0310.1.
20 Page (1911) 142–6. See also Richards (1999) 205–6.
21 Blake-Roberts (2011).
22 Jewitt (1972 [1878]) xxiii.
23 Richards (1999) 206.
24 Hancarville (1766–1767).
25 Richards (1999) 206.
26 Wedgwood (1973) 302.
27 Bőttiger (1792); translated by Richards (1999) 207.
28 Jewitt (1972 [1878]) 89.
29 Buckley (1990) 5.
30 Notably Alfred Morgan's 'Pottery Shop' (1870s) in the V&A, Henry Tooth's 'Ceramic Artists at Work, Bretby Art Pottery', in Sharpe's Pottery Museum, Victor Strange's undated 'Classical Scene', now on display in the Potteries Museum and Lawrence Alma-Tadema's 'Etruscan Vase-painters' (1871) in the Manchester Art Gallery.
31 Jewitt (1972 [1878]) 48; Young and Jenkins (1963) 218–19.
32 Jewitt (1972 [1878]) 59–60 with figure 15 and plate 36.
33 Jewitt (1972 [1878]) 73 with plate 45, which is reproduced from an advertisement in the *Pottery Gazette* of 1898.
34 Jewitt (1972 [1878]) 79 with plate 47.
35 Jewitt (1972 [1878]) 110 with plate 62.
36 Jewitt (1972 [1878]) 123 with figure 24.
37 Jewitt (1972 [1878]) 132 with plate 78.
38 See Greenslade (1963) 149.

39 See the fascinating study by Edwards (1996).
40 'K' (1809).
41 On the references to the pottery industry in Bennett's works, especially the 'Clayhanger' novels, see Warrillow (1966).
42 See Arlidge (1864); Anon (1898); Board of Trade (1913).
43 Nash (1898).
44 Swain (2006) 6.
45 Warrillow (1960) 240.
46 Warrillow (1960) 242.
47 Warrilow (1960) 244–5.
48 See James (2015) 143–4 and above pp. 278 and 408.
49 Burchill and Ross (1977) 3; Warburton (1931).
50 Boyle (1838).
51 Burchill and Ross (1977) 57–109. There is an excellent collection of documents relating to the Chartist activism in the Potteries compiled in Fyson (1981).
52 Briggs (1993) 136–7.
53 Turton (1993) 157.
54 Warrillow (1960) 25.
55 Edwards (1996) 45.
56 Neale (2011) 9.
57 Jewitt (1972 [1878]) xxv–vi.
58 See http://edithorial.blogspot.com/2016/03/open-classics-on-pots-and-online.html.
59 Wedgwood (1973) 18.
60 See Hall and Macintosh (2005) 104–27; Wedgwood (1973) 9, 5–6, 54
61 Dyer (1916) 542–3.
62 Wedgwood (1973) 177. On the contents of the oven books, where the notices show deep knowledge but are often badly spelt, see Miller (1982).
63 Wedgwood (1973) 237.
64 Clark (1995) 53–4 with plate.
65 On Flaxman's designs for Etruria see Blake-Roberts (2014) 32–3.
66 Smith (1995) 9.
67 Gray (1894) 3–6.
68 Gray (1894) 20–32.
69 Andromeda, Mars, Venus, Roman Emperors, Gorgons, the Graces, Roman Republicans, Jove, Leucippus, Phocion, Helen, Omphale, Hippocrates, the Farnese Hercules and Atlas. See Smith (1995) 50–7.
70 Montgomery (1930) 357–8. Class politics were to play their own role in the controversy when the original vase was smashed by a drunken Irish visitor to the British Museum in 1845. There was much discussion as to the social background and income level of the perpetrator, whether his name was William Lloyd or William Mulcahy. See Brooks (2004) 16–18.
71 McKendrick (1961) 31.
72 Wedgwood Museum manuscripts, Etruria Collection I8299–25 (letter to Thomas Bentley of 12th May 1770), quoted in McKendrick (1961) 32.
73 Wedgwood Museum manuscripts, Etruria Collection I8271–25 (letter to Thomas Bentley of 1st December 1769), quoted in McKendrick (1961) 32.
74 Wedgwood Museum manuscripts, Etruria Collection 28409–39 (Commonplace Book, 1790–1794) 7–17. Quoted in McKendrick (1961) 33.
75 Wedgwood Museum manuscripts, Etruria Collection 18455-25 (letter of 9th April 1773), quoted in McKendrick (1961) 35.
76 Wedgwood Museum manuscripts, Etruria Collection. 27820–36 (letter to Wedgwood of 27th July I776).
77 Plot (1677) 251.
78 Hyland (2005) 36.

79 Hyland (2005) 43–4 with figure 15.
80 Jewitt (1972 [1878]) 188-9 with figure
81 Jewitt (1972 [1878]) 227.
82 Fleming (1926) 7.
83 Fleming (1926) 13–14.
84 Wedgwood Museum manuscripts, Etruria Collection I8302–25 (letter to Bentley of 23rd May 1773), quoted in McKendrick (1961) 35–6.
85 Wedgwood Museum manuscripts, Etruria Collection I8278–25 (letter to Bentley of 28th December 1769; I8523–25 (letter to Bentley of 13th March 1774); see Macht (1957) xv.
86 Macht (1957) 96–7 with plate 55.
87 Macht (1957) 12–18.
88 McKendrick (1961) 38.
89 Wedgwood Museum manuscripts, Etruria Collection I8479–25 (July 1773).
90 Wedgwood (1783) 17–18.
91 Wedgwood (1973) 305.
92 Wedgwood (1973) 313.
93 Wedgwood (1973) 236.
94 Wedgwood (1973) 238.
95 Wedgwood (1973) 244.
96 Wedgwood (1973) 272; 280.
97 Wedgwood (1973) 280.
98 Wedgwood (1973) 295.
99 V&A museum no. 414: 71/A–1885.
100 Reproduced in Appendix 3, chapter 11, of Leishman (2006).
101 See the library catalogue dated 1891 described in Leishman (2006) ch. 22.
102 British Museum no. 2010,8009.1.a–c.
103 On Moyr Smith's designs for Minton's see further Stapleton (1996) and Dennis (2015).
104 Haggar (1953) 3.
105 Sproll (1994).
106 Haggar (1953) 4–6.
107 Minute Book of the Pottery Mechanics' Institute 1848–1854, entry for 29th July 1851, quoted in Haggar (1953) 7 no. 1.
108 Haggar (1953) 9.
109 Haggar (1953) 10–11.
110 Haggar (1953) 11, quoting James Astley Hammersley in the *Staffordshire Advertiser* 29 (January 1859).
111 Haggar (1953) 13, no. 1, quoting the Minton Testimonial Fund.
112 Haggar (1953) 28–9.
113 Swale (1987) 21–4; Haggar (1953) 15–17, 38.
114 Edgar and Kipling (1864).
115 See Morgan (forthcoming).
116 All this information is derived from Morgan (forthcoming).
117 See Clifford (1992).
118 It is in the library of the National Portrait Gallery.
119 Anon. (1833b); see further the excellent discussion at www.npg.org.uk/research/programmes/plaster-figure-makers-history.
120 Published 31st December 1815. National Portrait Gallery no. D40098, viewable online at www.npg.org.uk/collections/search/portrait/mw201568/Unknown-man-selling-plaster-figures-Very-Fine-Very-Cheap.

22

CLASSICS AMONGST THE MINERS

Emancipation via self-education

In the Welsh coalmining village of Mountain Ash, Glamorgan, the future novelist Joseph Keating (1871–1934), born into a mining family of Irish immigrants, worked his way up from collier boy to haulier, reading every book he could get his hands on. Classical authors were comparatively accessible to the intellectually thirsty poor because they were out of copyright and available in cheap reprints.[1] Keating recalled in his autobiography *My Struggle for Life* (1916) that he was fascinated by a 'book about old Greek philosophers',[2] especially the maxim 'Know thyself', *gnōthi seauton*, inscribed in the forecourt of the Apollo temple at Delphi (Pausanias 10.24.1).[3] Perhaps the book was *The Greek Philosophers* (1882) by Alfred William Benn, who discussed the aphorism in these terms:

> Let us suppose that each individual has a sphere of activity marked out for him by his own nature and his special environment, then to discern clearly the limits of that sphere and to keep within them would be *Sôphrosynê*.[4]

Keating had a dawning desire to change his 'sphere of activity'.

His job was to extract coal and other minerals from the earth's crust and transport them by shovels, trams and horses. But Keating did not know how his self-education would shape his future self. 'Euclid, French, shorthand, or Greek philosophy would be of little use in "cutting" coal, and certainly, no thought of ever doing any other kind of work had entered my mind'.[5] Keating was, however, not physically suited to hard labour: 'My youthful body had not matured, and the strain began to be unbearable. I was a boy doing, not a man's work, but an elephant's'.[6] He gradually navigated his way towards gentler occupations around the pit and landed a perfect job tending to a pumping engine.

DOI: 10.4324/9781315446608-26

> Now I tasted joy. In a little shed with a brown canvas top, down at the water's edge, I oiled my engine, regulated valves and levers, and pumped the river into boilers, to make the steam for all the engines of the pit, on the surface and underground.

Since no one inspected him, he turned the engine hut into 'a study, library, and a university'. He read all day and his mind was free.[7] Not long after, Keating left his hut and the pit to complete his education and become a journalist.

Miners have featured in previous chapters not only as self-educators who read Pope's Homer, Plutarch and Aesop, but as Dissenters, Chartists, lecturers, activists, volunteer soldiers, commissioners of Trade Union banners, amateur archaeologists, founders of the Independent Labour Party and adult education initiatives; as future parliamentarians, poets, autobiographers and journalists; as audiences of Greek tragedy and purchasers of mass-produced ceramics. But mining communities, historically the backbone of industrial Britain, merit a chapter devoted to classical presences amongst them.[8] The large concentrations of mining activity in the coal regions of South Wales and north-eastern England have so far been best researched, rather than the Cornish tin and copper mines and the collieries of Scotland, especially the Clyde and Ayrshire regions.[9] Our discussion opened with Keating's story because it introduces a recurrent theme in miners' representation of educational experience. Keating escaped what he perceived as the bondage of the pits: his first novel, *Son of Judith: A Tale of the Welsh Mining Valleys* (1900), depicted the lives of the miners accurately and without sentimentality. After World War I he became a member of the Irish Self-Determination League and a prominent voice in local politics, working as a Labour Party councillor until his death.[10]

The peculiarly dark, dangerous and oppressive atmosphere of pit life resulted in the common articulation of miners' engagement with books and culture as a form of manumission, as a process in which chains were discarded and freedom embraced. This was partly a consequence of the actual serfdom which, in Scotland, disgracefully remained legal until 1799 and continued to haunt the national memory long afterwards. Acts of 1606, 1641, 1661 and 1672 had allowed coal-masters who could not hire voluntary recruits to arrest vagrants and force them to work for life down mines.[11] In 1751, Lord Bankton learnedly compared colliers with 'the *coloni adscripticii* among the Romans'.[12] Coal-owners granted 'arles' (recruitment 'bounty') in return for a period of colliers' time, often a lifetime, and usually laid a contractual claim to any children born to them as well.[13] Scottish miners absconded to English coalfields, bringing their enslavement narratives with them, but if arrested were subject to criminal convictions: 'Bondage, like the mark of Cain, was difficult to expunge'.[14] Floggings and other cruel punishments were common: at its worst,

> mining serfdom was a system of labour open to acts of studied humiliation by the master or his agents and to depths of personal degradation, most

> graphically seen in the work of the female members of the colliery communities in eastern Scotland.[15]

These miners were strictly speaking bound serfs rather than slaves, but once G. Booth had translated Diodorus Siculus in 1700, protests at their suffering and that of other miners were informed in the English-speaking world by the ancient historian's account (V.38) of the Roman mines in Spain in the 1st century BCE:

> Now though these Slaves that continue as so many Prisoners in these Mines incredibly inrich their Masters by their Labours, yet toyling Night and Day in these Golden Prisons, many of them being over-wrought, dye under Ground. For they have no rest nor intermission from their Labours; but the Task-masters by Stripes force them to intollerable hardships, so that at length they dye most miserably.[16]

Mineworkers have often taken an interest in ancient mining, identifying themselves with their ancient forebears (as can be seen in the NUM banner from the Lanchester division which serves as the frontispiece to this book), becoming amateur archaeologists and from the 1880s onwards enrolling in university extension courses in Roman Britain (see below).[17]

On the other hand, the ancient evidence of the importance of mining in wealth acquisition, economic development and empire-building has inspired rulers and owners of mines ever since the publication of Georg Bauer's much-read treatise *De Re metallica* (1556); there was an intimate historical relationship between the rediscovery of the ancient mines and mining technology in the Renaissance and Early Modern worlds. Mining prospectors identified with Pliny the Elder, who administered those Roman mines in Spain. Opening or re-opening apertures into the world beneath has also often coincided with or precipitated archaeological investigations and collecting activities. The leisure that made possible Athenian philosophy, drama and architecture was crucially funded by the vast revenues produced by the silver mines of Laureion discussed in the *Ways and Means* of Xenophon (c. 355 BCE), a popular text in the late 17th and early 18th centuries when mining activity intensified in the run-up to the industrial revolution.[18] The re-opening of the Laureion mines as commercial operations in the 19th century went in tandem with a dynamic new archaeological interest in the outlying areas of ancient Attica.[19]

Our view of miners' intellectual lives is however in danger of being skewed by the prevalent tropes of enslavement and escape from the pit, since numerous self-educating miners did not want to change their occupations or leave their native communities. It also risks distortion by stressing Greek and Roman Classics, since they were usually not central to autodidactic miners' reading lists. Jonathan Rose's account of the thriving atmosphere of the Miners' Libraries in the South Wales coalfields shows that classical reading in English translation was but one strand in a vibrant fabric of self-education.[20] The unique mixture of relatively paternalist mining companies, tight-knit communities energised by Nonconformist religious conviction, an organised and politically engaged workforce and the 'peculiar cultural environment of the region' created a Rhondda oasis of autodidacticism.[21] Other British mining regions, especially those in the Great Northern coalfield around Newcastle-on-Tyne and Durham, in the late 19th century became cultural as well as commercial and industrial hubs, and the intersection of Hadrian's Wall and various Roman settlements fired miners' imaginations.[22]

Classical images of confinement

The positive image of the highly literate miner must not obscure the grim realities of life in many pit villages: half the employees at the 'colony' attached to Annbank Colliery in Ayrshire were illiterate as late as 1867.[23] This was despite the general understanding that reading competence, unlike writing, was essential to mine safety,[24] and the national impact of the realisation that the deaths of 15 men at Lletty Shenkin Colliery near Aberdare had been caused by the failure of an illiterate overman named John Johns to understand company instructions.[25]

Acute poverty, danger, ill-health and undernourishment (in every sense) were suffered by adult and child miners in the earlier, unregulated period of its history, which along the Firth of Forth extends back from 1842 to the 16th century. Since the 18th century and the onset of deep shaft mining, British miners have worked at and indeed beyond the limits of our habitable world. With the huge demand for coal that fuelled the Industrial Revolution, and the technology that came with it, miners went ever deeper underground to labour with unusual physical severity. Until it was normalised locally, minework attracted only the starving and dispossessed, thus creating a new and visibly identifiable class of the working poor.[26] Like all 'the lowest forms of heavy and dirty manual labour—from general labouring and casual dockside occupations to toiling in the fierce heat of the coking works or in the poisonous atmosphere of the early chemical factories', mining attracted large numbers of desperately poor Irish immigrants,[27] of whom Joseph Keating's family were examples.

Conditions improved significantly following the Mines and Collieries Act 1842 (passed despite intense opposition from mine-owners[28]), which protected all females and males under 10 from underground work. It was triggered in 1838 by a catastrophe at the Huskar Colliery in Silkstone, where 26 working boys and girls (from 8 to 16 years of age) were killed when a ventilation shaft was flooded after a thunderstorm. The tragedy caused a national outcry and Queen Victoria demanded an inquiry.[29] But the darkness, claustrophobia and danger remained unavoidable. Disasters scar the history and contemporary experience of mining worldwide. A painting by Samson Gilbert Daykin (1886–1939), a miner born in Barnsley, south Yorkshire, entitled 'Symbolic: The Miner Enslaved' (1938) (Figure 22.1) is perhaps the most poignant example in the long iconographic tradition which equates miners, slaves and other manual labourers with the fettered Prometheus, also echoing the crucifixion of Jesus. The Aeschylean Prometheus counts mining as one of the technologies crafts he bestowed upon humankind (*Prometheus Bound* lines 500–3).

FIGURE 22.1 'Symbolic: The Miner "Enslaved"', 1938, reproduced by courtesy of the Science Museum/Science & Society Picture Library. Gilbert Daykin © Science Museum/Science & Society Picture Library.

Gilbert Daykin, as he was known, was born in Platts Common, near Barnsley. He was one of 12 children of a miner at Hoyland Silkstone Colliery, close to the site of the 1838 disaster. He worked down the pit from the age of 13, first running errands and tending to the pit ponies.[30] As an adult, he was employed at Warsop Main Colliery, a few miles north of Mansfield, and became a specialist in dangerous jobs. The mythical undertext distinguishes this painting amongst Daykin's works, most of which portray miners in a dispassionate and realistic idiom. Daykin had once spent two weeks in London, courtesy of Winifred Anna Cavendish-Bentinck, the duchess of Portland, who was an advocate of the Miners' Support Association in Nottinghamshire.[31] He used the time to study masterpieces in art galleries. Daykin even featured on the front page of the *Daily Mail* for 3rd August 1931; a photograph shows him wearing a flat cap. Some of his paintings had been shown then to the first Labour Prime Minister, Ramsay MacDonald, in Downing Street. Not that being patronised by aristocrats and leading politicians did Daykin much good. As an artist, he said that he had 'lived in eternal dread of injury to my eyes or hands in the pit, but that has been my lot in life'.[32] He was among six men killed in Warsop Main on his last shift before Christmas in 1939: as he said, 'There is a siren at the pits, and it rules my life'.[33]

Mining, especially shaft mining, has always had a conceptual relationship with the ancient world which goes far beyond material experience. Descent down a mineshaft is a *katabasis* par excellence. Many have not returned. It is a journey to the world of the dead, repeated continuously. For the families of mineworkers, their katabatic bread-winner is in effect a daily *revenant*. From Renaissance infernos to Zola's *Germinal* (1885), Tony Harrison's feature-length film/poem *Prometheus* (1998) and the contemporary artist Peter Howson's *Sons of Pluto* (2002), the mineshaft has been reconceived as the place of descent to the Underworld, and the caverns and corridors which corrugate the infernal world from which gold or lead or coal is extracted have provided the imaginary architectural plans of many of our culture's vision of the world of the dead. It has recently been argued that Karl Marx's own model of the system of political economy, based on raw forces of production at work in mines and cavernous foundries, by drawing on Dante's *Inferno* reveals its debt to the katabatic tradition.[34]

Martha Vicinus has argued that mineworker poets have felt a particular need to reveal the human cost of their labour,[35] and often present it in underworld terms, speaking of themselves as 'shades', 'ghosts' and 'wraith-like figures' operating within the land of the dead, never sure that they will return, 'enslaved' by various time-keeping devices, the clock, the caller, or knocker-upper, and in Daykin's more modern case 'the siren'.[36] Sid Chaplin (1916–1986) (Figure 22.2)

FIGURE 22.2 Sid Chaplin, reproduced by courtesy of Tudhoe & Spennymoor Local History Society and George Teasdale.

wrote about his day's labour in katabatic terms.[37] Working as a colliery blacksmith and then later an underground belt-fitter, he was an avid self-educator. He received no formal secondary education, but attended the 'pit university' of the Spennymoor Settlement, where he attended WEA courses and was mentored by its warden Bill Farrell (Figure 22.3).[38] In 1939 he won a scholarship to Fircroft Working Men's College, in Selly Oak, Birmingham, to study economics and political theory. After a year or so of struggling to meet the academic require ments made of him, the onset of war sent him back to Durham and the pit life he thought he had escaped. Chaplin's papers contain the manuscript poems of a coalman in his early 20s dreaming of a literary life.[39] Most are typewritten and a number have critical comments and metrical notation scribbled over and around the text by Farrell.

Among pages with titles such as 'Poems of an Unprivileged Poet' and 'Where Gorki Died' can be found the poem 'Miner', which uses the figure of Atlas, Prometheus' fellow Titan, to convey the unseen effort expended daily by workers underground:

> I am the inner Atlas of this spinning globe.
> At the dark centre of your green circumference
> I crouch, the crawling wonder of my darker world,
> The sweating surgeon of the strata depths,
> The probing, blasting hero of my diamond doom.[40]

The imminence of death crowds the short claustrophobic poem and its protagonist has the impossible task of carrying the weight of the world from within. Another poem in the folder is 'Miners at Work', which Chaplin wrote in

FIGURE 22.3 Bill Farrell 1954, reproduced by courtesy of Tudhoe & Spennymoor Local History Society and George Teasdale. Reproduced by permission of Tudhoe & Spennymoor Local History Society and George Teasdale.

response to drawings by another son of a Yorkshire coal miner, the artist and world-famous sculptor, Henry Moore (1898–1986):

> Unreal men in their inner Hades,
> But look, ah!
> See the pinpoint glowing of eyes,
> The eyes of the dead who live
> And in their life attain the mastery
> Of blood and sweat.

In December 1941, Moore visited Castleford and drew 'Britain's underground army' at the coalface down the pit at Wheldale, where his father had been an overseer.[41] Chaplin drew on his own experience of subterranean toil and landed in an 'inner Hades' occupied by the living dead. After John Lehmann published Chaplin's work in Penguin's 'New Writing' series in 1941, the reluctant miner's star steadily rose, and he became an established author, journalist and arts worker—for which service he was awarded an OBE in 1977.

A reason why miners find it difficult to escape the infernal world is that they can rarely acquire the expertise in the arcane ancient tongues which distinguish the ruling-class male, as Siegfried Sassoon points out in 'The Case for the Miners', written in 1921:

> "Why should a miner earn six pounds a week?
> Leisure! They'd only spend it in a bar!
> Standard of life! You'll never teach them Greek,
> Or make them more contented than they are!"
> That's how my port-flushed friends discuss the Strike.
> And that's the reason why I shout and splutter.[42]

But there *is* scattered evidence for serious classical encounters in British mining communities even beyond the near-legendary holdings of the South Wales miners' libraries. At the time of the bitter strike of 1844, when some mine-owners and politicians began to see the potential of using education as a means of social control, a few colliery schools introduced such diverse subjects as Greek and Roman history, Greek, Latin and French, as well as general history and mechanical drawing.[43]

Books in Wanlockhead and other mining communities

The earliest example we have found is in an isolated lead-mining village in Dumfries and Galloway, Scotland, at the turn of the 19th century. In this period, and especially in remote rural locations, working-class education required philanthropic landowners. In Wanlockhead and neighbouring Leadhills, the philanthropic model worked well for generations.[44] On the 19th August 1803 Dorothy

Wordsworth climbed up through the grey glen of the Lowther Hills. As they ascended she, her brother William and fellow poet Samuel Taylor Coleridge encountered three young boys. 'One', she noted in her *Recollections of a Tour made in Scotland in 1803*, 'carried a fishing-rod, and the hats of all were braided with honeysuckles; they ran after one another as wanton as the wind'. Soon the three

> were joined by some half-dozen of their companions, all without shoes and stockings. They told us they lived at Wanlockhead, the village above, pointing to the top of the hill; they went to school and learned Latin, Virgil, and some of them Greek, Homer, but when Coleridge began to inquire further, off they ran, poor things! I suppose afraid of being examined.[45]

These children of a relatively deprived lead-mining community were benefitting from a traditional classical education. Wanlockhead was owned by Henry Scott, the 3rd Duke of Buccleuch and 5th Duke of Queensberry (born in 1746), who supported the miners' endeavour to establish and run a lending library in the village. But he cannot take all the credit. The spirit of education is likely to have been nourished previously by the Quakers who ran the mines before the Duke's tenure. By 1750 there was already a thriving school in the village, with an excellent reputation by the time of the Wordsworths' visit; for 4 decades afterwards, the Minister of Wanlockhead Free Church, the Reverend Thomas Hastings, educated many working-class boys who went on to transcend their class origins to become lawyers, physicians, teachers, poets and ministers.[46] In the Sanquhar parish to which the lead-miners in and around Wanlockhead belonged, as well as workers in a carpet factory and handloom weavers, there were 3,268 inhabitants; 350 could not write, but 2 in every 15 could not read.[47]

From November 1756, 32 of the adult villagers of Wanlockhead also had access to their Miners' Library (founded in emulation of that opened at Leadhills in 1741[48]), originally entitled the Society for Purchasing Books in Wanlockhead.[49] Members included miners, lead-washers and engineers as well as middle-class individuals.[50] It eventually housed more than 3,000 volumes.[51] In the library (which may now be visited as part of the excellent Museum of Leadmining, Wanlockhead) there are shelves upon shelves of religious texts; numerous volumes of self-improvement literature; several journals and magazines collected and bound in leather.[52] The printed catalogues which survive from 1829 to 1925 constitute a record of the reading habits of a well-educated and religious working-class rural community.[53]

Novels abound, notably by Scott, Dickens, Fielding, Kingsley and Thackeray and Fénelon's *Adventures of Telemachus*; there are also books on foreign travel, adventure stories, scholarly treatises on agriculture, science and, of course, mining.[54] They subscribed to the best periodical literature of the day, including both the more accessible *Chambers' Edinburgh Journal* and *Chambers' Information for the People*, the *Penny Magazine* and Cassell's *Popular Educator* and the more serious literary journals, teeming with classical erudition, such as the *Edinburgh* and

Quarterly Reviews, *Blackwood's Magazine* and the *Athenaeum*.[55] In translation, however, were available the works of Plato and Aristotle's *Ethics* and *Politics*;[56] there are two versions of Josephus.[57] Reference works with classical content included Dionysius Lardner's *Cabinet Cyclopaedia* (1831) and the SDUK's 11-volume *Library of Useful Knowledge* (1834).[58]

Ernest Rhys (1859–1946) would have delighted in Wanlockhead miners' library. The socialist poet and literary editor is best known now as the indefatigable founding editor of Joseph Malaby Dent's hugely influential *Everyman's Library* (discussed above pp. 64–9). He began his working life as a coal viewer (engineer) at Langley Park, County Durham. In the few years before he moved to London to live by his pen, he sought to enrich the leisure conditions and intellectual lives of his co-workers. When compared to South Wales, this northern coal village was lagging behind the times.[59] To the consternation of his conservative line manager, who considered mineworkers to be interested only in drinking and gambling, he established a library in a derelict worker's cottage. Plato's *Republic* was on the inaugural reading list.[60]

Jack Lawson (1881–1965) would also have gazed longingly at the shelves of the miners' library in Wanlockhead. He began life destined to be only a 'two-legged mule of industry', as one of ten children of an illiterate mother and John Lawson, a County Durham merchant seaman turned miner. He followed his father down Bolden Colliery mineshaft, County Durham, at the age of 12.[61] By the time he died he had been MP for Chester-le-Street, 1st Baron Lawson, Financial Secretary to the War Office in the first Labour government and, to his great pride, the first Lord Lieutenant of County Durham.

His ascent from the pits was facilitated by joining the Methodists, and friendships with other bookish miners,[62] some of whom even taught themselves ancient Greek and Latin.[63] But his turning point was the moment when his penchant for gambling as an adolescent miner gave way to his passion for books. To his father's dismay he built a library of second-hand books, shelved in empty orange crates.[64] A favourite was Gibbon's *The Decline and Fall of the Roman Empire*.[65] Lawson spent his penniless weekends 'in following the Goths over Europe, right into old Rome, or marching with Attila's "Huns"'.[66] His father worried for his mental health. The passion he conceived for the ancient world endured throughout the life he presents as an unmitigated success; as a father he would tell his children the tale of the wooden horse of Troy.[67]

When he was not reading them, he also liked to talk books. This he did with fellow collier Jack Woodward:

> I can see Jack now … I can see the wraith-like figure of him as he talked books. The shovel squealed against the hard stone floor, then leaped over the tub its burden of coal, coming back for more almost before it had started … The pick was biting the coal as though driven by a machine. Thus we worked and talked, swallowing our peck of dust every minute … I timidly turned the subject to Ruskin, who was just at that time receiving

> my homage. His plea for art, education, and a decent life for the toiler aroused mutual enthusiasm in us.[68]

He progressed to the newly formed Ruskin College, Oxford,[69] and was soon enjoying the privilege Ruskin men had recently won to attend Oxford University lectures. Lawson declined post-graduate education, despite every encouragement. He preferred to return to the pit, from where he would begin his successful political career.

Lawson was not alone in his educational quest in Bolden. Besides Jack Woodward, he recalls an unnamed man, whose wife had taught him to read in his 30s and who would wait after work to walk home from the pit with Lawson so that they could discuss his reading. This long-illiterate collier spoke memorably to Lawson about his passionate appreciation of Nietzsche and had taught himself 'to read the New Testament in Greek, and oratorios are easy to him as the latest song is to the man in the street'.[70]

In his early 30s, Harold Laski (1893–1950), soon to be appointed professor of Political Science at the London School of Economics and co-founder of the influential Left Book Club, used to give educational talks to groups of workers. He developed a special bond with one group of miners in the pit village of Ashington in Northumberland. In September 1924 he visited the longstanding Ashington Debating and Literary Improvement Society. Since its formation in 1898, classical Greek and Roman authors were included on the reading list and discussed at its regular meetings. After his second visit, in autumn the following year, Laski wrote to his friend, the American jurist, Oliver Wendell Holmes:

> I gave them four lectures, but I learned more from them than I could ever teach. It was sometimes grim talk, for there are hard times ahead for the mining community in England. But, in general, it was of books and men … There was one … who had learned Greek in order to read Homer in the original … These twelve every Friday for thirty-six years have met to read and discuss a book. They argue grimly with text and counter-text and you have to know your piece to get by them. They were saddened, while I was there, by the death of a miner who was found killed by a fall of coal; in his coat was found a translation of Thucydides with the page turned down at the Periclean speech.[71]

In the 1930s the colliery community at Ashington also saw the rise of a tradition of painting facilitated by Robert Lyon, then master of painting at Armstrong College, Newcastle-upon-Tyne. It all began with the formation of an art appreciation group. The unlikely voyage of a group of colliers to artistic discovery, and a certain amount of fame, has been well documented by William Feaver in his book *The Pitmen Painters* (first published in 1988), which in turn inspired Lee Hall's successful play by the same name.[72]

FIGURE 22.4 Image by Harry Wilson (linocut c. 1934), reproduced by courtesy of William Feaver. Courtesy of William Feaver.

Eschewing the traditional educational approach of their tutor, the group learned by painting scenes of life in the pit village. One of the first pieces of work produced was the linocut by Harry Wilson. This image (Figure 22.4) resembles Daykin's Promethean miner. They are both enslaved by their oppressive occupation, symbolised by the miner's literally being chained to the pithead winding gear, and the illuminated clock slowly ticking the moments away until his release. The pitmen painters' group bore little resemblance to the Debating and Literary Improvement Society. It was a different era. But although they avoided the traditional lessons offered initially by Lyon, they soon began to appreciate classical sculpture and mythological reference in European art since the Renaissance.[73] In return, they brought the previously invisible or sentimentalised working-class experience into the canon of modern art.

University extension and County Durham miners

The story of miners' Classics extends well beyond our book's chronological scope, especially around Durham, to Joe Guy, a miner from Sacriston, who in 1952 studied Greek on a course set up by the National Union of Mineworkers and Durham Colleges' Board of Extra-Mural Studies,[74] and a Yorkshire miner's daughter named Barbara Taylor who was awarded a scholarship to read 'Latin at London University'.[75] From tentative beginnings in 1886, the University Extension Lectures in Durham often included classical subject matter. The lecture series aimed 'to bring some of the benefits of University teaching within the reach of persons, of either sex and of every class, who have been unable to join the University as Matriculated Students'.[76] Alongside others, courses on Roman poetry, Ancient Drama, Ancient History and Greek Philosophy were offered.[77] In 1911, Durham University joined forces with the WEA, and in 1916 the extra-mural teaching was directed by Revd. E.G. Pace, for whom 'one major ambition ... [was] to interest more pitmen in Extra-mural work'.[78] He was sensitive to 'suspicion both from University and the Miners' side', which he thought 'probably goes back a long way'.[79] In 1924, 45% of students in the tutorial classes were manual labourers and 33% colliers. These tutorials were conducted in many mining communities. 1934 saw the presentation of a wonderful WEA/University Tutorial Class in the Council School, Easington Colliery, entitled 'Utopias'. Before any mention of Thomas More, the tutor, Ralph Todd MA, ran three classes on Ancient Athens and Plato's *Republic*.[80]

Ever popular were classes that incorporated local Roman history, drawing on a thoughtful balance of the latest scholarship and more populist publications, such as those published in Allen Lane's excellent Pelican Books series (from 1936), which 'cost no more than a packet of cigarettes'; since they were 'aimed at the true lay reader, Pelicans combined intellectual authority with clear and accessible prose'.[81] These classes provided abundant opportunity for day trips to nearby Corbridge and Housesteads, where lecturers in raincoats could point at (and declaim earnestly from) bits of Hadrian's Wall, before admiring crowds of students.[82] (Figure 22.5 and 22.6). In the late 1940s, Walter Taylor's extra-mural *Social History* course covered the Roman Occupation of Durham County, and his evening classes (1957–1958), entitled *Archaeology and History of Roman Britain*, were well attended at Billingham Technical College.[83] A certain H.W. Harbottle also taught a course in *Ancient History* from 1954–1956, in the pit communities of

FIGURE 22.5 Walter Taylor and extension students, reproduced by courtesy of Durham University Library Archives and Special Collections. Courtesy of Durham University Library Archives and Special Collections (UND/DB15/IB/68).

FIGURE 22.6 J.P. Gillam and extension students, reproduced by courtesy of Durham University Library Archives and Special Collections. Courtesy of Durham University Library Archives and Special Collections (UND/DB15/IB/59).

Langley Park and Chester-le-Street.[84] It is a shame that so few British universities today pay serious attention to the provision of cost-free education for the less privileged members of society.

Notes

1 See above pp. 49–53 and 60–9.
2 Keating (1916) 65.
3 Pausanias (10.24.1)
4 Benn (1882) 1. 62. Sophrosyne (Σωφροσύνη) is an ancient Greek concept meaning 'prudence and moderation'.
5 Keating (1916) 66; see also Rose (2001) 121.
6 Keating (1916) 77.
7 Keating (1916) 99. On the difference that being transferred to a job above ground could make to a worker in the mining industry, see Preece (1998) 12–13.
8 This chapter builds upon Stead (2018b).

9 For example, the Cornish miner, John Harris, whose fifteen collections of poetry published between 1853 and 1884 are peppered with classical tropes alongside descriptions of the miner's labour, included a *recusatio* ('Dolcoath Man-Engine') in his first book, *Lays from the Mine, the Moor and the Mountain* (1853), explaining why he will not sing of epic deeds of battle; Harris (1856, 2nd ed.) 154. He worked as a manual sorter and crusher of copper ore at Dolcoath mine, Camborne, from the age of 10 and went down the mine at 12. Since he could not afford paper and ink for his poetry, he improvised with blackberry juice on discarded tea packaging. Harris (1882) 29; Harris (1853, 1856) 154–5; Keegan and Goodridge (2013) 226–37; Stephan (2004) *ODNB*.
10 O'Leary (2011) *ODNB*.
11 Galloway (1969) 179–80; Whatley (1989).
12 Macdouall (1751) vol. I, 69.
13 Galloway (1969) 182.
14 Galloway (1969) 185.
15 Galloway (1969) 186.
16 Translated by Booth (1721) 192. See Handelsman (2009) 115 and Davies (1955).
17 See also above pp. 195–202. Edith Hall was told about Roman finds collected by County Durham miners in Lanchester and other pit villages when conducting informal interviews with the wife of a former miner and the curators of the Durham Light Infantry Museum in 2003–2005.
18 Hall and Macintosh (2005) 40; Davenant (1698).
19 Hopper (1968).
20 Rose (2001) 237–55.
21 Rose (2001) 238.
22 See further Stead (2018b) 144–6.
23 Hassan (1980) 74–5.
24 *Durham Advertiser*, 14th Aug. 1857.
25 Morris and Williams (1958) 187–91; Heesom and Duffy (1981) 140.
26 Williams (2008) 184 extends this new 'subterranean' class to workers of all mechanical industrial trades, including factory work. Before the common availability of pithead baths, supported by revenues following the 1919 Sankey Commission (see below on Glasier, pp. 479–80), miners travelled home soaked with mine water and sweat, and caked in coal dust.
27 Smith and MacRaild (2009) 37.
28 Heesom (1980).
29 Roggins (2008).
30 Barnsley (2014).
31 Hammond (2004) *ODNB*.
32 *The Argus* (Melbourne) 22 December 1939, 1.
33 *The Argus* (Melbourne) 22 December 1939 p.1.
34 Roberts (2005). See also Thesing and Wojtasik (2000).
35 Vicinus (1974) 82–6.
36 Artistic and written depictions of mining as slavery associated with modes of time keeping are relatively common, including, e.g.: the 19th-century Geordie folk song 'The Caller', Anon (1891) and Harry Wilson's linocut at Figure 22.4, p. 471 of this volume.
37 Barstow (2004) *ODNB*.
38 The term 'pit university' was used in reference to the Settlement by Tisa Schulenburg in her unpublished autobiographical 'Sketches from the life' held in the Newcastle University's Robinson Library, Special Collections, GB 186 SC/8/7/13. For more on the Spennymoor Settlement see McManners and Wales (2008) and Stead (2018b).
39 Chaplin (Sid) Archive at Newcastle University's Robinson Library, Special Collections, GB 186 SC/4.
40 Chaplin (Sid) Archive at Newcastle University's Robinson Library, Special Collections, GB 186 SC/4.
41 Wilkinson (2009) *ODNB*
42 Sassoon (1921) 715.

43 Heesom and Duffy (1981) 140.
44 For more on the miners' library at Leadhills see its website: www.leadhillslibrary.co.uk.
45 Wordsworth (1874) 15.
46 Crawford (1978) 1–16.
47 Anderson (1995) 131
48 Crawford and James (1981) 2.
49 Crawford and James (1981) 5–6.
50 Crawford and James (1981) 18–19.
51 For the full catalogue, see James (1979).
52 See Crawford (1978) for a general description.
53 Analysed in Crawford and James (1981) 26–46.
54 James (1979).
55 Crawford and James (1981) 43–4, 39.
56 Crawford and James (1981) 37; the edition of Plato was Dacier (1749), and of Aristotle, Gillies (1804).
57 Wanlockhead Miners' Library (1829); the translations are those of L'Estrange (1752) and William Whiston (1865).
58 Crawford and James (1981) 39.
59 On Rhys and Classics see Stead (2018b) 148–50.
60 Rhys (1940) 56.
61 Lawson (1932) 50.
62 Lawson (1932) 93.
63 Lawson (1932) 112.
64 Lawson (1932) 119–20. 123–5, 131.
65 Lawson (1932) 79.
66 Lawson (1932) 80.
67 Lawson (1932) 185.
68 Lawson (1932) 94.
69 Lawson (1932) 158–70.
70 Lawson (1932) 70.
71 Holmes, Laski and Howe ed. (1963) 1. 448.
72 Hall, Lee (2008).
73 Stead (2018b) 153; Feaver (1988) 17.
74 *COAL*, Vol. 5 (January 1952), 6.
75 *COAL*, Vol. 13 (January 1960), 6. In 1957 there were also two CISWO classical scholarships awarded to F. Joy Roberts and John Brammah: *COAL* Vol.11 (September 1957), 10–11.
76 Anon (1897) 5.
77 Durham University, Special Collections, UND/DB15.
78 Pace (undated) 13.
79 Pace (undated) 13.
80 '1934 WEA Syllabus for University Tutorial Class (Under the control of the University of Durham Joint Board) to be held in the Council School, Easington Colliery …' Durham University, Special Collections, UND/DB15/F7.
81 The scholarly and cross-over publications included R.G. Collingwood and John Nowell Linton Myres, *Roman Britain and the English Settlements* (London: Oxford at the Clarendon Press, 1937) and Collingwood and Myres (1937) and Ian A. Richmond, *Roman Britain* (London: Collins, 1947).
82 In addition to Figure 22.5, depicting Walter Taylor in action (UND/DB15/IB 68), photographic evidence includes Durham University, Special Collections, UND/DB15/IB 70 (Walter Taylor) and UND/DB15/IB 58 (J. P. Gillam), both reproduced in Stead (2018b)145–6.
83 Durham University, Special Collections, UND/DB15/F7.
84 More names come up in the archive, and the whole enterprise calls out for closer scrutiny.

23

SOCIALIST AND COMMUNIST SCHOLARS

Introduction

In the late 19th and early 20th centuries, working-class activism changed in nature and increased in scale along with the rise of the Labour Movement, institutionalised workers' and women's education, the professionalisation of politics and the impact of the 1905 and 1917 Russian revolutions. Two contributory factors in the gradual opening of the academic profession to women, and to men who would previously have been excluded, were the opening of new universities, and the abolition in the 19th century of requirements that fellows of Oxbridge colleges should be ordained and members of the Anglican Church. This chapter excavates the classical interests of three groups committed to the cause of the working class, most of whom we have discussed at greater length elsewhere:[1] the women amongst the socialists and labour organisers of the late 19th century who founded the Independent Labour Party, the classical scholars active in the first decades of the Communist Party of Great Britain and two classically trained communists, Christopher Caudwell and Jack Lindsay, who used the medium of scholarship to further the working class' cause in the 1930s and (in Lindsay's case) beyond.

Early labour classicists

Three intellectual streams converged in the late Victorian labour and socialist movements, two of which were indigenous and the third (Marxism) to an extent developed in London, where Marx and Engels worked from 1849. The oldest was the Utilitarianism of Jeremy Bentham and John Stuart Mill, which emphasised the creation of conditions in which a maximum number of citizens could flourish. Blended with the anti-metaphysical, empirical historical methods developed in

DOI: 10.4324/9781315446608-27

France by Auguste Comte, this produced the socialist Positivism of, for example, Edward Spencer Beesley (1831–1915). A classical graduate of Wadham College, Oxford, Beesley was appointed Professor of Latin at University Hall (an organisation attached to UCL) and Bedford College for Women. It was almost certainly at Beesley's suggestion that the African American campaigner for the abolition of slavery in the USA, Sarah Parker Remond (Figure 23.1), studied Latin at Bedford in the early 1860s.[2] Beesley was also a friend of Karl Marx. But he did not adopt dialectical materialism, his book *Catiline, Clodius, and Tiberius* (1878) being a paradigm of Positivist thought. He chaired the First International (1864), which had led to the formation of the International Working Men's Association (IWA), and attended meetings of the Democratic Federation in 1881, but soon returned to the Liberal Party, standing for Parliament as a Liberal candidate.

The second indigenous tradition was the spiritual conservatism and moral individualism of Thomas Carlyle. As we have seen previously, this found articulation in the extraordinary prose of *Past and Present*, where the classical myth of Midas crystallises the relations of production under capitalism, and the Sphinx's riddle is recast as the problem of class struggle which exploded at Peterloo.[3]

FIGURE 23.1 Sarah Parker Remond (1826–1894) by unknown photographer. Public Domain image from Wikimedia Commons.

FIGURE 23.2 'Theseus asks the answer to the Riddle of the Sphynx', by Walter Crane (1887), a compositional study, reproduced by courtesy of the Museum of New Zealand.

Carlyle's questioning proletarian-Sphinx was portrayed by Walter Crane in his (untraced) 1887 oil painting 'The Riddle of the Sphinx', for which a compositional study mercifully survives.[4] (Figure 23.2) Crane submitted the painting to the Grosvenor Gallery exhibition in 1887, but withdrew it soon afterwards. He believed that its overtly socialist content had upset the organiser, Sir Coutts Lindsay, who had concealed it behind a pillar.[5]

The answer to the Sphinx's question was to be articulated rather differently by each of the various Labour and Socialist organisations which soon emerged: the early members of the Independent Labour Party (founded 1893), the Fabians (1884) and the Labour Party (1900) to which the ILP affiliated in 1906, along with charitable and philanthropic organisations, such as the Salvation Army, that were adamantly against revolutionary change.[6] The Fabian Society was founded in response to the work in London of New Yorker Dr. Thomas Davidson, a classical scholar and author of *Aristotle and Ancient Educational Ideals* and *The Parthenon Frieze*.[7] Some members of the utopian group 'The Fellowship of the New Life', which gathered around Davidson, split from it and established the Fabian Society. It was named after Quintus Fabius Maximus Verrucosus, the Roman general honoured as 'Delayer' (*Cunctator*) after his strategy, recorded in Livy XXII, of gradually wearing down Hannibal's army rather than confronting it in pitched battle. The title page of the Fabians' first pamphlet declared,

> For the right moment you must wait, as Fabius did most patiently, when warring against Hannibal, though many censured his delays; but when the time comes you must strike hard, as Fabius did, or your waiting will be in vain, and fruitless.[8]

The name was suggested by Frank Podmore (biographer of Robert Owen) who had studied Classics at Pembroke College, Oxford, and explained it at the society's first meeting 'in allusions to the victorious policy of Fabius Cunctator'.[9]

The early members of the Fabian Society included Beatrice and Sidney Webb, who were to play crucial roles in the Co-operative movement, Trade Unionism and the London School of Economics. They were both suspicious of the upper-class tradition of university education in Classics:[10] Sidney was a hairdresser's son who left school at 15, and Beatrice, although middle-class, like the ardent socialist and secularist Annie Besant, did not study at university. Sidney nevertheless studied ancient civilisation—in translation—assiduously, publishing an unusual sociological interpretation of Roman history which praised the submission of individuals to the collective good even under the worst emperors.[11] In the ILP and the Labour Party, on the other hand, there emerged the striking new phenomenon of radical women activists—lower-middle- or working-class—proud of their patrician university qualifications in Greek and Latin.

Women classicists and the ILP

One of the 15 members elected to the ILP's first National Administrative Council was former Classics teacher Katharine St. John Conway (on marriage, Glasier). Glasier wrote continuously for the socialist press, including the *Manchester Sunday Chronicle*, the *Clarion*, and *Woman Worker*,[12] and became Editor of the ILP's newspaper, *Labour Leader*, in 1916. She collaborated with her husband, whom she met in 1892, John Bruce Glasier (Keir Hardie's associate, born illegitimate and forced to work as a child shepherd in south Ayrshire). A vicar's daughter, she had been classically educated at the new Girls' Public Day School Company school at Hackney Downs.[13] At Newnham College, Cambridge, she scandalised tutors by striking up a romance with a postman she taught on the University's Extension scheme.[14] She then became Classics mistress at Redland High School for Girls in Bristol and mixed with the local Fabians (through whom she met the Webbs) and Christian Socialists. Under her tutelage, the schoolgirls' results improved dramatically: she successfully prepared 11 girls for Latin matriculation within 18 months of her arrival.[15]

Glasier inspired Enid Stacy, whose father was an artist friend of William Morris and Eleanor Marx. After excelling in her senior Cambridge examination at the age of 16, Stacy won a scholarship to University College, Bristol, from which, in 1890, she passed the exams for a London BA in Arts (open to women since 1878).[16] She took a tutoring position at the same school as Glasier, joined the Gasworkers and General Labourers' Union in 1889 and supported the Bristol cotton workers' strike of 1890, becoming Secretary of the Association for the Promotion of Trade Unionism among Women. This strike also changed the life of her mentor Glasier, who joined the Bristol Socialist Party.[17] They both resigned from Redlands during the Redcliff Street strike of 1892 to work full-time for the cause, speaking on the 'Clarion Van' and in dozens of provincial halls.

Glasier suffered serious poverty after bearing two children.[18] Yet she never forgot that she was a trained classicist. One of her most impressive pamphlets is *The Cry of the Children*, exposing the need for radical reform of the education system, abolition of child labour and state support for all children and mothers. It was published by the Labour Press in Manchester in 1895. She argues from a long historical perspective which adds both intellectual authority and—because she can show that attitudes have differed across cultures—the sense that the current predicament of children is a problem that can be solved. She discusses Sparta, Plato's *Republic* and ancient chattel slavery. Like most members of the ILP, Katharine was opposed to the British treatment of the Boers in the Boer War: amongst the lectures she gave on the circuit in Lancashire and Yorkshire was one entitled 'Roman imperialism and our own'. She was influenced by her close friend Edward Carpenter, also a founding member of the ILP. She cites his important *Civilization: its Cause and Cure* (1889) in her own visionary tract *The Religion of Socialism*, in which a white-haired old man, a fusion of Socrates, Aesop and the Christian god, converts her to socialism.[19] But the influence went two ways. After a traditional education including Classics at Brighton College, Carpenter had studied mathematics at Cambridge and lectured on astronomy for the University Extension Movement. But he became fascinated by the ancient Greeks, especially Plato and Sappho, as authors who helped him to think cross-culturally about homoerotic relationships. He probably discussed with Glasier the ancient sources on same-sex relationships gathered in his much-reprinted *Iolaus: An Anthology of Friendship* (1902). This father of British socialist-gay activism also translated both Apuleius and the *Iliad* in 1900.

Glasier discussed literature and culture with her husband, who remained sceptical of the value of university education, believing that academic professionals always try to appoint right-wingers to top posts; they prefer 'an uninformed political reactionary because … they want to set up as stiff a political guard as they can for the protection of their class privileges'.[20] But he instrumentalised information about the ancient world. One source was his friend William Morris, whom he regarded as a quasi-spiritual leader, invited regularly to lecture in Glasgow and visited in his Hammersmith home, Kelmscott House.[21] Morris, despite his disingenuous claim 'I loathe all classic literature',[22] 'devoted several of the most fruitful years of his poetic life to the retelling of the stories' found in ancient texts,[23] even if he gave *The Life and Death of Jason* a medieval colouring. But it was to his wife that Glasier owed his interest in ancient Greek oratory and Platonic aesthetics, and his belief that the ten great thinkers of the world included Aeschylus and Socrates, as well as Shakespeare, Milton and Shelley.[24]

The other great classically trained woman lecturer in the early ILP, Mary Bridges Adams, emerged through election to a non-parliamentary body, the School Board for London (LSB).[25] It had been created as one of many school boards by the Elementary Education Act 1870, which for the first time provided for the education of all children in England and Wales. Crucially, in the LSB women were allowed to vote and stand for election.[26] Adams was elected to the Greenwich district seat in 1894, her campaign supported by many other women including Enid Stacy.[27] An outstanding biography by Jane Martin has clarified Adams' achievements. Her parents were Welsh and working-class. Her father was an engine fitter. She studied towards an external degree at the University of London, and matriculated from the College of Science in Newcastle-upon-Tyne. In January 1882 she enrolled at Bedford College to study History, Maths, English and French as well as Latin and Greek. In the summer she passed the Intermediate London BA examinations, in the second division but with Distinctions in Maths and in Greek.[28]

Her academic prowess stood Adams in good stead, being cited by the gas workers who supported her election to the LSB in 1897,[29] and impressing men in the top echelons of the socialist intelligentsia, who supported and bankrolled her cultural initiatives in the radical Woolwich of the 1890s. She persuaded many eminent speakers to lecture, wrote in the socialist-feminist magazine *Shafts* (see above p. 385) appealing for financial help for the labouring classes, and in 1899 organised an exhibition of loaned pictures called 'Art for the Workers' in Woolwich Polytechnic, opened by Walter Crane himself.

When widowed in 1900, Adams became a full-time propagandist for socialism. From 1903 she worked as a political secretary for Lady Warwick, whom she recruited for the Socialist Democratic Federation. She believed that working class adults needed a specific curriculum which would educate them politically. She therefore objected to the classical and liberal educational philosophy which underlay the foundation of both Ruskin College in Oxford (1899) and the Workers' Educational Association, under the aegis of Albert Mansbridge, in 1903 (see above pp. 195–8). Adams was convinced that there was no alternative but for all the universities—Oxford and Cambridge included—to pass into state ownership and come under popular control. The endowed seats of learning, she argued, were 'the rightful inheritance of the people'.[30]

Adams was at the centre of the conflict between the WEA 'liberals' and the rebellious Marxist socialists who formed the revolutionary Plebs League and Central Labour College in Earl's Court, London. Adams immediately responded by opening an equivalent establishment for women nearby, the Women's College and Socialist Education Centre in Bebel House, into which she moved as Principal.[31] Along with the working-class Manchester novelist Ethel Carnie, she taught women workers literacy and numeracy and, through the Bebel House Rebel Pen Club, how to write propaganda.[32]

Glasier and Adams must have been delighted by the election of Mary Agnes Hamilton, a Newnham classicist, as Labour MP for Blackburn in 1929.

Hamilton was employed in 1913 as a correspondent on women's suffrage and reform of the poor law at *The Economist*, earning extra money from writing high-end 'popular' books about ancient Greece and Rome for OUP's Clarendon Press. Her *Greek Legends* (1912) is a well-written prose retelling of the Hesiodic *Theogony* and the stories of Theseus, Thebes, Perseus, Heracles, the Argonauts, Meleager, Bellerophon and the Trojan War. Her accessible history of the ancient world (1913) covers the entire history of the Greeks and Romans from Hissarlik (supposed site of Troy) to Julius Caesar. In the 1920s she wrote, for a general audience, *Ancient Rome: the Lives of Great Men* (1922) and a new book about Greece (1926). Being an acknowledged expert in the history of the classical world lent authority to her biographies of Abraham Lincoln, John Stuart Mill, Thomas Carlyle and Ramsay MacDonald, as well as a lucid textbook *The Principles of Socialism*, published 'with notes for lecturers and class leaders' as the second in the ILP's series of study courses.

Classical scholars in the CPGB

The third intellectual strand in British socialism was the thought of Marx and Engels that underlays revolutionary Communism; Marx had himself been a more than competent classicist, whose ideas drew to an extent, hitherto inadequately acknowledged, on the Chartist Bronterre O'Brien's detailed study of ancient slavery.[33] The Communist Party of Great Britain was founded in 1920. Inspired by the Russian revolution, the four major Marxist political groups which combined to form it were the British Socialist Party (BSP), the Socialist Labour Party (SLP), the Prohibition and Reform Party (PRP) and the Workers' Socialist Federation (WSF).[34] Although the CPGB never became a mass party like its equivalents in France or Italy, it exerted an influence out of proportion to its size, partly because there were always links between its members and those of the mainstream Labour Party. At the time of the General Strike in 1926, the CPGB had about 10,000 members. Its first MP, William Gallacher, was elected by the miners of West Fife in Scotland in 1931. Although by 1936 the leaders were divided over support for Joseph Stalin and reports of his purges, the situation in Spain to an extent diverted the membership's attention. British Communists were crucial in the creation of the International Brigades which went to fight for the Republicans in the Spanish Civil War.

While the Fascists gained power in both Germany and Italy, the membership of the CPGB steadily increased. When Germany invaded the Soviet Union in 1941, and Churchill announced that Britons and Russians were now close allies, party membership soared to 56,000. At the end of the war, two communists were elected to parliament in the General Election. This was the historic moment at which the CPGB enjoyed its greatest popularity.

During the party's first two and a half decades, it was joined by many leading intellectuals. Christopher Hill has argued that English Literature was their dominant original interest.[35] But the British Marxist intellectual tradition was founded just as much on literature in Latin and Greek: Eric Hobsbawm regards the Classicists as 'the most flourishing group' amongst the CPGB intellectuals.[36] The earliest of the classical scholars who were members of the CPGB was Benjamin Farrington. He graduated in Classics from University College, Cork, and then moved to Trinity College, Dublin, to take another degree in Middle English. As Atkinson has pointed out, Farrington would have been in Dublin in 1914, when the new Provost of TCD, the renowned historian of ancient Greece J.P. Mahaffy, banned a meeting of the Trinity College Gaelic Society because one of the speakers was to be an opponent of recruitment, Patrick Pearse.[37] Mahaffy later wrote that he had loathed Farrington; there was no love lost between the high-handed Provost and his left-leaning undergraduate.[38]

Farrington's political views were shaped by the plight of the working class in Ireland, which came to a head in the Dublin 'lock-out' of 1913, a traumatic industrial dispute between factory owners and thousands of slum-dwelling Dubliners fighting for the right to form trade unions. Farrington was affected by the speeches of James Connolly, a Scottish Marxist of Irish descent. His radicalism received an academic focus when, in 1915–1917, including the period of the 1916 Easter Rising, he was reading for his Master's degree in English from University College, completing his thesis in 1917 on Shelley's translation from the Greek.[39] After lecturing in Classics at Queen's University, Belfast, he moved to the University of Cape Town in South Africa, where he studied the racist and nationalist legacies of European imperialism at first hand. In four articles he wrote for the Afrikaans newspaper *De Burger* between 15th and 24th September 1920, he tried to foster Afrikaner support for Sinn Féin and the Republican wing of the new Dublin-based national government.[40]

But Farrington's interest in Marxism, opposition to racism and an increasing distrust of both the Boer cause and the de Valera administration in Ireland, soon led him to give up active participation in politics. He preferred working on what Marxists call 'the intellectual plane' to rewrite the world, including the ancient world, from a materialist and labour-focussed perspective. He was promoted to the Chair of Latin in 1929, but left Cape Town in 1935 as the first steps towards institutionalised Apartheid were taken. He worked at the University of Bristol for a year before becoming Professor at University College, Swansea, in the heart of the Welsh industrial and mining region, where he remained for 21 years.

Farrington achieved a high profile in the UK and Ireland, his major academic contribution being to the history and philosophy of ancient science, expressed in a series of pioneering if controversial books. *The Civilization of Greece and Rome* (1938) was an important attempt to make ancient history available to working people beyond the Academy. Farrington's lively, lucid materialist analyses of the relationship between the ancient economy and ideas were often derided by mainstream classical scholars, but they were (and still are) widely read by the more open-minded among them. His commitment to Communist ideals, born in the chaos leading up to the Easter Uprising, was lifelong. He taught on socialist summer schools and to working men's educational societies. His pamphlet *The*

Challenge of Socialism resulted from a series of lectures he delivered at weekend schools in Dublin in August 1946.[41] In England, some of the younger members of the CPGB in the 1930s only later went on to become prominent academic classicists. Frank William Walbank (1909–2008) was born in Bingley, West Yorkshire. He received his classical education at Bradford Grammar School and Peterhouse, Cambridge, and from 1951 to 1977 was Rathbone Professor of Ancient History and Classical Archaeology at the University of Liverpool. His name is inseparable from that of Polybius, on whose *Histories* he wrote the definitive commentary, published in three volumes in 1957, 1967 and 1979. He became increasingly sympathetic to the cause of the working class in the 1920s; along with his politically active wife he joined the CPGB in 1934. Yet the implicit Marxist element in his views of history and historiography has never been properly investigated.[42] The Marxism is more explicit in the case of Geoffrey de Ste. Croix (1910–2000). He had been trained in Classics at Clifton College, a fee-paying private school in Bristol, but left school at 16 and did not go straight to university, training instead as a lawyer. During the 1930s he practised in London and was a member of the CPGB and the Labour Party; unlike Walbank, he was one of many who left in 1939 after the Nazi–Soviet pact. It was not until he was released from the RAF in which he had served during the war, that he entered London University to study Classics; he then pursued a brilliant academic career, took up a position at New College, Oxford, in 1963, and wrote his two 'classics' of Ancient History from a Marxist analytical perspective, *The Origins of the Peloponnesian War* (1972) and *The Class Struggle in the Ancient Greek World* (1981). His two youthful periods of exposure to classical education therefore preceded and followed his period of intense exposure to Marxist ideas as a lawyer and CPGB member in the 1930s.

Robert Browning (not related to the famous poet), born in 1914, was de Ste. Croix's junior by four years. Although he never achieved the same fame (or notoriety), his books were and still are widely read, usually by scholars who have no idea that he was a lifelong idealistic Communist Party member. Brought up in Glasgow during the terrible poverty on Clydeside in the 1920s and 1930s, he studied Humanities at Glasgow University, and may have joined the CPGB at that time. He was certainly a member soon after he arrived at Balliol College, Oxford in 1935. There he won almost every available prize and scholarship for his performances in Latin and Greek, even as he immersed himself in CPGB activities and Marxist theories of history. He spent most of his working life at London University, first at UCL until 1965 and thereafter until 1981 as Professor of Classics and Ancient History at Birkbeck College. He was still lecturing at the CPGB headquarters on Marxism and History in the mid-1980s, when Edith Hall attended.

The fifth 1930s CPGB classicist was George Derwent Thomson (1903–1987), who studied Classics at King's College, Cambridge but then moved to the National University of Ireland (Galway), where he was swiftly promoted to the professorship. In western Ireland in the 1920s he became radicalised by contact with the Gaelic-speaking population, newly liberated from British imperialism. He learned to speak their ancient language, translating works by Plato

(1929), Aeschylus (1933) and Euripides into it (1932). His first scholarly commentary, published in 1932, was on the favourite ancient play of radicals since the 18th century, the Aeschylean *Prometheus Bound*. By the time he moved back to a lectureship at King's College, Cambridge, in 1934, he was an ardent socialist, and he joined the CPGB in 1936, when he also accepted the chair of Greek at Birmingham University. An industrial city with a large automobile industry, Birmingham offered him many opportunities to teach working-class men as well as full-time university students.[43]

Thomson was intellectually restless and enjoyed controversy. By the early 1950s he had come into conflict with the leadership and ideological programme of the CPGB. He became increasingly interested in China and Maoism. In the intervening period, from 1936 onwards, he produced a stream of publications which were informally blacklisted at Oxford, but widely read outside the Classics establishment in Britain, and indeed were on the syllabus of many departments of Anthropology and Sociology as well as the reading lists circulated by workers' educational organisations. In 1938 he published his impressive two-volume commentary on Aeschylus' *Oresteia*, which still needs to be consulted by any scholar working on that text. But the work of classical scholarship with which he will always be primarily associated was his 1941 *Aeschylus & Athens*, a Marxist anthropological study of early Greek tragedy, published by the press most closely associated with the CPGB, Lawrence & Wishart. In 1949 he followed this with *The Prehistoric Aegean*, and in 1954 with *The First Philosophers*, making a 'trilogy' of Marxist interpretations of ancient Greek civilisation from the Bronze Age to Periclean Athens. Generally derided in British, classical circles, *Aeschylus and Athens* nevertheless became well-known internationally, being translated into Czech, Modern Greek, Polish, Russian, Hungarian and German.

Erudite activists

Besides the Communist Classics dons, there was a substantial group of CPGB intellectuals who did not operate within the 'Ivory Tower' but in the public world of letters. In the 1920s and 1930s they were often associated in the public imagination with 'fellow-traveller' poets and authors such as Siegfried Sassoon (see above p. 467), W.H. Auden, Louis MacNeice and Naomi Mitchison. Sassoon's socialist activism has often been overlooked.[44] Auden's politics are clear enough from the beggars, the 'lurcher-loving collier, black as night' and the lonely Roman soldier on Hadrian's Wall in 'Twelve Songs', composed in the 1930s.[45] MacNeice, the public-school-educated Anglo-Irish lecturer in Classics at the University of Birmingham between 1930 and 1936, ironically pondered the relationship between the ancient languages and social privilege in his autobiographical poem *Autumn Journal* (1938):

> Which things being so, as we said when we studied
> The classics, I ought to be glad

> That I studied the classics at Marlborough and Merton,
> Not everyone here having had
> The privilege of learning a language
> That is incontrovertibly dead,
> And of carting a toy-box of hall-marked marmoreal phrases
> Around in his head.[46]

Naomi Mitchison (1897–1999), a convinced Socialist and in 1935 a Labour candidate for parliament, had studied Classics at the Dragon School in Oxford, and even performed in a production of Aristophanes' *Frogs* as a teenager;[47] her first two novels were experimental works of historical fiction responding to the carnage of World War I, set respectively during Caesar's campaign against the Gauls (*The Conquered*, 1923) and Athens during the Peloponnesian War (*Cloud Cuckoo Land*, 1925). Her masterpiece is *The Corn King and the Spring Queen* (1931), set in Hellenistic times on the northern coast of the Black Sea in a half-Hellenised barbarian community. It is written under the influence of radical feminism, Euripides' *Iphigenia in Tauris* and Frazerian ritualism.[48]

None of these famous authors took out membership of the CPGB, despite sympathy with its aims, but other literary figures did. Christopher Caudwell (1907–1937) was an energetic party activist, poet and the author of a work of literary theory influential in British left-wing circles, *Illusion and Reality*, published after his death in the Spanish Civil War in 1937. His real name was Christopher St John Sprigg, and he was a member of the educated Roman Catholic middle class. At 15 he was forced to leave his Benedictine school, where he had learned both Greek and Latin; he soon became radicalised when his father lost his job as literary editor of the *Daily Express* newspaper, joining the CPGB in London.[49]

There is a debt to Classics in Caudwell's poetry. He translated Greek epigrams. His finest poem, 'Classic Encounter', laments recent war fatalities. The 'I' voice meets the Athenians who had died miserably in Syracuse in 413 BC (described in tragic detail in Thucydides' *History of the Peloponnesian War* book VII) after the military debacle that concluded Athens' disastrous invasion of Sicily. The speaker mistakes them for those fallen in the Gallipoli campaign of 1915–1916, when combined British and Anzac fatalities alone are estimated at 76,000. The poem thus draws a parallel between the victims of warmongering generals in the Mediterranean at distances of more than two millennia.[50] 'Heil Baldwin!' (1936), a satire on the Anglo–German Naval Agreement of 1935, is framed as a *pastiche* of the *Aeneid*, opening 'Arms and the man I sing'.[51]

Yet Caudwell's poetry, like the classical foundations of his major work on aesthetics and society, has largely been ignored. Chapter 2 of *Illusion and Reality*, 'The Death of Mythology', is essentially a study of Aristotle's *Poetics*. Caudwell's fundamental thesis is inspired by the argument between Plato and Aristotle on the relationship between the empirically discernible world (reality) and the worlds conjured up in art (mimesis). Caudwell writes that 'Aristotle's theory of mimesis, as our analysis will show, so far from being superficial, is fundamental for an understanding of the function and method of art'.[52] He is here linking Aristotle's theory that all art was fundamentally mimetic of reality with his theory that *tragic* art's aim is the production of a socially beneficial function by somehow *addressing* the painful emotions aroused in tragedy. His teleological model of the evolution of genres resembles Aristotle's teleological description of the development of tragedy and comedy in the *Poetics*. But other things have impressed Caudwell about Aristotle: he analyses literature as a social product—a body of cultural data to be analysed for what it can tell us in its own right, rather than as an expression of the individual writer's subjectivity.[53] There were other influences on Caudwell, besides Marx and Engels, including I.A. Richards and Nikolai Bukharin. But Aristotle's *Poetics* shaped both the *form* taken by the questions Caudwell asked and his answers.

Caudwell worked in isolation from other CPGB literary figures. His posthumous reputation was established by Professor George Thomson. But several other party members saw the maintenance of a debate on the role of the arts in society as a collective enterprise. The *Left Review*, first published in October 1936, was a response to the rise of fascism in Europe and a platform for the development of Marxist literary criticism and socialist literature and art. One of the founding editors was the writer and activist, Edgell Rickword, also instrumental in the formation of the Left Book Club and the British Section of the Writers' International. Before its final issue (May 1938) the *Left Review* was the mouthpiece of the British Left and attracted impressive contributors' reviews of literature, poems, short stories and songs on communist themes, some even for mass declamation. Satiric cartoons and jocular advertisement campaigns served to lighten the tone. The democratisation of culture was an important goal, and therefore one of the key preoccupations of the early contributors was the British education system and the role of the classical education within it.

Cecil Day-Lewis (1904–1972), poet laureate in the 1960s and now known mainly by his accessible translations of Virgil, was a regular contributor to the *Left Review* and a CPGB member from early 1936.[54] He wrote—in an article entitled 'An Expensive Education'—that just as capitalism in its earlier phases was a progressive force … necessary for the higher development of the means of production, so was the classical education … necessary for the development of the human mind.[55]

Now, he explained, both forces had become reactionary, and the teaching of the Latin language, in particular,

> with its emphasis on syntax, its constant appeal to the past, its abstraction from contemporary issues, its combination of intellectual snobbery and imagination-deadening drudgery–may well be the most effective "mental discipline", but only when by "mental discipline" was meant: "the maintenance of the capitalist system.[56]

Not to be outdone, the poet Randal Swingler (1909–1967), editor of the *Daily Worker* (1939–1941), regular contributor to the *LR* and a CPGB member since 1934, claimed that 'the present state of classical education is the most efficient method designed for arresting the development of the individual mind'. He argued that 'to boys whose minds have been hammered out on the anvil of grammar' a knowledge of classical literature is nothing more than a knowledge of texts, and that culture, by extension, became a thing divorced of life, the 'possession' of a gentleman and no longer a 'function, or rather the condition of a function' of man.[57] Swingler had been expensively and classically educated at Winchester and then New College, Oxford.

The traditional British method of classical education, which had indeed often functioned to exclude the lower classes from accessing middle-class careers and institutional power,[58] had always been considered, by some in the British Labour movement, an enemy of socialism. Attempts made by writers to engage with the material of classical culture in ways that bypassed the socially corrosive landscape of the classical education were welcomed. One of the most prolific of the writers associated with the *Left Review* was Jack Lindsay (Figure 23.3), the Australian-born classicist awarded a *znak pocheta* (badge of

FIGURE 23.3 Jack Lindsay (1900–1989), Author's photo, Henry Stead's private collection.

honour) by the Soviet government in 1968. He wrote a biography of Mark Antony, about which the scholar George Thomson effused:

> What he has given us is of considerable value, suggestive and stimulating, especially to those who have not yet succeeded in shaking off the stultifying effect produced on their minds by the sort of Roman history they learned at school.

Thomson called the Late Roman Republic 'an excellent field for Marxist research' and explained that the great merit of Lindsay's book was that he 'exposes the real nature of the forces that brought about the fall of the Republic'.[59]

Lindsay, the son of the famous Australian artist Norman Lindsay (1879–1969), was born in Melbourne in 1900, brought up from the age of 5 in Sydney, and won scholarships to Brisbane Grammar School and the newly founded University of Queensland. There he studied Classics under the Scottish Professor John Lundie Michie, developing the skills in translation he would exploit for the rest of his life. Michie was the son of an Aberdeenshire blacksmith and a celebrated beneficiary of the north-eastern Scottish educational system discussed in Chapter 11.[60] After university, Lindsay continued to write and translate poetry, while eking out a living as a Workers' Educational Association of Australia lecturer. He arrived in London in 1926, the year of the General Strike. He met left-leaning middle-class literary men, including Rickword, Douglas Garman and Alec Brown.[61]

His relationship with Rickword (1898–1982) was intellectually intense. Rickword had studied Classics amongst other subjects at Colchester Royal Grammar School, before fighting on the Western Front briefly in 1918. He later commented on his experience of the war, in *Literature and Society* (1940), 'It was not the suffering and slaughter in themselves that were unbearable, it was the absence of any conviction that they were necessary, that they were leading to a better organisation of society'.[62] In his poem, 'Fatigue', the fetishisation of ancient Greek culture represents the lost dreams of obsolete ruling classes resisting human progress towards a better world.[63] His political views intensified when he could not live on his disability benefit after losing an eye, and he was an ardent supporter of the General Strike. He became convinced that Marxist theory was the best way to understand the world during a conversation with Lindsay about Aristophanes and Athens, and in 1934 he joined the CPGB. Rickword gave up poetry, and worked for Lawrence and Wishart. He subsequently edited a prominent left-wing review called *Our Time*, and was convinced that classicism was not good for poetry, criticising the Imagists thus: 'All that Grecian business, a Greece that never had been'.[64]

A colleague of both Rickword and Lindsay, Douglas Garman won a scholarship in Classics to Gonville and Caius College, Cambridge, spent the 1920s between London and Paris, and was in Leningrad in 1926. With Rickword, he edited and wrote for a journal, *The Calendar of Modern Letters*, which briefly appeared from March 1925 as a monthly literary review. A committed activist, Garman was Education Organiser of the CPGB from 1934 until at least 1950, and remained a member until he died in 1969. Lindsay, meanwhile, did not become a convinced socialist until around New Year 1936, after the editor of his book *Rome For Sale* (1934) added a preface in which he compared the Catilinarian revolt with Fascism and the start of the Spanish Civil War.[65] He then embarked on a lifelong and somewhat gruelling struggle with Marxism and the increasingly dogmatic postwar Communist Party.

In the mid-1930s Lindsay's writing changed ideological gear. There is a Marxist line running through his book for a broad popular audience *The Romans* (1935), part of the 'How-and-Why Series', edited by Gerald Bullett. Lindsay explicitly did not 'seek to tell the story of her [Rome's] wars and all the romance of her long adventurous career', but instead preferred, 'to unravel some of the main qualities that made a small Italian hill-town the most important factor in the building of modern Europe'.[66] In a chapter entitled *The End of Farmer-Aristocracy* he writes,

> As always when a landed aristocracy is broken up by the advent of a commercial class to power, there was great misery and uncertainty. All the old ideas of duty and social service were gone, and nothing seemed to take their place.[67]

The New Zealand-born classicist Ronald Syme reviewed *The Romans* from Trinity College, Oxford. Aside from a couple of points of detail, the review is entirely positive:

> Mr Jack Lindsay has won repute for his translations from the Latin poets and his novels of Roman life and politics. He has now set himself a more difficult task—to delineate in this brief compass of a hundred pages the spirit and character of the Roman people. This little book may be called a success: it is written with knowledge, with sympathy and with passion.[68]

Subscribing to the *Daily Worker* and plunging into the politics he had previously avoided, Lindsay realised that his old London friends, Rickword, Garman and Brown were following the same path, and that 'in *Left Review* there was a rallying-point of the movement'.[69] Lindsay's first piece for the *Left Review* was a seven-page declamatory poem called 'Who are the English?'[70] It was reprinted, circulated as a pamphlet[71] and performed by the recently formed Unity Theatre, the dramatic limb of the CPGB. Rickword asked him to write a similar poem on the Spanish Civil War, which produced the famous song 'On Guard for Spain'. This poem was quickly developed into a text designed for mass declamation all over England by socialist theatre groups.[72]

In his autobiography, Lindsay explains that if he were asked to summarise what his work since 1933 was about, he would answer: 'The Alienating Process (in Marx's sense) and the struggle against it'.[73] Such words from the mouth of a committed Marxist are no surprise, but it *is* notable that his own 'struggle against it' took a predominantly classical form. He published 11 historical novels based in the Greco-Roman world, the majority in late Republican Rome. One, *To Arms* (1938), was aimed at young people and set in ancient Gaul. He produced seven book-length translations from Greek and Roman literature, mainly poetry; some were anthologies, including the accessible and cheaply printed collections *Ribaldry of Rome* and its twin *Ribaldry of Greece* (1961). Amongst his historical non-fiction are his biography of Mark Antony (1936), *The Romans were Here* (1956), *Our Roman Heritage* (1967) about Roman Britain and *Leisure and Pleasure in Roman Egypt* (1965). *Song of a Falling World* (1948), probably his most well-received contribution to scholarship, is a Marxist history of the declining Roman Empire based on discussion of the period's poetry.

Lindsay produced around 160 books in his lifetime.[74] His classical output, in terms of books of which he was principal author, amounts to over 40 titles between 1925 and 1974. From the beginning of his writing career he expressed little interest in ancient authors who had, through the 19th and earlier 20th centuries, gained the 'classical' stamp of academic authority (especially Virgil and Cicero). He preferred to work with what he regarded as ancient 'popular literature' and especially that written by those he considered outsiders. He is now occasionally acknowledged as having usefully popularised the ancient novel, mime and everyday social world of the Oxyrhynchus papyri.[75] He was drawn to the poetry and prose of the spoken word, not the 'deadening side of the tradition', which he considered to have been fetishised by traditional 'academic criticism'.[76]

His favourite classical authors included the demotic and obscene Herodas (whom he first translated in 1930), Petronius (whose *Satyricon* and poems he translated in 1927), Apuleius (whose *Golden Ass* he translated first in 1932), Longus (whose *Daphnis and Chloe* he translated in 1948), and Aristophanes (whose *Lysistrata* and *Ecclesiazusae* he translated in 1925 and 1929 respectively). He was especially fond of Theocritus, whose poetry he first translated in 1929 and saw (as he said in an article advocating mass declamation as a political instrument) as being beautifully alive 'because it is tissued in a poetry derived in large part from popular Mimes'.[77] His lifelong passion, however, was for the poetry of Catullus, which produced not only two different full translations of his works, the first as an exclusive fine press edition in 1929, and then in 1948 as an affordable commercial edition,[78] but also his first trilogy of historical fiction, i.e. *Rome for Sale* (1934), *Caesar is Dead* (1934), *Last Days of Cleopatra* (1935c); also *Despoiling Venus* (1935), which is a narrative delivered in the first-person voice of Caelius Rufus, and finally *Brief Light* (1939), a fictionally embellished biographical account of Catullus.

Lindsay's Marxism gave him an ideological bedrock from which he could spring into the ancient world and an intellectual method of socio-economic analysis into which he could pour his substantial literary experience and his powerful imagination. The new angle on the ancient world that the hopeful, creative Marxism of the 1930s offered simultaneously repelled the traditional Ivory Tower classicists from his work, and attracted other Marxist intellectuals, like Browning and Thomson, who could see how such pioneering work could re-energise the traditional 'stultifying' realm of Classics. Lindsay's skill as a translator of Greek brought him right to the foot of the Ivory Towers, if never through the door, when he contributed translations to *The Oxford Book of Greek Verse in Translation* (1938), edited by T. F. Higham and C.M. Bowra, which accompanied *The Oxford Book of Greek Verse* (1930). The neglect of Lindsay in mainstream cultural history offers one of the most spectacular examples of the absence of people's Classics from our histories of the discipline.

FIGURE 23.4 Will Crooks, portrait in *Vanity Fair*, 6 April 1905. Public domain image from Wikimedia Commons.

Two factors have contributed to this occlusion. First, the traditional suspicion of linguistic classical education on the British Left. This was best articulated by Will Crooks, son of a ship's stoker from Poplar, East London, and close friend of Ben Tillett,[79] who became only the fourth ever Labour MP in 1901 (Figure 23.4). He famously asked the Conservative Prime Minister 1902–1905, Arthur Balfour, to refrain from speaking in Latin in parliament.[80] The other factor is the continuing discomfort, both inside and beyond the Ivory Tower, with excavating the history of British communism. There remains much work to be done investigating the instrumental presence of classical ideas and texts across the different political constituencies that made up the British Labour and Socialist movements, especially via the intellectual work at the heart of the CPGB. One way of continuing this project would be to investigate Andy Croft's fascinating collection of novels featuring CPGB members, written by card-carriers including Upward, Brown and Lindsay, many fellow travellers and also some writers more hostile to the cause.[81] It is fascinating to learn from Croft, for example, that in the first draft of *Lady Chatterley's Lover* by the classically educated Nottinghamshire miner's son D.H. Lawrence, Oliver Mellors the gamekeeper was secretary to his local cell of the Communist Party in Sheffield.

Notes

1 Hall (2015c); Hall and Stead (2016); Hall (forthcoming c); Stead (forthcoming). See also *Brave New Classics*, a web platform for collaborative research into classics and communism, bravenewclassics.info.
2 See Salenius (2016) 112–13.
3 Mendilow (1984).
4 Reproduced as O'Neill (2008) 34 as no. 35.
5 See O'Neill (2008) 35, 4, 17.
6 William Booth, for example, who was inspired by Carlyle: see Woodall (2005) 25–7.
7 McBriar (1962) 1; see further Knight (1907).
8 McBriar (1962) 9.
9 *Minutes of the First Meeting of the Fabian Society* cited in Pease (1925) 34, 39; McBriar (1962) 3.
10 Harrison (1987) 57.
11 Webb (1888); see Harrison (1987) 57.
12 Soldon (1978) 59. Katharine Glasier's diary, along with the 49 boxes of Glasier papers, remained for many years in the possession of the Glasier family, and were used and quoted from extensively by Thompson (1971). They can now be consulted in the Special Collections and Archives of the University of Liverpool.
13 See NSWS (1879) 48, where Pearse writes, 'I cannot see why, if women desire the Franchise, they should not have it, particularly as they are now eligible to vote for School Board candidates'.
14 Hamilton (1936) 140.
15 Thompson (1971) 64.
16 See *The Bristol Mercury and Daily Post* for Tuesday, November 25 (1890), issue 13272.
17 Thompson (1971) 65.
18 Thompson (1971) 134–7.
19 Glasier (1894) 1; Carpenter (1889).
20 J.B. Glasier (1921) 102.

21 On the exceptional importance of Morris to the thought of the new socialists of the 1880s and 1890s; see Levy (1987b) 92–3.
22 Mackail (1890) vol. II, 171.
23 Kermode (1912) 158–9.
24 J.B. Glasier (1921) 45, 67–8, 81, 99–100, 166.
25 For a wonderfully detailed account of women's involvement in local government before they became eligible to take part in parliamentary politics, see Hollis (1989), who (most unusually) is aware of the significance of Mary Bridges Adams (see 14, 66, 123 and 125, with the comments of Martin (2010a) 8).
26 On the importance of the School Boards and Board Schools to the rise of working-class women after 1870, see Liddington (2006) 20–3.
27 Martin (2010a) 83.
28 Martin (2010b) 25 n. 13.
29 London School Board Minutes, 2nd May 1895,1128 (London Metropolitan Archive), quoted in Martin (2010a)83–4.
30 Martin (2010b) 13.
31 See Bridges Adams (1912).
32 Martin (2010b) 14–15.
33 O'Brien (1885); see further Chapter 13 pp. 284–7. On Marx and antiquity, see especially Sullivan (1975); Cartledge and Harvey (1985); McCarthy (1990); Lekas (1988); Rose (1992); and the essays in Morley (1999); Hall (2011c) and (2018f); on Marx's debt to Aristotle, see McCarthy (1992).
34 See Arnot (1967) 185–6 and Klugmann (1968) 13–74.
35 Hill (1990) 11. See also the emphasis on authors of literature in English in Kettle (1975) 2. There are useful biographies and bibliographies of most of these figures in Paananen (2000).
36 Hobsbawm (1978) 23.
37 Atkinson (2010) 673.
38 Mahaffy's thinking is cited in a letter by Yeats dated 10th November 1914, as quoted by Foster (2003) 523.
39 Farrington (1919).
40 Atkinson (2010) 671 and *passim* with further bibliography; for the impact made by the radical young Irishman's arrival on the Cape Town political scene, see Hirson (2001) 122–53.
41 See Hall and Stead (2016).
42 See further Lister (2019), with his citations from Walbank's unpublished memoir.
43 This information was given to Edith Hall in a private interview held at Thomson's Birmingham home in 1987. On Thomson, see also 'Conversations on Communism', podcast with Richard Seaford, Ben Harker, Elinon Taylor and Henry Stead, via bravenewclassics.info.
44 Higbee (2007).
45 Auden (1991) 137, 143–4.
46 Macneice (1979) 125.
47 Benton (1990) 23, with figure 9.
48 Hall (2013a) 253–4.
49 See Hall (2015d) 235–51.
50 Caudwell (1986) 125–6. 'Classic Encounter' is his only poem which has appeared in several anthologies, beginning with the Everyman's Library volume *Poems of Our Time* ed. Church and Bozman (1942) 276.
51 Caudwell (1986) 99.
52 Caudwell (1986) 58.
53 Caudwell (1946) 58. After a digression on Plato, he returns to this theme: Aristotle, he writes, is uninterested in the poet's mind, and does not concern himself with whether or not the creation and appreciation of poetry is a conscious function.

54 See Stead (forthcoming).
55 Day-Lewis (1937) 43.
56 Day-Lewis (1937) 45.
57 Swingler (1937) 7.
58 Stray (1998); Vasunia (2013); Hall (2008a), ch. 10, (2008b), (2008c) and (2008d); Hall and Stead (2013); Stead and Hall (2015).
59 Thomson (1937) 185.
60 On Michie see Thomis (1986). At the University of Queensland there is a Michie building, named in the Aberdonian's honour.
61 Hall and Stead (2016) 21 with further references.
62 Quoted in Jay (2012) 103.
63 Rickword (1991) 117.
64 Young and Schmidt (1973).
65 See Lindsay (1962) 228–9.
66 Lindsay (1935b) 8.
67 Lindsay (1935b) 28.
68 Syme (1936) 40.
69 Lindsay (1962) 252.
70 Lindsay (1935a).
71 Lindsay (1936a). The price was 1d.
72 Lindsay (1937a). See Hall and Stead (2016) 24–5.
73 Lindsay (1962) 271n. On Lindsay's 'alienation' see Harker (2016).
74 A detailed bibliography exists online as part of *Jack Lindsay: writer, Romantic, revolutionary*, a web-based project led by Anne Cranny-Francis, University of Technology Sydney—jacklindsayproject.com.
75 See Lindsay (1929b) and full bibliography at Cranny-Francis' *Jack Lindsay: writer, Romantic, revolutionary* [c.f. preceding note].
76 Lindsay (1937b) 513.
77 Lindsay (1937b) 512.
78 Lindsay (1929) and (1948a). These two publications form the basis of Stead's project, 'A communist Catullus?' which examines how ideology makes its stamp on literary translation, part of 'Brave New Classics', for which see bravenewclassics.info.
79 Tillett (1931) 171.
80 Crooks (1907) 17–18. See also p. 16: 'The man trained as I have been amid the poor streets and homes of London, who knows where the shoe pinches and where there are no shoes at all, has more practical knowledge of the needs and sufferings of the people than the man who has been to the recognised Universities. I am the last to despise education. I have felt the need of more education all my life. But I do protest against the idea that only those who have been through the Universities or public schools are fit to be the nation's rulers and servants. Legislation by the intellectuals is the last thing we want'.
81 See Croft (n.d.) and also Croft (1998).

24

SOLDIERS

Dai and Diomedes on the Somme

Introduction

The World War I fatalities lists compiled by the British War Office record the names of somewhat over 41,000 officers and 660,000 British soldiers (Other Ranks).[1] One commissioned officer died for every 16 sergeants, corporals and privates. Before mid-1916, clear class divisions separated non-officer and officer ranks. Financial considerations excluded men with no independent income from seeking a commission; it was not possible to live on army pay. But the command style of trench warfare, which depended on junior officers leading platoons on the front lines, produced unprecedented casualty rates amongst young commissioned officers, who were mostly from the upper-middle classes. From the summer of 1916, the army offered commissions to men whose class would previously have debarred them from being considered 'officer material'.[2]

A bizarre new term, 'temporary gentleman', designated the working-class soldiers who suddenly found themselves with commissions.[3] But they now faced great danger as junior officers on the front line. The ratio of working-class men who were killed in proportion to those of higher classes was therefore ultimately higher even than 16 to 1. But when it comes to the 'War Poets', the ratio is reversed.

On 11th November 1985, a memorial to the poets of the First World War was unveiled in at Westminster Abbey by Ted Hughes, the Poet Laureate. The list contained 16 names: Richard Aldington, Laurence Binyon, Edmund Blunden, Rupert Brooke, Wilfred Gibson, Robert Graves, Julian Grenfell, Ivor Gurney, David Jones, Robert Nichols, Wilfred Owen, Herbert Read, Isaac Rosenberg, Siegfried Sassoon, Charles Sorley and Edward Thomas. All had fought in the war and all except Robert Graves were by this time dead. Poems by 14 of the 16 were read out at the ceremony. The two who were omitted were Blunden and Jones.[4]

DOI: 10.4324/9781315446608-28

FIGURE 24.1 'Private David Jones', reproduced by courtesy of the David Jones Society.

Jones was the only one not of officer class (Figure 24.1). The presence of classical ideas in the understanding of non-officers in the British army is a topic that deserves much further investigation. This chapter provides a starting-point by offering a class-conscious reading of Jones' harrowing epic *In Parenthesis* (1937), which forged a radically new form and language for the representation of the common soldier's subjective experience of the trenches of World War I.[5]

Private David Jones

By 1985, *In Parenthesis* had fallen out fashion. It was a product of trauma suffered in a manmade death-trap of barbed wire, vermin, machinegun fire and mud—where imperial nations slaughtered each other's menfolk as they struggled to secure the peripheral edges of their territorial power, or, as Jones put it in the language of Roman fortifications, to hold 'their crumbling limites intact'.[6] *In Parenthesis* shares with some other World War I poems the use of classical material, but is otherwise different. It unwaveringly looks at the war from the proletarian perspective of the lowest ranks of soldier, is book-length, collides realistic and supernatural elements, is aesthetically experimental and linguistically obscene. It implicitly questions the legitimacy of writing poetry about war, yet dispassionately withholds both a coherent critique of militarism or a partisan political view.

It is also graphic about violence. Jones, whose *In Parenthesis* doppelgänger is Private Ball, was injured in action:

> And to Private Ball it came as if a rigid beam of great weight flailed about his calves, caught from behind by ballista-baulk let fly or aft-beam slewed to clout gunnel-walker below belowbelow.
>
> When golden vanities make about,
> you've got no legs to stand on.
>
> He thought it disproportionate in its violence considering the fragility of us.[7]

Jones was never strong. There is even humour underlying his perception of the force which took him down as disproportionate 'considering the fragility of us'. Jones also watched several close friends die.

The son of a Welsh-speaking printer, Jones' lower-middle-class family lived in suburban London. He attended state school. He was backward academically and struggled to read; his sister read Macaulay's *Lays of Ancient Rome* aloud to him.[8] At 13, in 1909, he enrolled at the Camberwell School of Art. He enlisted in the 15th battalion of the Royal Welch Fusiliers (the 'London Welsh') on 2nd January 1915. He was newly 19 and had previously been rejected by the army twice. Jones' father wrote to David Lloyd George; soon the inarticulate teenaged art student was being trained at Llandudno.[9] The whole 38th (Welsh) Division embarked at Southampton in December 1915, trained for a fortnight at Warne, before moving to the front line at Neuve Chapelle. The battalion moved south in preparation for the Somme offensive of July 1916, when Jones, like his poetic doublet John Ball, was shot in the attack on Mametz Wood.[10]

This engagement was brutal, with prolonged machine gun fire and bayonet fighting at close quarters. Jones' division suffered a staggering 4,000 casualties. Robert Graves also fought in the battle, remembering the site as 'full of dead Prussian Guards, big men, and dead Royal Welch Fusiliers and South Wales Borderers, little men. Not a single tree in the wood remained unbroken'.[11] Graves' poem on Mametz Wood, 'A dead Boche' (written in 1916), is conventional in form, yet conveys the same physical disgust as Jones' much later work.[12]

By late October 1916 Jones had returned to the front, seeing action again in 1917 in the north-west of Ypres. A new bond had developed between the front-line fighters on both sides. All enmity was directed towards officers and politicians; the dedication to *In Parenthesis* honours 'the enemy front-fighters who shared our pains against whom we found ourselves by misadventure'.[13] Jones had no interest in institutional politics. But the poem's focalised viewpoints and subject-matter relate to the experience of the ordinary soldier, making *In Parenthesis* inescapably political with a small 'p'. Hirst has defined the distinction between Jones and the officers Owen and Sassoon as lying in the common soldier's pride in his gun and his regiment.[14] Cohen argues that Jones 'forces the reader to protest rather than doing it for him', in a manner 'unlike any other World War I poet'.[15] He held only generals and statesmen accountable, men whom he despised: 'Damn them all, all who rule and all who counsel', he was to write later in *The Dying Gaul*.[16]

A new form for working-class War Poetry

The commitment to representing the world of regular, usually working-class soldiers—turning their squalid everyday rituals into a sacrament which has been repeated since the dawn of time—extends to Jones' extreme colloquialism. In the preface to *In Parenthesis* he deplores the prudish restrictions which in 1937 circumscribed the poet's freedom to represent the swear-words of soldier-speak accurately. He saw them as a ritualised reiterative language or Homeric formula. He has felt hampered (xii),

> because the whole shape of our discourse was conditioned by the use of such words. The very repetition of them made them seem liturgical, certainly deprived them of malice, and occasionally, when skilfully disposed, and used according to established but flexible tradition, gave a kind of significance, and even at moments a dignity, to our speech. Sometimes their juxtaposition in a sentence, and when expressed under poignant circumstances, reached real poetry.[17]

Jones fought in the opening stages of Passchendaele. But in February 1918, Trench Fever invalided him home again. He was demobilised on 15th January 1919.

The poem follows Private Jones' own experiences from mid-1915 to mid-1916. The first three of the seven sections recount the gathering of his division and their first deployments after the Iliadic opening of Part 3, in which a spectacular sunrise is followed by a military parade. Part 4, Christmas 1915, is spent behind the lines. Part 5 telescopes the events of spring 1916, including an officer's reading of the 'good news' of the initial British success of July 1st, when the infantrymen were 'permitted to cheer'.[18] Part 6 correlates to the confused marching which robbed the battalion of sleep and brought it to battle exhausted, with a Homeric-style simile comparing it to a ship's crew watching another ship depart while they must beach their vessel, 'turn their eyes from the white in-swell and get down to some job of work'.[19] Part 7 is the assault on Mametz Wood on July 10th and the shooting of Private John Ball. This merges with the final hallucinatory sequence, initiated by the Queen of the Woods, who bestows branches on 12 of Jones' dead comrades.[20]

Ypres haunts the conversations of the men in the poem, for the protracted butchery of the first Ypres battle had already changed the way people talked about war. During the 7 weeks between 14th October and November 30th 1914, the British had suffered 58,155 casualties (7,960 dead, 29,562 wounded and an enormous 17,873 missing). The poison gas of the second battle of Ypres in the following May then made its terrifying impression.[21] Jones drew the strange world he found around him,

> as well as the machine-gun and the howitzer, the aeroplane, the 1917 version of the tank and the rather primitive system devised to warn of gas attacks. These drawings are truly the work of "the man who was on the field".[22]

Jones was interested in technology. He asked whether art could or should respond to the industrialisation of war. Can lethal chemicals be aesthetic?

> It is not easy in considering a trench-mortar barrage to give praise for the action proper to chemicals—full though it may be of beauty. We feel a rubicon has been passed between striking with a hand weapon as men used to do and loosing poison from the sky as we do ourselves. We doubt the decency of our own inventions, and are certainly in terror of their possibilities.[23]

In 1942 Jones was to write a fine study, 'Art in relation to war'.[24] But in the *In Parenthesis* preface he writes that poets, who had always faced the same challenge, are finding it difficult to make chemical weapons glamorous: 'It would be interesting to know how we shall ennoble our new media as we have already ennobled and made significance our old—candle-light, fire-light, Cups, Wands, and Swords, to choose at random'.[25]

We feel him struggling to 'ennoble' the new media of destruction stockpiled in the trench dugout he calls home:

> Picks, shovels, dredging-ladles, carriers, containers, gas-rattles, two of Mrs. Thingumajig's patent gas-dispersing flappers, emptied S.A.A. boxes, grenade boxes, two bales of revetting-wire, pine stakes ...[26]

The unique style of *In Parenthesis* is exemplified by this epic catalogue of military equipment. The poem was held, by W.B. Yeats, T.S. Eliot (who wrote a complimentary 'Note of Introduction' to preface the first edition), W.H. Auden, Graham Greene and Peter Levi to be the most important literary response to World War I.[27] It won the prestigious Hawthornden Prize in 1938. Yet it has suffered incomprehensible neglect. No scholar except Oswyn Murray has appreciated its idiosyncratic classicism, its 'obsession with the frontier walls of the Roman empire and their prefigurement of the trenches'.[28] Elizabeth Vandiver omits Jones from her 2010 study of the relationship between Classics and the War Poets, *Stand in the Trench, Achilles*.

Perhaps the neglect results from Jones' fame as an artist. *In Parenthesis* sometimes uses classical allusions as an invitation to visualise an artwork: the cadaver of lance-corporal Aneirin Lewis is 'more blistered' than 'painted Troy Towers'.[29]

The poem began as a series of pictures rather than words.[30] The ink-and-watercolour frontispiece offers a route into understanding Jones' verbal technique: its thick texture pulses with activity, implying chaos only just under aesthetic control. It straddles figurative/realist art and symbolism or abstract-expressionism. The figure is a half-naked soldier, with an injured leg, whose limbs fuse with the jagged branches of the menacing wood. They both crucify him and enfold him. The suggestion of crucifixion lends the image an icon-like religious dimension, an aspiration to offer a universal meaning. What it represents is not glorious but nor is it despicable: it is men doing and suffering. It subverts celebrated War Poets across all cultural history by asking how war can legitimately have a poetics, if at all. The picture complements his description of taking the first of the two hits he received in the battle at Mametz Wood:[31]

> You know the bough hangs low, by your bruised lips and the smart to your cheek bone.
> When the shivered rowan fell
> you couldn't hear the fall of it.
> Barrage with counter-barrage shockt
> deprive all several sounds of their identity,
> what dark convulsed cacophony
> conditions each disparity
> and the trembling woods are vortex for the storm …

The phrase 'dark convulsed cacophony' reminds us that calling *In Parenthesis* a 'poetic' response is problematic: much of the text is printed as syntactically disjointed prose.

Critics have been reluctant to designate it a prose poem, but by the 1930s the genre was well established.[32] The earliest manifestations of the form are the passages in prose *within* poetic texts which feature in early bible translations. The name John Ball is an adaptation of the canonical character who had represented typical Englishmen in cartoons since the 18th century; yet it is also the name of a Lollard rebel priest during the 1381 Peasants' revolt, a rhyming preacher who invented the couplet, 'When Adam delved and Eve span, / Who was then the Gentleman?' This John Ball used the English translations of the Vernacular Latin Bible (the Wycliffe Bible), which feature both verse and prose. Jones may have encountered Ball in the novel by William Morris (whom he admired), *A Dream of John Ball* (1888). During a scene in a bar in *In Parenthesis*, Ball's companion asks a 'ma'm'selle' in prose for drinks. Then, swaying his pelvis 'like a corner-boy', he launches into song:[33]

> *He shall die*
> *he shall die*
> *with one*
> *mighty swipe I*

will I will
diss-lo-cate his bloody jaw.

At this point Jones' omniscient narrator, intermittently merged with John Ball, tells us:

> He reverts to the discipline of prose.

Jones draws attention to his jarring formal hybridity. He is going beyond the limits of poetry as the other War Poets understood it—as rhyming verse in conventional stanzas. He finds these limits constricting. He revered James Joyce, and it shows. He combines free indirect discourse, fragmentary dialogue, description, sensory evocation and dense allusiveness. This fusion requires, the 'discipline of prose' if it is to do justice to the psychic and physiological bombardment he underwent as a soldier, as well as presumably during his first nervous breakdown of 1932, when the poem was half-finished.

Jones understood the impossibility of reconciling the unprecedented experience of World War I to inherited poetic forms. Amongst the War Poets, only Jones welds the aesthetic revolution we call Modernism—the ideological expression of the economic and socio-political contradictions of the late 19th and early 20th centuries—to the historical events in which those contradictions exploded in military conflict. World War I and Modernism are inseparable, as military and aesthetic instantiations of the same crisis in the global order. This involved the apocalyptic collision of forces unleashed by new technologies (internal combustion engines; aviation; telecommunications; chemical munitions), Germany's industrialisation, pressure on internal European geopolitics, the rise of Proletarian radicalism, and cracks in British, French, Ottoman and Austro-Hungarian imperialism. It is unsurprising that the older literary forms—lyricism and realism in fiction, metre and rhyme in poetry—failed to delimit the aesthetic expression of such a crisis. Yet amongst the so-called War Poets, Jones is (with the arguable exception of Rosenberg) the sole Modernist. *In Parenthesis* assumes the innovations of Pound in metre and Eliot's *The Waste Land* (1922) in atmosphere. More famous War Poets used traditional poetic structures inherited from the Victorians, and conventional, even obsolescent diction.

Their generic form keeps the terrible experiences they aesthetically process safe, sealed in a box labelled 'The Past'. This past is a formal category which makes World War I close an old cultural epoch (the Victorian Age, the British Empire and the world before women and workers were liberated, unironic patriotism morphing into guilt-laden pacifism) rather than the foundation stone of a new epoch (global war, the industrialisation of death, nuclear weapons and terrifying racism/nationalism). *In Parenthesis* is an arduous experience. Reading it after Sassoon is like tackling Joyce's *Ulysses* after Thomas Hardy. Yet, as Dudley puts it, Jones explodes a 'tension at the heart of modernity: the seeming failure to find a poetic or narrative mode adequate to control and convey the extent and gravity of the problems of the modern world.[34] The tonal strangeness of *In Parenthesis* was a unique achievement, even if it explains why it has not appeared on GCSE syllabuses or been recited in Westminster Abbey.

Jones only refers once to any other War Poet. In Part 6, the soldiers are waiting, terrified, for the Mametz assault.[35] Jones strains to remember what they discussed: John Ball is talking to his closest companions, a man with the Lewis guns (a newly invented light machine gun), and the most educated of those we meet, Signaller Olivier.

> They talked of ordinary things ... Of the dissimilar merits of Welshmen and Cockneys. Of the diverse virtues of Regular and Temporary Officers. Of if you'd ever read the books of Mr. Wells. Of the poetry of Rupert Brooke ... Of the Lloyd George administration, of the Greek, who Olivier said was important, of whom John Ball had never previously heard.[36]

The mention of Brooke is historically accurate. He had come to sudden fame on 11th March 1915 when the *Times Literary Supplement* published two sonnets ('IV: The Dead' and 'V: The Soldier'). 'The Soldier' was read on Easter Sunday in St Paul's Cathedral, shortly before Brooke died on Skyros. Brooke's *1914 & Other Poems*, containing the 5 famous sonnets, was published the following month and reprinted no fewer than 11 times before the end of 1915. His verses were in the minds of the men on the Somme. But verses like his no longer satisfied an emotionally honest trenches survivor like Private Jones.

Classical banter in the trenches

A similar point can be made by about the poem's classical presences, which sit alongside the presentation of John Ball and his companions as the Arthurian heroes of knightly legend. In the first part, the only certain invocation of Classics comes when Ball and his comrades are on parade before embarkation. The band plays. 'Broken catches on the wind-gust came shrilly back: *Of Hector and Lysander and such great names as these*—the march proper to them'.[37] This well-known line belongs to 'The British Grenadiers', the traditional 18th-century marching song of all British fusilier companies, following 'Some talk of Alexander, and some of Hercules'. The proper names *Hector* and *Alexander* later crop up in banter between the men: 'When did they pass you out Hector-boy'. 'They get warmed to it—they're well away in tactics and strategy and the disciplines of the wars—like so many Alexanders'.[38]These classical warriors are part *both* of the realistic fragmentary soundscape Jones evokes *and* of his diachronic vision of World War I as an unavoidable, ritualised confrontation replaying an atavistic human urge going back to antiquity. The evocations of the past generations of warriors are fundamental to the poem's objective humanism, even if that humanism is fused, in Jones' unique manner, with sacramental mystery.

Some classical allusions are deployed in a comic vein, absurdly appearing in passages where the sentiment and language are bathetically unheroic: when Jones lists men resented by because they offload some of the contents of their kit bags onto the officers' transport vehicles, a reference to Julius Caesar's favoured bodyguards jostles with army slang and 20th-century nicknames:

> there's a whole lot of them that work it: the Pox-Doctor's Clerk, for one, the chitties, and types of scullion bummers up, specialist details, all of Caesar's household, chlorination Daniel, Private Miles who warms the Old Man's water.[39]

But the classical material also emphasises the tragic dimensions of army life. Trench runners in action were in mortal danger, and in Part 5 'hairy' Runner Herne is ominously summoned by a peremptory officer when dozing in the sunshine. Jones accumulates quasi-Homeric epithets in—unusually—verse-like colometry to describe the sleepy youth's sudden awakening:

> Runner Herne,
> where he lay sunned outside
> where he lay like Romany kral
> reposing and rook-hair disordered
> like fleet-foot messengers would sleep
> on windy plains
> who waked rosy-cheek
> remembering those deep-bosomed—to worry eyes with screwed fists.[40]

In pitched combat, Homerically calling the signallers 'clear-voiced heralds', who 'leg it to a safe distance', fuses the eternal procedures and personnel of combat with demotic slang.[41]

As the men wait tensely for orders, the wind ruffles the dust 'like Punic sands',[42] evoking the foul Libyan sandstorm in Lucan's epic on the Roman civil war (*Pharsalia* 9.411–.510). Calling the routes out of the dugouts into no-man's land *parodoi* creates a spatial sense of this ancient, distorted *theatre* of war; the 'unfathomed passion' of trench life contorts 'the comic mask of these tragic japers' and the 'masked face' of a dying soldier in Mametz Wood.[43] When Jones differentiates an unusually educated lance-corporal, Aneirin Lewis, from humble private Watcyn, we hear that Watcyn knew nothing of epic lays, 'was innocent of his descent from Aeneas, was unaware of Geoffrey Arthur and his cooked histories, or Twm Shon Catti for the matter of that—which pained his lance-corporal friend, for whom Troy still burned, and sleeping kings return'. At the climactic conclusion of Part 2, Jones is being reprimanded for failing to address his superior officer correctly, when he experiences his first exploding shell. The notion of the weapon as 'Pandoran' adds a mythic resonance: 'Out of the vortex, rifling the air it came—bright, brass-shod, Pandoran; with all-feeling screaming the howling crescendo's up-piling snapped'.[44] Latterly, he muses on the terrible injuries suffered by survivors, and compares the march-pasts of war veterans with the military processions of ancient Rome: 'Give them glass eyes to see and synthetic spare parts to walk in the Triumphs, without anyone feeling awkward and O, O, O, it's a lovely war with poppies on the up-platform for a perpetual memorial of his body'.[45]

In the third section, Jones describes the way that the 'rat of no-man's-land' and birds 'whose proud eyes watched the broken emblems droop and drag dust' join the soldiers in a process of Ovidian physical transformation as they acclimatise to the distorted world of the trenches and 'suffer with us this metamorphosis'.[46] The richest classical allusions of *In Parenthesis* are delayed until the section which is also the most formally 'poetic', with abbreviated colometry and sustained rhetorical flow. This is the boast of Dai Greatcoat, Jones' homage to the 'flyting' speech of Diomedes to Glaucus in *Iliad* VI.119–43 as well as an ironic salute to David Lloyd George. Dai proclaims his qualifications for the status of warrior, citing the participation of himself and his forefathers in the entire history of biblical and European warfare, mingling his Hebrew, classical and Welsh historical narratives with dizzying abandon. His fathers, he tells us, fought with the Black Prince of Wales, with Abel against Cain. Dai himself 'built a shithouse for Artaxerxes', the Persian King from 404 until 358 BCE who vanquished his brother in Xenophon's *Anabasis* and was famous for initiating architectural projects at Susa and Ecbatana.[47] Dai fought with the biblical Saul, who was armed like Saint Derfel of Wales; he fought 'in the standing wheat in Cantium' (Kent, where Julius Caesar landed in 55 BCE).[48] A passage mostly consisting of a list of Arthurian battles at places with Latin names (e.g. in regione Linnuis), drawn from the 9th-century *Historia Brittonum*, opens with a reference to Socrates, barefoot at Potidaea. Dai associates himself with the Trojan exile Brutus who 'digged the outer vallum' at 'Troy Novaunt', and with the giant-king Brân of Welsh mythology. He fought with the Archangel Michael in the war described in Revelation 12:7–13 but he also 'served Longinus that Dux bat-blind and bent; the Dandy Xth are my regiment'.[49] Longinus was the blind soldier who, according to Roman Catholic tradition, pierced the crucified Jesus' side with a spear; the Tenth Legion were favoured by Julius Caesar during the Gallic War.

Into the dark wood

Dai's uncommon aria on past military exploits anchors the action at a point in a transhistorical process which stretches back to the earliest conflicts recorded in European literature and even beyond. This diachronic perspective is bound up with Jones' identity as an Anglo-Welshman fighting in the Welsh Fusiliers. In the preface, he says that he fought alongside Londoners and Welshmen, who bore together in their bodies 'the genuine tradition of the Island of Britain ... . Those are before Caractacus was'.[50] The Caractacus allusion recalls the use of the defiant Briton Caractacus, celebrated by Tacitus, in early 20th-century British imperial propaganda (see Chapter 12). The climax of *In Parenthesis* contains the most emotionally intense engagements with classical War Poetry, in a sequence which places the *Aeneid* before us. John Ball, who shares Jones' skill at draughtsmanship, contemplates the wooded grove chosen for the engagement. He becomes an avatar of Virgil's Aeneas on his quest for the golden bough. It grows on a tree within the sanctuary of Diana of the Wood, Diana Nemorensis, at her sanctuary near Aricia in the Alban hills (*Aeneid* VI.136–8). Aeneas' mythical journey inspired Sir James Frazer's *The Golden Bough* (1890):[51]

> Keep date with the genius of the place—come with a weapon or effectual branch—and here this winter copse might well be special to Diana's Jack, for none might attempt it, but by perilous bough-plucking … .
>
> In the mirror: below the wood, his undulating breastworks all along, he sees and loses, thinks he sees again, grey movement for the grey stillness, where the sand-bag wall dipped a little.[52]

Jones implies that terrible violence is about to take place. At Aricia, each priest of Diana, each 'King of the Wood' (Rex Nemorensis) was replaced in the cult when a runaway slave mounted a challenge and then killed the incumbent priest in single combat. The grey 'mirror' which Ball thinks he sees beneath the sand-bag walls alludes to the circular Lake Nemi at Aricia.

The 'golden bough' sequence of *In Parenthesis* now segues into another classical vision at the wood: 'great strippings-off hanged from tenuous fibres swaying, whitened to decay—as swung immolations for the northern Cybele'.[53] The descent into the lethal Underworld of Mametz Wood is accompanied by the image of vegetation swinging from trees like sacrifices for a northern Cybele, the near-eastern goddess for whom men voluntarily castrated themselves. Jones' reference to the German foe as coming from places beyond 'Hercynia' and the description of the gateway to the trenches as 'this gate of Mars armipotente, the grisly place, like flat painted scene in top-lights' crude disclosing' are both informed by W.F. Jackson Knight's translation of *Aeneid* VII.601–.5, on the opening of the twin Roman Gates of War (as a fellow Roman Catholic, Jones was influenced by this classical scholar and expert on Virgil and Augustine): the custom applied 'when Romans first stir Mars to engage battle, alike if they prepare to launch war's miseries with might and main on Getae, Hyrcanians, or Arabs, or to journey to India'.[54] For Jones, World War I was a sacrificial offering to both Diana of the Wood and Cybele of the North, but also the latest in the perpetual re-opening of the primordial Gates of War, consecrated to Mars.

The poem's *nekuia* reminds us that the descent to the Underworld had become 'the single most important myth for Modernist authors'.[55] T.S. Eliot said that Tiresias was the unifying figure of the nightmarish *The Waste Land* (1922), at 'the evening hour that strives / Homeward, and brings the sailor home from sea'.[56] In 1935 Ezra Pound, whose first *Canto* begins with Tiresias, said that the *nekuia* was an atavistic remembering of primeval rites capable of putting us in touch with the earliest Mediterranean sensibilities.[57] Joyce, in the Hades chapter of *Ulysses*, 'represented the material and spiritual dislocations produced by Western capitalism as an infernal condition'[58] which led directly to the hellish trenches of World War I. And Jones' poem portrays a katabasis with no corresponding anabasis, except the unachievable goal of 'ascendancy' over the enemy after climbing upwards from a trench and 'over the top':[59]

> it all went west with the tin-hat—that harbinger of their anabasis, of these latter days, of a more purposed hate, and the establishment of unquestioned ascendancy in no-man's-land.

Mametz Wood is in the final, seventh section finally called simply 'the dark wood',[60] in a resounding echo of the *selva oscura* of the second line of the *Inferno* of Dante Alighieri. It is at the dark wood that John Ball is injured and his comrades die. This climactic section opens in Latin, with allusions to the vulgate Latin Bible: *Invenimus eum in campis silvae*, 'we have found it in the fields of the woods', which in Psalm 131.6 refers to the tabernacle David vows to build for God. Then come the evocative words from the Vulgate version of the Lamentations of Jeremiah for the fall of Jerusalem, '*Matribus suis dixerunt: ubi est triticum et vinum? Cum deficerent quasi vulnerati … cum exhalarent animas suas in sinu matrum suarum*'. 'They say to their mothers, Where is grain and wine? When they swoon as the wounded … / When their soul is poured out into their mothers' bosom'.

Despite the classicism of the katabasis and Dai Greatcoat sequences, Jones' *In Parenthesis* is a profoundly Christian poem, partly structured on the ritual sequence of the Eucharist.[61] But its classicism reveals Christianity as an outgrowth of an earlier, pagan theology. The 'Christmas' sequence is introduced thus:[62]

> It was yet quite early in the morning, at the time of Saturnalia, when men properly are in winter quarters, lighting His birthday candles—all a green-o.
>
> When children look with serious eyes on brand-new miracles

The antique conjurings underlie the poem's strangely objective tone, its gaze like children 'with serious eyes'. It is not patriotic. It is not a protest poem. It is not a pacifist poem. The war may have been senseless, even absurd, but the lower-ranking men who fought in it were not.

Jones defines what he is trying to do while describing the unsuitability of the damp lowlands around the trenches to combat:[63]

> It was a bad country to contend in, when such contention most required a way of life below the ground. Yet by fascined track they come to within their walls. They labour with the bulging gabions, they ladle and wattle … Two armies face and hold their crumbling *limites* intact. They're worthy of

> an intelligent song for all the stupidity of their contest. A boast for the dyke keepers, for the march wardens.

In Parenthesis is an 'intelligent song' to celebrate the deeds of the trench-digging lower-class warriors of the Somme; 'the stupidity of their contest' is not the point. The infantrymen's varied voices, and Ball's intermittently prominent consciousness, along with the subdued, Homerically non-judgemental omniscient narrator, present the appalling events with a curious detachment. Despite its use of epigraphs to each of its seven sections taken from *Y Gododdin*, a medieval Welsh poem attributed to the bard Aneirin, and consisting of elegies to the men who fell at the battle of Catraeth (600 CE), *In Parenthesis* is not elegiac.[64] Nor is its vision exactly tragic: there is investigation of the *causes* of the suffering and no emotive lingering on trauma. There is, however, a reference to Melpomene, Muse of Tragedy, towards the end. The wounded Ball's thoughts veer between the stretcher-bearers and the hospital, where 'Mrs. Willy Hartington has learned to draw sheets and so has Miss Melpomené; and on the south lawns, men walk in red white and blue under the cedars and by every green tree and beside comfortable waters'.[65]

The eternal goddesses of war

Miss Melpomené enters not battle but the future of the wounded soldier, his recuperation. She was one of the figures from the poem whom Jones sketched in the manuscript—one of his many instantiations of an eternal goddess-figure, alluring, mythic, part Helen of Troy, part Diana of the Woods and part Virgin Mary. She prefigures the Ur-matriarchal divinity proposed in *The White Goddess* (1948) by that other Mametz Wood survivor, Robert Graves.[66]

In Parenthesis does lend war, although no sentimental, elegiac or tragic overtones, a *metaphysical* aspect in its relationship between the men who wage it and its abstraction as a mysterious, eternal feminine principle, simultaneously mother, lover and female *genius loci*.[67] Dai Greatcoat's speech had fused into one female 'toast of the Rig'ment' a woman called 'Helen Camulodunum' (at the Battle of Camulodunum, the British Iceni massacred the Roman Ninth Legion in 61 CE), the Virgin Mary under her Roman Catholic title 'Mediatrix', a figure from a popular rhyme, and the Welsh folktale heroine Elen Luyddawg, alias Saint Helen of Caernarfon:[68]

> She's the girl with the sparkling eyes, she's the Bracelet Giver, she's a regular draw with the labour companies, whereby the paved army-paths are hers that grid the island which is her dower. Elen Luyddawg she is—more she is than Helen Argive.

Jones' eternally recurring feminine principle also appears in the form of Argive Helen's sister Penelope, waiting at home with her dog: the 'mademoiselle at

Croix Barbée' waits for her man to return, one of the 'green girls in broken keeps' who 'have only mastiff-guards'.[69]

Men have always offered themselves up to the feminine archetypal figure, half gentle nun and half lascivious whore:[70]

> But sweet sister death has gone debauched today and stalks on this high ground with strumpet confidence, makes no coy veiling of her appetite but leers from you to me with all her parts discovered.

As a thoroughgoing Modernist poem on World War I, and by a non-officer combatant, the poem is unique. Robichaud has shown that Jones' response to the Middle Agesis profoundly innovative;[71] it marks a violent break with pre-Raphaelite medievalism by seeing the chivalric age through a Modernist lens. The same, as we have seen, can be said of Jones' classicism. By 1937 his book collection included many on classical mythology and Roman Britain. There is also a large group of translations from and studies of classical authors: a Latin grammar, a Latin dictionary, a Greek grammar, a dictionary of New Testament Greek, Aristotle's *Nicomachean Ethics*, Augustine's *Confessions*, Gilbert Murray's translation of Euripides' *Trojan Women* (1905), all of Caesar's writings, the *Aeneid*, the *Iliad*, the *Odyssey*, Horace, Lucretius and a volume of Warmington's *Remains of Old Latin*.[72]

Jones' self-education, between fighting and publishing *In Parenthesis*, transformed its allusive depth and cultural complexity. He explained its title as indicating the way that war takes place between outbreak and peace treaty, and life takes place between the brackets constituted by birth and death.[73] But the poem was also created in the parenthesis between the two world wars. The new order which emerged from the first created the circumstances which made the second inevitable. Old monarchies were replaced by shaky republics and governments with extended powers which became breeding grounds for ethnic nationalism and resentment about the national boundaries demarcated under the Versailles Treaty. The crumbling of the European world empires abroad seemed reflected in the financial ruin and demoralisation of the European continent at home. And in a picture which Jones completed just after the beginning of the Blitz in 1941, and which has powerful correspondences with the frontispiece to *In Parenthesis*, the connection between the two wars is crystallised.[74] (Figure 24.2.) It depicts a full-bodied, Rubens-esque female nude of a type he had drawn before. But this one he entitled simply 'Aphrodite', after considering titles reflecting his belief in a universal type of the goddess 'Aphrodite Pandemos: The Triple Goddess', 'Turan' (the Etruscan love goddess) and 'The Lady'.[75] A friend suggested 'Aphrodite in Aulis' in 1949, and Jones embraced the implicit allusion to the sacrifice of Iphigenia enthusiastically.

Aphrodite is depicted with the crescent moon and stars belonging to the Madonna of Revelation 12, a figure in whom Jones wrote that he wanted to embrace 'all female cult figures, all goddesses rolled into one, mother-figure and virgo inter virgines, the pierced woman and mother and all her foretypes'.[76] She

FIGURE 24.2 'Aphrodite at Aulis' by David Jones (1940–1941), reproduced by courtesy of the Tate Modern.

is shackled to the sacrificial altar on which she stands, as the statue of Aphrodite was shackled in her temple at Sparta (Pausanias 3.15.22). Like the soldier in the frontispiece, she seems trapped within a chaotic frame crammed with disturbing detail. A crumbling edifice with four columns, in each of the classical orders, represents the disintegration of civilisation. The barrage balloon in the top left-hand corner signals the new technology of the new war, and there are soldiers and arms from many periods of history. But the most prominent, in the foreground, are the British and German soldiers with the uniform and equipment of World War I. This Aphrodite, a signifier of the transhistorical lust for war drawn from the ancient Greek world, occupies the parenthetic space on the canvas between the brackets constituted by the men in the trenches and the barrage balloon respectively. As in *In Parenthesis*, Jones employs artistic form and the diachronic depth offered by classical imagery to crystallise the acute turmoil undergone by soldiers across time.

Conclusion

Jones insisted in 1962 that no critic had ever yet understood

> the altogether different point of departure of my stuff "from the writing or poetry" or "prose" as conceived by "writers", whether good or bad, from blokes like Rupert Brooke right on through Sassoon and even Owen … It is next to impossible for me to indicate what the difference is.[77]

If we listen hard to *In Parenthesis* we can hear that difference at work in its class perspective, use of Classics and the innovative Modernism required to distinguish that perspective from the War Poets of the officer class. It is a painstaking, Herculean, craftsmanlike attempt to use words to evoke authentically the sustained extremes of trench warfare as experienced by its lowest-ranking combatants, and find in that act of authentic evocation a poetics—even a metaphysics—of human courage. These working-class men are worthy of an intelligent song despite the stupidity of the contest.

Notes

1 www.greatwar.co.uk/research/military-records/ww1-war-dead-records.htm.
2 Root (2006) n.p.
3 See Root (2006). The term was in use in Britain by 1916, when Dawson (1916), a book of letters, was published by the War Department under the title *A 'Temporary Gentleman' in France*.
4 See Westminster Abbey (2017). The problematic category 'War Poetry' is usually said to have been established in 1931 with the publication of Edmund Blunden's edition of Wilfrid Owen (Owen [1931]): see Bergonzi (1965) 5.
5 Another version of this chapter is also published as Hall (2018h).
6 Jones (2014 [1937] 89. For this sense of the Latin noun *limes*, *limitis* see e.g. Tacitus, *Agricola* 2.7 and *Germania* 29.
7 Jones (2014 [1937]) 183. The layout of the text throughout this chapter reproduces that specified by Jones in this edition; as an engraver, he saw the look of the printed page as contributing to its meaning. See Hills (1997).
8 Aldritt (2003) 9–13.
9 Hyne (1995) 11.
10 The authoritative study of Jones' military experiences is now Dilworth (2012).
11 Graves (1929) 175.
12 First published in Graves (1917).
13 See Hyne (1995) 12.
14 Hirst (2007) 53.
15 Cohen (1982) 47.
16 David Jones (1978) 132.
17 Jones (2014 [1937]) xii.
18 Jones (2014 [1937]) 123.
19 Jones (2014 [1937]) 150.
20 Jones (2014 [1937]) 185–6.
21 See Moore (1987).
22 Hyne (1995) 13. On the implementation of chemical weapons in World War I see Moore (1987).

23 Jones (2014 [1937]) xiv.
24 Not published until after his death, in David Jones (1978).
25 Jones (2014 [1937]) xiv.
26 Jones (2014 [1937]) 90.
27 Yeats praised it in a conversation reported in Dilworth (2012) 217; Eliot pronounced it 'a work of genius' in David Jones (2014 [1937]) vii; Auden (1962); Greene (1980) 28; Levi (1967).
28 Murray (1997) 3. On the classical figures in Jones' other major poem *Anathemata*, see chapters 8 and 9 of Miles (1990).
29 Jones (2014 [1937]) 155.
30 See the letter of 15th–19th July 1973 to René Hague, quoted in Hague (1975) 9.
31 Jones (2014 [1937]) 179.
32 See especially Robert Bly's essay 'The Prose Poem as an Evolving Form' in Bly (1986).
33 Jones 2014 [1937]) 179.
34 Dudley (2013) 107.
35 Jones (2014 [1937] 135.
36 Jones (2014 [1937]) 179. Eleftherios Venizelos was at that time Prime Minister of Greece.
37 Jones (2014 [1937]) 6.
38 Jones (2014 [1937]) 7.
39 Jones (2014 [1937]) 118.
40 Jones (2014 [1937]) 127–8.
41 Jones (2014 [1937]) 160.
42 Jones (2014 [1937]) 120.
43 Jones (2014 [1937]) 91, 167, 60, 166.
44 Jones (2014 [1937]) 88, 24.
45 Jones (2014 [1937]) 176.
46 Jones (2014 [1937]) 54.
47 Jones (2014 [1937]) 78–9.
48 Jones (2014 [1937]) 80.
49 Jones (2014 [1937]) 81, 82, 83–4.
50 Jones (2014 [1937]) x.
51 See Hall (2013a) 135–42.
52 Jones (2014 [1937]) 66–7.
53 Jones (2014 [1937]) 67.
54 Jones (2014 [1937]) 44; Jackson Knight (1956) VI.606ff.
55 Smith (2001) 7. See Hall (2008) chapter 15 *passim*.
56 *The Waste Land* 3.220–1, with the note on 3.228; Eliot (1974) 71, 82.
57 Pound (1971) 274, quoted in Kenner (1971) 147.
58 Falconer (2005) 27.
59 Jones (2014 [1937]) 114.
60 Jones (2014 [1937]) 165.
61 See further Query (2013).
62 Jones (2014 [1937]) 65.
63 Jones (2014 [1937]) 88–9.
64 Dilworth (1988) 42.
65 Jones (2014 [1937]) 186.
66 Dilworth (1988) 140–1.
67 Dilworth (1988) 149–52.
68 Jones (2014 [1937]) 80–1.
69 Jones (2014 [1937]) 35.
70 Jones (2014 [1937]) 162–3.
71 Robichaud (2007).

72 H.C. Jones (1995).
73 David Jones (2014 [1937]) xv.
74 Tate Gallery T02036.
75 Tate Gallery T02037. This information is derived from the article 'Aphrodite in Aulis 1941' on the Tate Gallery website, www.tate.org.uk/art/artworks/jones-aphrodite-in-aulis-t02036, last accessed 24th June 2017.
76 A letter quoted in Hague (1975) 38.
77 Letter of 22nd May 1962, in David Jones (2015). See Murray (1997).

25

THEATRE PRACTITIONERS

Introduction

No people's history of classics in Britain would be complete without describing the class-conscious and sophisticated classical theatre pioneered by Theatre Workshop. Founded by the working-class communists Joan Littlewood (1914–2002) and Ewan MacColl (1915–1989), this radical group of theatre-makers, especially in their interbellum incarnations as Theatre of Action and Theatre Union, fought bravely in the cultural wars of the 1930s for the rights of the working classes. Their engagement with classical, and especially Greek, theatre was informed by the public-facing, but cutting-edge scholarship discussed earlier, in Chapter 23.

A man called Jimmie Miller discovered a copy of Aristophanes' comedies in a secondhand bookshop in Leeds in 1936. Miller (Figure 25.1) was an unemployed motor mechanic turned communist theatre-maker from Salford.[1] Two years previously he had met Littlewood, who was to become his long-term creative collaborator and the most influential female British theatre director to date. Within a decade, Miller transformed himself. He proved himself to be a gifted playwright and a charismatic performer. With the assured theatrical knowledge of Littlewood and a head full of Marxist scholarship, he toured the UK and Europe with radical left-wing theatre troupes, gave Marxist lectures on theatre history and workshops on Stanislavsky's system; he was invited to study at the Soviet Academy for Theatre and Cinema in Moscow.[2] At the onset of World War II, he was drafted into the British Army, deserted after just six months, grew a beard, swore that he had been born in Scotland and changed his name to Ewan MacColl.[3]

A decade or so later, MacColl would even become the celebrated folk-singer and activist of the same name, who sang with and married Peggy Seeger, the half-sister of the even more widely celebrated US folk musician and communist,

DOI: 10.4324/9781315446608-29

FIGURE 25.1 Jimmie Miller [Ewan MacColl] Courtesy of The National Archives, KV 2/2175.

Pete Seeger. But this chapter closes our book by exploring the creative engagement of Littlewood and MacColl with Aristophanes' *Lysistrata* and how the rising tide of international communism in the 1930s influenced their responses to the ancient play.[4] Their work on *Lysistrata*, which they both performed and adapted into a new musical drama, *Operation Olive Branch*, was indispensable preparation for the ensemble's path-breaking satirical-epic musical of 1963, *Oh, What a Lovely War!*

MacColl was brought up in Salford, Lancashire, in an atmosphere thick with factory grime and class politics. His parents were Scottish socialists. His mother worked tirelessly as a charwoman and his father, Will Miller, was an iron moulder, often unemployed, who suffered from chronic bronchial asthma. He was also a trade unionist, supporter of the Socialist Labour Party, and fiery advocate for the broad syndicalism espoused by Daniel De Leon (see above pp. 199–201) and his followers.[5] MacColl's family was thus intellectually and politically active, but in financial difficulty. He qualified for the 'annual poor children's outing' which, organised by local charities, helped children from the poorest families take a trip out of the city.[6] Growing up in a blend of class-shame and class-consciousness, as Ben Harker's fine biography details, a 'red haze' covered the teenager's eyes, which would only develop over time and crystallise into increasingly clear vision of a revolutionary future.[7]

MacColl joined the Young Communists League, the British branch of the Young Communist International, after leaving school at 14. It was 1929, when the still small but rapidly growing Communist Party of Great Britain (CPGB) was launching its 'Class Against Class' campaign; this resonated with the young MacColl's anger at growing up in poverty, joblessness and boredom.[8] Harker explains that, for MacColl,

> communist analysis supplied a structural explanation for poverty and unemployment–the sources of his class-shame–and a revolutionary solution. Its culture of intellectual enquiry and debate provided a forum in which his hitherto secretive learning could be given an airing.[9]

On 11th October 1939, an MI5 report states that 'James Henry Miller is a Communist with very extreme views'.[10] MacColl's parents' cottage at the time was considered the headquarters of a secret communist espionage ring. Yet it was the headquarters of nothing more than MacColl and Littlewood's fledgling theatre company, 'Theatre Union'. The young artists were hell-bent on overthrowing capitalism and changing the world. But rather than as spies for the Soviet Union, they wanted to change it as revolutionary dramatists bringing the best of world theatre to the slumbering proletariat.

Littlewood was the daughter of an unmarried showroom assistant of a brush manufacturer in Stockwell, London. With the help of scholarships, she made it through school and the Royal Academy of Dramatic Art (RADA). In 1934 she packed it all in and tramped northwards, planning to stow away on a ship for America. She got as far as Manchester, where she met her match in MacColl.[11] It was an ideal partnership. They were in tune not only politically but also in terms of their artistic ambitions. Theatre Union, which crystallised around them, was their first joint offensive on the cultural plane. Their manifesto read,

> We live in times of great social upheaval; faced with an ever-increasing danger of war and fascism, the democratic people of the world have been forced into action. Their struggle for peace and progress manifests itself in many forms and not the least important of these is the drama.[12]

British socialist theatre in the 1930s

Among such groups, especially before the Nazi–Soviet Pact of 1939, there was a belief in the Soviet programme. Whatever our worldview, we need to bear in mind that while our privileged historical vantage point allows us to see the horrors lurking below the surface, it also demands that we handle with due sensitivity the inspirational dreams that captivated a whole generation. This included those under-celebrated intellectuals (discussed in Chapter 23) who were instrumental in forging a new relationship between the British public and 'high culture', not least ancient Greek and Roman literature and theatre, as well as artists. The creative individuals were less enthused by economic theory than by what Alick West called 'heighten[ing] men's consciousness', a process which they believed revolutionary socialism promised.[13]

Many socialists became disillusioned by the end of the 1930s. C. Day Lewis wrote in 1940 that the events in Spain were 'a death to us, Munich a mourning'.[14] But MacColl and Littlewood remained revolutionaries, even if their relationship with the CPGB over the years was intermittently distant and volatile. Both earned substantial MI5 folders, in which can be found files, photos and press cuttings that record the activities of these two 'known' and 'active' communists. There is correspondence between MI5 operatives and BBC officials that documents Littlewood and MacColl's blacklisting from most jobs in the Corporation, even before they were finally and literally barred from their place of work in 1940.[15] They sustained consistent creative dialogues with the political causes and cultural movements of the CPGB, even though their views could rarely be said to have been completely 'in tune' with other CPGB-affiliated theatrical organisations, such as the Workers' Theatre Movement (WTM) and New Theatre League (NTL).

The idea of 'being in tune' suggests a more consistent and uncontested communist cultural policy than ever materialised in practice during the turbulent 1920s and 1930s. Those socially diverse and opinionated individuals who served on the various CPGB boards were generally committed to the Leninist organisational method of 'democratic centralism', and in Britain there was especially fiery debate surrounding cultural policy. But stakes were considerably lower than they were in the Soviet states. By speaking their minds and challenging their political allies' interpretations of the Marxist scriptures, British communists may have been jeopardising their position in the Party, but they were rarely risking their lives.[16] MacColl and Littlewood's relationship with the CPGB was mutually beneficial, but frequently strained. Their theatrical development was rarely far out of line with the directions of other theatre groups of the left, but technically they were streets ahead.

In 1931 MacColl formed an Agit-Prop theatre troupe called the 'Red Megaphones', who (like the WTM, whose scripts they sometimes used) saw their art as a weapon in the class struggle. 'Agit-Prop' was a self-consciously revolutionary style pioneered in improvised performances outdoors or in factories in the Soviet Union, and in Germany by Erwin Piscator and Bertolt Brecht.[17] Like some of their German, Czechoslovakian and Italian counterparts, the Red Megaphones performed in the streets and made appearances at open-air rallies, protesting against the evils of capitalism and, more specifically, the unfair treatment of workers in Lancashire's textile industry.[18] MacColl adopted the slogan of the London-based WTM troupes, 'A Propertyless Theatre for the Propertyless Class'.[19] Both Littlewood and MacColl, in later life, likened Agit-Prop to the outdoor theatrical activity of past cultures, and especially ancient Greek drama, which they both presented as proto-communist drama. MacColl, for example, wrote: 'It was what it must have been like in the time of Aeschylus in great popular theatre. Crude? Yes, but as honest as we knew how to be'.[20]

The 1930s witnessed a general shift in Communist International, or 'Comintern', policy from what is usually dubbed the 'Class Against Class' strategy (which called for Communist Parties to distance themselves from and fight against other left-wing parties) to the so-called 'Popular Front' (PF) strategy. This encouraged a unified stance with other liberal political parties to combat directly the rising fascism across Europe.[21] The movement was officially endorsed by the Comintern, in the Seventh World Congress in Moscow, 1935.[22] Comintern head Georgi Dimitrov's speech argued that fascism had to be defeated in the cultural as well as the political sphere:[23]

> Communists who do nothing to enlighten the masses on the past of their people ... voluntarily hand over to the fascist falsifiers all that is valuable in the historical past of the nation ... The proletariat of all countries has shed much of its blood to win bourgeois-democratic liberties, and will naturally fight with all its strength to retain them.[24]

The Marxist left responded resoundingly to Dimitrov's call to promulgate the often-submerged historical exempla of popular radicalism. As Elinor Taylor notes, Dimitrov's speech 'seemed to enter the bloodstream of the left almost immediately'.[25]

This was then a pivotal moment in British cultural history, and triggered a frenzied exploration of the potential of culture, only a few years after MacColl and others advocating political theatre had been rebuked as time wasters by CPGB pundits. It set in motion a snowball of publications through the 1930s displaying the historical struggles against and victories of the people over vested interest. Jack Lindsay and Edgell Rickword, for example, in 1939 printed *A Handbook of Freedom: A Record of English Democracy through Twelve Centuries*, surveying British popular radicalism from serfdom to socialism.[26] The book is a prime example of the PF's so-called 'national turn', since it is concerned with the portrayal of distinctly English proto-communism. But the British left by no means restricted itself to British history: the classically trained communist writers of the 1930s trawled the outer margins of the Western tradition from its ancient Greek origins to the present day. It was not only expensively educated Communists and sympathisers who reached back to Greece and Rome, but also working-class young men and women, like MacColl, who used translations of the ancient writers and engaged with an impressive amount of classical scholarship.

As we have seen, in 1934 Joan Littlewood left the Royal Academy of Dramatic Arts (RADA), marched Northwards and settled in Manchester, where she was attracted by the militant and mesmerising MacColl. The historian Raphael Samuels (1934–1996) too was astounded by MacColl's fiery personality and energy. Samuels reflected in the 1980s, that MacColl was

> the first real revolutionary I had ever met, terrifyingly well organised, whether engaged in tracing the etymology of a word in a Scottish tinker's

> song, or … organising a production of Aristophanes' *Frogs* from a minesweeper in the Pacific with the putative cast … spread out in the Royal Navy halfway across the world.[27]

Sadly, no trace of MacColl's *Frogs* survives. Perhaps it was never made.

Theatre Union and the Greeks

Fascism was taking hold across Europe and global war looked ever more likely. MacColl began to consider Agit-Prop theatre too blunt an instrument in the increasingly high-stakes cultural war, but also aesthetically too 'crude in the age of Appia. Don't discount beauty'.[28] Fringe theatre in Britain was also inspired by the London publication in 1931 of Léon Moussinac's *The New Movement in the Theatre*, with its scintillating photographs of Russian and Soviet experimental non-naturalist productions and modernist set designs by Pablo Picasso and George Grosz. MacColl and Littlewood revelled in the copy in Manchester Central Library, finding it 'a veritable treasure-trove of concepts and ideas'.[29] Besides Piscator's production of *The Good Soldier Schwejk*, it was in this book that they discovered Alexander Tairov's *Phèdre* and, most importantly, Vladimir Nemirovich-Danchenko's polemical *Lysistrata*, first performed in the Art Theatre, Moscow in 1923.[30]

1936 heralded the pair's first joint theatrical project, Theatre Union, with their tagline 'The Theatre of the People'. Their manifesto boldly proclaimed:

> The theatre must face up to the problems of its times; it cannot ignore the poverty and human suffering which increases every day … If the theatre of to-day would reach the heights achieved four [*sic*] thousand years ago in Greece and four hundred years ago in Elizabethan England it must face up to such problems. To those who say that such affairs are not the concern of the theatre or that the theatre should confine itself to treading in the paths of "beauty" and "dignity", we would say "Read Shakespeare, Marlowe, Webster, Sophocles, Aeschylus, Aristophanes, Calderón, Molière, Lope-de-Vega, Schiller and the rest".

Their commitment to their own theatrical development and the depth of study undertaken were extraordinary.

Theatre Union's manifesto closed with a combative statement that the theatre of the future 'will not be born in the genteel atmosphere of retirement and seclusion, but rather in the clash and turmoil of the battles between oppressors and the oppressed'.[31] The overtly communist activities of Theatre Union, which would in 1945 become the famed Theatre Workshop, have been downplayed in most recent accounts. Stead's ongoing research into recently declassified MI5 files of cultural figures of the period shows that a number of those revered cultural figures were viewed by the contemporary authorities as enemies of the state.[32]

Some of their views appear crude or misguided, but we need to resist the urge to create narratives which obscure their true allegiances, the product of social crisis and imminent war.

On 28th July 1940, for example, Theatre Union performed at Manchester's Free Trade Hall, as part of a Communist Party anniversary celebration. We know this because a Manchester policeman submitted a memo to MI5 the following day:

> After Gallagher's speech, a short play depicting the progress of the Communist Party during the past twenty years was given by members of "Theatre of Action", led by Joan Miller (née LITTLEWOOD).[33]

Another report from the Lancashire Constabulary, dated 1st February 1939, states that Littlewood 'is said to be highly intellectual and a keen communist'.[34] At this time neither Littlewood nor MacColl appears to have been taking precautions to conceal their political inclinations. Even though MacColl was supposed to be serving in the 10th Battalion (Home Defence) of the King's Regiment (and was even on a Special Observations List for his known communist sympathies[35]), he and Littlewood were living at his parents' home in rural Lancashire and playing lead roles in performances at political rallies and celebrations of overtly communist organisations, including the *Daily Worker* and the Friends of Russia Society.[36] Theatre Union even for a time rehearsed their plays and sketches in the Communist Party Headquarters at 88 Rusholme Road, Manchester.

James Smith reminds us that their revolutionary politics opened as well as closed doors to the company since there were sympathisers in influential positions.[37] The picture that emerges from the now-declassified MI5 records—even when treated with due scepticism—is one of a theatre group actively involved in a semi-subterranean communist network throughout the cultural Cold War. It is a stark reminder that, in Britain, those suspected of being communists were under close surveillance, blacklisted from jobs and hounded by the secret services and their informants. It is difficult now to fathom the depths of the government's paranoia at the time. Not only were people encouraged to inform on their friends and neighbours if they suspected them of communism, but even local policemen were sent to stake out and eavesdrop on the conversations of a group of young men and women sitting in a cottage in rural Lancashire, planning their next theatrical production. The tightening surveillance of the regional police and the escalating audacity of Theatre Union came to a head in March 1940, when the troupe performed their politically inflammatory 'living newspaper' *Last Edition* in Manchester, without sufficiently working around the licensing restrictions.[38] The play was shut down by local police, who called it 'thinly-veiled communist propaganda', and MacColl and Littlewood were both prosecuted and fined.[39]

MacColl and Littlewood's meeting was one of kindred spirits. They developed in each other a shared understanding of what theatre could and *should* do. Part of what a grass-roots revolutionary communist theatre troupe should do, as far as they were concerned, was to produce Athenian drama. Despite the immediate associations of ancient Greek and Roman classics with 'bourgeois' culture—generated by centuries of instrumentalisation in the consolidation of social division—MacColl and Littlewood simply identified much classical culture as constituting the 'best' and most beautiful art for modernity, whatever our politics.[40] Their thinking echoes the seminal 4th thesis of V.I. Lenin's resolution for the first all-Russia Congress of the Soviet artistic institution Proletkult (1920), where he argued that Marxist ideology had been victorious 'because, far from rejecting the most valuable achievements of the bourgeois epoch, it has, on the contrary, assimilated and refashioned everything of value in the more than two thousand years of the development of human thought and culture'. Lenin had announced that only

> further work on this basis and in this direction, inspired by the practical experience of the proletarian dictatorship as the final stage in the struggle against every form of exploitation, can be recognised as the development of a genuine proletarian culture.[41]

Lenin was reacting to ultra-left proposals put forward since 1917 that the art of non-socialist societies of the past needed to be jettisoned as ideologically retrograde.[42] MacColl and Littlewood seem to have interpreted this directive as meaning that only the best, the most valuable remains of 'more than two thousand years of the development of human thought and culture', was good enough for British workers. As we saw in Chapter 23, there were numerous publications from British Marxist intellectuals that promoted this view of the classical world.[43] MacColl himself was fond of quoting an observation which they (it seems apocryphally) attributed to Engels; 'The bourgeoisie have raised monuments to the classics. If they'd read them, they'd have burned them'.[44]

After the *Last Edition* debacle mentioned above, the group (struggling with the fine) resolved to settle down to an intensive period of study. They considered themselves to be 'part of a world-wide movement to create a people's art'.[45] To do this they drew up a reading list, which became mandatory for members of Theatre Union, and later Theatre Workshop.[46] The list (a copy of which remains in the Theatre Royal archive[47]) is a window into leftist popular classical scholarship and translations. It contains several works by the leading communist classicists discussed in Chapter 23, along with The German Jewish musicologist Curt Sach's *World History of Dance* (1937). Other standard works of accessible criticism and classical translations are given, along with them Bukharin's *Historical Materialism* (1925), *The Communist Manifesto*, and Engels' *The Origin of the Family*. 'To be read concurrently with' the Roman comedies of Plautus and Terence, and various medieval plays through to Shakespeare, are works by Lenin on *Imperialism* and *State and Revolution*, Engels' *Dialectics of Nature* and the *Condition of the Working Class in England*, Hyman Levy's *Philosophy for a Modern Man* (1938) and Arthur Rothstein's *From Chartism to Labourism* (1929).[48]

Rosalie Williams, then an English Literature student in Manchester, who became a key member of Theatre Workshop and a celebrated TV actor,[49] recalled the intensity with which the members of Theatre Union were expected to educate themselves, alongside practical exercises:

> we studied the periods of popular theatre and their dramaturgy—the Greeks, Molière, the Elizabethans, the Spanish theatre of Cervantes, trying to find out what they had in common that had appealed to ordinary people and which might provide some basis for our own work in theatre. We discovered that they all had a progressive approach to topical themes in their plays.[50]

Each member would pick one area of special interest and present their findings to the rest. Their first port of call was the Manchester Reference Library, which Littlewood would later call 'our Alma Mater'.[51] Both Littlewood and MacColl followed George Thomson in approaching classical literature in new ways, adapted in part from the Cambridge ritualists, especially Gilbert Murray, and social anthropology. Sharpened by their Marxist ideology, their view of Greek drama was of a primitive form of popular performance, the epitome of proto-communist theatre.

The company's reception of the Greeks and their drama—largely unfettered as it was by associations with formal classical education and traditional classical scholarship—was more attractive to them than the 'bourgeoise' theatre of the West End, and indeed what they saw as the predominately pessimistic, conventional British socialist drama of the time.[52] But it was not only to the Greeks that they turned their attention, in the search for a people's theatre. In the Theatre Workshop manifesto (1945) they were to tell the public:

> The great theatres of all times have been popular theatres which reflected the dreams and struggles of the people. The theatre of Aeschylus and Sophocles, of Shakespeare and Ben Jonson, of the Commedia dell'Arte and Molière derived their inspiration, their language, their art from the people. We want a theatre with a living language, a theatre which is not afraid of the sound of its own voice and which will comment as fearlessly on Society as did Ben Jonson and Aristophanes.[53]

The group followed the examples of both Nemirovich-Danchenko in Moscow and the Provincetown Players in New York,[54] in working with Aristophanes' *Lysistrata*, twice, and differently.

Lysistrata in Manchester

The first production was performed under the banner of Theatre Union in a cluster of plays responding directly to the outbreak of the Spanish Civil War and the rise of fascism. Other than *Lysistrata* the group staged performances of Lope de Vega's *Fuente Ovejuna* (or *The Sheep-well*) and an adaptation of Hasek's *Good Soldier Schwejk*. The *Lysistrata* script, first performed in and around Manchester from circa 1938 to 1941,[55] was closely based on a readable, unexpurgated and anonymous translation, found in the *Eleven Comedies of Aristophanes*, first published privately in 1912 for the Athenian Society in London.[56] MacColl's copy, however, may have been the 1936 reprint by Tudor Publishing Company, New York.[57] We can tell from the scene breakdown, shown in the 1938 programme (Figure 25.2), that there is little digression from the original plot. Those original scenes of the play remain relatively close to the 1912 translation, even when it was rewritten with additional scenes, as in *Operation Olive Branch* nearly a decade later.

After the outbreak of war, when their usual rehearsal space in the Manchester Communist Party HQ was commandeered in the name of the war effort, Theatre Union found rent-free rehearsal space in the crypt of All Saints' Church.[58] The vicar, Etienne Watts, believed that 'communists were the only true Christians'.[59] He decorated the crypt with two banners, one red with a golden hammer and sickle, and the other bearing the symbol of the cross. As the men in the play were called up to the front, Joan Littlewood and her dwindling troupe rehearsed Aristophanes beneath the hammer and sickle and surrounded by the dead.[60] Some members of the company were literally buried for a time, when the Blitz directed its destructive gaze northwards, and All Saints' Church was damaged beyond repair.[61]

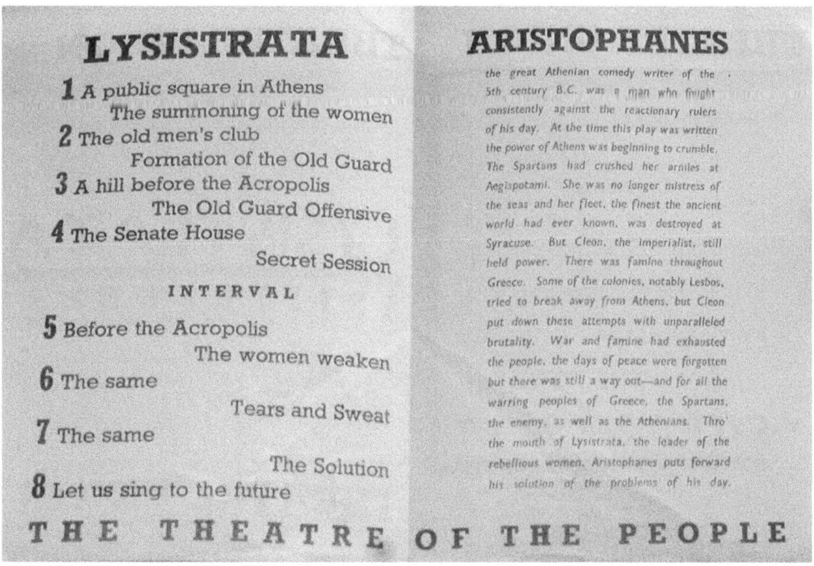
LYSISTRATA

1 A public square in Athens
The summoning of the women
2 The old men's club
Formation of the Old Guard
3 A hill before the Acropolis
The Old Guard Offensive
4 The Senate House
Secret Session

INTERVAL

5 Before the Acropolis
The women weaken
6 The same
Tears and Sweat
7 The same
The Solution
8 Let us sing to the future

ARISTOPHANES

the great Athenian comedy writer of the 5th century B.C. was a man who fought consistently against the reactionary rulers of his day. At the time this play was written the power of Athens was beginning to crumble. The Spartans had crushed her armies at Aegispotami. She was no longer mistress of the seas and her fleet, the finest the ancient world had ever known, was destroyed at Syracuse. But Cleon, the imperialist, still held power. There was famine throughout Greece. Some of the colonies, notably Lesbos, tried to break away from Athens, but Cleon put down these attempts with unparalleled brutality. War and famine had exhausted the people, the days of peace were forgotten but there was still a way out—and for all the warring peoples of Greece, the Spartans, the enemy, as well as the Athenians. Thro' the mouth of Lysistrata, the leader of the rebellious women, Aristophanes puts forward his solution of the problems of his day.

THE THEATRE OF THE PEOPLE

FIGURE 25.2 Centrefold of 1938 programme of *Lysistrata* by Theatre Union, reproduced by courtesy of Theatre Royal Stratford East Archives Collection, London.

MacColl referred to the pre- and early war *Lysistrata* as 'a spirited romp with lots of bawdy jokes and amusing horseplay'.[62] Its official opening at the Lesser Trade Hall, Manchester, coinciding with the Munich Agreement, or 'Munich Betrayal' (September 1938), was marred by 'the rising tide of fear and confusion' which accompanied that episode. MacColl recalled,

> We had passed the point where events could be influenced by a reference to the Peloponnesian War ... It's not enough, we said, to have plays which make a generalised exposure of the nature of Capitalism, they must have specific objectives and they must be about events which are taking place now.[63]

Operation Olive Branch

The post-war *Lysistrata*, opening in 1947 under the new name of *Operation Olive Branch*, did just this. It challenged the motives behind the war, presenting it as an extension of the class war by other means. It also hinted that the government was colluding with arms traders (or the Shield and Spear Manufacturers' Federation at Pylos).[64] The company had expressed this view explicitly in *Last Edition* (1940). MacColl grew to regret it, which is perhaps why both these plays still languish in archives. Theatre Union, by virtue of their strong counter-capitalist and anti-war conviction, rather than any kind of blind subservience to 'the [Stalinist] line', found themselves on the 'wrong side of history' in this period.

MacColl said *Operation Olive Branch* was

> a more radical reworking of the text in which soldiers' scenes were interpolated between scenes of striking women and where recondite references to obsolete religious practices were cut out in favour of lines and short sequences borrowed from *The Acharnians*, *The Thesmophoriazusae* and *The Peace*.[65]

Amphitheus crashes in as a deus ex machina and there are other, more subtle Aristophanic imports. The Theatre Royal archive holds a sound desk copy of the script, probably from the 1953 staging when it was rebranded as *Lysistrata*, 'the sauciest classic ever written'.[66] *Operation Olive Branch* opened in Middlesbrough in January 1947, and toured numerous towns in northern England (as was the company's common practice of bringing theatre to the people).[67]

Preparation for every element of the play had been intense. The Theatre Royal Archives hold a folder of materials produced by the artist and life-long CPGB member Ernest 'Ern' Brooks (1911–1993), who painstakingly sketched visual interpretations of the comedy's characters (Figure 25.3), drawing on his study of the scholarship chosen for the group by MacColl and Littlewood (Figure 25.4). As can be seen in the few remaining production photographs (e.g. Figure 25.4),

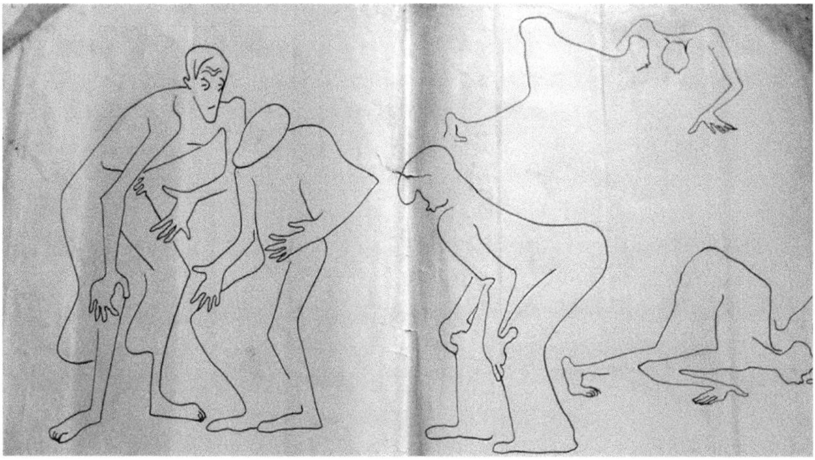

FIGURE 25.3 Early character sketches of Aristophanes' old men by Ern Brooks, reproduced by courtesy of Theatre Royal Stratford East Archives Collection, London.

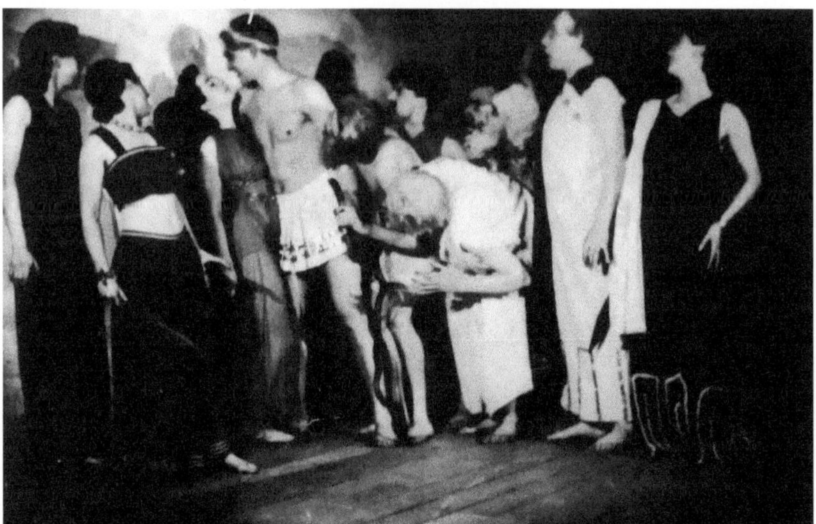

FIGURE 25.4 Production photograph from *Lysistrata*, Theatre Royal, Stratford East, 1953, reproduced by courtesy of Theatre Royal Stratford East Archives Collection, London.

Brooks' designs were taken seriously; the actors' bodies and faces were contorted into the other-worldly stoops and grimaces of the artist's sketchbook.

When Jean Newlove, a student of the famed dance artist and theorist Rudolf Laban, joined the company, her new techniques enabled the actors to sharpen character through posture and movement, complemented by the Appia-style lighting and stage design by John 'Camel' Bury (1925–2000), and classicising costumes designed by Brooks' wife and artistic collaborator Barbara Niven (died 1971). The hard work paid off. *Operation Olive Branch* (1947) made waves, winning for Littlewood her first London run—playing at the Rudolf Steiner Theatre in Northwest London.[68] The staging of the play was reported to 'take one's breath away … The pictorial beauty is astonishing'.[69] Nevertheless, it was no commercial success; the show was pulled before its fortnight's run played out.[70]

Operation Olive Branch was quickly translated into German and performed in East Berlin, where it became popular enough to be brought out in paperback in 1948,[71] and then restaged in 1961 under the joint direction of Littlewood and Horst Schönemann.[72] This production at the Maxim-Gorki-Theater was also filmed and broadcast by the state TV broadcaster DFF.[73] Littlewood encouraged the actors to improvise, drawing on their own experiences of the war:

> I added a scene where soldiers shuffled away from the Front, their feet swathed in sacking, as at Stalingrad, and those actors were magnificent. As it turned out they had all been anti-Hitler, some had been in camps, some had been through the hell of winter soldiering in Russia, but of course they hadn't expected to use their experience in a Greek comedy.[74]

Her bold direction and commitment to the sanctity of satire were not in the least bit hindered by the austere theatrical atmosphere she felt surrounded by at the Maxim Gorki Theatre. In her autobiography, she recalls how she

> had fun with Lampito, the girl from Sparta … First, I gave my impression of the tough C[ommunist] P[arty] rep, who attended my East-West press conference. It went down very well. All the actresses were dying to play the part.
>
> "Mocking a Party member?" said Walter, who was the Party representative in the company.
>
> "Why not? Is the Party above satire?"

As can be seen from Littlewood's recasting of the Spartan Lampito as an East German CP rep, there was at the heart of Theatre Workshop a fearless, urgent and irreverent responsiveness to the present. The performed script could end up diverging from the rehearsal script. We are extremely fortunate to have a sound desk copy of MacColl's script (Theatre Royal Archives, probably 1953) since this copy needed to be constantly updated and true to the actual performance.

MacColl recast the title role, Lysistrata, as a British champion of the working classes. He put contemporary socialist political terminology in her mouth:

> This is no time for tears and lamentations. We have work to do. Lampito, you hurry back to Sparta, and start things moving there. The rest of you will cover Boeotia, Corinth, and the Peloponnese. Work as you've never worked before. Organise all the women in your own districts. Form area committees and rural groups. Organise! Organise![75]

Aristophanes' doddering old men became British World War I veterans, and their scenes (at least in the 1947 version) echoed the Westminster ritual of the House of Commons, which members of the group had visited. One of the old men (mis) quotes Tennyson's *Charge of the Light Brigade* when he explains to a questioning youth 'Ours is not to reason why, ours is but to do and die'.[76] Another old man (Philocleon, the name borrowed from the elderly democrat in Aristophanes' *Wasps*) exhorts a younger man, 'Things change, boy, change! The people you praise yesterday you have to fight to-day. You've got to keep up with the times'. [77]

This is a reference to the altered attitude of Britain towards the Soviet Union after the Anglo–Soviet Agreement, the formal military alliance against Germany signed on 12th July 1941. The friendly relationship was notoriously celebrated in Winston Churchill's 'Sinews of Peace' speech in Fulton, Missouri, on 5th March 1946, in which he praised 'the valiant Russian people' and 'my wartime comrade, Marshal Stalin'.[78] The role of the Magistrate was explicitly recast as Winston Churchill (played by Howard Goorney in 1947 and Joby Blanshard in 1953), as shown by MacColl's skilful imitation of Churchillian apocalyptic speech patterns. The connection was made stronger still by the actor in question mimicking Churchill's gestures and cadences:

> Everywhere the barbarians are on the march; yesterday the slaves in the cobalt mines were revolting for more food. Last week colonial savages were revolting for home rule and today the women are asking, nay … demanding peace. Need I say, gentlemen, that immorality can hardly go further! My friends, the democracy is in the balance! We must defend it, if needs be, with our lives.
>
> (SUSTAINED APPLAUSE)[79]

The palpable allusions to Churchill are further confirmed by Littlewood, who recalled that the old men bore 'a distinct resemblance to Churchill, Pétain, Patton and their crew'.[80] MacColl himself stated on BBC Radio in 1978 that the audience immediately recognised the 'cant phrases' of hypocrisy.[81]

The justification for war had been questioned at the end of Act 2. The Magistrate insists that 'This war is a war of the people in defence of our ancient way of life', but Lampito answers: 'It is a war carried on for private interest at public expense'.[82]

MacColl also included what he called 'interpolated' soldier scenes,[83] original scenes for the beginning of Act 3, which depicted Allied working-class soldiers, mostly Scotsmen, killing time at the Front. They chatted and played cards, balancing the women's struggle in Athens and creating emotive dramatic irony. The Scottish Myrrhine's beloved husband, for example, who—unbeknownst to her—is under guard as a deserter, is stabbed to death on stage by a fellow soldier. The role of the Deserter was a mouthpiece for MacColl's pacifist views:

> Whit's Athens to me that I should fecht for't? Whit has Athens ever brocht to Anagyra but dule [grief] and greetin' [crying]? Athens to me means the wastit croft and the fell evictions o' sib fowk.[84]

The Deserter's lines were written by MacColl in Lallans, a literary version, invented by the Communist Scottish poet Hugh MacDiarmid, of lowland Scottish dialect.[85] The 'fell evictions' he speaks of are the Highland Clearances of the 18th to 19th centuries, for which the English will perhaps never be forgiven. The fourth soldier responds unconvincingly to the Deserter's question, 'We brought you civilisation',[86] before killing him in a rage. He is reprimanded pointedly by his comrade: 'You killed him out of envy; because he loved life more than your twisted death'.[87]

MacColl had intended to the play the role of Deserter himself. The week before the opening of *Operation Olive Branch* (July/August, 1947), however, two plain-clothes policemen—operating on an anonymous tip-off—arrested James H. Miller (i.e. MacColl) for desertion.[88] The show went on, but MacColl had to wait until 1953 to play the Deserter, in the newly permanent home of Littlewood's Theatre Workshop, the Theatre Royal, Stratford East, London.

In the creative hands of Theatre Workshop the seams of Aristophanes' *Lysistrata* were unpicked and a new play was skilfully woven together, uniting the company's political vision and world-changing historical events taking place around them. The company's commitment to their art as an active social instrument was remarkable. The theatre critic Kenneth Tynan would later describe Littlewood's dramatic contribution as the 'pursuit of a dream of theatre as a place of communal celebration, a Left wing shrine of Dionysus dedicated to whipping the Puritan frown from off the popular image of Socialist art'.[89] But the techniques of *Operation Olive Branch*, and *Oh, What a Lovely War!* were developed in the earlier phase in the work of Theatre Workshop in the 1930s, when classical civilisation, especially Greek literature, was inspiring every aspect of British left-wing intellectual and cultural life.

Notes

1 Goorney and MacColl (1986) xliii.
2 Harker (2007) 14–35; Ewan MacColl in Samuel, MacColl & Cosgrove (1985) 251–2; Rankin (2014) 28–35. His and Littlewood's visas required for travelling to Moscow never materialised.

3 Harker (2007) 5.
4 Henceforth, for clarity, I use the name Ewan MacColl, even when he was still known as James Henry (Jimmie) Miller.
5 Harker (2007) 8–9.
6 Harker (2007) 10–11.
7 Harker (2007) 13–14.
8 From 1929 to 1931 the party doubled its membership from 3,500 in January 1929. See Harker (2007) 18 and Thorpe (2000) 284.
9 Harker (2007) 19.
10 The National Archives KV 2/2175.
11 Rankin (2014) 28–31.
12 Goorney and MacColl (1986) xxxix.
13 West (1969) 167.
14 Day-Lewis (1940) 7.
15 E.g. The National Archives, KV/2/2175, from 12th October 1939 to 4th August 1943, when Littlewood had supposedly 'renounced her communist opinions and her husband'. Concurrent and later MI5 intelligence relating to her active relationship with the CPGB overrides this report and she continues to be blocked from roles within the BBC and ENSA, although she was occasionally employed as an actor. Before March 1940 MacColl and Littlewood contributed to numerous programmes for BBC radio, but following their conviction for staging an unlicensed and communist play, were no longer trusted to broadcast. See also Rankin (2014) 44–9. Heightened restrictions were placed on both Littlewood and MacColl in this period. As evidenced by BBC internal memos, e.g. BBC WAC/James Miller/Artist file/1935–62, MacColl would in the 1950s have these further reinforced for taking a militant line on working-class music; see Harker (2007) 129 for a nuanced account. MacColl's military desertion also made him a persona non grata among such national organisations.
16 There were notable exceptions, e.g. Rose Cohen; see Beckett (2004).
17 On agit-prop see Goorney & MacColl (1986) x–lvii; Styan (1981) 128–9.
18 Other British Agit-Prop troupes outside of London included 'The Dark Lamp', who worked the Wigan coalfields, and 'The Red Cops' worked the Rossendale Valley, once the heart of the British cotton industry. For useful introduction to Workers' Theatre Movement in Britain see Samuel, MacColl & Cosgrove (1985) 33–64; and Goorney & MacColl (1986) x–lvii.
19 Goorney (1981) 1–2.
20 Ewan MacColl in Samuel, MacColl & Cosgrove (1985) 238.
21 Morgan (1989) 196; Taylor (2017) 6–7.
22 Morgan (1989) 20; Morgan (1995) 142; Taylor (2017) 6–11.
23 Dimitrov (1935) 69–70.
24 Dimitrov (1935) 70, 98–99.
25 Taylor (2017) 10.
26 For British communist writing and the English radical tradition, see Taylor (2017) and Bounds (2012) 179–233. On Jack Lindsay see Taylor (2017) 103–35; Bounds (2016) and on Lindsay's classicism see Chapter 23, pp. 488–93 and Hall and Stead (2016) 20–8.
27 Samuel, MacColl and Cosgrove (1985) x.
28 Littlewood (1994) 91. Adolphe Appia was a pioneering Swiss lighting designer, famous for his 'living' three-dimensional sets.
29 Goorney and MacColl (1986) xxxiv.
30 See Given (2015) 304–9.
31 Goorney and MacColl (1986) ix.
32 Stead (forthcoming) as part of *Brave New Classics* project.
33 The National Archives, KV/2/2175/2.
34 The National Archives, KV/2/2175/2.

35 The National Archives, KV/2/2175/2.
36 The *Daily Worker* meeting, organised in part by the Communist Party, Manchester, was held in the city's Free Trade Hall, where 3,000 people watched the performance and listened to speakers including the recently resigned and not-yet-reinstated General Secretary of the CPGB, Harry Pollitt. The National Archives, KV/2/2175/2.
37 Smith (2013) 109.
38 Theatre Union were accustomed to performing their unlicensed plays to members clubs, but on this occasion must have let down their guard.
39 The National Archives, KV/2/2175/2. Another radical production of *Lysistrata* was banned as late as 1950. It was the initiative of Ronald Willetts (1915–1999), who would become Professor of Greek at Birmingham University and publish widely in Cretan studies, after active service in World War II and working as research assistant to the communist Professor George Thomson. We only know about it because it was proscribed by the Birmingham Watch Committee, and notice of this was recorded in a letter to the retired diplomat but still prominent 'cold war warrior' Lord Vansittart of Denham (The Papers of Lord Vansittart of Denham (1881–1957), VNST II/1/46. 'Judith' to Vansittart, 20 March 1950').
40 On the use of Classics in social division see *inter alia* Stray (1998a) and Waquet (1998), and for the development of this model, see classicsandclass.info, and Stead and Hall eds. (2015), esp. 1–5.
41 Lenin (1970) 155.
42 See Mally (1990), especially 30–1, 105–6, 144–5. For a discussion of classics in early Soviet Russia, see Stead and Paulouskaya (forthcoming) with full bibliography.
43 See Chapter 23 and Hall & Stead (2016) 3–31.
44 Rankin (2014) 45. Littlewood too used this quotation in a lecture, following it up with: 'We can find truth of this statement when we go to the great writers of theatre like Aristophanes, Aeschylus, Marlowe, Shakespeare, Webster'. Holdsworth (2011) 80.
45 *Bulletin: Monthly Organ of Theatre Union*, Theatre Royal Stratford East Archives Collection: 'Joan Littlewood's Theatre Workshop' section. The collection is not large and is uncatalogued; more specific referencing is therefore unavailable.
46 MacColl in Goorney & MacColl (1986) xlvii–viii; MacColl in Samuel, MacColl and Cosgrove (1985) 253–4.
47 'Theatre Workshop – Reading List' (dated: March 24th 1946 [original] and June 15th 1951 [typed copy]), Theatre Royal Stratford East Archives Collection: 'Joan Littlewood's Theatre Workshop' section. A similar list appears in Appendix One of Littlewood (1994) 763–64, where it bears the title: 'Theatre Union Study Course, 1940. Each company member should prepare a paper or photomontage on their chosen subject'.
48 'Theatre Workshop – Reading List' (dated: 24th March 1946 [original] and 15th June 1951 [typed copy]), Theatre Royal Stratford East Archives Collection: 'Joan Littlewood's Theatre Workshop' section.
49 Williams would famously play Mrs. Hudson in *The Adventures of Sherlock Holmes* alongside Jeremy Brett in the titular role (Granada, 1984–1994).
50 Williams quoted in Goorney (1981) 21.
51 Littlewood (1994) 281.
52 E.g. the plays of Upton Sinclair and George Bernard Shaw, to which MacColl had been exposed in his short time with the Clarion Players.
53 We do not know if this manifesto was written by MacColl or Littlewood, or by both. In any case, long after MacColl left Theatre Workshop, it formed the basis of what is now considered Littlewood's personal manifesto for theatre making, which continues to inform the productions of Theatre Workshop in Stratford.
54 Hall (2018g).
55 Goorney & MacColl (1986) xliii–iv.
56 Aristophanes (1912); Aristophanes (1936).

57 A typewritten copy of the full play (verbatim) exists in the Theatre Royal Stratford East Archives Collection: 'Joan Littlewood's Theatre Workshop' section. N.b. It is the Tudor Press edition that is given on the 'Theatre Workshop – Reading List' (1946/1951).
58 Littlewood (1994) 120–1; Rankin (2014) 47.
59 Littlewood (1994) 121.
60 Littlewood (1994) 122.
61 Littlewood (1994) 128; Rankin (2014) 47.
62 MacColl in Goorney and MacColl (1986) xliii.
63 MacColl in Goorney and MacColl (1986) xliii–xliv.
64 *Operation Olive Branch* (sound desk copy) 39, Theatre Royal Archives.
65 MacColl in Goorney and MacColl (1986) xliii.
66 Other versions of the script exist in the National Library of Scotland and the Ewan MacColl and Peggy Seeger Archive, Ruskin College, Oxford.
67 Holdsworth (2011) 54.
68 Littlewood (1994) 293.
69 *Theatre Newsletter*, printed on Theatre Workshop promotional material, Theatre Royal Archives.
70 Harker (2007) 84; Littlewood (1994) 295.
71 MacColl (1948), translated by Annemarie Weber and Ita Maximowna.
72 *Unternehmen Ölzweig* (1961).
73 The actors included: Manfred Borges, Albert Hetterle, Walter Jupe, Helmut Müller-Lankow, Willi Narloch, Heinz Scholz and Kurt Steingraf.
74 Littlewood (1994) 499.
75 *Operation Olive Branch* (sound desk copy) 16, Theatre Royal Archives.
76 *Operation Olive Branch* (sound desk copy) 21, Theatre Royal Archives.
77 *Operation Olive Branch* (sound desk copy) 18, Theatre Royal Archives.
78 The full speech can be heard at https://winstonchurchill.org/resources/speeches/1946-1963-elder-statesman/the-sinews-of-peace/
79 *Operation Olive Branch* (sound desk copy) 42, Theatre Royal Archives.
80 Littlewood (1994) 226.
81 BBC Radio 1978, Ruskin Archive, quoted in Leach (2006) 51.
82 *Operation Olive Branch* (sound desk copy) 44, Theatre Royal Archives.
83 MacColl in Goorney and MacColl (1986) xliii.
84 *Operation Olive Branch* (sound desk copy) 50, Theatre Royal Archives
85 In *Unternehmen Ölzweig* (East Berlin, 1961) the Deserter used the Swabian dialect.
86 *Operation Olive Branch* (sound desk copy) 50, Theatre Royal Archives.
87 *Operation Olive Branch* (sound desk copy) 52, Theatre Royal Archives.
88 Littlewood's sensitive and moving account of MacColl's desertion can be read in Littlewood (1994) 228–39.
89 Tynan (1967) 317.

AFTERWORD

Classics, the study of the languages and civilisation of ancient Greece and Rome, is usually assumed to have functioned historically as the curriculum of the British elite. This is the first substantial enquiry into the presence of ancient Greek and Roman culture in British working-class communities ever to have been conducted. It alters our understanding of the history of Classics irrevocably by examining evidence for the diverse working-class experience of the classical world between the Bill of Rights in 1689 and the outbreak of World War II. The evidence includes autobiographies, poetry, fiction, visual and material culture in museums, galleries and the civic environment, theatrical ephemera, records of Trade Union activities, self-education publications, mass-market inexpensive 'classic' series, archives relating to Poor, Free, Workers', Adult and Dissenting educational establishments and to political parties that supported the working class. This book asks how workers gained access to classical texts, ideas and materials, and how the contact affected their lives and attitudes.

Although there was a significant amount of working-class engagement with the ancient Greeks and Romans, most of which has hitherto been overlooked, it was often hard-won. The time-consuming study of the Greek and Latin languages was adopted as the core of 'Classics', the education of the newly redefined British 'gentleman', at the dawn of the 18th century, whether his fees were paid by landed estates or commerce. It symbolised his fitness for a profession, a marriage into the gentry, a career in prestigious educational institutions or government, or advancement in the civil or colonial services. By the end of the second decade of the 18th century, the battle-lines which still shape debates over Classics had been drawn up. Britons who were unable or unwilling to bankroll their sons' classical educations fought back. The Greeks and Romans could be approached by other routes which did not require years glued to grammars and dictionaries. They could increasingly be read in mother-tongue translations, by great poets like Dryden and Pope, even though this was obviously derided as a vulgar mode of access to the Classics by those who had purchased the linguistic training. The material covered in ancient authors could be enjoyed even by the completely illiterate in accessible entertainments such as fairground shows.

Part I asks what Classics-related cultural media and literary genres were accessed and in turn used as vehicles by working-class subjects. In the 18th century, some autodidacts in lowly occupations succeeded in learning classical languages against the odds, while others accessed classical authors via increasingly abundant translations. In the 19th century, widening literacy and inexpensive literature, especially the many educational publications of John Cassell, expanded access to Classics exponentially. Although Homer, Virgil and Caesar were universally popular, the authors prioritised by working-class readers differed from those read in expensive schools and elite colleges: the Greek New Testament, Aesop, Plutarch, Epictetus, Josephus, Plato, Livy and a particular canon of historians of antiquity (e.g. Rollin, Gibbon, Osborne Ward) recur on working-class reading-lists.

Labouring-class poets, both male and female, such as Stephen Duck and Mary Collier, published collections which display knowledge of classical forebears; some used it to flatter their rich patrons and others to challenge social injustice. Life-writing by workers reveals a similar gulf between those who embraced what they perceived as their escape from their natal class and those who never ceased to work in its cause; what unites many working-class autobiographies is a youthful encounter with Classics which transforms the subject's life trajectory, whether by inspiring a programme of self-education or by proving to him (and almost all the 19th-century worker-autobiographers were male) the extent of his educational deprivation.

Until the later 19th century, a large proportion of the British working class, especially women, remained illiterate. This book explores their engagement with the visual media which informed them about classical culture—the windows of print shops, aristocratic and civic architecture and internal decoration, museums, spectacles and illustrated educational periodicals. Since drawing, painted decoration and modelling often attracted apprentices from impoverished backgrounds, the visual understanding of sites such as Pompeii and the Athenian Acropolis was often provided by originally working-class men. Theatrical performances provided another route to the classical world, although the censorship of stage plays limited the use of rousing ancient stories in plays exploring the iniquities of the class system. The case of a censored tragedy about the Gracchi produced just before and after Peterloo provides a vivid example.

Contact with Classics varied between different communities. Section II explores religious identity, adult educational groups, and the national experiences in Ireland, Scotland and Wales. Dissenters of all denominations were crucial in making classical authors available to Britons across the lower end of the class spectrum. Dissenters also often led major educational initiatives offering opportunities to the working classes to study subjects including Classics:

Mutual Improvement Societies, Adult Schools, Mechanics Institutes, University Extension schemes, the Workers' Educational Association (WEA) and the Labour Colleges.

The relationship between the Irish and the Greco-Roman world was intense, as their literature in both Gaelic and English reveals. Competence in Latin was fostered across even some of the lowest classes by Roman Catholicism and informal education at 'hedge schools'. But political allegiances were complicated; along with classically skilled Irish working-class Catholics, who supported Irish rebellion, some ardently opposed it. Two radical Irish classicists campaigning in the interests of the Irish working classes were Protestants; Robert Tressell, author of the Plato-influenced working-class novel *The Ragged-Trousered Philanthropists* (1914), was of mixed religious parentage. In Scotland, the proud tradition of the 'lad o' pairts' boasts a longstanding reputation for good working-class education. There were indeed remarkable resources for studying and teaching the Classics in the counties around Aberdeen, which furnished hundreds of educated men to work in the furthest outposts of the British Empire; cheap and popular publishing ventures were founded by Scotsmen, especially the Chambers brothers; two of the most important books in British Labour History were Thomas Carlyle's classically informed *Past and Present* and Lewis Grassic Gibbon's *Spartacus*. Wales had a distinct Nonconformist tradition of classical education, but it also had Caractacus, the ancient British leader who, according to Tacitus, had fought against the ancient Romans in Wales and was paired in the public imagination with David Lloyd George. There was an Edwardian craze in Wales for amateur theatrical performances by school children starring Caractacus, and once World War I broke out, they became transparently connected with recruitment, morale and fund-raising for the war effort.

Individual working-class subjects teetering on or below the edge of respectability are put at the centre of the radar in section III. Between the French revolution and the collapse of the Chartist movement, diverse British radicals—republican revolutionaries of the 1790s, men incarcerated for sedition in the aftermath of Peterloo, Chartists, workplace organisers and freethinkers, some working-class and some from more prosperous backgrounds—were motivated by the ancient Greeks and Romans. They used Classics to enliven their journalism, inform arguments at the trials, and explore religious questions that took them far beyond the limits of Anglican theology. A few outstanding autodidacts harnessed Classics to assist a meteoric rise to university chairs, where most of them relinquished class anger to become quietist professionals. The attempts of other extraordinary working-class boys to escape poverty by self-education never quite got off the ground; some ended their days as itinerants, alcoholics or suffering from acute mental disorders.

The aura surrounding the ancient cultures did not signify gentlemanliness and financial security everywhere. Alongside the gentry enjoying their Palladian mansions and expensive school curriculums, there always existed more commercial, demotic, subterranean and secretive groups in British society who used imagery from the Greek and Roman worlds to communicate and self-identify: salesmen, imposters, criminals, prostitutes, circus and fairground performers, showgirls, libertines, madmen and participants in recreational activities ranging from the merely vulgar to the illegal. Ancient Greek appeared in a variety of recherché contexts such as accusations of witchcraft, caricatures of Jesuits, the slang dialects of the criminal underclass, the display of prodigiously intellectual dogs and pigs, fairground freaks including satyrs and centaurs, the lives of notoriously uncouth Scotsmen, Welsh dream divination and down-market pharmaceuticals and sex manuals. A few classicists unambiguously joined the underclass in being convicted of violent crimes and/or confined in asylums. Most beauty and strength performers in the long 19th century—dancers, actresses, strongmen, contortionists, strongwomen, wrestlers, boxers, novelty performers, artists' models and posers of all kinds—used draped fabric, leather straps and bared flesh to identify their acts with Greco-Roman antiquity. They almost always came from working-class families.

The final Part, IV, examines the presence of classical material in other working lives. The figures from antiquity with whom the working classes identified, or were identified with by others, were male martyrs, rebels, slaves and labourers, largely distinct from the heroes and gods instrumentalised by those higher up the social scale, such as Alexander, Aeneas, Augustus, Jove and Juno, Leto, Apollo, Diana, Venus and Mars. Sources including workers' newspapers and Trade Union art show that workers identified with Aesop, both Brutuses, the Gracchi, Solon, Caractacus, Boadicea, Spartacus, Prometheus, Vulcan, Hercules' labours, Atlas, the Cyclopes and Neptune. Hercules and Atlas were violently contested, being used to symbolise both ruling-class/imperial dominion and the physical power of the proletariat. Shoemakers, often radical Nonconformists, although sometimes espousing conservative views, were well-read and conversant with classical authors, inspired by the examples of learned cobblers they found in ancient sources. Pottery workers were familiar with ancient artefacts and with books visually reproducing and discussing them. Miners, especially in Scotland and Wales, enjoyed some of the best workers' libraries, well stocked with Classics, in the nation.

As working-class activism increased with the rise of the Labour Movement, classically self-educated professional politicians rose from the working classes, and their cause was espoused by newly university-trained socialist women, the academic Classicists who joined the Communist Party of Great Britain, and classically trained fulltime activists and intellectuals such as Christopher Caudwell and Jack Lindsay. Accessing the experience of working-class soldiers is exceptionally difficult, but one War Poet, David Jones, was not of officer rank. His neglected epic prose poem *In Parenthesis* (1937) forged a radically new Classicism, Modernist form and demotic language for the representation of the common soldier's subjective experience of the trenches, which are prefigured by the frontier walls of the Roman empire. *A People's History of Classics* closes with the class-conscious and sophisticated classical theatre pioneered by Theatre Workshop, founded by the working-class communist theatre-makers Joan Littlewood and Ewan MacColl, who used Greek drama to fight the cultural wars of the 1930s for the rights of the working classes.

The British working classes were almost universally excluded from institutionalised Classics, and from study of ancient languages, but a few overcame the obstacles; many more engaged with the ancient Greeks and Romans in myriad creative ways. The classical world aided their careers, expanded their horizons, improved their rhetoric, informed their politics, alleviated their boredom, inspired them to read, write, paint, draw, sculpt, act, perform, teach, publish, organize Trade Unions, join debating societies, read the Gospels in the original or question the existence of God altogether. They used Classics to prove their intellectual calibre, to express their plight and signal their consciousness of the class system; they also used it to subvert and undermine the authority of the classes that ruled them and to entertain themselves during leisure hours.

The heroes of People's Classics we have met were gardeners, stonemasons, circus acrobats, factory operatives, engravers, cutlers, domestic servants, brewers, weavers, tramps, beggars, prisoners, thieves, inmates of mental hospitals, plasterers, painter-decorators, cabin-boys, milkmaids, washerwomen, wool-sorters, drummers, butchers, grocers, mechanics, carpenters, errand-boys, tailors, pill-sellers, janitors, porters, dockers, hatters, fishermen, sailors, comb-makers, bakers, bricklayers, navvies, shepherds, threshers and grave-diggers. They deserve honoured places in the gallery of People's Classics simply because they struggled so hard to get access to the ancient world. But they also offer us a new ancestral backstory for a discipline sorely in need of a democratic makeover.

REFERENCES

Aberdeen Grammar School (1807–1855) 'Annual dinner record', University of Aberdeen, Special Collections MS 633.

Abrams, Lynn (1992) *Workers' Culture in Imperial Germany: Leisure and Recreation*. London and New York: Routledge.

Acworth, H.A. (1894, trans.) *Ballads of Marathas, Rendered into English Verse from the Marathi Originals*. London and New York: Longmans, Green and Co.

Adams, J.R.R. (1987) *The Printed Word and the Common Man: Popular Culture in Ulster 1700-1900*. Belfast: Institute of Irish Studies.

Adams, W.E. (1903) *Memoirs of a Social Atom*, 2 vols. London: Hutcheson & Co.

Addison, Joseph (1719) *Poems on Several Occasions: With a Dissertation upon the Roman Poets. By Mr: Addison*. London: E. Curll.

Aesop (1780) *Æsop's Fables*. [A chapbook]. London: No Publisher Indicated.

Aiken, J. (1810) 'An account of Gilbert Wakefield' *The Belfast Monthly Magazine* 4 (June 30th), 437–444.

Ainsworth, Robert (1736) *Thesaurus Linguae Latinae Compendarius*. London: J. & P. Knapton.

Ainsworth, Robert (1758) *An Abridgment of Ainsworth's Dictionary of the Latin Tongue*, by Mr. [N.] Thomas. London: Mount and Page.

Akenside, Mark (1781) *The Poetical Works of Mark Akenside*. Edinburgh: Bell and Daldy.

Albright, Ann Cooper (2010) 'The Tanagra Effect: Wrapping the modern body in the folds of ancient Greece', In: Macintosh (ed.), 57–76.

Aldred, Guy (1908) *From Anglican Boy-Preacher to Anarchist Socialist Impossibilist*. London: Bakhunin Press = 'Pamphlets for the Proletarian' no. 5, accessed in Special Collections, the Mitchell Library, NRA(S) (1410).

Aldred, Guy (1923) 'History for prudists', In: *The Commune*, G. Aldred (ed.), vol I, no. 3, 21, accessed in Special Collections, The Mitchell Library, NRA(S)1410.

Aldred, Guy (1955–1963) *No Traitor's Gate!* Glasgow: Strickland Press, British Library.

Aldred, Guy (1966) *Guy Alfred Aldred, 1886–1963*. [With excerpts from his writings and a portrait.] Glasgow BLL01000045045: The Strickland Press.

Aldridge, A. Owen (1968) 'Thomas Paine and the classics', *Eighteenth-Century Studies* 1(4), 370–380.

Aldritt, Keith (2003) *David Jones: Writer and Artist*. London: Constable.

Allan, D. (2011) 'The age of Pericles in the modern Athens: Greek history, Scottish politics and the fading of enlightenment', *Historical Journal* 44(2001), 391–417.

Allen, Robert C. (1991) *Horrible Prettiness: Burlesque and American Culture*. University of North Carolina Press.

Altick, R.D. (1957) *The English Common Reader: A History of the Mass Reading Public 1800–1900*. Chicago, Illinois: Chicago University Press.

Altick, R.D. (1978) *The Shows of London*. Cambridge, Massachusetts; London: Belknap Press.

Altick, R.D. (1998) *The English Common Reader*. 2nd edition. Columbus, Ohio: Ohio State University Press.

Amber Film and Photography Collective: Landscapes and lives of NE England, since 1968. www.amber-online.com.

Anderson, Alexander (1873) *A Song of Labour*. Dundee: Office of Dundee Advertiser.

Anderson, Alexander (1912) *Surfaceman's Later Poems*, ed. with a biographical sketch by Alexander Brown. Glasgow: Fraser, Asher & Co.

Anderson, Robert (1983) *Education and Opportunity in Victorian Scotland*. Oxford: OUP.

Anderson, Robert (1995) *Education and the Scottish People 1750–1918*. Oxford: Clarendon Press.

Anderson, Linda (2001) *Autobiography*. London: Routledge.

Andreas, Johannes (1469, ed.) *Auli Gellii Noctium Atticarum libri XX*. Rome: Petrus de Maximis.

Andrews, David (1991) 'Welsh indigenous! and British imperial?—Welsh rugby, culture, and society 1890–1914', *Journal of Sport History* 18, 335–49.

Andrews, Kerri (2013), *Ann Yearsley and Hannah More, Patronage and Poetry*. London: Pickering and Chatto.

Anon. (1700a) *Lucian's Charon: Or A Survey of the Follies of Mankind. Translated from the Greek, With Notes, and A Prefatory Dialogue in Vindication of Translations*. London: Farrow.

Anon. (1700b) *The Famous or Renowned History of Hector Prince of Troy. Chapbook*. No Publisher or Place of Publication Indicated.

Anon. [i.e. Richard Bentley] (1751a) *A True and Faithful Account of the Greatest Wonder Produced by Nature These 3000 Years, in the Person of Mr Jehan-Paul-Ernest Christian Lodovick Manpfendt, the Surprizing Centaur*. London: M. Cooper.

Anon. (1751b) 'An authentick account of the surprising CENTAUR, the greatest wonder produced by nature these 3000 years, later proposed to be exhibited to public view', *The Gentleman's Magazine*, (April), 153–54.

Anon. (1762) *Homer Travestie: Being a New Translation of the Four First Books of the Iliad. By Cotton, Junior. To Which Is Prefix'd*. London: Some Small Account of the Author: R. Marriner.

Anon. (1773a) *Baratariana. A Select Collection of Fugitive Political Pieces, Published During the Administration of Lord Townshend in Ireland*. 2nd Corrected Edition. Dublin: No Publisher Indicated.

Anon. (1773b) 'Theatrical intelligence', *Gentleman's and London Magazine*. (March). London, 176–77.

Anon. [Honestus] (1788) 'Ne sutor ultra crepidam: Cobbler, stick to your last', *The American Museum or Repository of Ancient and Modern Fugitive Pieces etc*, vol. III, No. 1, 528–30. Philadelphia, PA: Mathew Carey.

Anon. (1802, ed.) *The Spirit of the Public Journals for 1797*, vol. I. 3rd edition. London: No Publisher Indicated.

Anon. (1813) 'Machinae gesticulantes, or the puppet-show', translated from the Latin of 'Addison', *The Edinburgh Annual Register for 1811*, vol. IV, part 2, lxxxvi–viii. Edinburgh: John Ballantyne.

Anon. (1819) 'Interesting account of the Reverend Samuel Lee' In *Imperial Magazine, or, Compendium of Religious, Moral, & Philosophical Knowledge*, vol. I, columns 177–89. Liverpool: Caxton Press.

Anon. (1822) 'On auto-biography', *The Scots Magazine* 89, 742–45.

Anon. (1829) 'Weekly newspapers', *Westminster Review* 10 (April), 478.

Anon. (1832a) 'A Roman city–Pompeii', *Chambers' Magazine* (Saturday February 25th) no. 4, 30.

Anon. (1832b) 'Ancient Pottery', *Chambers' Magazine* (Saturday March 31st) no. 9, 70.

Anon. (1832c) 'Grecian philosophers and Christianity compared', *Chambers' Magazine* (Saturday April 14th) no. 11, 81–82.

Anon. (1832d) 'Wine', *Chambers' Magazine,* (Saturday May 5th) no. 14, 111.

Anon. (1832e) 'Pompeii and Herculaneum', 1. *Chambers' Magazine* (Saturday November 17th) no. 42, 330–331; 2. *Chambers' Magazine* (Saturday December 1st) no. 44, 350; 3. *Chambers' Magazine* (Saturday December 22nd) no. 47, 376.

Anon. (1832f) 'Popular information on history: Athens and Sparta', *Chambers' Magazine* (Saturday December 15th) no. 46, 366.

Anon. (1832g) 'Dick Aberdaron', *North Wales Chronicle* (Bangor, September 11th) 3.

Anon. (1833a) 'Popular information on history: Romans': 1 'The monarchy and republic', *Chambers' Magazine* (Saturday January 19th) no. 51, 401–402; 2. 'The Empire, its decline and fall', *Chambers' Magazine* (Saturday January 26th) no. 52, 411–12.

Anon. (1833b) 'Wandering Italians', *Penny Magazine* (February 2nd) no. 54, 42.

Anon. (1838) 'On the proportion of persons in England capable of reading and writing', *The Penny Magazine*, (August 18th and 25th).

Anon. (1840) *History of Eugene Aram*. Newcastle: W. and T. Fordyce.

Anon. (1843) 'Dick of Aberdaron, alias 'Dirty Dick'', *Liverpool Mercury*, (December 29th).

Anon. (1849) *Wright's Patent Vulcan Chimney Sweeping Machines, the Only Efficient Supporters of the Law against Climbing Boys*. Derby: W. Hobson.

Anon. (1850) 'No. XXI Books and reading (Part V)', In: *Working Man's Friend, and Family, Instructor*, vol. II, London: John Cassell, 257–60.

Anon. (1851) 'Shopkeeper's Greek', *Chambers Edinburgh Journal* 15, 358–59.

Anon. (1862) 'Songs relating to Sheffield, Saturday night', In: *The Songs of Joseph Mather, to Which Are Added a Memoir of Mather and Miscellaneous Songs Relating to Sheffield*. Sheffield: Pawson and Brailford.

Anon. (1867) 'First visit of English workmen to Paris (by one of themselves)', *The British Lion*, (June 29), 12.

Anon. (1870) 'Ancient classics for English readers', *Quarterly Literary Adviser.*

Anon. (1871) 'Useful versus ornamental learning', *The Huddersfield Chronicle and West Yorkshire Advertiser*, (Saturday, October 28), no. 1319, 8.

Anon. (1884) 'Obituary: Henry George Bohn', *The Academy* 26: 137. J. London: Murray.

Anon. (1890) 'Sandow in Bristol', *Bristol Mercury*, (Friday 7th February).

Anon. (1891) *'The caller', Allan's Illustrated Edition of Tyneside Songs and Readings*. Newcastle: Tom and George Allan, 392–93.

Anon. (1896) *Newsagents' Chronicle*. London: William Dawson & Sons.

Anon. [Jevons, F.B.?] (1897) *General Information, Instructions to Centres, and Lecture List for Session 1897–1898*. Durham University Archives and Special Collections, UND/DB15/F6.

Anon. (1898) 'Lead poisoning in the Potteries', *BMJ* 2 (July 23rd), 245–46.

Anon. (1903) 'Taken as read', *The Academy and Literature*, c.1 v. 64, (January–June). London.

Anon. (1904) *The Welsh Historical Drama and How to Produce it. Being the Actual Experience of the Abergele County School Company in the Production of "Caractacus" (CARADOG). Illustrated by Flash-light Photographs Taken during an Actual Performance. Reprinted from "The Welsh Leader" February and March 1904.* Caernarvon: Welsh Leader Office.

Anon. (1906a) 'The royal national eisteddfod. Held at Carnarvon, August 22, 22, 23 and 24', *The Musical Times*, (September 1st).

Anon. (1906b) 'The modern Venus: The female form as it was in the days of ancient Greece', *Sandow's Magazine of Physical Culture*, vol. 16, 18, (3rd May). London: Thomas and Burchell, Ltd, 560–563.

Anon. (1913) *'Lecture Note-book' Apparently the Work of Mrs I. Dawson,* University of Aberdeen, Special Collections, MS 3817/1.

Anon. (1914a) 'The legend of Pygmalion: a free rendering from Ovid's *Metamorphoses*', *Plebs* volume 6, No. 4 (May) 95.

Anon. (1914b) 'Oldest story of the flood', *Plebs* volume 6, number 10 (November) 234.

Anon. (1917) 'Review of R.W. Livingstone's A Defence of Classical Education (1916)', *The Highway* 19(101), 91.

Anon. (1928) *Carlisle Historical Pageant, August 6th–11th 1928. Book of Words.* Carlisle: Historical Pageant Committee.

Anon. (1939) 'Miner who showed in London killed in mine', *The Argus (Melbourne),* (December 22nd), 1.

Anon. (1948) 'Mysterious saint', *Milwaukee Sentinel*, (January 18th), 28.

Anon. (2014) 'A brief biography: Samson Gilbert Daykin, 1886–1939', http://barnsley artonyourdoorstep.org.uk/wp-content/uploads/2014/02/Brief-Biography-Gilbert -Daykin.pdf.

Arch, Joseph (1986 [1898]) *From Ploughtail to Parliament: An Autobiography*, with a Preface by Norman Willis and an Introduction by Alun Hawkins. London: Cresset Library.

Archard, Cary, Sandra Anstey and Gwyneth Lewis (1982, eds.) *The Achievement of David Jones* [= *Poetry Wales* special edition, vol. 17.4, Spring]. Swansea: Swansea University.

Archer, W. (1890) *William Charles Macready*. London: Kegan Paul.

Archer, Stuart and Nigel Shepley (1995) *Josiah Wedgwood and the Industrial Revolution.* Edinburgh: Tyke Publications.

Aristophanes (1912) *The Eleven Comedies: Complete and Unabridged*, trans. Anon. London: Athenian Society.

Aristophanes (1936) *The Eleven Comedies: Complete and Unabridged*. New York: Tudor Publishing Co.

Arlidge, J.T. (1864) *On the Sanitary State of the Staffordshire Potteries, with Especial Reference to That of the Potters as a Class, Their Mortality, and the Diseases Present among Them.* Worcester, Massachusetts: Sanitary Institute.

Arnold, Matthew (1882) *Irish Essays, and Others*. London: Smith, Elder & Co.

Arnot, R.P. (1967) *The Impact of the Russian Revolution in Britain*. London: Lawrence and Wishart.

Aron, Paul (2006) *La Littérature Prolétarienne en Belgique Francophone Depuis 1900.* Loverval: Éditions Labor.

Ashton, John (1882) *Social Life in the Reign of Queen Anne Taken from Original Sources*, 2 vols. London: Chatto & Windus.

Ashton, John (1883) *Social Life in the Reign of Queen Anne*. New edition. London: Spottiswoode & Co.

Aspinall, Arthur (1946) *The Circulation of Newspapers in the Early Nineteenth Century.* London: OUP.

Aston, Miles (1728) *An Heroick Poem on the Powerful and Commanding Art of Brewing.* Dublin: Edward Waters.

Atkinson, John (2010) 'Benjamin Farrington: Cape Town and the shaping of a public intellectual', *South African Historical Journal* 62(4), 671–92.

Aubagne (1996) *À Aubagne, l'abbé Barthélemy, de l'Académie française, savant et homme de lettres.* Aubagne: M. Crombez de Montmort.

Auden, W.H. (1962) 'The Geste says this and the man who was on the field', *Mid-Century Review* 39 (March), 12–13.

Auden, W.H. (1991) *Collected Poems*, ed. Edward Mendelson. Revised edition. London: Faber & Faber.

Autobiography (1826) *Autobiography: A Collection of the Most Instructive and Amusing Lives Ever Published, Written by the Parties Themselves.* London: Hunt and Clarke.

Avlami, Chryssanthi (2000) *L'Antiquité Grecque à la Française: Modes d'appropriation de la Grèce au XIXe Siècle.* Paris: L'Harmattan.

Ayres, Philip (1997) *Classical Culture and the Ideal of Rome in Eighteenth-Century England.* Cambridge: CUP.

Azoulay, Vincent (2014) *Pericles of Athens,* Translated by Janet Lloyd with a Foreword by Paul Cartledge. Princeton, New Jersey: Princeton University Press.

Backhouse, Ann (2015, ed.) *Malvern in the Great War 1915: A Study of a Worcestershire Town in Wartime Britain.* Great Malvern: Malvern Museum.

Bain, Alexander (1865) 'Grote's Plato', *Macmillan's Magazine*, (July), 193–208.

Bain, Alexander (1904) *Autobiography.* London: Longman's. Green & Co.

Baldwin, E. [pseudonym Godwin, W.] (1805/2014) *Fables Ancient and Modern. Adapted for the Use of Children from Three to Eight Years of Age* – A Romantic Circles Electronic Edition edited by Barnett, Suzanne L. and Gustafson, Katherine Bennett. www.rc.umd.edu/editions/godwin_fables.

Baldwin, E. [pseud- Godwin, W.] (1806/1810) *The Pantheon: Or Ancient History of the Gods of Greece and Rome. For the Use of Schools, and Young Persons of Both Sexes.* London: Thomas Hodgkins, at the Juvenile Library, M. J. Godwin.

Ball, F.C. (1973) *One of the Damned: The Life and Times of Robert Tressell, Author of the Ragged-Trousered Philanthropists.* London: Lawrence and Wishart.

Bamford, Samuel (1967 [1849]) *The Autobiography of Samuel Bamford*, 2 vols. New edition edited and with an introduction by W.H. Chaloner. London: Frank Cass & Co. Includes reprint of edition of 1849, London: Simpkin, Marshall & Co.

Bamford, T.W. (1967) *The Rise of the Public Schools.* London and Edinburgh: Thomas Nelson.

'Bangoriensis' (1844) 'Richard Robert Jones', Obituary in, *North Wales Chronicle*, (January 2nd).

Banister, James (1791) *A Translation of all the Pythian, Nemean, and Isthmian Odes of Pindar (1791), Except the fourth and fifth Pythian Odes, and those Odes which have been Translated by the Late Gilbert West, Esq.* London: G. and T. Wilkie.

Bankes, Jonathan (1679) *Januae Clavis: Or, Lilly's Syntax Explained.* London: Benjamin Clarke.

Barclay, Tom (1934) *Memoirs and Medleys: The Autobiography of a Bottle-Washer.* Leicester: Edgar Backus.

Barnsley (2014) 'Samson Gilbert Daykin (1886–1939) brief biography', online article at http://barnsleyartonyourdoorstep.org.uk/wp-content/uploads/2014/07/Gilbert-Daykin.pdf.

Barker, E.H. (1852) *Literary Anecdotes and Contemporary Reminiscences, of Professor Porson and Others*. London: J.R. Smith.

Barker, Hannah (1998) *Newspapers, Politics and Public Opinion in Late Eighteenth Century England*. Oxford: OUP.

Barker, Joseph (1880) *The Life of Joseph Barker*. London: Hodder and Stoughton.

Barnett, Samuel (1898) 'On the *lampadēphoria* of Aeschylus, *Ag.* 314', summary of paper, *Proceedings of the Cambridge Philological Society* 49, 15.

Barnett, S.L. and K.B. Gustafson (2014) 'Introduction: The radical Aesop: William Godwin and the Juvenile Library, 1805–1825' William Godwin[1805] 'Fables Ancient and Modern', In: *Romantic Circles*, S.L. Barnett and K.B. Gustafson (ed.), https://romantic-circles.org/editions/godwin_fables.introduction.

Barrell, John (2017) 'Reform and revolution: James Barry's writings in the 1790s', In: *James Barry, 1741–1806,* Tom Dunne and William L. Pressly (eds.), Farnham: Ashgate, 127–43.

Barringer, T.J. (2005) *Men at Work: Art and labour in Victorian Britain*. New Haven and London: Paul Mellon Centre for Studies in British Art by Yale University Press.

Barros, Carolyn A. (1992) 'Figura, persona, dynamis: Autobiography and change', *Biography* 15(1), 1–28.

Barros, Carolyn A. (1998) *Autobiography: Narrative of Transformation*. Ann Arbor, MN: University of Michigan Press.

Barstow, S. (2004) 'Chaplin, Sidney (1916–1986)', *ODNB*. Oxford. OUP.

Bass, Marisa (2011) 'Jan Gossaert's Neptune and Amphitrite reconsidered', *Simiolus: Netherlands Quarterly for the History of Art* 35, 61–83.

Bath (1909) *Bath Historical Pageant: Book of Words*. Bath: Bath Historical Pageant Committee.

Batt, Jennifer (2015) 'Stephen Duck', In: G. Day and J. Lynch (eds.), *The Encyclopeadia of British Literature, 1660–1789.* Oxford: Wiley Blackwell.

Bauer, Georg (1546) *De Re metallica*. Basel: Frobenius.

Baumgarten, Maria (1977) *Professoren und Universitäten Im 19. Jahrhundert*. Göttingen: Vandenhoeck & Ruprecht.

Bavande, William (1559) *A Worke of Ioannes Ferrarius Montanus, Touchynge the Good Orderynge of a Common Weale*. London: John Kingston.

Bayne, Thomas Wilson (1885–1900) 'Murray, Alexander (1775–1813)', *DNB*. 39, 346–47.

Bayne, Thomas Wilson (2004) 'Graham, James (1765–1811), rev. Douglas Brown', reverend Douglas Brown, *ODNB*. Oxford: OUP. www.oxforddnb.com/view/article/11229.

Beale, J.M. (1983) *A History of the Burgh and Parochial Schools of Fife*. Edinburgh: Scottish Council for Research in Education.

Beard, John Relly (1853) *The Life of Toussaint L'Ouverture, the Negro Patriot of Hayti: Comprising an Account of the Struggle for Liberty in the Island, and a Sketch of Its History to the Present Period*. London: Ingram, Cooke & Co.

Beard, John Relly (1856) *Cassell's Lessons in Greek. From the 'Popular Educator'*. London: Cassell.

Beard, Mary (2002) *The Invention of Jane Harrison*. Cambridge, Massachusetts; London: Harvard University Press.

Beasley, Jerry C. (1973) 'English fiction in the 1740s: Some glances at the major and minor novels', *Studies in the Novel* 5, 155–75.

Beavan, Brad (2005) *Leisure, Citizenship and Working-Class Men in Britain, 1850–1945.* Manchester and New York: Manchester University Press.

Beck, Horace (1973) *Folklore and the Sea.* Middletown, Connecticut: Wesleyan University Press.

Beckett, J.V. (1980a) 'The disinheritance of Sir Christopher Lowther in 1701', *Transactions of the Cumberland and Westmorland Antiquarian and Archaeological Society* 80, 131–36.

Beckett, J.V. (1980b) 'Illness and amputation in the eighteenth century: The case of Sir James Lowther (1673–1755)', *Medical History* 24(1), 88–92.

Beckett, J.V. (2004) 'Lowther, Sir James, fourth baronet', *ODNB.* doi:10.1093/ref:odnb/37692.

Beckett, Francis (2004) *Stalin's British Victims.* London: The History Press.

Beckett, J.C. (1976) *The Anglo-Irish Tradition.* London: Faber & Faber.

Beddoes, Thomas and Lovell ['Unus Solus'] (1800) *A Letter, Addressed to the Rev. R. Polwhele, Vicar of Manaccan.* Bristol: W. Bulgin.

Beers, Laura (2016) *Red Ellen.* Cambridge, Massachusetts: Harvard University Press.

Beesley, Edmund Spencer (1878) *Catiline, Clodius, and Tiberius.* London: Chapman Hall.

Begbie, Harold (1918) *Living Water: Being the Romance of the Poor Student.* London: Headley Bros.

Behn, Aphra (1688) *Oroonoko.* London: Will. Canning.

Behrendt, Stephen C. (1989) *Shelley and His Audiences.* Lincoln and London: University of Nebraska Press.

Bell, Edward (1924) *George Bell, Publisher: A Brief Memoir.* London: Chiswick Press (privately printed).

Bell John ed. (1812) *Rhymes of Northern Bards: Being a Curious Collection of Old and New Songs.* Newcastle: Graham.

Beness, J.L. and T.W. Hillard (2001) 'The theatricality of the deaths of C. Gracchus and friends', *The Classical Quarterly* 51(1), 135–40.

Benn, Alfred William (1882) *The Greek Philosophers*, 2 vols. London: Kegan Paul, Trench, & Co.

Bennett, Scott (1984) 'The editorial character and readership of "the Penny Magazine": An analysis', *Victorian Periodicals Review* 17, 127–41.

Bensley, Edward (1930) 'The Library at Moor park', *The New Quarterly* 159, 48.

Bentley, Gerald Eades (1941–1968) *The Jacobean and Caroline Stage.* Oxford: Clarendon Press.

Bentley, Nicolas (1968) *The Victorian Scene.* London: Spring Boks.

Benton, Jill (1990) *Naomi Mitchison. A Biography.* London: Pandora.

Bergonzi, Bernard (1965) *Heroes' Twilight: A Study of the Literature of the Great War.* London: Constable.

Bertenshaw, Mary (1991) *Sunrise to Sunset. An Autobiography.* Bury, Lancs: Printwise Publications.

Bewick, T. (1791) *A General History of Quadrupeds. The Figures Engraved on Wood by T. Bewick.* Text by Ralph Beilby. Newcastle upon Tyne: Beilby and Bewick.

Blackburn, Elizabeth, K (1980). *In and Out the Windows: A Story of the Changes in Working Class Life 1902–1977 in a Small East Lancashire Community.* Burnley: E.K. Blackburn.

Blackie, J. (2004) 'Bell, Andrew (1753–1832), Church of England clergyman and educationist'. www.oxforddnb.com/view/10.1093/ref:odnb/9780198614128.001.0001/odnb-9780198614128-e-1995.

Blacklock, Thomas (1756) *Poems by Mr. Thomas Blacklock. To which Is Prefix'd, an Account of the Life, Character and Writings of the Author by ... Mr. Spence*. 3rd edition. London: R and J Dodsley.

Blackwall, Anthony (1718) *An Introduction to the Classics; Containing a Short Discourse on Their Excellencies and Directions How to Study Them to Advantage*. London: George Mortlock.

Blackwall, Anthony (1725) *The Sacred Classics Defended and Illustrated; or, An Essay Humbly offer'd towards Proving the Purity, Propriety, and true Eloquence of the Writers of the New Testament*. London: C. Rivington.

Blake-Roberts, Gaye (2011) *Wedgwood Jasperware*. Oxford: Shire Publications.

Blake-Roberts, Gaye (2014) *Wedgwood: The Illustrated History of an Iconic Name in Pottery*. Stamford, Lincolnshire: Key Publishing Ltd.

Blanchard, E.L. (1891) *The Life and Reminiscences of E.L. Blanchard / with Notes from the Diary of Wm. Blanchard*, ed. Clement Scott and Cecil Howard. 2 vols. London: Hutchinson.

Blaney, Roger (1996) *Presbyterians and the Irish language in Belfast*. Ulster: Historical Association.

Blanning, T.C.W. (2000) *The Eighteenth Century*. Oxford: OUP.

Blanshard, A. (2005) *Hercules: A Heroic Life*. London: Granta Books.

Blanshard, A. (2014) 'Hellenic fantasies: Aesthetics and desire in John Addington Symonds', In: *Dialogos: Hellenic Studies Review*, D. Ricks and M. Trapp (eds.), Hoboken, New Jersey: Taylor and Francis, 99–123.

Blanshard, Thomas W. (1870) *The Life of Samuel Bradburn: The Methodist Demosthenes*. London: Elliot Stock.

Bloomfield, Robert (1827) *Poems*, 2 vols. London: W. Wilton.

Bly, Robert (1986) *Selected Poems*. New York: Harper & Row.

Board of Trade (1913) *Report of an Enquiry by the Board of Trade into the Earnings and Hours of Labour of Workpeople of the United Kingdom: VIII*. London: Board of Trade.

Boase, George Clement (1885–1900) 'Cann, Abraham', *Dictionary of National Biography*, 8, 410–411.

Bobrick, Benson (2001) *The Making of the English Bible*. London: Weidenfeld and Nicholson.

Bondeson, Jan (2008) *Animal Freaks*. 2nd edition. Stroud: Tempus.

Bondeson, Jan (2011) *Amazing Dogs*. Stroud: Amberley.

Booth, G. (1721, trans.) *The Historical Library of Diodorus the Sicilian*. 2nd edition. London: W. Taylor.

Bopp, Franz (1816) *Franz Bopp über das Conjugationssystem der Sanskritsprache In Vergleichung mit Jenem der Griechischen, Lateinischen, Persischen und Germanischen Sprache*. Frankfurt am Main: Andreäischen Buchhandlung.

Bossu, Rene Le (1695) *Treatise of the Epick Poem*. London: Tho. Bennet.

Boswell, J., F.A. Pottle and S. Johnson (1936, eds.) *Boswell's Journal of a Tour to the Hebrides with Samuel Johnson*. London: Heinemann.

Bőttiger, C.A. (1792) 'Ueber die Prachtgefässe der Alten', *The Journal des Luxus und der Moden* June, 286–87.

Bounds, Philip (2012) *British Communism and the Politics of Literature 1928–1938*. London: Merlin.

Bounds, Philip (2016) 'Science, art and dissent: Jack Lindsay and the Communist theory of culture', In: *British Marxism and Cultural Studies: Essays on a Living Tradition*, David Berry and Philip Bounds (eds.), Farnham, Surrey: Ashgate, 21–43.

Bourdieu, P. (1984) *Distinction: A Social Critique of the Judgement of Taste* translated by Richard Nice. London: Routledge.

Bourdieu, P. (1986) 'The forms of Capital', In: *Handbook for Theory and Research for the Sociology of Education*, J.G. Richardson (ed.), New York: Greenwood Press, 241–58.

Bourdieu, P. (1992) *Language and Symbolic Power*. Cambridge: Polity.

Bouwsma, William (1981) 'From history of ideas to history of meaning', *Journal of Interdisciplinary History* 12(2), 279–91.

Boyle, John (1838) 'An account of strikes in the potteries, in the years 1834 and 1836', *Journal of the Statistical Society of London* 1(May), 37–45.

Bradley, J.E. (1990) *Religion, Revolution, and English Radicalism: Nonconformity in Eighteenth-Century Politics and Society*. Cambridge: CUP.

Bradley, John L. (1965, ed.) *Rogue's Progress: The Autobiography of 'Lord Chief Baron' Nicholson*. London: Longmans.

Brake, Laurel (2012) 'Stead alone: Journalist, proprietor, and publisher 1890–1903', In: Brake, King, Luckhurst and Mussell (eds.), 77–97.

Brake, Laurel, Ed King, Roger Luckhurst and James Mussell (2012, eds.) *W.T. Stead: Newspaper Revolutionary*. London: The British Library.

Brauer, Fae (2017) 'Virilizing and valorizing homoeroticism: Eugen Sandow's queering of body cultures before and after the Wilde trials', *Visual Culture in Britain* 18(1), 35–67.

Brecht, Bertolt (1976) *Gesammelte Gedichte*, vol. 2. Frankfurt: Suhrkamp.

Brewer, John (1986) *The Common People and Politics, 1750s–1790s*. Cambridge: Chadwyck-Healey.

Brewer, Richard J. (1987) *Caerleon-isca. The Roman Legionary Museum*. Caerleon: The Museum.

Bridges, Thomas (1771) *Dido a Comic Opera. As It Is Performed at the Theatre Royal in the Hay-Market*. London: T. Davies.

Bridges, Thomas (1797) *A Burlesque Translation of Homer*, 2 vols. 4th edition. London: G.G. and J. Robinson.

Briggs, Asa (1967) 'The language of "class" in early nineteenth-century England', In: *Essays in Labour History*, A. Briggs and J. Saville (eds.), MacMillan, 43–73.

Briggs, Asa (1994) *A Social History of England*. London: BCA.

Briggs, Charles F. (2002 [1855]) *A Literary Martyrdom*. Charlottesville, Virginia: University of Virginia.

Briggs, J.H.Y. (1993) 'Urban institutions and administration', In: Phillips (ed.), 130–44.

British Museum (1833) *Elgin and Phigaleian Marbles*. London: Charles Knight for the British Museum Department of Greek and Roman Antiquities.

Broadbent, R.J. (1908) *Annals of the Liverpool Stage, from the Earliest Period to the Present Time: Together with Some Account of the Theatres and Music Halls in Bootle and Birkenhead*. New York and London: Benjamin Blom.

Brockwell, Maruice W. (1915) *Catalogue of the Pictures and Other Works of Art in the Collection of Lord St. Oswald at Nostell Priory*. London: Constable & Co.

Brodribb, Arthur Aikin (1885–1900) 'Wakefield, Gilbert', *Dictionary of National Biography* 58, 452–455.

Brooks, M. (2004) 'Aikin, John (1747–1822), physician and writer', *ODNB*. Oxford. OUP.

Brooks, Robin (2004) *The Portland Vase: The Extraordinary Odyssey of a Mysterious Roman Treasure*. New York: HarperCollins.

Brougham, Henry (1840) *The Oration of Demosthenes upon the Crown: Translated into English, with Notes, and the Greek Text, with Various Readings Selected from Wolff, Taylor, Reiske and Others*. London: Knight.

Brougham, Henry (1893) *The Oration of Demosthenes upon the Crown. Translated into English with Notes by Henry, Lord Brougham*. Revised edition. London: George Routledge & Sons.

Brown, F.C. (1910) *Elkanah Settle: His Life and Works*. Chicago, Illinois: University of Chicago Press.

Brown, Michael (2016) *The Irish Enlightenment*. Cambridge, Massachusetts: Harvard University Press.

Brown, Thomas (1705) 'The contents of the first part of the comical view of London and Westminter', In: *A Legacy for the Ladies or, Characters of the Women of the Age*, London: S. Briscoe, 109–29.

Brown, Thomas (1707) *The Second Volume of the Works of Mr. Tho. Brown*. London: B. Bragg.

Brown, Thomas (1709) *The Fourth Volume of the Works of Mr. Thomas Brown, Serious, Moral, Comical, and Satyrical*. London: B. Bragg.

Browne, Thomas (1646) *Pseudodoxia Epidemica*. London: Tho. Harper.

Bründl, Sonja (2003) *The Gentleman Ideal*. Gőttingen: Cuvillier.

Buckley, Cheryl (1990) *Potters and Paintresses*. London: The Woman's Press.

Bullinger, Heinrich (1533) *Ein schönspil von der geschicht der Edlen Römerin Lucretiæ/ und wie der Tyrannischküng Tarquinius Superbus von Rhom vertriben/ vnd sunderlich von der standhafftigkeit Junij Bruti/ des Ersten Consuls zu Rhom*. Basel: Wolff.

Bunyan, John (1666) *Grace Abounding to the Chief of Sinners*. London: Ponder.

Burchill, Frank and Richard Ross (1977) *A History of the Potters' Union*. Hanley: Ceramic and Allied Trades Union.

Burke, Edmund (1790) *Reflections on the Revolution in France*. London: J. Didsley.

Burke, Edmund (1889) *The Works of the Right Honourable Edmund Burke*, 12 vols, 9th edition. Boston, Massachusetts: Little and Brown.

Burke, Peter (1985) 'Popular culture in Seventeenth-Century London', in *Popular Culture in Seventeenth-Century England*, Barry Reay (ed.), New York: St. Matin's Press, 31–58.

Burke, Peter (2001) *Eyewitnessing: The Uses of Images as Historical Evidence*. Ithaca, New York: Cornell University Press.

Burn, J. (1846). *An Historical Sketch of the Independent Order of Oddfellows M.U.* Manchester: A. Heywood.

Burn, James Dawson (1856) *Autobiography of a Beggar Boy*. 2nd edition. London: Tweedie.

Burn Murdoch, W.G. (1894) *From Edinburgh to the Antarctic: An Artist's Notes and Sketches during the Dundee Antarctic Expedition of 1892–1893*. London: Longmans, Green and Co.

Burnand, F.C. (1863) *Ixion; or, the Man at the Wheel*. London: Lacy.

Burnett, John (1974) *Useful Toil. Autobiographies of Working People from the 1820s to the 1920s*. London: Allen Lane.

Burnett, John, David Vincent and David Mayall (1984–1989) *The Autobiography of the Working Class*. Brighton: Harvester.

Burns, Robert (1840) *The Works of Robert Burns with Life by Allan Cunningham*. London: Tegg.

Burns, Robert (2001) 'Epistle to J. Lapraik', In: *The Canongate Burns: The Complete Poems and Songs of Robert Burns*, Andrew Noble and Patrick Scott Hogg (ed.), Edinburgh: Canongate, 133–37.

Burrow, R.W. (1987) 'Swift and Plato's political philosophy', *Studies in Philology* 84, 494–506.

Burt, Thomas (1924) *An Autobiography*. London: T. Fisher Unwin Ltd.

Burton, Vicki Tolar (2001) 'John Wesley and the liberty to speak: The rhetorical and literacy practices of early Methodism', *College Composition and Communication* 53(1), 65–91.

Butler, Sarah (2013) 'The Gracchi, reform, and the nineteenth-century press', In: *Classics in the Modern World: A Democratic Turn?* Lorna Hardwick and S. Harrison (eds.), Oxford: OUP, 301–18.

Byron, George Gordon Byron Baron (1810) *English Bards and Scotch Reviewers*. London: Cawthorn.

Byron, Lord George (1839) *Life, Letters and Journals of Lord Byron, with Notes,* ed. T. Moore. London: John Murray.

Calamy, Edmund (1713) *An Account of the Ministers, Lecturers, Masters, and Fellows of Colleges and Schoolmasters: Who Were Ejected or Silenced after the Restoration in 1660, By or Before, the Act of Uniformity; Design'd for the Preserving to Posterity the Memory of Their Names, Characters, Writings, and Sufferings*. London: Journal Lawrence.

Calder, William III (1972) 'Schliemann on Schliemann: A Study in the Use of Sources', *GRBS* 13, 335–53.

Callaway, Anita (2000) *Visual Ephemera: Theatrical Art in Nineteenth-Century Australia*. Sydney: UNSW Press.

Cameron, Kenneth Neill (1945) 'Shelley and the reformers', *ELH* 12(1), 62–85.

Cameron, William (1823[?]) *The Prophecies of Hawkie, the Wonderful Fifeshire Cow*. Glasgow: W. Carse.

Cameron, William (1888) *Hawkie: The Autobiography of a Gangrel*, ed. John Strathesk. Glasgow: David Robertson & Co.

Camp, J.M. (1992) *The Athenian Agora*. Revised edition. London: American School of Classical Studies at Athens.

Cannon, John (1743) *Memoirs of the Birth, Education, Life and Death of: Mr. John Cannon. Sometime Excise Officer & Writing Master at Mere Glastenbury & West Lydford in the County of Somerset*, Somerset Record Office, Ms. DD/SAS C/1193/4, now published as *The Chronicles of John Cannon, Excise Officer and Writing Master,* ed. John Money. Oxford: The British Academy by OUP.

Capp, Bernard (2004) 'Taylor, John [called the Water Poet] (1578–1653), poet', *ODNB*. Oxford: OUP. www.oxforddnb.com/view/10.1093/ref:odnb/9780198614128.001.0001/odnb-9780198614128-e-27044. doi:10.1093/ref:odnb/27044.

Carden-Coyne, Anna Alexandra (1999) 'Classical heroism and modern life: Bodybuilding and masculinity in the early twentieth century', *Journal of Australian Studies* 23(63), 138–49.

Carey, John (1992) *The Intellectuals and the Masses*. London and Boston, Massachusetts: Faber & Faber.

Carlile, Richard (1819) *A defence of Mr Cobbett, against the Intrigues of Sir Francis Burdett, and his Partisans*. London: R. Carlile.

Carlyle, Thomas (1836) *Sartor Resartus*. Boston, Massachusetts: James Munroe and Co.

Carlyle, Thomas (1843) *Past and Present*. London: Chapman and Hall.

Carnall, Geoffrey (2013) 'Moore, Thomas (1779–1852), poet', *ODNB*. Oxford. OUP.

Carpenter, Andrew (2018) 'Working-class writing in Ireland before 1800: "some must be poor—we cannot all be great"', In: Pierse (2018a), 72–88.

Carpenter, E. (1889) *Civilization: Its Cause and Cure*. London: Swan Sonnenschein & Co.

Carter, Charles (n.d. but in 1950s) *Alexander Macdonald 1837–1884, Aberdeen Art Collector*. Aberdeen: Aberdeen Art Gallery.

Carter, Thomas (1845) *Memoirs of a Working Man*. London: Charles Knight & Co.

Cartledge, Paul (1995) 'Vindicating Gibbon's good faith', *Hermathena* 158, 133–47.

Cartledge, Paul (1996) '"We are all Greeks"? Ancient Greek (especially Herodotean) and modern contestations of Hellenism', *Bulletin of the Institute of Classical Studies* 40, 75–82.

Cartledge, Paul (2004) 'What have the Spartans done for us?: Sparta's contribution to western civilization', *Greece and Rome* 51(2), 164–79.

Cartledge, Paul (2016) *Democracy: A Life*. Oxford: OUP.

Cartledge, Paul and David Harvey (1985, eds.) *Crux: Essays in Greek history presented to G.E.M. de Ste Croix on His 75th Birthday*. London: Duckworth.

Cassell John ed (1851) *The Working Man's Friend, and Family Instructor*. London: John Cassell.

Castronovo David (1987) *The English Gentleman. Images and Ideals in Literature and Society*. New York: Ungar.

Caudwell, C. (1946) *Illusion and Reality: A Study of the Sources of Poetry*. London: Lawrence and Wishart.

Caudwell, C. (1986) *Collected Poems 1924–1936*, ed. with an Introduction by A. Young. Manchester: Carcanet.

Caulfeild, James (1894) *The Manuscript and Correspondence of James, First Earl of Charlemont*, vol. II. London: Eyre and Spottiswoode.

Caute, D. (1966) *The Left in Europe Since 1789*. London: Weidenfeld and Nicolson.

Cavenagh, F.A. (1929) 'Lord Brougham and the society for the diffusion of useful knowledge', *The Journal of Adult Education* 4, 3–37.

Çelikkol, Ayşe (2011) *Romances of Free Trade: British Literature, Laissez-Faire, and the Global Nineteenth Century*. New York: OUP.

Cervantes, Miguel (1741) *Two Humorous Novels, Viz. I. A Diverting Dialogue Between Scipio and Bergansa, Two Dogs Belonging to the Hospital Of The Resurrection, in the City of Valladolid; Giving an Account of their Lives and Various Adventures; Interspers'd wtih their Reflexions and Sentiments on the Lives, Characters, Humours and Employments of the Different Masters they liv'd with. II. The Comical History of Rinconete and Cortadillo*. London: H. Kent.

Chalmers, George (1794) *The Life of Thomas Ruddiman*. London: John Stockdale.

Chambers, Ephraim (1728) *Cyclopædia; Or, An Universal Dictionary of Arts and Sciences ... Compiled from the Best Authors*. London: James & John Knapton.

Chambers, Colin (1989) *The Story of Unity Theatre*. New York: St. Martin's Press.

Chambers, Robert (1835) *A Biographical Dictionary of Eminent Scotsmen*, vol. IV. Glasgow: Blackie and Son.

Chambers, Robert (1862–1864) *The Book of Days: A Miscellany of Popular Antiquities in Connection with the Calendar*, 2 vols. London and Edinburgh: W. and R. Chambers.

Chambers, William (1872). *Memoir of Robert Chambers*. Edinburgh and London: W. and R. Chambers.

Chambers, William (1884) *Memoir of William and Robert Chambers*. 13th edition. London and Edinburgh: W. and R. Chambers.

Chambers, William and Robert Chambers eds. (1832–1834) *Chambers Edinburgh Journal*, vol. 1–2. London: William Orr.

Chapman, D.L. (1994) *Sandow the Magnificent*. Urbana, Illinois: University of Illinois Press.

Chapman, D.L. (2010) *Venus with Biceps*. Vancouver: Arsenal Pulp Press.

Chorley, H. (1847) 'George Lovell', *The Athenaeum* 1009 (27th February), 223–24.

Christmas, William J. (2001) *The Lab'ring Muses: Work, Writing, and the Social Order in English Plebeian Poetry 1730–1830*. Newark and London: University of Delaware Press and Associated University Presses.

Christmas, William J. (2009) '"From threshing corn, he turns to thresh his brains" Stephen Duck as laboring-class intellectual', In: Krishnamurthy (ed.), 25–48.

Church, Richard and Mildred May Bozman (1942) *Poems of Our Time 1900–1942*. London: Dent.

Cibber, Theophilus (1753) *The Lives of the Poets of Great Britain and Ireland*. London: R. Griffiths.

Claeys, Gregory (1995) *The Politics of English Jacobinism: Writings of John Thelwall*. Philadelphia, PA: Pennsylvania State University Press.

Clark, Garth (1995) *A Complete History of Pottery in Britain*. London: Phaidon.

Clarke, Alured (1847) '"The Rev. Dr. Alured Clarke to Mrs. Clayton", letters regarding Stephen Duck between August 18th and October 25th, 1730', in *Memoirs of Viscountess Sundon, Mistress of the Robes to Queen Caroline, Consort of George II; Including Letters from the Most Celebrated Persons of Her Time*. 2 Vols, Thomson, A.T. (ed.), London: Henry Colburn, 181–206.

Clarke, G.W. (1989, ed.) *Rediscovering Hellenism The Hellenic Inheritance and the English Imagination*. Cambridge: CUP.

Clarke, John S. (1918) *Young Workers' Book of Rebels*, vol. I. Glasgow: Andrew Fleming.

Clarke, Martin Lowther (1937) *Richard Porson. A biographical Essay. With a Portrait, Facsimiles and a Bibliography*. Cambridge, CUP.

Clarke, Martin Lowther (1940) 'Charles James Fox and the classics', *Greece and Rome* 9 (26), 81–87.

Clarke, Martin Lowther (1945) *Greek Studies in England 1700–1830*. Cambridge: CUP

Clarke, W. (1809) *The Authentic and Impartial Life of Mrs. Mary Anne Clarke: Including Numerous Original Letters and Anecdotes of Persons Deeply Interested, Never Before Published: With a Compendious View of the Whole Proceedings, Both Public and Private, Illustrative of the Late Important Investigation of the Conduct of His Royal Highness, the Duke of York, &c., &c.* London: T. Kelly.

Clarke, William B. (1831–1832) *Pompeii*. 2 Vols. London: Charles Knight.

Clarkson, Thomas (1786) *An Essay on the Slavery and Commerce of the Human Species, Particularly the African*. London: T. Cadell: J. Phillips.

Claxton, Timothy (1839) *Memoir of a Mechanic*. Boston, Massachusetts: George W. Light.

Clemit, Pamela (2000–1) 'Philosophical anarchism in the schoolroom: William Godwin's Juvenile Library, 1805–25', *Biblion* 9, 44–70.

Clemit, Pamela (2009) 'William Godwin's Juvenile Library', *The Charles Lamb Bulletin*, (July), 90–99.

Clifford, Brendan (1997) *Thomas Russell and Belfast, with Thomas Russell's Letter to the People of Ireland (1796)*. Belfast: Athol Books.

Clifford, Timothy (1992) 'The plaster shops of the Rococo and Neo-Classical era in Britain', *Journal of the History of Collections* 4(1), 39–65.

Clubbe, W. (1801) *Ver: de Agricolæ puero, anglicano poemate celeberrime excerptum et in morem latini georgici redditum*. Ipswich: M. Jermyn.

Coates, S. (1992) 'Manchester's German gentlemen: Immigrant institutions in a provincial city 1840–1920', *Manchester Region History Review* 5, 21–30.

Cobbett, William (1816) 'To the people of the United States of America', *Cobbett's Weekly Political Register* 31.12(September 21st), 353–66.

Cobham, A. (1920) 'A student's experience', In: *Cambridge Essays on Adult Education,* R. St. John Parry (ed.), Cambridge: CUP, 206–23.

Cockburn, Henry (1856) *Memorials of His Time.* Edinburgh: Adam and Charles Black.

Cockburn, Henry (1888) *An Examination of the Trials for Sedition*, 2 vols. Edinburgh: David Douglas.

Coffey, John (2013) 'Church and state, 1550–1750: The emergence of Dissent', In: *T & T Clark Companion to Nonconformity*, Robert Pope (ed.), London: Bloomsbury, 47–74.

Cohen, David (1982) 'Depth and control in David Jones' *In Parenthesis*', Archard et al. (eds.) 46–52.

Cole, G.D.H. (1943) *Richard Carlile 1790–1843.* London: Fabian Society.

Colman, G. and B. Thornton (1755, ed.) *Poems by Eminent Ladies: Particularly, Mrs. Barber* London: R. Baldwin.

Coleman, Stephen (1990) *Daniel De Leon (Lives of the Left).* Manchester: Manchester University Press.

Coleman, Terry (2001) *Nelson.* London: Bloomsbury.

Collier, Mary (1739) *The Woman's Labour: An Epistle to Mr. Stephen Duck; in Answer to His Late Poem, Called the Thresher's Labour.* London: J. Roberts.

Collier, Mary (1762) *Poems, on Several Occasions ... With Some Remarks on Her Life.* Winchester: Mary Ayres.

Cone, Carl B. (1982) 'The Molineaux-Cribb fight, 1810: Wuz Tom Molineaux robbed?' *Journal of Sport History* 9, 83–91.

Conolly, L.W. (1976) *The Censorship of English Drama, 1737–1824.* San Marino, California: Huntington Library.

Contogouris, Ersy (2018) *Emma Hamilton and Late Eighteenth-Century European Art.* London: Routledge.

Cooke, Thomas (1728, trans.) *The Works of Hesiod.* London: T. Green.

Cooney, Sondra Miley (2014) 'Chambers, William (1800–1883), publisher', *ODNB.* Oxford: OUP.

Cooper, Thomas (1845) *Wise Saws and Modern Instances*, vol. II. London: Jeremiah How.

Cooper, Thomas (1872) *The Life of Thomas Cooper, Written by Himself,* ed. Stephen Roberts. London: Hodder & Stoughton.

Cooper, Thomas (1877) *The Poetical Works.* London: Hodder & Stoughton.

Cordier, Mathurin (1568) *Colloquiorum scholasticorum Libri Quatuor. Ad Pueros in Sermone Latino Paulatim Exercendos. Nuper recogniti, & Multò quàm Antea & Politiores, & Ornatiores.* Paris: Buonius.

Corkery, Daniel (1924) *The Hidden Ireland: A Study of Gaelic Munster in the Eighteenth Century.* Dublin: M.H. Gill and Son.

Corner, G.W. (1948, ed.) *The Autobiography of Benjamin Rush.* Philadelphia, PA: American Philosophical Society.

Cornforth, M. (1978, ed.) *Rebels and their Causes: Essays in Honour of A.L. Morton.* London: Lawrence and Wishart.

Couper, Sarah (2004) 'Nicoll, Robert (bap. 1814, d. 1837)', *ODNB.* Oxford: OUP.

Couper, William James (1914) *The Millers of Haddington, Dunbar and Dunfermline; a Record of Scottish Bookselling.* London: T.F. Unwin.

Courtney, W. (2004a) 'Riley, Henry Thomas (1816–1878), literary scholar and translator', *ODNB.* Oxford: OUP.

Courtney, W. (2004b) 'Watson, John Selby, scholar and murderer', revised by H.C.G. Matthew, *ODNB.* Oxford. OUP.

Coutu, Joan (2015) *Then and Now: Collecting and Classicism in Eighteenth-Century England.* Montreal and London: McGill-Queen's University Press.

Cowan, Edward J. and Mike Paterson (2007) *Folk In Print: Scotland's Chapbook Heritage, 1750–1850.* Edinburgh: John Donald.

Cowan, Steven (2012) *The Growth of Public Literacy in Eighteenth-Century England.* PhD Dissertation. Institute of Education, University of London.

Cowper, W. (1782) *The Entertaining and Facetious History of John Gilpin = the Public Advertizer* (November 14th). London: Henry Woodfall.

Cox, Jeffrey N. (1998) *Poetry and Politics in the Cockney School: Keats, Shelley, Hunt, and their Circle.* Cambridge: CUP.

Craik, W.W. (1910a) 'General economic and social development in Greece', *Plebs* volume 2 no. 3 (April) 67–72.

Craik, W.W. (1910b) 'General economic and social development in Greece (continued)', *Plebs* volume 2 no. 4 (May) 94–120.

Craik, W.W. (1910c) 'General economic and social development of Rome' *Plebs* volume 2, no. 5 (June) 120–124.

Craik, W.W. (1910d). 'General economic and social development of Rome (continued)' *Plebs* volume 2, no. 6 (July) 144–148.

Craik, W.W. (1910e) 'General economic and social development of Rome (further continued)' *Plebs* volume 2, no. 7 (August) 170–176.

Cranfield, J.L. (2012) 'Chivalric machines: The Boer War, the male body and the grand narrative in the *Strand Magazine*', *Victorian Literature and Culture* 40(2), 549–73.

Crane, Walter (1887) *The Baby's Own Æsop.* London and New York: G. Routledge & Sons.

Crane, Walter (1896) *Cartoons for the Cause, 1886–1896.* London: Twentieth Century Press.

Crane, Walter (1911) *William Morris to Whistler: Papers and Addresses on Art and Craft and the Commonweal.* London: Chiswick Press (Charles Whittingham & Sons).

Crawford, John C. (1978) *Wanlockhead Miners' Library: A Guide Book.* Wanlockhead (Dumfries & Galloway): Wanlockhead Museum Trust.

Crawford, John C. and Stuart James (1981) *The Society for Purchasing Books in. Wanlockhead, 1756–1979.* Glasgow: Scottish Library Association.

Crawford, Robert (2009) *The Bard: Robert Burns, A Biography.* London: Jonathan Cape.

Creech, Thomas (1682) *T. Lucretius Carus the Epicurean Philosopher, His Six Books De Natura Rerum: Done into English Verse, with Notes.* Oxford: L. Lichfield.

Croft, Andy (1998) *A Weapon in the Struggle: The Cultural History of the Communist Party in Britain: Cultural History of the British Communist Party.* London: Pluto Press.

Croft, Andy (n.d.) 'The Communist Party in literature'. www.letterpressproject.co.uk/media/file/THE_COMMUNIST_PARTY_IN_LITERATURE_by.pdf.

Cronin, Maura (1994) *Country, Class or Craft? The Politicisation of the Skilled Artisan in Nineteenth-Century Cork.* Cork: Cork University Press.

Crooks, Will (1907) *From Workhouse to Westminster.* London: Cassell.

Crossick, Geoffrey (1977) 'The emergence of the lower middle class in Britain: A discussion', In: *The Lower Middle Class in Britain 1870–1914,* Crossick (ed.), London: Croom Helm, 11–60.

Croxall ([1722] 1790) *Fables of Æsop and Others: Translated into English With Instructive Applications; and a Print before Each Fable.* London: T. Longman et al.

Cruickshank, Dan (2009) *The Secret History of Georgian London: How the Wages of Sin Shaped the Capital.* London: Random House.

Cruickshank, Marjorie (1967) 'The Argyll commission Report 1865–8: A landmark in Scottish education', *British Journal of Educational Studies* 15 (June 1st), 133–47.

Crummell, Alexander (1898), 'The attitude of the American mind toward the negro intellect', *The American Negro Academy Occasional Papers* (3), 8–19. Washington, D.C.

Crust, Linda (2016) *Thomas Cooper*. Potterhanworth, Lincoln: CRB Associates.

Cueva, Edmund P., Shannon N. Byrne and Frederick Benda (2009, eds.) *Jesuit Education and the Classics*. Newcastle-Upon-Tyne: Cambridge Scholars Publishing.

Currie, James (1838) *The Life of Robert Burns*. Edinburgh: William and Robert Chambers.

Curtin, Nancy J. (1994) *United Irishmen: Popular Politics in Ulster and Dublin, 1791–1798*. Oxford: OUP.

Cust, Lionel Henry (1885–90) 'Stuart, James (1713–1788)', *Dictionary of National Biography*, 55, 66–68.

Cuthbertson, David (n.d.) *The Life-History of Alexander Anderson ("Surfaceman")*. Roseville, Midlothian: Privately Printed.

Dacier, Anne (1683, ed. under her maiden name) *Eutropii Historiæ Romanæ breviarium notis et emendationibus*. Paris: 'Widow of A. Cellier'.

Daley, Caroline (2003) *Leisure and Pleasure: Reshaping and Revealing the New Zealand Body*. Auckland: Auckland University Press.

Daley, Victor J. (1911) *Wine and Roses*, ed. with a memoir by Bertram Stevens. Sydney: Angus and Robertson; London: the Australian Book Company.

Daly, Nicholas (2012) 'Fiction, theatre and early cinema', In: *The Cambridge Companion to Popular Fiction,* David Glover and Scott McCracken (eds.), Cambridge: CUP, 33–49.

Daly, Nicholas (2015) *The Demographic Imagination and the Nineteenth-Century City*. Cambridge: CUP.

Dalzel, Andrew (1821) *Substance of Lecture on the Ancient Greeks, and on the Revival of Greek Learning in Europe*, 2 vols. Edinburgh: Archibald Constable & Co.

Dalzel, Andrew (1862) *History of the University of Edinburgh from Its Foundation, with a Memoir of the Author*, 2 vols. Edinburgh: Edmonston and Douglas.

Damrosch, Leo (2013) *Jonathan Swift: His Life and World*. New Haven, Connecticut: Yale University Press.

Dancy, J.R. (2015) *The Myth of the Press Gang: Volunteers, Impressment and the Naval Manpower Problem in the Late Eighteenth Century*. Suffolk: Boydell Press.

Danet, Pierre (1700) *A Complete Dictionary of the Greek and Roman Antiquities, Explaining the Obscure Places in Classic Authors and Ancient Historians*. London: John Nicholson.

Daniel, Stehen H. (1984) *John Toland*. Kingston and Montreal: McGill-Queen's University Press.

D'Arnay, Jean Rodolphe (1761) *The Private Life of the Romans*. Edinburgh: A. Donaldson.

Darnton, Robert (1980) 'Intellectual and cultural history', In: *The Past Before Us: Contemporary Historical Writing in the United States*, Michael Kammen (ed.), Ithaca, NY,: Cornell U.P, 327–48.

Darnton, Robert (1981) 'From history of ideas to history of meaning', *Journal of Interdisciplinary History* 12(2), 279–91.

Dart, Gregory (2012) *Metropolitan Art and Literature, 1810–1840: Cockney Adventures*. Cambridge: CUP.

Davies, J.G. (1955) 'Diodorus Siculus, iii. 12–14; v. 36–8', *Journal of Hellenic Studies* 75, 153.

Davies, Rachel Bryant (2019) *Victorian Epic Burlesques*. London: Bloomsbury.

Davis, Rose Mary (1926) *Stephen Duck, the Thresher-poet*. The Maine Bulletin. University of Maine Studies: Series 2 No.8. Orono. University Press.

Davis, Tracy C. Davis (1991) *Actresses as Working Women*. London and New York: Routledge.

Day-Lewis, Cecil (1940) 'Dedicatory stanzas, to Stephen Spender', In: *Virgil's Georgics*. London: Journal Cape, 7.

De Leon, Daniel (1908) *Two Pages from Roman History*. Edinburgh: Socialist Labour Party.

Dent, Joseph Malaby (1938) *The Memoirs of James Malaby Dent 1849–1926*. Letchworth: Dent.

Dent, J.M. and H.R. Dent (1938) *The House of Dent 1888–1938*. London: Dent & Sons.

Davenant, C. (1698) *Discourses on the Publick Revenues*. London: J. Knapton.

Davey, Richard (1906) *The Pageant of London*, vol. I, with Forty Illustrations in Colour by John Fulleylove. London: Methuen.

Davies, Ceri (1995) *Welsh Literature and the Classical Tradition*. Cardiff: University of Wales Press.

Davies, Ceri (2009) 'Classics and Welsh cultural identity', In: *British Classics Outside England*, Judith P. Hallett and Christopher Stray (eds.), Waco, TX: Baylor University Press, 35–47.

Davis, Michael T. (2004) 'Gerrald, Joseph (1763–1796)', *ODNB*.

Dawson, A.J. (1916) *A Temporary Gentleman in France: Home Letters from an Officer in the New Army*, with a Foreword by A.J. Dawson. London: Cassell.

Day-Lewis, Cecil (1937) 'An expensive education', *Left Review* 3, 43–5.

de Brún, P. (2009) *Scriptural Instruction in the Vernacular: The Irish Society and Its Teachers 1818–1827*. Dublin: Dublin Institute for Advanced Studies.

De Quincey, Thomas (1897) *The Collected Writings*, vol. XI. ed. David Masson. London: A. and C. Black.

Delany, Paul (1969) *British Autobiography in the Seventeenth Century*. London: Routledge and Kegan Paul.

Dellarosa, Franca (2018) 'Teaching the illegitimate: A London Street Scene and other stratagems', *Romantic Textualities: Literature and Print Culture, 1780–1840*. Online Journal Article. www.romtext.org.uk/teaching-romanticism-xxviii-drama-part-4/.

Dennis, Richard (2015) 'The John Scott collection at the Jackfield tile museum', *The Journal of the Decorative Arts Society 1850 - The Present*, 39, 140–67.

Derry, Warren (1966) *Dr. Parr: A Portrait of the Whig Dr. Johnson*. Oxford: Clarendon Press.

des Maizeaux, Pierre (1726) 'Some memoirs of the life and writings of Mr John Toland', In: Toland, iii–xcii.

Deutsch, Helene (1973) *Conversations with Myself: An Epilogue*. New York: Norton.

Dickens, C. (1850) *David Copperfield*. London: Collins.

Dickinson, Edward Ross (2017) *Dancing in the Blood: Modern Dance and European Culture on the Eve of the First World War*. Cambridge: CUP.

Dickinson, H.T. (1986) *Caricatures and the Constitution, 1760–1832*. Cambridge: Chadwyck-Healey.

Didot, Jules (1828) *The Catholic Question Considered in Its Various Relations Religious and Political*. Paris: J. Didot.

Dillon, John (1979) 'Some reflections on the Irish classical tradition', *The Crane Bag = Anglo-Irish Literature: Perspectives* 3(2), 28–32.

Dilworth, Thomas (1982) 'In Parenthesis as chronicle', In: Archard et al. (eds.), 37–45.

Dilworth, Thomas (1988) *The Shape of Meaning in the Poetry of David Jones*. Toronto, Buffalo/ and London: University of Toronto Press.

Dilworth, Thomas (2012) *David Jones and the Great War*. London: Enitharmon.

Dimitrov, Georgi (1935) *The Working Class Against Fascism*. London: Martin Lawrence.

D'Israeli, Isaac (1809) 'Memoirs of Percival Stockdale', *Quarterly Review* I(2), 371–86.

Doddridge, P. (1829) *The Correspondence and Diary of Philip Doddridge*, vol. 2, ed. J.D. Humphreys. London: Colburn and Bentley.

Dodds, John Wendell (1933) *Thomas Southerne, Dramatist*. New Haven and New London, Connecticut: Yale U.P.

Donnelly, T. (1979) *Structural and Technical Change in the Aberdeen Granite Quarrying Industry, 1830–1880*. London: OUP.

Doody, Margaret Anne (1985) *The Daring Muse: Augustan Poetry Reconsidered*. Cambridge: CUP.

Dowling, P.J. (1935) *The Hedge Schools of Ireland*. Dublin: Longmans *Green*.

Draper, W.H. (1923) *University Extension, 1873–1923: A Survey of Fifty Years, 1873–1923*. Cambridge: Cambridge University Press.

Dryden, John (1903) *The Works of Virgil*. London: Grant Richards.

Drennan, William (1785) *Letters of an Irish Helot, Signed Orellana*. Dublin: Constitution Society of the City of Dublin.

Dresser, Madge (2007) *Slavery Obscured: The Social History of the Slave Trade in Bristol*. London: Continuum.

Drew, Jacob Halls (1834) *The Life, Character, and Literary Labours, of Samuel Drew, by His Eldest Son*. London: Longman et al.

Driscoll, Lawrence (2009) *Evading Class in Contemporary British Literature*. New York and Basingstoke: Palgrave Macmillan.

Drucker, Tibor (2000) *A Csepeli Munkásotthon Története*. Budapest: Emlékek Budapest Multjából.

Dryden, John (1697) *The Works of Virgil: Containing his Pastorals, Georgics, and Aeneis, Translated into English Verse by MR. Dryden; Adorn'd with a Hundred Sculptures*. London: Jacob Tonson.

Duck, Stephen (1730) *Poems on Several Subjects*. 5th edition. London: J. Roberts.

Duck, Stephen (1736) *Poems on Several Occasions*. London: W. Bickerton, at Lord Bacon's Head, near Temple-Bar.

Duck, Stephen (1741) *Every Man in His Own Way: An Epistle to a Friend*. London: J. Roberts and R. Dodsley.

Duck Stephen (1750) 'From Stephen Duck, Kew. December 5, 1750', (Appendix XXVII.) in *Anecdotes, Observations, and Characters, of Books and Men*, Joseph Spence (1820, ed.), London: W. H. Carpenter and A. Constable and Co. Edinburgh, 436–37.

Duck, Stephen and Mary Collier (1989) *The Thresher's Labour & the Woman's Labour*. Edited and with Introduction by Thompson, E. P. London: Merlin Press.

Dudley, Jack (2013) 'Transcendence and the end of Modernist aesthetics: David Jones's *in Parenthesis*', *Renascence* 65(2), 103–24.

Duffy, C.G. (1845) *The Spirit of the Nation: Ballads and Songs by the Writers of 'The Nation'*. Dublin: J. Duffy.

Dunbar, George (1822) *Exercises on the Syntax, and Observations on Most of the Idioms of the Greek Language*. 3rd edition. Edinburgh: Stirling and Slade.

Dunbar, George (1824) *A Concise General History of the Early Grecian States Appendix in Archaeologia Graeca, or the Antqiuities of Greece, by John Potter*, a new edition with a Life of the Author by Robert Anderson, 2 vols, vol. II. Edinburgh: Stirling and Kenney.

Dunbar, Zachary (2010) 'From à la carte to convergence: Symptoms of interdisciplinarity in reception theory', In: *Theorising Performance*, Edith Hall and Stephe Harrop (eds.), London: Bloomsbury, 85–94.

Duncan, William James (1831) *Notices and Documents Illustrative of the Literary History of Glasgow, During the Greater Part of the Last Century*. Glasgow: Hutchison and Brookman.

Dunster, S. (1729, ed.) *Horace's Satires Epistles, and Art of Poetry, Done into English, with Notes*. London: W. Mears, F. Clay, and D. Browne.

Dutton, K.R. (1995) *The Perfectible Body: The Western Ideal of Physical Development*. London: Cassell.

Dyche, Thomas (1709) *Vocabularium Latiale: Or, a Latine Vocabulary*. London: S. Butler.

Dyer, George (1793) *Complaints of the Poor People of England*. London: Ridgway.

Dyer, Walter (1916) 'Creators of English styles: VIII. Josiah Wedgwood', *Arts & Decoration* 6, 541–44 and 564–66.

Eakin, Emily (2001) 'The intellectual class struggle', *The New York Times*, (January 6th).

Earle, John (1630) *Microcosmographie*. London: Robert Allot.

Earnshaw, Graham (2017) *The Formosa Fraud*. Hong Kong: Earnshaw Books.

East, John M. (1971) 'Andrew Ducrow: The world's greatest equestrian performer', *Theatre Quarterly* 1, 37–39.

Eastlake, Laura (2019) *Masculinity and Ancient Rome in the Victorian Cultural Imagination*. Oxford: OUP.

Eaton, D.I. (1795) *The Philanthropist, or, Philosophical Essays on Politics, Government, Morals and Manners*, vol. 1–43. (March 16, 1795–January 25, 1796).

Ebbatson, Roger (2010) '"A Thickness of Wall": Hardy and class', In: *A Companion to Thomas Hardy*, Keith Wilson (ed.), Oxford: Blackwell, 162–77.

Echard, Laurence (1715) *The Classical Geographical Dictionary*. London: J. Torson.

Echard, Laurence (1716) *Plautus's Comedies, Amphitryon, Epidicus, and Rudens, Made English: With Critical Remarks upon Each Play*. London: Timothy Child and William Taylor.

Edgar, Robert and John Lockwood Kipling (1864) 'Wedgwood Memorial Institute competition', *The Builder* 22 (October 8th), 736–37.

Edson, Michael (2012) '"A Closet or a Secret Field": Horace, protestant devotion and British retirement poetry', *Journal for Eighteenth-Century Studies* 35(1), 17–41.

Edwards, Catherine (1999, ed.) *Roman Presences: Receptions of Rome in European Culture, 1789–1945*. Cambridge: CUP.

Edwards, Francis (1985) *The Jesuits in England: From 1580 to the Present Day*. Tunbridge Wells: Burns and Oats.

Edwards, Hywel Teifi (2009) *The National Pageant of Wales*. Llandysul: Gomer.

Edwards, Lewis (1865) 'Yr hen brifysgolion a'r brifysgol I Gymru', *Y Traethodydd [The Essayist]* 20, 133–43.

Edwards, Mervyn (1996) *Potters at Play*. Leek: Churnet Valle Books.

Egan, Pierce (1828–1829) *Boxiana*, 5 vols. London: G. Virtue.

Egan, Pierce (1832) *Pierce Egan's Book of Sports, and Mirror of Life: Embracing the Turf, the Chase, the Ring, and the Stage*. London: T. Tegg and Son.

Elgar, Edward (1898) *Caractacus: A Cantata for Soprano, Tenor, Baritone, and Bass Soli, Chorus and Orchestra, the Words Written for Music by H.A. Acworth, the Music by Edward Elgar (Op. 35), Choruses Only, with Words of Solos, Translated into Tonic Sol-Fa Notation by W.G. McNaught*. London and New York: Novello.

Elias, A.C. (1987) 'A manuscript book of Constantia Grierson's', *Swift Studies* 2, 33–56.

Eliot, George (1996 [1861]) *Silas Marner, the Weaver of Raveloe*, ed. Peter Mudford. London: J.M. Dent.

Eliot, T.S. (1922) *The Waste Land*. New York: Boni & Liveright.

Eliot, T.S. (1974) *The Waste Land: A Facsimile and Transcript of the Original Drafts*. San Diego, California: Harcourt Brace Jovanovich.

Ellis, Ellis Owen (1844) *Illustrated Life of Richard Robert Jones (Aberdaron)*. MS held in National Library of Wales, Aberystwith. Drawing Volume Collection. 99239259002419; Drawing vol. 51.

Emerson, Ralph Waldo (1843) 'Past and present', *The Dialog* IV(July), 96–102.

Epstein, James (1982) *The Lion of Freedom: Feargus O'Connor and the Chartist Movement, 1832–1842*. London: Croom Helm.

Epstein, James and David Karr (2007) 'Playing at revolution: British "Jacobin" performance', *The Journal of Modern History* 79(3), 495–530.

Erasmus, D. (1753) *The Apophthegms of the Ancients*. London: A. Millar.

Evans, Beriah Gwynfe (1892) 'The Welsh language in education', *Welsh Review*, (March), 507–13.

Evans, Beriah Gwynfe (1904) *Caradog: Drama Hanesyddol*. Caernarfon: Cyhoeddedigganyrawdwr.

Evans, Beriah Gwynfe (1915) *The Life Romance of Lloyd George*. London: Everyman.

Evans, Gwyn and David Maddox (2010) *The Tonypandy Riots 1910–1911*. Plymouth: University of Plymouth Press.

Evelyn, J. (1667) *Publick Employment and an Active Life Prefer'd to Solitude and All its Appanages*. London: H. Herringman.

Eyres, Patrick (1985) *Studley Royal and Hackfall: The Classical and Sublime Landscapes of North Yorkshire*. Leeds: New Arcadians.

Factory Girl (1853) *The Unfortunate Genius, by a Factory Girl*. London: Israel Holdsworth.

Falconer, Ruth (2005) *Hell in Contemporary Literature. Western Descent Narratives Since 1945*. Edinburgh: Edinburgh University Press.

Farrant, John H. (2009) 'Grose, Francis', *ODNB*, Revised Version of Article First published 2004.

Farrell, William (1985). 'The Role of Mandeville's Bee Analogy in "The Grumbling Hive"', *Studies in English Literature, 1500-1900* 25(3), 511–27.

Farrington, Benjamin (1919) 'The text of Shelley's translation of the Symposium of Plato', *MLR* 14, 325–26.

Faxon, A.C. (2004) 'Preserving the classical past: Sir William and Lady Emma Hamilton', *Visual Resources* 20(4), 259–73.

Feaver, William (1988) *Pitmen Painters: The Ashington Group 1934–1984*. London: Chatto and Windus.

Felton, Henry (1713) *A Dissertation on Reading the Classics, and Forming a Just Style Written in the Year 1709, and Addressed to the Right Honourable, John Lord Roos, the Present Marquis of Granby*. London: Jonah Bowyer.

Ferguson, Christopher (2016) *An Artisan Intellectual: James Carter and the Rise of Modern Britain, 1792–1853*. Baton Rouge, Louisiana: Louisiana University Press.

Ferguson Moira ed. (1985) *First Feminists: British Women Writers, 1578–1799*. Bloomington, Indiana: Indiana University Press.

Ferguson, Moira (1995) *Eighteenth-Century Women Poets: Nation, Class, and Gender*. New York: State University of New York Press.

Fieldhouse, R. (1977) *The Workers' Educational Association: Aims and Achievements, 1903–1977*. Syracuse, NY: Syracuse University, Publications in Continuing Education.

Fieldhouse, Roger (1983) 'The ideology of English adult education teaching 1925–1950', *Studies in Adult Education* 15 (September), 29–30.

Fielding, Henry (1742) *The History of the Adventures of Joseph Andrews, and His Friend Mr. Abraham Adams. Written in Imitation of the Manner of Cervantes, Author of Don Quixote*, 2 vols. 2nd edition. London: A. Millar.

Fielding, Henry and William Young (1742, trans.) *Plutus. The God of Riches. A Comedy. Translated out of the Original Greek*. London: T. Waller.

Findlater, Richard (1967) *Banned: A Review of Theatrical Censorship in Britain*. London: Macgibbon Kee.

Filon, Augustin (1907) *The English Stage*, translated by Frederic Whyte with an Introduction by Henry Arthur Jones. London and New York: John Milne and Dodd, Mead & Co.

Findlater, Richard (1967) *Banned: A Review of Theatrical Censorship in Britain*. London: MacGibbon and Kee.

Finegan, Joanna (1996) 'Georgian Drogheda and the printed word', In: Long (ed.), 33–50.

Fissell, Mary (2015) 'When the birds and the bees were not enough: Aristotle's *Masterpiece*', *The Public Domain Review*, (August 19th). https://publicdomainreview.org/2015/08/19/when-the-birds-and-the-bees-were-not-enough-aristotles-masterpiece/.

Fitzgerald, Percy (1870) *Principles of Comedy and Dramatic Effect*. London: Tinsley.

Fitzgerald, William (1996) 'Labor and laborer in Latin poetry: The case of the *Moretum*', *Arethusa* 29(3), 389–418.

Flanagan, Thomas (1979) *The Year of the French*. London: Macmillan.

Fleming, J. Arnold (1923) *Scottish Pottery*. Glasgow: Maclehose, Jackson & Co. Ltd.

Fleming, J. Arnold (1926) *Modelling and Pottery Painting in Glasgow*. Jackson, MS: Wylie & Co.

Flexner, Helen Hudson (2014) *The London Mechanics' Institution: Social and Cultural Foundations 1823–1830*. PhD Thesis, University College London.

Fontaine, Charles (1546, trans) *Epitome des trois premiers livres de Artemidorus ancien autheur traictant des songes*. Lyon: J. de Tournes.

Foote, Jesse (1811) *The Life of Arthur Murphy, Esq*. London: J. Faulder.

Forbes, Atholl (1897) *Curiosities of a Scots Charta Chest, 1600–1800: With the Travels and Memoranda of Sir Alexander*. Edinburgh: W. Brown.

Fordyce, Christian James (1921) *Gaisford Greek Prose: Herodotus in Ireland, Being Part of the Third Book of His Account of Britain*. Oxford: Basil Blackwell.

Forrest, Martin (2003) 'The abolition of compulsory Latin and Its consequences', *Greece and Rome* 50 (Supplement 1), 42–66.

Fosbroke, Thomas Dudley (1825) *Encyclopædia of Antiquities, and Elements of Archaeology: Classical and Mediæval*, 2 vols. London: John Nichols and Son.

Fosbroke, Thomas Dudley (1833–1835) *A Treatise on the Arts, Manufactures, Manners, and Institutions of the Greeks and Romans*. London: Longman, Rees, Orme, Brown, Green, and Longman, Paternoster-Row; and John Taylor, Upper Gower Street.

Foster, R.F. (2003) *W.B. Yeats, a Life*, vol. I. Oxford: OUP.

Fowell, Frank and Frank Palmer (1913) *Censorship*. London: Frank Palmer.

Fox, R.M. (1930) *Drifting Men*. London: Leonard and Virginia Woolf at the Hogarth Press.

Fox, R.M. (1937) *Smoky Crusade*. London: Socialist Book Club.

Fraistat, Neil (1994) 'Illegitimate Shelley: Radical piracy and the textual edition as cultural performance', *PMLA* 109(3), 409–23.

Frank, D.L. (1972) 'Llewellyn Jewitt's view of the Stamford Brick and Terra-Cotta works with comments by D.L. Franks', *Lincolnshire Industrial Archaeology* 7, 49–54.

Fraser, Flora (1986) *Beloved Emma: The Life of Emma Lady Hamilton*. London: Weidenfeld and Nicolson.

Fraser, W. Hamish (1999) *A History of British Trade Unionism 1700–1998*. Basingstoke: Macmillan.

Frazer, James George (1890) *The Golden Bough: A Study in Comparative Religion*. London: Macmillan & Co.

Freedman, L. (1995) 'Neptune in classical and renaissance art', *IJCT* 2, 219–38.

Freeman, John (1888) *Lights and Shadows of Melbourne Life*. London: Sampson Low.

Freeman, Kathleen (1926) *The Work and Life of Solon, with a Translation of His Poems*. Cardiff: University of Wales Press Board.

Freeman, Philip (2001) *Ireland and the Classical World*. Austin, TX: University of Texas Press.

Friedman, Sam and Daniel Laurison (2019) *The Class Ceiling: Why It Pays to Be Privileged*. Bristol: Bristol Policy Press.

Friel, Brian (1980) *Translations*. London: Faber & Faber.

Fry, Carole (2003) 'Spanning the political divide: Neo-Palladianism and the early eighteenth-century landscape', *Garden History* 31(2), 180–92.

Fryer, Michael (1842) *The Trial and Life of Eugene Aram*. Richmond, Virginia: M. Bell.

Furuland, Lars and Johan Svedjedal (2006) *Svensk Arbetarlitteratur*. Stockholm: Atlas.

Fussell, Paul (1983) *Class. A Guide Through the American Status System*. New York: Summit Books.

Fyfe, Aileen (2012) *Steam-Powered Knowledge: William Chambers and the Business of Publishing, 1820–1860*. Chicago, Illinois: University of Chicago Press.

Fyson, R. (1981) *Chartism in North Staffordshire*. Burton-on-Trent: SCC.

Gagnier, Regenia (1991) *Subjectivities: A History of Self-Representation in Britain, 1832–1920*. New York and Oxford: OUP.

Galloway, Robert Lindsay (1969) *A History of Coal Mining in Great Britain*. A reprint with a new introduction, bibliography and index by Baron F. Duckham. Newton Abbot: David & Charles.

Galt, John (1978) 'The mem', In: *Selected Short Stories*, Ian A. Gordon (ed.), Edinburgh: Scottish Academic Press, 1–9.

Gardiner, Leslie (1968) *The British Admiralty*. Edinburgh: William Blackwod.

Garratt, Walter Vero (1939) *A Man in the Street*. London: J.M. Dent & Sons, Ltd.

Gaskell, Philip (1964) *A Bibliography of the Foulis Press*. London: Hart-Davis.

Geggus, David P. (2001) 'The French slave trade: An overview', *The William and Mary Quarterly* 58(1), 119–38.

'Gentleman' (1715) *The Gentleman's Library, Containing Rules for Conduct in All Parts of Life. Written by a Gentleman*. London: W. Mears.

Gepp, C.G. (1871) *Progressive Exercises in Latin Elegiac Verse*. London: Rivingtons.

Gerrald, Joseph (1794) *The Trial of Joseph Gerrald, Delegate from the London Corresponding Society, to the British Convention. Before the High Court of Justiciary, at Edinburgh, on the 3d, 10th, 13th, and 14th of March, 1794. For Sedition. Taken in Short-hand by Mr. Ramsey*. Edinburgh: James Robertson.

Gerrald, Joseph and 'Porcia' (1812) 'Letter from Joseph Gerrald to Gilbert Wakefield', *The Belfast Monthly Magazine* 9 (November 30th), 372–74.

G.F.R.B. (1885) 'Homer, *Travestie*', *Notes and Queries* series 6, no. 11 (February 7th), 115.

Gibbon, Edward (1779–1789) *The History of the Decline and Fall of the Roman Empire*, 6 vols. London: W. Strahan and T. Cadell.

Gibbon, Edward (1796) *Miscellaneous works of Edward Gibbon, Esquire: With Memoirs of his Life and Writings, Composed by Himself*, 2 vols, ed. John Lord Sheffield. London: printed for A. Strahan, T. Cadell Junior and W. Davies.

Gibbon, Lewis Grassic (1996 [1933]) *Spartacus*. London: Redwords. First published under the author's real name, James Leslie Mitchell.

Gibson, John (1842) 'Table showing, 1, the numbers present at the Time of Inspection; 2, the various Branches taught; 3, the Proportion of Pupils learning each Branch', *Special Report on Schools Inspected in the Presbyteries of Haddington and Dunbar.* Appendix to Minutes of Committee of Council on Education (1841–2) 63. Haddington: John Gray Centre, ES13, A25, 5.

Giddens, A. (1973) *The Class Structure of the Advanced Societies.* London: Hutchinson.

Gideon, John (1845) *Jack Hornet; or, the March of Intellect.* London: Richard Bentley.

Gifford, William and Juvenal (1802) *Juvenal, Satires* ['translated into English verse by Wm. Gifford']. London: G. and W. Nicol; and R. Evans.

Gifford, William (1803) *The Satires of Decimus Junius Juvenalis, Translated into English Verse by Wm. Gifford. Esq. with Notes and Illustrations*, vol. 1. New York: J. Morgan and Ezra Sergeant.

Gifford, William (1810) *The Baviad and Maeviad.* 8th edition. London: S. Tipper et al.

Gilbert, Ann Margaret (1922) *The Work of Lord Brougham for Education in England.* Chambersburg, Pennsylvania: Franklin Repository.

Gilbert, Bentley B. (1985) 'Pacifist to interventionist: David Lloyd George in 1911 and 1914. Was Belgium an issue?' *The Historical Journal* 28(4), 863–85.

Gill, Ellen (2016) *Naval Families, War and Duty in Britain, 1740–1820.* Rochester, New York: Boydell and Brewer.

Gillies, J. (1804, trans.) *Aristotle's Ethics and Politics: Comprising His Practical Philosophy.* London: J. Cadell and W. Davies.

Gilmour, Robin (1993) *The Victorian Period: The Intellectual and Cultural Context of English Literature 1830–1890.* London and New York: Longman.

Given, John (2015) 'Aristophanic Comedy in American Musical Theatre, 1925–1969', in *The Oxford Handbook of Greek Drama in the Americas.* Kathryn Bosher, Fiona Macintosh, Justine McConnell, Patrice Rankine (eds.), Oxford: Oxford University Press.

Glasier, J.B. (1921) *William Morris and the Early Days of the Socialist Movement, with a Preface by May Morris.* London: Longmans, Green and Co.

Glasier, K.B. (1894 As Katharine St John Conway) *The Religion of Socialism.* Manchester: The Labour Press.

Goadby, Robert (1768) *An Apology for the Life of Mr Bampfylde-Moore Carew Commonly called the King of the Beggars.* London: Goadby, Owen and Lee.

Godwin, William (1794a) *Cursory Strictures on the Charge Delivered by Lord Chief Justice Eyre to the Grand Jury, October 2, 1794.* London: C. and G. Kearsley.

Godwin, William (1794b) *Things as They Are; Or, the Adventures of Caleb Williams, etc.* London: B. Crosby.

Godwin, William (1992) *Collected Novels and Memoirs of William Godwin*, vol. 1, ed. Mark Philp, with an Introduction by Marilyn Butler and Mark Philp. London: Pickering.

Goff, Barbara (2014) *'Your Secret Language': Classics in the British Colonies of West Africa.* London: Bloomsbury.

Goff, Barbara (2015) 'The Greeks of the WEA: Realities and Rhetorics in the First Two Decades', *Greek and Roman Classics and the British Struggle for Social Reform.* Stead and Hall (eds.), London, Bloomsbury, 216–34.

Goff, Barbara and Michael Simpson (2007) *Crossroads in the Black Aegean.* Oxford: OUP.

Goldhill, Simon (2002) *Who Needs Greek? Contests in the Cultural History of Hellenism.* Cambridge: CUP.

Goldman, Lawrence (1995) *Dons and Workers.* Oxford: Clarendon Press.

Goldsmith, Oliver (1764) *An History of England in a Series of Letters from a Nobleman to his Son.* London: J. Newbery.

Goldsmith, Oliver (1769) *The Roman History: from the Foundation of the City of Rome, to the Destruction of the Western Empire*, 2 vols. London: S. Baker, G. Leigh, T. Davies and L. Davis.

Goldsmith, Oliver (1774a) *An Abridgment of the History of England: From the Invasion of Julius Cæsar, to the Death of George II.* London: B. Law; G. Robinson; G. Kearsly; T. Davies; T. Becket, T. Cadell and T. Evans.

Goldsmith, Oliver (1774b) *The Grecian History, from the Earliest State to the Death of Alexander the Great.* London: J. and F. Rivington.

Goodridge, John (1995) *Rural Life in Eighteenth-Century English Poetry.* Cambridge: CUP.

Goodridge, John (2006) *Nineteenth Century English Labouring-Class Poets: 1800-1900*, Vol. 3. London: Pickering & Chatto.

Goodwyn Barmby, J. (1842a) *The Promethean; or, Communitarian Apostle.* no. 1 (January). G. Barmby.

Goodwyn Barmby, J. (1842b) *The Promethean; or, Communitarian Apostle.* no. 2 (February). G. Barmby.

Goodwyn Barmby, J. (1842c) *The Promethean; or, Communitarian Apostle.* no. 3 (March). G. Barmby.

Goorney, Howard (1981) *The Theatre Workshop Story.* London: Methuen.

Goorney, Howard and Ewan MacColl (1986) *Agit-Prop to Theatre Workshop: Political Playscripts, 1930–1950.* Manchester: Manchester University Press.

Gorman, John (1973) *Banner Bright: An Illustrated History of the Banners of the British Trade Union Movement.* London: Allen Lane.

Gould, Frederick James (1906) *The Children's Plutarch.* London: Watts & Co.

Gould, Frederick James (1913) *Pages for Young Socialists: with Prefaces by H.M. Hyndman and J. Keir Hardie, and Illustrations by Walter Crane.* Manchester: National Labour Press Ltd.

Gould, Frederick James (1932) *Bright Lamps of History and Daily Life. A Junior Reading Book of Stories from Many Countries and Times.* London: Watts & Co.

Grafton, Anthony (2006) 'The history of ideas: Precept and practice, 1950–2000 and Beyond', *Journal of the History of Ideas* 67(1), 1–32.

Graham, Dougal (1777) *Witty and Entertaining Exploits of George Buchanan, who was commonly called 'The King's Fool'.* Glasgow: J. and J. Robertson.

Graham, T.B. (1983) *Nineteenth Century Self-Help in Education – Mutual Improvement Societies*, vol. 2. Nottingham: Department of Adult Education: University of Nottingham.

Grant, Anne MacVicar (1815) *Popular Models, and Impressive Warnings for the Sons and Daughters of Industry.* Edinburgh: Longman, Hurst et al.

Graver, Bruce (2006) 'Illustrating the farmer's boy', In: *Robert Bloomfield: Lyric, Class, and the Romantic Canon*, S. White, J. Goodridge and B. Keegan (eds.), Lewisburg, Pennsylvania: Bucknell University Press, 49–69.

Graves, Robert (1917) *Goliath and David. [Poems].* London: Charles Whittingham & Co.

Graves, Robert (1929) *Goodbye to All That: An Autobiography.* London: Cape.

Gray, John M. (1894) *James and William Tassie: A Biographical and Critical Sketch.* Edinburgh: Walter Greekoak Patterson.

Gray, Rockwell (1982) 'Autobiography now', *The Kenyon Review* 4, 31–55.

Greene, Graham (1980) *Ways of Escape.* Toronto: Lester and Orpen Dennys.

Greenslade, M.W. (1963) 'A history of Hanley', In: *Victoria County History of Staffordshire*, vol. VIII, 142–75. Stafford: Staffordshire Libraries, Arts and Archives

Greenwood, Emily (2010) *Afro-Greeks: Dialogues Between Anglophone Caribbean Literature and Classics in the Twentieth Century.* Oxford: OUP.

Gregory, Lady A. (1903) *Poets and Dreamers: Studies and Translations from the Irish*. Dublin: Hodges Figgis.

Grierson, C. (1730, ed.) *Tacitus*, 3 vols. Dublin: Grierson.

Griffiths, Antony (1992) 'Sir William Musgrave and British biography', *The British Library Journal* 18, 171–89.

Grose, Francis (1785) *Classical Dictionary of the Vulgar Tongue*. London: Hooper & Co.

Grose, Francis (1786) *A Treatise on Ancient Armour and Weapons*. London: S. Hooper.

Grose, Francis (1791) *The Grumbler: Containing Sixteen Essays*. London: S. Hooper.

Gross, John (1969) *The Rise and Fall of the Man of Letters*. Harmondsworth: Penguin.

Grossek, Mark [Paul Selver] (1937), *First Movement*. London: Geoffrey Bles.

Grote, George (1865) *Plato, and the Other Companions of Sokrates*. London: John Murray.

Grote, George (1873) *The Minor Works of George Grote. With Critical Remarks on His Intellectual Character, Writings and Speeches*, ed. Alexander Bain. London: J. Murray.

Grote, George (1880) *Aristotle*. 2nd edition. ed. Alexander Bain and G. Croom Robertson. London: John Murray.

Grote, George (1906) *A History of Greece*, vol. 1. London: J. M. Dent.

Grubgeld, Elizabeth (2004) *Anglo-Irish Autobiography: Class, Gender and the Forms of Narrative*. New York: Syracuse University Press.

Grugel, Lee E. (1976) *George Jacob Holyoake: A Study in the Evolution of a Victorian Radical*. Philadelphia: Porcupine Press.

Gulick, C.B. (1899) 'The attic Prometheus', *Harvard Studies in Classical Philology* 10, 103–14.

Gummere, Richard M. (1965) 'Thomas Paine: Was he really anticlassical?' *American Antiquarian Society* (October), 254–69.

Gurney, Peter (2014) 'The democratic idiom: Languages of democracy in the Chartist movement', *The Journal of Modern Histor* 86(3), 566–602.

Gusdorf, George (1980 [1956]) 'Conditions and limits of autobiography', translated by James Olney, in Olney (1980) 28–48. Originally Published as *Conditions et limites de l'autobiographie*. Berlin: Duncker and Humblot.

H.H.B. (1659) *The World's Idol or, Plutus the God of Wealth, A Translation from Aristophanes by, H. H. B.* London: W. G.

Haan, Estelle (2005) *Vergilius Redivivus: Studies in Joseph Addison's Latin Poetry*. Philadelphia, Pennsylvania: American Philosophical Society.

Habermas, Jürgen (1989 [1962]) *The Structural Transformation of the Public Sphere: An Inquiry into a Category of Bourgeois Society*, translated by Thomas Burger. Cambridge, Massachusetts: The MIT Press. Originally published in 1962 as *Strukturwandel der Öffentlichkeit: Untersuchungen zu einer Kategorie der bürgerlichen Gesellschaft*. Berlin: Luchterhand.

Hackett, Nan (1985), *XIX British Working-Class Autobiographies: An Annotated Bibliography*. New York: AMS.

Haggar, Reginald G. (1953?) *A Century of Art Education in the Potteries*. Stoke on Trent: Webberley Ltd.

Hague, René (1975) *David Jones*. Cardiff: University of Wales Press.

Hale, Elizabeth (2010) 'Sickly scholars and healthy novels: The classical scholar in Victorian fiction', *International Journal of the Classical Tradition* 17(2), 219–43.

Hall, Edith (1977) *Canary Girls and Stockpots*. Luton, Bedfordshire: Workers' Educational Association.

Hall, Edith M. (1997) 'Talfourd's ancient Greeks in the theatre of reform', *IJCT* 3, 283–307.

Hall, Edith M. (1999a) 'Medea & British legislation before World War I', *Greece and Rome* 46(1), 42–77.

Hall, Edith M. (1999b) 'Classical mythology in the Victorian popular theatre', *IJCT* 5(3), 336–66.

Hall, Edith M. (1999c) '1845 and all that: Singing Greek tragedy on the London stage', In: *The Use and Abuses of Antiquity,* M. Biddiss and M. Wyke (eds.), Leiden: Brill, 37–53.

Hall, Edith M. (2002) 'The singing actors of antiquity', In: *Greek & Roman Actors: Aspects of an Ancient Profession*, co-ed. with Pat Easterling. Cambridge: CUP, 3–38.

Hall, Edith M. (2005a) 'Aeschylus' Clytemnestra versus her Senecan tradition.' In: *Agamemnon in Performance*, F. Macintosh, P. Michelakis, E. Hall and O. Taplin (eds.), Oxford: OUP, 53–76.

Hall, Edith M. (2005b) 'Iphigenia and her mother at Aulis: A study in the revival of a Euripidean Classic', In: *Rebel Women: Staging Ancient Greek Drama Today*, S. Wilmer and J. Dillon (eds.), London: Methuen, 3–41.

Hall, Edith M. (2006) *The Theatrical Cast of Athens*. Oxford: OUP.

Hall, Edith M. (2007a) 'The English-speaking Aristophanes', In: *Aristophanes in Performance*, Edith Hall and Amanda Wrigley (eds.), Oxford: Legenda, 66–92.

Hall, Edith M. (2007b) 'Subjects, selves, and survivors', In: *Classical Subjects and Modern Subjectivities*, Barbara Goff (ed.), 125–160. [= Helios Special Issue 34.2]. Texas Tech University.

Hall, Edith M. (2008a) *The Return of Ulysses. A Cultural History of Homer's Odyssey.* Baltimore, Maryland: John Hopkins University Press.

Hall, Edith M. (2008b) 'Putting the class into classical reception', In: Hardwick and Stray (eds.), 386–97.

Hall, Edith M. (2008c) 'Navigating the realms of gold: Translation as access route to the Classics', In: *Translation and the Classic*, A. Lianeri and V. Zajko (eds.), Oxford: OUP, 315–41.

Hall, Edith M. (2010a) 'Mughal princes or Greek philosopher-kings? Indian and neoclassical styles in British mansions built by East Indiamen, 1790–1805', In: Hall and Vasunia (eds.), 31–32.

Hall, Edith M. (2010b) 'Refractions of India and the 1857 'Mutiny' through the prism of ancient Greece and Rome', In: Hall and Vasunia (eds.), 33–49.

Hall, Edith M. (2011a) 'Introduction: A valuable lesson', In: Hall, Alston and McConnell (eds.), 1–40.

Hall, Edith M. (2011b) 'The problem with Prometheus: Myth, abolition, and radicalism', In: Hall, Alston and McConnell (eds.), 209–46.

Hall, Edith M. (2011c) 'Karl Marx and the ruins of Trier', In: *Antiquity and the Ruin* (Special Issue of *ERH*, no. 18), Ahuvia Kahane (ed.), 783–97. Taylor and Francis.

Hall, Edith M. (2013a) *Adventures with Iphigenia in Tauris: A Cultural History of Euripides' Black Sea Tragedy*. New York: OUP.

Hall, Edith M. (2013b) 'Mob, cabal or utopian commune: The political contestation of the ancient chorus, 1789–1917', In: *Choruses, Ancient and Modern*, Joshua Billings, Felix Budelmann and Fiona Macintosh. Oxford: OUP, 281–307.

Hall, Edith M. (2014) 'Is the study of Greek and Latin elitist?' *The Journal of Classical Teaching* 29, 10–12.

Hall, Edith M. (2015a) 'The migrant muse: Greek drama as feminist window on American identity, 1900–1925', In: *The Oxford Handbook to Greek Drama in the Americas*, K. Bosher, F. Macintosh, J. McConnell and P. Rankine (eds.), Oxford: OUP, 149–65.

Hall, Edith M. (2015c) 'Classically Educated Women in the early Independent Labour Party', In: Stead and Hall (eds.), 197–215.

Hall, Edith M. (2015d) 'Christopher Caudwell's Greek and Latin classics', In: Stead and Hall (eds.), 235–55.

Hall, Edith M. (2015e) 'Classics for the people', *Guardian Review*, (June 20th). www.theguardian.com/books/2015/jun/20/classics-for-the-people-ancient-greeks.

Hall, Edith M. (2015f) 'Making it really new: Dickens versus the Classics', In: Stead and Hall (eds.), 99–115.

Hall, Edith M. (2016a) 'Xenophon: Magician and friend', In: *The Cambridge Companion to Xenophon*, Michael Flower (ed.), Cambridge: CUP, 449–60.

Hall, Edith M. (2016b) 'The reception of ancient Greek literature and western identity', In: *A Companion to Greek Literature*, Martin Hose and David Schenker (eds.), Oxford: Wiley Blackwell, 511–33.

Hall, Edith M. (2017) '"Master of those who know": Aristotle as role model for the twenty-first century academician', *European Review* 25(1), 3–19.

Hall, Edith M. (2018a) 'Aesop the morphing fabulist', In: *Classical Reception and Children's Literature*, Owen Hodkinson and Helen Lovatt (eds.), London: I.B. Tauris, 89–107.

Hall, Edith M. (2018b) 'Classics in our ancestors' communities', In: *Forward with Classics*, A. Holmes-Henderson, S. Hunt and M. Musie (eds.), London: Bloomsbury, 243–61.

Hall, Edith M. (2018c) 'Verbal and visual witnessing: Tony Harrison's Euripides', In *New Light on Tony Harrison*, E. Hall (ed.), Oxford: OUP for the British Academy, 111–35.

Hall, Edith M. (2018d) 'The boys from Cydathenaeum: Aristophanes versus Cleon again', In: *How to Do Things with, History*, D. Allen, P. Christesen and P. Millett (eds.), Oxford: OUP, 339–63.

Hall, Edith M. (2018e) 'Classical epic and the London fairs, 1697–1734', In: Macintosh, McConnell, Harrison and Kenward (eds.), 439–60. Oxford: OUP.

Hall, Edith M. (2018f) 'Materialisms old and new', In: *The Materialities of Greek Tragedy*, Mario Telò and Melissa Mueller (eds.), London: Bloomsbury, 203–17.

Hall, Edith M. (2018g) 'American Communist idealism in George Cram Cook's *the Athenian Women* (1918)', In: *Classical Theatre on Communist Stages*, D. Movrin and E. Olechowska (eds.), Warsaw: Warsaw University Press, 7–25.

Hall, Edith M. (2018h) 'Beyond the limits of art and war trauma: David Jones' *in Parenthesis*', In: Richardson (ed.), 115–35.

Hall, Edith M. (2018i) 'Hephaestus the hobbling humorist: The club-footed god in the history of early Greek comedy', In: *Morbid Laughter [= Illinois Classical Studies 43.2]*, George Kazantzidis and Natalia Tsoumbra (eds.), 366–87. Illinois University Press.

Hall, Edith M. (2019) 'How can Aristotle's example help public philosophy today?' https://aeon.co/essays/how-aristotles-example-can-help-public-philosophy-today.

Hall, Edith M. (forthcoming a) 'Sinn Féin and Ulysses: Between Professor Robert Mitchell Henry and James Joyce', In: Torrance and O'Rourke (eds.).

Hall, Edith M. (forthcoming b) 'Secular ethics for junior socialists: F.J. Gould on ancient history, 1906–1932', In: *Our Mythical History*, K. Marciniak (ed.), Warsaw: Warsaw University Press.

Hall, Edith M. (forthcoming c) 'Crises of excess and succession: Herodotus, Cambyses and the Early Modern Stage', In: *Reaching the Ancient Near East in Early Modern Europe*, Jane Grogan (ed.), OUP.

Hall, Edith M. (forthcoming d) 'Classics invented: Gentlemen and their Schools 1689–1750', In: *Festschrift for Christopher Stray*, S.J. Elsner, S. Harrison and C. Pelling (eds.), OUP.

Hall, Edith M. (forthcoming e) 'Late Victorian musical Odysseys, scholarship and translation: The curious case of Samuel Butler', In: *Performing Homer*, Wendy Hiller (ed.), Princeton, New Jersey: Princeton University Press.

Hall, Edith M. (forthcoming f) *Classics in British Advertising, 1830–1914*.

Hall, Edith M. (forthcoming g) 'Caractacus in the long 19th century', In: *Celts, Romans, Britons: Classical and Celtic Influence in the Construction of British Identities*, Francesca Kaminski-Jones and Rhys Kaminski-Jones (eds.), Oxford: OUP.

Hall, Edith M. (forthcoming h) 'How much did British pottery workers know about Classics?' In: Petsalis-Diomedis (ed.).

Hall, Edith M. (Forthcoming i) '"Romantic poet-sage of History": Herodotus and his Arion in the long 19th century', In: *Herodotus in the Long 19th Century*, Tom Harrison and Joseph Skinnner (eds.), CUP, 46–70.

Hall, Edith, Richard Alston and Justine McConnell (2011, eds.) *Ancient Slavery and Abolition*. Oxford: OUP.

Hall, Edith, Arlene Holmes-Henderson and James Corke-Webster (Forthcoming) *Classical Civilisation and Ancient History in British Secondary Education*. Liverpool: Liverpool University Press.

Hall, Edith and Fiona Macintosh (2005) *Greek Tragedy and the British Theatre 1660–1914*. Oxford: OUP.

Hall, Edith and Henry Stead (2013) 'Is the study of Greek and Latin elitist?' *Proceedings of the Manchester Literary and Philological Society* 152, 14–26.

Hall, Edith and Henry Stead (2016) 'Between the party and the ivory tower: Classics and Communism in 1930s Britain', In: *Classics & Class: Greek & Latin Classics & Communism at School*, D. Movrin and E. Olechowska (eds.), University of Warsaw and Ljubljana University Press, 3–31.

Hall, Edith and Phiroze Vasunia (2010, eds.) *India, Greece & Rome 1757–2007* (*BICS* suppl. 108). London: ICS.

Hall, Edith and Amanda Wrigley (2007, eds.) *Aristophanes in Performance*. Oxford: Legenda.

Hall, Edith and Rosie Wyles (2008, eds.) *New Directions in Ancient Pantomime*. Oxford: OUP.

Hall, Edith and Rosie Wyles (2018) 'The censoring of Plutarch's Gracchi on the revolutionary French and reformist English stages, 1792–1823', In: *The Afterlife of Plutarch* (*BICS* Supplement), John North and Elizabeth Potter (eds.), 127–46. London: CUP form ICS

Hall, John Hall (1652, trans.) *Longinus*. London: Francis Eaglesfield.

Hall, Lee (2008) *The Pitmen Painters*. London: Faber & Faber.

Hall, Owen (1898) *A Greek Slave: Musical Comedy* with lyrics by Harry Greenbank and Adrian Ross and music by Sidney Jones. London: Hopwood and Crew.

Hamilton, Mary Agnes (1936) *Newnham. An Informal Biography*. London: Faber & Faber.

Hamlyn, Robin (1984) 'Henry Wallis, the Stonebreaker', In: *The Pre-Raphaelites*, Leslie Parris (ed.), London: Tate Gallery Publications, 167.

Hammond, Nicholas (2004) 'Bentinck, Winifred Anna Cavendish- [née Winifred Anna Dallas-Yorke], duchess of Portland (1863–1954)', *ODNB*. Oxford. OUP.

Hancarville, Pierre d' (1776–1777) *Collection of Etruscan, Greek and Roman Antiquities from the Cabinet of the Honble. W. Hamilton His Britannick Maiesty's Envoy Extraordinary at the court of Naples*. Naples: François Morelli.

Handelsman, Simon Joseph (2009) *Realities and Perceptions of Human Rights and the Mining Industry: A Case Study*. PhD Diss. University of British Columbia.

Hans, Nicholas (2014 [1951]) *New Trends in Education in the Eighteenth Century Paperback Edition*. London: Routledge.

Hardie John L. (1979) *Scottish Aspects of Child Education a Century Ago: Elizabeth Lipp*. Aberdeen: Rainbow Books.

Hardwick, Lorna and Christopher Stray (2008, eds.) *A Companion to Classical Receptions*. Oxford: Blackwell.

Hardwick, Lorna and Carol Gillespie (2010, eds.) *Classics in Post-Colonial Worlds*. Oxford: OUP.

Hardy, Thomas (1877) *A Pair of Blue Eyes*. London: S. King & Co.

Hardy, Thomas (1994 [1895]) *Jude the Obscure*. London: Penguin.

Harker, Ben (2007) *Class Act: The Cultural and Political Life of Ewan MacColl*. London: Pluto Press.

Harker, Ben (2016) 'Jack Lindsay's alienation', *History Workshop Journal* 82(1), 83–103.

Harker, Dave (2003) *Tressell: The Real Story of the Ragged-Trousered Philanthropists*. London: Zed Books.

Harker, Dave (2018) *Billy Purvis: The First Professional Geordie*. Newcastle upon Tyne: Wisecrack Publications.

Harris, B. (2011) 'The enlightenment, towns and urban society in Scotland, c.1760-1820'. *The English Historical Review* 126(522), 1097–136.

Harris, John (1856 [1853]) *Lays from the Mine, the Moor, and the Mountain*. ['By John Harris, A Cornish Miner'. 2nd Edition 'with several additional poems'] London: Alexander Heylin.

Harris, John (1882) *My Autobiography*. London and Penryn: Hamilton: Adams and Co.

Harrison, J.F.C. (1954) *A History of the Working Men's College, 1854–1954*. London: Routledge and Kegan Paul.

Harrison, J.F.C. (1957) *Workers Education in Leeds*. Leeds: Workers' Educational Association.

Harrison, J.F.C. (1971) *The Early Victorians, 1832-1851*. London: Weidenfeld and Nicolson.

Harrison, Royden (1987) 'Sidney and Beatrice Webb', In: Levy (ed.), 35–89.

Harrison, Stephen (2017) *Victorian Horace: Classics and Class*. London: Bloomsbury.

Harrison, Tony (1998) *Prometheus*. London: Faber.

Hartwell, Clare and Nikolaus Pevsner (2009) *Lancashire: North*. New Haven, Connecticut: Yale University Press.

Harvey, Cyril P. (1931) *Solon: Or, the Price of Justice*. London: Kegan Paul, Trench, Trubner & Co.

Hassan, J.A. (1908) 'Paternalism and the Coal Industry in Midlothian, 1800-1880', *The Scottish Historical Review* 59, 73–91.

Haw, G. (1917) *The Life of Story of Will Crooks, MP*. London: Cassell.

Hawker, Henry Edward (1919) *Notes of My Life, 1870–1918*. Stonehouse, Gloucestershire: W.G. Davis, Star Press.

Hawkins, George (1781) *An Essay on Female Education. Containing an Account of the Present State of the Boarding Schools for Young Ladies in England*. London: G. Wilkie.

Hawlesworth, John (1754) *The Adventurer*, vol. 1. 2nd edition. London: J. Payne.

Haydon, Benjamin (1960) *The Diary of Benjamin Robert Haydon*, ed. W.B. Pope. Cambridge, MA: Harvard UP.

Hazlitt, William (1902–1906) *The Collected Works of William Hazlitt*, ed. A.R. Waller and A. Glover. London: J.M. Dent.

Hazlitt, William (1932) *The Complete Works of William Hazlitt*, vol. 9, ed. P.P. Howe (after the edition of A.R. Waller and Arnold Glover). London: Dent and Sons.

Heesom, A.J. (1980) 'The northern coal-owners and the opposition to the coal mines act of 1842', *International Review of Social History* 25, 236–71.

Heesom, A.J. and Brendan Duffy (1981) 'Coal, class and education in the north-east', *Past & Present* 90, 136–51.

Henderson, Emma (2015) 'Miners march in final farewell to last British deep coal mine', *The Independent* (December 20th). www.independent.co.uk/news/uk/home-news/kellingley-colliery-miners-march-in-final-farewell-to-the-last-coal-mine-and-british-mining-a6780301.html.

Henry, Paul (1951) *An Irish Portrait*. London: W.B. Batsford.

Henry, Robert Mitchell (1905) *Livy. Book XXVI, Edited, with Introduction, Notes and Appendices by Robert Mitchell Henry*. London: Edward Arnold.

Henry, Robert Mitchell (1920) *The Evolution of Sinn Féin*. Dublin: Talbot and New York: Huebach.

Henry, Robert Mitchell (1924–1925) 'The ideal city', in *The Voice of Labour*, issues 51 (December) and 52 (January).

Heringman, Noah (1998) 'Stones so wonderous cheap', *Studies in Romanticism* 37(1), 43–62.

Hernon, Ian (2015) *Robert Tressell—A Life in Hell*. Spalding: Red Axe Books.

Herzog, Don (1998) *Poisoning the Minds of the Lower Orders*. Princeton, New Jersey: Princeton University Press.

Hess, Scott (2005) *Authoring the Self: Self-Representation, Authorship, and the Print Markets in British Poetry from Pope through Wordsworth*. London: Routledge.

Hewitt, John (1974, ed.) *Rhyming Weavers and Other Country Poets of Antrim and Down*. Belfast: Blackstaff Press.

Hibbert, Julian (1828) *Περί Δεισιδαιμονίας. Plutarch and Theophrastus on Superstition*. London: No Publisher Stated.

Hicks, Philip (2012) 'The ancient historians in England', In: *Oxford History of Classical Reception in English Literature*. Volume 3: 1660-1790, David Hopkins and Charles Martindale eds. Oxford: OUP, 569–92.

Higbee, Douglas (2007) 'Siegfried Sassoon, fellow-traveler: Poetry, socialism, and the British veterans' movement', *War, Literature and the Arts* 19, 296–98.

Hill, Christopher (1972) *The World Turned Upside Down*. London: Temple Smith.

Hill, Christopher (1990) 'The people's historian', In: *History and the Imagination: Selected Writings of A.L. Morton*, M. Heinemann and W. Thompson (eds.), London: Lawrence and Wishart, 11–17.

Hill, Robert (1775) *Christianity the True Religion: An Essay in Answer to the Blasphemy of a Deist*. Chester.

Hills, Paul (1997, ed.) *David Jones Artist and Poet*. Aldershot: Scholar Press.

Hindle, Maurice (1988) 'Introduction', in *Things as They Are or the Adventures of Caleb Williams*. Harmondsworth: Penguin.

Hinks, John, Catherine Armstrong and Matthew Day (2009, eds.) *Periodicals and Publishers The Newspaper and Journal Trade 1740–1914*. London: Oak Knoll Press and the British Library.

Hirson, Baruch (2001) *The Cape Town Intellectuals: Ruth Schechter and Her Circle, 1907–1934*. Maitland, Cape Town: Merlin Press.

Hirst, Desirée (2007) 'The two Davids: Jones and Rosenberg', *The David Jones Journal* Spring/Summer, 53–59.

Hiscock, Matthew (2010) 'The politics of classical allusion at the end of the eighteenth century: Radical or redundant?' *The Cambridge Classical Journal* 56, 95–139.

Hiscutt, Allan (2018) *The Miniature Moulds of John Henning: Their Genesis, Development, Production and Reception*. PhD Thesis. University of Reading.

Hobbes, Thomas (1651) *Leviathan, or, the Matter, Forme, and Power of a Common Wealth, Ecclesiasticall and Civil*. London: Andrew Crooke.

Hobsbawm, E.J. (1978) 'The historians' group of the Communist Party', In: Cornforth (ed.), 21–47.

Hobsbawm, E.J. (1990) *Nations and Nationalism Since 1780*. 2nd edition. CUP.

Hobsbawm, E.J. (1992) *Nations and Nationalism since 1780: Programme, Myth, Reality*. Cambridge: Cambridge University Press.

Hobsbawm, E.J. and J.W. Scott (1980) 'Political shoemakers', *Past and Present* 89(1), 86–114.

Hodkinson, Stephen and Edith Hall (2011) 'Appropriations of Spartan helotage in British anti-slavery debates of the 1790s', In: Hall, Alston and McConnell (eds.), 65–102.

Hogarth, William (1833) *Anecdotes of William Hogarth*. London: J.B. Nichols.

Hoggart, Richard (1957) *The Uses of Literacy: Aspects of Working Class Life*. London: Penguin.

Hogg, Graham (2009) 'Later struggles in the life of a provincial bookseller and printer: George Miller of Dunbar, Scotland', In: Hinks, Armstrong and Day (ed.), 139–160.

Holcroft, Thomas (1784) *The Noble Peasant*. London: George Robinson.

Holdsworth, N. (2006) *Joan Littlewood*. London: Routledge.

Holdsworth, N. (2011) *Joan Littlewood's Theatre*. Cambridge: CUP.

Holiday, Henry (1914) *Reminiscences of My Life*. London: William Heinemann.

Hollis, P. (1989) *Ladies Elect: Women in English Local Government 1865–1914*. Oxford: Clarendon Press.

Holmes, George (1801) *Sketches of Some of the Southern Counties of Ireland, Collected During a Tour in the Autumn, 1797*. London: Longman.

Holmes, O.W., H.J. Laski and M.D.W. Howe (1963, eds.) *Holmes-Laski Letters: The Correspondence of Mr. Justice Holmes and Harold J. Laski, 1916–1935*. New York: Atheneum.

Holmström, Kirsten Gram (1967) *Monodrama, Attitudes, Tableaux Vivants*. Translated by Richard Cox. Stockholm: Almqvist and Wiksell.

Hood, Thomas (1839) *Hood's Own; Or, Laughter from Year to Year*. London: Ward, Lock & Co.

Hooke, Nathanial (1727) *The Travels of Cyrus: In Two Volumes. To Which is Annex'd, A Discourse upon the Theology and Mythology of the Ancients / By the Chevalier Ramsay*. 2nd edition. London: T. Woodward and J. Peele.

Hooke, Nathanial (1738–1771) *The Roman History, from the Building of Rome to the Ruin of the Commonwealth*. London: James Bettenham.

Hoole, Charles (1657) *Maturini Corderii Colloquia scholastica Anglo-Latina: In varias clausulas distributa; observato utriusque linguæ idiomate, quò sc. ope vernaculi, in quotidiano sermone Latino pueri feliciùs exerceantur*. Londini: S[arah] G[riffin] pro Societate Stationariorum.

Hooper, Charles (1867) 'Cabinet making', In: *Reports of Artisans Selected by A Committee Appointed by the Council of the Society of Arts to Visit the Paris Universal Exhibition*. London: Bell and Daldy, 1–25.

Hopper, R.J. (1968) 'The Laurion mines: A reconsideration', *The Annual of the British School at Athens* 63, 293–326.

House of Commons (1816) 'House of Commons', *The Examiner* 441(Monday June 10th), 357.

Houston, R.A. (1985) *Scottish Literacy and the Scottish Identity: Illiteracy and Society in Scotland and Northern England 1600–1800*. Cambridge: CUP.

Howarth, J. (2004) 'Sidgwick, Arthur (1840–1920), educationist and classical scholar', *ODNB*. Oxford: OUP.

Howe, P.P., A.R. Waller, A. Glover and J. Thornton (1930– 1934, eds.) *The Complete Works of William Hazlitt*, 21 vols. London: J.M. Dent and Sons, Ltd.

Hughes, Brian (2016, ed.) *Eoin MacNeill Memoir of a Revolutionary Scholar.* Dublin: Irish Manuscripts Commission.

Hughes, J.L. (1922) *The Real Robert Burns.* London: W. and R. Chambers.

Hunnings, Leanne (2007) 'Spartacus in nineteenth-century England: Proletarian, Pole and Christ', In: *Remaking the Classics: Literature, Genre and Media in Britain 1800–2000,* Christopher Stray (ed.), London: Bloomsbury, 1–19.

Hunt, Henry (1820) *Memoirs of Henry Hunt, Esq., Written by Himself in His Majesty's Jail at Ilchester.* London: T. Dolby.

Hunt, Jane (2004) 'Vulcana and Atlas', *Home Truths.* Interview with John Peel. BBC Radio 4, August 30th.

Hunt, Jane (2016) 'Post 2, 1890 onwards – professional appearances and Sandow's Magazine', *Vulcana: Victorian Wonder Woman!.* Digital source: vulcanaonline.com.

Hunt, Leigh (1823) *Ultra-Crepidarius; A Satire on William Gifford.* London: John Hunt.

Hunt, L. (1983) 'Hercules and the radical image in the French Revolution', *Representations* 2(1), 95–117.

Hunt, Nadine (2012) 'Remembering Africans in diaspora: Robert Wedderburn's "freedom narrative"', In: *Slavery in Africa and the Caribbean: A History of Enslavement and Identity Since the 18th Century,* Olatunji Ojo and Nadine Hunt (eds.), London: I.B. Tauris, 175–98.

Hunt, Tamara L. (2003) *Defining John Bull: Political Caricature and National Identity in Late Georgian England.* Aldershot: Ashgate.

Hunter, Jack (2014) *Alexander Murray: Galloway's Self-Taught Genius.* Stranraer: Stranraer Local History Trust.

Hurst, Isobel (2006) *Victorian Women Writers and the Classics: The Feminine of Homer.* Oxford: OUP.

Hutchinson, Horace (1914) *Life of Sir John Lubbock, Lord Avebury,* 2 vols. London: Macmillan.

Hutchinson, W.M.L. (1901) *Aeacus: A Judge of the Underworld.* Cambridge: Macmillan and Bowes.

Hutchinson, W.M.L. (1907) *The Golden Porch.* London: E. Arnold.

Hutchinson, W.M.L. (1909) *Orpheus with His Lute.* London: E. Arnold.

Hutchinson, W.M.L. (1911) *The Sunset of the Heroes: Last Adventures of the Takers of Troy.* London: Dent.

Hutchinson, W.M.L. (1912, 1914) *The Muses' Pageant: Myths & Legends of Ancient Greece.* London: Dent.

Hutchinson, W.M.L. (1920) *Evergreen Stories.* London: Dent.

Huxley, David (2013) 'Music hall art: La Milo, nudity and the pose plastique, 1905–1915', *Early Popular Visual Culture* 11(3), 218–36.

Hyland, Peter (2005) *The Herculaneum Pottery: Liverpool's Forgotten Glory.* Liverpool: Liverpool University Press.

Hyman, Richard (1966) *Oxford Workers in the Great Strike.* Oxford: Centre for Socialist Education.

Hyne, Anthony (1995) *David Jones: A Fusilier at the Front.* Bridgend: Poetry Wales Press.

Inch, Thomas (1923) *Inch on Fitness.* London: G. Newnes.

Inglis, Lucy (2014) *Georgian London: Into the Streets.* London: Penguin.

Inman, Philip (1952) *No Going Back.* London: Williams and Norgate.

Innes, N. (1861) *Memoir of Andrew Dalzel: Professor of Greek in the University of Edinburgh.* Edinburgh: T. Constable.

Irwin, M. Eleanor (2016) 'An unconventional classicist: The work and life of Kathleen Freeman', In: Wyles and Hall (eds.), 313–34.

Jackson, Holbrook (1930) *The Anatomy of Biblomania*, 2 vols. London: Soncino.
Jackson Knight, W.F. (1956, trans.) *The Aeneid. Virgil*. Harmondsworth: Penguin.
James, Felicity and Ian Inkster (2012, eds.) *Religious Dissent and the Aikin-Barbauld Circle, 1740-1860*. Cambridge: Cambridge University Press.
James, Paula (2015) 'Hercules as a symbol of labour: A nineteenth-century class-conflicted hero', In: Stead and Hall (eds.), 138–54.
James, Stuart (1979) *Catalogue of the Wanlockhead Miners' Library*. Paisley: Paisley Museums Trust.
Jardine, William (1843, ed.) 'Memoir of Thomas Bewick', In: *The Naturalist's Library*, vol. XVIII. Edinburgh: W.H. Lizars, 17–51.
Jay, Basil (2012) *The Soldier Poets of the Great War*. Bloomington, IN: Authorhouse.
Jefferson, Thomas (1784 [1782]) *Notes on the State of Virginia*. Paris: Henry Stevens.
Jenkyns, Richard (1980) *The Victorians and Ancient Greece*. Oxford: Blackwell.
Jenkyns, Richard (1991) *Dignity and Decadence: Victorian Art and the Classical Inheritance*. London: HarperCollins.
Jennings, Bernard (2002) *Albert Mansbridge: The Life and Work of the Founder of the WEA*. Leeds: University of Leeds with the Worker's Educational Association.
Jewitt, Llewellynn (1972 [1878]) *Jewitt's Ceramic Art of Great Britain 1800–1900*. 3rd edition revised by Geoffrey A. Godden. London: Barrie and Jenkins.
Johnson, James William (1958) 'Tertullian and "A modest proposal"', *Modern Language Notes* 73(8), 561–66.
Johnson, Marguerite (2019) 'Black out: Classicizing indigeneity in Australia and New Zealand', In: *Antipodean Antiquities*, Marguerite Johnson (ed.), London: Bloomsbury, 13–28.
Johnson, Samuel (1755) *A Dictionary of the English Language*. London: J. & P. Knapton.
Johnson, Samuel (1958) *The Yale Edition of the Works of Samuel Johnson: Poems*. New Haven, CT: Yale University Press.
Johnston, John (1828, ed.) *The Works of Samuel Parr*. 8 vols. London: Longman, Rees, Orme, Brown and Green.
Johnston, John (1990) *The Lord Chamberlain's Blue Pencil*. London: Hodder & Stoughton.
Jones, David (2014 [1937]) *In Parenthesis, with a Note of Introduction by T.S. Eliot*. London: Faber & Faber.
Jones, David (1955) *The Sleeping Lord and Other Fragments*. London: Faber & Faber.
Jones, David (1959) *Epoch and Artist*, ed. Harman Grisewood. London: Faber & Faber.
Jones, David (1978) *The Dying Gaul, and Other Writings*. London: Faber.
Jones, D. (2004) 'Aikin, John (1713–1780), tutor and theological scholar', *ODNB*. Oxford. OUP.
Jones, David (2015) *Dai Greatcoat: A Self-Portrait of David Jones in His Letters*. London: Faber & Faber.
Jones, E. (1857) *The Revolt of Hindostán; or. The New World*. London: Effingham Wilson.
Jones, Henry (1745) *The Bricklayer's Poem to the Countess of Chesterfield, on Her Ladyship's Saving the Soldiers from Being Shot*. Dublin: No Publisher Named.
Jones, Henry (1751) *An Epistle to the … Earl of Orrery, Occasion'd by Reading his Lordship's Translation of Pliny's Epistles*. London: No publisher.
Jones, Henry (1758) *The Patriot Enterprize: Or An Address to Britain. A Poem. Inscribed to the Right Hon. William Pitt*. London and Dublin: William Whitestone.
Jones, Henry (1924) *Essays on Literature and Education*, ed. H.J.W. Hetherington. London: Hodder & Stoughton.

Jones, Hugh Ceiriog (1995) *The Library of David Jones (1895–1974): A Catalogue.* Aberystwyth: National Library of Wales.

Jones, Peter d'Alroy (1968) *Christian Socialist Revival, 1877–1914.* Princeton, NJ: Princeton University Press.

Jones, Sidney (1898) *Souvenir of A Greek Slave.* London: Daly's Theatre.

Jones, Stanley (1991) *Hazlitt: A Life.* Oxford: OUP.

Jones, Thomas (1698, trans.) *Gwir ddeongliad breuddwydion* by Artemidorus Daldianus. Shrewsbury: T. Jones.

Jones, Thomas (1942) *Leeks and Daffodils.* Newtown: Welsh Outlook Pres.

Jones, Thomas (1970) *Rhymney Memories Reprint of 1936.* 1st edition. Llandysul: Gwasg Gomer.

Jones, Trevor (1970) *Street Literature in Birmingham: A History of Broadside and Chapbook.* Oxford: Oxford Polytechnic.

Jones, Victor Pierce (1988) *Saint or Sensationalist? The Story of W.T. Stead.* East Wittering: Gooday Publishers.

Jonson, Ben (1641) *The Workes of Beniamin Ionson.* London: Richard Meighen and Thomas Walkley.

Jowett, B. (1884) *Lectures on the Industrial Revolution in England: Public Addresses, Notes and Other Fragments, Together with a Short Memoir.* London: Rivington's.

Jowett, Benjamin (1892) *The Dialogues of Plato: Translated into English with Analyses and Introductions.* Oxford: Clarendon Press.

Joyce, James (1922) *Ulysses.* Paris: Shakespeare and Company.

Judson, Barbara (2001) 'The politics of Medusa: Shelley's physiognomy of revolution', *ELH* 68(1), 135–54.

'K.' (1809) 'Potteries of Staffordshire', *The Belfast Monthly Magazine* 2 (June 30th), 417–18.

Kahane, Henry and Renée Kahane (1957) 'Pearls before wine? A reinterpretation of Matt. 7.6', *Traditio* 13, 421–24.

Kay, John (1877) *A Series of Original Portraits and Character Etchings*, 2 vols. Edinburgh: Adam and Charles Black.

Kaye, F.B. (1921) 'The writings of Bernard Mandeville: A bibliographical survey', *The Journal of English and Germanic Philology* 20(4), 419–67.

Keane, John (1995) *Tom Paine: A Political Life.* London: Bloomsbury.

Keating, Joseph (1916) *My Struggle for Life.* London: Simpkin, Marshall & Co.

Keats, John (1863) *Keatsii Hyperionis libri tres. Latine reddidit Carolu Merivale. Eng. & Lat.* Cambridge and London: Macmillan.

Keefe, Joan (1977) *Irish Poems from Cromwell to the Famine: A Miscellany.* Lewisburg, Pennsylvania: Bucknell University Press.

Keegan, Bridget and John Goodridge (2013) 'Modes and methods in three nineteenth-century mineworker poets', *Philological Quarterly* 92, 225–50.

Keevak, Michael (2004) *The Pretended Asian: George Psalmanazar's Eighteenth-Century Formosan Hoax.* Detroit, MI: Wayne State University Press.

Keightley, Thomas (1836) *The History of Rome.* London: Longman, Rees, Orme, Brown, Green, and Longman.

Kellett, Arnold (2004) 'Wright, Joseph', *ODNB*. doi:10.1093/ref:odnb/37036.

Kelly, Thomas (1966) *Early Public Libraries: A History of Public Libraries in Great Britain before 1850.* London: Library Association.

Kelly, Thomas (1992 [1962]) *A History of Adult Education in Great Britain.* Liverpool: Liverpool University Press.

Kennedy, Brian (1989–1990) 'Paul Henry: An Irish portrait', *The GPA Irish Arts Review Yearbook*, 43–54.

Kennedy, M. (2009) 'William Flynn (1740–1811) and the readers of Munster in the second half of the eighteenth century', In: Hinks, Armstrong and Day (eds.), 73–94.

Kenner, Hugh (1971) *The Pound Era*. Berkeley, California: University of California Press.

Kennerley, Eija (1975) *The Jenkins Story* [= Gwent Local History No. 39]. Newport: Gwent Local History Society.

Kennett, Basil (1696) *Romæ Antiquæ notitia: Or, the antiquities of Rome*. London: A. Swall and T. Child.

Kennett, Basil (1713) *The Idylliums of Theocritus...To Which Is prefix'd, the Life of Theocritus. By Basil Kennet*. London: E. Curll.

Kenyon, F.G. (1891, ed.) *Aristotle on the Constitution of Athens*. London: British Museum.

Kermode, H. Sybil (1912) 'The classical sources of Morris's *Life and Death of Jason*', In: *Primitive; Essays in English Literature by Students of the University of Liverpool*. Liverpool: Liverpool University Press, 158–82.

Kersey, John (1757) *New Classical English Dictionary*. Dublin: S. Powell.

Kettle, A. (1975) 'Foreword' to A. West *Crisis and Criticism and Selected Literary Essays*. London: Lawrence and Wishart, 1–3.

Kidd, Thomas (1815) *Tracts and Miscellaneous Criticisms. (An imperfect outline of the life of R. Porson)*. London: Payne and Foss.

Killen, John (1990) *A History of the Linen Hall Library 1788–1988*. Belfast: Linen Hall Library.

King, C.E. (1981) 'A hoard of clipped siliquae in the Preston Museum', *The Numismatic Chronicle* 141, 40–64.

King, Clifford (1920) *New Poems*, 3 vols. London: Drane's Ltd.

King, W. (1708, trans.) *The Art of Love: In Imitation of Ovid de Arte Amandi*. London: Bernard Lintott.

Kingsley, Charles (1898 [1850]) *Alton Locke*, 2 vols. New York and London: The Co-Operative Publication Society.

Kinkel, Sarah (2018) *Disciplining the Empire: Politics, Governance and the Rise of the British Navy*. Cambridge, MA: Harvard University Press.

Klaus, H. Gustav (1993, ed) *Tramps, Workmates and Revolutionaries: Working-Class Stories of the 1920s*. London and Boulder, Colorado: Journeyman Press.

Klein, Alan M. (1993) *Little Big Men: Bodybuilding Subculture and Gender Construction*. New York: State University of New York Press.

Klugmann, J. (1968) *History of the Communist Party of Great Britain*, vol. I. London: Lawrence and Wishart.

Knapp, Charles (1923) *The Classical Weekly* (October 15th). vol. XVII (no. 3) (whole no. 453) 24.

Knight, Charles (1984 [1847]) 'The Staffordshire Potteries', reproduced from *The Land We Live in* (London: Charles Knight, 1847) in *Staffordshire County Council Education Department Local History Source Book* L 48, Burton-On-Trent: SCC, 13–45.

Knight, Charles (1865) *Shadows of the Old Booksellers*. London: Bell and Daldy.

Knight, Helen (1853) *Lady Huntingdon and Her Friends*. New York: American Tract Society.

Knight, William (1907, ed.) *Memorials of Thomas Davidson*. London: T. Fisher Unwin.

Knowles, J.S. (1815) *Caius Gracchus: A Tragedy, in Five Acts*. London: J. Dicks.

Knowles, J.S. (1820) *Virginius*. London: J. Dicks.

Knowles, J.S. (1823) *Caius Gracchus*. Glasgow: Reid and Henderson.

Knowles, J.S. (1825) *William Tell*. London: J. Dicks.

Knowles, J.S. (1856) *Dramatic Works*. London and New York: G. Routledge & Co.

Knowles, J.S. (1873a) *Lectures on Dramatic Literature (Delivered Belfast in 1830 and Liverpool in 1848)*. London: James McHenry.

Knowles, J.S. (1873b) *Lectures on Oratory, Gesture and Poetry*. London James McHenry.

Knowles, R.B. (1872) *The Life of James Sheridan Knowles*. London: Privately Printed.

Knox, Vicesimus (1783/4) *Elegant Extracts, of Useful and Entertaining Passages in Prose, Selected for the Improvement of Scholars at Classical and Other Schools in the Art of Speaking, in Reading, Thinking, Composing, and the Conduct of Life*. London: Charles Dilly.

Knox, Vicesimus (1789) *Elegant Extracts: Or, Useful and Entertaining Pieces of Poetry*. London: Charles Dilly.

Kocmanová, Jessie (1980) 'Hugh MacDiarmid, Grassic Gibbon, and the Class Commitment of Scottish Literature in the 20s and 30s', *Angol Filológiai Tanulmányok / Hungarian Studies in English* 13, 59–69.

Konstan, David (1994) 'The classics and class conflict', *Arethusa* 27, 47–70.

Krevens, N. ed. (2001) 'Class and classics: A historical perspective', Forum, *Classical Journal* 96, 293–334.

Krishnamurthy Aruna ed. (2009a) *The Working-Class Intellectual in 18th and 19th Century Britain*. London: Routledge.

Krishnamurthy, Aruna (2009b) 'Introduction', In: Krishnamurthy (2009a), 1–24.

Kumar, Krishan (1990) 'Utopian thought and communal practice: Robert Owen and the Owenite communities', *Theory and Society* 19(1), 1–35.

Kurtz, Donna (2000) *The Reception of Classical Art in Britain: An Oxford Story of Plaster Casts from the Antique*. Oxford: The Beazley Archive and Archaeopress.

Lackington, James (1791) *Memoirs of the First forty-five Years of the Life of James Lackington: The Present Bookseller in Chiswell-Street, Moorfields, London / Written by Himself. In a Series of Letters to a Friend. With a Triple Dedication. 1. To the Public. 2. To Respectable Booksellers. 3. To Sordid Booksellers*. London: Lackington and Bristol: W. Bulgin.

Lackington, James (1792) *Memoirs of the Forty-Five First Years of the Life of James Lackington*. 2nd edition. London: Lackington.

Lada-Richards, Ismene (2003) '"Mobile Statuary": Refractions of Pantomime Dancing from Callistratus to Emma Hamilton and Andrew Ducrow', *International Journal of the Classical Tradition* 1, 3–37.

Lada-Richards, Ismene (2010) 'Dead but not extinct: On reinventing pantomime dancing in eighteenth-century England and France', In: Macintosh (ed.), 19–38.

Laing, Alastair (2000) 'Sir Rowland and Lady Winn: A conversation piece in the library at Nostell', *Apollo*, (April), 14–18.

Lalor, James Fintan (1895) *The Writings of James Fintan Lalor*. Dublin: T.G. O'Donohue.

Lamb, Charles (1808) *The Adventures of Ulysses*. London: The Juvenile Library.

Lamb, Charles (1820) 'Oxford at the vacation', *London Magazine* 2(October), 365–69.

Lamb, Charles (1833) 'Amicus redivivus', In: *Essays of Elia*. London: Moxon, 237–41.

Lamb, Charles and Mary A. Lamb (1975 and 1978) *The Letters of Charles and Mary Anne Lamb*, vol. 1 and 2, ed. Edwin W. Marrs. Ithaca, NY: Cornell University Press.

Lambert, Michael (2011) *The Classics and South African Identities*. London: Bloomsbury.

La Mothe le Vayer, Francis (1678) *Notitia Historicorum Selectorum, or Animadversions upon the Antient and Famous Greek and Latin historians: Written in French by the Learned Francis La Mothe le Vayer, Councellor of State to the Present French King. Translated into English, with Some Additions by W.D. B.A. of Magd. Hall, Oxon*. Oxford: Leon. Lichfield.

Landry, Donna (1987) 'The resignation of Mary Collier: Some problems in feminist literary history', In: *The New Eighteenth Century*, Felicity Nussbaum and Laura Brown (eds.), New York: Methuen, 99–120.

Landry, Donna (1990) *The Muses of Resistance: Laboring-Class Women's Poetry in Britain, 1739–1796*. Cambridge: CUP.

Langhorne, John and William Langhorne (1770) *Plutarch's Lives: Translated from the Original Greek*, 6 vols. London: Edward and Charles Dilly.

Larson, Victoria Tietze (1999) 'Classics and the acquisition and validation of power in Britain's "imperial century" (1815–1914)', *International Journal of the Classical Tradition* 6(2), 185–225.

Lathrop, Henry Burrowes (1933) *Translations from the Classics into English from Caxton to Chapman, 1477–1620*. Madison, Wisconsin: University of Wisconsin.

Lauro, Pietro (1547, trans.) *Dell' interpretatione de sogninouamente di Greco in Uolgare tradotto*. Vinegia: Gabriel Giolito de Ferrari.

Lawley, G.T. (1868) *History of Bilston*. Bilston: Price and Beebee.

Lawson, Jack (1932) *A Man's Life*. London: Hodder and Stoughton.

Lawton, Denis (1975) *Class, Culture and the Curriculum*. London and Boston, Massachusetts: Routledge and Kegan Paul.

Layard, Austen Henry (1903) *Autobiography and Letters from His Childhood*. London: John Murray.

Laycock, Samuel (1908) 'Quality row', In: *The Collected Writings of Samuel Laycock*. London: Simpkin & Co., 59–61.

Leach, Robert (2006) *Theatre Workshop: Joan Littlewood and the Making of Modern British Theatre*. Exeter: University of Exeter Press.

Leask, W. (1854) *Struggles for Life: Autobiography of a Dissenting Minister*. Philadelphia, Pennsylvania: Lindsay and Blakiston.

Leatherland, J.A. (1862) *Essays and Poems, with a Brief Autobiographical Memoir*. A Cassell Prize Essay. London: W. Tweedie.

Lee, Charles E. (1955) *St. Pancras Church and Parish*. London: Church of Saint Pancras.

Lee, Matthew (2016) 'Birkbeck, George (1776–1841), physician and educationist', *ODNB*. Oxford: OUP.

Lee, Ying S. (2007) *Masculinity and the English Working Class in Victorian Autobiography and Fiction*. New York: Routledge.

Leech, Sarah (1828) *Poems on Various Subjects, by Sara Leech, a Peasant Girl, with a Biographical Memoir*. Dublin: J. Charles.

Leed, Eric (1979) *No Man's Land: Combat and Identity in World War 1*. Cambridge: CUP.

Lekas, P. (1988) *Marx on Classical Antiquity*. London: Palgrave Macmillan.

Lemon, Mark (1856). *Medea: A Tragedy in One Act*. British Library Add. MS 52960 L.

Lenhart, Gary (2006) *The Stamp of Class*. Ann Arbor, Minnesota: University of Michigan Press.

Lenin, V.I. (1970) *On Literature and Art*. Moscow: Progress.

L'Estrange, Sir Roger (1678) *Seneca's Morals: By Way of Abstract of Benefits*. London: Henry Broome.

L'Estrange, Sir Roger ([1702] 1720) *The Wars of the Jews in Two Books*. 2nd edition. Glasgow: Thomas Crawford.

L'Estrange, Sir Roger (1752) *A Compleat History of the Wars of the Jews, Written in Greek by Flavius Josephus*. Edinburgh: Gray.

Lessenich, Rolf (2012) *Neoclassical Satire and the Romantic School 1780–1830*. Bonn: Bonn University Press.

Levi, Peter (1967) 'The poetry of David Jones', *Agenda* 5, 80–89.

Levine, Joseph (1991) *The Battle of the Books: History and Literature in the Augustan Age*. Ithaca, New York: Cornell University Press.

Levine, Joseph (1999) *Between the Ancients and the Moderns: Baroque Culture in Restoration England*. New Haven, Connecticut and London: Yale University Press.

Levy, Carl (1987*a*, ed.) *Socialism and the Intelligentsia 1880–1914*. London: Routledge Kegan Paul.

Levy, Carl (1987b) 'Education and self-education: Staffing the early ILP', In: Levy (1987a, ed.), 135–210.

Lewis, Jayne Elizabeth (1996) *The English Fable: Aesop and Literary Culture 1651–1740*. Cambridge: CUP.

Lewis, Richard (1993) 'Starr, Mark (1894–1985) workers' educationist', In: *The Dictionary of Labour Biography*, vol. 9, Joyce M. Bellamy and John Saville eds. London: Macmillan.

Lewis, Sian (1998–1999) 'Slaves as viewers and users of Athenian pottery', *Hephaistos* 16/17, 71–90.

Liddington, Jill (2006) *Rebel Girls: Their Fight for the Vote*. London: Virago.

Lieber, Francis (1863) *Plantations for Slave Labor: The Death of the Yeomanry*. Philadelphia, PA: C. Sherman, Son & Co.

Leishman, Douglas A. (2006, ed.) online version of Henry Kelly's *The Glasgow Pottery of John and Matthew Preston Bell*. www.bellsglasgowpottery.com/fileuploads/Bells%20Appendix%20III.pdf.

Lindsay, Jack (1927) *The Complete Works of Petronius*. London: Fanfrolico Press.

Lindsay, Jack (1929a) *Catullus, the Complete Poetry of Gaius*. London: Fanfrolico Press.

Lindsay, Jack (1929b) *The Mimiambs of Herondas*. London: Fanfrolico Press.

Lindsay, Jack (1932) *The Golden Ass of Apuleius*. New York: Limited Editions Club.

Lindsay, Jack (1935a) 'Not English? A reminder for May Day', *Left Review* 1, 353–57.

Lindsay, Jack (1935b) *The Romans*. London: A. and C. Black.

Lindsay, Jack (1935c) *Last Days with Cleopatra*. London: Ivor Nicholson & Watson.

Lindsay, Jack (1935d) *Despoiling Venus*. London: Nicholson & Watson.

Lindsay, Jack (1936a) *Who Are the English?* [pamphlet] London: Left Review.

Lindsay, Jack (1936b) *Marc Antony: His World and Contemporaries*. London: George Routledge.

Lindsay, Jack (1937a) 'On Guard for Spain! A poem for mass declamation', *Left Review* 3, 79–86.

Lindsay, Jack (1937b) 'A plea for mass declamation', *Left Review* 8, 511–17.

Lindsay, Jack (1948a) *Catullus, the Complete Poems*. London: Sylvan Press.

Lindsay, Jack (1948b) *The Daphnis & Chloe of Longus*. London: Daimon Press.

Lindsay, Jack (1956) *The Romans Were Here: The Roman Period in Britain and Its Place in Our History*. London: Muller.

Lindsay, Jack (1962) *Fanfrolico, and After*. London: Bodley Head.

Lindsay, Jack (1965) *Leisure and Pleasure in Roman Egypt*. London: Muller.

Lindsay, Jack (1967) *Our Roman Heritage*. London: Weidenfeld and Nicolson.

Linebaugh, Peter and Marcus Rediker (2000) *The Many Headed Hydra: Sailors, Slaves, Commoners and the Hidden History of the Revolutionary Atlantic*. London: Verso.

Lister, Robert (2019) 'A people's history of F.W. Walbank'. www.classicsandclass.info/.

Littleton, Adam (1678) *Linguæ Latinæ liber dictionarius quadripartitus*. London.

Littlewood, Joan (1994) *Joan's Book: The Autobiography of Joan Littlewood*. London: Methuen.

Lloyd George, David (1918) *Lloyd George's Message*. London: National War Aims Committee.

Llwyd, Alan (2008, ed.) *Out of the Fire of Hell: Welsh Experience of the Great War 1914–1918 in Prose and Verse.* Llandysul: Gomer.

Locke, John (1913 [1693]) *Some Thoughts Concerning Education*, ed. R.H. Quick. Cambridge: CUP.

Lockhart, John Gibson (1827) 'The life and times of Frederick Reynolds', *The Quarterly Review* 35(69), 148–65.

Lockhart, John Gibson (1839) *Memoirs of the Life of Sir Walter Scott, Bart*, vol. 1. Edinburgh: Robert Cadell.

Lockwood, T. (2013) 'W.T. Stead's 'Penny Poets': Beyond Baylen', *Interdisciplinary Studies in the Long Nineteenth Century* 19. doi:10.16995/ntn.655.

Loeber, R. and M. Stouthamer-Loeber (1999) 'Fiction available to and written for cottagers and their children', In: *The Experience of Reading: Irish Historical Perspectives*, R. Cunningham and M. Kennedy (eds.), Dublin: Economic and Social History Society of Ireland, 124–72.

Loftis, John (1963) *The Politics of Drama in Augustan England.* Oxford: Clarendon Press.

Loftus, Belinda (1978) *Marching Workers: An Exhibition of Irish Trade Union Banners and Regalia.* Belfast: Arts Councils of Ireland/Irish Congress of Trade Unions.

Long, Gerard (1996, ed.) *Books Beyond the Pale: Aspects of the Provincial Book Trade in Ireland before 1850.* Dublin: Rare Books Group of the Library Association of Ireland.

Loraux, N., P. Vidal-Naquet and R. Bolgar (1979) 'La formation de l'Athènes bourgeoise: Essai d'historiographie 1750–1850', In: *Classical Influences on Western Thought ad 1650–1870.* Cambridge: CUP, 169–222.

Lovett, William (1920 [1876]) *Life and Struggles of William Lovett in his Pursuit of Bread, Knowledge, and Freedom*, with an Introduction by R.H. Tawney. New York: Alfred A. Knopf.

Lowe, N.F. (1997) 'James Barry, Mary Wollstonecraft and 1798', *Eighteenth-Century Ireland / Iris an dá chultúr* 12, 60–76.

Lowe, R. (2007) 'Jones, Thomas (1870–1955), civil servant and benefactor', *ODNB.* Oxford: OUP.

Luard, Henry R. (1857), *Porson.* London: Parker.

Lubbock, John (1887) *The Pleasures of Life*, vol. 1. 2nd edition. London and New York: Macmillan and Co.

Lucas, C.P. (1885) 'The Working Men's College', *Charity Organisation Review* 1, 161–63.

Lydenberg, Harry (1977) *Crossing the Line.* New York: New York Public Library.

Lynch, Jack (2005) 'Forgery as performance art: The strange case of George Psalmanazar', In: *1650–1850: Ideas, Aesthetics, and Inquiries in the Early Modern Era*, vol. 11, 21–35.

Lyons, Israel (1735), *The Scholar's Instructor: An Hebrew Grammar.* Cambridge: CUP.

Mably, Gabriel Bonnot de (1751) *Observations on the Romans.* London: R. Griffiths.

MacAdam, Henry (2015) 'Dramatizing Roman History: Spartacus in fiction and film', *The RAG* 10 (2) (November), 1–5.

MacAloon, John J. (1981), *This Great Symbol: Pierre de Coubertin and the Origins of the Modern Olympic Games.* Chicago, Illinois: University of Chicago Press.

Macaulay, Thomas Babington (1895) *The Lays of Ancient Rome, and Other Poems by Lord Macaulay.* The Penny Poets 1, the Masterpiece Library. London: 'Review of Reviews' Office.

MacCarthy, Denis Florence (1872) *Shelley's Early Life, from Original Sources. With Curious Incidents, Letters, and Writings, Now First Published or Collected.* London: John Camden Hotten.

MacColl, Ewan (1990) *Journeyman: An Autobiography.* London: Sidgwick and Jackson.

MacColl, Ewan, Annemarie Weber and Ita Maximowna (1948) *Unternehmen Ölzweig. Komödie in einem Vorspiel und drei Akten*. Berlin: Verlag Bruno Henschel und Sohn.

MacDiarmid, Hugh (1970) *Selected Essays of Hugh MacDiarmid*, Duncan Glen (ed.), Berkley: University of California Press.

Macht, Carol (1957) *Classical Wedgwood Designs*. New York: Medicine Barrows & Co.

Macintosh, Fiona (2010, ed.) *The Ancient Dancer in the Modern World: Responses to Greek and Roman Dance*. Oxford: OUP.

Macintosh, F., J. McConnell, S. Harrison and C. Kenward (2018, eds.) *Epic Performances from the Middle Ages into the Twenty-first Century*. Oxford: OUP.

Mack, Maynard (1988) *Alexander Pope*. 2nd edition. New York and London: Norton.

Mackail, J.W. (1890) *The Life of William Morris*, 2 vols. London: Longmans, Green.

Mackenzie, Peter (1868) *Old Reminiscences of Glasgow and the West of Scotland*, vol. 3. Glasgow: J. Tweed.

MacNeice, Louis (1979) *The Collected Poems of Louis MacNeice*. 2nd edition. ed. E.R. Dodds. London: Faber.

Madden, R.R. (1846) *The United Irishmen: Their Life and Times*, 3 vols. Dublin: James Duffy.

Madden, R.R. (1887, ed.) *Literary Remains of the Untied Irishmen*. Dublin: James Duffy & Sons.

Mahaffy, J.P. (1898) *Social Life in Greece*. New York: Macmillan and Co.

Mahl, Mary R. and Helene Koon (1977, eds.) *The Female Spectator*. Bloomington, Indiana: Indiana University Press.

Maidment, Brian (1987) *The Poorhouse Fugitives: Self-Taught Poets and Poetry in Victorian Britain*. Manchester: Carcanet.

Maidwell, Lewis (1684, ed.) *A Breviary of Roman History. From the Building of Rome, to the Year 1119 … Translated into English by Several Young Gentlemen, Privately Educated in Hatton-Garden*. London: Jo. Hindmarsh.

Malamud, Margaret (2018) 'Receptions of Rome in debates on slavery in the USA', In: *Roman Error: Classical Reception and the Problem with Rome's Flaws*, Basil Dufallo (ed.), Oxford: OUP, 97–126.

Malcolm, J.P. (1808) *Anecdotes of the Manners and Customs of London During the Eighteenth Century*. London: Longman's.

Malcolm, William (1984) *A Blasphemer and Reformer: A Study of James Leslie Mitchell/Lewis Grassic Gibbon*. Aberdeen: Aberdeen University Press.

Malcolmson, Robert W. (1973) *Popular Recreations in English Society, 1700–1850*. Cambridge: CUP.

Malden, J. (1977) *John Henning 1771–1851, '… a Very Ingenious Modeller'*. Renfrew District Council Museum and Art Galleries Department. Paisley: Browns.

Malden, J. (2008) 'Henning, John (1771–1851), sculptor', *ODNB*. Oxford: OUP doi:10.1093/ref:odnb/9780198614128.001.0001/odnb-9780198614128-e-12945.

Mally, Lynn (1990) *Culture of the Future: The Proletkult Movement in Revolutionary Russia*. Berkeley: University of California Press.

Mandelbrote, Scott (2004) 'Ramsay, Andrew Michael [Jacobite Sir Andrew Ramsay, baronet] (1686–1743), philosopher and Jacobite sympathizer', *ODNB*. Oxford: OUP.

Mansbridge, Albert (1920) *An Adventure in Working-Class Education*. London: Longmans, Green & Co.

Mansbridge, Albert (1940) *The Trodden Road: Experience, Inspiration and Belief*. London: J.M. Dent & Sons Ltd.

Mansbridge, Albert (1944) 'University tutorial classes [1913]', In: *The Kingdom of the Mind; Essays & Addresses, 1907–1937*, ed. Leonard Clark with an introduction by G.M. Trevelyan. London: J.M. Dent & Sons Ltd, 28–33.

Mansfield, Nick (2013) 'Military radicals and the making of class, 1790–1860', In: *Soldiering in Britain and Ireland 1750–1850: Men at Arms*, Catriona Kennedy and Matthew McCormack (eds.), London: Palgrave Macmillan, 57–75.

Mark-All, Martin (1610) *Martin Mark-All, Beadle of Bridewell; His Defence and Answere to the Belman of London. Discouering the Long Concealed Originall and Regiment of Rogues.* London: John Budge and Richard Bonian.

Marston, W. (1888) *Our Recent Actors*, 2 vols. London: Sampson Low.

Martin, Benjamin (1749) *Lingua Britannica Reformata*. London: No Publisher Indicated.

Martin, Augustine (1980) *Anglo-Irish Literature*. Dublin: Ormond Printing Co.

Martin, J. (2010a) *Making Socialists: Mary Bridges Adams and the Fight for Knowledge and Power, 1855–1939*. Manchester: Manchester University Press.

Martin, J. (2010b) *Radical Connections: A Journey through Social Histories, Biography and Politics*. London: Institute of Education.

Marwick, Arthur (1990) *Class: Image and Reality*. 2nd edition. Basingstoke: Macmillan.

Marx, Karl [tr. De Leon, Daniel] (1907) *The Eighteenth Brumaire of Louis Bonaparte*. Chicago, IL: Kerr, C.H. & Co.

Marx, Karl and Friedrich Engels (2010) *Collected Works, vol. 40, = Letters 1856–1859*. London: Lawrence and Wishart.

Mason, T. (2004) 'Veitch, Colin Campbell McKechnie (1881–1938), footballer and journalist', *ODNB*. Oxford: OUP. doi:10.1093/ref:odnb/9780198614128.001.0001/odnb-9780198614128-e-64560.

Maurer, Shawn Lisa (1998) *Proposing Men: Dialectics of Gender and Class in the Eighteenth-Century English Periodical*. Stanford, California: Stanford U.P.

Maurice, John Frederick Denison (1968) *Learning and Leisure: A Lecture*, ed. H.P. Smith. *Adult Education and Society Series*. Documentaries No. 13. Oxford: O.E. Smith.

Mavor, William (1800) *A Selection of the Lives of Plutarch Abridged: Containing the Most Illustrious Characters of Antiquity; for the Use of Schools*. London: R. Phillips.

Mavor, William Fordyce (1802–1804) *Universal History, Ancient and Modern: From the Earliest Records of Time, to the General Peace of 1801*. London: R. Phillips.

May, Thomas (1635) *The Victorious Reigne of King Edvvard the Third Written in Seven Bookes*. London: John Beale for T. Walkley and B. Fisher.

Mayer, David (1971) 'Billy Purvis: Travelling showman', *Theatre Quarterly* 1, 27–34.

Mayer, David (1994) *Playing Out the Empire*. Oxford: OUP.

Mayes, Stanley (2003) *The Great Belzoni: The Circus Strongman Who Discovered Egypt's Treasures*. Tauris Parke.

Mayhew, Robert A. (2011, trans.) *Problems. Aristotle*. Cambridge, Massachusetts: Harvard University Press.

Mays, Kelly J. (2001) 'Slaves in heaven, laborers in hell: Chartist poets' ambivalent identification with the (black) slave', *Victorian Poetry* 39(2), 137–63.

McBriar, A.M. (1962) *Fabian Socialism and English Politics 1884–1918*. Cambridge: CUP.

McCalman, Iain (1986) 'Anti-slavery and ultra-radicalism in early nineteenth century England: The case of Robert Wedderburn', *Slavery and Abolition* 7(2), 99–117.

McCalman, Iain (1988) *Radical Underworld. Prophets, Revolutionaries and Pornographers in London, 1795–1840*. Cambridge: CUP.

McCarthy, George E. (1990) *Marx and the Ancients*. Savage, Maryland: Rowland and Littlefield.

McCarthy, George E. (1992, ed.) *Marx and Aristotle: Nineteenth-Century German Social Theory and Classical Antiquity*. Savage, Maryland: Rowman and Littlefield.

McCarthy, William (2016) 'Barbauld [née Aikin], Anna letitia [Anna Laetitia] (1743–1825), poet and essayist', *ODNB*. Oxford: OUP.

McCleery, Alistair (2005) 'Defining characters', *Textualities: Scottish Book Collector,* 10–14. http://textualities.net/author/alistair-mccleery.

McConnell, Justine (2013) *Black Odysseys: The Homeric Odyssey in the African Diaspora Since 1939.* Oxford: United Kingdom OUP.

McCrie, Thomas (1812) *The Life of John Knox*. Edinburgh: John Ogle and William Blackwood.

McDonald, Marianne and Michael Walton (2002, eds.) *Amid Our Troubles: Irish Versions of Greek Tragedy*. London: Methuen.

McGuire, Charles Edward (2007) 'Elgar and Acworth's *Caractacus*: The druids, race and the individual hero', In: *Elgar Studies,* J.P.E. Harper-Scott and Julian Rushton (eds.), Cambridge: CUP, 50–77.

McKendrick, Neil (1961) 'II. Josiah Wedgwood and factory discipline', *The Historical Journal* 4(1), 30–55.

McManners, R. and G. Wales (2008) *Way to the Better: The Spennymoor Settlement*. Bishop Auckland: Gemini Productions.

McManus, Antonia (2004) *The Irish Hedge School and its Books, 1695–1831*. Paperback edition. Dublin: Four Courts Press.

McManus, Barbara (2017) *The Drunken Duchess of Vassar: Grace Harriet MaCurdy, Pioneering Feminist Classical Scholar,* foreword by Judith P. Hallett and Christopher Stray. Columbus, OH: The Ohio State University Press.

McMinn, Joseph (2001) 'Swift and theatre', *Eighteenth-Century Ireland / Iris an dáchultúr* 16, 35–46.

Measom, George S. (1861) *The Official Illustrated Guide to the Great Northern Railway*. London: Griffin and Bohn.

Medwin, Thomas (1832) *Prometheus Bound, A Tragedy, Translated from the Greek of Aeschylus, into English Verse*. London: William Pickering.

Mee, Arthur (1906, ed.) *The Harmsworth Self-Educator,* vol. I. London: Amalgamated Press.

Mee, Arthur (1907, ed.) *Harmsworth History of the World*. London: Carmelite Press.

Mellor, G.J. (1970) *The Northern Music Hall: A Century of Popular Entertainment*. Newcastle upon Tyne: Graham.

Melville, Jennifer (2010) *Aberdeen Art Gallery: A History*. Aberdeen: Aberdeen City Council.

Melvin, Murray (2007) *The Art of the Theatre Workshop*. London: Oberon.

Melvin, Murray (2009) *The Theatre Royal: A History of the Building*. Stratford: Stratford East Publications.

Mendilow, J. (1984) 'Carlyle, Marx and the ILP: Alternative routes to socialism', *Polity* 17(2), 225–47.

Merivale, Charles (1850–1862) *A History of the Romans under the Empire*. Cambridge and London: MacMillan.

Merivale, Charles (1863) *Keatsii Hyperionis Libri Tres (1853)*. Cambridge and London: MacMillan.

Merivale, Charles (1912) *History of Rome to the Reign of Trajan*. London: J.M. Dent and sons.

Meyer, Jessica (2009a) *Men of War: Masculinity and the First World War in Britain*. Basingstoke: Palgrave.

Meyer, Jessica (2009b) 'Separating the men from the boys: Masculinity and maturity in understandings of shell shock in Britain', *Twentieth Century British History* 20(1) (January 1, 2009):, 1–22.

Micchiavelli. N. (1531) *Discorsi di Nicolo Machiauelli*. Rome: Antonio Blado.

Michelakis, P. and M. Wyke (2013, eds.) *The Ancient World in Silent Cinema*. Cambridge: CUP.

Millar, Andrew (1743) *An Historical, Genealogical, and Classical Dictionary*. London: A. Millar.

Miller, Frank (1907) 'An unpublished topical poem by Dr. Blacklock', *Scottish, Historical Review* 4, 205–12.

Miller, George (1821) *Popular Books: Including a choice Variety of FAMILY AND POCKET BIBLES, and the Greater Part of our MOST ESTEEMED MODERN PUBLICATIONS, To commence on Monday the 8th October current, At 7 o'clock Evening,—Door open at half past 6, IN THE TOWN-HALL, DUNBAR, Being the only one for this Season*. John Gray Centre.

Miller, George (1833) *Later Struggles in the Journey of Life*. Edinburgh: James Colston.

Miller, Hugh (1993 [1854]) *My Schools and Schoolmasters, or, the Story of My Education*. Edinburgh: B and W Publishing.

Miller, Hugh (1869) *My Schools and Schoolmasters: Or, The Story of My Education*. 14th edition. Edinburgh: W.P. Nimmo.

Miller, Lynn (1982) 'The oven books: Oddities and incidentals', *Proceedings of the Wedgwood Society* 11, 163–72.

Miller, Thomas P. (1997) *The Formation of College English*. Pittsburgh, Pennsylvania: University of Pittsburgh Press.

Miles, Jonathan (1990) *Backgrounds to David Jones: A Study in Sources and Drafts*. Cardiff: University of Wales Press.

Millgate, M. (2006) 'Hardy, Thomas (1840–1928), novelist and poet', *ODNB*, (May 25). Oxford: OUP. doi:10.1093/ref:odnb/9780198614128.001.0001/odnb-9780198614128-e-33708.

Milne, Anne (2001) 'Gender, class, and the beehive: Mary Collier's "the Woman's Labour" (1739) as nature poem', *Interdisciplinary Studies in Literature and the Environment* 8, 9–129.

Milne, Anne (2008) *'Lactilla Tends her Fav'rite Cow': Ecocritical Readings of Animals and Women in 18th-Century British Labouring-Class Women's Poetry*. Lewisburg, Pennsylvania: Bucknell University Press.

Milner, Andrew (1999) *Class*. London: Sage.

Minerva (1795) *A Catalogue of the Minerva General Library, Leadenhall-Street, London*. London: Minerva Literary Repository, Library and Printing-Office.

Mitchell, R. (2004) 'Cassell, John (1817–1865), publisher', *ODNB*. Oxford: OUP. doi:10.1093/ref:odnb/9780198614128.001.0001/odnb-9780198614128-e-4861.

Mitford, William (1784) *The History of Greece*. London: J. Murray, and J. Robson.

Moncrieff, W.T. (1830) *The March of Intellect: A Comic Poem*. London: William Kidd.

Monod, Paul Kléber (2009) *Imperial Island: A History of Britain and Its Empire, 1660–1837*. Malden, MA and Oxford: Wiley-Blackwell.

Monrós Gaspar, Laura (2011) *Cassandra, the Fortune-Teller: Prophets, Gipsies and Victorian Burlesque [= Le rane. Studi, 56]*. Bari: Levante.

Montague, C.J. (1904) *Sixty Years in Waifdom, or, the Ragged School Movement in English History*. London: Charles Murray & Co.

Montesquieu, Charles (1752) *Reflections on the Causes of the Rise and Fall of the Roman Empire*, 2 vols. 2nd edition. London: W. Innys in Pater-Noster Row, C. Davis against Gray's-Inn Gate, Holborn, R. Manby on Ludgate-Hill, and H. S. Cox in Pater-Noster Row.

Montesquieu, Charles (1826) *Ouevres*, ed. L. Parrelle, vol. VIII. Paris: Lefèvre.

Montgomery, Evelyn M. Vernon (1930) 'Josiah Wedgwood, James Tassie and the Portland vase', *American Magazine of Art* 21, 557–59.

Moore, Jane (2013) 'Thomas Moore, Anacreon and the romantic tradition', *Romantic Textualities* 21, 30–52.

Moore, Lindy (1984) 'Invisible scholars: Girls learning Latin and mathematics in the elementary public schools of Scotland before 1872', *History of Education Journal* 13(2), 121–39.

Moore, Thomas (1853–1856) *Memoirs, Journal and Correspondence of Thomas Moore*, 8 vols. ed. Lord John Russell. London, Brown, Green and Longmans.

Moore, William (1987) *Gas Attack! Chemical Warfare 1915–1918 and Afterwards*. London: Cooper.

Moores, John Richard (2015) *Representations of France in English Satirical Prints 1740–1832*, Houndsmills: Palgrave Macmillan.

Morgan, Janett (forthcoming) 'A Greek tragedy? Why Dillwyn's Etruscan ware failed', In: Petsalis-Diomedis (ed.)

Morgan, Kenneth O. (1981) *Rebirth of a Nation: Wales, 1880–1980*. Oxford: OUP.

Morgan, Kevin (1989) *Against Fascism and War: Ruptures and Continuities in British Communist Politics, 1935–1941*. Manchester: Manchester University Press.

Morgan, Kevin (1995) 'The Communist Party and the Daily Worker, 1930–56', In: *Opening the Books: Essays on the Social and Cultural History of the British Communist Party*, K. Morgan, N. Fishman and G. Andrews (eds.), London: Pluto, 142–59.

Moritz, Charles P. (1795) *Travels, Chiefly on Foot, Through Several Parts of England, in 1782*. London: G. G. and J. Robinson.

Morley, Henry (1866) *Journal of a London Playgoer from 1851 to 1866*. London: Routledge.

Morley, Neville (1999, ed.) *Marx and Antiquity* = *Helios*. Special Issue, 26.2, Buffalo University.

Morley, Neville (2018) *Classics: Why It Matters*. London: Polity.

Morris, J.H. and L.J. Williams (1958) *The South Wales Coal Industry 1841–1875*. Cardiff: University of Wales Press.

Morris, John (2007) 'The Scottish chapmen', In: *Fairs, Markets and the Itinerant Book Trade*, Robin Myres, Michael Harris and Giles Mandelbrote (eds.), Oak Knoll Press and British Library, 159–86.

Morris, R. and G. Morton (1994) 'Where Was Nineteenth-Century Scotland?' *The Scottish Historical Review* 73(195), 89–99.

Mortimer, Peter (2018) *Rainbird: The Tragedy of an Artist*. North Shields: Iron Press.

Morton, A.L. (1952) *The English Utopia*. Lawrence and Wishart.

Morton, A.L. (1964 [1938]) *A People's History of England*. London: Lawrence and Wishart.

Morton, A.L. and George Tate (1956) *The British Labour Movement*. London: Lawrence and Wishart.

Mottley, John and Thomas Cooke (1728) *Penelope: A Dramatic Opera*. London: Thomas Green.

Müller [-Straten] Christian (1977) *James Sharples und das Zertifikat der Amalgamated Society of Engineers: Studien zur Bildkultur britischer Gewerkschaften*. Diss: Munich.

Munro, Ian S. (1966) *Leslie Mitchell: Lewis Grassic Gibbon*. Edinburgh and London: Oliver and Boyd.

Murphy, Paula (2010) *Nineteenth-Century Irish Sculpture*. New Haven and London: Yale U.P.

Murphy, Paul Thomas (1994) *Towards a Working-Class Canon: Literary Criticism in British Working-Class Periodicals, 1816–1858*. Columbus, OH: Ohio State University Press.

Murray, Alexander (1812) *Copy of Documents in Favour of the Rev. Alexander Murray, Minister of Urr, as Candidate for the Professorship of Oriental Languages.* Edinburgh: George Ramsay.

Murray, Alexander (1823) *History of the European Languages*, 2 vols. Edinburgh: Archibald Constable & Co.

Murray, Gilbert (1889) *The Place of Greek in Education: An Inaugural Lecture Delivered in the University of Glasgow November 6th, 1889.* Glasgow: James Maclehose & Sons.

Murray, Gilbert (1905, trans.) *The Trojan Women of Euripides.* London: George Allen.

Murray, Gilbert (1911, trans.) *Oedipus, King of Thebes.* London: George Allen.

Murray, Gilbert (1913) *Euripides and His Age.* London: Home University Library.

Murray, Oswyn (1997) '"It was a dark and stormy night ...": David Jones and history', In: *David Jones: Artist and Poet*, Paul Hills (ed.), Aldershot: Scholar Press, 1–17.

Mussell, James (2012) '"Characters of blood and flame": Stead and the tabloid campaign', In: Brake, King, Luckhurst and Mussell (eds.), 22–36.

Musurillo, Herbert (1954, ed.) *The Acts of the Pagan Martyrs = Acta Alexandrinorum.* Oxford: OUP.

Myers, Victoria, David O'Shaughnessy and Mark Philp eds. (2010) *The Diary of William Godwin.* Oxford: Oxford Digital Library. http://godwindiary.bodleian.ox.ac.uk.

Naerebout, Frederick (2010) '"In search of a dead rat": The reception of ancient Greek dance in late nineteenth-century America', In: Macintosh (ed.), 39–56.

Nairn, Thomas (1981) *The Break-Up of Britain: Crisis and Neo-Nationalism.* 2nd, expanded edition. London: Verso.

Nash, Rosalind (1898) *Life and Death in the Potteries.* Manchester: The Labour Press.

National Gallery (1850) *Report from the Select Committee on the National Gallery.* London: House of Commons.

National Trust (1981) *Stourhead.* London: National Trust.

Neale, William (2011) *More Old Theatres in the Potteries: An Appendix.* Stoke: Stoke on Trent City Archives.

Nelson, Eric (2004) *The Radical Tradition in Republican Thought.* Cambridge: CUP.

Neuburg, Victor E. (1964) *Chapbooks: A Bibliography of References to English and American Chapbook Literature of the Eighteenth and Nineteenth Centuries.* London: The Vine Press.

Neville, Robert G. (1976) 'The Yorkshire miners and the 1893 lockout: The Featherstone "massacre"', *International Review of Social History* 21(3), 337–57.

Newman, John Henry (1994 [1864]) *Apologia Pro Vita Sua*, ed. Ian Ker. New York: Penguin.

Newton, K.M. (1997) *Twentieth-Century Literary Theory.* 2nd edition. London: Palgrave.

NíChinnéide, S. (1978) 'A journey from Mullingar to Loughrea in 1791', *Journal of the Old Athlone Society* 5, 15–23.

Nicholas the Fisherman (1794) *Oppression Unmasked, Being a Narrative of the Proceedings in a Case between a Great Corporation and a Little Fishmonger, Relative to Some Customs for Fish.* Dublin: No Publisher Indicated.

Nicholson, John (1827) *The Lyre of Ebor; the Fall of Belshazzar; Genius and Intemperance; and Other Poems.* London: Seeley and Son.

Nicholson, John (1876) *The Poetical Works of John Nicholson.* London: Simpkin, Marshall, & Co.

Nicolson, Angus (1979) 'An interview with Sorley MacLean', *Studies in Scottish Literature* 14(1), 23–36.

Nicolson, Benedict (1968) *Joseph Wright of Derby: Painter of Light. Text and Catalogue.* London: Paul Mellon Foundation for British Art; Routledge and Kegan Paul.

Norbrook, David (1999) *Writing the English Republic.* Cambridge: CUP.

North, Dudley (1645) *A Forest of Varieties*. London: Richard Coates.

Nostell (1954) *Nostell Priory, Yorkshire*. London: National Trust.

Nostell (2001) *Nostell Priory, Yorkshire*. London: National Trust.

Nowell-Smith, S. (1958) *The House of Cassell, 1848–1958*. London: Cassell.

NSWS (1879) *Opinions of Women on Women's Suffrage*. London: Central Committee for the National Society for Women's Suffrage.

Nussbaum, Felicity (1989) *The Autobiographical Subject: Gender and Ideology in Eighteenth-Century England*. Baltimore, MD: Johns Hopkins University Press.

O'Brien, James Bronterre (1859) *A Dissertation and Elegy on the Life and Death of the Immortal Maximilian Robespierre*. London: G.J. Holyoake & Co.

O'Brien, James Bronterre (1885) *The Rise, Progress and Phases of Human Slavery: How It Came into the World and How It Shall Be Made to Go Out*. London: William Reeves.

O'Brien, P. (1989) *Warrington Academy, 1757–1786*. Wigan: Owl Books.

Ó'Coigligh, C. (1987, ed.) *Raifteiri*. Dublin: AnClóchomhar.

O'Faoláin, Seán (1947) *The Irish*. Harmondsworth: Penguin.

Ogilby, John (1654) *The Works of Publius Vergilius Maro*. London: Thomas Warren.

O'Higgins, Laurie (2017) *The Irish Classical Self: Poets and Poor Scholars in the Eighteenth and Nineteenth Centuries*. Oxford: OUP.

O'Leary, P. (2011) 'Keating, Joseph (1871–1934), novelist', *ODNB*. Oxford: OUP. doi:10.1093/ref:odnb/9780198614128.001.0001/odnb-9780198614128-e-101153.

Oldfield, J.R. (1992) 'The London Committee and mobilization of public opinion against the slave trade', *Historical Journal* 35(2), 331–43.

Olney, James (1972) *Metaphors of Self: The Meaning of Autobiography*. Princeton, NJ: Princeton University Press.

Ó'Néill, E. (2000) *The Golden Vale of Ivowen*. Dublin: Geography Publications.

O'Neill, Morna (2008) *'Art and Labour's Cause is One': Walter Crane and Manchester, 1880–1915*. Manchester: Whitworth Gallery.

Orrells, Daniel, Gurminder K. Bhambra and Tessa Roynon (2011, eds.) *African Athena New Agendas*. Oxford: OUP.

Osler, Alan (1967) 'Keats and Baldwin's *pantheon*', *The Modern Language Review* 62(2), 221–25.

O'Sullivan, Carol (2009) 'Translation within the margin: The 'Libraries' of Henry Bohn', In: *Agents of Translation*, vol. 81, J. Milton and P. Bandia (eds.); *Benjamins Translation Library*, EST subseries. Amsterdam and Philadephia, PA: John Benjamins Pub, 107–29.

Owen, Robert (1818) *Two Memorials on Behalf of the Working Classes: The First Presented to the Governments of Europe and America, the Second to the Allied Powers Assembled in Congress at Aix-La-Chapelle*. London: Longman, Hurst, Rees, Orme, and Brown.

Owen, Wilfred (1931) *The Poems of Wilfred Owen. A New Edition*. London: Chatto and Windus.

Owenson, Sydney (i.e. Lady Morgan) (1807) *Patriotic Sketches of Ireland, Written in Connaught*. London: Phillips.

Paananen, V.N. (2000, ed.) *British Marxist Criticism*. New York and London: Garland Publishing.

Pace, E.G. (undated [1930s]) 'The Durham miners', In: *The Extra-mural Work of the Durham Vision of the University of Durham*. Durham University Library and Special Collections, UND/DB15/K, 13.

Page, Denys (1960) *Richard Porson (1759–1808)*. London: OUP for the British Academy.

Page, Judith W. (2003) '"Hath not a Jew eyes?": Edmund Kean and the sympathetic Shylock', *The Wordsworth Circle* 34(2), 116–19.

Page, William (1911, ed.) *A History of the County of Middlesex*, vol. II. London: Victoria County History.

Paget, Derek (1990) *True Stories? Documentary Drama on Radio, Screen, and Stage*. Manchester: Manchester University Press.

Paine, Thomas (1776) *A Dialogue between the Ghost of General Montgomery just Arrived from the Elysian Fields and an American Delegate: In a Wood near Philadelphia*. Philadelphia, Pennsylvania: R. Bell.

Paine, Thomas (1783) *A Letter Addressed to the Abbé Raynal on the Affairs of North-America*. Philadelphia, Pennsylvania: Melchior Steiner.

Paine, Thomas (1787) *Prospects on the Rubicon: Or, an Investigation into the Causes and Consequences of the Politics to be Agitated at the Meeting of Parliament*. London: J. Debrett.

Paine, Thomas (1788) *The American Crisis. Number V. Addressed to General Sir William Howe*. Hartford, CT: Watson and Goodwin.

Paine, Thomas (1792) *Rights of Man. Part the Second*. Carlisle, Pennsylvania: George Kline.

Paine, Thomas (1795) *Dissertation on First Principles of Government*. London: 'The Proprietors'.

Paine, Thomas (1796a) *The Age of Reason, being an Investigation of True and Fabulous Theology*. London: 'The Proprietor'.

Paine, Thomas (1796b) *The Age of Reason. Part the Second*. London: Daniel Isaac Eaton.

Paine, Thomas (1796c) *The Decline and Fall of the English System of Finance*. Paris: Hartley, Adlard and Son.

Paine, Thomas (1797) *A Letter to the Honourable Thomas Erskine, on the Prosecution of Thomas Williams, for Publishing The Age of Reason*. Paris: 'Printed for the Author'.

Paine, Thomas (1817) *The Political Works of Tom Paine*. London: W.T. Sherwin.

Paine, Thomas (1824) *The Theological Works of Thomas Paine*. London: Richard Carlile.

Parker, H.T. (1937) *The Cult of Antiquity and the French Revolutionaries: A Study in the Development of the Revolutionary Spirit*. Chicago, Illinois: Chicago University Press.

Parker, Irene (1914) *Dissenting Academies in England: Their Rise and Progress and Their Place among the Educational Systems of the Country*. Cambridge: CUP.

Parr, Samuel (1828) *The Works of Samuel Parr, LL.D.*, vol. VIII, ed. John Johnstone. London: Longman, Rees, Orme, Brown and Green.

Pascal, Roy (1960) *Design and Truth in Autobiography*. Cambridge, Massachusetts: Harvard UP.

Payne, John Howard (1818) *Brutus; or, the Fall of Tarquin*. London: T. Rodwell.

Peacock, Sandra J. (1988) *Jane Ellen Harrison: The Mask and the Self*. New Haven: Yale University Press.

Pearsall, R. (1973) *Victorian Popular Music*. Newton Abbot: David and Charles.

Pease, E.R. (1925) *The History of the Fabian Society*. London: Allen and Unwin.

Pellow, Thomas (1740) *The History of the Long Captivity and Adventures of Thomas Pellow, in South-Barbary, written by Himself*. London: R. Goadby.

Pérez Rodríguez, Eva M. (2003) 'Education, conversation, and history: Godwin's search for style in "the Enquirer" and "of History and Romance"', *Atlantis* 25, 81–90.

Perkins, W. (1604) *A Commentarie or Exposition, vpon the Fiue First Chapters of the Epistle to the Galatians*. Cambridge: John Legat.

Perry, Benjamin (1952) *Aesopica: A Series of Texts Relating to Aesop or Ascribed to Him or Closely Connected with the Literary Tradition That Bears His Name*. Urbana, Illinois: University of Illinois Press.

Petersen, Lauren Hackworth (2006) *The Freedman in Roman Art and Art History*. Cambridge: CUP.

Petrie, George (2002 [1903]) *Ancient Music of Ireland*, reprint (of original 1903 edition published by C.V. Stanford), ed. David Cooper. Cork: Cork University Press.

Petsalis-Diomedis, Alexia (forthoming, ed.) *Ancient Greek Vases in C18th-C19th Britain: Access, Reproduction and Consumption. BICS* special issue.

Pfeiffer, Rudolf (1968) *History of Classical Scholarship from 1300 to 1850*. Oxford: Clarendon Press.

Phillip, Mark (2012) 'Godwin, William (1756–1836)', in *ODNB*. Oxford: OUP.

Phillips, A.D.M. (1993, ed.) *The Potteries: Continuity and Change in a Staffordshire Conurbation*. Stroud: Alan Sutton.

Pierse, Michael (2018a, ed.) *A History of Irish Working-Class Writing*. Cambridge: CUP.

Pierse, Michael (2018b) 'Was it us in the coffin? Writing death on the margins in twentieth-century Irish working-class writing', In: Pierse (ed.), (2018a), 168–94.

Pilkington, Laetitia (1748) *The Memoirs of Mrs. Laetitia Pilkington, Wife to the Rev. Mr. Matt. Pilkington. Written by Herself*, 2 vols, Dublin: 'Printed for the Author'.

Pimlott, John Alfred Ralph (1935) *Toynbee Hall: Fifty Years of Social Progress, 1884–1934, etc.* London: J. M. Dent & Sons.

Place, Francis (1972) *The Autobiography of Francis Place*, ed. Mary Thale. Cambridge: CUP.

Plato (2007) *Complete Works. Edited, with Introduction and Notes, by John M. Cooper.* Indianapolis, IN/Cambridge: Hackett Publishing Company.

Plebs (1909a) 'Editorial', *Plebs* volume 1, no. 2 (March) 21–25.

Plebs (1909b) 'Editorial', *Plebs* volume 1, no. 1 (February) 1–4.

Plot, Robert (1677) *The Natural History of Oxford-Shire, Being an Essay toward the Natural History of England*. Oxford: The Theatre.

Plot, Robert (1686) *The Natural History of Stafford-Shire*. Oxford: The Theatre.

Plummer, Alfred (1971) *Bronterre: A Political Biography of Bronterre O'Brien 1804–1864*. Toronto: University of Toronto Press.

Podmore, Frank 'Robert Owen and cooperation', *The Economic Journal* 15(58), 257–265.

Pointer, John (1718) *Miscellanea in Uusum Iuventutis Academicae*. Oxford: A.Peisley.

Pollard, A. (2004) 'Geddes, Sir William Duguid (1828–1900), classical scholar', *ODNB*. Oxford: OUP. doi:10.1093/ref:odnb/9780198614128.001.0001/odnb-97801986141 28-e-10492.

Pollard, M. (1989) *Dublin's Trade in Books 1550–1800*. Oxford: OUP.

Pomey, François (1659) *Pantheum mythicum; seu, Fabulosa deorum historia, hoc primo, epitomes eruditionis volumine, breuiter dilucidéque comprehensa*. Lyons: A. Molin.

Pomey, François (1694) *The Pantheon Representing the Fabulous Histories of the Heathen Gods, in a Short, Plain and Familiar Method by Way of Dialogue. For the Use of Schools.* Translated by J.A.B. London: Benj. Motte for Robert Clavel, and Charles Harper.

Pomey, François (1698) *The Pantheon: Representing the Fabulous Histories of the Heathen Gods and most Illustrious Heroes, in a Short, Plain and Familiar Method by Way of Dialogue.* Another Edition. London: Charles Harper.

Poole, Steve (2000) *The Politics of Regicide in England, 1760–1850*. Manchester: Manchester University Press.

Pope, Alexander (1711) *An Essay on Criticism*. London: W. Lewis; W. Taylor, T. Osborn, J. Graves.

Pope, Alexander (1715–1720, trans.) *Iliad of Homer*. London: Bernard Lintott.

Pope, Alexander (1903, trans.) *The Odyssey of Homer*. London: Grant Richards.

Porson, Richard (1815) *Tracts and Miscellaneous Criticism of the Late Richard Porson, Esq.*, ed. Thomas Kidd. London: Payne and Foss.

Porson, Richard (1818) *A Catechism for the Swinish Multitude, Necessary to be Had in All Sties*. London: 1, Shoe-Lane, Fleet Street.

Porter, J.I. (2008) 'Future reception studies', In: Hardwick and Stray (eds.), 469–81.

Potter, John (1697) *Archæologiæ Græcæ: Or, the Antiquities of Greece*. Oxford: Abel Swall; London. St. Pauls Church: Unicorn-yard.

Pound, Ezra (1971 [1950]) *Selected Letters of Ezra Pound, 1907–1941*, ed. D.D. Paige. New York: New Directions.

Preece, Rosemary (1998) *Coal Mining and the Camera*. Overton: National Coal Mining Museum for England Publications.

Price, Richard N. (1971) 'The Working men's club movement and Victorian social reform ideology', *Victorian Studies* 15, 117–47.

Prichard, J.C. (1831) *Eastern Origin of the Celtic Nations*. Oxford.

Priestley, Joseph (1970) *Autobiography of Joseph Priestley*. Introduction by Jack Lindsay. Bath: Adams and Dart.

Prins, Yopie (2017) *Ladies' Greek: Victorian Translations of Tragedy*. Princeton, New Jersey: Princeton University Press.

Prochaska, F.K. (1973) 'English state trials in the 1790s: A case study', *Journal of British Studies* 13(1), 63–82.

Prothero, Iorwerth (2013) *Artisans and Politics in Early Nineteenth-Century London: John Gast and His Times*. London: Routledge.

Proust, J. (1681, ed.) *Auli Gellii Noctes Atticae Interpretatione et notis illustravit Jacobus Proust e Soc. Jesu. Jussu Christianissimi Regis, ad usum serenissimi Delphini*. Paris: Simon Bénard.

Psalmanazar, George (1704) *An Historical and Geographical Description of Formosa, an Island subject to the Emperor of Japan. Giving an Account of the Religion, Customs, Manners, &c. of the Inhabitants*. London: Dan. Brown.

Psalmanazar, George (1764) *An Historical and Geographical Description of Formosa, an Island subject to the Emperor of Japan. Giving an Account of the Religion, Customs, Manners, &c. of the Inhabitants*. London: 'Printed for the executrix'.

Pyke, E.J. (1973) *A Biographical Dictionary of Wax Modellers*. Oxford: Clarendon Press.

Quarrell, W.H. and W.J.C. Quarrell (1928, eds.) *Oxford in 1710 From the Travels of Zacharias Conrad Von Uffenbach*. Oxford: Basil Blackwell.

Query, Patrick R. (2013) *Ritual and the Idea of Europe in Interwar Writing*. Aldershot: Ashgate.

Quinet, Edgar (1838) *Prométhée*. Paris: F. Bonnaire.

Quinn, Josephine Crawley (2018) 'Time to move on', *TLS* (September 18th).

Raath, Andries and Shaun de Freitas (2005) 'Rebellion, resistance, and a Swiss Brutus?', *The Historical Journal* 48(1), 1–26.

Radcliffe, Christopher (1997) 'Mutual improvement societies and the forging of working-class political consciousness in nineteenth-century England', *International Journal of Lifelong Education* 16(2), 141–155.

Ragon, Michel (1974) *Histoire de la Littérature Prolétarienne en France*. Paris: Albin Michel.

Rankin, Peter (2014) *Joan Littlewood: Dreams and Realities*. London: Oberon.

Rankine, Patrice (2006) *Ulysses in Black: Ralph Ellison, Classicism, and African American Literature*. Madison, Wisconsin and London: University of Wisconsin Press.

Rapple, Brendan A. (2017) *Matthew Arnold and English Education*. Jefferson, NC: MacFarland.

Rauch, Alan (2001) *Useful Knowledge: The Victorians, Morality, and the March of Intellect*. Durham, North Carolina and London: Duke University Press.

Ravenhill-Johnson, Annie (2013) *The Art and Ideology of the Trade Union Emblem, 1850–1925*, ed. Paula James. London: Anthem Press.

Ravenhill-Johnson, Annie (2015) 'Vulcan—a "Working-class" god'? In: Stead and Hall (eds.), 155–164.

Rawson, Joseph (1889–1895, ed.) *Chronicon Henrici Knighton, vel Cnitthon, Monachi Leycestrensis*. London: H. M. S.O. by Eyre and Spottiswoode.

Ray, M. (1995) 'Thomas Hardy in Aberdeen', *Aberdeen University Review* 56, 58–69.

Raynal, Guillaume (1770) *Histoire philosophique et politique des établissemens & du commerce des Européens dans les deux Indes*, 6 vols. Amsterdam

Rayner, Samantha (2009) 'Death and the grimly voice in David Jones' *in Parenthesis*', In: *The Arthurian Way of Death: The English Tradition*, Karen Cherewatuk and K.S. Whetter (eds.), Cambridge: D.S. Brewer, 226–40.

Reading Experience Database. Open University. www.open.ac.uk/Arts/reading/UK.

Real, Hermann J. and Heinz J. Vienken (1985) 'A catalogue of an exhibition of imprints from Swift's library', *Proceedings of the First Minster Symposium on Jonathan Swift*. Minster, 351–88.

Reid, Ivan (1981) *Social Class Differences in Britain*. 2nd edition. London: Grant McIntyre.

Reid, J.C. (1971) *Bucks and Bruisers: Pierce Egan and Regency England*. London: Routledge.

Reynolds, Margaret (2003) *The Sappho History*. Basingstoke: Palgrave Macmillan.

Rhys, Ernest (1940) *Wales England Wed: An Autobiography*. London: J.M. Dent & Sons Ltd.

Richards, Sarah (1999) *Eighteenth-Century Ceramics: Products for a Civilised Society*. Manchester and New York: Manchester University Press.

Richardson, Edmund (2015a) 'Political writing and class', In: *Oxford History of Classical Reception in English Literature*. Volume 4: 1790-1880…, N. Vance and J. Wallace (eds.), Oxford: OUP, 103–29.

Richardson, Edmund (2015b) 'The harmless impudence of a revolutionary: Radical Classics in 1850s London', In: Stead and Hall (eds.), 79–98.

Richardson, Edmund (2018, ed.) *Classics in Extremis: The Edges of Classical Reception*. London: Bloomsbury.

Richardson, John (1777–1780) *A Dictionary, Persian, Arabic, and English*. Oxford: Clarendon Press.

Richardson, Jonathan (1722) *An Account of Some of the Statues, Bas Reliefs, Drawings and Pictures in Italy*. London: J. Knapton.

Richardson, Keith P. (1977) 'Polliwogs and shellbacks: An analysis of the equator crossing ritual', *Western Folklore* 36(2), 154–59.

Rickword, Edgell (1991) *Collected Poems*, ed.Charles Hobday. Manchester: Carcanet.

Ridgway, C. (2004) 'Howard, George James, ninth earl of Carlisle (1843–1911), artist and politician', *Oxford Dictionary of National Biography*. Oxford: OUP.

Ritchie, J. and Ewing (1857) *The Night Side of London*. London: William Tweedie.

Rivers, Isabel and Mark Burden (forthcoming, eds.) *A History of the Dissenting Academies in the British Isles, 1660–1860*, 4 vols. Cambridge: CUP.

Rizzo, Betty (1990) 'The patron as poet-maker: The politics of benefaction', *Studies in Eighteenth-Century Culture* 20(1), 241–66.

Roberts, I. (2002) 'Working-class studies', *International Journal of Labor & Working-Class History* 61, 177–79.

Roberts, John (1961) *The Sheffield Educational Settlement (1918–1955)*. PhD thesis. 3 vols. University of Sheffield: Division of Education.

Roberts, R. (1923/1991) *A Wandering Scholar: The Life and Opinions of Robert Roberts*, Introduced by John Burnett and H.G. Williams. Cardiff: University of Wales.

Roberts, William Clare (2005) 'Marx in Hell: The critique of political economy as katabasis', *Critical Sociology* 31(1–2), 39–55.

Roberts, W. Rhys (1892) *British Universities: Notes and Summaries Contributed to the Welsh University Discussion by Members of the Senate of the University College of North Wales.* Manchester: J.E. Cornish.

Roberts, W. Rhys (1913) 'Greek and Latin in a young university', *The Classical Review* 27(8), 289–91.

Roberts, W. Rhys (1914) 'Prose rhythm in Welsh and English: With special reference to the Latin cursus', *The Classical Review* 28(5), 151–56.

Roberts, W. Rhys (1916) 'Greek civilization as a study for the people', *Proceedings of the British Academy* 7, 505–17.

Robichaud, Paul (2007) *Making the Past Present; David Jones, the Middle Ages, and Modernism.* Washington, DC: Catholic University of America Press.

Robins, Edward (1898) *The Palmy Days of Nance Oldfield.* London: William Heinemann.

Robinson, Robert (1887) *Thomas Bewick: His Life and Times.* Newcastle: R. Robinson

Robson, Joseph Philip (1849) *The Life and Adventures of the Far-famed Billy Purvis.* Newcastle-Upon-Tyne: J Clarke.

Roe, N. (1992) *Politics of Nature: Wordsworth and Some Contemporaries.* London: Palgrave Macmillan.

Roe, N. (2004) 'Dyer, George (1755–1841)', *ODNB.* Oxford. OUP.

Roe, N. (2012) *John Keats: A New Life.* New Haven, CT and London: Yale University Press.

Rogers, Samuel (1856, ed.) *Recollections of the Table Talk of Samuel Rogers. [Edited by A. Dyce.] To which is added Porsoniana. [By W. Maltby.]* London: Edward Moxon.

Roggins (2008) *The Huskar Disaster 1838.* Silkstone: Roggins Local History Group.

Rollin, Charles (1731) *The Ancient History of the Egyptians, Carthaginians, Assyrians, Babylonians, Medes & Persians, Macedonians, and Grecians.* London: George Virtue.

Rolph, C.H. (1980) *London Particulars.* Oxford: OUP.

Ronnick, Michele (2004) 'Twelve black classicists', *Arion* 11, 85–102.

Ronnick, Michele (2005, ed.) *The Autobiography of William Sanders Scarborough,* with a foreword by Henry Louis Gates Jr. Detroit: Wayne State University Press.

Ronnick, Michele (2006, ed.) *The Works of William Sanders Scarborough,* with a foreword by Henry Louis Gates Jr. Oxford and New York: OUP.

Ronnick, Michele (2016) 'Classical education and the advancement of African American women in the nineteenth and twentieth centuries', In: Wyles and Hall (eds.), 176–93.

Root, Laura (2006) '"Temporary gentlemen" on the western front: Class consciousness and the British Army ffficer 1914–1918' *The Osprey: Journal of Ideas and inquiry* 72. (UNF Digital Commons; https://digitalcommons.unf.edu/ojii_volumes/72/).

Root, Robert L. (1981) *Thomas Southerne.* Boston, Massachusetts: G.K. Hall.

Roscoe, William (1855 [1822]) *Memoirs of R. R. J. (Dick of Aberdaron), the Cambrian Linguist,* eds. John Kent, Hugh Maurice and John Goodwin, etc. http://access.bl.uk/item/viewer/ark:/81055/vdc_100024131976.0x000001.

Rose, John Holland (1911) *William Pitt and the Great War.* London: G. Bell & Sons.

Rose, Jonathan (1993) '"Everyman": An experiment in culture for the masses', *Victorian Periodicals Review* 26, 79–87.

Rose, Jonathan (1994) 'Workers' journals', In: *Victorian Periodicals and Victorian Society,* J. Don Vann and Rosemary T. Van Arsdel (eds.), Toronto and Buffalo: Toronto University Press, 301–10.

Rose, Jonathan (2001/2010) *The Intellectual Life of the British Working Classes.* 2nd edition. New Haven, CT and London: Yale University Press.

Rose, Jonathan (2004) 'Dent, Joseph Malaby (1849–1926)', *ODNB*. Oxford: OUP doi:10.1093/ref:odnb/9780198614128.001.0001/odnb-9780198614128-e-32788.

Rose, Peter W. (1992) *Sons of the Gods, Children of Earth: Ideology and Literary Form in Ancient Greece*. Ithaca, NY: Cornell University Press.

Rosenfeld, Sybil (1960) *The Theatre of the London Fairs in the 18th Century*. Cambridge: CUP.

Rosenfeld, Sybil (1977) 'Muster Richardson the great showman', In: *Western Popular Theatre*, David Mayer and Kenneth Richards (eds.), London: Methuen, 105–21.

Rosenheim, James M. (1998) *The Emergence of a Ruling Order: English Landed Society, 1650–1750*. London: Longman.

Rowntree, J.W. and H.B. Binns (1903) 'The organization of the class', In: *A History of the Adult School Movement*, chapter 5. London: Headley Brothers. Available in the informal education archives: www.infed.org/archives/e-texts/rowntree_and_binns.htm.

Rubin, J.H. (1976) 'Painting and politics, II: J.-L. David's patriotism, or the Conspiracy of Gracchus Babeuf and the Legacy of Topino-Lebrun', *The Art Bulletin* 58(4), 547–68.

Rubinsohn, Wolfgang Zeev (1987) *Spartacus' Uprising and Soviet Historical Writing*, translated by John G. Grifith. Oxford: Oxbow Books.

Ruddiman, Thomas (1714) *Rudiments of the Latin Tongue*. Edinburgh: Mr. Robert Freebairn.

Runge, Jörn E. (2009) *Olga Desmond: Preussens nackte Venus*. Friedland: Steffen.

Rupp, Gordon (1986) *Religion in England 1688–1791*. Oxford: Clarendon.

Russell, P. (2008) 'Babeuf and the Gracchi: A comparison of means and ends', *Melbourne Historical Journal* 36, 41–57.

Russell, Thomas (1796) *A Letter on the State of the Parties*. Dublin: No Publisher Indicated.

'R.W.' (1606) *The Iudgement, or Exposition of Dreames, Written by Artimodorus, an Antient and Famous Author*. London: R. Braddock for William Iones.

Ryan, Deborah Sugg (2007) '"Pageantitis": Visualising frank Lascelles' 1907 Oxford historical pageant', *Visual Culture in Britain* 8, 63–82.

Ryff, Walther Hermann (1540, trans.) *Warhafftige* by Artemidorus Daldianus. Straßburg: Balthasar.

Salenius, Sirpa (2016) *An Abolitionist Abroad: Sarah Parker Remond in Cosmopolitan Europe*. Amherst, Massachusetts; Boston, Massachusetts: University of Massachusetts Press.

Salmon, Thomas (1758) *A New Geographical and Historical Grammar*. 6th edition. London: William Johnston.

Saltzman, Rachelle H. (1994) 'Folklore as politics in Great Britain: Working-class critiques of upper-class strike breakers in the 1926 general strike', *Anthropological Quarterly* 67(3), 105–21.

Sambrook, James (2010) 'Spence, Joseph', *Oxford Dictionary Of National Biography*, revised Version of Article Originally published 2004. doi:10.1093/ref:odnb/26111.

Samuel, Irene (1976) 'Swift's reading of Plato', *Studies in Philology* 73, 440–62.

Samuel, Raphael, Ewan MacColl and Stuart Cosgrove (1985) *Theatres of the Left: Workers' Theatre Movements in Britain and America*. London: Routledge and Kegan Paul.

Sancroft, Willian (1694) *Occasional Sermons Preached by the Most Reverend Father in God, William Sancroft*. London: Thomas Bassett.

Sanders, Mike (2017) 'The guilty game of human subjugation', In: *A History of British Working Class Literature*, John Goodridge and Bridget Keegan (eds.), Cambridge: CUP, 226–47.

Sanders, Mike (2009) *The Poetry of Chartism*. Cambridge: CUP.

Sandford, Margaret E. (1888) *Thomas Poole and His Friends*, 2 vols. London: Macmillan.

Sandiford, Keith (1988) *Measuring the Moment: Strategies of Protest in Eighteenth-Century Afro-English Writing*. London and Toronto: Selinsgrove.

Sandow, E. (1919) *Life Is Movement*. London: Simson & Co.

Sandow, E. and G.M. Adam. (1894) *Sandow on Physical Training*. London: Gale and Polden.

Sandow, E. and G.M. Adam (1897) *Strength and How to Obtain It*. London: Gale and Polden.

Sandys, John Edwin (1906–8) *A History of Classical Scholarship*. Cambridge: CUP.

Sassoon, Siegfried (1921) 'The case for the miners', *The Nation (New York)*, (May 18th), 715.

Saunders, Peter (1990) *Social Class and Stratification*. London: Routledge.

Savage, M. et al. eds. (2015) *Social Class in the 21st Century*. London: Pelican.

Savile, Gertrude and Alan Savile ed. (1997) *Secret Comment: The Diaries of Gertrude Savile, 1721–1757*. Nottingham: Kingsbridge History Society.

Saville, John (1952, ed.) *Ernest Jones Chartist: Selections from the Writings and Speeches*. London: Lawrence and Wishart.

Sayer, Andrew (2005) *The Moral Significance of Class*. Cambridge: Cambridge University Press.

Sayers, Frank (1823) *Collective Works of the Late Dr Sayers*, ed. W. Taylor. Norwich: Stevenson and Matchett.

Scally, John (2012) 'Cheap print on Scottish streets', In: *The Edinburgh History of the Book in Scotland*, vol. II, S. Brown and W. McDougall (eds.), Edinburgh: Edinburgh University Press, 372–81.

Scatcherd, Norrison (1875) *Memoirs of the Celebrated Eugene Aram*. 3rd edition. Harrogate: T. Rollins.

Schmidt, Wilhelm (1899, ed.) *Herons von Alexandria Druckwerke und Automatentheater = Pneumatica et Automata*. Leipzig: Teubner.

Schoenfield, Mark (2015) 'Periodical auto-biography: Theories and representations', *The Wordsworth Circle* 46(2), 93–102.

Schofield, R.E. (2004) *The Enlightened Joseph Priestley: A Study of His Life and Work from 1773–1804*. Philadelphia, Pennsylvania: Penn State Press.

Schofield, R.E. (2013) 'Priestley, Joseph (1733–1804), theologian and natural philosopher', *ODNB*. Oxford. OUP.

Schwab, U. (1993) *The Poetry of the Chartist Movement = Studies in Social History*, vol. 13. Dordrecht and London: Kluwer Academic Publishers.

Scot, David (1823) 'Life of Alexander Murray D.D.', In: Murray (1823) vol. I, xxix–cxix.

Scotland (1969) *Education (Scotland) Act, 1969*. London: H.M.S.O.

Scott, A. and Miss Bratton (No initial supplied) (1925) *Catalogue of the Ceramic Library*. Hanley: Webberley Printers.

Scott, J.W. Robertson (1952) *The Life and Death of a Newspaper*. London: Methuen.

Scott, Robert (1801) *The Life of Robert Scott, Journeyman Wright ... in Verse; Written by Himself*. Dundee: T. Colville and Sons.

Scrivener, Michael (1993) 'Shelley and radical artisan poetry', *Keats-Shelley Journal* 42, 22–36 [= Bicentenary Tribute to the Achievement of Percy Bysshe Shelley].

Sellars, John (2003) 'Simon the shoemaker and the problem of Socrates', *Classical Philology* 98(3), 207–16.

Senelick, L. (1997, ed.) *Tavern Singing in Early Victorian London: The Diaries of Charles Rice for 1840 and 1850*. London: The Society for Theatre Research.

Settle, Elkanah (1666) *Cambyses*. London: William Cademan.

Settle, Elkanah (1707a) *The Siege of Troy: A Dramatick Performance. Presented in Mrs. Mynns's Booth. Over against the Hospital-gate in the Rounds in Smithfield, during the Bartholomew-Fair.* London: B. Bragge.

Settle, Elkanah (1707b) *The Siege of Troy: A Dramatick Performance, Presented in Mrs. Mynn's Great Booth, in the Queen's-Arms-Yard near the Marshalsea-Gate in Southwark.* London: Lee and Morphew.

Seymour-Smith, Martin (1994) *Hardy.* London: Bloomsbury.

Shattock, C.H. (1958, ed.) *Bulwer and Macready,* ed. C.H. Shattock. Urbana, Illinois: University of Illinios Press.

Shaw, Charles (published under name 'An Old Potter') (1903) *When I Was a Child.* London: Methuen.

Shaw, John Stuart (1999) *The Political History of 18th-Century Scotland.* Basingstoke: Macmillan.

Shelford, April G. (2007) *Transforming the Republic of Letters: Pierre-Daniel Huet and European Intellectual Life, 1650–1720.* Rochester, NY: University of Rochester Press.

Shelley, Percy Bysshe (1817) *A Proposal for Putting Reform to the Vote.* London: C. and J. Ollier.

Shelley, Percy Bysshe (1820a) *Oedipus Tyrannus, or, Swellfoot the Tyrant: A Tragedy in Two Acts.* London: J. Johnston.

Shelley, Percy Bysshe (1820b) *Prometheus Unbound: A Lyrical Drama in Four Acts.* London: C. and J. Ollier.

Shepherd, T.B. (1966) *Methodism and the Literature of the Eighteenth Century.* New York: Haskell.

Sherbo, Arthur (1963, ed.) *New Essays by Arthur Murphy.* East Lansing, Michigan: Michigan State University Press.

Shershow, Scott Cutler (1995) *Puppets and "Popular" Culture.* Ithaca, New York and London: Cornell University Press.

Shewan, Alexander (1905) *Meminisse juvat: Being the Autobiography of a Class at King's College in the Sixties.* Aberdeen: University of Aberdeen Press.

Shewan, Alexander (1935) *Homeric Essays.* Oxford: Blackwell.

Shiach, M. (1989) *Discourse on Popular Culture: Class, Gender and History in Cultural Analysis, 1730 to the Present.* London: Polity.

Shiman, Lilian Lewis (1992) *Women and Leadership in Nineteenth-century England.* London: Macmillan.

Shouldice, Frank (2015) *Grandpa the Sniper: The Remarkable Story of a 1916 Volunteer.* Dublin: The Liffey Press Ltd.

Shroff, Homai J. (1983) *The Eighteenth Century Novel: The Idea of the Gentleman.* London: Edward Arnold.

Shumaker, Wayne (1954) *English Autobiography: Its Emergence, Materials, and Form.* Berkeley, California: University of California Press.

Shuttleton, David E. (2013) '"Nae Hottentots": Thomas Blacklock, Robert Burns, and the Scottish vernacular revival', *Eighteenth-Century Life* 37(1), 21–44.

Sidgwick, A. and F.D. Morice (1883) *An Introduction to Greek Verse Composition with Exercises.* London, Edinburgh: Rivington's.

Sidgwick, Arthur Hugh (1920) *The Oxford Magazine*, vol. 38 (5 March). Oxford, Horace Hart. British Library shelfmark P.P.6118.k. Vol. 1, no. 1 (1883); Vol. 91, no. 4 (1973).

Sinclair, Jenny (2000) *A Walking Shadow: The Remarkable Double Life of Edward Oxford.* Melbourne: Arcade Publications.

Smedley, Constance (1929) *Crusaders: The Reminiscences of Constance Smedley (Mrs Maxwell Armfield)*. London: Duckworth.

Smelser, Neil J. (1991) *Social Paralysis and Social Change: British Working-Class Education in the Nineteenth Century*. Berkeley, California: University of California Press.

Smith, A. (1996) *The Victorian Nude: Sexuality, Morality and Art*. Manchester: Manchester University Press.

Smith, Charles Manby (1853) *Curiosities of London Life*. London: William and Frederick G. Cash.

Smith, Charles Manby (1854) *The Working-man's Way in the World: Being the Autobiography of a Journeyman Printer*. New York: Redfield.

Smith, Eunice (2004) 'Blacklock, Thomas (1721–1791)', *ODNB*. Oxford: OUP.

Smith, Evans Lansing (2001) *The Descent to the Underworld in Literature, Painting, and Film, 1895–1950: The Modernist Nekyia*. Lewiston, Maine, Queenston and Lampeter: Edwin Mellen.

Smith, Greg and Sarah Hyde (1989, ed.) *Walter Crane 1845–1915*. London: Lund Humphries.

Smith, John P. (1995) *James Tassie 1735–1799, Modeller in Glass: A Classical Approach*. London: Mallett.

Smith, James (2013) *British Writers and MI5 Surveillance, 1930–1960*. Cambridge: CUP

Smith, Joshua Toulmin (1836) *A Popular View of the Progress of Philosophy among the Ancients*. London: Longman, Rees, Orme, Brown, Green, and Longman.

Smith, J.W.A. (1954) *The Birth of Modern Education: The Contribution of the Dissenting Academies, 1660–1800*. London: Independent Press.

Smith, M.K. (2004) 'Adult schools and the making of adult education', *Encyclopaedia of Informal Dducation*. www.infed.org/lifelonglearning/adult_schools.htm.

Smith, L. and H. Matthew (2013) 'Smith, Joshua Toulmin [formerly Joshua Smith] (1816–1869), publicist and lawyer', *Oxford Dictionary of National Biography*. Oxford: University Press.

Smith, Malcolm and Don MacRaild (2009) '*The origins of the Irish in Northern England: An isonymic analysis of data from the 1881 census*', *Immigrants and Minorities* 27, 152–77.

Smith, Neil, Ianthi Tsimpli, Gary Morgan and Bencie Woll (2010) *The Signs of a Savant: Language Against the Odds*. Cambridge: CUP.

Smith, Tyler Jo (2010) 'Reception or deception? Approaching Greek dance through vase-Painting', In: *The Ancient Dancer in the Modern World Responses to Greek and Roman Dance*, Fiona Macintosh (ed.), Oxford: OUP, 77–98.

Smith, William (1753) *The History of the Peloponnesian War, Translated from the Greek of Thucydides*, 2 vols. London: John Watts.

Soldene, Emily (1897) *My Theatrical and Musical Recollections*. London: Downey & Co.

Soldon, N.C. (1978) *Women in British Trade Unions 1874–1976*. Dublin: Gill and MacMillan.

Solly, Henry (1898) *The Life of Henry Morley*. London: Edward Arnold.

Solon (1834) *Corn-Law Prose: Containing the Old Sow and Her Litter of Pigs: Look before You Leap; and a Letter to the Author of "Thoughts on the Corn Laws"*. Sheffield: A. Whitaker & Co.

Somerville, Alexander (1848) *The Autobiography of a Working Man: By One Who Has Whistled at the Plough*. London: Charles Gilpin.

Southerne, Thomas (1721) *The Spartan Dame. A Tragedy*. London: W. Chetwood.

Spacks, Patricia Meyer (1976) *Imagining a Self: Autobiography and Novel in Eighteenth-Century England*. Cambridge, Massachusetts and London: Harvard UP.

Spateman, Thomas (published anonymously) (1742) *The School-Boy's Mask, Design'd for the Diversion of Youth and their Excitement to Learning.* London: J Roberts.

Speaight, George (1952) 'Powell from the Bath: An 18th-century London puppet theatre' In: *Studies in English Theatre History in Memory of Gabrielle Enthoven, O.B.E.* London: Society for Theatre Research, 38–51.

Speck, W.A. (1998) *Literature and Society in Eighteenth-Century England.* London and New York: Longman.

Spector, Robert Donald (1979) *Arthur Murphy.* Boston, Massachusetts: G.K. Hall.

Spence, Joseph (1726) *An Essay on Pope's Odyssey: In Which some Particular Beauties and Blemishes of that Work are Considered.* London: J. and J. Knapton.

Spence, Jospeh (1731) *A Full and Authentick Account of Stephen Duck, the Wiltshire Poet.* London: J Roberts.

Spence, Joseph (1771) *Fugitive Pieces on Various Subjects.* 3rd edition. London: J. Dodsley.

Spence, Joseph (1794) 'The marine republic', *Pigs' Meat* 2, 68–72.

Spirit (1802) *The Spirit of the Public Journals for 1797*, vol. I. 3rd edition. London: James Ridgway.

Sproll, Paul (1994) 'Matters of taste and matters of commerce: British Government intervention in art education in 1835', *Studies in Art Education* 35(2), 105–13.

Spurr, John 'The Church of England, comprehension and the 1689 Toleration Act', *English Historical Review* 104, 927–46.

Squire, M. (2011) *The Art of the Body: Antiquity and Its Legacy.* London: I. B. Tauris.

St Clair, William (1989a) 'William Godwin as children's bookseller', In: *Children and Their Books: A Celebration of the Work of Iona and Peter Opie*, G. Avery and Julia Briggs (eds.), Oxford: Clarendon Press, 165–79.

St Clair, William William (1989b) *The Godwins and the Shelleys: A Biography of a Family.* New York: W.W. Norton.

St Clair, William (1998) *Lord Elgin and the Marbles.* 4th edition. Oxford: OUP.

Stafford, Emma (2012) *Herakles.* London: Routledge.

Stallings, A.E. (1996) '"The time you won your town the race": "A Shropshire Lad" and the modern Olympics', *The Classical Outlook* 73, 113–16.

Stamper, Joseph (1960) *So Long Ago.* London: Hutchinson.

Stamper, Kory (2017) *Word by Word: The Secret Life of Dictionaries.* Pantheon Books.

Stanford, W.B. (1976) *Ireland and the Classical Tradition.* Dublin: Allen Figgis.

Stanford, W.B. and R.B. McDowell (1971) *Mahaffy: A Biography of an Anglo-Irishman.* London: Routledge and Kegan Paul.

Stanhope, P. (1892) *The Letters of Philip Dormer Stanhope, Earl of Chesterfield.* London: Sonnenschein.

Stanhope, P. (1932) *Letters to His Son on the Art of Becoming a Man of the World and a Gentleman.* New York: Viking Press.

Stanley, Brian (2004) 'Carey, William (1761–1834), orientalist and missionary', *ODNB.* Oxford: OUP.

Stanyan, Temple (1707) *The Grecian History: Volume the First. Containing the Space of about 1684 Years.* London: Jacob Tonson.

Stapleton, Anamarie (1996) 'John Moyr Smith 1839–1912', *Journal of the Decorative Arts Society 1850-the Present* 20, 18–28.

Starobinski, Jean (1980) 'The style of autobiography', In: *Autobiography: Essays Theoretical and Critical*, James Olney (ed.), Princeton, New Jersey: Princeton University Press, 73–83.

Starr, G.A. (1965) *Defoe and Spiritual Autobiography.* Princeton, New Jersey: Princeton UP.

Starr, Mark (1918) *A Worker Looks at History: Being Outlines of Industrial History Specially Written for C.L.C. Plebs Classes*. London: Plebs' League/Fox, Jones & Co.

Stauffer, Donald (1941) *The Art of Biography in Eighteenth Century England*. Princeton, New Jersey: Princeton UP.

Stead, Henry (2013) 'Seneca's Oedipus–by hook or by crook', *Canadian Review of Comparative Literature* 40, 88–104.

Stead, Henry (2015a) 'Swinish classics; a conservative clash with cockney culture', In Stead and Hall, 55–78.

Stead, Henry (2015b) *A Cockney Catullus*. Oxford: OUP.

Stead, Henry (2018a) 'Classical epic in early musical theatre: The case of Kane O'Hara's Midas', In: Macintosh, McConnell, Harrison and Kenward (eds.), 461–75.

Stead, Henry (2018b) 'Classics down the mineshaft: A buried history', In: Richardson (ed.), 136–56.

Stead, Henry (forthcoming) *Cecil Day-Lewis and Virgil*. London: Bloomsbury.

Stead, Henry (forthcoming) 'Sandow the modern Hercules: Or the twelve labours of the class-conscious historian of British Classics', in: *Hercules Performed*, Output from 'Hercules: a Hero for All Ages' Project. https://herculesproject.leeds.ac.uk/publications/hercules-performed.

Stead, Henry and Edith Hall (2015, eds.) *Greek and Roman Classics in the British Struggle for Social Reform*. London: Bloomsbury.

Stead, Henry and Hanna Paulouskaya (forthcoming, 2020) 'Classics, crisis and the Soviet experiment: Russia, 1917–1939', In: *Classicizing Crisis*, B. Goff and M. Simpson eds. London: Bloomsbury.

Stead, W.T. (1885) 'The maiden tribute of modern Babylon'. https://attackingthedevil.co.uk/pmg/tribute/.

Stead, W.T. (1901) 'The World's Classics; or bound books for the million. The last word in cheap literature', In: *Wake Up! John Bull. An Illustrated Supplement to The Review of Reviews*, W.T. Stead (ed.), no. 5.24 (November 15th). London: Stead, 544–45.

Stead, W.T. (1906) 'Impressions of the theatre, XXII', *The Review of Reviews* 34(201), 255–58.

Stedman Jones, Gareth (1972) 'History: The poverty of empiricism', In: *Ideology in Social Science*, R. Blackburn (ed.), London: Fontana, 96–115.

Stephan, M. (2004) 'Harris, John (1820–1884), poet and miner', *ODNB*. Oxford: OUP. doi:10.1093/ref:odnb/9780198614128.001.0001/odnb-9780198614128-e-12403.

Stephen, L. and W. Jones (2004) 'Duck, Stephen (1705?–1756), poet', *Oxford Dictionary of National Biography*. Oxford: Oxford University Press.

Stephens, J.R. (1980) *The Censorship of English Drama 1824–1901*. Cambridge: CUP.

Stephens, W.B. (1964, ed.) 'Economic and social history: Social history since 1815', in *A History of the County of Warwick: Volume 7, The City of Birmingham*. The Victoria History of the Counties of England. London: published for the Institute of Historical Research by the Oxford University Press, 223–45. Accessed online at *British History Online* http://www.british-history.ac.uk/vch/warks/vol7/pp223-245 (accessed 14 December 2019).

Stephens, W.B. (1990) 'Literacy in England, Scotland, and Wales, 1500–1900', *History of Education Quarterly* 30(4), 545–57 [= Special Issue on the History of Literacy].

Stevens, Elena (2013) 'Making a spectacle of themselves: Art and female agency in 1890s music hall', *Reinvention* 6(2). https://warwick.ac.uk/fac/cross_fac/iatl/reinvention/issues/volume6issue2/stevens/.

Stewart, C. (1818, ed.) *Cornelii Nepotis excellentium imperatorum vitæ*. Edinburgh: Mundell & Son.

Stewart, D.M. (1928) 'The Scottish conference on adult education', *The Journal of Adult Education* 3, 6–25.

Stewart, J.A. (1905) *The Myths of Plato; Trans., with Introductory and Other Observations*. London: Macmillan.

Stone, L.C. (1925) 'Letter to the editor', *Highway* 18 (November), 30.

Stonehouse, Samuel (1736) *A Rational Method of Fitting Youth for Business*. London: J. Purser.

Strachan, John (2007) *Advertising and Satirical Culture in the Romantic Period*. Cambridge: CUP.

Strachan, John and Alison O'Malley-Younger (2010, eds.) *Ireland Revolution and Evolution*. Berlin and London: Peter Lang.

Stray, Christopher (1998a) *Classics Transformed: Schools, Universities, and Society in England 1830–1960*. Oxford: OUP.

Stray, Christopher (1998b) 'Schoolboys and gentlemen: Classical pedagogy and authority in the English public school', In: *Pedagogy and Power: Rhetorics of Classical Learning*, Yun Lee Too and Niall Livingstone (eds.), Cambridge: CUP, 29–46.

Stray, Christopher (1999, ed.) *Classics in 19th- and 20th-Century Cambridge Curriculum, Culture and Community*. Cambridge Philological Society Supplement, 24.

Stray, Christopher (2018) *Classics in Britain: Scholarship, Education, and Publishing 1800–2000*. Oxford: OUP.

Strickland, S. (1822) *Spartacus: A Roman Story*. London: A.K. Newman & Co.

Strong, Michele M. (2014) *Education, Travel and the "Civilisation" of the Victorian Working Classes*. New York: Palgrave Macmillan.

Stuart, Charles Douglas and A.J. Park (1895) *The Variety Stage*. London: Fisher Unwin.

Stuart, James (1911) *Reminiscences*. London: Printed for private circulation at the Chiswick Press.

Stuart, Matthew (2017) *Locke's Metaphysics*. Oxford: Clarendon Press.

Stubley, Peter (2015) *A Pauper's History of England*. Barnsley: Pen and Sword History.

Styan, J.L. (1981) *Modern Drama in Theory and Practice: Volume 3, Expressionism and Epic Theatre*. Cambridge: CUP.

Sullivan, J.P. (1975, ed.) *Marxism and the Classics* [Arethusa special issue 8.1]. Buffalo: University of Buffalo Press.

Svetlov, Valerian (1904) 'Duncan', *Birzhevyie Vedomosti (Биржевые Ведомости)*, (Wednesday December 15), no, 649. St Petersburg. P5.

Swain, Stanley W. (2006) *A Potteries Lad*. Norfolk: Copydiss.

Swale, Alan (1987) 'The terracotta of the Wedgwood Institute, Burslem', *Journal of the Tiles and Architectural Ceramics Society* 2, 21–27.

Swift, Jonathan (1726) *Travels into Several Remote Nations of the World. In Four Parts. By Lemuel Gulliver, First a Surgeon, and then a Captain of Several Ships*, 2 vols. London: Benj. Motte.

Swift, Jonathan (1729) *A Modest Proposal for Preventing the Children of Poor People from Being a Burthen to Their Parents, or the country, and for Making Them Beneficial to the Publick*. Dublin: S. Harding.

Swift, Jonathan (1963–1965) *The Correspondence of Jonathan Swift*, 5 vols. ed. Harold Williams. Oxford: Clarendon Press.

Swindells, Julia (1985) *Victorian Writing and Working Women*. Cambridge: Polity.

Swingler, Randall (1937) 'Apropos of translation', *Greece and Rome* VII(19) (October), 1–10.

'Sylvanus Urban' [pseud. editors of *Gentleman's Magazine*] (1884), 'Table Talk: Bohn's Libraries and the Purchase of Books.' *Gentleman's Magazine* 257: 413–14. London.

Syme, Ronald (1936) 'Review of Jack Lindsay, *The Romans*', *Classical Review* 50(1), 40–41.

Synge, J.M. (1907) *The Playboy of the Western World. A Comedy in Three Acts. Theatre Edition*. Dublin: Maunsel.

Taaffe, Dennis (1798) *The Probability, Causes, and Consequences of an Union between Great Britain and Ireland*. Dublin: J. Hill.

Tacitus (1730) *C. Cornelii Taciti Opera quae extant ex recensione et cum animadversionibus Theodori Ryckii*, 3 vols. Dublin: George Grierson.

Tanner, R.G. (1962) 'Ancient history and the modern citizen', *Greece and Rome* 9(1), 62–66.

Taylor, Elinor (2017) *The Popular Front Novel in Britain, 1934–1940*. Leiden: Brill; Chicago: Haymarket Books.

Taylor, Ellen (1792) *Poems, by Ellen Taylor, the Irish Cottager*. Dublin: G. Draper.

Taylor, George (1989) *Players and Performances in the Victorian Theatre*. Manchester and New York: Manchester University Press.

Taylor, Miles (2003) *Ernest Jones, Chartism and the Romance of Politics 1819–1869*. Oxford: OUP.

Terrill, Ross (1973) *R.H. Tawney and His Times: Socialism as Fellowship*. Cambridge: Harvard University Press.

Thackeray, William Makepeace (1849–50) *The History of Pendennis*, 2 vols. London: Bradbury and Evans.

The Dissenting Academies Project. www.qmulreligionandliterature.co.uk/research/the-dissenting-academies-project/dissenting-academies.

Thelwall, John (1795) *The Natural and Constitutional Rights of Britons to Annual Parliament*. London: Thelwall.

Thelwall, John (1796a) *The Rights of Nature against the Usurpations of Establishments*. London: H.D. Symonds.

Thelwall, John (1796b) *Prospectus of a Course of Lectures, Delivered during the Season of Lent, in Strict Conformity with Mr. Pitt's Convention Act*. 2nd edition. London: H.D. Symonds.

Thesing, William B. and Ted Wojtasik (2000) 'Poetry, politics and coal mines in Victorian England', In: *Caverns of Night*. Columbia, South Carolina: University of South Carolina Press, 32–49.

Thom, William (1841–1963) *William Thom, Poet and Weaver: Papers*. University of Aberdeen, Special Collections MS 2304, MS 2497 and MS 3089.

Thom, William (1880) *Rhymes and Recollections of a Hand-Loom Weaver*, ed. W. Skinner. Paisley: A. Gardner.

Thomas, Claudia N. (1994) *Alexander Pope and His Eighteenth-Century Women Readers*. Carbondale, IL and Edwardsville, IL: Southern Illinois University Press.

Thomas, John (1936) 'Pottery in England's industrial history', *Journal of the Royal Society of Arts* 84, 521–46.

Thomas, M. Wynn (2016) *The Nations of Wales 1890–1914*. University of Wales Press.

Thomas, R.S. (1987) *Welsh Airs*. Bridgend, Mid Glamorgan: Poetry Wales Press.

Thomas, Zoe (2017) 'Historical pageants, citizenship, and the performance of women's history before second-wave feminism', *Twentieth Century British History* 28(3), 319–43.

Thomis, M.I. (1986) 'Michie, John Lundie (1882–1946)', *Australian Dictionary of Biography*. Melbourne: Melbourne University Press.

Thompson, D.B. (1960) 'The house of Simon the shoemaker', *Archaeology* 13, 234–40.

Thompson, Elbert N.S. (1917) 'Tom Brown and eighteenth-century satirists', *Modern Language Notes* 32(2), 90–94.

Thompson, E.P. (1968) *The Making of the English Working Class, with Revisions.* Harmondsworth: Penguin Books.

Thompson, E.P. (2013) *The Making of the English Working Class.* London: Penguin.

Thompson, Judith (2009) 'Citizen Juan Thelwall: In the footsteps of a free-range radical', *Studies in Romanticism* 48, 67–100.

Thompson, Judith (2015, ed.) *John Thelwall: Selected Poetry and Poetics.* New York: Palgrave Macmillan.

Thompson, L. (1971) *The Enthusiasts: A Biography of John and Katharine Bruce Glasier.* London: Gollancz.

Thompson, Paul (1988) *The Voice of the Past: Oral History.* Oxford: OUP.

Thomson, George (1720) *Tetradymus.* London: J. Brotherton and W. Meadows.

Thomson, George (1726) *A Collection of Several Pieces of Mr. John Toland, Now First Publish'd from his Original Manuscripts: With Some Memoirs of his Life and Writings.* London: J. Peele.

Thomson, George (1937) 'Class struggles in the Roman world', *Left Review* III, 185–86.

Thomson, George (1975) *Marxism and Poetry.* London: Lawrence and Wishart.

Thorpe, Andrew (2000) *The British Communist Party and Moscow, 1920–1943.* Manchester and New York: Manchester University Press.

Thorpe, Vanessa (2009) 'The Ragged Trousered Philanthropists Leads Surge in Popularity for Leftwing Books', www.theguardian.com/books/2009/may/02/ragged-trousered-philanthropists-left-wing-bestsellers.

Tillett, Ben (1931) *Memories and Reflections.* London: John Long.

Tilley, Arthur (1938) 'Greek Studies in England in the early sixteenth century', *The English Historical Review* 53(CCX), 221–39.

Tilly, Chris (2005) *Popular Contention in Britain 1758-1834.* Paperback Edition. Boulder, CO and London: Paradigm.

Tilton, Theodore (1871) *Victoria C. Woodhull: A Biographical Sketch.* New York: The Golden Age.

Timperley, Charles Henry (1839) *A Dictionary of Printers and Printing.* London: H. Johnson.

Toby (1805) *The Life and Adventures of Toby, the Sapient Pig; with his Opinions on Men and Manners. Written by Himself.* London: Nicholas Hoare.

Todd, Janet (1984) *A Dictionary of British and American Women Writers 1660–1800.* London: Methuen.

Todd, Margot (2002) *The Culture of Protestantism in Early Modern Scotland.* London and New Haven: Yale University Press.

Toland, John (1714) *Reasons for Maturalizing the Jews in Great Britain and Ireland: On the Same Foot with all Other Nations. Containing also, a Defence of the Jews against all Vulgar Prejudices in all Countries.* London: J. Roberts.

Tomalin, Claire (1992) *The Life and Death of Mary Wollstonecraft.* London: Penguin.

Tompson, R. (2004) 'Clarke, John (1757–1820), schoolmaster', *ODNB.* Oxford. OUP.

Tone, Theobald Wolfe (1826) *Life of Theobald Wolfe Tone: Founder of the United Irish Society,* ed. W.T.W. Tone. Washington, D.C.: Gales and Seaton.

Torrance, Isabelle and Donncha O'Rourke (forthcoming, eds.) *Classics and Irish Politics 1916-2016.* Oxford: OUP.

Touchette, Lori-Ann (2000) 'Sir William Hamilton's 'pantomime mistress': Emma Hamilton and her attitudes', In: *The Impact of Italy: The Grand Tour and Beyond,* Clare Hornsby (ed.), London: British School at Rome, 123–46.

Treadwell, James (2005) *Autobiographical Writing and British Literature, 1783–1834*. Oxford: OUP.

Tressell, Robert (2008 [1914]) *The Ragged-Trousered Philanthropists*, ed. Peter Miles. Oxford: OUP.

Treue, Wilhem (1978) 'Zur Gesellschafts- und Berufgeschichte des deutschen Ingenieurs', *Technikgeschichte* 43, 27–36.

Trewin, J.C. (1955) *Mr Macready: A Nineteenth-Century Tragedian and his Theatre*. London: George G. Harrap & Co.

Tucker, Bernard (1996, ed.) *The Poetry of Laetitia Pilkington (1712–1750) and Constantia Grierson (1706-1733)*. Lewiston, ME/Queenston/Lampeter: Edwin Mellen Press.

Tuckwell, F.W. (1907) *Reminiscences of Oxford*. 2nd edition. London: Smith, Elder & Co.

Tumblety, Joan (2012) *Remaking the Male Body*. London: Routledge.

Turner, Frank (1991) *The Greek Heritage in Victorian Britain*. New Haven, Connecticut and London: Yale University Press.

Turner, H.E., Herbert Longhurst and Geo. G. Lewis (1924) *Caractacus: A Juvenile Operetta for Boys and Girls and Infants. Words by H.E. Turner. Music by Herbert Longhurst and Geo. G. Lewis*. London and Philadelphia, Pennsylvania: J. Curwen/Curwen Inc.

Turner, Thomas and David Vaisey ed. (1984) *The Diary of Thomas Turner*. Oxford: OUP.

Turton, B.J. (1993) 'The potteries in the interwar period', In: Phillips (ed.), 145–63.

Tylecote, Mabel (1957) *The Mechanics' Institute of Lancashire and Yorkshire before 1851*. Manchester: Manchester University Press.

Tynan, Kenneth (1967) *Right and Left*. London: Longmans.

Tyrrell, A. (1969). 'Political economy, whiggism and the education of working-class adults in Scotland 1817–1840'. *The Scottish Historical Review* 48(146), 151–65.

Tyson, Nancy Jane (1981) *Eugene Aram: A Study in the Literary History and Typology of the Scholar-Criminal*. PhD Diss. Ohio State University.

Urie, John (1908) *Reminiscences of Eighty Years*. Paisley: A. Gardner.

Vaisey, D. (2004) 'Turner, Thomas (1729–1793), diarist and shopkeeper', *ODNB*. Oxford: OUP.

Valpy, Richard (1788) *Delectus sententiarum et historiarum: in usum tironum accommodatus*. London: G. Robinson and J. Pridden.

van Amerongen, J.B. (1926) *The Actor in Dickens*. London: Cecil Palmer.

Vandiver, Elizabeth (2010) *Stand in the Trench, Achilles: Classical Receptions in British Poetry of the Great War*. Oxford: OUP.

Van-Hagen, Steve (2009) 'The life, works and reception of an evangelical radical: James Woodhouse (1735–1820), the "Poetical Shoemaker"', *Literature Compass* 6(2), 384–406.

Vasunia, Phiroze (2005) 'Greek, Latin and the Indian civil service', *Cambridge Classical Journal* 51, 35–71.

Vasunia, Phiroze (2013) *The Classics and Colonial India*. Oxford: OUP.

Veitch, Norman (1950) *The People's: Being a History of the People's Theatre*. Northumberland: Northumberland Press.

Vernon, Sally (1977) 'Trouble up at t'mill: The rise and decline of the factory play in the 1830s and 1840s', *Victorian Studies* 20, 117–39.

Vertot, Abbé de (1720) *The History of the Revolutions that Happened in the Government of the Roman Republic. Written in French by the Author of the History of the Revolutions in Sweden and in Portugal. English'd by Mr. Ozell and Others*. London: printed for W. Taylor at the Ship in Pater-Noster-Row, J. Pemberton at the Buck in Fleet-Street, and E. Symon in Cornhill.

Vicinus, M. (1974) *The Industrial Muse: A Study of Nineteenth Century British Working-Class Literature*. London: Croom Helm.

Victor, Benjamin (1761) *The History of the Theatres of London and Dublin, from the Year 1730 to the Present Time*, 2 vols. London and Dublin: G. Faulkner and J. Exshaw.

Vidal-Naquet, P. (1990) 'La Place de la Grèce dans l'immaginaire des hommes de la Révolution', In: *La Démocratie Grecque Vue d'ailleurs*. Paris: Flammarion, 211–36.

Vince, Ronald W. (1988) *Neoclassical Theatre: A Historiographical Handbook*. New York, Westport, Connecticut; London: Greenwood Press.

Vincent, D. (1981) *Bread, Knowledge and Freedom: A Study of Nineteenth-Century Working-Class Autobiography*. London: Europa.

Vincent, D. (1989) *Literacy and Popular Culture: England 1750–1914*. Cambridge: CUP.

Vincent, D. (2016) 'Working-class autobiography in the nineteenth century', In: *A History of English Autobiography*, A. Smyth (ed.), Cambridge: CUP, 165–78.

Volney, C.-F. (1791) *The Torch; or, A light to Enlighten the Nations of Europe in their Way towards Peace and Happiness: Extracted from De Volney's Ruins*. London and Dublin: no Publisher Indicated.

Volney, C.-F. (1792) *The Ruins: Or a Survey of the Revolutions of Empires*. English translation. London: J. Johnson.

Volpilhac-Auger, Catherine (1997) 'La collection Ad usum Delphini: entre érudition et pédagogie', *Histoire de l'éducation* 74(1), 203–14.

Volpilhac-Auger, Catherine (1999, ed.) *La collection Ad usum Delphini l'antiquité au Miroir du Grand Siècle*. Grenoble: ELLUG.

von Wilamowitz-Moellendorff, Ulrich (1921) *Geschichte der Philologie*. 3rd edition. Leipzig: B.G. Teubner.

von Wilamowitz-Moellendorff, Ulrich (1982) *History of Classical Scholarship Translated from the German by Alan Harris*, edited with introduction and notes by Hugh Lloyd-Jones. London: Duckworth.

Wahrman, Dror (1995) *Imagining the Middle Class: The Political Representation of Class in Britain, c. 1780–1840*. Cambridge: CUP.

Wakefield, G. (1792) *Memoirs of the Life of Gilbert Wakefield, B.A. Late Fellow of Jesus College*. London: J. Johnson.

Wakefield, G. (1798) *A Reply to Some Parts of the Bishop of Landaff's Address to the People of Great Britain*. Hackney, London: The Author.

Waldron, Mary (1996) *Lactilla, Milkwoman of Clifton*. Athens, Georgia: University of Georgia Press.

Waldron, Mary (2004) 'Yearsley [née Cromartie], Ann (bap. 1753, d. 1806), poet and writer', *ODNB*. Oxford. OUP.

Walker, George (1894) *Aberdeen Awa': Sketches of its Men, Manners, and Customs as Delineated in Brown's Book-stall, 1892–1894*. Aberdeen: Brown.

Walker, Keith (2003, ed.) *John Dryden: The Major Works*, Oxford World's Classics. Oxford: OUP.

Wallace, Jennifer (1987) *Shelley and Greece*. London: Macmillan.

Wallach, Jennifer Jensen (2006) 'Building a bridge of words: The literary autobiography as historical source material', *Biography* 29(3), 446–61.

Walpole, Horace (1961) *Horace Walpole's Correspondence with Hannah More ...* , vol. 31, ed. W.S. Lewis et al. New Haven, Connecticut and London: Yale University Press.

Walvin, James (1986) *England, Slaves and Freedom, 1776–1838*. Basingstoke and London: Macmillan.

Waquet, Françoise (1998) *Le Latin, ou, L'empire d'un Signe*. Paris: Albin Michel.

Warburton, W.H. (1931) *The History of Trade Union Organisation in the North Staffordshire Potteries*. London: Allen and Unwin.

Ward, C. Osborne (1887) *A History of the Ancient Working People and the Ancient Lowly to the Adoption of Christianity by Constantine*, 2 vols. New York: Charles H. Kerr.

Warden, Claire (2011) 'Politics, war, and adaptation: Ewan MacColl's Operation Olive Branch, 1947', *Comparative Drama* 44/5(Spring), 536–38. MI: Western Michigan University Press.

Warren, Samuel (1841) *Ten Thousand A-Year*. London: Ward and Lock.

Warrillow, E.J.D. (1960) *A Sociological History of the City of Stoke-On-Trent*. Hanley: Etruscan Publications.

Warrillow, E.J.D. (1966) *Arnold Bennett and Stoke-On-Trent*. Hanley: Etruscan Publications.

Waterfield, Giles (2015) *The People's Galleries: Art Museums and Exhibitions in Britain, 1800-1914*. New Haven, Connecticut and London: Yale University Press.

Watkin, David (1982) *Athenian Stuart: Pioneer of the Greek Revival*. London: Allen and Unwin.

Watkinson, Ray (1987) *Fighting Spirits: Peter Peri and Cliff Rowe*. Journeyman in association with the London Borough of Camden.

Watson, Eric R. (1913) *Eugene Aram: His Life and Trial*. London, Sydney, Wellington and Calcutta: Butterworth & Co.

Watson, John Selby (1861) *The Life of Richard Porson, Professor of Greek in the University of Cambridge from 1792–1808*. London: Longman Green Longman and Roberts.

Watson, Richard (1798) *An Address to the People of Great Britain by … Lord Bishop of Landaff*. London and Cork: A. Edwards.

Watson, Robert Spence (1897) *The History of the Literary and Philosophical Society of Newcastle-Upon-Tyne (1793–1896)*. London: Walter Scott.

Watts, Michael Robert (1978) *The Dissenters: From the Reformation to the French Revolution*, vol. 1. Oxford: Clarendon Press.

Waugh, Colin (2009) *'Plebs', the Lost Legacy of Independent Working-Class Education*. Sheffield: Post-16 Educator.

Whatley, Christopher A. (1989) *Serfdom: A Species of Slave. Serfdom in Scottish Coal Mines, c.1606–1799*. Dalkeith: Scottish Mining Museum.

Wearmouth, R.F. (1937) *Methodism and the Working-Class Movements*. London: Epworth Press.

Webb, Alfred (1878) 'Barry, James', In: *A Compendium of Irish Biography*. Dublin: M. H. Gill and Son, 11–12.

Webb, R.K. (1955) *The British Working-Class Reader (1790–1848)*. London: Allen and Unwin.

Webb, Sidney (1888) 'Rome: A sermon in sociology', *Our Corner* 12, 53–64 and 79–89.

Webb, Timothy (1977) *Shelley: A Voice Not Understood*. Manchester: Manchester U.P.

Weber, M. (1952) *Essays in Sociology*, eds. H. Gerth and C.W. Welsh. London: Routledge and Kegan Paul.

Webster, David P. (2000a) 'The Flemish Hercules'. *Iron Game History* 6(2). Access via www.starkcentre.org.

Webster, David P. (2000b) 'The Atlas and Vulcana group of society athletes', *Iron Game History* 6(3), 26–29. www.starkcenter.org/igh/igh-v6/igh-v6-n3/igh0603l.pdf.

Wedderburn, Robert (1820) *The Trial of the Rev. Robt Wedderburn*, ed. Erasmus Perkins. London: Perkins.

Wedderburn, Robert (1824) *The Horrors of Slavery*. London: R. Wedderburn.

Wedgwood, Josiah (1783) *Address to the Workmen in the Pottery on the Subject of Entering into the Service of Foreign Manufacturers*. Newcastle-under-Lyme: No Publisher Indicated.

Wedgwood, Josiah (1973) *Letters of Josiah Wedgwood, 1762 to 1770* (originally ed. by Katherine Euphemia, Lady Farrar, in three volumes 1903–1906 and privately circulated) New One-Volume Edition. Manchester and Barlaston: E.J. Morten and The Wedgwood Museum.

Weightman, Alfred E. (1957) *Heraldry in the Royal Navy*. Aldershot: Gale and Polden.

Welsh Carlyle, Jane Baillie (1889) *Early letters of Jane Welsh Carlyle, Together with a Few of Later Years, and Some of Thomas Carlyle*, ed. D.G. Ritchie. London.

Wesley, John (1831) *The Works of John Wesley*, ed. Thomas Jackson. 3rd edition. London: John Mason.

West, Alick (1969) *One Man in His Time*. London: Allen and Unwin.

Westgate, R.I.W. and Paul Lachlan MacKendrick (1942) 'Swift and Juvenal', *The Classical Journal* 37, 468–82.

Westminster Abbey (2017) 'Poets of the First World War', article on the official website of Westminster Abbey, last accessed June 23rd 2017, www.westminster-abbey.org/our-history/people/poets-of-the-first-world-war.

Whelan, Kevin (1996) 'The republic in the village: The dissemination and reception of popular political literature in the 1790s', In: Long (ed.), 101–40.

Whiston, William (1865) *The Works of Flavius Josephus*. Edinburgh: W.P. Nimmo.

Whitaker, G.H. (1986) *Glasgow and the Classical Tradition*. Glasgow University Library.

White, Rachel (2019) 'Australia as underworld: Convict classics in the 19th century', In: *Antipodean Antiquities*, Marguerite Johnson ed. London: Bloomsbury, 29–39.

Whitehead, Catherine S. (1989) *The Third Programme: A Literary History*. Oxford: OUP.

Whitehead, Maurice (2016) *English Jesuit Education: Expulsion, Suppression, Survival and Restoration, 1762–1803*. London: Routledge.

Whitehouse, Tessa (2015) *The Textual Culture of English Protestant Dissent 1720–1800*. Oxford: OUP.

Wise, Sarah (2013) *Inconvenient People: Lunacy, Liberty and the Mad Doctors in Victorian England*. London: Vintage.

Whyte, Frederic (1925) *The Life and Letters of W.T. Stead*, 2 vols. London: Jonathan Cape.

Wiener, Joel H. (1983) *Radicalism and Freethought in Nineteenth Century Britain*. Westport, CT and London: Greenwood Press.

Wilberforce, R.I. and Samuel Wilberforce (1843) *The Life of William Wilberforce*. Abridged edition. London: Seeley, Burnside and Seeley.

Wilde, John (1793) *An Address to the Lately Formed Society of the Friends of the People*. London and Edinburgh: T. Cadell, and Peter Hill.

Wilkie, William (1757) *The Epigoniad. A Poem. In Nine Books*. Edinburgh: Hamilton, Balfour and Neill.

Wilkinson, A. (2009) 'Moore, Henry Spencer (1898–1986), sculptor', *ODNB*. Oxford: OUP.

Wilkinson, R. (1964) *The Prefects*. Oxford: OUP.

Wilkinson, Tate (1790) *Memoirs of His Own Life*, 4 vols. York: Wilson, Spence and Mawman.

Williams, Harold (1932) *Dean Swift's Library*, With a Facsimile of the Original Sales Catalogue. Cambridge: CUP.

Williams, Luke G. (2015) *Richmond Unchained: The Biography of the World's First Black Sporting Superstar*. Stroud: Amberley Publishing.

Williams, Marjorie, ed. (1939) *The Letters of William Shenstone. Arranged and Edited with Introduction, Notes and Index*. Oxford: Basil Blackwell.

Williams, Raymond (1973) *The Country and the City*. New York: Oxford University Press.
Williams, Raymond (1975) *The Country and the City*. St. Albans: Paladin.
Williams, Raymond (1976) *Keywords*. London: Croom Helm.
Williamson, Gillian (2016) *British Masculinity in the Gentleman's Magazine, 1731 to 1815*. Houndmills, Basingstoke, Hampshire: Palgrave Macmillan.
Willis, J.F. (1928) 'The Y.M.C.A. and adult education', *Journal of Adult Education* 3, 36–46.
Wilson, David M. (2002) *British Museum: A History*. London: British Museum.
Wilson, J. (1684) *A Discourse of Monarchy More Particularly of the Imperial Crowns of England, Scotland, and Ireland*. London: Jos. Hindmarsh.
Wilson, John Henry (1804) *Swiftiana*, 2 vols. Dublin: Richard Phillips.
Wilson, Joseph Havelock (1925) *My Stormy Voyage through Life*. London: Nat. Sailors' & Firemans Union.
Wilson, Penelope (2012) 'The place of Classics in education and publishing', In: *Oxford History of Classical Reception in English Literature*. Volume 3: 1660-1790, David Hopkins and Charles Martindale eds. Oxford: OUP, 29–52.
Winks, William Edward (1882) *Lives of Illustrious Shoemakers*. London: Sampson Low & Co.
Wood, A. Skevington (1969) *Captive to the Word: Martin Luther: Doctor of Sacred Scripture*. Exeter: Paternoster Press.
Wood, Alexander, and Alice Engholm (1907) 'Ancient barbarous sports', *Folklore* 18(3), 336–38.
Woodall, Ann M. (2005) *What Price the Poor? William Booth, Karl Marx and the London Residuum*. Aldershot: Ashgate.
Woodhouse, James (1764) *Poems on Sundry Occasions*. London: W. Richardson and S. Clark.
Woodhouse, James (1766) *Poems on Several Occasions: By James Woodhouse, Journeyman Shoemaker*. London: Printed for the Author, and Sold by Messrs. Dodsley et al.
Woodhouse, James (1803) *Norbury Park, a Poem; with Several Others, etc.* London: Watts and Bridgewater.
Woodhouse, James (1896) *Life and Poetical Works of James Woodhouse*, 2 vols. London: Leadenhall Press Ltd.
Woodhouse, James and Steve Van-Hagen ed. (2005) *The Life and Lucubrations of Crispinus Scriblerus: A Selection*. Cheltenham: The Cyder Press.
Woodhouse, W.J. (1938) *Solon the Liberator: A Study of the Agrarian Problem in Attika in the Seventh Century*. London: Humphrey Milford.
Woods, C.J. (1991) *Journals and Memoirs of Thomas Russell, 1791–1795*. Belfast: Irish Academic Press and Linen Hall Library.
Wooler Jack [= Frank Sikes] (1851) *Jason and Medea: A Comic. Heroic. Operatic. Burlesque-Spectacular Extravaganza* (British Library Add. MS 43036, fos. 276–307).
Woolrich, A.P. (2004) 'Ruddiman, Thomas (1674–1757), printer, classical scholar, and librarian', *ODNB*. Oxford: OUP.
Wordsworth, Dorothy (1874) *Recollections of a Tour Made in Scotland A.D.* 1803, ed. J.C. Shairp. New York: G.P. Putnams & Sons.
Wormald, J. (1991) *Court, Kirk, and Community: Scotland, 1470–1625*. Edinburgh: Edinburgh University Press.
Wright, Anthony (1987) *R.H. Tawney*. Manchester: Manchester University Press.
Wright, D.G. (1988) *Popular Radicalism: The Working-Class Experience, 1780–1880*. London: Longman.
Wright, Elizabeth Mary (1932) *The Life of Joseph Wright*. London: OUP.

Wright, John Henry (1906) 'The origin of Plato's cave', *Harvard Studies in Classical Philology* 17, 131–42.

Wright, Joseph (1905) *English Dialect Grammar.* Oxford: Oxford University Press.

Wright, Thomas (1922) *The Romance of the Shoe: Being the History of Shoemaking in All Ages, and Especially in England and Scotland.* London: C.J. Farncombe.

Wrigley, Amanda (2015) *Greece on Air.* Oxford: OUP.

Wyke, M. (1996) 'Herculean muscle! the classicizing rhetoric of bodybuilding', *Arion* 4(3), 51–79, reprinted in J.I. Porter (ed), *Constructions of the Classical Body.* Ann Arbor: Michigan University Press, 355–79.

Wyles, Rosie (2007) 'Publication as intervention: Aristophanes in 1659', In: Hall and Wrigley (eds.), 94–104.

Wyles, Rosie (2016) 'Ménage's learned ladies: Anne Dacier (1647–1720) and Anna Maria van Schurman (1607–1678)', In: Wyles and Hall (eds.), 61–77.

Wyles, Rosie and Edith Hall (2016, eds.) *Women Classical Scholars: Unsealing the Fountain from the Renaissance to Jacqueline de Romilly.* Oxford: OUP.

Yagoda, Ben (2009) *Memoir: A History.* New York: Riverhead Books.

Yearsley, Ann (1787) *Poems on Various Subjects, by Ann Yearsley, Milkwoman of Clifton, near Bristol.* London: G. G. J. and J. Robinson.

Yearsley, Ann (1788) *A Poem on the Inhumanity of the Slave-Trade.* London: G. G. J. and J. Robinson.

Yearsley, Ann (1793) *Catalogue of the Books, Tracts, &c. Contained in Ann Yearsley's Public Library, No. 4, Crescent, Hotwells.* Bristol: printed for the proprietor.

Yearsley, Ann (1796) *The Rural Lyre.* London: G G. and J Robinson.

Yeats, William Butler (1913) *Stories of Red Hanrahan.* London and Stratford-upon-Avon: A.H Bullen.

Yoshino, Ayako (2011) *Pageant Fever: Local History and Consumerism in Edwardian England.* Tokyo: Waseda University Press.

Young, Alan and Michael Schmidt (1973) 'A conversation with Edgell Rickword', *Poetry Nation 1.* www.pnreview.co.uk/cgi-bin/scribe?item_id=3979.

Young, Barbara and J.G. Jenkins (1963) 'A history of Fenton and Longton', *Victoria County History of Staffordshire* VIII, 205–46.

Young, Douglas F. (1973) *Beyond the Sunset: A Study of James Leslie Mitchell (Lewis Grassic Gibbon).* Aberdeen: Impulse Books.

Youngkin, Molly (2007) *Feminist Realism at the Fin de Siècle: The Influence of the Late-Victorian Woman's Press on the Development of the Novel.* Columbus, OH: Ohio University Press.

Youings, J. (2008) 'Blundell, Peter (c. 1520–1601), clothier and philanthropist', *ODNB.* Oxford: OUP. doi:10.1093/ref:odnb/9780198614128.001.0001/odnb-9780198614128-e-2714.

Ziolkowski, Theodore (2000) *The Sin of Knowledge: Ancient Themes and Modern Variations.* Princeton, New Jersey and Oxford: Princeton University Press.

Zweiniger-Bargielowska, Ina (2010) *Managing the Body: Beauty, Health, and Fitness in Britain 1880–1939.* Oxford: OUP.

INDEX